I0091696

Gemini and the Sacred

Also Available from Bloomsbury

The Bloomsbury Reader in the Study of Myth,
Edited by Jonathan Miles-Watson and Vivian Asimos

Goddesses in Myth and Cultural Memory
Emilie Kutash

The Roman Mithras Cult,
Olympia Panagiotidou with Roger Beck

Gemini and the Sacred

Twins and Twinship in Religion and Mythology

♊

Edited by
Kimberley C. Patton

BLOOMSBURY ACADEMIC
LONDON • NEW YORK • OXFORD • NEW DELHI • SYDNEY

BLOOMSBURY ACADEMIC
Bloomsbury Publishing Plc
50 Bedford Square, London, WC1B 3DP, UK
1385 Broadway, New York, NY 10018, USA
29 Earlsfort Terrace, Dublin 2, Ireland

BLOOMSBURY, BLOOMSBURY ACADEMIC and the Diana logo are trademarks of
Bloomsbury Publishing Plc

First published in Great Britain 2023
Paperback edition published 2024

Copyright © Kimberley C. Patton and Contributors, 2023

Kimberley C. Patton has asserted her right under the Copyright, Designs and
Patents Act, 1988, to be identified as Editor of this work.

For legal purposes the Acknowledgments on p. xvi constitute an extension of
this copyright page.

Cover design: Maria Rajka

Cover image: 'Gemini', folio 3r, detail from the Hunterian Psalter,
Glasgow University Library MS, Hunter 229 (U.3.2) Circa 1170. Anonymous
Hunterian Psalter c. 1170 Gemini
(© The Picture Art Collection / Alamy Stock Photo)

All rights reserved. No part of this publication may be reproduced or transmitted in any
form or by any means, electronic or mechanical, including photocopying, recording, or
any information storage or retrieval system, without prior permission in writing from the
publishers.

Bloomsbury Publishing Plc does not have any control over, or responsibility for, any third-
party websites referred to or in this book. All internet addresses given in this book were
correct at the time of going to press. The author and publisher regret any inconvenience
caused if addresses have changed or sites have ceased to exist, but can accept no
responsibility for any such changes.

A catalogue record for this book is available from the British Library.

Library of Congress Control Number: 2022932161

ISBN: HB: 978-1-8488-5931-9
PB: 978-1-3503-2041-3
ePDF: 978-1-7867-3591-1
eBook: 978-1-7867-2591-2

Typeset by Deanta Global Publishing Services, Chennai, India

To find out more about our authors and books visit www.bloomsbury.com and
sign up for our newsletters

for

Jacob Kẹ́hìndé and Isaac Táyéwò
Jacob Atta and Essau Atta
The Nabeysil and Salvador
Jaya and Uma
Laurie and Kathy
Erik and Katrina
Joseph and Philip
Ben and Natalie

& for

Lee and Caitlyn

always

Figure TC.1. Zodiac mosaic, Beit Alpha Synagogue.
Beit She'an Valley, sixth century CE, N. Israel.
Detail: Gemini (*teomim*).
Courtesy Israel Antiquities Authority.

Contents

♊

Illustrations

ⅠⅠ

Figures

Plates

Ọ̀rọ̀ tó rin méjì o ò   Spirit Children who walk in pairs!

—Yorùbá *Orin Ìbejì* (twin songs)

Dancing Round in a Ring

"You've begun wrong!" cried Tweedledum. "The first thing in a visit is to say 'How d'ye do?' and shake hands!" And here the two brothers gave each other a hug, and then they held out the two hands that were free, to shake hands with her.

Alice did not like shaking hands with either of them first, for fear of hurting the other one's feelings; so, as the best way out of the difficulty, she took hold of both hands at once: the next moment, they were dancing round in a ring. This seemed quite natural (she remembered afterward); and she was not even surprised to hear music playing; it seemed to come from the tree under which they were dancing, and it was done (as well as she could make it out) by the branches rubbing one across the other, like fiddles and fiddlesticks.

"But it certainly *was* funny" (Alice said afterward, when she was telling her sister the history of all this) "to find myself singing *'Here we go round the mulberry bush.'* I don't know when I began it, but somehow I felt as though I'd been singing it a long, long time!"

— from "Tweedledum and Tweedledee"
Lewis Carroll, *Through the Looking-Glass*

Acknowledgments

♊

"Twins are always a harder birth," Ayodeji Ogunnaike reminded me during the last year of work on *Gemini and the Sacred*, as a pandemic shrouded the world and all its doings. As the co-editor of three other books in comparative religious studies, in the past I had worked in tandem with trusted colleagues with whom I could share intellectual dialogue, as well as the myriad months or even years of labor required to deliver a multi-contributor volume. Ironically, for *Gemini,* no twin appeared: nor, after a point, did I look for one. Nevertheless there were many helpmates along the way, not all of them visible, and my debt of gratitude to each one runs deep.

My heartfelt thanks belong first and foremost to the contributors to this volume: Jacob Kẹ́hìndé Olúpọ̀nà, Pashington Obeng, Adam Michael McGee, John Grim, Vincent Stanzione, Wendy Doniger, Vijaya Nagarajan, Lauren Talalay, Gregory Nagy, Douglas Frame, James Skedros, Oktor Skjærvø, Gregory Riley, Charles Stang, Stephen Mitchell, Miranda Aldhouse-Green, Joseph Garrity, and Philip Garrity. They have been not only supernaturally patient, but also dedicated in their commitment to the research, writing, and comparative revision of their work in light of the other chapters. Every chapter in this book is unique, yet each multiply resonates with the others, often at startling junctures. The contributors to *Gemini* have what Moshe Halbertal calls "a shared biography." From the time of the book's inception in three successive panels sponsored by the Comparative Religions Section at the annual meetings of the American Academy of Religion, to the date of its publication, two contributors—Vincent Stanzione and Charles Stang—wrote entire books inspired by their chapters, happily requiring them to footnote themselves in the pages that follow.[1,2] In particular I am indebted to Jacob Olúpọ̀nà, who lost his twin brother Isaac when they were both only seven years old. His brilliant account of that loss and the yearning that ensued, and of Ìbejì in the Yorùbá tradition, treated in depth for *Gemini* for the first time in his extensive body of work, generated some of the book's most important comparative themes.

Phil Garrity was a student in one of two seminars I taught at Harvard Divinity School on twinship in 2012 and 2016, and through him I met his brother Joe, creator of the 2016 short film *Twinsburg* that is the centerpiece of their jointly written chapter, the coda to *Gemini*, "Epilogue: Dialogue." The graduate and undergraduate students who participated in these seminars—many of them twins, their missing doubles neither present nor entirely absent—thought creatively, wrote rigorously, and shared openly about twinship in our discussions. Of these, Eric Jarrard who is now my colleague at Wellesley College, Ayodeji Ogunnaike now at Bowdoin College, Jason Smith now at Mercer University, and Funlayo Wood-Menzies recently at the University of

California at Santa Barbara Santa Barbara, later joined by Kyrah Malika Daniels now at Emory University, have kept alive my engagement with the topic of twinship in sacred history and religious practice. The work of William Viney at the University of London continues to inspire me, and I was delighted to set *Gemini* in conversation with his recent book *Twins: Superstitions and Marvels, Fantasies and Experiments*.[3]

Gregory Nagy heroically read, proofread, and offered invaluable criticism on the introduction and my own chapter on Achilles's immortal twin horses. Without complaint, he set aside his own work to do this, and I will always remember his kindness, encouragement, and patient intervention.

Of my many companions in the life-story of *Gemini*, one shines brightest: the editor with whom I began this work, Alex Wright,[4] former Executive Editor at I.B. Tauris, Ltd., the book's original publishing house, came under the wing. Alex was enthusiastic about the concept of the book from its genesis, supporting it at every turn. He immediately asked for a title change; startled, I agreed. *The Mirror of Twinship* became *Gemini and the Sacred*. Through our many conversations over the years, Alex has become a true friend. Although he has moved on to become Head of Humanities & Senior Executive Publisher at Cambridge University Press, his angelic, unswerving loyalty strengthened me. Never complaining, he is the reason I was able to persist and "never give up," even if Churchill didn't say it.

After I.B. Tauris came under the wing of Bloomsbury Academic Publishers in 2019, some smiling fortune brought us Publisher Lalle Pursglove. She offered nothing but encouragement, backlit by her own keen interest in the topic. When the Garrity twins' searing "Epilogue" was complete, I sent the chapter to her to read, just because I thought she would find it fascinating. And she read it—and did. What editor, even an academic one, takes the time to do that now? Though her Oxford days are now past, Lalle remains an engaged independent scholar of history, religion, and literature, a passion for which no forced attention to the bottom line has robbed her. In the home stretch of *Gemini,* Lalle and I spoke over Zoom and many emails about new motherhood (hers), childhood memories of moors and tors and bluebells (mine, from when Devon was still Devonshire), and the uncanny bond between twins: my brother's children; and one of her closest friends and that friend's twin sister, now separated by an ocean. As progress on the book moved like a snail and deadlines melted in the blast furnace of the life-threatening, decade-long illness of one of my own children, my anxiety about the fate of *Gemini* became chronic guilt and something like despair. Lalle, however, breathed calm and wisdom. Throughout the soul-crushing year of 2020 and up to the nearly fireless Nowruz of 2021, she neither scolded nor threatened; a good thing, else *Gemini and the Sacred* might have been stillborn. I owe a special debt to Lily McMahon, Editorial Assistant at Bloomsbury, whose skillful oversight was invaluable throughout the last stages of production and to Megan Jones, Production Editor, and her successor Elizabeth Kellingley, both knowledgable and kind voices of reason. Publisher Stuart Hay took over for Lalle during her leave and shepherded *Gemini*, a complex project, through to its final publication. Venkat Perla Ramesh at Deanta Global Publishing Services in Chennai was the soul of patience as he oversaw a volume of nineteen chapters with myriad authors, editors, languages, fonts, diacriticals, and corrections. Matippiṟkuriyatu Venkat! I cannot thank them enough.

Thanks to Faculty Support/Team Leader Jennifer Conforti at Harvard Divinity School for her help with administrative and financial matters related to *Gemini*. Matthew Rogan offered expert assistance in acquiring illustrations and permissions from museum collections from London to Boston to Oklahoma to Queensland, a task he interwove with his demanding position as Curatorial Assistant for Special Exhibitions and Publications in the Division of Asian and Mediterranean Art at the Harvard Art Museums. I am indebted to the Office of the Academic Dean at Harvard Divinity School for a special grant to support the publication of the splendid color plates that illustrate this volume.

The love of my kind husband Bruce, my radiant, funny daughters Christina and Rosemary, and our weird and wonderful dogs Shine, Pippi, Mollie, and Jax sustained me throughout this lengthy project.

The wellspring of my interest in twins comes from my role as the aunt of my brother Geoffrey and sister-in-law Karen's children, identical twins Lee and Caitlyn. From their birth they were both joy and enigma to our family, who had at the time no history of twins, and in hindsight almost no understanding of them. Their parents and all of us learned in the fire. Loving and caring for them in their "distributed personhood" made them more familiar and yet also at the same time more confounding with each passing year. The enigma that was "our" twins eventually led me to begin *Gemini and the Sacred*, as I kept pulling on the thread of twinship through the labyrinth. What I discovered was that much of what we found uncanny and unclassifiable about Lee and Caitlyn was not personal but transpersonal: twinship has always been a preoccupation of religion, sacred history, orature, folklore, mythology, and iconography. But to "our" two, twinship was their *habitus*: nothing anomalous, except by contrast with everything that surrounded them. "I think about Lee all the time," Caitlyn said to me recently. "But I don't think about being a twin all the time." Lee lives a thousand miles away from their twin sister and has for years. Such "all the time" awareness of a sibling is in fact a defining trait of twinship. We were theirs more than they were ours, because they knew our world, plus their own—a world of only two that we barely knew at all.

Thank you, Lee and Caitlyn, for this journey, and for your willingness to share your feelings about it as you each evolved. I hope this book will remind you of the laughter we three shared long ago, "dancing round in a ring."

Notes

1 Vincent Stanzione, "Translating the Mayan Popol Wuj," *ReVista* 20, no. 2 (2021), 3.9.21. https://revista.drclas.harvard.edu/translating-the-maya-popol-wuj/. Accessed 5.29.22.
2 Charles M. Stang, *Our Divine Double* (Cambridge, MA: Harvard University Press, 2016). It should also be noted that original material presented at the first AAR panel by historian of religion Henry John Walker appeared in his *The Twin Horse Gods: The Dioskouroi in Mythologies of the Ancient World* (I.B. Tauris, Ltd., 2015), a book that has been of great value to the editor.
3 William Viney, *Twins: Superstitions and Marvels, Fantasies and Experiments* (London: Reaktion Books, 2021).
4 During the *Gemini* journey, Alex Wright also wrote and published *Exploring Doubt: Landscapes of Loss and Longing* (London: Darton, Longman, and Todd, 2016; repr. Minneapolis: Augsburg, 2020).

1

A Mirror

Reflecting on *Gemini and the Sacred*

♊

Kimberley C. Patton

Starbirth in Gemini

In the second green season of Gemini, in the wake of the ghastly Upside Down that was 2020—a "twinned" calendar year of vast misery and few blessings—a new collection on the theme of twinship in religion, myth, and lived experience may come at the right time. At the summer solstice in 2021 and then again in 2022, the sun moved westward—in our line of sight—from the constellation Taurus to stand in front of Gemini. Anchored by two bright stars that appear quite close in the Northern night sky, Gemini is one of the twelve constellations through which the sun traveled each

Figure 1.1 Zodiac mosaic, Beit Alpha Synagogue. Beit She'an Valley, sixth century CE, N. Israel. Detail: Gemini (*teomim*). Courtesy Israel Antiquities Authority.

Figure 1.2 "Gemini" (*al-Jawzā'*) from *Kitāb al-Bulhān* ("Book of Wonders"), Ms. Bodl. Or. 133, fol. 5b, *c.* 1400 CE. Compiled by Abd al-Ḥasan Al-Iṣfāhānī. By permission of the Bodleian Library Oxford.

year when the tropical zodiac was first developed in Western astrology.[1] The stars are the heads of two imagined star-bodies that clasp hands, joined by a single bright but "variable" star known as Propus or Eta Geminorum, a triple star 380 light-years from Earth.

Of the eighty-five visible stars that make up the asterism Gemini ("twins" in Latin), Pollux is the brightest. It is a giant star of orange hue, thirty-four light-years from Earth, with an orbiting extrasolar planet (β Geminorum in the 1603 *Uranometria* of Johann Bayer). The blue-white Castor (α Geminorum), second brightest, is a system of six stars, fifty-two light-years away. The pulsar star Geminga is part of Gemini. Every December a major meteor shower known as "the Geminids" from the rock asteroid 3200 Phaethon, one of Gemini's minor stars, brightens the darkness. On March 8, 2021, as the coronavirus washed the globe in death and the fear of death, the orbiting Hubble Telescope sent back a photo, which NASA called "a beautiful stellar nursery located in the constellation of Gemini (The Twins). At the centre . . . , a massive star is forming and blasting cavities through the clouds with a pair of powerful jets, extending to the top right and bottom left of the image. Light from this star is mostly escaping and reaching us by illuminating these cavities, like a lighthouse piercing through the storm clouds."[2] On earth, the twin giant telescopes (8.1 m.) under the auspices of the National Science Foundation and its counterparts in Canada, Chile, Brazil, and Argentina—Gemini North on Mauna Kea, Hawaii, and Gemini South in Cerro Pachón, Chile—comprise the Gemini Observatory. Apart from two areas near the celestial poles, they can survey the entire sky. The Gemini still generate.

In many parts of the ancient Mediterranean, the star-brothers were named after Leda's sons, the Argonaut heroes Kastor (Castor), whom Homer calls "breaker of horses," and Polydeukes (Pollux), "strong boxer."[3] The *Iliad* knows the brothers as already dead and buried at Therapne in Sparta by the time of the Trojan War.[4] In the *Odyssey*, Odysseus sees them both in Hades, sons of the king Tyndareos, to whom Leda "bore two strong-hearted children" (κρατερόφρονε γείνατο παῖδε); the use of the long-obsolete dual number in Greek reminded the hearer of their double birth and twinned nature.[5] They are miraculously both alive one day and both dead the next.[6] As Pindar centuries later describes their eschatology in *Nemean Ode* 10, they are half-brothers, of the mixed paternity common to hero twins.[7] Kastor is the son of a mortal father, and Polydeukes of an immortal one, the greatest: "Changing in succession, they spend one day with their dear father Zeus, the other deep under the earth in the hollows of Therapna, as they fulfill an equal fate, because Polydeu[k]es chose that life rather than being wholly divine and living in heaven, when [K]astor was killed in war [or: battle]."[8] Gregory Nagy calls this a "mystical deal" that complicates the original pure "counterbalancing of absolute immortality with absolute mortality," through this admixture creating a path for them both to become gods. But in votive inscriptions as early as the sixth century BCE and on into Late Antiquity, Castor and Pollux were called "Dioskouroi": "sons of Zeus."[9] "Saviors of men" in their afterlife, like their Vedic cousins the Aśvins who were horse-riding sky-doctors, the Dioskouroi rescued sailors in distress, rushing "through the air on dark wings,/and at once they stop the blasts of the dreadful storm-winds,/ . . . beautiful signs to sailors from their trouble."[10] They would descend in the form of eerie twin lights, later called St. Elmo's fire in medieval

Christian times, playing on the masts and spars of ships as they pitched in night-storms at sea—the visit of only one light, called "Helen," appropriately spelled disaster.[11] In Acts 28:11, four centuries after the probable date of their *Homeric Hymn*, we read that Paul sailed to Rome on a ship they protected: "Three months later we set sail on a ship that had wintered at the island, an Alexandrian ship with the Twin Brothers as its figurehead."[12]

The brother heroes were especially revered in Rome, where their cult spread from Magna Graecia. They were enshrined early in the history of the new Roman Republic in a tall west-facing temple in the Forum built by the consul Aulus Postumius Albus Regillensis and dedicated by his son in 484 BCE.[13] The dictator had promised Castor and Pollux this cultic home in exchange for their help in achieving victory over Lucius Tarquinius Superbus, the last king of Rome, at the Battle of Lake Regillus in 495–6 BCE. The Twins mysteriously appeared as *equites* among Aulus Postumius's troops to fight, and then were seen watering their horses at the healing Spring of Juturna as they rode through the Forum to announce the victory. In a parade of Roman cavalry held annually thereafter on the Ides of July, two young men rode white horses in tandem as the Dioskouroi. The divine pair were assimilated to Caesar Augustus's two sons Gaius and Lucius, then after their deaths, to Tiberius and his brother Drusus.

In Rome, the principal stars of Gemini were also known as Romulus and Remus; in Arabia, as twin goats; in ancient Egypt, as twin peacocks—or the older and younger Horus. In Northern Babylonia, whose constellations were adopted and Hellenized by the Greeks, they had been called "the Great Twins" (MAŠ.TAB.BA.GAL.GAL), perhaps as far back as the Bronze Age. Originally both were minor gods of death: Lugal-irra, "The Mighty King," and Meslamtaea, "the One who Has Arisen." They are believed to have been absorbed by the Old Babylonian underworld god Nergal as two of his names: dual dimensions of one infernal deity. During the neo-Assyrian period in Kisiga, which was their cultic stronghold, their figurines were buried on either side of doors and gateways. The first millennium series of incantations *Maqlû* describes the pair as "guard-gods who tear out the heart and compress the kidneys."[14] The sibling stars in the Babylonian night sky stood neither for the salvation of mortals nor for any remedy of their afflictions, but for the opposite: the fierce, annihilating curse of mortality.

Perpetual Entanglement

Just as the stick star figures of the constellation Gemini were thought to clasp hands at one marked point—the star Propus—so their particular iconography, and that of many other sacred twinned pairs, has always shown their interlocking being. In their homeland of Sparta, the Dioskouroi were venerated in the form of the aniconic *dókana*, two wooden posts spanned by two crossbeams, which Plutarch called a "common and indivisible . . . offering," an appropriate emblem of brotherly love.[15] The *dókana* was a dual symbol whose religious power derived from how it joined two parallel singletons and made them into a whole exponentially stronger than its parts. Like twinship, it was not a single solid mass. It comprised both space and the fixed double span of that space. Both were fundamental to how it "worked" as a sign of the Dioskouroi.

A renowned sixth century CE mosaic centrally placed in the floor of the Beit Alpha Synagogue in Northern Israel offers another striking example of such connectedness. A zodiac encircles a solar figure, the frontal-facing driver of a quadriga [Plate 1]. One of several similar programs from the Late Antique period, these synagogue zodiacs still challenge historians of Late Antique Judaism, their cosmology located somewhere between the Hellenization of the Galilee and *hekhalot* mysticism.[16] In the Beit Alpha one, the sign of Gemini is represented as a pair of twins (*teomim*): identified, like the other signs, by their Hebrew inscription set in tesserae: תאומים. At first glance they look like a single-bodied, two-headed individual, belonging to the region's ancient arc of cryptic doubles discussed by Lauren Talalay in her chapter in this volume.[17] A closer look reveals the pair's differently colored hemmed tunics and eight limbs: the Gemini are two separate people, but only barely, and the artist has gone out of her way to confuse. Their arms are thrown around one another's shoulders, each twin drawing the other so tight to his own body that they are deeply intertwined, hands appearing to rest on one other's hearts.

Eight hundred years later the Gemini (*al-Jawzā'* الجوزاء)[18] appear very differently posed, but just as entangled, in a spectacular late-fourteenth-century Islamic codex from Baghdad known as *Kitāb al-Bulhān* ("Book of Wonders" or "Book of Surprises"), now held in the Bodleian Library at Oxford [Pl. 3; Figure 1.2]. Compiled and possibly also illustrated by the polymath Abd al-Ḥasan Al-Iṣfāhānī during the reign of Jalayirid Sultan Ahmad, it teaches astrology, astronomy, geomancy, and other forms of divination.[19] One of a series of illuminated full pages, the Gemini are shown among the planets that surround their constellation in the night sky, while the planet that governs them, Mercury, looms nearby as an astronomer. He wears an emerald robe and holds a quadrant. The Gemini are shown in a seated, yogic position, *but with only two legs visible*; although their torsos are distinct, they are entirely fused. They seem to arise from one body. Their heads turn toward one another. Their mutual gaze appears unbreakable.

The persistently interlocking depiction of the sign of Gemini is reflected in its glyph, which, along with Virgo and Libra, is one of the only zodiacal signs not depicted by an animal. It resembles the Roman numeral 2: II. As in the *dókana*, two signs for the numeral "1" are joined together at the top and the bottom by transverse lines:[20]

$$\text{Ⅱ}$$

As will emerge from several of the chapters in this book, perhaps the most appropriate expression of this aspect of twinship may be the yoke, *zugón* [ζυγόν] in Greek: found in the Homeric lexicon of the chariot in the *Iliad* and resurfacing in Plato's *Phaedrus*, the apocryphal "Acts of Thomas," the *Cologne Mani Codex*, and the Irish epic cycles of Cú Chullain. One who is yoked to another is guaranteed never to be alone, but also never to escape the other, who is equally constrained to be so close.

The unusual relationship between twins—and those who are *made into twins* in myth or in life by mutually creating (or recognizing) the kind of relationship that twins have—entails a field of binding, symbiotic energy. This adds a third element to their two-ness. As a convergence—or incomplete differentiation—the "third" can be symbolized by images that merge two ordinarily separate individuals (human, animal, or magical creature) into a kind of dual singular. This can take the form of one body with two heads serenely gazing; two horses running beneath one yoke; or two Norman knights holding one shield, as on the cover of the volume, who stand for the sign of Gemini in the twelfth-century illuminated *Hunterian Psalter* [Cover; Pl. 2]). The relationality between twins can be represented as clasped hands merged into one star. It can range from a barely signaled resonance to a graphic depiction of intertwined bodies, as in the prehistoric cruciform figurines from Cyprus who wear one another, or the Attic cup tondo by Sosias from 500 BCE showing Achilles tenderly binding the wound of Patroklos. Even when twins are distinguished from one another in art, this is often achieved in a complementary, rather than a disjunctive, way (e.g., symmetrical clothing designs using the same colors reversed, as in the icon of Ss. Cosmas and Damian [Pl. 11; Figure 12.1]). This "third field" shown between twins is quasi-autonomous; it seems to arise from both of them, but at the same time to subsume and define each one. Both in how they construe themselves "in real life" and in how their lived realities have been mythologically "seen" and distilled, twins remain connected. But "connection" is not enough to describe the otherness of their bond. They are existentially braided, interwoven, or, shading darker, interlocked, entangled. In life they share experience; in sacred history, they also share fate. The best way to name this might be to bring to bear on twinship some of the dimensions implied by Thich Nat Hanh's word "interbeing."[21]

Taken as a whole, the eighteen studies in *Gemini and the Sacred* suggest that this resonant relationship itself, rather than the duality of twins—the mystique of their number: two, or their similar appearance—ultimately defines twinship. This widening of the categorical parameters is afforded by the twins found in these chapters who are not siblings, not carried by one mother, not born at one time. Twins inter-are. This is neither necessarily beneficial nor bad for them. But it is a given that always organizes their stories.

An Ideal State of Being

Divine twins often occupy themselves with the healing and repair of what mortals suffer and gods destroy—including even the wrecked sacrifice itself. In a Vedic story the gods fruitlessly try to make a Soma sacrifice without Makha's head. Frustrated, they demand of "the twin horse-gods," the Aśvins:

"You are doctors, put back the head of the sacrifice."
The two [Aśvins] said:
"Let us choose a favor. Let a cup be filled here for us also."
[The gods] filled the Aśvin cup for the two [Aśvins].

(Taittirīya Saṃhitā 6:4, 9).

The two [Aśvins] put back the head of the sacrifice; the head is the *Pravargya*.
When they [the gods] sacrificed with that sacrifice, including its head, they
   received all their wishes, they won the world of heaven."

                                                    (*Taittirīya Āranyaka* 5:1)[22]

Conceived by Saranyū with the sun god Surya while both were in the shape of horses
in the liminal forest, the solar twins' heritage is one of both power and exile. As divine
but socially marginalized physicians who heal the impure diseases of mortals and thus
by extension can "heal" the sacrifice, the Aśvins thereby leverage cultic recognition
for themselves from the distraught gods.[23] They restore not only the *Pravargya* but
also the efficacy of all sacrifice. They show a path forward for a human sacrificer to
re-capitate the Soma:

   If someone puts the *Pravargya*-pot on the fire, he puts back the head of the
      sacrifice.
   When he sacrifices with that sacrifice, including its head, he receives all his
      wishes, he wins the world of heaven.
   Therefore it seems to provide strength to the Aśvins; it is the *Pravargya.*
                                                    (*Taittirīya Āranyaka* 5: 6–7)[24]

The tradition of twin healers may arise from the idea that in the treatment of
disease or wounds, two are much more effective than one. It was then and is now a
highly desirable goal to double healing powers. But twins also afflict and wound,
including one another, like Jacob and Esau in Genesis, or battle to the death,
like Eteocles and Polyneices in Sophocles's *Antigone*. Beyond basic ambiguity,
beyond double vision, oscillation and paradox often mark twinship. The binaries of
linguistic structuralism, even when taken as complex relationships among formal
elements, cannot fully account for how twins inter-are. In sacred histories but also
in lived experience, twins inhabit multiple, at times contradictory, realms. They
strain the boundaries of what is expected, because they are each other's instigators.
They can pivot as one, wherever they are summoned, because they are each other's
accomplices. The positive air sign Gemini is said to preserve these characteristics
of strategic mutability, as do twins in mythological traditions, ritual practices, and
philosophical frameworks. As Wendy Doniger writes, "Of all the things made with
words, myths span the widest of human concerns, human paradoxes."[25] Outside of
myth, on earth, the twinned condition may be perceived with fascination, envy, or
unease by outsiders—in other words, as a mystery—but it is rarely perceived as
other than an ideal state by twins themselves.
   In his chapter in this book, Vincent Stanzione lifts up the regard in which twinship
is held for the Ki'che' Maya of Guatemala, through the long cord binding them to the
Twin Heroes of the *Popol Wuj*:

   It is a blessing to be a . . . twin who knows what one's twin longs for in life and
   can, together with her, him [or them], follow a twinned calling. . . . Twins have a
   great advantage over the rest of humanity, since their identical nature, emerging

from a shared womb, enables them to double up their efforts so as to bring their lives to fruition. According to Maya myth, it is a great gift to be born a twin—and if lacking that gift, one must listen to one's inner voice as if one had an inborn twin.[26]

Twins do not just double a singleton's powers, gifts, or troubles; they reduplicate these and amplify them, creating their own pleroma. They embody contestation, but even when that struggle has cosmic consequences, it takes place within a kind of hermetic seal. As in the ever-expanding adventures of the Twins of the Winnebago cycle *waikan*, twins keep widening their range. In "Epilogue: Dialogue," Joseph Garrity writes to his identical twin brother Philip,

> You were my terrible influence, and I was yours, but this grew into our greatest strength: boundless, leapfrogging curiosity. Taking one step further than the other, inventing and mutually defying boundaries, we mapped a vast territory. We asked foolish questions of our world and together, foolishly answered them. No single child could have deviated so far from common sense. We created and amplified our own rules, those foundational myths that were more convincing than anything that came afterwards in our lives.[27]

That élan, expanding up and outward, strains against the uncanny entanglement that begins for them in the womb and never ends. We now know that some bigeminal twins, like all mammalian mothers and fetuses, permanently exchange groups of cells called *microchimera* while in utero.[28] As they grow and negotiate the world together, they continue to co-create their original shared existence. This can be true to the point that twins, especially but not exclusively "identical" (monozygotic) twins, sometimes cannot psychologically or even physically separate as adults. The death of one is devastating for the other—the other who is both the self and not the self.[29]

Twins share an ideal love that transcends romance, a kinetic unity to which lovers can aspire but which they can never match. Of the Vodou Marasa, twin *lwa* (intermediary beings between Bondye ["Bon Dieu"] and humanity), Adam McGee observes,

> In [Edwidge] Danticat's *Breath, Eyes, Memory*, the Marasa as the perfect union between two bodies—because they share a soul—is contrasted with Sophie's mother's disappointing love affairs, which she hopes will achieve a similar union between lovers. She says, "When you love someone, you want him to be closer to you than your *Marassa*. Closer than your shadow. You want him to be your soul."[30]

But he never can be. Lovers can never be as close as twins, unless the inflamed power of what they share makes them into twins. But if that happens, the erotic distance that lovers need to maintain between themselves is lost. Their separate identities melt and fuse. Their love becomes something beneath and beyond love: what Gregory Nagy calls the "uncanny mix of intimacy and alienation that only twins will ever truly understand."[31]

Dangerous Twinship

For the mothers who conceive, carry, and bear them, the arrival of twins may not realize an ideal. Rather, it may cause deep ambivalence. In the traditional Yorùbá song cited by Jacob Kẹ́hìndé Olúpònà in the first chapter of this book, a woman asserts—and repeats—to herself, to her community, to the òrìṣà, that she is unafraid to become the mother of twins.[32]

Bí mo bí 'Bejì n ó gbe o, e o	If I have twins, I will care for them,
Bí mo bí 'Bejì n ó gbe o, e o	If I have twins, I will care for them,
Àyà mi ò jáá, ó ó ye,	I am not afraid, never,
Àyà mi ò já láti bí 'Bejì	I am not afraid to have twins
Bí mo bí 'Bejì n ó gbe o, e o.	If I have twins, I will care for them.[33]

Why would a potential future mother of two living children—a blessing and a sign of divine favor—sing a song like this? As Vijaya Nagarajan writes, in twinship there is "superabundance."[34] Just as potent is what Ugo Bianchi calls its "problematical nature," an equal through-line in *Gemini and the Sacred*.[35] Afusat Ganiyu and Ganiyatu Adesope are the sororal (dizygotic) daughters of Suliat Ogunjimi. In this photo taken in Afolabi Sotunde in Igbo Ora, Nigeria [Pl. 4; Figure 1.3], a town that has the highest rate of twin births in the world (45–50 sets per 1,000 annually)—a distinction attributed by the residents themselves to be a direct gift of God—their mother encircles and grounds them in her embrace, sustaining them in her gaze.[36]

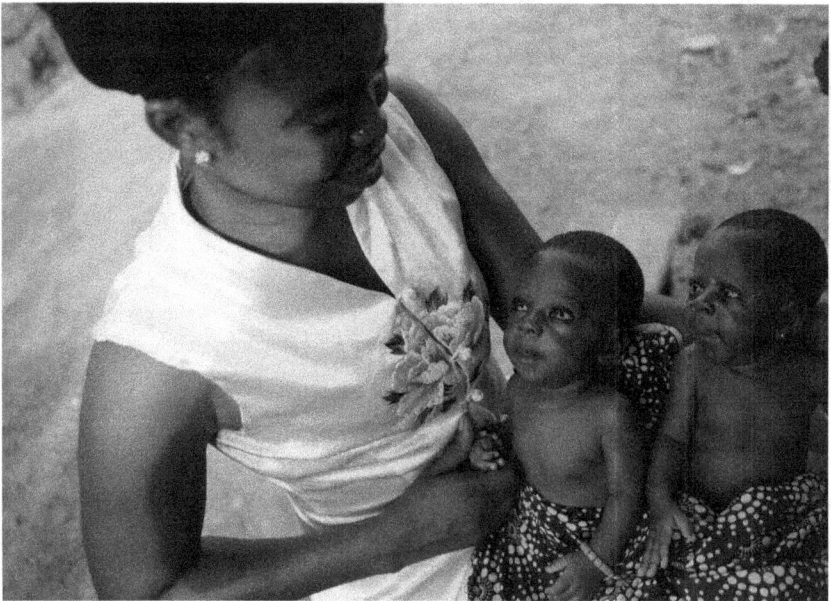

Figure 1.3 Suliat Ogunjimi holds sororal twins Afusat Ganiyu and Ganiyatu Adesope in Igbo Ora, Oyo State, Nigeria—April 3, 2019. Reuters/Afolabi Sotunde.

As the studies in this volume show, twins both mortal and immortal are invariably fused by, contained in, and defined by a third entity. The original "third" (or first) is the womb they shared, whether or not their mother raises them. If she must care for older children; if she lacks access to birth control; if she is afflicted by hunger, scarcity, domestic or civic violence, homelessness, postpartum depression, or mental illness; or if her community is nomadic, the advent of twins may signal not superabundance but an acute threat, making what had once been possible now impossible. One or both of the twins become debilitating to her.

Because of the commonplace use of in vitro fertilization in wealthier countries, twins and triplets seem to be everywhere now, whereas once they were rare. Medical re-evaluation of the abnormally high rate of multiple births resulting from intervention is a reminder that such births remain risky and therefore undesirable: not to be clinically normalized. Twins are often born prematurely, arriving smaller and weaker than single babies, and their mothers have more complications during childbirth.[37] Strangely, women who have twins are more likely to have single babies after birth that are heavier than average, hence more likely to survive. Twins may "prime the womb" and increase blood flow to it. But when women have a single baby preceding the birth of twins, they are *also* more likely to have heavier than average babies. Women who bear twins have a higher rate of a protein called IGF-1: "The protein, which circulates in the blood, can cause the ovaries to release multiple eggs, thus increasing the chance of twins. It also regulates how much a fetus grows during development."[38] Why did twinning evolve? Counterintuitively, bearing two children during the same pregnancy may never have been the evolutionary "goal" of human reproduction but rather the biologically weaker byproduct of an endocrinological condition that favors more viable siblings.

Myths and epics don't feature those robust infants who precede or follow twins, however. Instead, the preoccupation of tradition is twins. They are also the vehicle for expressing a vast range of social values, tensions, and ideologies. Rarely have twins been treated neutrally in any cultural context. The appearance of two human beings from the same womb when normally only one is expected can catalyze anxiety that can only be ritually resolved, including by infanticide; twins can ontologically link worlds that single children cannot, or embody signs, auspicious or suspicious. Twins may be allied with the celestial or animal realms. They are often construed as "extra-human." But these stories and functions can swing or flip, even within a single tradition, presenting challenges for comparative analysis. Twins can be allied with benign or malignant ethical poles, or both, depending on the circumstances. What seems to matter most to twins both legendary and biological, as I have said, is connection. Not who they are, not what they can do, but what they share and *whether or not they can stay connected*. The twin relationship is so fundamental as to be irreducible: it stands for nothing other than itself.

Craniopagus Siamese twins Krista and Tatiana Hogan, born in British Columbia in 2006 sharing a thalamus, nervous system, and the ability, among many, to see out of one another's eyes, should be a tragic story: they can never be surgically separated. Yet despite their heavily documented lives, their vibrant spirit breaks through any story about them. Krista and Tatiana, joined at the head, share a twinned connection that is medically pathological and socially anomalous; yet for them it is the opposite of tragedy: a story of inseparable connection that brings inexhaustible joy. Susan

Dominus's 2015 "The Mixed-Up Brothers of Bogotá" is about two sets of identical Colombian twins, one of each pair having been switched at birth at the Materno Infantil Hospital into families of an entirely different social class and environment. It should be a story of joy, recognition, and relief when after twenty-six years through a chance encounter the four young men discovered the truth and were able to meet one another.[39] Instead, the account of Jorge Enrique Bernal Castro, William Cañas Velasco, Carlos Alberto Bernal Castro, and Wilber Cañas Velasco is shot through with shock, pain, resentment, alienation, and a kind of grief that breaks the heart of their story's hearer in involuntary communion with those who lived through it. Even though the truth restores the "right sons to the right families," at least in knowledge, and reunites long-lost identical twins, Jorge's, William's, Carlos's, and Wilber's story is one of severed connection and ongoing relational rupture that can never be fully restored. "Rightness" in the world for twins is defined through realized relationship with one another, and all meaning proceeds from this.

Dioscurism Revisited

The heroic twinship of the Dioskouroi was so persistent a theme in the devotion of antiquity, especially crisis religion, as to become an eponymous, quasi-universal category in the Western study of mythology. "Dioscurism" was a term coined by the English biblical scholar J. Rendel Harris in his ambitious 1906 work *The Cult of the Heavenly Twins.* Harris postulated that the human response to twinship was always one of dread, so primordial that it

> may be described as the oldest religion in the world; a religion which is still extant in some of its simplest and most primitive forms, though, of course, it will very soon disappear. We have shown that in all parts of the world and all parts of history, there is a taboo of extraordinary force upon twin children and their mother. We have traced the modification of this taboo from its more cruel forms to a milder cult. We have shown how twin-asylums were formed, how the taboo was gradually restricted from the mother and the children to a single child, and how the belief arose that one of the children was of spirit-ancestry and not really normal. We found that at a later stage both children were credited with sky-parentage, and were known as Children of the Sky. . . . this is exactly the Greek belief, as disclosed by Castor and Polydeuces, the Children of the Sky-God.[40]

Along with Harris's unsurprisingly Eurocentric and racist depictions of modern African twin traditions that (wrongly) predicted their erasure, his assertion that "there are certain universal features shared by all twins in the mythical and religious views of every culture"[41] is symptomatic of that the comparative study of religion has been forced to confront in the past few decades. Harris claimed that his list of features were shared by twins in the traditions of *every* culture, including not only the evolution of their celestial paternity (ascribed at first to neither, then to only one of the pair, then finally to both, e.g., "sons of Zeus"), but their role as "sources of fertility" and rainmakers, at a later stage becoming "the healers of diseases, the great saviors of the distressed, the protectors . . . of sick persons, those that travel by land and water . . . they are the patrons of truthfulness, and punish perjury."[42] In other words, Harris derived the sacralization of twins in myth from the dread of twins born into living communities. He then mapped the Dioskouroi, a particular Indo-European pair of twins with Vedic and Indo-Iranian relatives, onto all cases of sacred twins throughout history.

Harris claimed to have traced the cult of the heavenly twins through Phoenicia and Mesopotamia, and ultimately to early Christian hagiography. This surfaced, Harris argued, in both the Western and Eastern churches; in the East, "twin religion" lay behind the veneration of saintly pairs such as Cosmas and Damian, Cyrus and John, Nearchus and Polyeuctes. As Henry Walker notes, part of Harris's agenda was to "unmask" the pagan sources of early Christianity: "The Calendar of the Christian Church is full of converted pairs of twins, of whom it is safe to say that hardly any are other than mythical."[43] But Harris's most radical claim concerned the twinship of Jesus: that he was worshipped along with his twin brother Judas in Edessa, and in Antioch with Thomas, replacing the Dioskouroi. The logic and habit of sacred twinship in the Greco-Roman world, North Africa, Mesopotamia, and the Levant required, he said, that a heavenly twin be provided for Christ, a singleton messiah—particularly one whose theology was rooted in divine paternity, mortal maternity, heavenly descent, incarnation, healing miracles, the salvation of humanity, and reascent to the heavenly father.

The forensics of Harris's "genealogy of all religions" show that he did not start with prehistoric evidence or even classical Mediterranean twinship and decide that it survived, thinly camouflaged, in Christian hagiography. Rather, as a biblical scholar renowned for his translation of the earliest known version of the Gospels on site at the Monastery of St. Catherine of Mt. Sinai, Harris's interest in the Dioskouroi and divine twinship began with a heterodox early Christian text that gave Jesus a twin. This was the *Acts of Thomas*, an early-third-century Christian novella concerning the travels of St. Thomas to India. The earliest versions, surviving in Greek (that most scholars think reflects the original Syriac) and in Syriac, show clear Encratic signs, purged in the later Syriac. Jesus and the Apostle Thomas Didymos "the twin," also named Judas, are called identical twins by a serpent, by a colt, and by Jesus himself, as Gregory Riley observes in his chapter: "In fact, Jesus is so like Thomas in appearance that he is mistaken for him; he must say, 'I am not Judas, who is also Thomas; I am his brother' [*Acts of Thomas*] (11)."[44] In this text we hear a twin responding to a common confusion caused by his resemblance to his sibling. He uses the words familiar to identical twins have had to use throughout history. But the speaker is Jesus, and startlingly, *the Lord is taken for his twin brother,* not vice versa.

It was apparently too much for Harris that the divine twinship found in the *Acts of Thomas* might have been sourced in early Christian gnostic theology—possibly with Indo-Iranian precedents and a roughly contemporaneous Manichaean analogue. He believed it had to have had a pagan backstory. He found this in the cult of the Dioskouroi, Castor and Pollux.

What drew Harris to the theme of "heavenly twins" in the first place? We know that he worked with identical Scottish twin sisters, Agnes Smith Lewis and Margaret Smith Gibson, learned independent scholars and intrepid white European explorers in the Middle East, in the rediscovery and translation of the oldest known manuscript of the Gospels from the Monastery of St. Catherine at Mt. Sinai. On Harris's advice, the sisters discovered in a small dark closet adjacent to the Archbishop's study—and with his permission—a set of Syriac manuscripts. One of these, later named the Sinaitic Palimpsest or Codex Sinaiticus Syriacus [Sinai Syriac ms. 30], was written over a fourth-century version of the Gospels that preserved an even earlier translation from the late second century CE: one in which the Book of Mark ended before the account of the Resurrection.[45] Unlike the Codex Sinaiticus discovered there in 1859, this text was not stolen from the monastery; Harris and the twin sisters would travel back to Sinai to photograph and transcribe it together, and their collaboration would be lifelong. Is it a coincidence that "primordial twinship" was the cynosure of Harris's most controversial work?

Harris's claims that heavenly twins were the universal key to the history of religions commanded respect for a century—and are a bane to scholars like Walker, who condemns his essentializing and universalism. In his 2015 study of "the twin horse-gods," the Aśvins and Dioskouroi, Walker blames Harris for having exaggerated a comparative theme to the degree that it has dominated analysis of any religious phenomenon in which twins appear, eclipsing other factors that may matter more. "According to many scholars who study the horse gods, the mere fact that they are twins explains everything about them."[46]

As a birth anomaly that juxtaposes compatibility alongside contrast and differen-tiation, even antagonism, twinship has figured prominently in both anthropology and mythography. Because white European and American anthropologists believed that twins, like animals, "are good to think," instantiating the most significant symbolic structures in a given society, they have been foregrounded in field research in indigenous African and Amerindian cultures. As medical anthropologist William Viney observes, "twins, much like the spirits that are said to possess them, are understood to the visible, manifest content of deeper, more latent structures of cultural meaning and social reproduction. The logic here is that, w[h]ere it was possible to find a prior cause for the classificatory anomalies that twins are understood to represent, then wider patterns and rationales of social organisation may become clearer."[47] In much colonialist anthropology, especially structuralist, twins have been seen as "the code-crackers."[48] This began with the work of Claude Lévi-Strauss, who believed that cultural themes, including stories and myths about twins, manifested a universal code that could be seen in linguistic principles. In the interviews he gave in *Myth and Meaning*, Lévi-Strauss expounded on the human need for order: "since, after all, the human mind is only part of the universe, the need probably exists because there is some order in the universe and the universe is not a chaos."[49] Influenced by Hegelian thought, Lévi-Strauss held that mythology follows universal laws, always expressing binary oppositions whose tensions must lead toward a stereoscopic end—namely to resolve the problems of classification, privilege, and power that binaries create. In their encoded dualism, mythic twins bore this burden. Reflecting on twinship traditions among the Séliš-speaking peoples (Salish), Kwakwa̱ka'wakw (Kwakiutl), and other First Peoples of the Pacific Northwest treated in his *Mythologiques*, as well as the Algonquian (Algonkian)-speaking peoples' myth of the harelip, he asserted that twinship expressed notions of splitting (the bodily fluids or the entire womb of the mother; the lip of the hare: "he is not twins, but he is incipient twins"), oppositional polarity, and mediation. "In all American mythology, and we could say in mythology the world over, we have deities or supernaturals, who play the roles of intermediaries between the powers above and humanity below. . . we have . . .characters of the type of a Messiah; we have heavenly twins."[50] In African anthropology, the work of non-African E. E. Evans-Pritchard and Victor Turner continued to focus on "these interstitial beings," as Elijah Renne and Misty Bastian would later call them.[51] According to Evans-Pritchard, the Nuäär (Nuer) believe that infant twin children share one soul. They are the children of the Sky-god Kuoth (Kwoth): "birds."[52] Developing Arnold van Gennep's paradigm of separation, liminality, and re-incorporation in the life cycle, Turner published a study of Ndembu twin ritual as a chapter in his *The Ritual Process: Structure and Anti-Structure.*[53] He argued that the contested occupation of one kinship niche by two children always requires ritual resolution—by treating two as one ritual entity, or made into one through infanticide:

> There is a classificatory assumption that human beings bear only one child at a time and that there is only one slot for them to occupy in the various groups articulated by kinship which that one child enters by birth. Sibling order is another important factor; older siblings exert certain rights over junior siblings . . . Yet twinship presents the paradoxes that *what is physically double is structurally single and what is mystically one is empirically two.*[54]

In a book published in May of 2021, a month before research concluded on this one, William Viney—himself an identical twin—criticizes something similar in popular culture. Whatever twins do, whatever happens to them, tends to be mystified, bathed in an aura of the uncanny that is reflexively produced by the category itself:

> The events themselves are ordinary or mundane, but the involvement of twins makes the mundane magical. The lives of twins are subject to a kind of amplified significance. They are special not simply for what they do or say but for what they are taken to be. The things that twins do or say are become tangled up in what their twinship represents, creating a self-fulfilling loop that keeps the world of media revolving.[55]

Like all human beings deemed anomalous, twins bear the projections of those around them; they are the focus of many fields: not only religion and mythology, but also anthropology, developmental psychology, and genetics.[56] Particularly through the impulse to compare twins—to identify what they share and what differentiates them—it somehow seems possible to determine what is essential and non-contingent about being human. For divine twins, the *agōn* of comparison is also their matrix.

Comparative Challenges

Although these eighteen studies span 8,000 years, the aspiration of *Gemini and the Sacred* is not to provide an exhaustive history of twinship in religion and myth. That has been a goal of earlier works, starting with Harris's *The Cult of the Heavenly Twins,* and it will certainly be tried again. Instead, each one of the eighteen chapters dives deep into a tradition in which twins—defined and treated as such within their respective contexts—are lionized: where their presence has been so central as to saturate both collective memory and future thought. Some chapters, such as Gregory Nagy's and Douglas Frame's, or Joseph Garrity's and Philip Garrity's, themselves record a consciously twinned dialogue. Many of the authors discussed their research in person at successive panels held at three annual meetings of the American Academy of Religion. They also read one another's chapters early on in the book's development, and again at a later stage before submission. Highly particular, culturally inflected dimensions of twinship surface in each chapter. But so do striking crosscurrents and resonances among twin traditions. What emerges in this collection is far from an essentialized list of features common to all sacred twins, as J. Rendel Harris proposed.[57] But neither does the juxtaposition of these various essays fail to support robust comparative analysis. Once the problematic history of the comparative enterprise is acknowledged, recurrent patterns nevertheless remain, and they are hard to ignore. It is not enough to attribute them to the arbitrary, subjective choices of the comparative scholar, as J. Z. Smith seemed to in "In Comparison a Magic Dwells."[58]

Methodologically, *Gemini* is inspired by the approach of Susan Starr Sered in her *Priestess, Mother, Sacred Sister: Religions Dominated by Women.*[59] In this study, remarkable for its intellectual humility, the author, an anthropologist of religion, closely analyzes twelve traditions in which "women . . . have control over their religious lives—women who lead or join women's religions (as opposed to women who have some freedom to maneuver within men's religious structures)."[60] In her analysis of "women's own concerns, ideas, and rituals," Sered saw that some themes consistently recurred, even if they were refracted very differently from case to case, or were in some cases almost entirely sublimated. They were not, however, the ones she expected or perhaps even sought. "When women have opportunities to express their own religious ideas and rites, themes peripheral to men's lives emerge as central to women's religiosity."[61] Rather than religious autonomy or female empowerment, maternal metaphors and concerns for the safety and well-being of children tend to dominate in genuinely female-controlled traditions. This is a finding that many feminist thinkers might find problematic. Yet Sered squarely faces what her research reveals: Successful motherhood seems to be the root metaphor and goal of most women's religions, even those that have been traditionally marked by rules of celibacy and transcendentalizing theologies.[62]

The authors in *Gemini and the Sacred* similarly challenge some of the tropes that have overlain twins in past studies, while validating and building on others. I expected to find two-ness emerge as a common theme in twin traditions, along with its range of expressions: harmony, contestation, and the chronic interplay between them, including dominance and corollary recessiveness. But the lack of much cultural elaboration around multiple births that are not *two* seemed strange, not entirely explicable by the infrequency of the birth of triplets or quadruplets; attention to multiple births is usually back-burnered or otherwise subsumed under the rubric of twinship. The ways in which biological twinship chronically influences cultural themes of sacred twinship—and vice versa—were also unsurprising, although I was impressed by the extent to which this was the case.

What *did* surprise me was the way in which twins are defined both in sacred history and in lived experience not so much by their shared, split, doubled, or mirroring identities, i.e. by the number "two," *as by the complex relationship between them.* Sered was honest enough to admit her surprise at how powerfully women's identities as *mothers*, literal or metaphorical, determined the applied theologies of religious groups that women controlled. In working on this volume, I came to change my own views of twins in myth and religion—and of the living twins I knew—as doppelgängers of one another. I came to see the magnetic, charged "space between" twins as what orients them to one another, to their purpose, and to their environment. This reflexive energy differs from what exists between any other beings, except for mother and child. Whether hostile or deeply bonded—or any degree between these modes—twins are bound up with one another. When the non-twinned world reacts oddly to twins, making them culture heroes, heavenly ambassadors, or dangerous threats, it reacts to this force field, interpreting it as a matter of anomalous number—because in Turner's words "what is mystically one is empirically two." But no matter the angle of approach, *the relationality of twins matters most of all.* Stories about them build out from this and continually circle back to it; their lived experience grows out of their relationality and creates the social world they inhabit. This is what I have learned from *Gemini and the Sacred*, and what surprised me as a singleton who thought I had a decent understanding of twinship.

Who Counts as Twins?

"Twins" can be defined in myriad ways. "Twinship" is a fluid taxon, and as Viney notes, its definition has not been historically stable, but has been pressed into service by the preoccupations of the day. Twins are defined and constrained by ideas of who they are. Twins themselves however, in turn, define these ideas: "knowledge is made with twins."[63]

Using any category as a lens for the cross-cultural study of religious phenomena is inescapably problematic. This is true for all the reasons that have been rehearsed—and responded to—with such energy over the past several decades in the field of the comparative study of religion.[64] Jettisoning the use of categories altogether, however, is equally problematic, and, instead of dissolving hegemony, can make it worse. Without category formation no complex thought or communication is possible; no language can evolve. The steps of responsible comparison proposed by Jonathan Z. Smith in his "Epilogue" to *A Magic Still Dwells: Comparative Religion in the Postmodern Age* offer a methodological path forward: comparison, rectification, and redescription, resulting in theorization. This must be a process that "churns" and is never static. Although Oliver Freiberger, Barbara Holdrege, and others endorse the comparative goal of "illumination" as over and against taxonomy, it is empirically impossible to avoid taxonomy when considering multiple data gathered from multiple sources. Nor perhaps is it even desirable. Rather, a "working taxonomy" is needed with each new study, as new comparanda arise, interrogating, modulating, rectifying or even potentially shredding the original taxon.

A further theoretical challenge arises in the comparative religious study of what is already by its nature inherently comparative—twinship. Smith wrote that "it is axiomatic that comparison is never a matter of identity. Comparison requires difference as the grounds of its being interesting, and a methodological manipulation of that difference to achieve some stated cognitive end."[65] This statement itself reveals the preoccupation of the fields of both religion and anthropology with alterity; ironically, the more we are able to recognize how we produce "otherness" in our thinking and behavior, the more we seem unable to stop. Especially at a time in history when corporately exported "globalism" is being countered by the assertion of particular identities, especially historically silenced ones, as well as by tribalism, polarization, fragmentation, and disintegration, is Smith right? Why *is* difference the grounds of what is interesting? Explicating identity or sameness arguably pose the greater and more interesting challenge. *Twins are always both the same and different.* Since most forms of twinship entail both life-nourishing similarity—to the point of interchangeability—and the kind of heart-tearing, kidney-compressing difference wrought by Lugal-irra and Meslamtaea, the task of considering twinship comparatively itself requires a degree of analytical reflexivity. Effective interpretation requires respect for the hall of facing mirrors that is twinship.

Who counts as twins? Junajpu and of the *Popul Wuj* are clearly twins, both born at the same time when the skull of Jun Junapu spit from a calabash tree into the palm of Blood Maiden in the underworld, Xibalba; but so were the orphaned Nabeysil (a Tz'utujil Maya rain-, cloud-, and mist-shaman well known to Vincent Stanzione) and his younger brother Salvador, a Deer-Jaguar companion, performing traditional Mayan dances in the Western Highlands of Guatemala "to bring the Sky's gifts to the Earth." Although not born at the same time, they lived and spoke as one until they succumbed to religious persecution, alcohol, and despair, and were un-twinned by the annihilation of one of them. Jacob Kẹhìndé and Isaac Táyéwò Olúpọnà of Òkè-Igbó were clearly twins, born of the same mother at the same time, but so were Achilles and Patroklos, the latter not related to the former by blood, but nevertheless destined to die in his stolen armor as his ritual substitute (*therapōn* (Greek)/*tarpanalli* (Hittite). Many other twins emerge from these studies whose biological twinship is ambiguous or else never given, but whom religious tradition understands as such: in early Christianity, Jesus, the Incarnate Logos and the apostle Thomas ("twin" in Aramaic, "who is called Didymos" ['twin' in Greek]); in the Indo-Iranian tradition, Gaiia Marətān, a cosmic fetus *who is twinned with his own placenta*; in the Old Norse tradition, Huginn and Munnin, who are ravens but have the names of abstract concepts, "Thought" and "Memory," and whom the shaman-god Óðinn dispatches each day to encircle Midgard and bring back news, enriching their keeper in wisdom and knowledge.

Who counts as twins? Twins are not copies or clones.[66] Yet in stories of conscious doubling, such as those told about Saṃjñā/Saraṇyū, twinship is attributed to the unhappy wife and the copy *of herself* that she creates to escape her marriage to the "too-hot" sun god Sūrya. The "real," self-occulting wife who is exiled to the forest in the form of a mare and the simulacrum, Chhaya ("shadow" or "reflection"), who is thrust into a domestic prison she never chose, are united in multiple versions of the stories—and in centuries of votive art—that make them both the consorts of Sūrya. As is so often the case in which twinship itself reduplicates, Saraṇyū herself has a twin brother, the god Triśiras, and is the mother of two sets of twins: Yama (death) and Yami (a river goddess) and then, in the form of a mare, the great Aśvins themselves. In *Splitting the Difference*, Wendy Doniger brilliantly exegetes this history of this tradition. In *Gemini and the Sacred*, commenting on Doniger's observation that the more co-wives Saraṇyū accumulates, the more she disappears,[67] Vijaya Nagarajan notes that self-splitting always constrains the integrity of the individual woman, even as it offers her social cover for escaping. "So the act of this doubling, though enabling her agency, initially, also acts as a brake to her intrinsic powers . . . from the beginning that there is an overlap between the categories of twin-ness and doubling, or even a kind of *shadowing of the main individual identity that is created by the very existence of the doubled version of the self.*"[68]

Especially germane to this book, Viney's interdisciplinary work argues from the outset that the conception of who "twins" are, or what constitutes "twinship" cannot be successfully essentialized throughout human history nor even across contiguous cultures. In a sense, "twins" are created, not born, within the stellar nursery of their own particular cultural constellation. Particular ideologies of "twinship" are mapped onto them, and those facets of their experience that fail to enact the archetype are often subtly or overtly suppressed. The degree to which twins double or mirror one another, the resonance or antagonism between them, whether they attract gifts for their families and communities or everlasting trouble—these psychosocial modes are determined by whatever is attributed to them, added on by the non-twinned world through which they move. And that "add," as we know, can vary radically depending on cultural situation, which is always infused with particular myths that have hardened into ideologies.

A recent work in twin studies exemplifies this. Should the "idea" of twins be construed as an exteriorization of the self, a living mirror for which everyone born alone secretly yearns? Developmental psychologist Vivienne Lewin suggests just this in her 2018 *The Twin Enigma*:

> There are . . . particular qualities that we project onto twins because of what twins represent to each of us at a deep unconscious level, psychically.. . . The extraordinary intimacy and closeness between twins represent the special factors in twin relationships that are highly prized by twins, and also by the parents of twins. Singletons envy this "special factor" as they perceive that twins have something exciting that they do not have, *and that we all long for.*[69]

The idea that a twin incarnates an *imago* of the self, in other words, that a twin is a ready-made soulmate, may seem natural to a Western reader, particularly a white European, Canadian, or American one. But this view may not be universally applicable to sacred twinship. It could instead reflect an individual-focused culture whose extreme pole is narcissism, refracted in the spheres of education, psychology, technology, sports, entertainment, the arts, the legal system, and politics, and publicly exacerbated throughout life at every stage by social media. On May 21, 2021, deep into the arc of the pandemic and the fervent hope for its end in mass vaccination, the late-night South African comedian Trevor Noah did a feature on "Zoom dysmorphia," the documented increase in negative body-image among the users of virtual meeting platforms caused by the unnatural mandate of *staring at oneself,* without relief, for so many hours.[70] "Zoom shouldn't make you feel bad about your looks. It should make you feel bad about your dirty-ass living room. But you have to remember, people, that this is a new phenomenon that we're dealing with. Humans didn't evolve to see their own faces all the time. That's not normal. I mean, except for twins. I guess. But they don't count, they're freaks! *There's like another one of you? What?*"[71]

This view of twinship, then, sees the twin as representing the "perfect best friend" who, like a living selfie, reflects one back to oneself. Lewin believes that is why people often ask whether young twins are identical, even when they are clearly not. But a twin is not created by flipping the black mirror; rather, she materializes in real space and time. Hence the ambivalence about twins as both ideals and "freaks." The twin as an exteriorization of the curated self, so perfectly suited to the present technophiliac age, is not the only one, nor even the definitive one cross-culturally.

Lewin herself finds such projections highly problematic, and is at pains to emphasize the differences between all pairs of twins, even identical twins: "I believe that no two people are identical, not even monozygotic (so-called 'identical' twins). To believe that they are identical feeds our phantasies about finding twin souls and is designed to avoid recognition of twins' separatenesses and differences, whatever the genetic make-up of the twins."[72] She cites the research showing that monozygotic and dizygotic twins may have a variety of different configurations of placental and umbilical configurations, and that even "monozygotic twins are genetically different in some aspects, despite having come from the same fertilized egg and the fact that most are very similar in appearance."[73] This has been dramatically borne out in an Icelandic study of 381 sets of identical twins published at the beginning of 2021 in *Nature Genetics*, which shows that genetic mutations can occur in one of two monozygotic twins very early in their development, as or even "before embryos form from the mass of cells inside the blastocyst, a structure that implants in the uterine wall. During this stage of development, this inner cell mass can split to form two separately developing embryos."[74] On average, twins studied differed by 5.2 average mutations, coming from "replication errors," although in some cases an identical twin descended entirely from one cell that had undergone an early mutation. The implications are significant, as coauthor Kári Stefánsson remarked in an interview, and directly challenges "the assumption that the differences between identical twins [are] always due to the environment."

> Take, for example, studies looking at autism in identical twins who are reared separately or apart. The classic interpretation of whatever differences [found] would be that the difference between them would be due to different environments. But before you can make that interpretation, you'd better make sure that one of them does not have a de novo mutation in an important gene that the other one does not. So this certainly places a new kind of burden on those who use identical twins to establish the separation between nature and nurture.[75]

Another cultural view sees twins as amplifying the range of one person, not simply replicating that one's features. As the Garrity brothers write, two together can travel further, create and evade more danger, solve problems more cleverly, dare and accomplish more than one alone. This is not unrelated to the first view, but there are subtle differences between the mirrored self and the doubled/dual individual. Such power surely describes the Apsaalooke (Crow) Lodge-boy and **Thrown-in-the-Spring**, who resurrect their own mother, or the Zuni twins Ahayuta and Matsilema who lead their people up from the underworld and kill the monsters they encounter, as John Grim recounts. In his chapter, Vincent Stanzione locates the origin of the Mayan hero-twins in the "psychospiritual phenomenon of the *coatl nahualli* or 'twinned double' among Mesoamericans." He argues that myths in which both the heroes and their rival were twinned "grew out of their chronic use of a 'double' or 'other' to overcome and destroy their enemies." In a landscape shared by prey and predator,

> it was imperative that one's "twin" was there to protect one's back while in quest for one's sustenance. In a world where human beings were shadowed or mirrored by their "twin," it was inevitable that the Maya should create sacred histories that reified the idea of the "twin" or *nahualli* on whom one could always count, especially in life-threatening danger. Thus it seems clear that the concept of the "double" or "twin" in Maya myth and religion is as much about an individual having an "other" as it is about two supernatural brothers who collaborate with one another in order to create a world of their own making and liking.[76]

On the flip side, twins may easily venture into trouble so deep that no one can rescue them; then, their heroic adventures become a cautionary tale:

> The errors of the ancestors are one of the principal ways of teaching in the *Popol Wuj*. You wouldn't want to do as the failed ancestors did and end up with your head sprouting out of a calabash tree in the underworld. The improvement of humanity is always founded on the mistakes of those who came before, something which the second set of twins takes to heart and puts into practice.[77]

As in an ancient theme reexamined by Prods Oktor Skjærvø in his chapter "Primordial Twins in Ancient Iranian Myth," the cosmic or heroic twin may be an evil or problematic "other" in relation to the self, rather than a beneficent, inspirational one. Their interlocking relationship is the plot of Nysien and Efnisien in the Welsh *Mabinogion*, treated by Miranda Aldhouse-Green in this book. The cosmogonic myth of the Haudenosaunee/Iroquois echoes this, as Grim shows, positing a primordial Good Twin (or Good Mind) and Evil Twin (or Bad Mind).[78] This old idea feeds the 2019 Jordan Peele horror film *Us*, where a family finds itself contending with its own doppelgängers. In the end, the mother's own "evil twin" is revealed to have long ago taken the place of her original self as a child, the latter choked in a funhouse hall of mirrors and dragged underground to a parallel world. There dwells in misery an entire race of government-created, twinned copies of every person in America, artficial beings called "The Tethereds" who plot their escape.[79] The horror of *Us*, showing Peele's genius, grows out of its unwillingness to let us be certain about which twin, the Good or the Evil one, is the (or our own) "authentic" self.

In the Yorùbà tradition, the birth of twins was believed, among other variant interpretations, to signify the uncanny, inappropriate birth of the spiritual twin of the earthly child: the divine double. As Ayodeji Ogunnaike remarks, however, that double was never meant to be pulled down: "They are dangerous because they are not supposed to be here.. . . . The only way to know which is which is if one of them dies, returning to her true home; but once there, she continually threatens to pull the other one back up with her."[80] The living twin is "stranded," like Fred Weasley, like Achilles, like Cú Chullain's horse Liath Macha when his chariot-mate Dub Sainglend breaks their shared yoke and flees back to the otherworldly pool of Linn Leith whence he came. If twins become separated from one another, as Douglas Frame has discussed, the "stranded twin" either absorbs the lost twin and takes on the attributes of both (like Nestor and Periklymenos, or arguably like Red and Adelaide in *Us*) or else tries to follow, but instead stalls the path of immortalization to which the Dioskouroi paved the way (like Herakles and Iphikles, or arguably like Voldemort and Harry Potter).

An ancient Near Eastern view on the other hand saw twinship as the *splitting of a self*, an archetypally different idea from the previous views of mirroring to reflect or doubling to augment. As explored in both Gregory Riley's and Charles Stang's chapters on Thomist Christian traditions, and in the revelations given to the prophet Mani, the yearned-for or epiphanic "other" may also be a spiritual rather than an earthly double, permanently living in heaven or a space that is the metaphysical counterpart of one's own, but constantly connected to it.[81] This is hypostasized in the prophet Mani's *syzygos*, his heavenly counterpart or companion in the Cologne Mani Codex, often translated as "Twin." The Greek invokes the state of being "yoked together": Συζυγία (σύν + ζυγία), as I consider at length in my chapter on the yoking and unyoking of the twin immortal horses of Achilles, Xanthos and Balios.[82] This is yet another example of the paradoxical nature of sacred twinship. Despite the joy of receiving "that most beautiful and greatest mirror-image of [myself] (*katoptron tou prosōpou mou*),"[83] Mani was also vulnerable thereafter, because without his *syzygos* he would be spiritually truncated. The idea of twins as "split selves" closely hews to what is known about the embryology of monozygotic twinship, whereby a solitary zygote, a eukaryotic cell formed through the process of yoking two gametes together—an ovum and a sperm—then divides asexually through mitosis to produce two identical fetal processes.

Who then counts as twins? Pace Harris, *Gemini and the Sacred* clearly shows that the biological reality of twinship, the "bottom-up," lived experience of twinship, was not a primordial starting point *away from which* later religiously elaborated pairs of twins evolved, but instead was *a condition always present* in the social reality of living bodies, continually informing sacred twinship and vice versa. Non-biologically related pairs who are presented as twins in anthropological, ritual, and mythological contexts are not "metaphors" of twins, somehow drawing from twinned experience and mapping this onto themselves like borrowed clothing. They, too, *are* twins.

Exceptional and Primordial

The chapters in *Gemini and the Sacred* additionally engage with the question posed by Ugo Bianchi in his "*Il dualismo come categoria*": What, if any, is the potential relationship in any given culture between "what is exceptional on earth"—that is, the biological event of twins—and the twins who animate myth and ritual? What meaning is attributed in a given context to the dual birth and "doubled" life of two living beings, and how is this culturally expressed? As a kind of afterthought concluding his overview of twins in religion, Bianchi highlights the interpretive challenge of exegeting the relationship between lived experience and sacred history—told about the past, yet "realer than real."

> Another issue concerning the twins motif in mythology concerns the direct impact of the physiological experience of twinship on the psychology of the relevant populations. According to Hultkrantz (1963), the 'superstitious' attention paid to the phenomenon of twinship could have been inspired by its appearance in the symbological language of myth. On the other hand, what is exceptional on earth could also be seen as primordial, so that the inauguration of the terrestrial (imperfect) status of humanity would have meant also the transition from (perfect) twinship to (imperfect singleness).. . .
>
> One could . . . venture that the typical ambivalence found in the disparities between twins (the second twin as bad, or simply as terrestrial, or, as part of a totality, destined for a sacrifice from which he is ultimately rescued . . .) is not unrelated to the problematical nature of physiological twinship, in which the different values of duality (completeness, but also distinction or even disparity) can put in motion a plurality of interpretations, both at the mythological and the ritual-sociological level.[84]

The apparent mandate to separate "twins in religion and mythology" from "twins in real life" (born to human mothers, raised in cultural specificity) in order to determine which sphere influenced which can only lead to interpretive trouble—trouble of the kind that Twins create and in which they revel. A "chicken and egg" problem is one that where neither of a pair can be determined to be the cause or the effect of the other. Bianchi nevertheless wonders whether the opposite could be true, that sacred twinship in a given culture could determine the social treatment (and therefore necessarily the social experience) of "real" twins, and reaches his own impasse.

> The reverse possibility, namely that the motif of twinship, which originally developed on the mythological level, could have motivated with its different expressions the contradictory nature of twinship on the ritual-sociological level, is perhaps too far-fetched.[85]

As suggested by the work of Adam McGee and Vijaya Nagarajan, among others in this volume, the possibility is by no means far-fetched. Rather, it represents one direction of a bidirectional flow that, as described earlier, moves between living twins and the telling of traditional stories about primordial twins (or the creation of doubled images) then back again. I argued in *Religion of the Gods* that this flow might best be understood as a kind of parabola, with the source of ritual traditionally understood to be located on the metaphysical side, where the gods are known to exist, act, and even themselves perform ritual, but then reiterated in human cultic performance.[86] *Gemini and the Sacred* shows how this model of mutual influence might illumine the relationship between supernatural and natural twins. What is characteristic of twins—or those identified as twins—in religious tradition, especially myth, is recognized in lived experience; but the experience of twinship then reinforces religious traditions, ideologies, and practices about twins.

"Real" twins and divine or archetypal twins might be seen more as members of a resembling family—to adapt Wittgenstein—than as a clear binary. The *Familienähnlichkeit* is saturated with characteristics of twinship, which clearly control its shape and function, but the family can be wider: for example, Obeng's "welcome and unwelcome" power of twinship can extend before and after twins in birth order and in wider societal significance. Or as McGee observes of Vodou,

> In the case of the Marasa, to have a relationship with them often means that one is, oneself, a Marasa—since the difference between human, still-living twins, dead twins, and "cosmic" or ancestral twins is one of degree rather than of kind. A number of our members are either Marasa De (what in English would properly be called "twins"), Marasa Dosou or Dosa (children born after Marasa who share and even exceed Marasa De's power)—or else have twins in their families. Marasa, though sometimes referred to as *jimo* (twins), in fact refers to an entire complex of children who are considered special, unusual, uncanny, and powerful. These include twins, triplets, and the next two children born after doubled or tripled births, as well as the child born before. All of these children, and more, have their role to play in the category of Marasa.[87]

In Vodou, *those who intersect the orbit of twins are in a sense made into them*, becoming part of the realm controlled by the powerful twin *lwa*, the Marasa.

What, if anything, informs the relationship between "real" twins and archetypal ones? From a birth that simultaneously produces both another "self" and a problematic "other," both a soulmate and an archrival in the same mirrored body, what existential conditions have characterized twin lives? Which conditions continue to arise, and how does enculturation affect these? In conversation with Walter Burkert, who defines myth as "a traditional narrative that is used as a designation of reality,"[88] Nagy writes, "Myth, in societies where it exists as a living tradition, must not be confused with fiction . . . Rather, myth represents a collective expression of society, an expression that society itself deems true and valid. From the standpoint of the given society that it articulates, myth *is* the primary reality."[89] The traditions in these studies center on some of the world's most storied twins. But their stories are not divorced by from the lives of twins—from concrete physical and psychological realities, in the "bottom-up" comparative approach based on "the raw material of human experience" Doniger advocates in *The Implied Spider*.[90] As an approach Dioscurism has its limits, because it retrojects a particular ancient Greek myth back into prehistory and then thence across all religious traditions about twins, and because *pace* Harris there is no "top-down," universal myth of twinship. At the same time, the tradition of the Dioskouroi can illuminate much about the category. "By extrapolating from what all the myths have in common, modified in the light of what . . . can be observed about the human situation in different cultures," however, Doniger suggests that one can arrive at something like a core.[91] But those who "arrive" cannot seek only to produce and consume knowledge concerning others, especially those whose epistemologies have been distorted. As Oludamini Ogunnaike has recently insisted, comparison should reject an "objective" vantage point that is unable interrogate its own biases, and instead seek a diverse one that includes the perspectives of those being analyzed.[92]

Structure, Scope, and Contents

Although *Gemini and the Sacred* is organized by historical-cultural complexes, the themes that arise out of its eighteen chapters recombine across cultural specificities. They show a kaleidoscopic interplay between personal and transpersonal twinship, between what Bianchi calls "the typical ambivalence found in the disparities between [mythological] twins" and "the problematical nature of physiological twinship."[93] By "problematical," he means that between twins, "the different values of duality (completeness, but also distinction or even disparity) can put in motion a plurality of interpretations."[94]

The volume begins with **Twins in Africa and the African Diaspora**, not to figure African indigenous or African diasporic religions as "primordial" but rather because twinship so often plays a major role in many African traditions—perhaps more than in any other historical-religious or geographical complex. Twinship rates run higher in Africa than in anywhere else in the world. The visible presence of twinship produces significance, reflecting the binary or complementary structure of the cosmos and creating a template for divinatory practices, ritual obligation and transgression, and concepts of spiritual protection.

The work of **Jacob Kẹ́hìndé Olúpọ̀nà** on animals as symbolizing beings in the Yorùbá tradition—in particular how certain animals can represent the highly charged category of twins (*ìbejì*) in the orature—opened a portal into the importance of twinship in the anthropology of religion.[95] In his chapter "The Code of Twins: Ìbejì in Yorùbá Cosmology, Ritual, and Iconography," Olúpọ̀nà explores twinship at length for the first time in his work, including the ways in which his own existential status as Kẹ́hìndé (second-born twin, but considered the older) to a Táyéwò (first-born twin, considered the younger) who died in childhood has affected his life. The sacrality of twins among the Yorùbá of West Africa, who have the highest rate of twinning among African and diasporic African populations, and in the world [Pl. 4], rivals that of Yorùbán kings—but, unlike twins, kings are not born sacred. Three or more births are not viewed as special by the Yorùbá. He asks, "So, why all the excitement over two? Why not one? Why not three?"

> [T]he Yorùbá accentuate multiples of two, both reflecting the structure of the human being and the cosmos and deriving from it. As such, in addition to replicating the revered *Èjì Ogbè* [divination] sign, the birth of two children at the same time embodies and enacts a salient universal principle.[96]

In treating the theme of twins in narrative, song, ritual, and iconography, Olúpọ̀nà considers the assimilation of twins to the animal world through their special relationship to the colobus monkey, a treetop-dweller surrounded by hunting and eating prohibitions and serving as the hero of a genre of songs called *orin ìbejì*. The crisis of the death of a twin like his own brother Isaac mandates the creation of a statuette of the lost child as a substitute (Ère Ìbejì: *èrè*: "statue; sacred image"; *ibi*: "born"; *ejì*: "two"): "If a twin dies, the Yorùbá believe that the twin has returned to where it came from. Twins have dual personalities; they belong both to this life and to the other world. Therefore, by their nature, even on death, a twin retains its beingness on earth. An icon must be made in the image (sex, lineage facial marks, etc.) of the deceased twin as a form of veneration."[97] A twin's *èrè* must be ritually maintained throughout life, cared for first by the mother, and then by the surviving twin. It is necessary that the spirit-twin, the one who has returned to heaven, be "grounded" by representing it on earth, lest the mother's fertility be blocked by the primordial rupture caused by the severing of the twin-bond. The Ère Ìbejì, whose conical heads are often washed in indigo, wear accessories such as glass-bead necklaces, iron armlets, cowry-shell waist strings [Pl. 5; Figure 2.1]. They are bathed, washed, dressed, fed, and carried along with the surviving twin by the bereaved mother, corresponding to the care that a spiritual mother provides on the other side. If she has had the misfortune to lose both twins, she traditionally commissions two Ère Ìbejì and cares for them both.

In other words, Yorùbá twins are in dual relationship whose potential is exponential, much as a zygote halves and then halves again. Born alive on earth, they mirror one another, but as a pair, they also mirror their celestial counterparts (who are also selves). If one of the living twins cannot remain on earth, this structural quaternity is revealed at once. This occurs when sacred art is commissioned and ritually curated.

There could be no clearer testimony of the continuum among philosophical superstructure, ritual obligation, and embodied culture than Olúpọ̀nà offers. The cultic attention paid to deceased twins concretely enacts the anthroposophical principle that elsewhere in this volume corresponds in many ways to "the divine double"; but it also is interlinked to ordering cosmological principles.

> Partly responsible for the misrepresentation of Yorùbá traditions in the literature is that a Durkheimian and Eliadian Western-imposed dichotomy of the sacred and the profane has been adopted in several theoretical and ethnographic works on African religions. However, this dichotomy disregards abundant evidence of an integrated Yorùbá cosmology—the realm of humans embraces the wild realm of forest and savanna and the spirit realm. A tangential approach imposing artificial boundaries on Yorùbá religious culture blurs the understanding of apparently liminal phenomena such as twinning.[98]

The idea of twins as both functionally threatening and politically ratifying of central interest to **Pashington Obeng**, who calls twins in the Akan tradition of Ghana and elsewhere in West and Central African cultures "welcome and unwelcome danglers." They are suspended in the normal human cultural matrix, potentially destabilizing it.[99] Like Olúpọ̀nà, Obeng affirms the historicity of the practice of infanticide in some African societies, grounded in anomaly—the appearance of two babies as a "deformity." This can be sadly played out when twins are orphaned, in Ghana necessitating a society dedicated to their protection. paradoxically, however, in Akyem (Akan) monarchical traditions in Southern Ghana, this anomalous twin "charge" is mystified and politicized. All twins, by virtue of their similarity to the first Akyem king, a twin, are symbolically assimilated into the royal family and his lineage, established in the eighteenth century.

> Nana Ofori Panin (Senior Twin Ofori) was the first political leader of the Akyem state. As Ofori Panin was a twin and the progenitor of the Akyem, *all twins are believed to belong to the royal family of the Akyem nation.*[100]

All twins participate in in royal twinship ceremonials (*Odwira*), which, Obeng writes, "clarify the notion that Akyem kings/chiefs are seen as twins, sharing in the legacy of the earlier Akyem lineage, because they occupy a seat or stool named after a twin. *That is, Akyem kings derive their powers from mystical twinship, not the other way around. The twins who appear at the Ohum festival do so symbolically to ratify his kingship and to remind the Akyem of its source.*"[101] Obeng's Obeng's research supports the intervention of Philip Peek, namely that "the doubling of souls/personalities alleged to be inherent in twinship allows Africans to draw attention to, as well as to ratify, the multiple selves and interlocking relationships that underscore social and religious realities."[102]

Turning the reader's attention to the African Diaspora in his "Marasa Elou: Twins and Uncanny Children in Haitian Vodou," **Adam Michael McGee** writes as both a scholar and an ordained *oungan*. Like the Nuäär (Sudanese Nuer) term for twins, "birds"—because children of the celestial Kuoth Nhial (God in heaven)—they have their own category, *Marasa*. Furthermore, this category contains more than twins, although twin *lwa* (spirits) and their characteristic powers control the category.

> Vodouisants also believe that an aura of spiritual power adheres to people who have unusual birth circumstances: . . . being born breach, with the face covered by a caul, with the umbilical cord wrapped around the neck, with a full head of hair, or webbed fingers or toes, or with a sixth finger.[103] In the last two cases, of webbing and polydactlylism, the child is considered to be *Marasa* because he or she is said to have devoured their twin in the womb, leaving only the extra finger or the excess skin. Finally, people with physical abnormalities—such as albinos, dwarves, and hydrocephalics—are considered spiritually powerful beings. Although not Marasa, strictly speaking, they are often honored in the same ceremonies that are made to honor Marasa . . . the Haitian Vodou concept of Marasa sees twins as inseparable from a much larger category of uncanny children and spirits.[104]

In light of the placement of Marasa at the head of the roster of *lwa* (spirits), McGee suggests that the prominence of the twinned Marasa has much to do with their twoness, a numerical field of central importance in Yorùbá and other African cosmologies (for example, in the division of the Ifà divination board). In the words of Odette Mennesson-Rigaud, the Marasa are "the divine principle of life."[105] McGee suggests that the way in which Marasa seem to be a kind of cosmic mirror, "which operates in Vodou as the hinge between the human world and the world of the spirits," is consonant in turn with a reflective surface of water—including "the glimmering surface of the primordial waters in which the dead dwell and through which one must pass to reach Ginen [a cosmic Africa where the *lwa* dwell]."[106]

Hero Twins in the Americas comprises two new in-depth studies of the many powerful pairs of divine twins from Native American traditions. In "Twins in Native American Mythologies: Relational Transformation," **John Grim** treats "the mythic motif of twinship" that is "extremely widespread among indigenous peoples of North America,"[107] and has also dominated Meso-american religions well before their classical periods. A stunning portrait of them was engraved on a conch shell gorget on the necklace of a prominent individual buried in the Spiro Mounds in Oklahoma, perhaps a version of the Hero Twins from the Mississippian Culture (1200–1350 CE). Two dancers face away from one another mid-step, holding shields, rattles, and raccoon pelts [Pl. 7a; Figure 5.1]. They are encircled by a four-armed quaternity that may relate to the Cross/Tree/or Milky Way found during the same period in classical Mayan iconography.

As Grim shows, themes that seem to bear a strong "family resemblance" often surface in non-contiguous Native American societies. Although the shared historical relationship of variant, but related, traditions can be inferred, it is difficult to trace. For example, the Diné twins from the American Southwest who slay monsters seem to have a very different mission from the cosmogonic twins of the Quechuan from the area of the Colorado River, embodying both creation and destruction. "[But] the Quechan are actually more similar to the Northeastern woodland Haudenosaunee/Iroquois than they are to more geographically proximate peoples; in a cosmogonic myth, the latter tell of Good Twin (or Good Mind) and Evil Twin (or Bad Mind), who make the world helpful and harmful for humans."[108] In ways that are reminiscent of Yorùbá and Indo-Iranian traditions, twinship expresses wider epistemology. As Seneca scholar Barbara Alice Mann has forcefully argued in *Spirits of Blood, Spirits of Breath: The Twinned Cosmos of Indigenous America*, the native American cosmos must itself be understood as "a halved and interdependent whole, particularly as expressed in the iconic Twinships of Blood/water/earth Serpents and Breath/air/sky Thunderbirds. These existed in harmony, not enmity, for the purpose of cosmic balance, in star patterns and earth-bound mirrors of those patterns."[109]

Grim shows that "twinship emerges as a root metaphor of Native American cognition, organizing both knowledge and experience: 'the Indigenous approach assumes that everything happens by matched sets, and not infrequently, by doubled matched sets.'"[110] These sets are not necessarily children of the same set of parents, but may be half-siblings. "They may be boyhood friends, or simply similar mythic forms who undertake the heroic journeys together as multiple expressions of a single enterprise."[111] The twins cycle in the Northern Haudenosaunee (Iroquois) confederation is a creation one, wherein Woman-who-fell-through-the-hole-in-the-sky has her fall broken by herons, sitting her on the back of Turtle Island, Earth. She bears a daughter (Earth Mother) who bears twins who, like the Avestan Ohrmazd and Ahrimen, quarrel in the womb (also in the Quechuan version). Between the antagonisms are what Grim calls "an interactive logic": "As with all living forms, then, what appears to be fixed in one moral camp may transform into another quite different than one expects. This transformative characteristic has strong cosmological implications, suggesting that movement between realms is at the heart of mythic twinship."[112]

The Crow/Apsaalooke story of the hero twins, Lodge-boy (*Bitàalasshiaalitc-hiasshiituuash*) and **Thrown-in-the-Spring** (*Bahàa Awúuaasshiituuash*) on the other hand belongs to a family of monster-slaying stories across the continent. These include the Zuni twins *Ahayuta* and *Matsilema* who lead the people during the cosmogonic time of Emergence from the interior up and onto the surface of the Earth; the native peoples of Acoma Pueblo tell of *Masewa* and *Uyuyewa* who also lead the people through the *shipapu*, or underground opening, onto the plane of this world. As sons of the Sun, both also journeyed up to their father and acquire powers of rain-making. The Stricken Twins of the Diné, who are entirely human, also have this capacity to cross realms, and "communicate with the *yei*/spirits and by this movement effect transformation of themselves."

> Whether a natural or supernatural doubling, twins often find themselves facing difficulties they did not create. One insight into doubling, then, is the nature of the difficulty faced and the ways in which twinship responds to that difficulty. In the Navajo-Diné story of the Stricken Twins this characteristic is especially poignant as the illness of the two is the vehicle for the powerful healing ceremony of the Night Chant, Klay'jih Hatal'.[113]

Thus the ordeals of the Hero Twins result in their people's most efficacious rituals. As with most traditions that concern twins, their suffering is never "stranded" in their tales without producing cultural meaning.

Vincent Stanzione has lived and worked among the Tzu'tujil Maya people of Santiago Atitlán in highland Guatemala for over thirty years. His lyrical essay, which he writes in the manner of a traditional storyteller, retells and reflects on the story of the two pairs of hero twins from the *Popul Wuj*: The Ahpu twins, One Junajpu and Seven Junajpu, and the twin sons of One Junaphu: Junajpu and XB'alamkiej. He considers duality and pairedness, and how these ritualized ways of being, surviving in continuity with are still intertwined with present-day Mayan epistemology. "The hero twins' story is the oldest Mesoamerican narrative that exists that is completely intact. It was likely told even before the people we know as the Maya existed as a people; we find what appear to be aspects of it on the Itzapan stela in Chiapas (300 BCE-100 or 50 BCE; possibly as late as 250 CE) that predate the formative Maya period. The Mayan sacred cycle of maize pairs the hero twins' life and death struggle for survival with the ordeal of their mirroring enemies, the twins known as 'One' and 'Seven Death,' also called 'the Lords of Death.'"[114]

Fluent in three Mayan languages, Stanzione shows how twins have existential affinities with both divine and human realms; these are both strategic and genetic. Divine twins are often culture heroes, bringing maize, medicine, or sacrifice to the human world. They can fly through the heavens or, in the case of the Mayan hero twins, travel to the underworld, and defeat the Lords of Death after the first set of twins has failed. As Stanzione writes, "Tricksters make the world" by which he means in part that tricksters make it possible for human beings to dwell in a world that in most, if not all, cosmogonies, was made by gods—and not for them.

> The twins Junajpu and XB'alamkiej are tricksters who make a world ready made for the maize-growing people known in this story as the K'iche' Maya. They will offer their ancestors, the hero twins, worship and sacrifice for the heroic deeds they performed *in illo tempore* in order to prepare the way.[115]

As his harrowing story of his beloved brother friends the Nabeysil and Salvador shows, human twins are often not left alone to their personal histories; they are instead enlisted into transpersonal vocations and modes of being, and sometimes in the end are destroyed if caught between indigenous and outsider socioreligious values.

> The story of the hero twins forms the central pillar of the sacred history of the Maya known as the *Popol Wuj*. That pillar might be thought of as two trees perfectly entwined around one another, an ancestral tree whose roots reach into the underworld and whose limbs branch out into the heavens. The *Popol Wuj* is not just a story of the K'iche' Maya. It is an ancient story they used to substantiate their claim of being an original and ancient people who are the rightful lords of the K'iche' kingdom.[116]

That claim has been challenged in ways that are increasingly lethal to Traditional Maya people.

In **South Asian Legacies**, chapters by **Wendy Doniger** and **Vijaya Nagarajan** encounter the Hindu tradition in different, yet sometimes intersecting, vectors from ancient Vedic to medieval epic texts. Working with the textual premise that "apparently twins in the womb already have individually differentiated souls"[117] in Hindu mythology, Wendy Doniger sheds light on how twins can be embroiled in lethal competition, symbiotic love, or alternate. The embryo is not only "sentient within the womb but already in possession of its own *karma*"; but embryonic bodies are neither alive nor differentiated. Hence intra-uterine "wars" can break out in Vedic and later texts, revealing a strange *agōn* between two quasi-incarnate souls who share a womb, and delineating another major theme in the study of twinship: "Each twin has . . . its own agenda, which often results in antagonism or at the very least competition within the womb."[118] Doniger also explores themes in myths of maternal choice between one or multiple offspring (Gandhārī and Sāgara); the transfer of embryos between wombs with personality intact (the birth narrative of Kṛṣṇa); and the paternal mutilation of the embryo, resulting in multiple viable pieces that may still emerge as siblings who remain at odds for life. The mythic viability of the fractured or dismembered embryo is contrasted with the strict Hindu prohibition against abortion, begging the question of how such dismemberment is not understood as "killing." Especially since Doniger's chapter looks at the role of the deceived, ambivalent, or destructive parent of twins in utero, there are suggestive parallels in the biblical story of Jacob and Esau, or in the war between Ohrmazd and

Ahrimen in the womb of Zurwān, god of Time, as Skjærvø discusses in the context of Zoroastrian "dualism."[119]

Vijaya Narayanan offers an ethnographic picture of the increasing presence of twins among Indian-Americans in northern California, focusing on religious beliefs regarding twins among the families in the context of Hindu mythology (e.g., Saraṇyū's motherhood of Yama-Yamī and the Aśvins, among others). She also considers contemporary Indian literature, as in Kirin Narayan's twin goddess family *kuladev* [family deity] in her *My Family and Other Saints*). Nagarajan observes that the explosion of multiple births in this population, paralleling that in the middle and upper classes of the US population at large, is an experience often construed as miraculous: the "nothing" of infertility becomes the surreal multiplicity of two or more children at once. In this context, she also considers issues of identity formation in relationship to acculturation. To Bianchi's skeptical question about whether divine twin traditions can influence the lived experience of "actual" twins in their families and cultures, Nagarajan's initial research seems to indicate that this is indeed possible. This can be intensified within diaspora communities for whom doubled births instantly augment the population and enhance the status of the parents—and, by extension, the status of the community within the host country. Most intriguingly, she presents her research through the lens of the experience of raising her non-identical twin children, Jaya and Uma, who found themselves at five years old receiving small gifts and sweets from fellow Hindus, and five years later were asked to represent the goddesses Saraswathi and Gayathri at a Navarathri Festival held by the Brahma Kumaris at the Sunnyvale Hindu Temple in California [Pl. 9a; Figure 8.1]. Pl. 9b shows the twins, dressed in complementary colors, performing a *Bharatanatyam Arangetram* in Bakersfield in 2018.

The vision of paleohistorian and museum curator **Lauren Talalay** anchors the next section, **Twins in the Ancient Mediterranean World**. In an original essay she both wrote and illustrated, Talalay attempts the most systemic analysis to date of a peculiar subset of "several thousand Neolithic and Bronze Age figurines from the eastern Mediterranean" that figure the human body.[120] "Entangled Bodies: Rethinking Twins and Double Images in the Prehistoric Mediterranean" treats the few but consequential "handful of items representing two identical portrayals, conjoined, merged, or encapsulated in some way."[121] These composite figurines depict dual identical images that emerge from one body, or intersect or incorporate one another. She suggests that "the concepts of twins and twinship provide a valuable optic through which to view these unusual images." Absent the textual evidence that gives us some kind of purchase on prehistoric twinship as a metaphor for harmonic unity, conflictual duality, or both, Talalay considers the material evidence on other terms, including cultural context and comparanda: "the twin-like figurines provide a good starting point for exploring the significance of human doubles in this region."[122]

Starting with the tall, single-bodied, double-headed Neolithic figurines at 'Ain Ghazal, Jordan, Talalay moves east to west to analyze and illustrate the "eye idols" of Tell Brak in Northern Syria; the strange evidence from Bronze Age Cyprus ("the two-headed plank figures, the cruciform images, the figure wearing itself as a pendant, and the twin cradle figures"); the two-headed, four-breasted figurines that may or may not be goddesses from Neolithic Çatalhöyuk and Hacilar in Anatolia; the double- and triple-headed stone figurines with stereo-staring "twins in the belly" from Kültepe; the double figurines of repoussé gold buried at Alaca Höyük; ending with the gender-fluid, arm-draping early Neolithic clay figurines from Larissa, and their double-headed, single-bodied cousins from the Balkans. Talalay points out that in these cryptic ancient figurines, not only are "the boundaries of *individual* identity . . . effectively blurred, replaced with a visual code suggesting shared or double identities," as might be expected, but also that "designation of sex is often submerged" in these small, portable figurines, which are found in "burials, 'shrines,' or caches" outside the domestic sphere, suggesting ritual activities or "enactments associated with their deposition in these contexts."[123]

Herself an identical twin, Talalay pushes the boundaries of archaeologist Colin Renfrew's essential question about prehistoric peoples: "What did they think?"[124]

> From our western vantage point, for example, even a casual study of the twin-headed and conjoined images engenders pointed questions: What does it mean to strongly resemble someone else? What if one possessed not a single and bounded body but a double and entangled one? How do we understand the notion of divided unity in human identity? Do all societies possess a sense of individual uniqueness and how is that mediated? These questions problematize, among other things, the notion of the self as bound to a single bodily entity.[125]

Perhaps the *teomim* (Gemini) mosaic figure at the Beit Alpha synagogue, with its apparently "double-wide" body that only on second glance reveals itself as two bodies, might be seen as further along a continuum that begins at 'Ain Ghazal. Its ambiguity might have been intentional, exemplifyng Strathern's notion of "dividuals" or Alfred Gell's notion of "distributed personhood": "Ancestral shrines, tombs, memorials, ossuaries, sacred sites, etc. all have to do with the extension of personhood beyond the confines of biological life via indexes distributed in the milieu."[126]

It is hard to escape that many in Talalay's corpus of "merged" or "entangled" figurines seem to be gendered female (or in a few cases are fluidly hard to categorize), whereas the majority of sacred twins considered in the chapters in this volume are male. In the ancient Mediterranean, divine female pairing or twinning may grow out of an older set of traditions that center on the reduplication of the female godhead. This could have lain at the root of powerful, iterative female "icons" like the mysterious ivory female figures found at Mycenae, sometimes called "the Twin Goddesses," carved as a contiguous pair with Minoan-style open bodices and flounced skirts, tending to a single small child between them, or the mother-daughter deities of death, fertility, and rebirth Demeter and Persephone (Korē, "the maiden"), called "the Twain" in archaic strata of the Eleusinian tradition and sometimes shown as iconographically identical.

"Twinned" chapters by longtime friends and mutual classicist muses **Gregory Nagy** and **Douglas Frame** continue this ancient Mediterranean theme of identities merged or interchanged between a famous pair of warriors whose story unfolds as the center of the *Iliad*.[127] The contemporary preoccupation with whether Achilles and Patroklos were or were not lovers is at best anachronistic—since erotic relationships between men were not only a given but a cultural fountainhead throughout ancient Greek civic and military history. At worst, it may have obscured our understanding of the depths of their relationship, making its more meaningful levels inaccessible. As Jung held in the course of his slow-moving break with Freud, such levels of human experience extend beyond the sexual, *which always eventually reveals its limits*, and into the religious, which is limitless in its potential complexity and significance. That the erotic can be a sign of the religious, or a portal into it, was no secret to the rabbis who wrote commentary on the biblical *Shir ha-Shirim* (Song of Songs), or to the practitioners of seventh-century CE Hindu tantric traditions, or the Sufi mystic Rumi inspired by his love for God through the dervish Shams of Tabriz, or the sixteenth-century Rajasthani poet Mirabai who wrote ecstatic, yearning hymns for Kṛṣṇa (Krishna). Nagy and Frame show how the most productive lens through which to view Achilles and Patroklos is that of Indo-European sacred twinship, which went deeper.

"Achilles and Patroklos as Models for the Twinning of Identity" argues that "the fused identity of mythical twins is at the same time a split personality," and that the heroes Achilles, who is half-god, and Patroklos, who is mortal, "are paired off in the Homeric *Iliad* in such a way as to resemble and even to duplicate such a model of twinning in myth."[128] Meditating on the terms *philos* "meaning 'friend' as a noun, and 'near and dear' or 'belonging to the self'" as an adjective," and *therapōn*, "attendant," Nagy makes a case for both as bearing with equal force on the warriors' relationship, inflecting, redeeming, and dooming them. *Philos* has its own capacious field of affectionate and even possessive bonds from the oldest Greek literature on. Patroklos and Achilles care more deeply about one another than anyone else. "Such mutual caring determines the identification of Patroklos as the virtual twin or body double of Achilles in Homeric mythmaking."[129] But *therapōn* is strange and terrible. Its Indo-European family includes the Hittite *tarpalli-/* tarpanalli- and *tarpašša-*, shown by Nadia van Brock to mean "ritual substitute" in Bronze Age inscriptions in which a figure called by this name is said to die for the once-sacrificed Hittite king "so that he may live."[130] This role carries with it a potent notion of transfer and absorption of pollution, but through the logic of ritual, it also has a kind of quasi-ontological meaning.

> Such a meaning, "ritual substitute," must be understood in the context of a Hittite ritual of purification that expels pollution from the person to be purified and transfers it into a person or an animal or an object that serves as a ritual substitute; the act of transferring pollution into the victim serving as ritual substitute may be accomplished either by destroying or by expelling the victim, who or which is identified as another self, un autre soi-même.[131]

When in *Iliad* 16 Patroklos steals the armor of Achilles, still angrily abstinent from the fighting, and goes to fight in his place, Achilles prays to Zeus,

> I shall send my companion into battle at the head of many Myrmidons,
> sending him to fight. Grant, O all-seeing Zeus, that victory may go with him;
> put boldness into his heart so that Hektor
> may find out whether he [Patroklos] knows how to fight alone,

[Patroklos,] my <u>attendant</u> [therapōn], or whether his hands can only then be so
   invincible
with their fury when I myself enter the war struggle of Ares.

—Iliad 16. 240–5[132]

Nagy's exposition of the role of the ritual substitute—*therapōn*—as a characteristic of
ancient twinship casts the Achilles-Patroklos relationship in an entirely different light
than an exclusively psychologizing one. He observes, "What makes the substitute
in ritual seem so intimately close to you is that he or she or it must die for you."[133]
Implicit in this is the hope and expectation that the god will accept the *therapōn* as an
acceptable substitute victim. But this is never guaranteed.

> As the other self who is ready to die for the self that is Achilles, Patroklos achieves
> an unsurpassed level of intimacy with the greatest hero of the Homeric *Iliad*.
> This intimacy is sacral, thus transcending even sexual intimacy. But this sacred
> intimacy has an uncanny other side to it, which is a kind of sacred alienation.
> As we saw in the case of the Hittite prisoner, about to be expelled into an alien
> realm, he must wear the clothing of the king, thus becoming ritually intimate
> with the body of the king. So too Patroklos wears the armor of Achilles when he
> dies; and he wears something else that is even more intimately connected with his
> best friend. Patroklos wears also the epic identity of Achilles, as expressed by the
> epithets they share. These heroic epithets, such as the one that makes them both
> "equal to Ares," will predestine both of them to live and die the same way. And the
> sameness of their shared life and death can be seen as an uncanny mix of intimacy
> and alienation that only twins will ever truly understand.[134]

Nagy's work reminds us that there is something else, something beyond "mutual
caring" that is sacrificial and substitutionary, which we can see in human twins
when one faints in the emergency room and a moment later the other is on the floor;
when one falls grievously ill and the other inevitably begins to languish; when one
becomes pregnant and then, unknowingly, so does the other the same week; when
a twin is desperate to take on the spiritual suffering of their twin; when a surgeon is
relieved in the knowledge that her patient in need of a new kidney or a bone marrow
transplant has a twin whose DNA is so close as to allow him to be a donor. It is not
enough to use analogies of long friendship to describe twinship, or of normal sibling
harmony and rivalry, or of romantic love and erotic attraction, although twinship has
dimensions of all of these. Because twins inter-are, they are also always potential
sacrifices for one another. If one is a half-god or sacred king, the other who is not can
or must give his life to save the king from the pollution of death that threatens him.
But it is not that Achilles flourishes for long when Patroklos dies; the sacrifice only
saves him to fulfill his destiny which is to destroy Hektor and Troy with him, then die
himself. Twins are, as Nagy writes of the hero Meleagar and the smoldering log who
was his twin, "fatally homeopathic with one other."[135]

    Douglas Frame's "Achilles and Patroklos as Indo-European Twins: Homer's
Take," also considers other modes of twinship in the Indo-European tradition, but

explores their solar lineage and their binary identities of warrior/healer and horse/ cattle. These modes grow out an aspect of sacred twinship that Harris saw as *a priori* in "Dioscurism": mixed fatherhood; therefore in some (Harris claimed "all") stories of "celestial twins," one is mortal and the other immortal. In the first mode, the story of Kastor and Polydeukes in crisis, the mortal twin dies but is resurrected by the immortal one, though intense negotiation. In order to do this, as Nagy writes and on which Frame expands, it is not enough for the god-brother to wish his corpse-brother back to life; he must sacrifice some part of his immortality to do so. The implication is clear—he must return it to the god who fathered him.

In the second form of the myth, Frame argues, "one twin again dies but his brother, instead of bringing him back to life, takes his place as a warrior. When Patroclus takes Achilles's place in battle Achilles is of course not dead, but only out of action. Patroclus's deed is nevertheless viewed in the *Iliad* through the prism of this second form of the twin myth."[136] Frame argues that in the epic Greek tradition, "Nestor and Patroclus are presented in parallel,"[137] whereby a separated or stranded twin assumes the attributes both of himself and of his lost double. Thinking through Frame's thesis, one might conclude that this second form of the twin myth still represents a form of resurrection.

Frame notes how in Book 11, the aging yet influential *gerōn* Nestor, king of Pylos, urges Patroklos either to rouse the dormant Achilles, or to take his place in the battle that is turning against the Achaeans. Of course, Patroklos chooses the latter, and is killed by the Trojan champions Euphorbos and Hektor after Apollo strikes a death-blow. But hidden in the Homeric account is the story of how Nestor had to take the place of his older brother Periklymenos, a horse-warrior, known from Hesiodic fragments and the *Odyssey*, who used his shape-shifting powers, to fight Heracles as he sacked Pylos. Periklymenos was killed, along with all the children of Neleus (himself the twin brother of Peleus of Iolkos).[138] Nestor himself rode out as a horse-warrior and became both brothers.[139] Just as the phenomenon of microchimerism makes it possible for one twin to absorb the other in the womb and become a kind of hybrid, so Nestor absorbs the attributes of his older brother, Periklymenos. The Aśvins, like the Dioskouroi, are almost always referred to as a pair. But a unique verse of the Rig Veda "says that only one of the twins was called the 'son of Dyaus,' and that the other was called the son of Sumakha, an otherwise unknown figure, but presumably a mortal like Tyndareus."[140] "Nestor carries out the cattle-raid single-handedly, no brother having survived at his side, and then, when his cattle-raid provokes a war, he becomes a warrior as well, taking his brother's place and in effect becoming two twins in one: the savior and the horseman."[141]

Frame's chapter also explores the way in which divine or heroic (and therefore semi-divine) twins are often cast as healers. As a pair, the Dioskouroi are *Dios kouroi*, "sons of Zeus," who have cognate twins in the Vedic tradition. Like Kastor and Polydeukes, they are called *divo napātā*, "off-spring of Dyaus [Sky]" and Aśvínā, "horse-possessors,"[142] but also *Nā́satyā* ("saviors"), an ancient epithet with cognates in Avestan.[143] Frame notes the meaning of the root **nes-*.

The Vedic twins have the characteristic functions of "saving" and "healing" distressed mortals, and this has suggested a connection with the Gothic verb *nasjan*, "save" and "heal," which contains this root. The underlying meaning of Gothic *nasjan . . .* is "bring back to life." A similar implication of the name *Nā́satyā* is indicated by the twins' rescue myths, in several of which they are said to bring mortals "back to life."[144]

This would be consonant with the magico-religious powers of the Mayan Hero Twins, who resurrect slain beings in the underworld, Xibalba. But it is also bound up in Nestor's own name:

> The idea that the "intelligence" of this twin is bound up with his bringing his brother back to life, as is implied by the combined epithets *dasrā bhiṣajau*, "skilled physicians," characterizing both twins as a pair, gains more precise definition in Greek, where the noun *noos*, "mind," is seen to be a close equivalent of the name *Nestōr* in terms of its etymology and semantics: if *Nestōr* is originally "he who brings back to life," the noun *noos* (reconstructed as **nos-os*, with the same verbal root as *nos-tos*, "return," but in the active sense seen in *Nestōr*) means a "bringing back to life," and originally probably designated "consciousness."[145]

> Through this complicated lens of fractured and reconstituted twinship by absorption, seen through the heritage of the figure of Nestor and the etymology of his name, Frame has a different take on the Achilles and Patroclus are "failed twins": they are a tragic failure both of the myth of the twin who brings his dead twin back to life, and of the myth of the twin who absorbs his lost brother.[146]

The tradition of doubled supernatural healers survived in the Late Antique Christian Mediterranean, as laid out in the chapter by **James Skedros**, "Ss. Cosmas and Damian: Synergistic Brother Healers": in both Western and Eastern Christian hagiography, called "unmercenary" (*anargyroi* [ανάγυροι], literally, "silverless") brothers who treated both ill human beings and sick animals without pay. As had troubled Harris, the early Church honored no less than three pairs of healing twin brothers by the same names in different regions and at different times before the Peace of the Church. The veneration of the saints was established by the fifth century in both the east and in Rome, blossoming into a notable healing cult that throve well into the Middle Ages. In Constantinople, a late-fifth-century CE extramural church that came to be known as "the Kosmidion" continued the form and function of earlier non-Christian healing shrines in antiquity: the practice of incubation by the ill in covered porticoes in the hope of a dream visit from the twins. The successfully healed included the emperor Justinian I. Skedros examines closely the six collections of healing miracles attributed to the saints, the majority an anonymous collection from the sixth century. But unlike the medical pilgrimage centers of antiquity like Epidauros or Oropos, where surviving votive inscriptions (*iamata*) testify to the names of the grateful healed patients and their households,

> the majority of the miracle stories from the Kosmidion do not give the *personal* names of those who were healed, nor their specific homelands . . . The apparent pattern of deliberate rhetorical choice for pilgrim anonymity and generic healings

. . . suggests that the *Miracles* were intended to sidestep or even quietly suppress local or ethnic affinities, thus imbuing themselves with a more universal appeal in order to enhance the prestige of the shrine.[147]

How did the duality of the holy physicians matter in the perception of their medical authority? Ss. Cosmas and Damian almost invariably work in tandem, in a kind of therapeutic symbiosis. Skedros notes that in the Byzantine iconographic tradition, they are never depicted separately, and in texts about their practice of medicine, they always act together, for example, in the case of "the Jewish woman with cancer who is healed through 'the prayer' of the saints, that is, one prayer that is offered by both saints together (2.33–34)."[148] The twinned saints' healing actions, such as the prayer, are always reported in the singular. "The tag-team, dynamic nature of the therapy provided by Ss. Cosmas and Damian" emerges in these *Miracula*, including one extraordinary account (30) wherein the saints debate with one another about the treatment of a man with a fistula in his hip:

> The account tells the hearer that the man has spent fifteen years in extreme pain, undergoing several surgeries and other remedies all to no avail. The encouragement of his friends and a nocturnal visit in a dream by Cosmas and Damian at his home leads the man to the saints' healing sanctuary. Once there, he is taken by the saints to the operating room located in the hostel where visitors to the shrine lodged. Seeing yet another operating room, the man tries to convince the saints not to operate. St. Damian agrees, and tries to prevent St. Cosmas from making an incision. Cosmas argues back to Damian, who then relents, allowing the surgery to proceed. . . The fistula and the wound from the surgery are healed, and the man offers praises and thanksgiving to the Lord and to his saintly healers Cosmas and Damian.[149]

Here the symbiosis between the brothers resembles more of a kind of clinical triage. Perhaps most significantly for the persistence of twinship, Skedros discusses an account of a pagan, desperately ill, whose friends believe they are taking him to an incubation shrine of the Dioskouroi, because "they had in view the names Castor and Pollux taken from accounts of them found in those empty and harmful mythical readings," mistakenly bring him to the church of Ss. Cosmas and Damian. Once laid in the shrine, the ill pagan sees the saints ministering to the sick and cries out to the brothers for healing. After Cosmas and Damian upbraid the man for thinking that they are to be identified with the ancient pagan pair, the man is healed and then receives Christian baptism."[150] As Skedros observes, the polemic behind this confusion of one pair of sacred twins for another is partly to disassociate the saints from the Dioskouroi—the saints reject the association repeatedly until the sick man calls them by their proper Christian names.[151] Yet ironically, this deliberate confusion of the saints for the Dioskouri only "doubles down" on the Dioscuric nature of Cosmas and Damian: "the association of the pair with the twin sons of Zeus suggests that the twinning of the Christian brothers was never far from the surface of their identity, and perhaps of their numinous powers."[152]

Skedros's research makes clear that the ancient vocation of the *Aśvins/Nāsatyā*, of Castor and Pollux, and of Makhaon and Podaleirios, persists in the Late Antique figures of Ss. Cosmas and Damian, whereby twinned brother-physicians—through their shared powers of triage, their intensive dialogue, and their miraculous cures, anchored in the rituals of cult—are more gifted at healing human affliction than one divine doctor acting alone.

Divine Twinship in the Ancient Near East and Early Christianity treats three related themes of religious twinship that developed in Indo-Iranian, early Christian, Gnostic, and Manichaean matrices in the long religious history of the Ancient Near East. In a watershed new view of Zoroastrian religion, the Indo-Iranianist **Prods Oktor Skjærvø** re-examines the genealogy of the "twin spirits" of Good and Evil who famously contest in its sacred texts. He proposes a stunning twist on its original radical dualism, recast over the centuries by the tradition itself—and often accepted by modern scholars—as ethical monotheism.

Skjærvø traces the "myth of the primordial twin spirits (*maniiu*) . . . found in the [ancient] *Gāθās*," through its elaboration in the *Young Avesta* and later Zoroastrian sacred and heterodox texts.[153] Ahura Mazdā is the principal "creator"—by thinking, not speaking—of an ordered cosmos, and performer of a primeval sacrifice. Achaemenid inscriptions merged the two divine names and in later Pahlavi texts, the supreme god became known as Ohrmazd. "The opposite principle was *drug/druj* (Old Persian *drauga*, cf. Old Indic *drúh*) commonly translated as 'the Lie', that is, the cosmic deception," later called Ahrimen, the evil twin of Ohrmazd.[154]

The ancient Avestan *Gāθā* 1.30.3 speaks of "those two spirits in the beginning, which have been renowned as the twin 'sleeps' (*yə̄mā xvafnā*) . . .". Skjærvø suggests that "sleeps" may metonymically refer to two "sleeping fetuses." The cosmogony in the Old Indic *Laws of Manu* (*Manusmṛti* 1.5) offers a possible comparand: "This (thing) was, *risen from darkness, unknown, with no distinguishing marks,/ inconceivable, incomprehensible, like asleep (*prasuptam*) all over." The first *Gāθā* continues, "From these arise ". . . two thoughts and two speeches; they (are) two actions, a better and an evil" (1.30.3). The *Gāθā* goes on to set up a mysterious contrast at verse 1.30.4:

> . . . whenever the two spirits come together one *determines (*dazdē*) for the first (time) both life (*gaiia*: for the good) and lack of living (*a-jiiāti*: for the wicked).[155]

In perfect incompatibility, the Life-giving Spirit says to the Dark Spirit:

> "Neither our thoughts, nor announcements (*sə̄ngha*), nor guiding thoughts, nor preferences (*varəna*), nor utterances, nor actions, nor vision-souls (*daēnā*), nor breath-souls (*uruuan*) go together."—*Gāθā* 2.45.2

The twins' mismatch is highly consequential for the believer who is called to choose between them, in particular for the human poet-sacrificers who are called to maintain the "cosmic/ritual Order [*aṣa*, Old Indic *ṛtá*]" on earth. As Skjærvø observes, "Thoughts, utterances, and actions obviously make up the entire ritual; there is nothing in the ritual that is not one of the three. In addition, the two 'triads' of good/evil thoughts, etc., form the basis of Zoroastrian ethics still today."[156] The twins are identified with light and darkness (day and night). Life-giving Spirit"/good thought," generally associated with the supreme god, Ahura Mazdā, also "represents the sunlit sky that is woven and stretched out every morning, whereas 'evil thought' and Wrath, the embodiment of the dark night sky, are cut back and removed from the cosmic loom."[157] This is in keeping with a powerful, millennia-old tradition of creation as a form of cosmic weaving, appearing in Indo-Iranian, Indo-European, and Semitic traditions, a theme which Skjærvø has developed elsewhere.[158] The process is mirrored in the divine creative weaving of the child in the womb. The first human being, a primordial creation, could not have been an exception.

In the Young Avestan texts, each of the two spirits performs sacrifices and produces their own creations, including the good and evil animals; later, in the *Videvdad*, the Evil Spirit will also create a myriad of illnesses. Their struggle continues, with Ahura Mazdā interdicting the Dark Spirit, quoting the Gāθic formula of incompatibility. Life-giving Spirit is usually identified with Ahura Mazdā, although in one striking text, Ahurā Mazdā seems to be sickened by the plagues unleashed on the world, and asks for help from Life-giving Spirit (*maθrō spəntō*) to heal him:

> Ahura Mazdā said to Zarathustra: I, Ahura Mazdā, I, who set in place (all) good things, when I made that house, beautiful, bright, luminous, then the Villain looked at me, then the Villain, the Evil Spirit full of destruction, made 99,999 illnesses. So now you must heal me, you my Life-giving Word. (*Videvdad* 22.1–2).

By the time of the Pahlavi writings of the priest Zādspram (fl. 900 CE), Ohrmazd himself opposes Ahrimen by wrestling him "in order to hold him back from his realm" (*Zādspram* 1.4).

A story developed at around the same time of how Ohrmazd (Ahura Mazdā) contended with Evil Spirit (Ahrimen) as a twin within the womb of Time, Zurwān, a paternal godhead said by the tenth-century *Bundhišn* (1.42) to be "stronger than both creations, the creation of Ohrmazd and that of the Foul Spirit." Known from Christian writings, Armenian history, and Muslim historians as late as the eleventh to twelfth centuries CE, in one version of the anathematized myth *Zurwāniyya*, Zurwān sacrifices for a thousand years "to conceive a son who would create heaven and earth." As the *yasna* appeared fruitless, he doubted his effort: the twin sons Ohrmazd and Ahrimen were conceived from his doubt. Zurwān thought to give primogeniture to Ohrmazd, but Ahrimen, hearing this from his brother, tore open his father's womb and claimed 9,000 years of stolen reign, after which Ohrmazd would rule. As in the *Gāθās*, both twins then began to create. "Zurwān-Time became identified with the cosmic egg or womb that had contained the two spirits," *thus exonerating Ahura Mazdā of having produced evil himself.* This provided a late, heretical solution to a problem of theodicy for a tradition that evolved into highly ethical directions.

Skjærvø believes that gestation and birth imagery has always characterized the myth of the two spirits. Through careful re-analysis of the textual tradition, with attention to Vedic and Manichaean comparanda, Skjærvø suggests that this cosmogony may have been inspired by the physical experience of live birth. Every living, embodied, differentiated infant comes into the world attached to its non-surviving, circular, undifferentiated "twin," the placenta—equal in size but lacking in dimensionality or the potential for life. Therefore every human birth is a dual birth of a living "twin" cord-bound to a dying one.

Skjærvø's thesis centers on the nature of the primeval man and progenitor of humanity, Gayōmard: The Pahlavi tradition understood "Gayōmard" as "dying (mortal) life," the first human being, to whom Ahrimen brought sickness (*Zādspram* 2.18); the *Bundahišn* 1A.15 says that he was "luminous, like the sun," understood to be circular.

> The name of Gaiia Marətān may . . . refer to the fact that he was the first human fetus, but never developed into human form; instead, he remained in the spherical form he would have had in the womb, containing both the living fetus and the dead placenta.[159]

Skjærvø points to how the Vedic *Kāṭhaka-saṃhitā* 11.6 recounts part of the myth of Mārtāṇḍa, the eighth and last of the solar offspring conceived by Aditi, in which he is expelled by his brothers, the Ādityas (mentioned by Doniger in her chapter as an example of a "war within the womb"):

> (Aditi) became pregnant (*gárbham adhatta*). The embryo, (still) within (her), spoke.. . The Ādityas [= his brothers] thought, "If this one will be born, he will thrive (*bhaviṣyati*) here." "They smashed (*níraghnan*) him out [= "aborted him"]. Expelled/aborted [*nírasto*, lit. "thrown out"] he lay there."

Returning to the crucial passage in the *Gāθā*s, and "reading *dhā* 'place' in the middle voice + *gárbham* to express 'become pregnant,'" then applying "this meaning to *dazdē* in the Old Avestan passage," he suggests that "we obtain a remarkable sense":

> 1.30.4
> . . . and when those two spirits come together (in someone), then one becomes pregnant (*dazdē*) for the first time with life and non-life.

In other words, the vitality of the fetus may have given rise to, or been assimilated with, the cosmic principle of light, truth, right, and order; the morbidity of the placenta may have been assimilated to Darkness, Evil, Deception, and "the Lie." Both would have had one creator, contained within one womb. Gayōmard's name is a sign that he contains both principles (*Gaiia Marətān* in Avestan; "dying (mortal) life" or "living and dying" [*zīndag ī mīrāg*] in the Pahlavi tradition). Skjærvø's thesis sources these principles in the physiology of reproduction. The meaning of Avestan Gaiia Martān from *gaiia marta-Han*, according to Skjærvø, seems to mean not, as Karl Hoffman argued, "what contains (*–Han-*) what is dead (*marəta*),"[160] but rather 'life with a dead thing." This, he writes, is "the perfect description of the products of the birth process: the living new human followed by the lifeless afterbirth, the (circular) placenta."[161]

Skjærvø concludes that "the element of birth that pervades the Iranian creation myth and the notion of two fetuses, a good and a bad, combined with the ancient Indo-Iranian myths of Gaiia Marətān and Mārtāṇḍa, finally permits us to take yet one step further":

I want to propose that the ancient Iranians viewed creation as a complete birth myth and that the "radical dualistic" element in it originated in the observation of the dual birth: of the new living being and of the afterbirth, which, although it was what kept the fetus alive, was now dead (and disposed of).[162]

We may also note that, in Persian, the afterbirth is called *joft* "twin."[163]

It is hard to overestimate the importance—and, in a sense, the strangeness—of Skjærvø's new intervention in these notoriously difficult questions. If he is right, one of the most complex of all historical theodicies may have its origin in the most corporeal and transitory of human organs, the placenta, whose usefulness is spent after nine months and which must be delivered by the laboring mother after delivering her baby ("after-birth"). The two spirits, both "life (*gaiia*: for the good) and lack of living (*a-jiiāti*: for the wicked)" may express how the neonate is to the placenta. Through this lens, every human being is born attached to her own twin, a twin that is her antitype; every newborn delivered alive is tethered to death itself. The umbilical cord—the connection between the two—must be cut for the infant to survive and thrive. This would have been sublimated as the ethical imperative to choose the right, sunlight, and order, and of severing oneself from the Lie, death, darkness, and anarchy. "Primordial Twins in Ancient Iranian Myth" reverses the lens of an ancient tradition that has distanced itself from its dualism:

> After the Muslim conquest of Persia and the exodus of many Zoroastrians to India and after having been exposed to both Muslim and Christian propaganda, some Zoroastrians, especially among the Parsis in India, went so far as to deny dualism and to view themselves as outright monotheists, and the dualist aspect of the religion is today often downplayed or explained away. Its origin in a myth of the primordial conception, gestation, and birth of cosmic twins and their struggle until the end of time was forgotten long ago.[164]

The twin of Jesus himself is the subject of "Didymos Judas Thomas: The Twin Brother of Jesus," in which **Gregory Riley** reflects on the early Christian apostolic tradition that is memorably intensified in the extracanonical "Gospel of Thomas." "The idea that all things are made after patterns became a Christian mode of thinking about God and Christ and the individual person. The goal of the spiritual life, in fact, was to join in the perfection of the pattern, to rejoin one's image and again become one with the ideal form that God had originally planned for each person."[165] Riley shows how both Platonic and biblical thought coalesce in the gnostic figure of Thomas, doubling the once-unique Savior by giving Him an eschatological twin. "For the Thomas Christians, every individual had been patterned after an individual heavenly image. The idea that Jesus had a twin brother Thomas expressed just this spiritual reality. The image, the twin according to which we all were created, proved that each of us was in the divine plan from the beginning, that each had a divine origin, and that each had the potential for a divine destiny."[166]

In "The Divine Double in Late Antiquity," **Charles Stang** takes up Riley's contemplation of the esoteric meanings of the Thomas tradition and finds in the

Gospel of Thomas a mandate for those who would follow Christ and "dwell in the light" to "become two" (§11).

> The light within the man of light is Jesus the transcendent, comprehending source of all. When one finds this light, one realizes that one is not entirely oneself, not entirely *one,* but has *another,* namely Jesus, already inside. This is the splitting, the doubling, the becoming two that marks the entry into the kingdom, the place of life, from which vantage point one rules over the all—not from a place of distance from the all, but from a place of intimacy within the all, paradoxically embedded in a world that issues forth from a source within you.[167]

Stang reiterates this theme in the history of the third-century CE prophet Mani, raised in a community of Baptists in Mesopotamia, twice visited by a divine "twin" or "double" that he referred to as his *syzygos,* sent by God and "[appearing in] great glory" (CMC a Greek word whose root metaphor is "yoked together." : . . . Then, at the time when my body reached its full growth, immediately there flew down and appeared before me that most beautiful and greatest mirror-image of [myself] (*katoptron tou prosôpou mou*)" (Cologne Mani Codex 17, 1–6).

> On this model, to assume that one is a single self is a form of false consciousness. Rather than overcoming division, the self must first be initiated into its constitutive division, the difference between the "I" and its double. The self is not one half of the pair—*either* the "I" or its double—but is rather the pair itself, somehow preserving that constitutive difference or division in a new self, a new "I."[168]

As the chapters in this section illumine, even originary oppositional principles, locked in struggle within the godhead as though inside a womb, can be understood as twins; their twinship can be expressed through the lens of cosmic birth, down to its most particular details, with the ancient view of the placenta as a kind of twin to the morally conscious infant, one that is not-alive, not-aware. Divine figures can be affiliated with mortal counterparts, who are then understood as a twinned pair with two different ontologies, one often understood to be a spiritual guide for the mortal of the two. This hidden gnosis automatically creates esoteric mandates for human beings. Correspondingly, singleton mortals can have divine twin counterparts, who inspire and inform them. In their hagiographies, the discovery of this "divine double" is often figured as revelation.

The chapters in **Powerful Twins in the Archaeology of Myth** contemplate the relationship between doubled figures and material culture. The presence of wise and magical twin animals in many traditional stories, re-presented in archaeological artifacts, may have amplified the power of the divine beings—including demigod heroes—they served, as well as protected their masters: the "dragon-pairs" of Iron Age swords; the tiny birds, possibly the ravens Huginn and Muninn ("Thought" and "Memory") who perch on opposite shoulders of an enthroned, tiny Óðinn in a silver amulet found only a few years ago in Lejre; the patient, tragic horses of Achilles, Xanthos and Balios, depicted on a black-figure vase fragment from the Athenian acropolis by Exekias. The last is part of a larger category of matching pairs of draft animals that pull the chariot of the deity and advertise her power. It is not only that the lions who flank the throne of the Anatolian mother goddess Cybele from the Neolithic period onward or pull her chariot in monumental Roman imperial bronze statues are fearsome; they also manifest a natural hierarchy, with their roots in her prehistoric role as "Mistress of Animals"—the one who subdues wild beasts with both hands, at the same time, and sits between them.[169]

Having previously explored in depth Celtic mythologies that feature twin births and doubles, particularly those found in animal metamorphoses, renowned archaeologist **Miranda Aldhouse-Green** turns her attention in this volume to ancient Gaulish and British evidence from the Iron Age. Her chapter is framed by the oppositional Welsh twins Nysien and Efnisien in the *Mabinogion*: "One of these was a good lad—he could make peace between two armies when they were most enraged; that was Nysien. The other could cause two of the most loving brothers to fight . . . The two brothers share almost the same name; in a sense, they are two halves of a single whole, reflecting the positive and negative traits that are hard-wired as part of the human condition."[170] As part of the larger theme of "the hostile twins" in Indo-European tradition, she argues that "close attention to the Mabinogen's two Welsh brothers surfaces concepts and principles of twins/twinning, doubles and pairs, oppositional identities, halves and wholes, partibility and completeness."[171] These principles are reflected in the medieval Irish tale of the ordeal of the queen-goddess Macha who is forced to race while pregnant because of her mortal husband's braggadocio, giving birth to twins and cursing any who heard her groans to suffer the pain of childbirth—save Cú Chullain, who is exempt from her curse, and who is gifted with the twin colts born at the same time. Aldhouse-Green believes that the geminal nature of the medieval texts resonates with Iron Age bog deposits of paired bronze cauldrons at Llyn Fawr and at the Scottish bog site of Blackburn mills, paired divination spoons from graves and marshes, or the paired male bodies in the marsh at Weerdinge, one of them violently disemboweled, "discovered close together and placed as though in an embrace, one resting on the arm of the other, leading to speculation as to whether they might have been brothers, comrades-in-arms, master and servant or even lovers."[172] At the end of life, such "kinship logic" created "twinned burials," whether sacrificial, battle, or familial.

Aldhouse-Green suggests that a cultural tendency to think in twinned pairs tended to impose itself on various aspects of this world, shaping ritual arrangements and aesthetics, at every stage of the life cycle. She locates the aesthetic of doubling or twinning in Iron Age ornamented "La Tène" metalwork; the Capel Garmon "fire-dog" that framed elite feasting with its mirrored, yet slightly different, heads [Pl. 13a; Figure 17.1]; the "dragon-pairs" elite of sword scabbards:

> The two "dragons" are presented as equal opponents, in a perpetual, never-to-be-resolved conflict, and so may have symbolised the craft of war and the unceasing strife for supremacy against an enemy. But, as 'twins' they may also, like Castor and Pollux of classical myth, have represented life and death, light and dark, the material and spirit worlds, all interdependent yet in opposition, as positive and negative dimensions of one state of being.[173]

Aldhouse-Green next turns to the stone sculptures of Roman-period Britain and Gaul, in which male and female deities are curiously depicted, *contra* normal human gendered proportions, as equivalent in size, as, for example, at Dijon, the god Sucellus and the goddess Nantosuelta, with attributes, or the stone reliefs of Mercury and Rosmerta from Glanum in Provence [Figure 17.2] and Bath. In these sculptures, emblems of power are shared, swapped, exchanged, or "hijacked," perhaps consonant with the isomorphism of the figures themselves in showing how indigenous and Roman cultural groups were negotiating relations in the same areas. Small white clay figurines made in France and exported to the Western British provinces show mothers nursing one or sometimes twin babies found in private homes, in shrines, and sometimes buried with the dead (*Deae Nutrices*; see Figure 17.3). They may be fertility images; they may be psychopomps, guarding the dead; or "the doubled symbolism could refer to the goddess's dual role in the material and spirit worlds."[174]

Finally, Aldhouse-Green contemplates the "contrapuntal interplay" between twos and threes in Romano-British and Gallo-Roman figural imagery in which tripled figures are depicted with one "odd-one-out"; she suggests that these themselves creates a kind of meta-dyad. Further exploring number symbolism and the significant tensions between triples and dyads, she points to the addition of a third horn to a normally two-horned animal in small Gallo-Roman bull figurines to create uncanniness, possibly resonant with the imposition of a dyadic schema on a tripartite color scheme among the Ndembu. Because symmetry is the hallmark both of the bilateral animal body, Aldhouse-Green notes the progression to extrapolate from natural two-ness "the notion of upside-down-ness and mutual reversal. It is tempting to relate this to ideas of double worlds: the material world and the realm of the spirits . . . Twinning and pairing appear to be a persistent method of referencing the supernatural world both in later western European prehistory and the Roman provincial period." However the deliberate attempt in votive art "for instance in the triple motifs identified in Gallo-Roman and Romano-British imagery" seems to have had as its goal "to destabilize and question symmetry."[175]

Animal twins, both mortal and immortal, protect and report to the god with whom they are totemically affiliated, thereby extending the scope of divine strategic knowledge and power. In "Óðinn's Twin Ravens, Huginn and Muninn," **Stephen A. Mitchell**, scholar of ancient Scandinavian literature and ritual, considers the pair of birds that belong to the notorious shape-shifter and highest god of the Norse pantheon, Óðinn. His chapter is inspired by the discovery in 2009, confirmed by two similar Viking Age figurines since found elsewhere, of a tiny silver amulet in a field at Gammel Lejre in Denmark depicting an elaborately robed figure with two birds perched on either arm of his or her throne, attentively watching a staring face that seems to be missing an eye. It most likely depicts Óðinn, "possibly a cross-dressed Óðinn, seated on Hliðskjálf, the throne from which the god can look into all the worlds."[176] The thirteenth-century Icelandic Prose Edda of Snorri Sturluson explains,

> Two ravens sit on his [i.e., Óðinn's] shoulders and speak into his ear all the news they see or hear. Their names are Huginn and Muninn. He sends them out to fly over the whole world at daybreak and they return at the morning-meal. From this he becomes wise about many things. For this [reason] he is called the Raven God.[177]

Always shown together, the ravens' names mean "Thought" and "Memory." Mitchell asks, "[W]hy should this deity need to have two such birds, rather than just a single one? Is the very existence of two such assistants itself of importance?"[178]

He offers three possible answers to this question, which may be interrelated levels of an extended metaphor that begins both with quarrelsome, curious, brilliant ravens, and also, as in Native American twin traditions, with a kind of obsession with complementary pairs. First, he shows how Huginn and Muninn are members of a family of famous Old Norse sibling dyads, such as Freyr and Freyja or Sigmund and Signý. Beyond that circle lies a rich spectrum of twinned figures with alliterative, antonymic, or rhyming names: Gautan ("Babbling") and Ógautan ("Not Babbling"); the giantesses Fenja and Menja who, laboring at a magical grinding-stone, create their own avenging army to march on the king on the king who enslaved them; the celestial horse Skínfaxi ('shining mane') who pulls Day across the sky and Hrímfaxi ("rime mane") who pulls Night. In this circle, "Even though we are not always explicitly told that they [the ravens Huginn and Munninn] are twins in the biological sense, there can be little doubt but that we are to interpret them as paired in a way similar to twins."[179]

Second, through their names, Mitchell exegetes the ravens as animate vehicles for some of the central preoccupations of medieval Icelandic culture, as, for example, in Snorri Sturluson's *Prose Edda*:

Huginn and Muninn fly each day
over the earth;
I fear for Huginn lest he not return,
yet I fear more for Muninn.[180]

"Beyond the most basic and literal sense of the text, one reading would be that the poet's is an anxiety which is at once both personal and universal, namely, that he fears the loss of reasoning, of mental ability, of cogitation, of thinking—but even more so the loss of memory, the on-set of dementia and the erosion of mental faculties that comes with age. This concern is natural and one which, as we know from other tales in *Snorra edda*, was current in thirteenth-century Iceland: in reflecting on Þórr's struggle with the old nurse, 'Age' (Elli), during his visit with Útgarða-Loki, the text explicitly comments on age-related decline, noting that no one reaches old age who is not ruined by it."[181]

Going further, Mitchell notes that the elegiac tone of the poem may represent a sorrowful concern for "pending cultural amnesia: combating this development . . . is, in fact, the very purpose for the mythological handbook that is the *Prose edda*. After all, the ultimate goal of Snorri's *ars poetica* is the preservation of the tradition of skaldic poetry, a dying native art form intimately tied to metaphors drawn from the pagan past."[182] Zeus's two eagles circumnavigated the whole earth to meet at its *omphalos* or navel at Delphi, the place of Apollo's oracle on Mt. Parnassos. This creates a fixed point on the globe, a foundation for the later seat of prophesy.[183] The mercurial Óðinn on the other hand, is always afoot, insatiably hungry for knowledge new and old, especially that gleaned from the dead—which another verse suggests his carrion-eaters are good at retrieving. So not just once but daily at dawn he imperils his ravens, and perhaps himself to deep anxiety in the process—just as he hanged himself on the windswept Tree in *Hávamál* 138, seeking the runes (and who is the "I" who fears for Huginn "lest he not return," yet fears more for the fate of Muninn? Is it Snorri, Óðinn, or a transpersonal voice that speaks for the whole dying world?).

Finally, as part of over a century of scholarly discussion on the topic of what the ravens represent, Mitchell suggests that the twins Huginn and Muninn show Old Norse thinking about on two modes of cognition and mentation. They may well represent the bicameral mind: "[V]iewing the mind in this way, as consisting of an active thinking component together with the power of recollection, has historical roots reaching back to Augustine (and even further back in time), as well as contemporary value."

> Twinning, on the one hand, cerebration, actual mental activity, "thinking," with, on the other hand, the capacity to recall past events, "memory," is thus one means of "thinking about thinking," a problem with manifestly deep roots in Indo-European linguistic and cognitive configurations. Seen in this broader historical perspective, Huginn and Muninn may then "simply" be Nordic visualizations of a much more general and much more archaic pattern for conceptualizing the human mind as necessarily twinned. [As Pernille Hermann asks], "what is thought without memory, which brings the past into the present?"[184]

Like all pairs of totemic animals who belong to gods—horses, birds, lions, serpents—directionality matters deeply to interpretation. Their mythologies tell of, or at least imply, their submission as wild animals, which extends the god's range of power. The two little ravens who perch on the throne-arms of the regally robed, staring Lejre figure face inward, looking up from either side, intently watching his face. They have news to tell him from the ends of the earth: news that he needs. But soon enough, when breakfast is over, they will both turn and fly in opposite directions once more—simultaneously *away from* and *toward* one another.

The visible and invisible "third" binding immortal twin horses both to another and to warrior mortals is realized in the symbol of the yoke of a chariot-team in "Yoking the Winds: The Tears of Xanthos and Balios" by **Kimberley C. Patton** (my own contribution). Beneath the war-charge of Achilles's immortal horses is the memory of their mother Pordarge, a harpy who bore them "beyond the streams of Ocean and the caves of Tethys" and their father Zephyros, the west wind summoned by Achilles to ignite the pyre of his *therapōn* Patroklos. As twins and as an epic chariot pair, the horses are yoked to one another; so too are they yoked to what is mortal, namely the heroes they serve and who die, breaking their one shared heart.

To conclude *Gemini*, I asked **Philip Garrity** and **Joseph Garrity** to reflect on the experience of reading the other chapters in the volume as adult identical twins. In "Epilogue: Dialogue," Joe writes, "Before our parents, before our older siblings, we were each other's teachers. Our definitions, limits, boundaries, were all determined by our committee of two, and were therefore porous, malleable, and subject to change."[185] Joe and Phil's contrapuntal account of their own life story/stories, seen through the looking-glass of the many twin traditions found here, is searing. Their chapter makes a case for the ongoing relevance of sacred history to human biography.

But did you know we are a fraction? To this day I haven't mastered this concept, how one human being can be divided into two halves and become two whole human beings. How can these once-halves who were so admired for their halfness, fawned over and ogled so persistently, magically assume their separate wholeness? I am still doing the math. I have learned this no-man's land between your personhood and mine is wired and treacherous.[186]

Their reflections are fascinating to compare with William Viney's, called by his teachers, like his brother, "Master Viney" when he started school at five years old in England.

Our teachers couldn't bear to mix us up but seemed unaware that they left us feeling like strangers to ourselves . . . As little boys we grew aware that not everyone had a twin and encountered these simple problems of recognition. We learned that an invisible hand could separate us from our companions. How this happened and when could take us by surprise. We were simply different for being two, different for looking alike. We tried our best to fit in . . . I have met twins who have impersonated each other for months, travelled on each other's passports, attended each other's classes. But I am at a loss when asked what devilish tricks we played on people, as our social world seemed constantly fooled of its own accord. Now the photos of young Master Viney leave me feeling fooled. This is the irony of these family albums. I am left unsure on whose navel I gaze.[187]

As children, Phil and Joe Garrity swapped identities, went adventuring, and wrought havoc in their household. William Viney and his brother did not seem to have done any of this; but in their experience, twinship itself was the joke played on them. Later in life, Joe and Phil suffered mightily in their efforts to differentiate, partly through separate yet intertwined life-threatening conditions, and partly in the meta-arena of Joe's original film, *Twinsburg*, which is set in the context of the annual August festival of twins in Twinsburg, Ohio.

Conclusion

The structural "splitting" Lévi-Strauss identified did not, as he thought, find its paradigmatic illustration in myths about twins. The arcs of twins in heaven, "divine twins," have, on the contrary, always been hard to disentangle from those of vulnerable twins on earth. Phenomenologically, each category intends the other, and is implicated in it: Adam McGee's observation that "the difference between human, still-living twins, dead twins, and 'cosmic' or ancestral twins is one of degree rather than of kind" can be extended concentrically outward from the Marasa, as it seems to obtain to all of these studies in some way.

Human twins are *de facto* born into the space of "exceptionalism," a mythically inflected heterotopia. They can never "blend in," either to established social structures, or to family systems. Their primary relationship throughout life is always with one another.

They can't escape the projections of others who don't understand their experiences. In family tropes or social discourse, they are "freaks," uncanny, an interpretive problem— *even to one another*, as Joseph Garrity's and William Viney's testimonies show. Always inseparable even when alienated or in outright conflict, they alone "get" one another. Their mutual identification can mimic narcissism, as they are one another's person, double, and "other self." Yet the twin remains other to their twin, not the same, and not *not* the same. Both their power and their torment derive from the sacred twin archetype and the way in which it is construed in their own contexts. Whether the mystery that seems to be their lot is superimposed or inherent is unclear, even, apparently, in the minds of twins themselves.

Twins are not one person split into two. They are neither fused nor doubled individuals. They are not exact clones of one other, either genetically or spiritually. On a spectrum of resemblance, they come much closer to being living mirrors than other people or animals born singly. But like the dual number, they are their own taxon, one that cannot be described in terms that belong to other taxa. That is the source of their troubles, at the same time offering its most chronic solution. Matthew and Michael Dickman, identical American twin brothers who are both distinguished poets, have published their work separately but also frequently collaborated, despite their very different voices. One of Matthew's most well-known poems is called "Slow Dance." It reads, in part,

> The slow dance doesn't care. It's all kindness like children
> before they turn four. Like being held in the arms
> of my brother. The slow dance of siblings.
> Two men in the middle of the room. When I dance with him,
> one of my great loves, he is absolutely human,
> and when he turns to dip me
> or I step on his foot because we are both leading,
> I know that one of us will die first and the other will suffer.[188]

Conversely, divine twins are de facto deeply implicated in the mortal realm, even in ways that threaten their status as gods, as well as their own flourishing. They have more dealings with human beings than other gods. Divine twins usually have mortal characteristics or are painfully constrained by mortal affairs, including mortal suffering. They move easily between heaven and earth. They cannot escape living a dual life as gods whose obsession is the protection of, or love for human beings. They heal them, save them, and fight for them; they bring them invaluable gifts. Their fate is flight—and often, in their histories, constant struggle.

I conclude with a puzzle from Apollo's oracle at Delphi. Who are the twin *kouroi* statues excavated there? In 1893 and 1894, they were found by the French School's Théophile Homolle dating from the High Archaic period c. 580 BCE and signed by "[Poly]medes the Argive (?)" Of Parian marble, they are over life-size, 2.16 and 2.18 m. respectively, although statue A (inv. 467) is far more complete than statue B (inv. 1524), which is damaged. Heavily muscled, nude and "highly symmetrical," they were found on the same pedestal, striding forward in travelers' boots.[189] To illustrate what the gods consider "the best thing for men," Herodotus (*Histories* 1.31.1–5) has Solon tell King Croesus of Lydia the story of the pious Argive brothers Kleobis and Biton, who pulled their mother the priestess of Hera six miles to the temple of Hera for a festival when her oxen were not yet back from the fields: "so the young men, being thus thwarted by lack of time, put themselves to the yoke (ὑποδύντες αὐτοὶ ὑπὸ τὴν ζεύγλην) and drew the carriage with their mother sitting thereon: for five and forty furlongs they drew it till they came to the temple." Overjoyed by the praise they received (ἡδὲ μήτηρ περιχαρὴς ἐοῦσα τῷ τε ἔργῳ καὶ τῇ φήμῃ), and she for bearing them—an intensely Greek kind of joy, in antiquity and to this day—their mother "prayed that the goddess might grant the best thing for man to her children Kleobis and Biton, who had given great honor to the goddess. After this prayer they sacrificed and feasted. The youths then lay down in the temple and went to sleep and never rose again; death held them there. The Argives made and dedicated at Delphi statues of them as being the best of men."[190] Solon's lesson? "Call no man blessed until he is dead."

These appear to be the matching archaic *kouroi* of which Herodotus speaks. That is how the Delphi Museum labels them: Kleobis and Biton [Κλέοβις καὶ Βίτων]. Although they retain the frozen symmetry and stability of archaic period sculpture with its Egyptian heritage, they each stride slightly forward on the left foot, wearing travelers' high boots, their muscular arms slightly flexed. But this traditional identification is disputed; more than one archaeologist sees the Dioskouroi, reading one of the partial inscriptions as FANAKΩN (*wanakōn*), "belonging to the rulers," a form of the conventional title for the divine twins in the Peloponnese, where their cult, especially in Argos, was strong.[191]

If this majestic archaic pair are the Dioskouroi, then where are Kleobis and Biton at Delphi? That uncertainty remains about whether these statues represent the devoted sons of Herodotus's account, funerary figures smiling in the apotheosis of heroic death—or Kastor and Polydeukes, smiling in the serenity of their shared immortality, illustrates a more complex idea: sacrificed brothers, solidly anchored in a version of historical memory, could easily shade into twin gods and vice versa.[192]

It is entirely possible, and even likely, that there never were two sets of archaic statues dedicated at Delphi. There may have been only one, which simultaneously figured two sets of twins. In commemorating the twins Kleobis and Biton who yoked themselves together as oxen and sacrificed themselves for their mother—but ultimately, for Hera—the Argives may have portrayed them as the Dioskouroi.[193]

Poignancy lies at the heart of the story of Kleobis and Biton: They aborted the suffering each would have felt had the other died before him. So did their marble *kouroi*, buried by time. Giving up the light of consciousness and returning to the womb-state of sleep in the dark earth, the earthly brothers, in a sense, sacrificed themselves for one another, reversing their birth. "Fatally homeopathic with one other," each could not have endured the other's death. The twin statues of Kleobis and Biton may well have been carved in the type of their divine twin ancestors—warrior horsemen who were the cousins of the Aśvins, who defended Sparta and Rome, who rode down the sky to save terrified sailors, who healed the dreaming sick, and who became the Gemini, star-brothers in the Northern night sky, hands clasped at the single shared point of a triple star.

But before they were the Gemini, they were Kastor and Polydeukes. Like Kleobis and Biton, when faced with the unending separation that death brings to all who love—but to twins is unbearable—they found a way to share one fate.

July 1, 2022

Feast of Ss. Cosmas and Damian of Rome, Holy Unmercenaries
"and by your miracles, heal the world"
—Kontakion

Notes

1 Now, because of axial precession, a cycle of 26,000 years, the traditional dates of the Western zodiacal constellations no longer correspond to the solar path. Hence the sun moved from Taurus into Gemini on June 21, 2021, rather than from Gemini into Cancer. A thirteenth constellation, Ophiuchus, was not part of the Babylonian zodiac.

2 AFGL 5180, "Nestled amongst the Vast Clouds of Star-Forming Regions Like This One Lie Potential Clues about the Formation of Our Own Solar System," NASA/ESA Hubble, "Through the Clouds," March 8, 2021. https://esahubble.org/images/potw2110a/.

3 *Odyssey* 11.298–300, in Homer, *The Odyssey of Homer*, trans. Richmond Lattimore, (New York: Harper Perennial, 1991, c. 1967).

4 *Iliad* 3.343–4.

5 *Odyssey* 11.299. Only a few modern Indo-European languages, among them Irish, Scots Gaelic, and Lithuanian, preserve the dual number. Modern Arabic and Hebrew also use dual forms. The dual barely survives in a few English words such as "both," "either," and "neither." As a result, modern English is impoverished; twins can be thought of either as "one split in two," or as "one times two." only as "one split into two," or as "one times two." In fact, neither is accurate: they are their own existential category. The dual number, like all linguistic elements, both reflects and determines thought.

6 *Odyssey* 11.301–4: "The life-giving earth holds both of them, yet they are still living, and, even underneath the earth, enjoying the honor of Zeus, they live still every other day; on the next day they are dead, but they are given honor even as gods are."

7 As with so much in myth, this phenomenon has a physiological correlative—not the same as a reductive explanation—at least for the possibility of twins gestated at the same time having two fathers: heteropaternal superfecundation.

8 Pindar, *Nemean Ode*, 10, 55–9, trans. William Race, with some amendments by the author for standardization and a better translation of ἐν πολέμῳ (Gregory Nagy calls it "more like a cattle-raid"). In Pindar, *Nemean Odes. Isthmian Odes. Fragments,* ed. and trans. William H. Race, Loeb Classical Library 485 (Cambridge, MA: Harvard University Press, 1997), 118–19. In Pindar's version of the myth, the moment that Kastor died in battle, Polydeukes chose Zeus's offer to forgo an afterlife in Olympus and to share his immortality with his brother, in turn sharing in his mortality rather than be separated. "As a result of this symmetrical sharing, both twins are now half-immortal, half-mortal. And it is this new half-mortality of Pollux that makes his original immortality recessive . . . Once Pollux is reunited or let us say recombined with Castor, however, the two twins together can now become dominantly immortal, since the

innate recessiveness of immortality is now canceled by the mystical deal that Pollux has made with Zeus. The divine father can now accept both twins as his own sons, and the combined immortality and mortality that the twins share with each other can hereafter become the dominant force of their existence. That is how the Dioskouroi, viewed together, are both gods." Gregory Nagy, "Helen of Sparta and Her Very Own Eidolon," *Classical Inquiries*, May 2, 2016. The Center for Hellenic Studies, https://classical -inquiries.chs.harvard.edu/helen-of-sparta-and-her-very-own-eidolon/.

9 In CEG 373, 391, 427, and IG XII 3, 359, a gymnasium inscription from archaic Thera; in 2020, Elena Martin Gonzalez argued that "a drawing like the ladder, if identified with the so-called *dokanon*, i.e. an aniconic representation of the Dioscuri, actually points to the idea that the Theran rock inscriptions, or at least part of them, belong to a ritual context," in "The Drawings on the Rock Inscriptions of Archaic Thera (IG XII 3, 536–601; IG XII 3 Suppl. 1410–93)," Annual Meeting of the Society for Classical Studies 2020, ttps://classicalstudies.org/annual-meeting/145/abstract/drawings-rock-inscriptions-archaic-thera-ig-xii-3-536-601-ig-xii-3-suppl. On the *dókana*, upright parallel bars joined by two other crossbeams as a symbol of the Dioskouroi in Sparta; see fn. 15 (Plutarch, *Moralia, De fraterno amore,* 2.478b, trans. W. C. Hembold, *Moralia* VI, Loeb Classical Library 337 (Cambridge, MA: Harvard University Press, 1997). Other accounts of their paternity evolved, overlapped, or may simply have been differently emphasized, ranging from both mortal (for both twins), to split between mortal and divine (for Castor and Pollux, respectively), to both divine.

10 *Homeric Hymn* 33 (to the Dioskouroi), 12–16, trans. Apostolos Athanassakis, *The Homeric Hymns*, 3rd ed. (Baltimore: Johns Hopkins, 2020). Consonant with their flexible paternity, they are also called Tyndaridai in the same hymn. J. Rendel Harris attached great importance to an evolutionary explanation of earthly to mixed to divine paternity in his provocative *The Cult of the Heavenly Twins* (Cambridge: Cambridge University Press, 1906), and the expansive manuscript that followed, *Boanerges*, which surveyed traditions of sacred twinship around the world (Cambridge: Cambridge University Press, 1913). Important contemporary scholarship on the Dioskouroi in relation to the Vedic Aśvins includes Douglas Frame, *Hippota Nestor*, Hellenic Studies 37 (Washington, DC: Center for Hellenic Studies, Trustees of Harvard University; Cambridge, Mass: Distributed by Harvard University Press, 2009), http://nrs.harvard.edu/urn-3:hul.ebook:CHS_Frame.Hippota _Nestor.2009 and Henry John Walker, *The Twin Horse Gods: The Dioskouroi in Mythologies of the Ancient World* (London: I.B. Tauris, Ltd. [Bloomsbury Academic], 2015).

11 Euripides, *Orestes*, 1636–7, and in a number of other classical authors. Helen's ancestry as the sister or shared wife of solar twins, "daughter of the sun" and perhaps a dawn-goddess in Baltic and Vedic mythology, is treated in Frame, *Hippota Nestor*, 72–3, and in Gregory Nagy, *Greek Mythology and Poetics* (Ithaka: Cornell University Press, 1990), 256–9. "The essence of the *Nā́satyau* theme is that the morning star, as it rises from the horizon, 'recovers' the light of the sun [Sūrya], represented by Sūryā [his daughter]. The night before, the evening star had dipped beyond the horizon, plunging after the sinking sun, in order to effect its recovery, another morning, by the alter ego, the morning star." 256. Nagy argues that like the Vedic Aśvins, the Dioskouroi may also manifest the Morning and Evening stars, alternating but never in sync. "By contrast, the cosmological visualizations of these twins show them coexisting in alternating times and places, as when they

represent the Morning Star and the Evening Star.. . . Such alternation would have to be initiated by Pollux, all lit up. Then, for Castor to light up in turn, Pollux must shut down. But then this twin will in turn light up again when the time comes for the other twin to shut down again. And so on it goes, forever. . . the Greek name of Pollux, *Poludeukēs* ["which means 'continuous' or 'leading many times' or even 'leading in many different ways'"] signals the recurrent action of this twin in initiating an eternally ongoing alternation with the other twin." Nagy, "Helen of Sparta and her very own Eidolon"; see also Gregory Nagy, *Poetry as Performance: Homer and Beyond* (Cambridge, Mass.: Harvard University Press, 1996).

12 New Revised Standard Version.

13 Livy, *Ab urbe condita* 2.42; see discussion in Michael Grant, *History of Rome* (London: Weidenfeld and Nicolson, 1978), 37; on their temple in the Roman Forum, see Birte Poulson and Pia Guldager, *The Temple of Castor and Pollux I and II* (Rome: L'Erma di Bretschneider, 2008).

14 W. G. Lambert, "Lugalirra and Meslamtaea," in *Reallexikon der Assyriologie und Vorderasiatischen Archäologie 7*, ed. Michael P. Streck (Berlin: de Gruyter, 1987–90), 145.

15 Plutarch, *Moralia, De fraterno amore*, 478 a-b. "The ancient representations of the Dioscuri are called by the Spartans "beam-figures"; they consist of two parallel wooden beams joined by two other transverse beams placed across them; and this common and indivisible (κοινὸν καὶ ἀδιαίρετον) character of the offering (τοῦ ἀναθήματος, used of votive dedications, emphasizing the divine nature of the twins as heroes) appears entirely suitable to the brotherly love of these gods" (*Moralia, VI*, trans. W. C. Hembold).

16 Rachel Hachlili, *Ancient Jewish Art and Archaeology in the Land of Israel* (Leiden: Brill, 1997), 308–9; Jodi Magness, "Heaven on Earth: Helios and the Zodiac Cycle in Ancient Palestinian Synagogues," *Dumbarton Oaks Papers* 59 (2005): 1–52, esp. 5–8 and Fig. 3; Eleazar Lipa Sukenik, *The Ancient Synagogue of Beth Alpha* (Piscataway: Gorgias Press, 2007). Despite the anti-iconic nature of rabbinical literature, Magness argues that the Helios (or Metatron) driving a quadriga and zodiac symbolism found in six synagogues in Late Antique Palestine reflect Jewish mystical *hekhalot* themes that survived and continued to be influential long after the destruction of the Temple.

17 Lauren E. Talalay, "Entangled Bodies: Rethinking Twins and Double Images in the Prehistoric Mediterranean," in *Gemini and the Sacred: Twins and Twinship in Religion and Mythology*, ed. Kimberley C. Patton, 247–67 (London: Bloomsbury Academic, 2022).

18 The dual constellation of Gemini was originally called *al-Jawzā'*, "the central one," by Arab astronomers, but later this name was given to Orion.

19 The authoritative work in English on this codex has been done by Stefano Carboni, "The 'Book of Surprises' (*Kitab al-bulhan*) of the Bodleian Library," *The La Trobe Journal* 91 (2013): 22–34.

20 The beautiful rendition of the astrological sign of Gemini used throughout *Gemini and the Sacred* is the work of Kyrill Veretennikov. Used by permission of the artist.

21 Thich Nhat Hanh writes, "About thirty years ago I was looking for an English word to describe our deep interconnection with everything else. I liked the word 'togetherness,' but I finally came up with the word 'interbeing.' The verb 'to be' can be misleading, because we cannot be by ourselves, alone. 'To be' is always to 'inter-be.' If we combine the prefix 'inter' with the verb 'to be,' we have a

new verb, 'inter-be.' To inter-be and the action of interbeing reflects reality
more accurately. We inter-are with one another and with all life." Thich Nhat
Hanh, *The Art of Living: Peace and Freedom in the Here and Now* (New York:
HarperOne, 2017). While it is important not to deracinate Hanh's new word from
its traditional Madhyamaka Buddhist matrix of principles such as *anattā,* or their
ethical imperatives, its emphasis on the impossibility of solitary being may be
helpful in understanding how twins experience their own relationship, and how it
is religiously represented.

22 For attention to these passages of *Taittirīya Saṃhitā* and *Pravargya Brāhmaṇa* of
the *Taittirīya Āranyaka,* which in turn acknowledge the work of Michael Witzel and
translations and commentaries by Jan E. M. Houben (1991), I am indebted to Walker
in *The Twin Horse Gods,* 107 and nn. 62 and 63.

23 Similar to ancient Greek notions of the role of the physician, the goal of ancient
Indian healing was not about "curing" per se but rather, the restoration of wholeness
and physical beauty, which curing a human malady—or fixing a ruined sacrifice—
might bring about.

24 See n. 22, above.

25 Wendy Doniger, *The Implied Spider: Politics and Theology in Myth* (New York:
Columbia University Press, 2011), 8.

26 Vincent Stanzione, "Junajpu and XB'alamkiej: The Maya Hero Twins of the *Popol
Wuj,*" in *Gemini and the Sacred: Twins and Twinship in Religion and Mythology*, ed.
Kimberley C. Patton (London: Bloomsbury Academic, 2022), 199.

27 Joseph Garrity and Philip Garrity, "Epilogue: Dialogue," in *Gemini and the Sacred:
Twins and Twinship in Religion and Mythology*, ed. Kimberley C. Patton (London:
Bloomsbury Academic, 2022), 484.

28 Małgorzata Waszak, et al., "Microchimerism in Twins," *Archives of Medical
Science: AMS* 9, no. 6 (2013): 1102–6. doi:10.5114/aoms.2013.39212.
Microchimerism, "the co-existence of two genetically different cell populations
in one organism," has a number of common sources, the most prevalent of which
is fetomaternal. Adults of either gender have a small population of their mother's
cells; most mothers host a population of fetal cells from each pregnancy which,
starting as stem cells, differentiate into her organs, possibly strengthening her
immune system.

29 J. K. Rowling has said that the killing of Fred Weasley, the more mischievous, bolder
twin brother of George, during the Battle of Hogwarts in *The Deathly Hallows* was
"the hardest death she wrote" in the *Harry Potter* series. She even tweeted an apology
on the anniversary of his death (May 2, 1998) in 2015. The Weasley brothers, who
true to the twin archetype were tricksters, possessed a Marauder's Map that could
show the whereabouts of anyone at Hogwarts. They planned to open a job shop after
their wizarding education. Fred and George were played by British actors James and
Oliver Phelps. They went on to do a number of joint projects, including a podcast with
guest interviews called "Double Trouble," now in its third season, called "Normal Not
Normal": "What is normal, and does it even exist?".

30 Edwidge Danticat, *Breath, Eyes, Memory* (New York: Soho, 1994), 84, cited in
Myriam J. A. Chancy, *Framing Silence: Revolutionary Novels by Haitian Women*
(New Brunswick: Rutgers University Press, 1997), 125. Adam Michael McGee,
"Marasa Elou: Twins and Uncanny Children in Haitian Vodou," in *Gemini and the
Sacred: Twins and Twinship in Religion and Mythology*, ed. Kimberley C. Patton
(London: Bloomsbury Academic, 2022), in this volume, n. 53.

31 Gregory Nagy, "Achilles and Patroklos as Models for the Twinning of Identity," in
    Gemini and the Sacred: Twins and Twinship in Religion and Mythology, ed. Kimberley
    C. Patton (London: Bloomsbury Academic, 2022), in this volume, 283.

32 Jacob Kẹ́hìndé Olúpọ̀nà, "The Code of Twins: Ìbejì in Yorùbá Cosmology, Ritual,
    and Iconography," in *Gemini and the Sacred: Twins and Twinship in Religion
    and Mythology*, ed. Kimberley C. Patton (London: Bloomsbury Academic, 2022),
    71–105.

33 Yorùbá traditional song, cited in the Appendix of *Orin Ìbejì* (Ìbejì [twin] songs)
    collected by Jacob Kẹ́hìndé Olúpọ̀nà, "The Code of Twins," 99.

34 Vijaya Nagarajan, "Twins in Hindu Mythology and Everyday Life in the California
    Diaspora," in *Gemini and the Sacred: Twins and Twinship in Religion and
    Mythology*, ed. Kimberley C. Patton (London: Bloomsbury Academic, 2022), in this
    volume, 236.

35 Ugo Bianchi, "Twins: An Overview," in *Encyclopedia of Religion*, 2nd ed., ed. Lindsay
    Jones (New York: Macmillan: 1987), 9418. For a psychoanalytic overview of twinship
    in development and archetypal experience, including the ways in which social
    views of twins reflect a universal experience for a "perfect soul-mate," see the work
    of Vivienne Lewin, *The Twin in the Transference*, 2nd ed. (London and New York:
    Routledge, 2016) and *The Twin Enigma: An Exploration of Our Enduring Fascination
    with Twins* (Karnac, 2016; repr. Routledge, 2018). Medical anthropologist William
    Viney's rich new study, *Twins: Superstitions and Marvels, Fantasies and Experiments*
    (London: Reaktion Books, 2021) argues that the very presence of twins contributes
    the aura of the supernatural or uncanny to events in a self-fulfilling loop: "The
    events themselves are ordinary or mundane, but the involvement of twins makes the
    mundane magical. The lives of twins are subject to a kind of amplified significance.
    They are special not simply for what they do or say but for what they are taken to be.
    The things that twins do or say become tangled up in what their twinship represents,
    creating a self-fulfilling loop that keeps the world of media revolving" (9–10).

36 Cf. the recent 2020 study by Akhere A. Omonkhua, et al., "Community perceptions
    on causes of high dizygotic twinning rate in Igbo-Ora, South-west Nigeria: A
    qualitative study," *PLoS One* 15, no.12 (2020): e0243169. https://doi.org/10.1371/
    journal.pone.0243169. In addition to acknowledging factors such as heredity and
    diet (yams, high in progesterone, and okra were most commonly named), "the
    majority of the participants attributed the high occurrence of dizygotic twins in
    Igbo-Ora to an act of God. Many of those who held this view believe it is a divine
    destiny—that God created Igbo-Ora people specially to give birth to twins. Others
    viewed the high prevalence of twins as a sign of God's special love and blessing to
    Igbo-Ora people. Attributing twinning in Igbo-Ora to an act of God was mentioned
    in 11 out of the 18 FGDs and KIIs: 'Igbo-Ora is a town of twins; I gave birth to
    twin[s]; my younger sister did; and in fact one of my sisters gave birth to twins
    twice. But the thing is, it is God that has blessed Igbo-Ora with twins because right
    now other villages around us eat the same thing we eat but it's only Igbo-Ora that
    gives birth to twins; so it's just a blessing from God (Respondent 3).'"

37 In 2011, Ian Rickard and his colleagues with the UK Medical Research Council
    published a study of 1889 single babies born to Gambian women over a thirty-year
    period showing that women who have twins also tend to have single babies that are
    heavier (226 grams) at birth than single babies born to mothers who have no twins,
    which makes them more likely to survive; this was the case not only after the birth
    of twins, but for children born *before* the arrival of twins (334 grams). Rickard and

his colleagues propose that "a protein called IGF-1 may underlie the benefits of twinning. The protein, which circulates in the blood, can cause the ovaries to release multiple eggs, thus increasing the chance of twins. It also regulates how much a fetus grows during development." Ian J. Rickard, Andrew M. Prentice, Anthony J. C. Fulford, and Virpi Lummaa, "Twinning propensity and offspring in utero growth covary in rural African women," *Biology Letters*, August 10, 2011, https://doi. org/10.1098/rsbl.2011.0598.

38 Sara Reardon, "Why Do Women Have Twins?" *Science*NOW, August 9, 2011.

39 Susan Dominus, "The Mixed-Up Brothers of Bogotá," *New York Times Magazine*, July 12, 2015. "Brian filmed the encounter on his phone. With the sound turned off, the nervous chatter muted, the video captures Jorge and William engaging in what looks like some kind of a highly choreographed, ritualized pantomime. William stares at Jorge, as Jorge looks off to the side; then William turns his head away, as if intuitively giving Jorge the chance to stare at his face, which he does, looking him up and down. The two stare directly at each other — there's a moment of eye contact that is shockingly intimate, and an exchange of smiles — and then they each look quickly away. As they keep stealing glimpses of each other, they look the way lovers might when they are on the brink of confessing, for the first time, to a mutual infatuation. Jorge pulls himself together, looks at William a bit more appraisingly; Jorge is chewing gum, and his jaw is working hard. He puts his hand on his cheek, pressing his own flesh: Yes, this is me. That person over there, that is him. William is quiet, shifting his weight so that he appears to be swaying from side to side. ('It was like staring through a mirror, and on the other side of the mirror, there's a parallel universe,' Jorge would say later.)" At the meeting of Wilber and Carlos, which Carlos resisted with some deep anxiety, "Carlos opened the door, and the group filed in, like a procession from a dream. There was Jorge, and there was his double—it was Jorge in a strange sweater; Jorge, only quiet; Jorge without the cool confidence. There was some woman, and some other guy. And then there he was—Carlos was staring at himself, an altered version of himself, a funny photocopy, a joke, a nightmare. Carlos looked at Wilber, his mirror image. They took a quick peek at each other—they both shouted 'Ay!' and turned their backs, covering their eyes, each turning red." https://www.nytimes.com /2015/07/12/magazine/the-mixed-up-brothers-of-bogota.html.

40 Harris, *The Cult of the Heavenly Twins*, 152.

41 Walker, *The Twin Horse Gods*, 4.

42 Harris, *The Cult of the Heavenly Twins*, 152.

43 Ibid., 153.

44 Gregory J. Riley, "Didymos Judas Thomas, the Twin Brother of Jesus," in *Gemini and the Sacred: Twins and Twinship in Religion and Mythology*, ed. Kimberley C. Patton (London: Bloomsbury Academic, 2022), 357. Riley uses G. Bornkamm's edition of "The Acts of Thomas," in Edgar Hennecke, *New Testament Apocrypha* (Wilhelm Schneemelcher, ed.; English trans. by R. McL. Wilson; Philadelphia: Westminster Press, 1963).

45 A fascinating account of the twin sisters in the context of their time has been written by philosophical theologian Janet Soskice, *The Sisters of Sinai: How Two Lady Adventurers Discovered the Hidden Gospels* (New York: Alfred A. Knopf, 2009).

46 Walker, *The Twin Horse Gods*, 4.

47 William Viney, *The Wonder of Twins*, https://thewonderoftwins.wordpress. com/2015/03/10/anthropologys-twins/.

48 This would seem automatically to objectify twins as other than multi-dimensional persons with agency.

49 Claude Lévi-Strauss, *Myth and Meaning: Cracking the Code of Culture* (New York: Schocken Books, 1978; repr. with Foreword by Wendy Doniger, 1995), 13. "The universe is not a chaos," a theologically consequential proposition from the founder of structural anthropology, bears more attention than it has received.

50 Lévi-Strauss, *Myth and Meaning*, 32 and 33, passim.

51 Elisha P. Renne and Misty L. Bastian. "Reviewing Twinship in Africa," *Ethnology* Winter 40, no. 1 (2001): 6. Renne and Bastian use this phrase to characterize contemporary Hausa-speaking beliefs about twinship in Dogondoutchi studied by Adeline Masquelier, where special powers are traditionally believed to be held by twins, "including the ability to harm their siblings (particularly other twins), to hold witch-like meetings in the wild, and to fly invisibly through the air to meet with their fellow interstitial beings." Despite these and associations with impoverishment and higher infant mortality, Masqualier found that twins were tolerated until the advent of a Muslim reformist movement called Izala. In the rhetoric of Izala, the first-born twins are cast as the product of immorality, "the product of morally suspect unions between married women and their lovers . . . Rather than both children having a soul or full personhood in contemporary Dogondoutchi, elder members of twin pairs are stigmatized as markers of improper, extraconjugal relations and are treated as abominable objects. The second-born are granted fill Muslim subjectivity because of the supposed legitimacy of their conception." In other words, twins are made to enact religious control of female sexuality. For the study itself, see Adeline Masquelier, "Powers, Problems, and Paradoxes of Twinship in Niger," *Ethnology* 40, 1 "Special Issue: Reviewing Twinship in Africa" (Winter, 2001): 45–62.

52 E. E. Evans-Pritchard, *Nuer Religion* (Oxford: Clarendon Press, 1956), 156.

53 Victor Turner, *The Ritual Process: Structure and Anti-Structure* (Chicago: University of Chicago, 1969). Turner's treatment of Ndembu twin ritual, as Renne and Bastian observe, attributes the group's treatment of twins to a "tensed unity of Ndembu society that contains all sorts of oppositions," in particular, matrilineal social structure vs. patrilocal residence. (see *The Ritual Process*, 83).

54 Turner, *The Ritual Process*, 45. In their watershed literature review, the anthropologists Elijah Renne and Misty Bastian bracketed these earlier anthropological models of African twinship that foregrounded binary tensions in polysemic symbolic structures ultimately leading to ritual resolution. Instead, they lifted up newer work that showed religious responses as reflecting "a certain awareness of dissonance in social life locally associated with these interstitial beings . . . including conflict between individual and group (house, lineage, village) interests, between religious and secular ideologies, with their use of associated symbols, and between the propertied rich and landless poor." Elisha P. Renne and Misty L. Bastian, "Reviewing Twinship in Africa," *Ethnology* Winter 40, no. 1 (2001): 1–11. Pashington Obeng's chapter in this volume is a more recent example of ethnography that "sees" these social tensions in sacred twinship in Africa (e.g., Ghana).

55 Viney, *Twins*, 9–10.

56 A benign example of such experimentation was the year-long NASA study of the long-term effects of space flight on the human body from March 2015 to March 2016 involving identical twin astronauts Scott and Mark Kelly, the former living for a year on the *Soyuz* spacecraft, the latter as a control on the ground. One of its most notoriously evil faces was the three-year program designed by the physician Josef Mengele on 3,000 Jewish and Roma children at Auschwitz-Birkenau, subjecting

one of a pair of twins to deliberate infection, amputations, torture, and murder while the other was held as a control; if one died, the other would be killed, and both then dissected and documented. The goal of this fanatical focus on twins, already decades old in the work of Mengele's Nazi mentor Otmar Freiherr von Verschuer, was to prove the genetic basis of racial "inferiority" and undesirable social behavior, even though by the 1940s environment had already been upheld as equally important in the formation of human personality traits. "Eugenics" itself was originated by Francis Galton, a cousin of Darwin, in 1883, who relied heavily on twin studies to promote notions of selective breeding: similarities between twins, he believed, were always due to genetics, and differences to environment.

57 Harris, *The Cult of the Heavenly Twins*, 152.

58 Jonathan Z. Smith, "In Comparison a Magic Dwells," in *Imagining Religion: From Babylon to Jonestown* (Chicago: The University of Chicago Press, 1983), x. For a range of responses see Kimberley Patton and Benjamin Ray, eds., *A Magic Still Dwells* (Berkeley: University of California Press, 2000).

59 Susan Starr Sered, *Priestess, Mother, Sacred Sister: Religions Dominated by Women* (New York: Oxford University Press, 1994).

60 Ibid., "Preface," unnumbered.

61 Ibid.

62 Other comparative volumes that followed, juxtaposing studies on broad themes from culturally and historically diverse contexts, have had similarly catalytic effects on how such themes might be theorized. *Thinking through Things: Theorizing Artefacts Ethnographically*, ed. Amiria Henare, Martin Holbraad, and Sari Wastell (London: Routledge, 2007) comes to mind, as does *Pain and its Transformations: the Interface of Biology and Culture*, ed. Sarah Coakley and Kay Shelamay (Cambridge: Harvard University Press, 2008); *Ritual Failure: Archaeological Perspectives*, ed. Vasiliki G. Koutrafouri and Jeff Sanders (Leiden: Sidestone Press, 2013); Lara Medina and Martha R. Gonzales, eds., *Voices from the Ancestors: Xicanx and Latinx Spiritual Expressions and Healing Practices* (Tucson: University of Arizona Press, 2019). There are a number of others.

63 Viney, *Twins*, 15. Viney's perspective is trenchant, and as it comes from an identical twin, carries authority. He writes, "The concepts and realities of twinning merge with world views, what we might call the animate clines and hierarchies that link natural and cultural, human and non-human, biological and environmental phenomena. A history of twins that highlights past, present and future understandings of twinning also addresses how twins have affected these broader categories of distinction and taxonomy. Twins are people who have been made to matter, and their bodies make matters of fact and matters of concern visible" (ibid.).

64 Jonathan Z. Smith, "The 'End' of Comparison: Redescription and Rectification," in *A Magic Still Dwells: Comparative Religion in the Postmodern Age*, ed. Kimberley C. Patton and Benjamin C. Ray (Berkeley: University of California Press, 2000), 237–41; Oliver Freiberger, "Modes of Comparison: Towards Creating a Methodological Framework for Comparative Studies," in *Interreligious Comparisons in Religious Studies and Theology: Comparison Revisited*, ed. Perry Schmidt-Leukel and Andreas Nehring (London: Bloomsbury Academic, 2016), 53–71. In the latter work, Freiberger modified J. Z. Smith's proposed four operations of comparison (description, comparison, redescription, and rectification) to change "comparison" to "juxtaposition" and to add a fifth, "theory formation." In contrast to a taxonomic model of comparison, Freiberger "aims at illuminating a particular

historical-empirical item, especially assumed blind spots, by drawing comparatively on other cases." See the discussion and application in Barbara Holdredge, "Interrogating the Comparative Method: Whither, Why, and How?" *Religions* 9, no.2 (2018): 58; doi:10.3390/rel9020058. I am indebted to Munjed M. Murad for this summary.

65 Jonathan Z. Smith, *To Take Place: Toward Theory in Ritual* (Chicago: University of Chicago Press, 1987), 13–14.

66 In American culture, however, twinship is often implicated in the preoccupation with copies. See Hillel Schwartz, *The Culture of the Copy: Striking Likenesses, Unreasonable Facsimiles* (Cambridge, Mass.: Zone Books, 1996), 50.

67 Wendy Doniger, *Splitting the Difference: Gender and Myth in Ancient Greece and India* (Chicago: University of Chicago Press, 1999), 50–1.

68 Nagarajan, "Twins in Hindu Mythology and Everyday Life," 229.

69 Vivienne Lewin, *The Twin Enigma: An Exploration of Our Enduring Fascination with Twins* (Karnac, 2016; repr. Routledge, 2018), xiii–xiv.

70 Viren Swami, George Horne, and Adrian Furnham, "COVID-19-Related Stress and Anxiety Are Associated with Negative Body Image in Adults from the United Kingdom," *Personality and Individual Differences* 170 (2021): 110426; doi:. "Because social interactions are now happening via video, there is an extra layer of scrutiny on appearance. Not only are people worried about what other people think of their appearance, but they're also watching their own appearance," "It can be upsetting for them in a way that is different from social anxiety associated with face-to-face interactions." Sophie Schneider, Psychiatry and Behavioral Sciences, Baylor College of Medicine, cited in Nicole Blanton, "How Do We Cope with Body Dysmorphia in the Zoom Era?" *Baylor College of Medicine Blog Networks*, May 17, 2021. https://blogs.bcm.edu/2021/05/17/how-do-we-cope-with-body-dysmorphia-in-the-zoom-era/.

71 Trevor Noah, "The Daily Social Distancing Show," *Comedy Central*, May 20, 2021. https://www.cc.com/episodes/myoihq/the-daily-show-with-trevor-noah-may-20-2021-jeremy-lin-season-26-ep-100.

72 Lewin, *The Twin Enigma*, xiv.

73 Ibid. "Chromosomal changes can be caused by epigenetic factors, various intra-uterine factors account for this differential development: the timing of the twinning process; initial differences in the number of cells at the time of separation of the egg into two; differences in blood flow to each twin; the amount of space for each twin in utero; hormones and chemical factors that influence the development of each embryo."

74 Hakon Jonsson et al., "Differences between Germline Genomes of Monozygotic Twins," *Nature Genetics*, January 7, 2021, doi:10.1038/s41588-020-00755-1, 2021.

75 Kári Stefánsson, in Catherine Offord, "Identical Twins Accumulate Genetic Differences in the Womb," *The Scientist,* January 7, 2021. https://www.the-scientist.com/news-opinion/identical-twins-accumulate-genetic-differences-in-the-womb-68324.

76 Stanzione, "Junajpu and XB'alamkiej," 179.

77 Ibid., 204, n. 35.

78 John Grim, "Twins in Native American Mythologies: Relational Transformation," in *Gemini and the Sacred: Twins and Twinship in Religion and Mythology*, ed. Kimberley C. Patton (London: Bloomsbury Academic, 2022), 158.

79 *Us,* directed by Jordan Peele (2019: Universal Pictures with Monkeypaw Productions), 1 hr. 56 min. https://www.netflix.com/gb/title/81026600. When asked

by Ariana Brockton whether the plot of a family's struggles with its own "evil twins" was intended to represent a microcosm or double of the United States, Peele responded, "There's a double meaning to everything . . . this movie is about duality and there's no choice that I'm not trying to layer. The state of this country inspired me. We're a country that is afraid of the outsider. Whether it's within our borders or outside of our borders. I think when we fail to point our finger inward, we're capable of really messing up in big ways." Brockton expands, "As for why Peele chose to mainly express these problems through doppelgangers, that reasoning *was* actually quite simple. Coming face to face with your evil twin is creepy. Yes, even Peele, a horror genius, has fears. He explained how these fears inspired the plot of Us on *Late Night with Seth Meyers.* 'I've been terrified of the idea of doppelgangers since I was a kid,' Peele revealed. 'I always had this vision of seeing myself across the subway platform and just kind of thought what if you saw yourself and if that's not creepy enough what if the other you sort of smiled at you.' Then, Peele's mind ran wild with ideas of an entire family of look-alikes." Ariana Brockton, "Does Jordan Peele's Us Have a Double Meaning?" *Refinery 29*, March 22, 2019. https://www .refinery29.com/en-us/2019/03/227592/what-does-jordan-peele-us-movie-title-mean.

80 Conversation with Ayodeji Ogunnaike, Department of Africana Studies, Bowdoin College, 6.1.21.

81 Riley, "Didymos Judas Thomas, the Twin Brother of Jesus," 354–67; Charles Stang, "The Divine Double in Late Antiquity," in *Gemini and the Sacred: Twins and Twinship in Religion and Mythology*, ed. Kimberley C. Patton (London: Bloomsbury Academic, 2022), 368–93. The connection is implied in the name of "The Tethereds" in *Us* who live in an underground network of tunnels; in other words, the twin does not simply mirror, but is connected to its twin.

82 Kimberley Patton, "Yoking the Wind: Achilles' Twin Horses," in *Gemini and the Sacred: Twins and Twinship in Religion and Myth*, ed. Kimberley C. Patton (London: Bloomsbury Academic, 2022), in this volume, 441–3.

83 *Cologne Mani Codex* 17, 1–16, in Ron Cameron and Arthur J. Dewey, eds. and trans., *The Cologne Mani Codex: Concerning the Origins of His Body* (Texts and Translations 15, Society of Biblical Literature; Missoula: Scholars Press, 1979). See the discussions in Riley, "Didymos Judas Thomas, the Twin Brother of Jesus," 360 and in Stang, "The Divine Double in Late Antiquity," 379. Stang questions whether *syzygos* should be translated "Twin" at all, as it is represents the prefix "together" (*syn-*) and the word "yoke" (*zygos*): "[A] *syzygia* is, at its most literal, a conjunction of two cattle 'yoked together,' forming a pair or a couple. The adjectival form, *syzygos* (often used as a noun), refers to one half of the conjoined pair, and can mean 'spouse,' 'comrade,' or 'companion.' I have refrained from translating *syzygos* as 'twin' largely because this seems to confuse matters." Stang, "The Divine Double in Late Antiquity," 379. Following François de Blois, Stang notes that in the Manichaean tradition, there are two clusters of titles for Mani's visitor: one having to do with twinning and one to do with partnership. In my own chapter on the horses of Achilles as yoke-mates, I argue the opposite: the state of being yoked to another is perhaps the most fitting metaphor for twinship, participating in the language of being "tethered" or "tied together."

84 Bianchi, "Twins," 9418.

85 Ibid.

86 Kimberley C. Patton, *Religion of the Gods: Ritual, Paradox, and Reflexivity* (New York: Oxford University Press, 2009).

87 McGee, "Marasa Elou," 131.

88 Walter Burkert, "Mythisches Denken," in *Philosophie und Mythos*, ed. Hans Poser (Berlin and New York: 1979), 16–39. Translation with modification by Gregory Nagy.

89 Nagy, *Greek Mythology and Poetics*, 8.

90 Doniger, *The Implied Spider*, 58.

91 Ibid., 56. For productive contemporary applications of Dioscurism, see Frame, *Hippota Nestor*, Hellenic Studies 37 (Washington, DC: Center for Hellenic Studies, Trustees of Harvard University; Cambridge, Mass.: Distributed by Harvard University Press, 2009), ; and Gregory Nagy, *Greek Mythology and Poetics* (Cornell University, 1990, repr. 1992); Nagy makes a rich short intervention in "Helen of Sparta and her very own Eidolon."

92 See Oludamini Ogunnaike's trenchant critique of Mikel Burley's *A Radical Pluralist Philosophy of Religion: Cross-Cultural, Multireligious, Interdisciplinary* in his "Expanding the Menu or Seats at the Table? Grotesque Pluralism in the (post) Colonial Philosophy of Religion," *Journal of the American Academy of Religion* 89, no. 2 (June 2021): 729–38. "The pluralism of a postcolonial or decolonial philosophy of religion should be 'on both ends' of the discipline; that is, both the phenomena and subjects considered . . . by the discipline should be diverse, but also the people, perspectives, and methods should come from diverse backgrounds" (734). This well expresses why it mattered to have so many twins and relatives of twins write for this volume, to enable a more contributory or even "entangled" perspective rather than one that Burley might extol as "rational" and "disinterested."

93 Bianchi, "Twins," 9418.

94 Ibid.

95 Jacob Kẹ́hìndé Olúpọ̀nà (Jacob Olupona in the original publication), "Some Notes on Animal Symbolism in Africa Religion and Culture," *Anthropology and Humanism* 18, no. 1 (1993): 3–12, esp. 4–5: "I was born a twin into an Anglican lineage from a long line of priests. I lost my twin brother in childhood and, in accordance with Yoruba custom in Nigeria, my grandparents and parents encouraged the development of my twin cult. By tradition, a statuette, *ere ibeji*, must be constructed as a substitute for the lost child. The Yoruba have the highest rate of twinning on the planet, and this has developed into an elaborate religious and artistic tradition concerning twinning that is unrivaled in the world. . . . Twins are regarded as sacred children related by birth to the colobus monkey (*edun*). We are forbidden to kill this animal or even smell its meat when it is killed by hunters. The close relationship between the colobus monkey and twins has given rise to the development of a considerable genre of oral texts called *orin ibeji* (*ibeji* songs) that runs into hundreds of verses. . . . These songs, along with other aspects of the twin tradition, are learned by parents and grandparents of twins, by diviners, and by medicine men and women, to be used in the weekly rituals for twins and also in the day-to-day life of the Yoruba people. However, the songs are also learned by hunters as part of another elaborate oral genre (hunters' dirges) sung whenever they are face-to-face with monkeys in the bush. . . . . [e.g.] 'Ejire, ki mi, ki ng pada lehin re/ mba tete mo o/ mba b' Edun de' sokun/ ile edun. . . Twin, call me by my *oriki* [personal praise poetry] so that I may turn aside from you/ Had I known you earlier, I should have accompanied you, Colobus, to Isokun, the home of monkeys.'"

96 Olúpọ̀nà, "The Code of Twins," in this volume, 74.

97 Ibid.

98 Olúpọ̀nà, "The Code of Twins," 7.

99 Pashington Obeng, "Twins: Welcome and Unwelcome Danglers in African Religions," in *Gemini and the Sacred: Twins and Twinship in Religion and Mythology*, ed. Kimberley C. Patton (London: Bloomsbury Academic, 2022), 106.

100 Ibid., 116. Italics in original.

101 Obeng, "Twins," 121. Italics in original.

102 Idem, describing the contribution of Philip M. Peek in his Introduction to *Twins in African and Diaspora Cultures*: *Double Trouble, Twice Blessed*, ed. Philip M. Peek (Bloomington: Indiana University Press, 2011), 27–8.

103 McGee, "Marasa Elou," in this volume, 131.

104 Ibid.

105 "*Les Marassas sont . . . le principe divin de la vie.*" Odette Mennesson-Rigaud, "Étude sur le culte des Marassas en Haïti," *ZAÏRE* 6, no. 6 (1952): 597.

106 McGee, "Marasa Elou," 132.

107 Grim, "Twins in Native American Mythologies," in this volume, 158.

108 Grim, "Twins in Native American Mythologies," 157; he notes that the various realms of the cosmos are involved in this story. It is the actions of Bad Twin that kill Earth Mother when he will not be born normally like his brother; but bursts through her side; but from her body grow corn, beans, and squash; just as through his actions, the healing society of "False Faces" comes into being.

109 Barbara Alice Mann, *Spirits of Blood, Spirits of Breath: The Twinned Cosmos of Indigenous America* (New York: Oxford University Press, 2016), 12.

110 Mann, *Spirits of Blood, Spirits of Breath*, 45. Grim says about this, "The result of the cultural misinterpretation of this twinship principle is, as Mann observes, that 'only Western observers are baffled to note such things as two creation stories per culture— one of descent from the sky and one of the emergence from the earth'" (Mann, idem, discussed in Grim, "Twins in Native American Mythologies," 172, n. 5.).

111 Grim, "Twins in Native American Mythologies," 158.

112 They are opposed by a mysterious stranger, usually Red Woman during their mothers' pregnancy, costing her life in a gruesome or cruel manner. Lodge-boy is eventually recognized and reclaimed by his grieving father, but only through a series of ordeals is the fierce water-being who was his brother caught by his twin and then brought by his father to the sweat lodge, where he is forced to call out for his father using a kinship. As Grim notes, having been violently ripped from the womb, before "Thrown-in-the-Spring can undertake his role as a twin he has to be transformed by the creative work of a ceremony, the sweat lodge," itself a microcosm of the cosmos that orders the world (ibid., 161). This unusual Apsaalooke backstory leads to a set of heroic monster-slaying adventures; the supernatural quarry are "a human-eating bear, cougar, and elk and, befitting their Plains ecology, a monster buffalo" (ibid., 163).

113 Ibid., 165–6.

114 Stanzione, "Junajpu and XB'alamkiej," 179.

115 Ibid., 179.

116 Ibid.

117 Wendy Doniger, *"Wars within the Womb,"* in *Gemini and the Sacred: Twins and Twinship in Religion and Mythology*, ed. Kimberley C. Patton (London: Bloomsbury Academic, 2022), in this volume, 219.

118 Ibid., 213.

119 Prods Oktor Skjærvø, "Primordial Twins in Ancient Iranian Myth," in *Gemini and the Sacred: Twins and Twinship in Religion and Mythology*, ed. Kimberley C. Patton (London: Bloomsbury Academic, 2022), in this volume, 332–4.

120 Talalay, "Entangled Bodies," in this volume, 247.
121 Ibid.
122 Ibid.
123 Ibid., 257.
124 Colin Renfrew, "What Did They Think? Cognitive Archaeology, Art and Religion," Chapter 10 in *Archaeology: Theories, Methods, and Practice*, 8th ed. (London: Thames & Hudson, 2019), 386–429.
125 Talalay, "Entangled Bodies," 258. "Although such reflections might seem more at home in a post-modern world of analysis, we should not discount that some semblance of them existed in these early societies. Members of early Mediterranean societies surely dealt with definitions of 'personhood' and how one's identity played out through the body."
126 Alfred Gell, *Art and Agency: An Anthropological Theory* (Oxford: Clarendon Press, 1989), 223.
127 Nagy, "Achilles and Patroklos as Models for the Twinning of Identity"; Douglas Frame, "Achilles and Patroklos as Indo-European Twins: Homer's Take," in *Gemini and the Sacred: Twins and Twinship in Religion and Mythology*, ed. Kimberley C. Patton (London: Bloomsbury Academic, 2022), in this volume, 268–88 and 289–99. respectively.
128 Nagy, "Achilles and Patroklos as Models for the Twinning of Identity," 268.
129 Ibid.
130 Nagy cites Nadia van Brock, "Substitution rituelle," *Revue Hittite et Asianique* 65 (1959): 117–46, and in particular here one of the ritual texts from Boghazköi she discusses, published in Hans Martin Kümmel, *Ersatzrituale für den hethitischen König* (Wiesbaden: Otto Harrassowitz, 1967), 188.

> nu-wa-at-ta ku-u-uš [tar-pa]-al-li-uš [
> . . . nu-wa ku-u-uš ak-kán-du am-mu-uk-ma-w[a le]-e ak-mi
>
> And for you, here are these ritual substitutes [tarpalliuš]
> . . . And may they die, but I will not die.
>
> (*Keilschrifturkunden aus Boghazköi* XXIV 5 I 15–16)

131 Nagy, "Achilles and Patroklos as Models for the Twinning of Identity" 273. "*Un autre soi-même*" is a phrase used by van Brock, "Substitution rituelle," 119.
132 Translation by Gregory Nagy; a longer passage is cited in his chapter.
133 Ibid., 274.
134 Nagy, "Achilles and Patroklos as Models for the Twinning of Identity," 283.
135 Diodorus of Sicily 4.34.6–7, discussed in Nagy, "Achilles and Patroklos as Models for the Twinning of Identity," 284, n. 5.
136 Frame, "Achilles and Patroklos as Indo-European Twins," 290.
137 Ibid., 296.
138 "[T]he twins' two names, *Aśvínā* and *Nā́satyā*, each originally designated a different twin, and the significance of this for Nestor struck me immediately: the 'horseman Nestor' combines the characteristics of both twins, and this is the essence of his myth. Nestor becomes a 'horseman' in order to take the place of a twin brother. This is the point of the story that Nestor tells Patroclus in *Iliad* 11, and Periklymenos is thus an essential part of this story. Nestor and Periklymenos are twin figures, but they are twins who separate.. . .." Frame, *Hippota Nestor*, 16. "If Nestor truly became *hippóta Néstōr* by separating from his brother and taking

his brother's place as a warrior, it is not without significance that his father Neleus was a twin who likewise separated from his brother. Nestor and Periklymenos are not called twins, but they follow the pattern of a pair of twins a generation before them" (ibid., 19–20).

139 In Hesiod, Frag. 35. 2–9, in *Greek Epic Fragments from the Seventh to the Fifth Centuries BC*, ed. Martin L. West, The Loeb Classical Library (Cambridge, Mass.: Harvard University Press, 2003). Nestor, the youngest, visiting the Gerenians, took his place as king; in the *Iliad*, though, he tells the story of how he had to go as a horse-riding warrior to save the city, replacing his brother Periklymenos in that role.

140 *RV* 1.181.4, "where only the son of Sumakha is characterized as a warrior" (Frame, *Hippota Nestor*, 64–5.)

141 Frame, "Achilles and Patroklos as Indo-European Twins," 293.

142 It is also impossible to overlook their conception in the Vedic by the sun god Vivasvat with his wife Saṃjñā/Saraṇyū when both were in the shape of horses.

143 Frame, "Achilles and Patroklos as Indo-European Twins," 290, and idem., *Hippota Nestor*, 59.

144 Frame, *Hippota Nestor*, 60–1.

145 Frame, "Achilles and Patroklos as Indo-European Twins," 290.

146 Ibid. Frame notes that Patroklos, urged by Nestor in Book 11 to return to the fight, thereby heading to his doom in Book 16, is called "horseman" (like Nestor) by Homer five times, by Achilles once, "and by a mocking Hector impersonating Achilles a final time, clearly evok[ing] the phrase 'horseman Nestor.'" Frame, "Achilles and Patroklos as Indo-European Twins," 295.

147 James C. Skedros, "Ss. Cosmas and Damian: Synergistic Brother Healers," in this volume, 300–13. Skedros refers to the critical edition by Ludwig Deubner, *Kosmas und Damian. Texte und Einleitung* (Leipzig: B.G. Teubner, 1907).

148 Skedros, "Ss. Cosmas and Damian," 306.

149 Ibid., on Miracle 30.54–82.

150 Miracle 9.37–60. "His friends together of one accord advised him [the ill man] to go to the house of the holy saints Cosmas and Damian, not sending him to the saints themselves . . . , but comparing (them) to the name(s) of those in the empty and harmful readings of the legends concerning Castor and Pollux." Translated by James Skedros.

151 Skedros, "Ss. Cosmas and Damian, Synergistic Brother Healers," 304.

152 Ibid.

153 Skjærvø, "Primordial Twins in Ancient Iranian Myth," in this volume, 318.

154 Ibid., 320.

155 Resonating with the Vedic themes in Doniger's "Wars in the Womb," Skjærvø writes, "Here, the verb "come together" (*hām . . . jasa-*) probably implies competition or fight (like Old Indic *sam-gam-*), as in 2.44.15 "when two armies come together." (322).

156 Skjærvø, "Primordial Twins in Ancient Iranian Myth," 322.

157 Ibid.

158 Prods Oktor Skjærvø, "Poetic and Cosmic Weaving in Ancient Iran: Reflections on Avestan *vahma* and Yasna 34.2," in *Haptačahaptāitiš: Festschrift for Fridrik Thordarson*, ed. D. Haug and E. Welo. Instituttet for Sammenlignende Kulturforskning: Serie B: Skrifter 116 (Oslo: Novus, 2005), 267–79, and elsewhere.

159 As Skjærvø notes, a passage from the tenth-century compendium *Denkārd* clearly shows the placenta to have been thought to have been dead, a source of pollution, but bound (tied) to what is living (translation and notes from Skjærvø's chapter, [342]):

> "Here we begin to talk about the pollution of the various parts that come apart from the body also in life, but especially from a dead body. Not only flesh, but also semen, blood, and all the other things that are called *hixr*. And the most severe of them is menstrual discharge and the *placenta (murdag, spelled <YMYTNtk'> = *murdag*), a part of what is attached to (*niwast*) to the child's *texture (*hambandagīh* or *hambandišnīh*, lit. "what is bound together") (*Dēnkard* 5.24.19b).

160 Karl Hoffmann, "Mārtāṇḍa und Gayōmart," *Münchener Studien zur Sprachwissenschaft* 11 (1957): 100 = idem, *Aufsätze zur Indoiranistik*, vol. 2 (Wiesbaden: L. Reichert, 1975), 435, discussed in Skjærvø, "Primordial Twins in Ancient Iranian Myth," 334.

161 Skjærvø, "Primordial Twins in Ancient Iranian Myth," 341.

162 Ibid., 340.

163 Ibid.

164 Skjærvø, "Primordial Twins in Ancient Iranian Myth," 344.

165 Riley, "Didymos Judas Thomas The Twin Brother of Jesus," 359.

166 Ibid., 364.

167 Stang, "The Divine Double in Late Antiquity," 373.

168 Ibid., 38.

169 One of the earliest enthroned goddesses on a lion throne is from Neolithic Çatalhöyük; her throne and chariot drawn by twin lions have well-known examples in a plate from the second to third centuries BCE from Ai Khanoum in Bactria now in the National Museum of Afghanistan in Kabul, or the bronze sculptural assemblage from the mid-Imperial period now in the Metropolitan Museum of Art (97.22.24).

170 Miranda Aldhouse-Green, "Twinning and Pairing: Rethinking Number in the Roman Provincial Religious Imagery of Gallia and Britannia," in *Gemini and the Sacred: Twins and Twinship in Religion and Mythology*, ed. Kimberley C. Patton (London: Bloomsbury Academic, 2022), 415.

171 Ibid., 416.

172 Ibid., 418. Aldhouse-Green notes that another such pair found in the Great Bog near Hunteburg dates from the third or fourth century CE.

173 Ibid., 420.

174 Ibid., 425.

175 Ibid., 427–8 *passim*.

176 Stephen Mitchell, "Óðinn's Twin Ravens, Huginn and Muninn," in *Gemini and the Sacred: Twins and Twinship in Religion and Mythology*, ed. Kimberley C. Patton (London: Bloomsbury Academic, 2022), in this volume, 398.

177 Translated by S. A. Mitchell from *Edda Snorra Sturlusonar*, ed. Guðni Jónsson (Akureyri: Íslendingasagnaútgáfan, 1954), 57.

178 Mitchell, "Óðinn's Twin Ravens, Huginn and Muninn," 399.

179 Ibid, 400.

180 Translated by S. A. Mitchell. Also known from the eddaic poem *Grímnismál*.

181 Mitchell, "Óðinn's Twin Ravens, Huginn and Muninn," 403.

182 Ibid.

183 Pindar Fr. 54, in Strabo, *Geography of Greece* 9.3.6: "They called the place the navel of the earth, having made up a story, which Pindar tells, that the eagles set

free by Zeus, one from the west, the other from the east, met there" (ὅτι συμπέσοιεν ἐνταῦθα οἱ αἰετοὶ οἱ ἀφεθέντες ὑπὸ τοῦ Διός, ὁ μὲν ἀπὸ τῆς δύσεως, ὁ δ' ἀπὸ τῆς ἀντολῆς.) Pindar Vol. 11, *Nemean Odes. Isthmian Odes. Fragments*, 302–3. In one account, the holy birds even impale one another to establish the spot, like the twin sons of Oedipus who contested at Thebes, Eteocles and Polyneices.

184 Stephen Mitchell, "Óðinn's Twin Ravens, Huginn and Muninn," 402; Stephen Mitchell and Pernille Hermann, "Key Aspects of Memory and Remembering in Old Norse-Icelandic Literature," in *Minni and Muninn: Memory in Medieval Nordic Culture,* ed. Pernille Hermann, Stephen A. Mitchell and Agnes S. Arnórsdóttir, Acta Scandinavica 4 (Turnhout: Brepols, 2014), 17.

185 Joseph O. Garrity and Philip S. Garrity, "Epilogue: Dialogue," in *Gemini and the Sacred: Twins and Twinship in Religion and Myth* (London: Bloomsbury, 2022), 484.

186 Ibid.

187 Viney, *Twins*, 9.

188 Excerpt from "Slow Dance," in Matthew Dickman, *All-American Poem*, (Port Townsend, WA: APR/Copper Canyon Press, 2008). "Slow Dance" first appeared in *All-American Poem* by Matthew Dickman (*The American Poetry Review*, 2008).

189 "Statue A (inv. 467) (on the right as displayed in the Delphi Museum) is well preserved and nearly complete, missing only the feet, although the soles are intact on the base, providing the stance. Statue B (inv. 1524) is much more fragmentary: a large fragment comprises the head through knees, several joining fragments comprise the left arm and part of the base. The lower legs and remainder of the base are restored. The right arm and left leg are missing. the surface is heavily eroded." Petros G. Themelis, *Delphi: The Archaeological Site and Museum* (Athens: Ekdotike Athenon 1991), 33. The Perseus Project: "Delphi, Kleobis and Biton", http://www.perseus.tufts.edu/hopper/artifact?name =Delphi%2C+Kleobis+and+Biton&object=Sculpture, accessed June 9, 2021.

190 Herodotus, *The Histories*, trans. A. D. Godley, 1.31.4–5; Loeb Classical Library (Cambridge, Mass.: Harvard University Press, 1920). In Plutarch, Frag. 133 (Stobaeus 4.52.43), the mother of the brothers, twinned in their *agōn*, was called Cydippe.

191 See Charles C. Chiasson, "Myth, Ritual, and Authorial Control in Herodotus' Story of Cleobis and Biton (Hist. 1.31)," *The American Journal of Philology* 126, no. 1 (2005): 41–64, esp. 41, n. 1; Claude Vatin, "Monuments votifs de Delphes V: Les couroi d'Argos," *Bulletin de Correspondence Héllenique* 106 (1982): 509–25; Paul Faure, "Les Dioscures a Delphes," *L'Antiquité Classique* 54 (1985): 56–65. Chiasson notes that David Sansone, in "Cleobis and Biton," *Nikephoros* 4 (1991): 121–32, "defends the traditional identification, considering it 'virtually impossible' that there were two pairs of kouroi dedicated at Delphi by Argive citizens in the first half of the sixth century, suggesting that the statues of the brothers were dedicated to the Dioscouroi." Chiasson notes the initiatory character of the deaths of Cleobis and Biton, and Sansone, its sacrificial nature: the brothers, physically perfect and young, die in the place of oxen, who were the preferred animal victims of Hera, but without polluting her sanctuary as would normally have been the ritual case, *since she herself sends their death as offerings to herself* (Sansone, "Cleobis and Biton," 123).

192 Sansone argues that the pious twins were understood in Herodotus to have been contemporary historical figures living at the time of Solon and Croesus, not heroes in the remote past. Ibid.

193 Catherine Keesling, *Early Greek Portraiture: Monuments and Histories* (Cambridge: Cambridge University Press 2017), 59.

Bibliography

"*Acts of Thomas*—Introduction and Translation." Edited and translated by Gunther Bornkamm. In *New Testament Apocrypha, vol. 2: Writings Related to the Apostles, Apocalypses and Related Subjects*, edited by Edgar Hennecke and Wilhelm Schneemelcher, translated by Robert McLachlan Wilson, Wilson, 425–53. Philadelphia: Westminster Press, 1963.

Aldhouse-Green, Miranda. "Twinning and Pairing: Rethinking Number in the Roman Provincial Religious Imagery of Gallia and Britannia." In *Gemini and the Sacred: Twins and Twinship in Religion and Mythology*, edited by Kimberley C. Patton, 413–44. London: Bloomsbury Academic, 2022.

Athanassakis, Apostolos N., trans. *The Homeric Hymns*, 3rd ed. Baltimore: Johns Hopkins University Press, 2020.

Bianchi, Ugo. "Twins." In *The Encyclopedia of Religion*, 2nd ed., edited by Lindsay Jones, 9411–19. Detroit: Macmillan, 2005.

Blanton, Nicole. "How Do We Cope with Body Dysmorphia in the Zoom Era?" *Baylor College of Medicine Blog Networks*, May 17, 2021. https://blogs.bcm.edu/2021/05/17/how-do-we-cope-with-body-dysmorphia-in-the-zoom-era/.

Brockton, Ariana. "Does Jordan Peele's Us Have a Double Meaning?" *Refinery 29*, March 22, 2019. https://www.refinery29.com/en-us/2019/03/227592/what-does-jordan-peele-us-movie-title-mean.

Burkert, Walter. "Mythisches Denken." In *Philosophie und Mythos*, edited by Hans Poser, 16–39. Berlin and New York: DeGruyter, 1979.

Carboni, Stefano. "The 'Book of Surprises' (*Kitab al-bulhan*) of the Bodleian Library." *The La Trobe Journal* 91 (2013): 22–34.

Chiasson, Charles C. "Myth, Ritual, and Authorial Control in Herodotus' Story of Cleobis and Biton (Hist. 1.31)." *The American Journal of Philology* 126, no. 1 (2005): 41–64.

"Delphi, Kleobis and Biton." *The Perseus Project*. Medford, MA: Department of the Classics, Tufts University, 2019. http://www.perseus.tufts.edu/hopper/artifact?name=Delphi,+Kleobis+and+Biton&object=sculpture.

Dickman, Matthew. "Slow Dance." In *All-American Poem*. Port Townsend, Washington: APR/Copper Canyon Press, 2008.

Dominus, Susan. "The Mixed-Up Brothers of Bogotá." *New York Times Magazine*, July 12, 2015.

Doniger, Wendy. *Splitting the Difference: Gender and Myth in Ancient Greece and India*. Chicago: University of Chicago Press, 1999.

Doniger, Wendy. *The Implied Spider: Politics and Theology in Myth*. New York: Columbia University Press, 2011.

Doniger, Wendy. "Wars Within the Womb." In *Gemini and the Sacred: Twins and Twinship in Religion and Mythology*, edited by Kimberley C. Patton, 213–23. London: Bloomsbury Academic, 2022.

Faure, Paul. "Les Dioscures a Delphes." *L'Antiquité Classique* 54 (1985): 56–65.

Frame, Douglas. *Hippota Nestor*, Hellenic Studies 37. Washington, DC: Center for Hellenic Studies, Trustees of Harvard University; Cambridge, MA: Distributed by Harvard University Press, 2009. http://nrs.harvard.edu/urn-3:hul.ebook:CHS_Frame.Hippota_Nestor.2009.

Frame, Douglas. "Achilles and Patroklos as Indo-European Twins: Homer's Take." In *Gemini and the Sacred: Twins and Twinship in Religion and Mythology*, edited by Kimberley C. Patton, 268–88. London: Bloomsbury Academic, 2022.

Freiberger, Oliver. "Modes of Comparison: Towards Creating a Methodological Framework for Comparative Studies." In *Interreligious Comparisons in Religious*

Studies and Theology: Comparison Revisited, edited by Perry Schmidt-Leukel and Andreas Nehring, 53–71. London: Bloomsbury Academic, 2016.

Garrity, Joseph O., and Philip S. Garrity. "Epilogue: Dialogue." In *Gemini and the Sacred: Twins and Twinship in Religion and Mythology*, edited by Kimberley C. Patton, 483–505. London: Bloomsbury Academic, 2022.

Gell, Alfred. *Art and Agency: An Anthropological Theory*. Oxford: Clarendon Press, 1989.

Gonzalez, Elena Martin. "The Drawings on the Rock Inscriptions of Archaic Thera (IG XII 3, 536–601; IG XII 3 Suppl. 1410–93)." Annual Meeting of the Society for Classical Studies 2020, https://classicalstudies.org/annual-meeting/145/abstract/drawings-rock-inscriptions-archaic-thera-ig-xii-3-536-601-ig-xii-3-suppl.

Grant, Michael. *History of Rome*. London: Weidenfeld and Nicolson, 1978.

Grim, John. "Twins in Native American Mythologies: Relational Transformation." In *Gemini and the Sacred: Twins and Twinship in Religion and Mythology*, edited by Kimberley C. Patton, 157–175. London: Bloomsbury Academic, 2022.

Hachlili, Rachel. *Ancient Jewish Art and Archaeology in the Land of Israel*. Leiden: Brill, 1997.

Herodotus, *The Histories*. Translated by A. D. Godley. Loeb Classical Library. Cambridge, Mass.: Harvard University Press, 1920.

Holdredge, Barbara. "Interrogating the Comparative Method: Whither, Why, and How?" *Religions* 9, no. 2 (2018): 58; doi:10.3390/rel9020058.

Homer. *The Iliad of Homer*. Translated by Richmond Lattimore. Chicago: The University of Chicago Press, 1951, 2011.

Houlberg, Marilyn. "Ibeji Images of the Yoruba." *African Arts* 7, no. 1 (1973): 20–7, 91–2.

Jonsson, Hakon et al., "Differences between Germline Genomes of Monozygotic Twins." *Nature Genetics*, January 7, 2021, doi:10.1038/s41588-020-00755-1.

Keesling, Catherine. *Early Greek Portraiture: Monuments and Histories*. Cambridge: Cambridge University Press, 2017.

Lambert, W. G. "Lugalirra and Meslamtaea." In *Reallexikon der Assyriologie und Vorderasiatischen Archäologie 7*, edited by Michael P. Streck, 145. Berlin: de Gruyter, 1987–90.

Lévi-Strauss, Claude. *Myth and Meaning: Cracking the Code of Culture*. New York: Schocken Books, 1978; Foreword by Wendy Doniger, 1995.

Lewin, Vivienne. *The Twin Enigma: An Exploration of Our Enduring Fascination with Twins*. Karnac Books, Ltd., 2016; repr. London and New York: Routledge, 2018.

Magness, Jodi. "Heaven on Earth: Helios and the Zodiac Cycle in Ancient Palestinian Synagogues." *Dumbarton Oaks Papers* 59 (2005): 1–52.

Masquelier, Adeline. "Powers, Problems, and Paradoxes of Twinship in Niger." *Ethnology* 40, no. 1, Special Issue: Reviewing Twinship in Africa (2001): 45–62.

McGee, Adam Michael. "Marasa Elou: Twins and Uncanny Children in Haitian Vodou." In *Gemini and the Sacred: Twins and Twinship in Religion and Mythology*, edited by Kimberley C. Patton, 127–53. London: Bloomsbury Academic, 2022.

Mitchell, Stephen. "Óðinn's Twin Ravens, Huginn and Muninn." In *Gemini and the Sacred: Twins and Twinship in Religion and Mythology*, edited by Kimberley C. Patton, 397–412. London: Bloomsbury Academic, 2022.

Mitchell, Stephen and Pernille Hermann, "Key Aspects of Memory and Remembering in Old Norse-Icelandic Literature." In *Minni and Muninn: Memory in Medieval Nordic Culture*, edited by Pernille Hermann, Stephen A. Mitchell and Agnes S. Arnórsdóttir, Acta Scandinavica 4. Turnhout: Brepols, 2014.

Nagarajan, Vijaya. "Twins in Hindu Mythology and Everyday Life in the California Diaspora." In *Gemini and the Sacred: Twins and Twinship in Religion and Mythology*, edited by Kimberley C. Patton, 224–44. London: Bloomsbury Academic, 2022.

Nagy, Gregory. *Greek Mythology and Poetics*. Ithaka: Cornell University Press, 1990.

Nagy, Gregory. *Poetry as Performance: Homer and Beyond*. Cambridge, MA: Harvard University Press, 1996.

Nagy, Gregory. "Helen of Sparta and Her Very Own Eidolon." *Classical Inquiries*, May 2, 2016. https://classical-inquiries.chs.harvard.edu/helen-of-sparta-and-her-very-own -eidolon/.

Nagy, Gregory. "Achilles and Patroklos as Models for the Twinning of Identity." In *Gemini and the Sacred: Twins and Twinship in Religion and Mythology*, edited by Kimberley C. Patton, 268–88. London: Bloomsbury Academic, 2022.

Nhất Hạnh, Thích. *The Art of Living: Peace and Freedom in the Here and Now*. New York: HarperOne, 2017.

Noah, Trevor. "The Daily Social Distancing Show." *Comedy Central*, May 20, 2021. https://www.cc.com/episodes/myoihq/the-daily-show-with-trevor-noah-may-20-2021 -jeremy-lin-season-26-ep-100.

Obeng, Pashington. "Twins: Welcome and Unwelcome Danglers in African Religions." In *Gemini and the Sacred: Twins and Twinship in Religion and Mythology*, edited by Kimberley C. Patton, 106–26. London: Bloomsbury Academic, 2022.

Offord, Catherine. "Identical Twins Accumulate Genetic Differences in the Womb." *The Scientist*, January 7, 2021. https://www.the-scientist.com/news-opinion/identical-twins -accumulate-genetic-differences-in-the-womb-68324.

Olúpọ̀nà, Jacob Kẹ́hìndé. "Some Notes on Animal Symbolism in Africa Religion and Culture." *Anthropology and Humanism* 18, no. 1 (1993): 3–12.

Olúpọ̀nà, Jacob Kẹ́hìndé. "The Code of Twins: Ìbejì in Yorùbá Cosmology, Ritual, and Iconography." In *Gemini and the Sacred: Twins and Twinship in Religion and Mythology*, edited by Kimberley C. Patton, 71–105. London: Bloomsbury Academic, 2022.

Patton, Kimberley C. "Yoking the Wind: The Tears of Xanthos and Balios." In *Gemini and the Sacred: Twins and Twinship in Religion and Myth*, edited by Kimberley C. Patton, 435–80. London: Bloomsbury Academic, 2022.

Peele, Jordan, director. *Us*. Universal Pictures with Monkeypaw Productions, 2019. 1 hr., 56 min. https://www.netflix.com/gb/title/81026600.

Pindar. *Nemean Odes. Isthmian Odes. Fragments*. Edited and translated by William H. Race. Loeb Classical Library 485. Cambridge, MA: Harvard University Press, 1997.

Plutarch. *Moralia, VI*. Translated by W. C. Hembold. Loeb Classical Library 337. Cambridge, MA: Harvard University Press, 1997.

Poulson, Birte, and Pia Guldager. *The Temple of Castor and Pollux I and II*. Rome: L'Erma di Bretschneider, 2008.

Reardon, Sara. "Why Do Women Have Twins?" *ScienceNOW*, August 9, 2011.

Renne, Elisha P., and Misty L. Bastian. "Reviewing Twinship in Africa." *Ethnology* Winter 40, no. 1 (2001): 6.

Rickard, Ian J., Andrew M. Prentice, Anthony J. C. Fulford, and Virpi Lummaa. "Twinning Propensity and Offspring in Utero Growth Covary in Rural African Women." *Biology Letters*, August 10, 2011, https://doi.org/10.1098/rsbl.2011.0598.

Riley, Gregory J. "Didymos Judas Thomas, the Twin Brother of Jesus." In *Gemini and the Sacred: Twins and Twinship in Religion and Mythology*, edited by Kimberley C. Patton, 354–67. London: Bloomsbury Academic, 2022.

Sansone, David. "Cleobis and Biton." *Nikephoros* 4 (1991): 121–32.

Schwartz, Hillel. *The Culture of the Copy: Striking Likenesses, Unreasonable Facsimiles*. Cambridge, MA: Zone Books, 1996.

Sered, Susan Starr. *Priestess, Mother, Sacred Sister: Religions Dominated by Women.* New York: Oxford University Press, 1994.

Skjærvø, Prods Oktor. "Primordial Twins in Ancient Iranian Myth." In *Gemini and the Sacred: Twins and Twinship in Religion and Mythology*, edited by Kimberley C. Patton, 317–53. London: Bloomsbury Academic, 2022.

Smith, Jonathan Z. "The 'End' of Comparison: Redescription and Rectification." In *A Magic Still Dwells: Comparative Religion in the Postmodern Age*, edited by Kimberley C. Patton and Benjamin C. Ray, 237–41. Berkeley, CA: University of California Press, 2000.

Soskice, Janet. *The Sisters of Sinai: How Two Lady Adventurers Discovered the Hidden Gospels.* New York: Alfred A. Knopf, 2009.

Stang, Charles. "The Divine Double in Late Antiquity." In *Gemini and the Sacred: Twins and Twinship in Religion and Mythology*, edited by Kimberley C. Patton, 368–97. London: Bloomsbury Academic, 2022.

Stanzione, Vincent. "Junajpu and XB'alamkiej: The Maya Hero Twins of the *Popol Wuj*." In *Gemini and the Sacred: Twins and Twinship in Religion and Mythology*, edited by Kimberley C. Patton, 176–209. London: Bloomsbury Academic, 2022.

Sukenik, Eleazar Lipa. *The Ancient Synagogue of Beth Alpha.* Piscataway, NJ: Gorgias Press, 2007.

Swami, Viren, George Horne, and Adrian Furnham. "COVID-19-Related Stress and Anxiety Are Associated with Negative Body Image in Adults from the United Kingdom." *Personality and Individual Differences*, February 15, 2021; 170: 110426; doi:10.1016/j.paid.2020.110426.

Talalay, Lauren E. "Entangled Bodies: Rethinking Twins and Double Images in the Prehistoric Mediterranean." In *Gemini and the Sacred: Twins and Twinship in Religion and Mythology*, edited by Kimberley C. Patton, 247–67. London: Bloomsbury Academic, 2022.

Themelis, Petros G. *Delphi: The Archaeological Site and Museum.* Athens: Ekdotike Athenon 1991.

Thompson, Robert Farris. *Black Gods and Kings: Yoruba Art at the University of California at Los Angeles.* Los Angeles: Museum and Laboratories of Ethnic Arts and Technology 13, 1, 1971.

Turner, Victor. *The Ritual Process: Structure and Anti-Structure.* Chicago, IL: The University of Chicago, 1969.

Vatin, Claude. "Monuments votifs de Delphes V: Les couroi d'Argos." *Bulletin de Correspondence Héllenique* 106 (1982): 509–25.

Viney, William. *The Wonder of Twins.* https://thewonderoftwins.wordpress.com/2015/03/10/anthropologys-twins/.

Viney, William. *Twins: Superstitions and Marvels, Fantasies and Experiments.* London: Reaktion Books, 2021.

Voisenat, Claudie. "La Rivalté, la separation et la mort: Destinées gémellaires dans la mythologie grecque. La fabrication mythique des enfants." *L'Homme* 28, no. 105 (1988): 88–104.

Walker, Henry John. *The Twin Horse Gods: The Dioskouroi in Mythologies of the Ancient World.* London: I.B. Tauris, Ltd., 2015.

Waszak, Małgorzata et al. "Microchimerism in Twins." *Archives of Medical Science: AMS* 9, no. 6 (2013): 1102–6. doi:10.5114/aoms.2013.39212.

Part One

Africa and the African Diaspora

2

The Code of Twins

Ìbejì in Yorùbá Cosmology, Ritual, and Iconography

⚇

Jacob Kẹ́hìndé Olúpọ̀nà

Orílàkí, ẹgbẹ́ ọ̀gbà	Twins, our kindred Spirit Children
Ó wu 'ni bí adé,	Whom we cherish as in the Sacred Kings
Ó wu 'ni bí ìlẹ̀kẹ̀	Twins, whom we adore as in the King's hallowed beaded ornaments
A-pọ̀-jọjọ-wọ̀lú	Twins enter the city so splendidly with wealth and riches

—Yorùbá oríkì (praise poetry)[1]

An older employee caught my attention as I checked into a hotel in the ancient Yorùbá city of Oǹdó, Nigeria, located in the southwestern rainforest belt. I heard her recite the above *oríkì*, or praise poetry and appellation for her fellow hotel worker who had helped me to my room, a twenty-seven-year-old twin. Despite my birth status as a twin and my upbringing in the Yorùbá tradition of twins, her uncommon *oríkì* was new to me, and gave me much to think about throughout that weekend. I had traveled home to my mother's town to bury my aunt, herself the grandmother and great-grandmother to four sets of twins. Everywhere I turned during the three-day celebrations I saw twins—twins of various ages, identical twins, fraternal twins both of the same and opposite genders—twins, twins, twins!

That family event brought back deep memories of my early childhood as a twin in the city of Òkè-Igbó, where my twin brother and I were born into this same twin family and were raised as twins in the traditional Yorùbá context. Although my identical twin brother, named Isaac Táíwò, died as a young child, I was fortunate to be pampered with the weekly traditional festivals and ceremonies associated with the upbringing of twins in the Yorùbá tradition. My other mother—that is, my mother's aunt—who was responsible for my day-to-day upkeep while my mother was serving as a schoolteacher in the same town, was very well versed in the traditions of twins because she was one of the wives of a chief priest of an indigenous religious deity in the town. Feasting with little kids, playing drums with music relating to twins (*orin Ìbejì*) were all things I grew up with as a child. They were regarded as tradition and part of the rites of passage rather than seen as a form of religious activity that would later be condemned by Islam and Christianity.

The frequency of *Ìbejì* (twins) among the Yorùbá indicates that both their numbers and the forms of *oríkì* praise poetry in their honor are so myriad that no one really knows the extent of the cultural influence of twinship in Yorùbá society.

This encounter with a twin and an unfamiliar *oríkì* brought back the deep-seated memory of my research experiences in the 1970s in Oǹdó, the city of women where Púpùpú was the legendary Woman-King and daughter of Odùduwà. Púpùpú was purportedly born a twin, the daughter of Odùduwà, the god-king and Yorùbá culture hero. Púpùpú was expelled with her twin brother from the city of Ilé-Ifè, only to become the founder and first king of Oǹdó City.[2] The *oríkì* above likens twins to the status of a sacred king (*ọba*), whose beaded crown is an object of honor and adoration. The beaded ornaments (*ìlèkè*) belong primarily to the sacred king, but also to any set of twins, here described and adored as sacred kings. Twins, in another *oríkì* and metaphor, are referred to as "kings" among children (*ọba ọmọ*), as *Erelú ọmọ*, the highest titled female chief in Yorùbá communities. Presented in both male- and female-gendered images, they are perceived as belonging to the highest echelon of religious and social circles. As spirit beings, twins share in the potent ontology of *àbíkú* children (*ẹgbẹ́ ọgbà*), born to die in infancy, as the Yorùbá say. Yet twins are not despised as *àbíkú* children are; the incessant deaths of the latter, the Yorùbá believe, may require the powerful medicine of female and male healers to intervene quickly to expel evil forces. Even then, the *àbíkú* often outsmart mere mortals, since their power can render the medicine of healers ineffective. After all, the *àbíkú* are also people of the Spirit World.[3]

This chapter will provide a fresh ethnographic interpretation of the phenomenon of twins among the Yorùbá of southwestern Nigeria. I will argue that properly interpreted, Ìbejì traditions offer a deep correlative understanding of the meaning, functions, and purpose of existence and life in Yorùbá society. However, we must view Ìbejì-twin traditions both comprehensively over time, and through the lens of religious space, to enable us to historicize the evolution of Yorùbá religious traditions and social life—including apparent contradictions. We might, for example, consider the Yorùbá preoccupation with immortality as a paradox. The Yorùbá experience the exact opposite: constant threats to long life, under extreme hardships of abject poverty and a high rate of child mortality. I suggest that the multifaceted Ìbejì tradition illustrates how the Yorùbá people respond religiously to the central challenge of poverty and—by corollary—seek to effect the ideals of wealth and well-being in individuals and the community.

Research into the Ìbejì phenomenon has spanned almost a century of Yorùbá studies as art historians, among others,[4] examined hundreds of twin statuettes, wooden carvings displayed in museums in Nigeria, Europe, and the United States. Although a few other scholars have focused on music, dance, and the genetic meaning of the Ìbejì-twins phenomenon, hardly a single case is published on Ìbejì traditions from the perspective of a comparative history of religions, which this chapter and, indeed, this volume aim to correct. Two important preliminary observations are pertinent here to achieve an unobstructed analysis of twins in Yorùbá culture. Some studies of agency in Yorùbá religion have adopted a Western perspective by focusing centrally on the principal deities in the pantheon of the *òrìṣà* (deities). Such a focus arbitrarily often dichotomizes between the realm of the sacred priests and diviners and the realm of the non-sacred. I wish to correct this Cartesian theoretical imposition by emphasizing that the Yorùbá hold much broader views of the sacred than Western philosophical thinking affords.

The sacred Ifá Divination orature—an ancient encyclopedia of oral compilations handed down over generations of Yorùbá culture and traditions—contains copious references to the liminal, from the Latin *līmen* or "threshold," the world of the Ìbejì, albinos, hunchbacks, and sacred kings. Up until very recently, there has been a lack of serious scholarship analyzing the phenomenon of twins in Yorùbá religious studies.[5] Partly responsible for the misrepresentation of Yorùbá religious traditions in the literature is that Durkheim's and Eliade's Western-imposed dichotomy of the sacred and the profane has been adopted in several theoretical and ethnographic works on African religions. However, this dichotomy disregards abundant evidence of an integrated Yorùbá cosmology—the realm of humans embraces the wild realm of forest and savanna and the spirit realm. A tangential approach imposing artificial boundaries on Yorùbá religious culture blurs the understanding of apparently liminal phenomena such as twinning. Such a superimposed approach undermines the very critical role twins play and the meaning twins have in the ontological, metaphysical world of Yorùbá people in which these three integrated realms—human, nature, and spirit—share similar cultural and social universes.

The Code of Ìbejì (Twins)

The "Code of Twins" here refers to the specific characteristics, myths, rituals, and iconography that pertain to the Ìbejì and describe their essence and point to the nature of their being and place in the cosmos. Without understanding those elements, we cannot fully understand who they are and what they represent. In other words, Ìbejì are regarded as kings and sacred spirits in their own right by humans, so the "code" in this case is the deep hermeneutics that is embedded or required in order to have a fuller understanding of who they are in Yorùbá culture and society. The Ìbejì tradition, properly speaking, consists of narrative, ritual, iconography, and mythic symbolism of first-born twins, whom the Yorùbá call Táyéwò (Táíwò), and the second-born, Kẹ́hìndé.[6] The twins' next siblings are called Ìdòwú and Àlàbá. If a second set of twins is born, the second twin siblings may be called Ẹdun and Àáyá, apparently names given to monkeys. Traditionally, all sets of twins share these common names, although in recent years, conversions to Christianity and other shifting cultural factors have caused some to abandon these names in an effort to normalize and desacralize twins.[7] Naming and narrative traditions present deep historical, sociocultural tenets and issues to explore and interpret. The beliefs and practices concerning twinning provide enormous insight into Yorùbá religious worldviews. Its traditions reflect the social evolution of Yorùbá society itself from its origins in the tenth century CE to the present period. More recently, we can show the influence of outside cultures, especially, Christianity and Islam, on these ancient traditions. An in-depth study of twins in Yorùbá tradition allows us to glimpse the depth of Yorùbá religious thought and traditions.

Ambiguity of Sacred Twins in the Yorùbá Worldview: A Phenomenological Interpretation

Among the Yorùbá of southwestern Nigeria, the incidence of Ìbejì, or twins, continues to generate scholarly reflections in the reproductive sciences and the humanities.[8] The Yorùbá have the highest rate of twining in the world. The enigmatic Yorùbá Ìbejì have attracted the attention of several disciplines, providing multifaceted explanations of why such a large number of twin births occurs in this part of Africa. Twinning itself has become the focus of interdisciplinary research.

The Yorùbá bestow honor and sacrality on certain individuals considered special and different through circumstances of birth and acquisition such as the special authority and power in the office of the king. Twins are considered similarly in Yorùbá social order and ranked as the *òrìṣà* or gods. Twins share rank with kings and witches (Àjẹ́), although twins are more powerful than Àjẹ́, who are believed to be invisible female spirits who regulate and control the world of humans. The Yorùbá imagine that twins, unlike single-birth children, can never be devoured by evil, nor can the king punish twins unnecessarily, as the Ọlọ́fin narrative indicates. "Orílàkí, ẹgbẹ́ ọgbà," that is, "Twins belong to the league of Spirit-Children." This saying refers to their high status in the pantheon of Yorùbá deities.

By extension, twinning offers the figure and metaphor of duality, as opposed to oneness; a duality that suggests double strength and multiple sources of power. The Yorùbá do not celebrate the birth of three, of *Ìyá Ìbẹta* (women who bear triplets). The Yorùbá see no special attribute in giving birth to three or more children. Why then are twin births so highly valued? Although the present-day technology of fertility medicine allows simultaneous births of four or five children at a time, multiple births fail to invoke similar emotional response as the Ìbejì birth.

So, why all the excitement over two? Why not one? Why not three? Ifá Divination provides an important primal, a cardinal sign, called *Èjì Ogbè*. It translates, "I am in support of two, not one," or "Èjì, èjì ni mo gbè, èmi ò gbe ẹnìkan." It is the most auspicious divination sign, comparable to the first *Sūrah* of the *Qur'ān, al-Fātiḥah*. The Yorùbá sign indicates good luck, goodness, peace, abundance, tranquility, integrity, and strength; in addition, it warns of danger. To replicate the *Èjì Ogbè* sign in birth is auspicious, and its appearance on the divination tray suggests good luck, prosperity, and long life to the clients who consult divination. Moreover, in everyday life, the Yorùbá accentuate multiples of two, both reflecting the structure of the human being and the cosmos and deriving from it. As such, in addition to replicating the revered *Èjì Ogbè* sign, the birth of two children at the same time embodies and enacts a salient universal principle.[9]

Status and Identity

As sacred twins, Ìbejì present a dilemma to the Yorùbá and their ethos of seniority; this is a form of the crisis posed by twins and noted by Victor Turner among the Ndembu, whereby two individuals occupy only one niche in the lineage web. In every lineage, clan, or family, the order of birth regulates social relations. Yorùbá society presents two ways of looking at this ranking. An individual is either ẹ̀gbọ́n (senior) or àbúrò (junior). It does not matter if the individual is female or male. The rules of seniority surpass those of gender. The senior-junior ranking is critical in ways the Yorùbá people organize themselves. Consequently, twinship creates a crisis in principle of rank, especially twins of a royal family. However, the Yorùbá myth of Ìbejì attempts to resolve this problem. The code of Ìbejì inexplicably pronounces the *second* child Kẹ́hìndé, forever "senior." The first may be called Táyéwò or Táíwò, which is "the first to taste the world," or one can say "the errand boy" or "the forerunner." Such designations resonate with the New Testament narratives of John the Baptist, a secondary figure whose appearance heralded the coming of the deity figure, Jesus Christ of Nazareth. Likewise, Yorùbá mythology holds that the second child, the one with greater status, sends the first one out to taste the world to determine whether the world is good enough for the senior child. If the junior child tastes the world and refuses to cry, then the second twin will not come out. In other words, the myth addresses the science of birthing.[10] In that sense, Kẹ́hìndé as the senior child places Táíwò in the junior position. Thus in the Yorùbá order of appearance, Kẹ́hìndé holds the more honorable first place. Likewise, how does this ranking order fit the general Yorùbá scheme of things and cosmology, considering the Yorùbá importance placed on seniority? As the Yorùbá say, "It is the oldest masquerade that is asked to dance last." It is taboo, for instance, for the elder to dance first. Accordingly, in all things, ways are created to place individuals in their proper rank of seniority. Such social proscription helps avoid conflict of seniority in social settings. Sociologist Erving Goffman described in superb detail the social dilemma facing Westerners in "the presentation of the self in everyday life," "relations in public," and "behavior in public places." Yorùbá culture has tried neatly to ascribe precise status to something that is such a bewildering dilemma to Westerners.

The Ìbejì myth resolves the potential social conflict constituted by sibling rivalry as exemplified in the Ambani family, co-owners of Reliance in Mumbai, India,[11] and many stories that came before and after it, a disastrous consequence in a system in which seniority is highly valued. The Táyéwò-Kẹ́hìndé story provides a formidable narrative of identity in its classic sense that affirms the sameness of the twins, yet circumscribes the individuality of each twin child. The *orí*, the personal destiny deity, bestows on the individual twin an identity quite dissimilar for Kẹ́hìndé and for Táyéwò. The *orí-destiny* leads each twin to accomplish a distinct course and separate results in life.

The Sacred Quest of the Yorùbá

No tradition better expresses and points to the immediacy of the meaning, purpose, and essence of the Yorùbá religious quest than does the twin tradition. The quest is illustrated in the three manifold blessings bestowed upon individuals—riches, children, and long life (*ire owó, ire ọmọ, ire àlàáfíà*). The Yorùbá sustain the teachings of the three manifest blessings of life. Their blessings encompass (1) the *ire owó* or the blessings of money, (2) the *ire ọmọ* or the blessings of children, and (3) the *ire àìkú* or the blessings of long life and immortality. The *ire àìkú* first signifies that an individual will not die during infancy (*àìkú èwe*), and once this has been achieved, *ire àlàáfìà* signifies peace of mind, total wellness, and longevity. Comparable to other indigenous traditions, Yorùbá religions hardly separate the essence, intrinsic meaning, and function of spirituality. The journey of individuals on earth emanates from a well-lived and fulfilled life aspiring to achieve status as a beloved ancestor through death. The journey entails both mundane and spiritual accomplishment all interwoven. The Yorùbá entertain no such notion of salvation in the afterlife as some would claim by converting to Islam or to Christianity. Such a conversion would bypass fulfilling the Yorùbá destiny on earth first. The ambiguous fact of twinning poses both a serious threat—and curiously, at the same time—a solution to this problem. I will provide evidence to show that the Yorùbá narratives, rituals, symbolism, and iconography of twins respond to this cardinal religious quest, which can be understood as Yorùbá culture's quintessential sacred purpose.

The Ìbejì-twin tradition responds to profound social and religious concerns, especially Yorùbá concerns with mortality. Yorùbá people perceive that a death in infancy comprises a serious social crisis. Such tragic premature death disrupts lineage continuity over generations and family unity, as well as communal and social networks and relations. The Yorùbá worldview of family kinship structure and clan is far more expansive than is found in the West. The Yorùbá extend family values and ties beyond present time and visualization. They incorporate and venerate the dead and the undead as constituents of the living contemporary family clan-community. The Yorùbá realize that death is inexorable—death will come. However, what they fear most is a death in infancy that prevents an individual from attaining a full life of accomplishment and self-actualization. Abraham Maslow described the concept as the ultimate achievement in his hierarchy of human needs in *A Theory of Human Motivation* (1943). As the Yorùbá say, "Bí a ò kú, ìṣe ò tán" ("If we live, then there's a chance for great accomplishment"). Consequently, the Yorùbá are driven to do everything possible to prevent an ill-fated death in infancy that would preclude their consummate priority in life. For example, they do not favor too long of a life, which they refer to as *awáyé-málọ* (one who comes and refuses to go). The Yorùbá believe that such a person is kept alive at the expense of the younger generation. They expect you to live your life fully and then to go. They dread child mortality. Perhaps the tradition and the code of twins engendered this interesting story tied to that whole notion of death and immortality. To manage the crisis of mortality, the Yorùbá created immortal images, or Ère Ìbejì, of deceased twins who act as partners to the living twin. Consequently, then, the images are produced in response to the quest to maintain life.[12] Twins are described as *ẹgbẹ́ ọgbà*, meaning "friends and kindred Spirit Children." This appellation in part suggests similar tutelary spirits such as Greek and Roman patron deities, Japanese Shinto *kami*, Islamic genies *(jinn)*, Catholic saints, and Christian guardian angels.

Twins in Yorùbá Names, Myth, and Cosmology

Numerous narratives and stories establish the significance of twins in Yorùbá society and their primal place of honor in kinship clan, communities, towns, and cities. Several

Ifá narratives talk about Ìbejì-twin origins, their relationship to the human and animal world, and the origin of their power that surpasses any other in the animal kingdom or human society. Twins share similar names to those of the sacred king, whom the Yorùbá consider a living deity. These narratives assist us in locating the status of Ìbejì in Yorùbá religious structure and social settings, as well as in understanding how this status relates to the Yorùbá religious worldview.

An Ifá narrative, *Ọ̀yẹ̀kú-dì*, tells us that at the time of creation of the world, monkeys and humans, who shared the same abode, were regarded as related beings. The monkeys were the first to be created before humans. The Yorùbá say that the monkey's procreative ability allowed monkeys to dominate colonies all over the world. Once the monkeys consulted their diviner to find out about the future, and they were warned to perform sacrifices so that "strangers" would never take over their homelands. True to Ifá's prediction, humans—the last to be created who lived with monkeys as cousins—began to give the monkeys a tough time. Consequently, the monkeys became fed up with human lifestyles, transgressions, and failures to maintain peaceful relations with animal beings. The monkeys decided to distance themselves by climbing into trees to escape into the forest away from the human aggression and menace. Their transformation and separation into the wilderness, and their ascent into a new abode, explain their superior status to contemporary human beings.

Today it is still common to find monkeys who are domesticated living with humans as "pet-objects." Babaláwo Fátóògùn observed that these monkeys are referred to in popular Yorùbá parlance as *ẹdun arìnlẹ̀*, that is, "monkeys that walk on the ground," as opposed to those that fly through the trees. The Yorùbá often invoke this metaphoric monkey to refer to someone who fails to become a high achiever, someone reduced from riches to rags. The metaphor speaks to the loss of the superior place and habitat space of a forest monkey, a monkey reduced to sharing a space of lesser status with humans. Fátóògùn refers to the domesticating process in which the monkey is ostracized from the forest and banished to city life. As we will see later in the narrative of how the forest monkey, such as a red colobus monkey (*Procolobus badius waldroni*), a primate endemic to West African forests, established its power and superiority over humans. However, such a domesticated monkey loses its "magical" power and dominance over humans. The Yorùbá often use "Ẹdun", or monkey(s), and "Ìbejì-Twins" interchangeably thereby linking the relationship between the two and showing why and how the Ìbejì acquired their sacred and magical prowess. Indeed, some of my elders call me Ẹdun, as well as Kẹ́hìndé. The story may reflect the Yorùbá imagination, a sacred genealogy that reflects biological evolution sourcing humans from animal species; in both forms of the story, human beings emerged from a monkey lineage.

Ẹdun is an uncommon family or lineage name, like the magnificent Ìrókò (*chlorophora excelsa*) or Àràbà (*ceiba pentandra*) or ceiba, a West African hardwood that may reach 160 feet. Tradition says that the massive Ìrókò Tree houses the spirit of an elder who lies in waiting at night to terrify forest inhabitants. Among the animal species is Ògìdán (leopard). Such a tradition serves to protect the species. As a family lineage name, Ẹdun reminds its bearer of the close relationship between humans and special species who dwell in nature.

Other cultures encourage special privilege for species found in their nearby natural habitats. On September 28, 2008, for example, "the people of Ecuador voted overwhelmingly for a new constitution that [gave] nature—its mountains, rivers, forests, air, and islands—legally enforceable rights to 'exist, flourish, and evolve.' It [was] the first country in the world to do so," changing the legal status of certain natural phenomena from mere property subject to mining, harvesting, and environmental degradation—to landforms and species endowed with rights of survival.[13]

The Ẹdun myth explains not only the fascinating relationship between twins and forest monkey lineages but also indeed why the two are interchangeable in Yorùbá society. More importantly, the narrative of Ẹdun and Twins suggests the parallel. Through their powers, twins could cause misfortune by spoiling the good fortune of those who have offended them. Even a twin's own parents are subject to retribution. Sharing similar oríkì with the monkey lineage, twins are forbidden to eat monkey flesh, known as bush meat, a special delicacy common in the Yorùbá diet. To eat monkey is tantamount to eating human flesh and indeed eating the flesh of one's own blood or kin.

Birth Names of the Ìbejì-Twins

The Ìbejì attain their power since they are born two of a kind from the same womb through the same birthing process, although the Yorùbá believe they have separate destinies (*orí*). There is a strong mythology behind them. Some children bring their natural names from heaven, from the other world. The circumstances of their birth depart from normal observable facts that explain the phenomena. For example, there are special names for various births, such as Òjó (male), and Àìná (female) which are given to children born with the umbilical cord around their necks. Infants born with natural dreadlocks, irrespective of their sex, are called Dàda. In the case of Dàda, like the biblical Samson, the child is never to cut its hair. This child is the recipient of elaborate ceremonies and ritual to ensure that it enjoys a peaceful life. Like twins, these children are considered extraordinary, having their own special oríkì-praise poetry to remind parents and relations of the special circumstances of their birth. As the Yorùbá would say, "orúkọ ọmọ ló ń ro ọmọ," "a child's acts according to his or her name." These remarkable children deserve names related to their *orí* (destiny). Forewarned, the Yorùbá control unforeseen crises brought about by unusual births.

The issue of identity is prevalent in the twinning tradition. The names of twins are bestowed on them by their *orí*, which are inherited from heaven, acquired only by virtue of being born twins. This birthright is partly what makes the twin tradition so special and significant. Unlike kings (*ọba*), who are made and not born, twins are born sacred beings. Twins are endowed from birth with a state of sacredness although destiny, the orí, guides both kings and twins equally. There is the question of why do certain lineages and families bear a twin surname when they themselves are not twins? Could be that their forebears or ancestors were twins? Surveys will have to supply the answers to these questions.

Ifá Divination Orature: Myth and Narratives of Ìbejì-Twins

We begin with the sacred narratives of origin in Ifá Divination orature. The vast body of knowledge and orature, known as Ifá, is an oral encyclopedia handed down generation after generation. Ifá narratives are replete with stories of Ìbejì-twins. Ifá contains significant resources for understanding the place of Ìbejì in Yorùbá cosmology, and illustrates the relationship of twinning to other minor and major deities. It stresses the important religious and social institution of sacred kingship, portraying all Ìbejì as powerful Spirit-Children whose influence and popularity among the gods and the animal kingdom is unsurpassed. Ifá often portrays the Ìbejì as spirit beings. In times of trouble, they emerge at a critical moment to avert impending disaster in the community and to provide wealth to impoverished parents.

In the *Ìrẹ̀tẹ̀ Àáyá* (also called *Ìrẹ̀tẹ̀ Ọ̀sẹ́*) divination text, we read about the origin of the propitiation of twins. An evolving relationship and kinship complex brings Ẹdun (monkey) and twins together as sibling spirits. The sacred narratives say:

Ifá ní Kókó-igi-mo-le-dain	Ifá says that Koko-igi-mo-le-dain (name of the Babaláwo)
A d'Ífá fún Ẹdun,	Performed Ifá Divination for Ẹdun (Monkey)
Ní'jó wọn tí ọrun bọ̀ wá sóde iṣálayé	While they were coming from heaven to the earth
Wọ́n délé ayé tán,	When they reached the world,
Wọ́n la igbó Orò	They struggled to pass through Orò's sacred forest
Wọ́n la igbó Ọpa	They struggled through Ọpa's sacred forest
Ni in wọ́n ti ń la ọnà gbòòròrò ní ibi ẹsẹ̀ ń tọ̀	They were able to discover a broad path where they could walk
Wọ́n ní Ilé ẹni tí kò ní ni àwọn yóò wọ̀ lọ	They resolved that they would enter the house of a destitute person to be born by the poor
Wọ́n ní àwọn yóò wọ ilé ẹni tí ó ń tiraka láti là,	They resolved that they would enter into the house of a person struggling to be prosperous in life
Láti lówó lọ́wọ́ àti láti ṣe orí ire ní ilé ayé	To be wealthy, to be successful in life, who would lack nothing
Ṣùgbọ́n tí kò ní	Who would never labor in vain
Wọ́n ní ara a rẹ̀ làwọn yóò gbà wá sí òde ayé	Through this category of persons they resolved to come into this world.[14]

The divination text relates how spirit beings, born as humans, choose a birth-path of poverty rather than a birth-path of wealth. However, the Ìbejì-Twins are unique as they chose a common path to this world, making the journey from heaven to this world as a pair. The birth-path they tread on earth is sacred, as they cross the sacred threshold of Orò and Ọpa Groves, two sacred forests exuding danger and fear. However, the success of their crossing transforms them from sacred spirit beings into human beings. They are then born to a house of poverty, which they in turn transformed to a house of assets and prosperity.

Another oral myth of Ìbejì origins speaks of a narrative of taboo. Ẹdun and Àáyá were two animal species living in heaven. The two made up their minds to come to the earth. Kẹ́hìndé was first to arrive. When Kẹ́hìndé reached the earth, he jumped inside a tree called the *ọmọ làárọ̀*. Ọmọ làárọ̀ is the name of Èjì Òkò, which in turn is the name of the òrìṣà Orísẹ̀-ń-wáyé. Orísẹ̀-ń-wáyé gave birth to all Ìbejì-Twins. All came through Orísẹ̀-ń-wáyé. It is she who gave birth to numerous twins on the earth. Ọmọkẹ́hìndé was the first person to come, after which Ọmọtáyé followed. When the two of them arrived on earth, they lived together as one family, demonstrating genuine love toward each other. Their mother took excellent care of them. She carried one on her back in a wrapper and the other in front of her when she danced. She made sure that they followed her wherever she went.

Once upon a time, their mother was given the taboo that she and her children should never eat Obì Ẹdun ("monkey" or Ẹdun's kola nut). But she was starving, and as she was passing a path within the forest, she saw Igi Ẹdun (a special Ìbejì tree) weighed down with so many fruits called Obì Ẹdun (Ẹdun's kola nut). Extreme hunger drove her; yet she remembered vividly the taboo forbidding it. She thought over it a while but decided to eat, reconsidering the premise that the taboo after all was not proscribed for her but only for her children. When she returned home, carelessly she put the remaining forbidden fruit on the bare floor. Her children were already growing as they could crawl and jump to pick things up. As they crawled around, the toddlers picked up the fruit and ate it. Immediately, Táyéwò or Táíwò was transformed into a monkey. Kẹ́hìndé became Ẹdun, another species within the monkey family. The two of them started to jump from tree to tree, particularly on the forbidden tree. These two types of monkeys were known as Àáyá and Ẹdun, and the two of them may be seen today jumping around together in the forest or bush.

The people started to sing:

Táyé wọn d'ọbọ	Táyé has become a monkey
Kẹ́hìndé wọ́n ló wa d'Ẹdun	Kẹ́hìndé has become a monkey
Ẹ ò rí ohun Ìyá a yín ṣe bí?	See what your mother has done?
Ẹ̀yin ò ri tí Ìyá a yín gbé ṣe	See what your mother has achieved
Ó léyin ò rí èèwọ̀ bí ó ti ń jà yín more	What heartache the breaking of taboo can cause.

Since that time, any mother of twins, and the twins themselves, are forbidden to eat Obì Ẹdun.

Since the first Ìbejì-Twin had already changed to the form of a monkey, Ifá explains how the transformation of Ẹdun, a monkey, to the human Ìbejì occurred, through divine rebirth by Ọrúnmìlà himself. According to this story, Ọrúnmìlà himself later gave birth to the Ìbejì-Twins that became the human Ìbejì. Ọrúnmìlà instructed further that it is taboo for any mother of a twin, and the twins themselves, to eat Obì Ẹdun. Ọrúnmìlà decreed that Ìbejì are by right divinities and should, therefore, be venerated. Ọrúnmìlà mandated that the Yorùbá must carve images in their remembrance. The images must be venerated by sacrifices offered to them from time to time. Ọrúnmìlà now decreed unequivocally:

Kí Àáyá tó ní ìrù gangan-an-gan gun àgbọn;	Let Àáyá (monkey) with its long tail climb a coconut tree;
Kí Ẹdun tó ní ìrù gangan-an-gan s'ọkalẹ̀;	And Ẹdun (monkey) with its long tail descends down the coconut tree;
Ó ní kí orí Ìbejì ó wá d'orí àpésìn.	The Ìbejì from this moment have become subjects of veneration and honor.

In *Ìrẹtẹ̀-Kànràn*, we read these praise verses.

Aṣẹ́gi ń'gbó a yayo	Trees are cut in the bush and savanna clearings
Aṣẹ́gi lọ́dàn, a ya ya	Trees are also cut in forest as well in the clearings
Àgbà'lapá ló ṣẹ́gi tán, tó fi'bi èyí wìnnì tẹ́lẹ̀	It was Àgbà'lapá who cut trees and used another parts to touch the ground
A d'Ífá fún Ìya Abéjìrẹ́	Perform Ifá Divination for the mother of twins
Tí yóò máa ṣe ẹ̀wà ọ̀sọ̀sọ̀ ẹ̀ kiri	Who will be making regular bean meals for her twins.

When she was young, it was predicted that the Ìyá Ìbejì (mother of twins) would bear twins. She was instructed that when these twins were born, she should prepare succulent beans to celebrate their arrival and later she should sell cooked beans as a trade. In addition, the prediction foretold that these children would bring her great prosperity and success. Thus, when she was put to bed, she bore twins. Obeying the counsel of the diviner, she prepared succulent beans for the twin children. As she continued the specialty cooking, her life became more prosperous and successful.

The Odù Ifá *Ogbè-Wẹ̀yìn* tells another story about the mysterious origin and birth of twins:

Ogbè-Wẹ̀yìn b'ájá a rẹ ó bá pa'kún	*Ogbè-Wẹ̀yìn*, if your dog is unable to kill ikún (a type of animal)
A d'Ífá fún wọn n'Ílà-odò	Perform Ifá Divination for those living at Ìla-odò town
Ní'lé Aláró	Where they carry out indigo dyeing
Ní'bi wọ́n gbé fi omi ojú s'ògbérè e tọmọ	And they cried out seeking blessings of the fruit of the womb (children)
Won n fi omi oju se gbore ire gbogbo	They were desirous of all the good things in life
Wọ́n wáre wáre wọn ò rí	They looked for success, but they could not find it
Wọ́n wá lọ rèé bá wọn	And they went to meet those living
Ní etí Ìdó níbi wọ́n gbé	In Ido town
Ṣe'tí ọpọ́n yẹrẹyẹrẹ	Where on a daily basis there are many divination sessions
Ní'bi wọ́n ti ń fi àtẹ ẹ́ sọ èjìká	And there are many Odù prints strewn all over town
Tí wọn ń fi máa pakájà	They flaunt expensive cloth over their shoulders
Tí wọn fi kun etí ọpọ́n'fá.	And splendidly? do they decorate their Ifá Tray.

This family from Ido suffered all kinds of challenges including barrenness, poverty, and merciless abuse from those around them. They became so impoverished that they started to cry profusely. In alarm, they sought divination, and the Odù who appeared was no other than Ogbèwẹ̀yìn. The Odù assured them that they would bear children, giving birth to sacred beings. If they venerated the Òrìṣà properly, they would prosper, and all their problems would be solved. The Odù asked them to offer sacrifice at the base of the magnificent Ìrókò Tree, offering food and various animals including a cock and hen, served with tasty fried beans, kola nut, and gin. In the vast forest of Agúnrégé-Jégé, the family received instructions that after offering this sacrifice at the base of the great tree, they should return home, but they must never look back at all. Mysterious Spirit Beings lurked inside the enormous Ìrókò Tree. They cannot be described as either human or spirit, having both human and spiritual personalities. Endowed with spiritual powers and magic, whatever they pronounce comes to pass. With *Àṣẹ*, they can ordain a pregnancy, even without sexual intercourse. Their power is so terrifying that they can turn day to night and night to day. There was only one warning. Whosoever nears this imposing Ìrókò to offer sacrifice must never glance backward for fear of sensing the expressions, movement, and powerful spoken words of the forest. Any person who looks backward can hear what the forces are saying. The utterances and ill wishes of these forces can stun them. Their only protection is never to look back, to ensure that no ill effects of any kind will occur.

Under the spreading arms of the massive Ìrókò Tree in Agúnrégé-Jégé Forest, the family offered a sacrifice to the spirits. Immediately the sky became black, storm clouds arose, and the wind blew. As they returned home, the woman among them, referred to as *àwọn tí wọ́n máa ń ti èyìn tọ̀*, "[one of] those who urinate through the back," inadvertently glanced backward although the man continued looking straight forward. Immediately, she heard the spirit forces inside this Ìrókò Tree. Inexplicably, the Tree Spirit impregnated her. When she was ready, she delivered a set of twins. It was surprising for a woman to bear two babies at the same time. Thus, the family consulted divination. The Babaláwo reminded them of the instruction never to gaze backward after performing sacrifice at the Ìrókò Tree. It was said that because she looked back, the sperm of the Tree-forest Spirit had mixed with the woman's ovum (*àtọ̀ ọmọ ènìyàn ti papọ̀ mọ́ ti Ọ̀rọ̀*). The Babaláwo instructed that the lives of the twin children should be spared, revered, and placated. By implication, Ìbejì is half human and half spirit, and therefore Ìbejì is a spirit being who desires propitiation. This duality explains why they are venerable beings, although not fully human. To retain their spirit nature, the parents were told to go to Agúnrégé-Jégé Forest. They were to take the wood of the noble Ìrókò Tree to carve a worthy image (Èrè Ìbejì) to propitiate from time to time with rat, fish, and all other edibles.

Ẹdun and the Sacred Kingship

The discourse of Ìbejì features prominently in the narratives of sacred kingship, especially in Ilé-Ifẹ̀, the sacred city of Ọlófin. Few narratives illustrate this as well as Ìbejì's encounter with Ọlófin, the sacred monarch and Ọ̀rúnmìlà, deity of Divination himself. In the first encounter narrative in Odù Ifá, Ìbejì rescued Ọlófin when the king lost his way in the forest. Ìbejì recognized Ọlófin, and accorded Ọlófin the honor and respect due a sacred king. Ìbejì led Ọlófin to safety. Later, when Ìbejì was denied his/their rightful place in the assembly of gods and humans, Ìbejì never hesitated to display his/their higher power over all other animals and humans.

The second set of narratives illustrates how Ìbejì intuitively averted the sudden death that Ọ̀rúnmìlà would suffer, turning Ọ̀rúnmìlà's bad fortune into good. Thus, Ìbejì provides an archetypal model of how and why Ifá Divination is consulted today as a maker of good fortune and redeemer of bad fortune. If there is any doubt about Ìbejì's superior power over all other sacred subjects—especially diviners, the sacred kings, and animal beings— the Ifá narrative in Odù *Èjì Ogbè* establishes the superiority of Ìbejì. The Ẹdun narrative provided in several versions refers to the journey to Ilé-Ifẹ̀, the sacred city of the Yorùbá people, a journey that demands rigor and stamina, which only the monkey could undertake successfully.

The Rescue of King Ọlọ́fin

In the first narrative, the palace diviner asks Ọlọ́fin, ruler of Ilé-Ifẹ̀, to perform sacrifice so that Ọlọ́fin would never become lost in the forest like a discarded sacrificial calabash (Igbá ẹbọ). Ọlọ́fin vowed that Ifá's utterances would never come to pass, proclaiming that he, Ọlọ́fin, was too knowledgeable and powerful to succumb to failure. Then one of Ọlọ́fin's children was sick, Ọlọ́fin went to the nearby forest to gather the indispensable medicinal herbs to prepare a healing herbal drink for the child. True to Ifá's statement, Ọlọ́fin became lost in the forest and wandered about to find the path to the city and palace. Ẹdun, the monkey, from the treetops spied the king in his predicament. Ẹdun shouted, "Ìwá nù, Ìwá nù"—"A great person is missing, a great person is missing." Ẹdun rescued the king using his long tail to clear a space for Ọlọ́fin to sit and rest. Ẹdun used his deep eye socket to fetch water for Ọlọ́fin to drink. After drawing himself up, Ẹdun asked the king to hold on to him while he jumped from tree to tree carrying the king to safety. Ẹdun left Ọlọ́fin at a spot where the King could recognize his way back home. In celebration of his discovery and return home, Ọlọ́fin threw a big party for his people, inviting many dignitaries from the neighboring towns and communities.

As news of the celebration reached the animal kingdom, they wanted to come to celebrate with Ọlọ́fin; recognizing the role played by Monkey, one of their own who had participated in the rescue mission. Elephant was first to attend, but on reaching the palace was turned back. The gatekeepers told Elephant: "No animal is allowed to dine and celebrate with the King" ("Ẹranko kì í bá Ọlọ́fin sọ̀sìn"). Subsequently, other animals arrived to join in, but they were all sent back with similar message. It was the turn of Ẹdun the Monkey to visit Ọlọ́fin. As he arrived, the palace officials gave him the spiteful message—animals are forbidden to join the king in celebration. However, Ẹdun reminded them that he was the one with the shinning eyes who found the lost king: "Remember, I used my long tail to clear a place for the king to rest, and with my eye sockets I fetched water for the king to drink."

Perfunctorily, the gatekeeper repeated the instructions he had received to turn back all animals. Noticing his persistence, however, the gatekeeper decided to take Ẹdun's message to the Ọlọ́fin. Ọlọ́fin then told the servant to allow Ẹdun entry. But before the message was conveyed, Ẹdun achieved the impossible! Summoning his innate sacred powers, his secret strengths, and his knowledge of compelling incantations—he decreed the door to open immediately. Here follows the celebrated compelling "words" Ẹdun chanted to unlock the door.

Ikereke gbọ́!	Oh, Door Key, hear me!
Àṣẹ gbọ́!	Àṣẹ, (potent sacred energy), hear me!
Omi ojú ní ṣílẹ̀kùn fún ẹkún	The eyelid opens before tears emerge
Agada ní ṣílẹ̀kùn fún egbo	It is a machete cut that opens the wound
Omira ṣílẹ̀kùn fún ọmọ	The water keg must break before a child in the womb emerges
Kó yọ fòò Ikekere ilẹ̀kùn	Let the door be opened!
Kó yọ fòò Ikekere ilẹ̀kùn	Let the door be removed!
Kó yọ fòò Ikekere ilẹ̀kùn	Let the door be opened!
Afínjú ọmọ kì í gbẹ́yìn ilẹ̀kùn	A beautiful handsome child cannot be locked outside the door of the house
Ọmọ Kẹ́hìndé, wọlé wá	Thus, Kẹ́hìndé (the senior twin) may enter the house
OmoTáyéwò, wọlé wá.	Let Táyéwò (the junior twin) enter the house.[15]

Babalawo Fátóògùn informed me that with the powerful incantation, the door itself opened permitting Ẹdun to pass into the presence of Ọlọ́fin to celebrate with him.

The Ifá narrative demonstrates many crucial issues about the Yorùbá concept of twins, the source of their power and energy, and the status they occupy in their religious worldview and social life. Ẹdun cleverly displayed his innate power in both the wild forest regions and the urban centers of human habitation. As a liminal figure, Ẹdun mediates between the two Yorùbá realms of social world and wilderness environment. Àṣẹ came into play; Àṣẹ is the sacred unconscious energy with which spoken words arise to influence events. Twins themselves embody Àṣẹ, which Ẹdun did not hesitate to display in such occasions when the test of strength was necessary. Rowland Abíọ́dún observes the power of twins is symbolized in the lone bird (*ẹyẹ kan*) which stands over and above other birds that adorns sacred Yorùbá emblems, including the sacred crown and the diviner's staff of office, called "Ọ̀pá Òṣòrò." It is a lone bird, a regal symbol of Àṣẹ in the crown, or as in the diviner's staff of office that represent other powerful sacred forces in the universe.[16] Ẹdun did not hesitate to prove his turf to the human gatekeepers by invoking his Àṣẹ.

Babalawo Fátóògùn informs me that these incantations bestowed to the humans by Ẹdun are vital to perform many difficult but effective rituals, such as those of child delivery or the initiation of a new Babaláwo (diviner). During childbirth, the medicine healer recites the prayer to ease difficult labor. During initiation, when a novice Babaláwo (Ìyàwó Ifá) emerges from the initiation forest (Igbó Odù) and is about to enter his own house, the females held a net cover as if they were blocking his entrance into the house. The novice Babaláwo must recite the incantations before the door is opened to him. This ritual of passage and the crossing of the threshold affirm his new authority and uncommon strength as a Babaláwo, who like the Ìbejì-Ẹdun, must not be kept waiting outside the door by any mortal, even the king. The chanting signifies the Babaláwo's authority in sharing the energy of the primordial Àṣẹ created by Ẹdun.

Twins, Ifá, and Olókun (Òrìṣà of the Sea)

The dialectic between the polar opposites of poverty and riches, death and longevity, childlessness and procreation represents central discourses in Yorùbá religious quests. They are mediated clearly in the following narrative portraying Ìbejì Spirit-Children. Through their foresight and remedial instructions, the Twins overpower the fate decreed by the all-powerful Aṣọmátàsé, and change the status of the great òrìṣà of wisdom, Ọ̀rúnmìlà.

Ifá relates a significant tale of a bad dream:

A-riri–arira, Ariri–arira;
A-rira–níí–gorí–agbára,
Ògbólógbòó-ònà-níí-hu-ẹ̀kan–ṣàṣà   *An old and overgrown road*
A d'Ífá fún Ọ̀rúnmìlà![17]   *Performed Ifá Divination for Ọ̀rúnmìlà*

One day, Ọ̀rúnmìlà slept and had a bad dream. He summoned his Ifá priests to consult divination on his behalf. He was told that the *Ogbè-Dí* signature was revealed. He was advised to perform a sacrifice, as he had only seven days to live. The Ifá priests were well known and highly respected since their revelations always came true. Ọ̀rúnmìlà asked what sacrifice was required. The priests responded that whether he performed sacrifice or not—he was going to die. Resigned to his fate, he prepared himself for death. Whenever any of the Irúnmọlẹ̀ pass through his house, they must greet Ọ̀rúnmìlà. When Ọ̀rúnmìlà's death was revealed, Ògún, riding on his horse, passed by Ọ̀rúnmìlà's house, but received no response. Ògún then dismounted from his horse to find out what was amiss. He asked, "Ọ̀rúnmìlà! Why did you not respond to my greeting?" Ọ̀rúnmìlà revealed the dreadful truth.

"A-riri–arira, Ariri–arira; A-rira–níí–gorí–àgbàrá, Ògbólógbòó-ọ̀nà-níí-hu-ẹ̀kan-ṣàṣà."[18] Ifá Divination revealed that he was going to die—reason enough to disregard anyone. When Ògún heard this revelation, Ògún sent Ọ̀rúnmìlà on errand in the world beyond, to look for Ògún's deceased parents. He said that Ọ̀rúnmìlà must tell them to do something to make life easy for him on earth. After this, Ògún left. Later Oòṣà (Ọbàtálá) came. Ọ̀rúnmìlà again told Oòṣà his story. Oòṣà also begged him to implore the residents of ọ̀run (heaven) to make things easy on earth, because things were so difficult here on earth. All the Irúnmalẹ̀—Eégún, Orò, Ọbàlùfọ̀n, Ọbàgèdè, and so on came to visit Ọ̀rúnmìlà and all left unable to render any solution to Ọ̀rúnmìlà's predicament. The parents of Ìbejì also came with their twins, but unlike other times when Ọ̀rúnmìlà gave them gifts of huge sums of money and food from the remnants of the sacrifices of goats, chicken and sheep in his house, on this occasion he refused to entertain the twins. When the twins asked Orunmila why they were not entertained, he again told them of his fate and he concluded that doing good would no longer benefit him. The parents of Ìbejì were surprised at him. The twins told him that although they were not diviners, he should take their words seriously. They demanded two hens and "egbèjìlélógún" (420 cowries) only and he gave it to them. Twin spirits being very perceptive, they told him to be obedient to their instructions: he should leave his town for another town in the land of Olókun (goddess [òrìṣà] of the sea). Ọ̀rúnmìlà immediately began to prepare for his journey. Ọ̀rúnmìlà used to visit a faraway town in the house of Olókun. He used to go there only on request.

By coincidence, one Abikókó–etí–aṣọ–sunmunu-létí-aṣọ, a very powerful diviner near Olókun, performed Ifá Divination for Olókun, the mighty ocean òrìṣà, when she languished over her childlessness. Olókun, Queen of the Sea, had no child of her own. All her Ifá priests had become very wealthy in her house by making divination for her. She asked why all their divinations failed to come true and promised to make them wealthier if only their divination was positive. She was asked to make a sacrifice but even at that, what she sought was not within their power. She performed the sacrifice. On the second day after the sacrifice, she was informed that an Ifá priest would come from another land without being sent for; Ọ̀rúnmìlà himself was the one who came. He was recognized as an Ifá priest from afar due to his priestly garb. Olókun remarked that "truly, Ifá priests do not lie." Ọ̀rúnmìlà was asked to perform a sacrifice on Olókun's behalf. He listed the materials needed, and on the next day he performed the sacrifice. The sacrifice continued daily and after some months Olókun became pregnant. She refused to allow Ọ̀rúnmìlà to return to his town until her child was delivered. While he waited, she built him several mansions, securing huge sums of money inside one room. She then told Ọ̀rúnmìlà to go back to his place in the sacred city of Otù Ifẹ̀, to bid them farewell and then return to Olókun with whomever he wanted, with a promise to return to Otù Ifẹ̀ occasionally on visits if he was needed. Ọ̀rúnmìlà returned to Otù Ifẹ̀ and explained everything to them. He told them of his newly acquired *oríkì* fame, which came about because of his divination performance in the far distant place and abode of Olókun, òrìṣà of the sea. It was as a consequence of this act that Ọ̀rúnmìlà acquired the following new appellation and *oríkì:*

> Ifá pẹ̀lẹ́ o!
> Olókun asọ̀rọ̀–dayọ̀

"This is why Ifá is called in the popular parlance 'Ifá Olókun asọ̀rọ̀–dayọ̀.' Ifá, the òrìṣà of the sea's diviner who turns bad fortune into a good one," remarked Babaláwo Fátóògùn. The appellation became an alternative praise name invoked by diviners in praise and honor of Ifá's skills and prowess.

> Babaláwo Fátóògùn remarked that this is one of the Ìbejì narratives in Ifá orature that talk about the mothers of Ìbejì who go from house to house and place to place, dancing the twin dance and collecting gifts. Initially Ifá commanded them to do so; it is still the practice today. The local residents freely give the dancers money similar to sacrificing and giving alms. Babaláwo Fátóògùn, the narrator, observed,

> "The Asọmátàsé (those Babaláwo whose predictions always come to fruition) proclaimed a death sentence on Ọ̀rúnmìlà, but the Ìbejì reversed the sentence to make Ọ̀rúnmìlà a king, a position he never expected. From the Ìbejì, Ifá acquired the name *Ifá Olókun Asọ̀rọ̀–dayọ̀*, a name he still bears today. As a sign of gratitude for Ọ̀rúnmìlà's compassion to Olókun, the goddess (òrìṣà) divided her kingdom into two and gave half to Ọ̀rúnmìlà just as a king would reward anyone who does good. Ọ̀rúnmìlà, in gratitude for the Ìbejì's help, likewise bestowed on them and their family great wealth and fine gifts."

Although the narrative was reenacted to explain to me that the Ìbejì acquired one of their major trades, dance performance as ordained by Ifá himself, the stories focused on Ìbejì's perceptive inner eye and ability to avert sudden death, to ordain wealth for the poor, and joy for the childless. All these are illustrated in the story of Olókun whose misfortune was overturned through Ọ̀rúnmìlà's ritual sacrifice and divination. The Ìbejì, the Spirit-Children, demonstrated higher power over the legendary diviners whose predictions always transpire. They are central players when Ọ̀rúnmìlà, god of Divination, reinvented himself and his fortune, averted death and earned for Ifá the most significant honorific title and oríkì: *Ifá Olókun asọ̀rọ̀dayọ̀.*

In the discourse on poverty, we must explain why Ìbejì's mother—her child tied on her back and a second one holding her hands—dances in the open marketplace apparently begging for donations. Yorùbá tradition discourages begging for money. Begging is viewed as a sign of poverty and destitution. But why then were the twins, described as *erelú* and *ọba ọmọ* (king among children), subjected to an apparently unwelcome embarrassment in Yorùbá culture? Alms-giving (*sàráà*), not alms-begging (*báárà/agbe*), is an honorable and gracious practice. As in the Muslim *sadaqah*, Yorùbá generosity bestows blessings on the goodhearted donor. Giving is a spiritual obligation. Ìbejì offerings correspond to informal sacrifices and gifts given in exchange for the anticipated reciprocal blessings of children, wealth, and prosperity.

An Australian scholar of indigenous religion, G. W. Trompf, provides useful understanding of the importance and meaning of reciprocity and payback in Melanesian society. Yorùbá society, too, honors the notion of reciprocity, which lends support to the exchange between the Ìbejì Spirit Beings and their devotees who offer them gifts. According to Trompf, as "embodiments of spiritual power beyond (yet within) human reach,"[19] twins are revered by the rest of the community. In exchange for their efficacious prayer and blessing, their devotees bestow on them precious gifts of food, goods, and money. It is little wonder that the Yorùbá love twins and call them *Ọba Ọmọ* (kings among children). Twins are capable of turning the misfortune of the destitute into the fortune of the wealthy, as one of their *oríkì* shows, "Orílàkí, o ṣọ alákísà di aláṣọ"—"The children who are adored and make one wealthy." Ìbejì-Twins can transform a ragged wardrobe into a wardrobe of new clothes.

Ìbejì-Twins: Narratives of Cities Ancient and Modern

Customarily in antiquity, the founding of Yorùbá towns and urban centers was associated with specific Ifá Divination narratives. Ifá narratives contain copious references to the origins of virtually all ancient Yorùbá cities and towns, including the ancient capital, Ilé-Ifẹ̀, the mythic seat of Olọ́fin Odùduwà, and Ọ̀yọ́-Ilé, the place of Aláàfin Ṣàngó, a king whose apotheosis is connected with the powerful deity of Ṣàngó, god (òrìṣà) of lightning and thunder. Such cities that were traditionally founded or inhabited by twins not only collectively honor twins, but their numerous praise poetry (oríkì-orílè) recount their founding myths and festivals, and rituals associated with the town, referencing Ìbejì. Perhaps the most ancient of these places is Ìṣokùn, a place that is now absorbed into the Ọyọ́ metropolis. Twins are greeted with these praises: "Èjìrẹ́ ará Ìṣokùn, Ẹní bá ń wá Ẹdun á dé Ìṣokùn, Ìṣokùn Ilé Ẹdun," meaning, "Twins, the people of Ìṣokùn place; whoever wants to see the colobus monkey should go to Ìṣokùn, the place of Twins."

Babaláwo Fátóògùn, my consultant and a diviner, informed me that Ìlobú, his hometown place, holds an annual festival of twins. Women who have given birth to deceased or living twins carry magnificently carved Ìbejì statuettes in procession around the town. They sing in unison, "Ẹdunjọbí, where indeed is your home?"[20] It is the town of Olúpọ̀nnà (not to be confused with my name), a town near Ìwó. It is the home and origin place of a twin called Ọ̀pẹ̀bẹ́, who established this town ritualized in their founding myths. The enchanting dance performance of the Ìlobú women indicates and celebrates not the founding of Olúpọ̀nnà Town as such, but the fact that the town was established in praise of twins. The authority of twins' tradition made it possible for such a town to be created. In Nigeria's Oyo State, the more contemporary town of Igbó Ọrà is home to the largest number of twins in Africa—if not in the world.[21]

Babaláwo Ọ̀jẹ́bọ̀dé, the Olú-Awo of Igbó Ọrà, offered a mythic narrative explaining the preponderance of twins in Igbó Ọrà, asserting that the Odù Ifá that established Igbó Ọrà was Ọ̀wọ́nrín-Sogbè. The Odù Ọ̀wọ́nrín-Sogbè prescribed the required sacrifice for the founding of this new place: About fifty-six years after its founding, the Great War called Ògún Idahomi (Dahomey-Yorùbá War) took place (Dahomey is in the present Republic of Bénin). The war scattered the people everywhere, but when it ended, people gathered again. To forestall an occurrence of another tragic war, two people were offered for sacrifice. As sacrifices are offered regularly on the spot where these two people were offered, they keep appearing as twins to the people of Igbó Ọrà. Ifá Divination then asked them to take Ìbejì matters seriously. The people of Igbó Ọrà are believed to be masters of the Ìbejì ritual as well as their taboos because of its significance in primordial times, and as a result of their mastery of and attention to Ìbejì rituals twins keep appearing to them. It is said that twins will not appear as often to those unskilled in, or ignorant of, caring for and venerating twins.

Ìbejì are also connected with the foundation myth of the Ọ̀yọ́ kingdom. An Ìbejì narrative traced the origin of the tradition to the reign of the legendary fourth Aláàfin of Ọ̀yọ́, Ṣàngó. Before the reign of Ṣàngó in the fifteenth century of Yorùbá history, Ìbejì were regarded as abominable children among the Yorùbá; whoever engendered or bore Ìbejì was equally regarded as an unfortunate person. It was held as abnormal for any woman to give birth to two children at the same time. Multiple deliveries were abominable, and the resulting twins were regarded as evil beings (ẹ̀ṣẹ ọmọ), hence dangerous. When twins were born, they must be killed. One of Ṣàngó's wives became pregnant and gave birth to twins. Since they were the children of a powerful king; it was difficult for the people to kill them. Immediately Ṣàngó idolized them. He asked for a special image to be carved for them, and he began to venerate them. He asked that the twins wear a special cloth of intricate design. Whenever he went out to war, he offered them sugarcane, àádùn, beans, èkuru, and other succulent edibles, which comprises the celebrated ritual meals of Ìbejì devotees today. Ṣàngó always returned victorious from the battlefield. Consequently, Ṣàngó became wealthier and stronger. It was said that the very source of Sango's power were his children, the Ìbejì. Thus twins are said to be "Àkọ́bí Aláàfin Ọ̀yọ́" (first-born of Aláàfin of Ọ̀yọ́), that is, Ṣàngó himself. As Ṣàngó metamorphosed into the god (òrìṣà) of thunder and lightning, twins were regarded as Children of Thunder,[22] an appellation and tradition that survived in Yorùbá traditions in Brazil.[23] The narrative also offers an etiology for the creation of Ìbejì statuettes. The Yorùbá Ṣàngó Ìbejì story is similar to the *Púpùpú* narrative of the founding of Oǹdó town to which I referred earlier in this work.[24] The Púpùpú events, however, happened much earlier in Yorùbá history; it is connected with Ilé-Ifẹ̀ civilization rather than with the later Ọ̀yọ́ Empire of the Ṣàngó myth. By the time of Ṣàngó's reign, twins—though still regarded as enigmatic children—had become subjects of veneration, whereas it seems clear that prior to this, as elsewhere in Africa, they were often killed.

Words, Images, and Movement: Ìbejì Iconography, Music and Dance

Ère Ìbejì (Ìbejì Images)

The creation of Ère Ìbejì came about mainly in the event of the death of one of the infant twins since the Ìbejì are no ordinary human beings. The statues are regarded as the incarnate of deceased twins. If a twin dies, the Yorùbá believe that the twin has returned to where it came from. Twins have dual personalities; they belong both to this life and to the other world. Therefore, by their nature, even on death, a twin retains its beingness on earth. An icon must be made in the image (sex, lineage facial marks, etc.) of the deceased twin as a form of veneration. In most cases, failure to make these images will thwart the mother of the twins in her desire to have more children. In some Yorùbá communities, it is a dreadful omen for a mother not to bear the Ìdòwú and Àlàbá, the sequential twin siblings that normally follow her initial set of twins children. In the making of the Ère Ìbejì statue, the Ìbejì-Twin who returned to the Spirit World is "to be brought down" (a ní láti rò kalè) to earth from its heavenly abode in order to inhabit the image and ensure the mother's sustained fertility. The propitiation of the image thereby draws more children into the lineage. Although space will not permit me to discuss the complex and elaborate rituals of fashioning an Ère Ìbejì, suffice it to say that the type of wood used in carving the ère as well as the rites performed while the wood is being turned into the sacred image illustrate the significance of Ìbejì statuettes as a spiritual replica and apotheosis of the deceased Ìbejì.

As observed earlier, the analysis of Ìbejì iconography is well developed in Yorùbá studies. I will begin here to document how Odù Ifá narratives prescribe the making of Ère Ìbejì for mothers of twins and their lineages. The following Ìwòrì-Bogbè divination text explains the origin of Ère Ìbejì.

Ifá ní ká mú'gbá bọ'gbá	Ifá says that when we place a calabash inside another calabash
Ká mú àwo bọ àwo	And likewise the deep china-plate inside another china-plate
Ká fì'wòrì bogbè mólẹ birikiti	If we divine Ìwòrì (an Odù Ifá) to supersede Ogbè (another Odù) completely
A díá fún Ẹdun, níjọ́ tó jí	Performed Ifá Divination for Monkey, when he woke up;
A díá fún Ọ̀rọ̀	And Ọ̀rọ̀ (a supernatural being)
Tí òun náà jí	When he also woke up
Tí àwọn méjèèjì jọ ń ṣe tọmọtìyá	And they related as brothers or sisters from the same mother
Wọ́n ní kí wọ́n ó yà wọ́n lére	It was said that their sacred image should be carved
Wọ́n ní kí wọ́n máa sìn wọ́n	And that they should be propitiated
Njẹ́ Àáyá, mo sìn ọ́ o	Behold, Àáyá (Monkey), I propitiate and honor you!
Ẹdun, mo sìn ọ́ o	Behold, Ẹdun (twins), I propitiate and pay you homage!
Ó léyin méjèèjì, kí ẹ wá yá wa léku	We have made images of both of you!
Nítorí pe eku lẹ yá 'mọlẹ	Because it is a mask (image) that you make to honor and propitiate a deity
B'áa bá sìn yín, gbogbo oore ni kẹ́ ẹ ṣe fún wa	If we propitiate you, you will bring all blessings unto us!

Here *sìn* translates as "to propitiate" as in worshiping a deity and as in paying homage and serving a master, a superior being. Whatever else they may be, twins are primarily òrìṣà (deities) whom the Yorùbá regard as supernatural beings, worth offering sacrifices to. The Yorùbá offer sacrifices only directly to deities who, although often silent, are present as represented in their iconic object (ère). Thus, Ère Ìbejì performs the dual role of representing a deceased twin deity as well as an iconic reference for the living twin, especially in Ìbejì regions where the Ojúbọ Ìbejì (Ìbejì Grove) is absent.

In the following text, 'Yẹkú-Àárín (also called Ọ̀yẹkú-Ọ̀wọ́nrín), Ọ̀rúnmìlà (the deity of Divination) promises to deify twins.

Ó rí omi ní'wájú ti ẹsẹ̀ bọ ẹrẹ̀;	Someone who saw water ahead yet sank his legs deep in marshy ground
A d'Ífá fún Ẹdun	Performed Ifá Divination for Monkey
Nígbà tí àwọn Ìbejì tí wọn ń ti Ìkọ̀lé ọrun, bọ wá sí Ìkọ̀lé ayé	As the twins were coming from heaven to this world
Wọ́n dé'lé ayé	They reached the world
Wọ́n ya'lé Ọ̀rúnmìlà	They stayed in Ọ̀rúnmìlà's house
Wọn sọ́ di ẹni ọlá	They caused Ọ̀rúnmìlà to receive very great wealth
Wọ́n sọ́ di ẹni iyì, wọn sọ́ di ẹni èyẹ	And to be honorable and respected.
Ọ̀rúnmìlà ní òun yóò sọ wọ́n di ẹni àpésìn	Ọ̀rúnmìlà promised to make the twins an object of worship.
Ó ní kí wọ́n lọ gé igi Ìrókò,	Ọ̀rúnmìlà therefore ordered an Ìrókò tree to be cut
Kí wọ́n gbẹ́ ẹ;	To carve delicate Ìbejì statuettes from it;
Kí wọ́n gbẹ́ e sí etí 'yàrá	To represent the twins' place of worship in the corner of a room.
Kí wọ́n sọ wọ́n di Òrìṣà síbẹ̀.	From that day forth Ìbejì became subjects of propitiation.

Ọ̀rúnmìlà, the archetypal diviner, as the Ifá source, features in another account of Ère Ìbejì origins as a spirit representation of twins and the relationship between the diviner and twins. Since their entry into his world spelled good fortune for the diviner and his trade, Ọ̀rúnmìlà saw the need to turn them into a permanent source of blessings and worship for all. The explanation is not far-fetched from what was known as Yorùbá ways of turning humans into gods.[25] If the twins' birth into Ọ̀rúnmìlà's house had ushered in misfortune, the legendary Code of Twins, an extensive source of splendid oral poetry in the Ifá divinatory corpus, would never have made it into Ifá's lexicon in such a grand way.

Let us assume for a moment that a divination consultation for a client produces such a text as we read above. It is highly likely that the diviner would predict that the clients would soon have a set of twins. The diviner would instruct the clients to carve Ère Ìbejì for their household as the birth of the twins will bring fortune and prosperity to the new home.

As I observed at the beginning of this chapter, art historical scholarship describing Ìbejì in museums and private collections worldwide far exceeds research on them in the history of religions. However insightful, much of this analysis lacks holistic perspective on how Ìbejì icons intersect with their mythic narratives in the realm of meaning. How do Ìbejì represent wider Yorùbá religious worldviews? How are the myths and rituals in which the fashioning of Ère Ìbejì are embedded in turn linked to larger Yorùbá cosmology and cosmogony? In the next part of this chapter, I will attempt to restore the icons to their religious contexts by reinstating the original relationship between sacred words and images.[26]

Èrè Ìbejì carved hardwood images almost certainly constitute the largest proportion of sculpture in Yorùbá art history and image-making. I make this observation from examining many catalogues of icons and images in museums and private collections.[27] These icons may outnumber other extant Yorùbá artworks such as Gẹ̀lẹ̀dẹ́ masks, Ifá Divination apparatus, sacred crowns, and other sculptures. Èrè Ìbejì icons are generally adorned with exquisitely beaded necklaces, bangles, bracelets, and at times beaded cloth, which appear in numerous photographs. This abundance of Ìbejì is surely a corollary to the evolution of specific mythic, historical, theological, cultural, and social factors.

First, one might consider the abundance of these icons as a product of mythical-historical evolution. A period in which twin infanticide was practiced, as reflected in Oǹdó founding stories of *Púpùpú*,[28] was gradually replaced by protective cultural attitudes in which twins gained pride and honor, replacing earlier abomination. The first period may belong to the classic era of Yorùbá history when kingdoms were founded as city-states, when people and lineages were dispersed from the sacred city of Ilé-Ifẹ̀ to the present Yorùbá regions. The second period may fall at the height of Yorùbá civilization in Ọ̀yọ́-Ilé, when Ṣàngó reigned as the patron of twins and god (òrìṣà) of thunder.[29] However, my concern here is to analyze some of the Ìbejì images as objects of divine veneration in the twins tradition.

Figure 2.1 Antique Male Èrè Ìbejì (Yorùbá twin statuettes, wood, cowrie shells). Property of Jacob Kẹ́hìndé Olúpọnà. Photo by Ian Choi. By permission of Ayọ̀dèjì Ògúnnáìkè.

Beading and beadwork are ornaments that mothers bestow on their girls for the purpose of beautification. Ìbejì icons are dressed and adorned, not as objects, but as reflections of traditional human attire, reflecting an attitude of cherishing. The same quality of craftsmanship and affection bestowed on a living Ìbejì-Twin are transferred to its iconic figurine; at the same time, the spiritualized and idealized qualities of the Twin are embodied. The icons thus represent human and spirit beings combined into one form, and are treated as such. Similarly, young children in Western culture adorn their own dolls, beautify, and feed them, not as simulacra of babies, but as real babies, cherished by their caregivers. *The Ìbejì are beautified because they are primarily perceived as children.* Similarly, the adornment of Ère Ìbejì means that they cannot be understood purely as *ọmọ láńgidi* (mere objects/human-like images), as Western art collectors have sometime mistakenly thought. On the contrary, the Yorùbá believe that the icons are human and spirit at the same time.

On a personal note, as a twin myself, the first time I came across a large number of Yorùbá twin images on display encased (for me, they were encaged) at the University of California Berkeley museum I almost went into a frenzy, imagining that my spirit-self had been imprisoned, displaced, and displayed for viewers to see! The Yorùbá, at times, can describe a human person as non-human being (*kì í ṣe ènìyàn*). Thus, the person so described ceases to be seen as human because his or her behavior does not confirm to certain expectations defined by the community. This was the only way I could express my thoughts after experiencing this inhumane treatment of the Ère Ìbejì: inhumane because the twin images were not treated humanely and because the people who had done this did not behave the way humans should.

Fertility and Fecundity

The carved hardwood icons we have of the Ère Ìbejì clearly show Yorùbá interests and its value system. The icons show the importance of fertility in the culture. This emphasis is visible in the well-developed penis, protracted buttocks, and large breasts often exaggerated far out of proportion in replicating the human figure. Perhaps this hyperbole indicates the ideals and deep desires to which the twins' parents aspire. Most significantly, the emphasis of procreation points to signs of the second blessing of the Yorùbá, *ire ọmọ*. The Yorùbá relate this tradition of twinning unequivocally to fertility. It raises the question of why twinning is so central to fertility in Yorùbá culture. We know that the Yorùbá women are very fertile and have the highest instance of twin births in the world. While genetic scientists have been analyzing their fertility rates extensively, in this chapter, we are interested in the Yorùbá cultural interpretations and perceptions of this tradition. Close to this notion of fertility is this notion of beauty, which takes us into the realm of aesthetics. Mothers adorn the statuettes, which become "human" rather than *ọmọ láńgidi* (mere images and toys carved from wood). We should add that several female Ìbejì icons represent girls specifically adorned with *bèbè* (waist beads), and they remind us of the personal affection and relationship that those mothers developed with their girls. The women transferred that same affection to the images, to the Ère Ìbejì. A Yorùbá proverb indicates accordingly, "One cannot say because one's own girl or child has a heavy buttock that they then go ahead and adorn the child of their neighbor with those beads as if their child needs no adornment."[30]

Wealth

The antique Ìbejì statues depicted wear belts of cowry shells, the form of money exchange in the Old Yorùbá kingdoms. Why are cowry shells used to decorate the Èrè Ìbejì? To the Yorùbá, cowries signify wealth and money. They are associated with Àjé, the Goddess (Òrìṣà) of Wealth, the daughter of Olókun, the òrìṣà of the seas; several Ifá narratives speak of the wealth ever present at her feet, and reveal much about the banking system of the Yorùbá and their notion of money and commerce. One of the Ìbejì oríkì says that twins bring wealth and money to parents. A twin might be praised: "Ò-dé-kílé-kún, ò-kún-dèdè-tẹrù-tẹrù": "He who comes into the house and fills it with gifts so that it overflows to the veranda." Twins are also praised as "Alaba oribi, erelú ọmọ," "precious child who eludes those with riches who desire them."

Poverty, Riches, and Ritual Power

The Yorùbá response and attitude to poverty, riches, and ritual power are vividly illustrated in the narratives and songs of Ìbejì. Twins figure prominently in the Yorùbá value system and cultural imagination, especially insofar as fecundity, riches, and a good life are both religious and social goals. Because twins are regarded as special children, surrounded by an aura of sacredness, the Yorùbá see them as capable of bestowing riches and benevolence on their parents, family members, and anyone who may encounter a twin. In my youth, it was common for local traders to ask me to assist them to place their wares on their head as they prepare to go to the market; they believed that my assistance would endow their wares with divine blessings. Ìbejì would help them sell those wares very quickly. A trader told me that twins are endowed with special magical power that ontologically bestows prosperity on whomever they interact with. The mere presence of a twin drives away the evil eye (àjẹ́) that may otherwise hinder good sales. Indeed, Ifá verses warn Àjẹ́ (the Witch) to avoid twins.

When I was a young boy on holiday in the 1960s in my mother's hometown, it was common for elderly women to greet me in a special manner not offered to other children. "Òrílakí, ẹgbẹ́ ọ̀gbà, ìwọ ni mo jí rí lónìí o, òní á san mí o" ("Twins, the mates and companion of Children of the Spirit World, you are the first person whom I see this early morning. May this day bring good luck and blessing to me").

Orin Ìbejì[31] provides a complex discourse on poverty and riches, that is, on alleviating the former and acquiring the latter. Through divination, twins can order and instruct their mothers to celebrate their existence by dancing in the open marketplace.[32] While these dancing mothers do not necessarily go begging for gifts and money, passers-by normally offer gifts because they consider it propitious to do so. But since begging is frowned upon in Yorùbá culture, as going against Yorùbá honor and dignity, Ìbejì songs provide the explanations and rationale for such ritual behavior. Carrying one twin baby on her back, holding one in her hand, the Ìbejì mother preempts such social criticism: "Òrílakí ló ní n kí gbogbo yín o, èmi ó sì kí gbogbo yín lókòòkan" ("It is the twins who ask me to greet you all one by one; and I will greet you one by one").[33] Thus, what might in other social contexts be perceived as undignified behavior, the twins' mother presents as divine instruction from the Spirit-Child. Of course, Ìbejì dances are undertaken with the diviner's instruction. As a twin mother, her material needs are plenty, especially food to fill her deep belly left by the emptying of twins occupying it for nine months of pregnancy. The public recognizes—and the mother of twins is teased—as one with a hollowed stomach. In an Ìbejì song, she is hailed, "Iya Ìbejì, abinú hàlo hàlo, ó jẹ ogún ẹkọ, kò yó, ó jẹ ọgbọ̀n ẹkọ, kò yó!" ("Behold the mother twins with a hollow belly! She eats twenty and thirty wraps of corn porridge yet complains of an empty stomach!").[34]

Dancing for the twins in the public marketplace gives rise to numerous gifts of food and money, which could easily fill the mother's room and overflow to her veranda. Hence, the twin is described as "Ò-dé-kílé-kún, ò-kún-dèdè-tẹrù-tẹrù" ("The one who returns home with material goods that fill the house, overflowing to the veranda for lack of space to keep them").[35] The typical consequence is that twins are capable of changing their parents' fortunes from poverty to riches. Twins are capable of turning an impoverished person wearing ragged clothing to an affluent person with a luxuriant wardrobe (Sọ alákísà di aláṣọ). As an *oríkì Ìbejì* attests:

Ò bẹ́ kìsì bẹ́ kẹ́sẹ́	One who jumps about like Monkey
Ó fẹsẹ̀ méjèèjì	Uses two legs to jump into the house of
Bẹ́ sílé alákísà	A person who wears ragged clothing about (a poor person)
Ó sọ alákísà di onígba aṣọ.	And made them to have plenty of cloth (200 pieces of cloth)

The purpose for which twins have come to the world must be fulfilled. When they enter the house of an impoverished family, especially the homes of parents who know how to venerate them in the proper manner, the Ìbejì will bring prosperity to the indigent parents. Those parents will then enjoy all the good things of life. Thus, the Yorùbá tradition supports the view that Ìbejì-Twins are Children of the Spirit World with particular responsibility to change an adverse destiny from poverty to prosperity.

Conclusion

Yorùbá traditions about Ìbejì reveal several important motifs. Twins share similar traits and characteristics with the colobus monkey; hence these particular monkeys feature not only as totemic partners of twins but are signified as associates and equals. Ifá orature juxtaposes twins and monkeys as beings sharing similar traits, names, and possessing *àṣẹ*, the divine command and its associated power, with which they make things happen. Ìbejì tradition illumines the Yorùbá notion of the sacred and of transcendence as centered on the quest for the good life and acquisition of wealth, children, and long life. Twins' myths, especially in the Ifá Divination orature, support twins' centrality in Yorùbá discourse on wealth, poverty, beauty, seniority, gender, sacred images, fecundity, and other aspects of the Yorùbá cultural and social system.

Appendix

Orin Ìbejì (Ìbejì songs)[36]

Kẹ́hìndé Táyéwò	Kẹ́hìndé and Táyéwò
Ọmọ máa gbẹ́sẹ̀ lọ́kọ̀ọ̀kan	Lift your legs one by one (walk leisurely)
Èjìrẹ́ orílà, ọmọ máa gbẹ́sẹ̀ lọ́kọ̀ọ̀kan.	Twins, lift your legs one by one
Ọlọ́run má jẹ́'yà ó jẹ wá	God, do not let us suffer
Ọlọ́run má jẹ́'yà ó jẹ wá	God, do not let us suffer
Ìyà é è é joní'bejì	Mothers of twins are not in want
Ọlọ́run má jẹ́'yà ó jẹ wá.	God, do not let us suffer.
Ẹni ti rí'bejì tó rojú	Whosoever that sees Ìbejì and looks moody
Ìyà ni yóò jẹ'lé ẹni ọhún	Will suffer
Ẹni ti rí'bejì tó rojú	Whosoever sees twins and looks moody.
Ọmọ́kẹ́hìndé o ò, ẹ dá mi lọ́lá;	Ọmọ́kẹ́hìndé, enrich me;
Èjì, mo ti bá ẹ dìbò	Twins, I have voted for you.
O wọlé oyè lọ́lá	You will be honored tomorrow
Táyélolú o ò, ẹ dá mi lọ́lá	Tayelolu, enrich me;
Èjì, mo ti bá ẹ dìbò	Twins, I have voted for you.
Ẹ fún mi lépo n ò lépo nílé	Give me palm oil; I have no palm oil at home.
Èjì, mo ti bá ẹ sẹ̀wà.	Twins, I have cooked delicious beans for you.
Táyélolú, má gbàgbé ilé	Táyélolú, never forget your home
Ibi o bá gbé wà, má sọnù o	Wherever you may be, home is home
Táyélolú, má gbàgbé ilé.	Táyélolú, never forget your home.
Táyélolú, rí mi bẹ́ẹ̀	Táyélolú sees me as I am
Tó yà 'dẹ̀dẹ̀ mi	And yet came to me (to be born)
Ọmọ́kẹ́hìndé ri mi bẹ́ẹ̀	Ọmọ́kẹ́hìndé also sees me as I am
Tó yà 'dẹ̀dẹ̀ mi	But he came to me (to be born)
Ìyá kò kọ́'lé	My mother could never build any house (too poor)
Bàbá kò ra'lẹ̀	Neither did my father buy any land
Tẹ́ẹ wá mi wá;	Yet you came to me;
Táyélolú rí mi bẹ́ẹ̀ tẹ́ẹ yà 'dẹ̀dẹ̀ mi.	Táyélolú sees me as I am, and he came to me.
Ọmọ ni Táyélolú o, e e e	Táyélolú is a good child
Ọmọni Kẹ́hìndé	Kẹ́hìndé also is a good son
K'órii Kẹ́hìndé ó má padà lẹ́hìn mi	Kẹ́hìndé's destiny (head) should continue to support me
Ọmọ ni Táyélolú.	Táyélolú is a good child.
Táyélolú lo lepo Èjìrẹ́o	Táyélolú owns palm oil
Ọmọ́kẹ́hìndé lo lepo Èjìrẹ́	Ọmọ́kẹ́hìndé owns palm oil
Táyé, Kẹhìn ló nikẹ̀tẹ́ o	Taye and Kẹ́hìndé own a special type of palm oil
Kẹ́hìndé ló lepo Èjìrẹ́ o.	Kẹ́hìndé owns palm oil.
Ò dé kílé kún,	One who comes to the house, and the house is filled up
Ò dé kílé kún	One who comes to the house, and the house is filled up
Ò dọ'dẹ̀dẹ̀ tẹrù-tẹrù	One who comes to the parlor with heavy load of gifts
Ò dé kílé kún	One who enters the house, and the house is filled up
Táyélolú dẹlẹ́wù ẹtù	Tayelolu has come with special kind of cloth (ẹtù)
Ò dé kílé kún, ò dé kílé dùn	One who comes to a house, and the house is filled up.
Ò dọ'dẹ̀dẹ̀ tẹrù-tẹrù	One who comes to the parlor with heavy load of blessing

Ò dé kílé kún	One who comes to the house, and the house is filled up
Táyélolú dẹlẹ́wù ẹtù	Táyélolú has come with special kind of cloth (ẹtù)
Ò dé kílé kún	One who comes to the house, and the house is filled up
Ò dọ́'dẹ̀dẹ̀ tẹrù-tẹrù	One who comes to the parlor with heavy load of blessing
Ò dé kílé kún.	One who comes to the house, and the house is filled up

Twins and Monkey (Ìgànná and Ìbejì)

Òkò ba'gi lẹ́ba padà sẹ́hìn	A stone thrown at a tree jumps back
A díá fún Àáyá[37]	Performed Ifá Divination for Monkey
A bù fún òwè	Performed Ifá Divination for Monkey
A díá fún Ẹdun 'Mẹ̀sí	Performed Divination for Ẹdun Mẹ̀sí
Ọmọ Mẹ̀sí mere	The son of Mẹ̀sí mere
Abi dorogbo Ìbejì,	The two tiny twin children
Òun náà níí múni sọ wọ́n ní Àáyá	That makes one name them Àáyá (Monkey).

Oríkì Ìbejì from Lálúpọn

Ọmọ sẹ̀jì wáyé ará Ìsokùn	Children who came into the world in twos
Ará Ìsokùn sọ́npọ́nná	Native of Ìsokùn City
Ẹdun jọbí Ẹdun máa dáa dókinni	Born collectively by Monkey
Ẹdun gbálájá ori igi	The strong and relaxing Monkey in the top of a tree
Ní'jọ́ Ejirẹ̀ ti dáyé kò jalè rí	Since the twins were born, they have never stolen anything
Ọmọ 're; mo kálá	Children who bring exceedingly good fortune
Ọmọ a-tikara-ẹ̀-káàgùn ikà	And with their power, remove evil charms from their surrounding
Ọmọ ò-sùn-sílé,	The children who lie down relaxing on the floor
F'orí jọ iyàwó Olúfọ̀rọ̀	Like Oluforo's wife
Ọmọ a-fàdín-mùkọ	Children who drink corn pap (ẹ̀kọ) with palm kernel oil
Ọmọ olóde àyúnrékọjá	Makes regular outings
Bú mi kí n bá ọ relé	Abuse me, and let me follow you home
Kì mi kí n padà lẹ́hìn rẹ.	Praise me, and let me retrieve my steps
Òjé lójú Ìbejì	The eyes of the twins are always shining like precious metal (òjé) as with the Monkey)
Akotopo lójú Ẹdun	And the face of the Ìbejì (Monkey) has a socket
Má fà mí ní ìrù	Do not pull my tail
Mi ò fi kótópó ojú sẹré	I do not joke about the socket in my eyes
Òyìnbó orí ìtẹ́	Oh beautiful one who is honored (like a king on the throne)
Afínjú ọmọ tí ń gba ikúnlẹ̀ iyá ẹ̀	Brave children whom their mother kneels down to greet,[38]
Afínjú ọmọ tí ń gba idòbálẹ̀ baba	Brave children whom their father prostrates to greet in the early morning;
Ọmọ fèjì wáyé mo kúnlẹ̀ẹ tèmi	Children who came in twos, I am also on my knees
Wínní-wínní lójú orogún	To their mother's co-wives, they are bewildering tiny children
Èjì-wọ̀rọ̀ lójú iyá ẹ̀	But to the mother of twins, they are two bountiful children
Ọmọ tó bẹ́ kìsi, bẹ́ kẹ́sẹ	Children who jump up and jump down, full of energy
Ó fẹsẹ̀ méjèèjì bẹ́ sílé alákísà	With their two legs, they jumped to be born into the home of a poor person
Ó sọ alákísà di onígba aṣọ	The twins turned the unfortunate person into one with abundant clothes and riches
Àkọ́bí Aláàfin Ọ̀yọ́.	The firstborn of Aláàfin Ọ̀yọ́.

Ẹdúnjọbi Ẹdun má ku lógun

Born by the Monkeys but daring at battle

Èèyàn tí ò m'Èjìrẹ́ ló lè kí Ìsokùn sọ́npọ́nná

A person who knows not twins speaks anyhow about the Children of Isokun City

Ẹni tí ò mọ Ẹdúnjọbí ló lè ki Erelú ọmọ

Those who know the Children of Ẹdun must venerate these special beings

Òrò tó rin méjì o ò

Spirit Children who walk in pairs!

Òrò tó rin méjì o ò

Spirit Children who act in pairs

Tí baálé ń tẹfá

And the head of the household consults Ifá Divination on their arrival

Ó délùú kanbi

Twins enter a city and are immediately recognized

Ó wọlú ko ará ẹ lọ́nà

They enter a city and quickly recognized their own people

Téńté lórí ìgbágó

Smallish looking at the top of dried palm frond (like a monkey)

Tìẹmì lórí Ìyeyè

And comfortably standing on the top of Ìyeyè tree

A-bí-jowú-orogún

Whose birth provokes rivalry and envy from their mothers' co-wives.

Ẹ bá n kí 'bejì kú eré

Join me to greet the twins' good outing!

Ẹ bá n kí 'bejì kú eré

Join me to greet the twins' good outing!

Èjìrẹ́ ọmọ méjì

Twins, two children born at the same time

Ẹ bá n kí 'bejì kú eré

Join me to greet the twins' good outing!

Ẹ bá n k'Ẹ́dúnjọbí

Greet the children born of Monkey!

Ọmọ onílé ọlá

Children who stay in the house of affluence!

Olórí akéwe o

Excellent above all children

Àwọn lolóríí wa

They are also greater than we are.

Èjìrẹ́ Táyé Kẹ́hìn tó m'Ẹdun òrò

Twins, Táyéwò and Kẹ́hìndé, who know the mysterious Monkey

Tó m'Ẹdun òrò

Twins who know the Enigmatic Monkey

À-rí-dunnú wa kò ní dẹkún

That which makes us so happy will never turn to tears (never lose the children)

Ẹ yáa bá mi sàmí n gbọ́

Please say a loud amen with me

Ẹ bá n b'Éléjìrẹ́ ṣeré

Help to play with Èjìrẹ́ (Táyéwò and Kẹ́hìndé)

Ẹ bá n b'Éléjìrẹ́ ṣeré

Help to play with Èjìrẹ́ (Táyéwò and Kẹ́hìndé)

Àùntí pa'ṣẹ́ rẹ tì

Sister, leave what you are doing!

Bùròdá pa'ṣẹ́ rẹ tì

Brother, leave what you are doing!

Ẹ bá n b'Éléjìrẹ́ ṣeré

And join me to play with twins!

Òrò Èjìrẹ́ o

The matter of twins

Òrò Èjìrẹ́ o

The business of twins

Èmi ò lè fọrọ̀ Èjìrẹ́ ṣàwàdà o

I dare not joke with matters pertaining to twins

Òrò Èjìrẹ́ o

The matters of twins are too important to me.

Epo ń bẹ, èwà ń bẹ o

I have enough palm oil and enough tasty beans

Epo ń bẹ, èwà ń bẹ o

I have enough palm oil and enough tasty beans

Àyà mi 'ò já, óó ye;

I am unafraid;

Àyà mi 'ò já láti bí 'Bejì,

I am unafraid to give birth to twins

Epo ń bẹ, èwà ń bẹ o

I have enough tasty beans and palm oil.

Bí mo bí 'Beji, n ó gbé e o,
If I have twins I shall carry them

Bí mo bí 'Beji, n ó gbé e o;
If I have twins I shall take good care of them

Àyà mi 'ò já, óó ye,
I am unafraid;

Àyà mi 'ò já láti bí 'Bejì;
I am unafraid to give birth to twins,

Bí mo bí 'Beji, n ó gbé e o o.
If I have twins, I shall carry them.

B'ọkọ gbé kan, èmi a gbé kan an o,
If my husband carries one, I shall carry the other

B'ọkọ gbé kan, èmi a gbé kan an o;
If my husband carries one, I shall carry one

Àyà mi 'ò já, óó ye,
I am not afraid;

Àyà mi 'ò já láti bí 'Bejì,
I am not afraid to have twins;

B'ọkọ gbé kan, èmi a gbé kan an o.
If my husband carries one, I shall carry one

Ẹ j'Ẹdun ó ná'wó,
Let the twins spend money,

Èjì ló lowó
They are the controllers of money.

Mo lẹni 'a pè pè, t'ó l'óun ò rójú
Person who was called to honor twins and said he has no time

Ẹdun gbójú ló'ọ rẹ
The twins took their eyes from them

Ẹdun gbà mí o; má gbojú lọwọ mi,
Twins save me; do not take my eyes from me

Mo ní kó o gbà mí o; má gbojú lọwọ ọ mi
I beg you to save me, do not take my eyes from me,

Ẹ gbà mí, ẹ má gbojú lọwọ ọ mi.
Please save me; do not take my eyes from me.

Mo lẹni a pè pè tó lóhun ò rọwọ o
The person who was called to honor twins and said he has no hand (too busy)

Ẹdun gbọwọ lọwọ rẹ
The twins took their hands from him

Ẹ gbà mí, ẹ má gbọwọ lọwọ ọ mi
Save me, do not take my hand from me;

Ọkọ ọ mi gbà mí, ẹ má gbọwọ lọwọ ọ mi
Oh, my husband—twins,[39] never take my hand from me.

Ọkọ ọ mi gbà mí
Oh, my husband, save me,

Ẹ má jẹ n tẹ láwùjọ
Never let me be humiliated publicly

Ẹ gbà mi, ẹ má jẹ n tẹ
Please save me; never let me be humiliated.

O! o! o! o!
Oh! Oh! Oh! Oh!

Ẹdun a bì'rù gbọọrọ
Monkey with the long tail

O! o! o! o!
Oh! Oh! Oh! Oh!

Ẹdun bì'rù gbọọrọ
Monkey with the long tail

Ọrọ a pò jọjọ wọlú
Spirits who come to a city with great awe

Ẹdun a bì'rù gbọọrọ
Monkey with the long tail

Àlàbá ò ri bí
Those who dream of having them, never have them,

Erelú ọmọ
Precious children

Ẹdun abì'rù gbọọrọ
Monkeys with long tails.

Ọlọrun, má jẹ'yà ó jẹ wá
Oh, God, do not let us suffer;

Ọlọrun, má jẹ'yà ó jẹ wá
Oh, God, do not let us suffer;

Ìyà kìí jẹ oníbejì
The parents of twins never suffer

Ọlọrun, má jẹ'yà ó jẹ wá
Oh, God, do not let us suffer.

Ẹni tó rí 'Bejì tó rojú,
Whoever sees the twins and feels moody,

Ìyà ni ó jẹni náà o.
Such a person will suffer.

Èjì, mo ti bá ẹ dìbò | Twins, I have voted for you (supported you)
N ó wọlé oyè lọ́la | Let me be made a chief tomorrow;
Táyélolú oo, ẹ dá mi lọ́lá | Táyélolú, please enrich me,
Kẹ́hìndé o, ẹ dá mi lọ́lá; | Kẹ́hìndé, please enrich me,
Èjì, mo ti bá ẹ dìbò | Twins, I have supported you,
N ó wọlé oyè lọ́la | Let me be made a chief tomorrow.

Ẹ fún mi lépo | Give me palm oil
N ò lépo nílé | I have no palm oil
Èjì, mo ti bá ẹ j'ẹ̀wà | Twins, I have eaten beans together with you
Ẹ fún mi lépo n bù sẹ́nu | Give me palm oil to drink.

Táyélolú, ma gbagbe ile | Táyélolú, never forget your home.

Táyélolú, ijó ọmọ là ń jó | Táyélolú, we are dancing for our children
Ijó ọmọ | The dance of children
T'ọmọdé t'arúgbó la ó jó | Both young and old will dance the dance;
Ijó ọmọ | The dance of children,
Ijó ọmọ là ń jó | We are dancing for our children,
Ijó ọmọ là ń jó o | We are dancing the dance of children
Kò síjó, Kò síjó ẹlẹ́yà lésẹ̀ wa, | This is no dance of shame
Ijó ọmọ là ń jó. | We are dancing the dance of children.

Táyé, Kẹ́hìn, ọmọ owó | Táyéwò and Kẹ́hìndé, children of prosperity
Èyin náà lẹ ẹ́ wo'ra a yín. | You are the ones to care for yourselves.[40]

Ẹ fún 'Bejì lówó o | Give twins a gift of money,
Ẹ fún 'Bejì lówó | Give twins a gift of money,
Ẹni bá ṣọ̀rẹ́ Ìdòwú o, | Whoever loves to be a friend of Idowu,
Ẹ fún 'Bejì lówó. | Give twins a gift of money.

Bí mo bí 'Bejì n ó gbe o, e o | If I have twins, I will care for them,
Bí mo bí 'Bejì n ó gbe o, e o | If I have twins, I will care for them,
Àyà mi ò jáá, ó ó ye, | I am not afraid, never,
Àyà mi ò já láti bí 'Bejì | I am not afraid to have twins
Bí mo bí 'Bejì n ó gbe o, e o. | If I have twins, I will care for them.

Ọmọkẹ́hìndé, mo so kele o, | Kẹ́hìndé, I tie my neck, wrist, and ankle bracelets
Mo so kele; | I tie my bracelets;
Táyélolú, mo so kele o, | Táyéwò, I tie my neck, wrist, and ankle bracelets
Mo so kele; | I tie my bracelets;
Ṣàngó, má so mí lókùn lọ́rùn, | Ṣàngó, do not tie rope on my neck,
Mo so kele. | I tie my bracelets.

Ìgànná (July 20, 2008)

From the council of Babálawo Fátóògùn in Ìgànná, I collected the myths of Ẹdun's preeminence in the animal kingdom and in the City of Ọlọ́fin Odùduwà in Ilé-Ifẹ̀. The domination of Ìbejì is exemplified in Ẹdun's story in Ifá Divination orature (another version of the story described on page 83): "There came a time of the need to elect the kind of personality that would rule Ifẹ̀ kingdom to bring back the glory of Ifẹ̀. All the big animals boasted of their abilities to do this, but all to no avail. However, when Ẹdun came out, he proved his ability and he entered into the house to rule Ifẹ̀. is the following praise poetry explains why twins are principal divinities among the Yorùbá."

Erin ló di gbọn gbọn "mo kàn"	Elephant says, "I am knocking!"
Wọ́n ní "taa ni ń kànkùn ọlá, ikẹ́kẹ́, ikẹ́kẹ́?"	They ask, "Who is knocking at our door?"
Ifá ni "taa ni ń kàn'kùn ọlà, ilẹ̀lẹ̀, ilẹ̀lẹ̀?"	Ifá asks, "Who is knocking repeatedly and forcefully at the door of honor?"
Wọ́n ní "taa ni ń kànkùn ọlá gbọn, gbọn, gbọn gbọn?"	Ifá asks, "'Who is knocking repeatedly and forcefully at the door of wealth?"
Erin l'óun ni	Elephant said, "I am the one knocking at the door!"
Òun ọmọ Olú-Igbó	Elephant himself, the Son of the Lord of the Forest
Wọ́n ní, "bá wo ni ọ̀nà Ilé Ifẹ̀ oòyè Lágbémoró ti rí?"	They ask, "What does the way to the sacred city of Ilé-Ifẹ̀ look like?"
Erin ní "bẹ́ẹ̀ ni wọ́n ń jẹ?"	Elephant asks, "'This is how they eat?"
Bẹ́ẹ̀ ni wọ́n ń mu	All are full of fun and merriment
Ó ní aboyún ilé ń bí wẹ́rẹ́,	Pregnant women deliver safely in the home!
Àgàn ń tọwọ́ àlà b'osùn	The barren also bear children!
Wọ́n l'érin kì í ṣe eléegun, kó máa lọ.	They say, "Elephant is not initiate; the type who could lead them to the great city. He should go back to his forest!

Ẹfọ̀n ló di gbọ̀n gbọ̀n mo kàn	Buffalo too came knocking at the door.
Wọ́n ní "taa ni ń kànkùn ọlá, ikẹ́kẹ́, ikẹ́kẹ́?"	They asked, "'Who is knocking at the door forcefully and repeatedly?"
Taa ni ń kàn'kùn ọlà, ilẹ̀lẹ̀, ilẹ̀lẹ̀?	Who is knocking at the door forcefully and repeatedly?
Taa ní í kànkùn ọlà nígbàkúùgbà?	Who is knocking at the door repeatedly?
Ẹfọ̀n ní òun Ẹfọ̀n, ọmọ Olú Ọ̀dàn ni.	Buffalo said, "Myself, King of the Lord of Ọ̀dàn!"
Àgbọ̀nrín ló di gbọ̀n, gbọ̀n, mo kàn	Àgbọ̀nrín also said, "He is knocking at the door!"
Àgbọ̀nrín l'óun àgbọ̀nrín òdògì-n̄-dogì	Àgbọ̀nrín said, "It was he who is òdògì-n̄-dogì
Ọmọ Onípolo Adaka (a town)	The child of Onipolo Adaka.
Ó ní "báwo lọ̀nà Ilé-Ifẹ̀ Oòyè Lágbémoró ti rí?"	They asked, "What does the way to Ilé-Ifẹ̀ look like?"
Wọ́n ní "bẹ́ẹ̀ ni wọ́n ń jẹ, bẹ́ẹ̀ ni wọ́n ń mu	All are full of merriment and fun!
Aboyún ilé ń bi wẹ́rẹ́,	Pregnant women give birth safely!
Àgàn ń tọwọ́ àlà b'osùn."	The barren bear children!
Wọ́n ní "ẹṣin ọba ń jẹko!"	They said, "The king's pets are grazing well!"
Wọ́n ní "wọn è é ṣeléegun oun won, kí wọn máa lọ!"	They answered, "He is incapable!" "He should go back to his forest!"
Etu ló di gbọ̀n, gbọ̀n, mo kàn	Antelope also said, "I am knocking at the door!"
Wọ́n ní 'taa ni ń kànkùn ọlá, ikẹ́kẹ́, ikẹ́kẹ́?'	They asked, "Who is knocking at the door forcefully and repeatedly?"
Taa ni ń kàn'kùn ọlà, ilẹ̀lẹ̀, ilẹ̀lẹ̀?	Who is knocking at the door forcefully?

Gbogbo ẹranko bá wá kànkùn títí tí	All other animals came and made the same claim!
Wọ́n rí pé àwọn náà è é ṣeléegun	And they too were found to be unqualified.

Ẹdun ló di gbọ̀n, gbọ̀n, mo kàn

Monkey (Ẹdun) came out and made the same claim.

Wọ́n ní "taa ni ń kànkùn ọlá, ikẹ́kẹ́, ikẹ́kẹ́?"
Taa ni ń kàn'kùn ọlà, ilẹ̀lẹ̀, ilẹ̀lẹ̀?

They asked, "Who is knocking at the door?"
Who is knocking at the door of honor forcefully and repeatedly?

Taa ní í kànkùn ọlà nígbàkúùgbà?
Ẹdun l'óun Ẹdun bélẹ́ńjé ni
Wọ́n ní "báwo lọ̀nà Ilé-Ifẹ̀ Lágbémoró ti ri?"

Who knocks at the door of wealth forcefully?
Ẹdun told them, "'It is I!'"
They asked, "'What does the way to Ilé-Ifẹ̀ look like?"

Ó ní "bẹ̀ẹ̀ ni wọ́n ń jẹ, bẹ̀ẹ̀ ni wọ́n ń mu"

The place is exceedingly pleasant.
Ẹdun told them, "I will make a difference!"
They began to chastise him.

Wọ́n ní "ọwọ́ ọ rẹ̀ wọ́lọwọ̀lọ

They abused him, saying, "'You with ugly hands!"[41]

Ìrù ẹ tiẹ̀mì
Ojú rẹ pókí, pókí, pókí"
Ó ní ọwọ́ òun wọ́lọ, wọ̀lọ
Ni òun fi ń sẹ́ obì fún ọmọ Eríwo Ọsìn jẹ.

You, with ugly tail!
You, whose eyes are full of holes!
He said, "It is with my ugly hands
That I cut precious kolanut for Eriwo Osin (the King of Ife) to eat!

Ojú òun pókí, pókí, pókí
L'òun fi í í pọn omi fún ọmọ Eríwo Ọsìn mu

He said, "It is with my eyesocket.
That I fetch drinking water for Eriwo Osin (the High Priest)

Ìrù òun tiẹ̀mì, tiẹmi, ni òun fi ń gbálẹ̀ fún ọmọ Eríwo Ọsìn jókòó sí

He said, "It is with my ugly tail that I sweep the ground so that the child of Eríwo Ọsìn can sit."

Lójú kan náà Ẹdun jẹ́wọ́
Ọ̀rọ̀ Ẹdun ò gbẹ́yin 'lẹ̀kùn Onílé, ẹ ṣílẹ̀kùn f'Ẹ́dun

Immediately, Ẹdun proved himself.
Ẹdun's matter is never a matter of backdoor, Open the door for me!

Ọ̀rọ̀ Ẹdun ò gbẹ́yin 'lẹ̀kùn Onílé, ẹ ṣílẹ̀kùn f'Ẹ́dun o

Ẹdun's matter is never a matter of backdoor, Please open the door for me to enter!

Ọ̀rọ̀ Ẹdun ò gbẹ́yin 'lẹ̀kùn Onílé, ẹ ṣílẹ̀kùn f'Ẹ́dun

Ẹdun's matter is never a matter of backdoor! So open the door for me to enter the Holy City of Ilé-Ifẹ̀!

Wọ́n kọ̀, ṣùgbọ́n Ẹdun lo agbára rẹ̀ ṣílẹ̀kùn fúnrarẹ̀, ó sì wọ ìlú Ọlọ́fin.

They refused, but he magically opened the door himself and entered the city of Ọlọ́fin.

Notes

1   A twins' *oríkì* (praise poetry) recited by an Oǹdó woman and heard by the author in the late summer of 2008, in Oǹdó town, Nigeria. All Yorùbá translations are my own with the kind and expert assistance of Dr. A. Adéọlá Fáléyẹ, Lecturer in the Department of Linguistics and African Languages, Obafemi Awolowo University.

2   Jacob K. Olupona [Olúpọ̀nà], *Kingship, Religion, and Rituals in a Nigerian Community: A Phenomenological Study of Ondo Yoruba Festivals* (Stockholm, Sweden: Almqvist & Wiksell International, 1991). I will return to this story later in the chapter.

3   A proverb refers to the *àbíkú*'s superior power over medicine men and women: "*àbíkú sọ olóògùn d'èké.*"

4   Among many studies, Babatunde Lawal, "Ejiwapo: The Dialectics of Twinness in Yoruba Art and Culture," *African Arts,* Spring 2008; Marilyn Houlberg, "Ibeji Images of the Yoruba," *African Arts* 7, no. (1973): 20–7, 91–2; Ladislas Segy, "The

Yoruba Ibeji Statue," *Acta Tropical* [Separation] 27, no. 2 (1970): 97–145; Eva L. R. Meyerowitz, "Ibeji Statuettes from Yoruba, Nigeria," *MAN* 44 (1944): 105–7.

5 See studies by Babatunde Lawal, "Sustaining the Oneness in Their Twoness: Poetics of Twin Figures (*Èrè Ìbèjì*) among the Yoruba," in *Double Trouble Twice Blessed: Twins in African and Diaspora Cultures*, ed. Philip M. Peek (Bloomington: Indiana University Press, 2011), 81–98, and Elisha Renne, "The Ambiguous Ordinariness of Yoruba Twins," in the same volume, 309–15.

6 It is not unusual to see the names also spelled as Taiwo and Keinde by those who do not follow the modern-day orthography.

7 See Renne, "The Ambiguous Ordinariness of Yoruba Twins," for discussion of these changes.

8 George Knox and David Morley, "Twinning in Yoruba Women," *Journal of Obstetrics and Gynecology of the British Empire* 67 (1960): 981–4; Percy P. S. Nylander, "The Frequency of Twinning in a Rural Community in Western Nigeria," *Annals of Human Genetics* 33 (1969): 41–4; Percy P. S. Nylander and Gerald Corey, "Placentation and Zygosity of Twins in Ibadan, Nigeria," *Annals of Human Genetics* 33 (1969): 31–40; Mitchell Creinin and Louis G. Keith, "The Yoruba Contribution to Our Understanding of the Twinning Process," *Journal of Reproductive Medicine* 34, no. 6 (1989): 379–87.

9 See Lawal, "Sustaining the Oneness in Their Twoness," for a synopsis of these various levels of duality and the place of twins within this configuration.

10 Ysamur Flores-Peña offers an interesting Lucumí explanation of this: the twin conceived first moves further up into the womb to make room for the one conceived second, and thus the first conceived is not born first, but is nevertheless the senior; see Ysamur Flores-Peña, "'Son Dos los Jimagüas' ('The Twins are Two'): Worship of the Sacred Twins in Lucumí Culture," in Peek, ed., *Double Trouble, Twice Blessed,* 106.

11 Saritha Rai, "A Family Rift Roils the Market in India," *New York Times*, November 23, 2004, https://www.nytimes.com/2004/11/23/business/worldbusiness/a-family-rift -roils-the-market-in-india.html

12 See Lawal, "Sustaining the Oneness in Their Twoness," and also Elisha Renne, "Twinship in an Ekiti Yoruba Town," *Ethnology* 40, no.1 (2001), "Special Issue: Reviewing Twinship in Africa" (Winter, 2001): 66–8 for an informative analysis of these images.

13 Karen Charman, "Ecuador First to Grant Nature Constitutional Rights," *Capitalism Nature Socialism* 19, 4 (2008): 131–3, https://doi.org/10.1080/10455750802575828

14 This and all subsequent traditional verses and mythologies from the Ifá oral corpus in this chapter were collected from Babaláwo Fátóògùn in Ilobu, Òṣun State, in July of 2008.

15 This fascinating story compares vividly with the ritual of investiture of a new Christian prelate. A bishop who is taking possession of his diocese will use his staff of office to knock on the door of the cathedral asking that the door be opened to him so he can enter it to worship the Lord.

16 Personal communication, September 25, 2008.

17 The first three lines are mythic and poetic names of the diviners, and while the third line can be translated, the first two are merely onomatopoeic iterations that cannot be effectively rendered in English.

18 The names of another legendary Babaláwo. Who was this and did he perform the divination? This is confusing.

19 Garry W. Trompf, *Payback: The Magic of Retribution in Melanesian Religions* (Cambridge: Cambridge University Press, 1994), 113.

20 In an interview carried out on my behalf by Dr. Fẹ́mi Jẹ́gẹ́dẹ́ in Igbó Ọ̀rà, June 2008.

21 Igbó Ọ̀rà town in Ìbàdàn suburb is the focus of fertility research. The research represents some of the most fascinating in the modern tradition of twins today (Nylander 1969, 1970; Nylander and Corey 1969).

22 Robert Farris Thompson, "Sons of Thunder: Twin Images among the Oyo and Other Yoruba Groups," *African Arts* 4, no. 3 (1971): 77–80.

23 Ibid.

24 Olupona, *Kingship, Religion, and Rituals in a Nigerian Community.*

25 See Karin Barber, "How Man Makes God in West Africa: Yorùbá Attitudes Towards the Orisa," *Africa* 51, no. 3 (1981): 724–45.

26 Rowland Abiodun, "Verbal and Visual Metaphors: Mythical Allusion in Yoruba Ritualistic Art of Ori," *Word and Images: A Journal of Verbal and Visual Enquiry* (1987): 252–70; "Yoruba Arts and Aesthetics: The Concept of Ase" (Memorial to William Fagg), *African Arts* 27, no. 3 (1994a): 68–125; "Verbalizing and Visualizing Creative Power through Art," *Journal of Religion in Africa* 24, no. 1 (1994b): 309–22.

27 Fausto Polo and Jean David, *Ibeji Catalogue* (Zurich: Galerie Walu, Vol. 1, 2001 & Vol. 2, 2005).

28 Olupona, *Kingship, Religion, and Rituals in a Nigerian Community*.

29 Although these two periods cannot be fixed with any great degree of certainty, the first period is likely to have fallen over a few centuries before 1000 CE, and the second period is likely to have begun around the fifteenth century and carried on through the eighteenth and beginning of the nineteenth centuries CE.

30 "Ọmọ ẹni kò ṣe ìdí bẹ̀bẹ̀rẹ̀, k'á fi ìlẹ̀kẹ̀ sí ìdí ọmọ ẹlòmíràn."

31 The *orin Ìbejì* genre emanates from this ritual practice of singing and dancing in praise of twins. See the appendix for the transcription and translation of close to ten *orin Ìbejì*. Val Olayemi's work *Orin Ìbejì* (University of Ibadan, 1971) still remains the most comprehensive text on Ìbejì songs. Òrìṣà devotees and lovers of twins never view the mothers as "beggars" but as protectors of their children, willing to go through this ritual, which under other circumstances would be humiliating. But set in the context of twinning, it is a tradition of singing and dancing to keep the children healthy and alive.

32 As she dances, she will be showered with gifts from admiring crowds, and through this process, she may acquire wealth.

33 This refrain from a traditional folk song places in context the role of the mother of twins, not as a beggar, but as someone responding to a traditional call to dance in the open market in honor of her twins. If the mother refuses to dance, the child could die. If the twins are sick, a diviner can advise the mother to dance for them in the open market.

34 This is yet another folk song related to the phenomenon of twin birth.

35 From traditional *oríkì* or "praising songs" recited to honor twins.

36 Unpublished folksongs collected from Babaláwo Fátóògùn in Ilobu, July 2008.

37 When Ìbejì are born more than once to a mother, the second set of Ìbejì is named after monkey (Àáyá or Ẹdun), indicating that the names are interchangeable. The two children born after Ìbejì bear the names Ìdòwú and Àlàbá.

38 A reference to the propitiation of a deity.

39 This is a reference to the twin children metaphorically described as her husband, that is, the one she adores.

40 Because they are Spirit-Children.
41 The people were castigating Ẹdun for claiming to be what they felt he was physically incapable of doing. They felt his physique was too small, and he should not claim to do what large animals accomplish.

Bibliography

Abiodun, Rowland. "Verbal and Visual Metaphors: Mythical Allusion in Yoruba Ritualistic Art of Ori." *Word and Images: A Journal of Verbal and Visual Enquiry* 3, no. 3 (1987): 252–70.

Abiodun, Rowland. "Yoruba Arts and Aesthetics: The Concept of Ase" (Memorial to William Fagg). *African Arts* 27, no. 3 (1994a): 68–125.

Abiodun, Rowland. "Verbalizing and Visualizing Creative Power through Art." *Journal of Religion in Africa* 24, no. 1 (1994b): 309–22.

Barber, Karin. "How Man Makes God in West Africa: Yoruba Attitudes Towards the Orisa." *Africa* 51, no. 3 (1981): 724–45.

Bulmer, Michael G. "The Twinning Rate in Europe and Africa." *Annals of Human Genetics*, 24 (1960): 121–5.

Charman, Karen. "Ecuador First to Grant Nature Constitutional Rights." *Capitalism Nature Socialism* 19, no. 4 (2008): 131–3. https://doi.org/10.1080/10455750802575828.

Creinin, Mitchell, and Louis G. Keith. "The Yoruba Contribution to Our Understanding of the Twinning Process." *Journal of Reproductive Medicine* 34, no. 6 (1989): 379–87.

Flores-Peña, Ysamur. "Son Dos los Jimagüas" ('The Twins are Two'): Worship of the Sacred Twins in Lucumí Culture." In *Double Trouble, Twice Blessed: Twins in African and Diaspora Cultures*, edited by Philip M. Peek, 99–115. Bloomington, IN: Indiana University Press, 2011.

Granzberg, Gary. "Twin Infanticide: A Cross-Cultural Test of a Materialistic Explanation." *Ethos 1*, no. 4 (1973): 405–12.

Houlberg, Marilyn. "Ibeji Images of the Yoruba." *African Arts*, 7, no. 1 (1973): 20–7, 91–2.

Jeffreys, Mervyn D. W. "Twin Births among Africans." South African *Journal of Science* 50 (1953): 89–93.

Knox, George, and David Morley. "Twinning in Yoruba Women." *Journal of Obstetrics and Gynecology of the British Empire* 67 (1960): 981–4.

Lawal, Babatunde. "Aworan Representing the Self and Its Metaphysical Other in Yoruba Art." *The Art Bulletin* 83, no. 3 (2001): 498–526.

Lawal, Babatunde. "Ejiwapo: The Dialectics of Twinness in Yoruba Art and Culture." *African Arts*, Spring 2008.

Lawal, Babatunde. "Sustaining the Oneness in Their Twoness: Poetics of Twin Figures (Èrè Ìbèjì) among the Yoruba." In *Double Trouble Twice Blessed: Twins in African and Diaspora Cultures*, edited by Philip M. Peek, 81–98. Bloomington, IN: Indiana University Press, 2011.

Meyerowitz, Eva L. R. "Ibeji Statuettes from Yoruba, Nigeria." *MAN* 44 (1944): 105–7.

Mobolade, Timothy. "Ibeji Custom in Yorubaland." *African Arts* 4, no. 3 (1971): 14–15.

Ngu, E. C. "Yoruba Ibeji Carvings, Ibadan." Unpublished Seminar Report, 1964.

Nylander, Percy P. S. "The Frequency of Twinning in a Rural Community in Western Nigeria." *Annals of Human Genetics* 33 (1969): 41–4.

Nylander, Percy P. S., and Gerald Corney. "Placentation and Zygosity of Twins in Ibadan, Nigeria." *Annals of Human Genetics* 33 (1969): 31–40.

Nylander, Percy P. S., and Gerald Corney. "Ethnic Differences in Twinning Rates in Nigeria." *Journal of Biosocial Science* 3 (1970): 151–8.

Olaleye-Oruene, Taiwo. "Cultic Powers of Yoruba Twins: Manifestation of Traditional and Religious Beliefs of the Yoruba." *Acta Geneticae Medicae et Gemellologiae* 32, no. 3–4 (1983): 221–8.

Olayemi, Val. *Orin Ibeji*. Institute of African Studies, University of Ibadan, Nigeria: 1971.

Olupona [Olúpọ̀nà], Jacob K. *Kingship, Religion, and Rituals in a Nigerian Community: A Phenomenological Study of Ondo Yoruba Festivals*. Stockholm: Almqvist & Wiksell International, 1991.

Peek, Philip M., ed. *Double Trouble, Twice Blessed: Twins in African and Diaspora Cultures*. Bloomington, IN: Indiana University Press, 2011.

Pison, Gilles. "Les jumeaux en Afrique au Sud du Sahara: fréquence, statut social et mortalité." In *Mortalité et société en Afrique au sud du Sahara*, edited by Gilles Pison, Étienne van de Walle, and Mpembele Sala Diakanda, 245–70. Paris: Institut national d'études démographiques, 1989.

Polo, Fausto, and Jean David. *Ibeji Catalogue*, Galerie Walu, Zurich, Vol. 1, 2001 & Vol. 2, 2005.

Rai, Saritha. "A Family Rift Roils the Market in India." *New York Times*, November 23, 2004. https://www.nytimes.com/2004/11/23/business/worldbusiness/a-family-rift-roils-the-market-in-india.html

Renne, Elisha. "Twinship in Ekiti-Yoruba." *Ethnology* 40, no. 1 (2001): 63–78.

Renne, Elisha. "The Ambiguous Ordinariness of Yoruba Twins." In *Double Trouble, Twice Blessed: Twins in African and Diaspora Cultures*, edited by Philip M. Peek, 309–15. Bloomington, IN: Indiana University Press, 2011.

Segy, Ladislas. "The Yoruba Ibeji Statue." *Acta Tropical* [Separatum] 27, no. 2 (1970): 97–145.

Thompson, Robert Farris. "Sons of Thunder: Twin Images among the Oyo and Other Yoruba Groups." *African Arts* 4, no. 3 (1971): 77–80.

Thompson, Robert Farris. *Black Gods and Kings: Yoruba Art at UCLA*. Bloomington, IN: Indiana University Press, 1976.

Trompf, Garry W. *Payback: The Magic of Retribution in Melanesian Religion*. Cambridge: Cambridge University Press, 1994.

Turner, Victor W. *The Ritual Process: Structure and Anti-Structure*. Chicago: Aldine Publisher, 1969.

3

Twins

Welcome and Unwelcome Danglers in Africa

♊

Pashington Obeng

Introduction

The apparent anomaly of twin births in African societies has evoked varying social and religious reactions. Historical responses have ranged from confusion—the perception of twins as humans who defy easy classification—or the embrace of twins as a blessing, to dislike, shame and such fear of the enigma that it has become stigma (e.g., among some of the Omotic-speaking Southern Ethiopian peoples, notably the Kara, Hamer, and Banna, where twins are still considered *mingi*; ritually impure and therefore dangerous to all).[1] Some people have resorted to twin infanticide, or the culturally sanctioned, even if euphemized, killing of one of a pair of twins. While twin rituals are either on the decline or being modified under socioeconomic and religious change, the Kedjom of the Cameroon Grassfields and the Ga and Akan Akyem of Ghana perform public rituals annually to enhance, reproduce, and propagate their society, people, animals, and nature. This chapter examines twin births in a number of African societies in order to shed light on the ambivalent attitudes to the sustained influence and relevance of mystical powers attributed to human beings with anomalous identities. We start with a brief survey of differing African responses to the paradox of multiple births in order to contextualize how the Ga and Akan Akyem draw on an ideology of extraordinary twin powers to reenact and ratify their foundational sacred history. By examining how twin mystical forces are implicated in sociopolitical and religious systems, we seek to clarify how African societies adopt ambiguous responses to humans who appear to have duplicated personalities within matching bodies. Finally, we foreground African religious ideologies that shape and are shaped by sociohistorical forces and actors to inflect twinship beliefs as a key aspect of religion in Africa.

Human twinning has dramatic impacts on the biological, physical, and social lives of the parents, families, and those who care for the twins.[2] This discussion uses Malian, South African, Cameroonian, Nigerian, and Ghanaian examples to explore the private and social responses to the idealized concepts as well as the fear and suspicion about duplication of living individuals. The chapter draws on these case studies to examine twins and their perceived mystical powers and the ambivalent responses they evoke in their families and larger societies. Even among African peoples whose notions represent twinning as "the ideal of a soul mate,"[3] twins may nevertheless be perceived as possessing mischievous, even malevolent tendencies if not appeased.

Twinship has been a focus of Africanist ethnographers and art historians from the 1920s to the present. Despite the fact that multiple births, especially twinship, are common in Africa, their occurrence has never been normalized, and African cultural responses to them, while varying across a spectrum, have never, to the present day, been neutral. Much has been written about ancestors, nature spirits, witches, sorcerers, and diviners,[4] but the literature on twinship tends to be scanty. However, twinship occupies an important domain in most African societies, that of ambiguous beings whose advent into normal lifeworlds is both welcome and unwelcome.

A critical aspect of indigenous African religion, often underdiscussed, is the role of ambiguous humans who embody the sacred for good or for ill, having the potential for both. Multiple births not only reduplicate the number of infants expected in any given childbirth; twins themselves have "duplicate personalities." Twins are in the category of paradoxical beings that, though human, are believed to possess extraordinary powers. The ambiguous social status of multiple births in African societies results in the attribution of unusual and special powers to twins. Though they are not usually labeled as witches, except in rare cases like the Omotic-speaking peoples (see fn. 1), where they are unambiguously seen as cursed and able to curse whole communities by their very existence, twins are universally believed to use their powers to wreak havoc or bring blessings on people. This has continued in Haitian Vodou, as discussed by Adam McGee in this volume. What appears to be exceptional in the biological event of twins and the social-religious constructions of twin or multiple births in Africa finds resonance in other societies, as ambiguous responses to twins are not an exclusively African or African diasporic phenomenon.

I begin by examining some of the reactions to the perceived auspiciousness and diabolical power of twins in Africa. I will then turn to specific case studies of the Akan Akyem and Ga of Ghana. I explore the religious, cultural, and political dimensions of how the Akyem and Ga have insinuated twinship, with its dual energies of auspiciousness and danger, recently to reimagine and repurpose their respective annual festivals.

A Pan-African Survey

Twinship in Mali

Among the Bamana (Bambara) and Maninka (Malinke) of Mali, twins are believed to derive directly from their Supreme Being, Faro.[5] Twins serve as Faro's functionaries among humans. Twinning, according to Imperato and Imperato, is regarded as normal.[6] While twins, albinos, and hermaphrodites are all regarded as having double beings, form of albinism and hermaphroditism are perceived as "genetic abnormalities."[7] As

God's representatives, twins and their parents are given respect and status in their society. People show their reverence toward the twins by offering them gifts. The gifts are seen as an expression of piety, and at times petition from those who are honoring the humans with "duplicate personalities."[8] In communities where rank and roles are as important as rights, privileges and responsibilities, twining presents a classificatory challenge.

The order in which twins are born, and how that birth order is construed, reflects aspects of Malian sociopolitical structure; this has analogies elsewhere in Western Africa (see the chapter by Jacob Olúpònà in this part of the book). The second twin born is considered the older because the first has been sent by the elder to give a report of what the world is out there. If the first-born does not give a favorable report about the world outside of the mother's womb, it is believed that the second to be born will not enter the world. Reversal of the birth order in determining seniority between twins helps us to understand the sociocultural underpinnings of Malian politics. In Malian political structure, senior members do not run errands for their juniors. According to this system of ultimogeniture, the twin born first is always junior to the second. The phenomenon of twins reinforces rank and status in Mali where elderly people by their advanced age are considered wise and thus wield more authority than young people. The second-born twin, the "older," also receives more status and respect. Twinning with its beliefs and practices impacts more than the twins. The mother, the family, and society at large can often face the challenges of twins equally and equability for twins.

Despite the euphoria surrounding twins and twin birth, as international obstetrician Alessandra Piontelli unsparingly observes, duplicate babies can "upset family life" and cause turmoil in societies.[9] Cases of risk in maternal deaths and complications are high for twin deliveries. Where systemic poverty runs deep, there may be a traditional pattern of preferential treatment given to a healthy twin, with a corollary neglect of the weaker twin less likely to survive after birth. The healthier of the two tends to receive most social interaction, while the "shadow" twin does not have the same opportunities for "face-to-face interactions" with the mother.[10] Piontelli argues that the scarcity of resources in Bamako, the capital of Mali, shapes how much affection and care a mother of twins can give her children, sometimes with the effect of parental favoritism.[11] Although neither Imperato nor Piontelli mentions infanticide in Mali, there is no question that neglect of a twin child can also lead to his or her death. The tradition of outright killing one of a pair of twins persists in parts of Benin and Madagascar.[12]

Twins and Challenges of Twinship in South Africa

Isaac Schapera's foundational study in 1927 interpreted twin birth within a larger corpus of cultural meanings, values, and notions. Schapera stressed both the auspiciousness and the malevolent powers of twins.[13] He argued that in some South African communities, twins were seen as unnatural and dangerous; mothers of twins were treated as guilty parties whose crime was being avenged. By interpreting twin birth as a spiritual punishment for a woman's alleged crime or antisocial act, "unnatural births" acquired a kind of cultural explanatory power. This calculus called for their killing, in order to rid the society of the crime and its consequences. In other South African contexts, however, Schapera noted how twins were treated as bearers of divine fortune, with their birth marked by celebrations. When the duplicate personalities of twins were seen as having divine origin, particular rituals were performed to conserve the "favor of the gods."[14] The applicability of Schapera's important work is limited, however, because it relies exclusively on a kind of static model of cultural logic. In fact, as we will see, societal response, even to instantiated ideas about a phenomenon such as twinship, can evolve. In South Africa, where twin infanticide used to be practiced, some volunteers are currently providing resources to support twins, orphans, and their families.

Present-day Response

Today the prevalence of HIV/AIDS in South Africa has undermined some of the indigenous parental and family support and rituals surrounding twinship. When parents die young, the orphan twins and singletons vie for the care, protection, and support that were previously guaranteed under the extended family networks that were underpinned by indigenous ritual practices.[15] Though not all rituals and beliefs about twinship have ended, the religious privileges that parents enjoyed with their twin children have been undermined or discontinued. In 1975, a group of South African volunteers founded the South African Multiple Birth Association (SAMBA) to assist parents and family members that might feel overwhelmed by the care that twins and other multiples need. SAMBA also provides nannies, night nurses, and support groups for the families.[16] SAMBA's response of care for twins, other multiples, and singletons expresses their awareness of the physical, economic, and social constraints that South Africa's children and adults face today. The SAMBA response to twinning reflects how they interpret twins or multiple births.

Sociocultural Interpretations of Twinship

In examining Ndembu twin rituals in light of the contradictions in people's social structure, Turner calls twins a "classificatory embarrassment" (1969). For Firth, twinship rituals reflect how humans symbolically pay respect to their creations and assets, as part of the process of asserting personal and collective identity.[17] Scholars such as Kilson (1973) and Oruene (1985) adopted a sociological perspective that focuses on the anomalous social status of twins and the larger society's ambivalence toward such anomalous beings. Neither Schapera's cultural interpretations of twinship nor the sociological explanations of Oruene (1985) about twinship are adequate. Such analyses fail to account for the complex motives informing twin-killings and other forms of neglect or abandonment that some twins suffer. Ball and Hill (1996) contend that twin infanticide could be parents' and societies' "biologically adaptive behaviors to invest resources in infants" that have a better chance of surviving.[18] Following this logic, as Piontelli later echoes from an epidemiological point of view, it is not only twins who are killed in some societies, but also other infants who are deemed to have less chances of survival; thus, cultural explanations have an underlying sociobiological component, with a significant concern for the relationship between survivability and scarce resources. The above approaches, though insightful, do not historicize religious practices and beliefs that surround twinship.

Sociohistorical Approaches to Twinship

As a corrective response to the overemphasis on social conflict and ahistorical approaches to twinning, some contemporary scholars examine twinship in sociohistorical contexts. The current focus presents theoretical models that "include the ambiguities of social and historical practices relating to multiple births" (Bastian 2001, 2003). Scholars address ongoing conflicts and competing worldviews that cover religious and ideological differences.

Gender Studies Approach

Bastian (2001) uses a gender studies lens to address how Igbo-speaking Nigerians dealt with twinship during the nineteenth and early twentieth centuries when Onitsha came under the Church Missionary Society's (CMS) influence. She points out that while the European and Nigerian men "conceptualize twins as abstract signifiers of personhood and/or moral worth, something to be saved or cast out," it was on the women that "the actual physical struggle over the care or destruction of twins and other multiples fell."[19] Bastian's analysis points to how the Igbo-speaking people used their notions of division of labor and religious understanding to rid their society of evil or to restore order. Twin infanticide existed in the Igbo society, according to Bastian, as one way to explain and eradicate misfortunes. While twin rituals may be on the decline in present-day Onitsha, the Kedjom of Cameroon have increased twinship rituals.

Resurgence of Twinship Rituals

Diduk (2001) notes that the Kedjom of the Cameroon Grassfields have increased their twinship rituals in spite of the presence of evangelical Christians' missionizing activities. She points out that twins' extraordinary powers were harnessed and augmented in the 1980s because the Cameroonians knew that Christian missionaries could not help with or did not have a satisfactory response to local peoples' understanding of the problem of evil. Since twins have mystical powers similar to those of "witches," the Kedjom people drew on the spiritual power of twins to tackle social and economic crises. For instance, since twins are humans with double personalities, some people consult them for spiritual assistance to improve their material conditions.

The people, according to Diduk, tap the powers of twins to address their daily needs. The Cameroonians use twinship rituals as an important religious weapon to deal with their contemporary concerns. Twin children wield social power because they are seen as possessing spiritual power to help the community in business, farming, for example. At the same time, twins are believed to have the capacity to change into animal familiars, invisibly moving among people to commit mischief. The prevalence of twinning with its attendant ritual practices inspires the adoption of various responses to twin birth.

Muslim Reform Response

Masquelier's work among the Hausa-speaking Mawri in Niger reveals how Mawri-Hausa cosmogony sees twinship as a gift from their Supreme Being. However, with the advent of the followers of Izala (a Muslim reformist movement in Dogondoutchi), twin births have been anathematized. According to the Muslim reformists, "twin pairs are invariably the product of morally suspect unions between married women and their lovers."[20] This position is similar to the prevalently held views in South Africa about twin birth. Twins who were once revered because they mediated between humans and God were reconceptualized and stigmatized to represent physical evidence of women's promiscuity. This also led to the killing or hiding of twins. It is only when a woman gives birth to a singleton after having had twins that the children can be granted full membership in the Muslim community. In their reconstruction of religious ethics, the Dogondoutchi Muslim reformists seem to discard some of their cosmogonic beliefs in favor of what they perceive as modern and morally appropriate religious attitudes and practices.

Christian Influence on Twinship

In southwestern Nigeria, the introduction of Christianity by Ekiti Yorùbá migrant workers who returned to their natal communities brought new ideas that helped to recast rituals and practices of twinship in Christian terms. The reassessment of twin beliefs made the Ekiti people perform twin rituals and set up twin shrines because twins were reconceived as beings with mystical powers given to them by God. It was believed that if people treated twins with love and care, their families and communities would be blessed with wealth, success, and abundance of animal, plant and human life. Recently, among some Ekiti communities, twins are perceived as ordinary humans given to them by God. The twins no longer need to have special rituals performed for them. Rather, they should "be raised, educated and taken to the hospital"[21] when they are ill. The new Ekiti sentiment toward twin birth, though it appears to be a break with the past, is rather a more universalizing continuation of their religious history: the belief that all children, be they twins or not, are gifts from God. The umbrella has simply been extended to erase the distinction twins bear among other Yorùbá peoples.

All the above ethnographers stress the local understandings of twinship within sociohistorical and economic contexts. Their analyses moreover point to changing notions and attitudes about twin births for the local people on the one hand, and researchers' positions on the other.[22] Although these scholars historicize religious beliefs and practices involved in twinship rituals, they do not address how religious ideas are constructed as people wrestle with the enigma of twin birth in present-day Africa. Ghanaian examples, notably the Ga and Akyem Akan, help us to understand the settings in which the exceptional powers of twins are amplified. This occurs through indigenous rituals, but also through the contemporary reconstruction of twinship, while at the same time hinting at the social and very real economic challenges that human twinning poses. As elsewhere in Africa, Ghanaian twinning is a social and symbolic category deployed in religious ritual; in Ghana specifically, it is also a trope of political power among the Ga and Akyem.

Ghanaian Twins and Alms

In Ghana, both the Ga of Accra and the Akan Akyem regard twinship as a special spiritual category. The Akan of Ghana call a male twin Atta, while a female twin is called Ataa. My late father Jacob Atta Adu Kumi, a twin, recalled, "When I was growing up, I remember my mother dressing my twin brother, Essau Atta Kuma, and me alike. We wore similar outfits and visited family members who gave us gifts. We did this until we started going to school. Since our parents were Christians, they didn't perform any rituals." There were times when he and his twin brother suffered from the same illness. He recalled that his twin brother would complain of similar ailments that he suffered from. He noted that twins in other households at Anum in the Eastern Region of Ghana received yearly elaborate rituals in their homes. He said there were rumors that twins could turn into animals to destroy crops on people's farms. In their non-human forms, they could travel to places far away from where they were physically situated.[23] Though he did not indicate that he was involved in any such antisocial or meta-empirical activity, Adu Kumi said other people in their community always dealt with his twin and him with reverence and a dash of fear or suspicion.

Some twins traditionally went around to receive gifts among the Ga of Accra and Akan ethnic groups in Ghana. Those who gave gifts believed that they would receive blessings from the twins; traditionally, many Ghanaians regarded twins as bearers of blessings from God. In the past, Akan couples sought multiple births by placing *akuaba* dolls (wooden images) of twins in special corners of homes where they were venerated. Some women carried the *akuaba* dolls on their back to foster the birth of twins. Also, among the Akyem Akan, numerical strength in families and lineages is interpreted as a blessing from the ancestors and God; thus, multiple births were sought.

Ghanaian twinship beliefs and practices shed light on the people's notions of social identity and personhood. Care for twins requires more resources than what is required for singletons. Doubling of personhood defies notions of the ordinary person and social order. Hence, the Akan and Ga attribution of mystical powers to twins helps us to understand the ordinary and mundane aspect of persons. Adu Kumi's testimony underscored the paradoxical nature of twins. If they receive what they want or need, they do not wreak havoc.

Twinship and Development

The traditionally elaborate rituals performed in Ghana when twins were born seem to have waned. However, the Akan saying *Baanu so a emmia* (Akan Twi meaning, "there is strength in numbers") has been recalibrated to involve twinship in new roles in Ghana. There is now a Ghana Twins Foundation headed by the identical twin sisters Zeena and Maya Aboujaoude of Accra, Ghana. The Akyem Abuakwa annual Odwira harvest festival, which incorporates twins' participants, is being expanded and modernized to be a tourist attraction in Ghana. Human twinning remains as a focus of continuing religious relevance as well as of ambiguity in Ghana.

Ghana Twins Foundation

The Ghana Twins Foundation has a membership of over 800 sets of twins from all over Ghana. Since 1999, the Foundation has since been organizing an annual National Twins Festival. The event, which is steadily gaining recognition among the Ghanaian public, has been adopted by the Ministry of Tourism and Modernization of the Capital City, Accra.[24]

Zeena and her twin sister Maya Abou-Jaoude reported by Owusu that they first conceived the idea of forming the Ghana Twins Foundation when they were growing up. "We always wanted to do something unique for the less privileged in society. At the time, we were members of the Red Cross Society and in 1999 we had an opportunity to conduct a research on street children while working at the at the Kwame Nkrumah Circle in the heart of Accra," said Zeena Abou-Jaoude. During the course of their work, they came across twins as young as four years old begging on the streets of Accra. "We were touched and the exposure we had after our interactions generated a lot of sympathy and concern," said Maya Abou-Jaoude. This is how the Foundation was born in 2000. They resolved to get the abandoned twin children off the streets. The Foundation started with about fourteen sets of twins, and its members now include a set of triplets and a set of quadruplets. Another objective of the celebration was that she, her twin sister, and others were assembling "all multiples and their hierarchies Atta (male) and Attaa (female), Tawia (one born after twins), Nyankomago (the next sibling) and the subsequent sibling is Atuakosan, followed by Damusaa,[25] to organize them by modernizing views about multiples and to use such persons with 'ambiguous identities' to bridge cultures and races of the world." Zeena and Maya Abou-Jaoude's ambitions are aimed at exploring how twins are treated in other societies and how adult twins could help educate their respective societies about the challenges and opportunities such people with dual personalities could provide for others.

Similar to SAMBA, the efforts of the Twins Foundation in Ghana might have been to counter some of the negative public valence around twins and twin birth in Ghana.

Zeena and her sister Maya Abou-Jaoude describe the importance of multiple births and their attendant rituals. Thus, they suggest that the mystical powers traditionally attributed to twins could be used to foster peace and understanding among all people. When the twin sisters include other siblings in the events, they are stressing an important aspect of twin ritual, which in traditional belief includes the sibling sisters and brothers.[26] Their approach, which involves the appropriation and re-direction of traditional African beliefs about the (benevolent) powers of twins, is the opposite of Lale Labuko's, which is to expose such beliefs when they are malevolent as untrue, although it is notable that when communicating with Karo elders prior to the cessation of infanticide in 2012, Labuko offered himself to absorb the *mingi* of condemned children rather than denying it.

Despite the reframing of the multiple birth event, it seems that the twin sisters do so in light of the paradoxical effects of two factors: the prestige of traditional beliefs in the extraordinary powers of twins and other multiples, coupled with the acknowledgment of the "stress and turmoil"[27] of multiple births that may lead to the abandonment of twins, particularly by impoverished women or families. The two women are constructing a pan-ethnic and global dimension of twinship celebration out of a religiously based festival that was traditionally limited to Ga communities in Ghana. The women's celebration of multiple births seems also to de-monopolize the traditional ritual role of indigenous priests/priestesses surrounding twin annual festivals. Today, instead, social workers and these philanthropist twin sisters mobilize notions of twinship to perform public service.

Zeena and Maya Abou-Jaoude were puzzled to see twin children in the streets, wearing similar outfits, begging. The sisters saw marginalized street children who might have been performing their traditional ritual role of developing their mystique to fend for themselves. The "abandoned" twins (from the perspective of Zeena and Maya), who were asking for alms in the streets of Accra, may also call attention to the perplexing roles and strain that twin births put on their families and communities. The financial and emotional hardships that the families of twins encounter may account for the reason some twins beg for alms. Also, not all multiple-birth families in Accra are Ga that hold religious beliefs about twins. Thus, economic, labor, and emotional stresses may compel some families to send their twin children to beg for alms. At the same time it is worth noting for those who believe that twins have extraordinary powers, twins are supposed to receive "hyper"-care because of their special status, and out of fear they might become displeased and malevolent. Twins are, therefore, to be treated and raised with special care. For instance, for Ga twins, there are special rituals that are observed, especially on Fridays when it is most propitious to cleanse their souls.[28] It is on Fridays that farmers rest, so that day is devoted to ritual bath that is given to twins.

Ga Twins and Animal Affairs

The Ga see twins as charismatic and desirable persons, although it is understood that such ambiguous personalities can also do harm. Cultural ambivalence toward twins in Ghana, as we have seen not unique in Africa, manifests in some children being left to fend for themselves: scarce resources and the emotional and psychological stress of twin care are surely causative, but so is the notion that twins can cause trouble in the mundane world. Just as the Nuer of the Sudan call twins birds, "children of Kwoth [the god of air]," so the Ga regard them in the category of spirits, as the locus of spirit being—as humans with special privileges but also as embodiments of malevolent forces. The Gamashie of Accra central, Ghana, regard twin birth as "desirable and anomalous."[29] They are both welcome and unwelcome danglers at the margins of normal life, yet also, curiously, at its center.

In the indigenous Ga symbolic and religious universe, the religious thought the bush cow is an abstract form of a twin.[30] The Ga identification of twins with plant or animal life is a "rallying point"[31] for the people to assert that what they believe and practice matters. In the plant world, twins have affinity with yams, while in the topographical realm, they are associated with the pond.[32] The Ga twin belief underscores their understanding of how humans and other aspects of nature share in the quality of being. Humans, they believe, are not, and should not, be seen as separate entities from other parts of creation. According to Marion Kilson, the symbol synonymy between animals and human beings may clarify why the Ga regard twin birth as anomalous and powerful. She argues that wild animals "reproduce several offspring at one time and are generically nonrational; they are dangerous to human beings not only because they may be ferocious, but because they do not control their sexuality."[33] Animals are believed to have multiple births because of the promiscuity of their females.[34] Schapera had also deployed a similar approach to that of Kilson and Chappel to interpret twin infanticide in South Africa. However, contra these interpretations, one might note that the Ga consider twin birth as a metaphor for potential, increasing the abundance of special powers and resources. The unclassifiable nature of twins helps the Ga to conceptualize and clarify such abundance in humans, plants, and animal life. The potential danger of twins, however, lies in their ability to inflict punishment on others in the society. Having multiple offspring is not due to lack of sexual control, nor does the uncanny meaning of twins originate there.

Ceremonies surrounding twin birth and twins are deployed to increase their special powers for humans. For instance, once a year, special rituals are performed for Ga twins to prolong their lives and make them happy. Their powers are kept alive and augmented through ceremonies during annual festivals. *Homowo* (hooting at, mocking, or chasing hunger) is one of the important festivals celebrated by the people of Ga (Accra) Traditional Area. Participants sprinkle *kpokpoi* (corn festival dish) to the gods and ancestors for spiritual protection and prosperity. Twins dressed alike are the major players, processing through the main streets of Accra. The festival is marked by a procession through the principal streets, accompanied by traditional drumming and dancing and general merrymaking. "A month before the celebration, there is a ban of noise making. A climax of the festival is that from 12 noon to 6:00pm any woman, no matter her status, should accept a hug from a man on the festival street."[35]

As they process, the Ga deploy twin powers to end hunger and to foster fecundity. One phase of such ceremonies includes twins carrying water bowls and swaying under the bowls; yet the water never spills, even when they stumble or become possessed by spirit. Such rituals, according to Kpobi, are meant to give a public demonstration of the boundless power of twins among the Ga people of Accra. The show of twin spiritual power also publicly reinforces the influence and status of the families to which twins belong. Twins are beckoned to increase fish catch, and fertility among humans and nature in Accra. As Mary Douglas famously argued of the pangolin, humans within an "unclassifiable class," through twinship rituals, wield spiritual power in Ga indigenous religion.

Religion and Politics

The religious, cultural, and political underpinnings of Akyem ritual ceremonies ratify the auspiciousness of twinship in either royal lineage or in priestly families. Also, as Imperato et al. argue, there is both a "dialogic" and "interactive"[36] relationship between twins that enable them to fully know each other because they intimately connected in the womb before they were born.[37] With the Akyem, the mystification of royal twins extends only to other twins. This mystification is not always a positive collective association, since twins are also perceived to have negative propensities.

The Akyem also use twinship rituals to harness the powers and blessings of twins, renew themselves, and ratify the society's foundational myth/history. The Akyem, a subgroup of the Akan, live in the southern part of Ghana. Their annual harvest festival, Odwira, contains a twinship ceremony called *abamhwie* (twinship ritual bath). The ritual bath involves the chief priest of the ceremony who uses water, cowries, and special leaves contained in a big calabash or basin to cleanse the twins. *Abam* also refers to the string of beads and cowries worn on the wrists of twins. The following brief history will be used to contextualize the sociopolitical and religious elements of Akyem *abamwhie*.

Twinship in Akyem History and Myth

Nana Ofori Panin (Senior Twin Ofori) was the first political leader of the Akyem state. As Ofori Panin was a twin and the progenitor of the Akyem, *all twins are believed to belong to the royal family of the Akyem nation.* In 1716, it is said that Ofori Panin and his army settled at Akyease as part of their expansionist endeavors. Ofori Panin was described as an "old, sagacious, and experienced" ruler in the 1700s.[38] It was under him that the Akyem Abuakwa capital was moved to Kyebi. There Ofori Panin built a palace which to this day is called Ofori Panin Fie. The Akyem Abuakwa royal stool was carved and consecrated in honor of the Okyehene (Akyem King) Ofori Atta Panin, and was referred to as Ofori Panin *akonwa* (Ofori Panin stool). The Akyem Abuakwa as a consolidated state therefore came into existence under Ofori Panin, although the Akyem people had lived in different segmentary groups dating back to the 1400s.[39]

Ofori Panin combined political strategy with military prowess and wisdom. Under his leadership the Akyem people were able to fight off the Asante and Akwamu who were other powerful Akan groups. When the Akwamu warriors threatened the Guans who resided in the Akwapem hills, Ofori Panin sent his nephew Ofori Kuma (junior Ofori) also called Safori (the brave warrior Ofori) to defend the Guans. With the combined forces of Guans, Akwapems and Akyems, the Akwamu fighters were routed. Oral historians assert that Ofori Panin (senior twin Ofori) used his twin spiritual powers to evade the enemies during the battles against the Asante. The legend highlights the people's belief in the extraordinary power of the king. In this case, the twin deployed his power to wage and win battles against the Asante.

Queen Mother, Bearer of Twins

When the Regent Nana Ohemaa Afia Dokuaa came into power as the Okyeman King/ Queen Mother of the Akyem state, twinship took on additional significance. She was the great-grandniece of Nana Ofori Atta Panin. In addition to her military skills, Nana Ohemaa Dokua was an extraordinary administrator. During her reign from 1817 to 1835, she divided the kingdom into administrative sections headed by chiefs who also held military roles as wing commanders. Nana Dokua's Akyem forces are said to have fought and defeated the Asante people on a number of occasions. She gave birth to twins, becoming known as *Owoo ntaa* (one who gives birth to twins), who ruled after her death. The birth of these royal twins is said to have led to the establishment and recognition of *abam* (twin ritual bath) celebrated on the first Friday of the annual Akyem Abuakwa Odwira festival. The Paramount Chief/King of the Akyem state celebrates the festival with the Queen Mother at her residence and along the banks of the Birim river. All twins in Akyem and the paramount stool's occupant celebrated the festival.

Rathbone contends that when Ofori Atta I came to the throne (1912–47), he was known as one of the most powerful kings and a "forceful modernizer."[40] He was seen as one who continued the legacy of Nana Ofori Panin. It was during Ofori Atta's reign that the Akan saying *tumi nyina wo asase so*—"land is the essence of power"—gained credence.

Covenant and Twinship

Ofori Atta I knew that in order to maintain a united Akyem state, he had to remind the citizens that family and royal lands had value beyond their market prices. He thus stressed that the integrity and the longevity of the kingdom's union depended on how office bearers and landholders maintained and honored their loyalty and obligation to the ancestors.[41] The king tied the people's identity to the collective obligations to one another and to the land and the spirit beings. Ofori Atta I strategically drew on and elaborated the ideology of a centralized royal power over the various ethnic populations. The king reminded his people about the covenantal links between the living and the dead and, thus, the significance of the ancestors in the Akyem worldview. Importantly, he constructed and renewed Akyem notions of citizenship to sustain and stabilize the Akyem state. It was his duty to continue the legacy of Nana Ofori Panin. King Ofori Atta I condensed and crystallized the religio-political concepts of Akyem identity around kingship and kinship by defusing conflicts and minimizing "the serious and growing cleavages in the kingdom whose roots lay, above all, in an economy making the rich richer while the "poor" suffered. Paramount in the kingship symbols was the mystical power of Ofori Panin (the elder twin), believed to hold the Akyem state together.

If twins have become an important component of the Akyem state annual festival, one of the reasons could be that the present-day rulers draw their authority from a long line of legendary royal twin rulers. By hereditary association, all Akyem kings are figuratively twins. Akan twins, with their extraordinary powers, are believed to foster material and spiritual energy for those who tap that resource. The Akyem therefore deploy twin ritual belief to enact and reenact the traditions that form the foundation of their nation during the Odwira festival.

Twins and the Ohum Festival

Ohum is the anniversary celebration in June/July of the founding of the Akyem nation; it is unique to the Akyem. Odwira is a larger pan-regional festival that is celebrated by most Akan communities. It is a ritual cleansing and thanksgiving in September/October that involves a two-week ban on drumming, dancing, and noise-making prior to the festival. During Ohum, twins follow the king, in whom political and religious powers cohere, in a procession to usher in the new harvest season. As one who occupies the royal twin stool (Ofori Panin *akonwa*), the king and twins are metaphysically linked. As twins, their extra-human powers are used by the Akyem to engender prosperity, longevity, and fertility. Just like indigenous Asante, all twins are considered royal household members and symbols of the king's fertility and sacrality. Parts of the Odwira/Ohum festivals are purification rites meant to castigate antisocial people as well as encourage people to abide by the injunctions of their forebears.

A critical component of the weeklong Odwira festival is the twinship ritual (*abamhwie*). Although belief in the extraordinary powers of people with duplicate souls or personalities predated the more recent forging of the Akyem Abuakwa nation, the celebration of this ritual illumines twins' continuing religious significance and status. *Abamhwie* is a ritual cleansing ceremony, observed on Friday as the final purificatory ceremony of the ritual cleansing week meant for the twins. Twins work in concert with the Supreme Being, river deities, and ancestors to orchestrate peace, success, harmony, and fertility for the Akyem people or, at times, misfortune. Their extraordinary ability to appear in doubling forms, as well as the superhuman military powers and administrative skills attributed to Ofori Atta Panin and his successors, is marshaled to buttress the foundational myth/history of the Akyem Abuakwa state.

We will first describe the phase during which twinship ritual (*abamwhie*) functions in the festival; second, address the importance of *abamhwie*; and third, show how Akyem notions about twins embedded in a larger Akan sociopolitical and religious framework are being reproduced in contemporary times.

Reformulation of Ohum Festival

In 2005, the Akyem festival was revived and modified; the Ghana News Agena wrote then, "As part of efforts by the Akyem Abuakwa Traditional Council to improve tourism in the area, the Council has decided that the Ohum festival will be celebrated annually to focus on tourism."[42] Traditionally, the Ohum festival had been celebrated only by individual towns located along the Birim river. During the Ohum festival, the Akyem thank the creator for blessing their land with the River Birim and to remember ancestors who struggled and persevered to consolidate the Akyem state. During the festival, citizens pledge to continue the tradition, to keep Okyenman (the name of the nation-state) strong and filled with peace and prosperity. They then pledge allegiance to the King (Okyehene) and his sub-chiefs and elders for their leadership and guidance. This ceremony of thanksgiving has two parts: the *Ohumkan* (starting with hooting at hunger and misfortunes) and the *Ohumkyire*. It is followed by the *Agyemperemuso Ko* (Sacred Gathering).

Ohum Huro (Hooting at Ohum)

On the evening of the festival called Ohum (Tuesday), drummers beat drums at the king's palace. At the sound of the drums, everyone hoots. Ohum marks the end of all misfortunes from the previous year: lack of jobs, difficulty passing qualifying exam, family members may be granted visas to travel abroad, and so on.

2. *Ohumkyire* (triumphant return of Ohum)

On Sacred Wednesday called *awukuadae*, palm fronds (*emmerenkenson*) are paraded through the towns to recall Ohum to bring fortunes of wealth, good health, fertility, hope, and confidence.

3. *Agyemperemuso Ko* (Sacred Gathering):

The most festive celebration is on Sacred Friday. The Akyem king and his subjects go to the state shrine, *Agyemperemuso*, to give thanks and offer a white sheep to the Almighty God and the ancestors. When the king and his twin siblings and the community go to the River Birim, for the next phase of Ohum, they perform *abamwhie* (twinship ceremonies). The River Birim lies in the Birim Valley; she is a goddess for the Akyem Abuakwa people, a source of life for humans, plants, and for livestock, as well as a conveyer of profound historical and spiritual significance. In the past, Akyem and non-Akyem mined gold and diamond in the Birim river basin. Thus the area with its rich deposits of diamond and gold has also been a source material wealth for the people.

At the *abamhwie* ceremony, on the last Friday of the weeklong Ohum/Odwira celebration, most of the twins (*abamfo*) in the region gather at the Akyem king's palace at Kyebi to participate in the annual Odwira festival. The twins are all dressed in white and smeared with white clay or powder. The twins carry their special miniature stools called *abam akonwa*. The white stool of the Okyehene (the Akyem king) is carried by the chief of the stool carriers. The king, leading all the twins, proceeds to the place of worship (*asoreso*) on the banks of the Birim river on the outskirts of Kyebi. The king's *okra* "soul" (or "soul bearer"), a special court attendant who accompanies Akan kings/chiefs all the time and embodies the soul of the ruler, also dresses in white and carries a white *abam akonwa* (the twin stool) in front of the king.

When the procession gets to the *asoreso* (place of worship), the king sits on his white stool and his *abam akonwa* (twinship ritual stool) is placed in front of him for his "soul bearer" to sit on. All the *abams* in the gathering arrange themselves in a circle around the king and his "soul bearer."

The children among them sit on their stools while the adult twins who are too big for their stools kneel behind them. A brass pan is taken to the river to fetch water. The pan of water from the Birim river is placed in front of the king. The indigenous chief priest (the king's appointed religious specialist) brings some *adwera* (*lonchocarpus cyanescens*, sacred herbs) in brass pan full of water and puts the pan in front of the king. By custom, the chief priest asks why the people have gathered on the banks of the Birim river on that Sacred Friday. The *okyeame* (the spokesperson for the king) announces that it is the end of the year. They are about to enter a new year, and as tradition demands, the occupant of the Ofori Panin stool, on behalf of all the twins in the state, has come to Birim Abenaa (name for a female born on Tuesday since Birim was believed to be born on Tuesday), to purify himself and his fellow twins, and ask for the blessings and protection for the state. The priest then pours a libation asking the spirit of the river to invite her brother and sister spirits, the royal ancestors, and all the Akyem ancestors to come and bless the ceremony and make it a success.

The priest sprinkles water thrice on a sheep so that it can vicariously bear all the misdeeds of the state. The sheep is then offered to propitiate the gods in order to wash away all the defilement that has come upon the king and his "twin siblings," namely, all the twins who are gathered as spiritual relatives of the king. At that stage, the priest sprinkles water on the twins and the king. He repeats this seven times—to represent the seven days of the week on which twins may have been born. Every one of these actions is accompanied with a petition to the spirits to wash away or cleanse the spirits of all the twins in the gathering. The sheep is then sacrificed.

All the twins in the gathering are then allowed to take a dip in the river to participate in a ritual swim or bath. At this point their parents, siblings, and well-wishers join them to perform this ritual cleansing. The Okyehene's (Akyem king) "soul bearer" takes the ritual swim on his behalf. Thus the "soul bearer" becomes a twin to enable him to represent the king by participating in the purification ceremony.

After the swim, the priest sprinkles water three times on all the people gathered on the banks of the river to close the ceremony. The ceremony ends when the *abamwhie* participants returning to Kyebi town in a procession behind the king and his brother and sister twins gather on the premises of the palace grounds during the Edwabo (gathering). This is the time when people pay homage to the king. In the evening the people attend a colorful *durbar* (gathering of paramount chief/king and sub-chiefs). A parade of chiefs occurs, during which sub-chiefs renew their allegiance to the king by swearing oaths in his presence. A variety of entertainment activities are held till sunset and the king declares Ohum ended.

The Akyem Traditional Council believed that the Ohum festival, repurposed as a tourist event, would have a broader, even an international appeal; Akyem and non-Akyem families would unite to participate in a ritual that is grounded in twinship beliefs. *Abamhwie* is an example of how Africans draw on their faith to renew themselves and to reengage with their forebears who are their sources of spiritual and political strength.

Such royal twinship ceremonials also clarify the notion that Akyem kings/chiefs are seen as twins, sharing in the legacy of the earlier Akyem lineage, because they occupy a seat or stool named after a twin. *That is, Akyem kings derive their powers from mystical twinship, not the other way around. The twins who appear at the Ohum festival do so symbolically to ratify his kingship and to remind the Akyem of its source.* Twinship powers, status, and privileges are transferable across time and space, as the South African and Akyem cases exemplify.

In reality, neither the twins nor their families necessarily live in a world of much power. While the Ga and Akan Akyem may include twins in annual festivals, the day-to-day nurturance of twins in their childhood is the responsibility, not of the royal family, but of their parents and extended families. Despite the desire of some Ghanaians to have many children, the reality of multiple births can create stress for the parents and the immediate family.

This is why my own father's observations may be relevant here. "When I was growing up . . . it seems the whole community contributed in cash and kind to care for twins."[43] While people contributed to ask for blessings, by the same token, contributors might be afraid of the potential mischief twins could commit against them (compare the Yorùbá evidence in Olúpǫnà's chapter). Here we have a kind of systemized, religiously grounded communal economy, whereby the parents and families of twins used such gifts to augment their own resources to raise the twins.

Infanticide practiced among the Akyem and Ga in the past could be interpreted in popular notions of misfortune, corresponding to ideas of homological malformation at the moment of birth. As Bleek observes, "a deformed infant was believed to bring [corresponding] misfortune to the environment."[44] Ghanaians conceptualized birth defects as potentially dangerous for the well-being of the lineage. Twins—the unwelcome appearance of a duplicated individual—were almost certainly believed to represent such a birth deformity. As in the case of Omo Mingi children in Ethiopia (see fn. 1) and elsewhere, the deformed infants could be drowned for the safety of all; the traditional euphemism used was *wasan awoye* ("the child died and returned"); *ba no anye yiye* ("the child did not survive"); *wawu nsuo mu* ("the child died in water"). There were various interpretations of deformities, including a baby with six fingers, or "two arms on one hand."[45] Could it be that they were not ready or equipped to deal with persons in a non-classifiable category? Perhaps multiple or twin births have posed a challenge not only to the classificatory systems and the mundane aspect of how to care for multiple mouths especially today when the close-knit extended families and values that sustained them are stretched to the breaking point.

The aforementioned responses elucidate the resilience and reproduction of beliefs and practices are found in all religions. While God is always assumed and addressed in African religions, corporeal humans with meta-empirical powers, "danglers" like twins are sources for empowerment, social and economic development, yet are at the same time, potentially malevolent spirits. Twins contain and control both beneficent and destructive forces.

Long-standing ambivalence toward twins in Ghana is not eased through the reframing or whitewashing of their auspicious powers. The Akyem Ohum festival, as well as Zeena and Maya Abou-Jaoude's reframing of mystical twinship as only positive, appropriating it for a collectively beneficial social agenda, is only a partial response to the perplexing character of twins and twinship. Pan-African ambivalence, suspicion, and fears of twins may occasion their abandonment in the streets of Accra. Twins remain anomalous in Ghana and are both auspicious and dangerous, both welcome and unwelcome danglers.

Having said that, doubling or twinning in Africa may be used as a model for conceptualizing African cosmologies. Twins may represent, among other things, the complementarity between the physical realm and the spiritual domain. Rather than producing a binary oppositionality between normal and abnormal births, Peek suggests that the doubling of souls/personalities alleged to be inherent in twinship allows Africans to draw attention to, as well as to ratify, the multiple selves and interlocking relationships that underscore social and religious reality.[46]

Conclusion

The ambiguity of twins seems to run very deep in Africa. I have tried to address the complex and varied responses some African societies give to twins and twinship, which are best understood in both sociohistorical and religious contexts. We have considered the reformulation of twinship rituals and the founding of twinship organizations in South Africa and Ghana, as well as how the Kedjom of Cameroon use twinship rituals and ideologies to negotiate socioeconomic forces in their society. The continuing reality of abandoned twins on the streets of Accra, and Adu Kumi's remarks about people's fear and suspicion of twins, make it clear that twins continue to be anomalous in Ghana. They can still be both dangerous and auspicious within the same culture, something like Otto's category of *fascinans*. The public ideologies of the revived Akyem Ohum festival convey the message that twins always bring blessings on people, reframing long-standing ambivalence toward twins by recasting the older, mystical twinship as only positive, thus appropriating it for particular collective social agenda. Despite the stress that twin births may bring on the family or community, twins continue in Ghana to be "linked to chieftancy and political authority—to the spiritual world and models of enhanced human interaction and communication."[47] In Accra, the capital of Ghana, the Twins Foundation has incorporated elements of indigenous beliefs about twins and used such ideas for public service. The Akyem of Ghana have deployed twin sacred and political powers to construct and sustain individual and collective well-being.

In examining these beliefs, I have tried to address the sociohistorical and political institutions, as well as the worldviews that Africans bring to bear on the enigma of twin births. When Ga and Akyem showcase twin sacred powers to perform public rituals to usher in the New Year, these African societies make a public statement about some of their religious ideas. Their responses are shaped by notions about the mystical powers of twins, albeit redeployed to serve new purposes. Contemporary Ohum and Homowo festivals, underscored by twin rituals, are promoted to foster peace and harmony, as well as to reinscribe royal status and serve as tourist attractions. The festivals are used to promote cultural tourism as well as renew important African indigenous beliefs and practices. In the popular imagination, twins, like ancestors and other spirit beings, may represent destructive forces as well as foster increase in fertility for land, animals, and humans.

My analysis has drawn attention to the quality of non-oppositionality in African twinship—that is, the lack of what might be called dualism—in the doubling, in some ways contrastive, yet in many others intertwining nature of twinship that is, on a larger scale, fundamental to life and reality.

Notes

1 *Mingi* is a complex word denoting ritual impurity deriving from culturally defined physical deformities that are believed to endanger the health and well-being of the community, especially drought; hence "curse" is not inappropriate as a descriptor. Among such specific anomalies are twin births (Twin Mingi), the eruption of baby teeth in the upper jaw before those in the lower or chipping a baby tooth (Tooth Mingi), or children born out of wedlock (Girl Mingi) or as the offspring of an unapproved marriage (Woman Mingi). See Gezahegn Petros, (Ababa: Addis Ababa University Dept. of Sociology, Anthropology and Social Administration, 2000), 57. Traditionally, they have been strangled, suffocated, exposed in the forest, or drowned in rivers. International attention was brought to this practice by Karo tribesman Lale Luboko, who lost two *mingi*-sisters before his own birth, Labuko's efforts to save *Mingi* children, sometimes endangering himself and his team, were the subject of the 2011 documentary *Drawn from Water* by John Rowe and later the documentary "Omo Child: The River and the Bush" (Little Pass Films in assoc. with Omo Child, 2015), as well as featured in National Geographic (https://www.nationalgeographic.org/find-explorers/lale-labuko), accessed March 4, 2022; . Video .nationalgeographic.com, accessed July 2, 2014), and in a CNN story, "" Matthew D. LaPlante (2011-05-11) and "Luboko and Rowe's Omo Child in Jinka works to rescue mingi children, but also to influence Omo religious and cultural attitudes." The rescued children live at Omo Child house; fourteen nannies care for the children on donations. On July 14, 2012, Luboko persuaded the Karo to ban the killing of *mingi* children in 2012; as his TED talk explains, Karo elders themselves proposed the sacrificial substitution of a lamb, which was performed, followed by a powerful rain-storm an hour later, interpreted as a sign of divine favor. Twin and other forms of *mingi*-child infanticide is still practiced among the Hamar. The fear of drought or sudden death of the entire family, brought on by the survival of dangerous *mingi*-children remains.

2   Helen L. Ball and Catherine Hill, "Twin Infanticide," *Current Anthropology* 37, no. 5 (1996): 856.

3   Alessandra Piontelli, *Twins in the World: The Legends They Inspire and the Lives They Lead* (New York: Palgrave Macmillan, 2008), 5.

4   E. Bọlaji Idowu, *Olódùmarè: God in Yoruba Belief* (New York: Praegar, 1963); cf. Geoffrey Parrinder, *African Traditional Religion* (Westport, CT: Greenwood, 1970); Blakely, et al., *Religion in Africa: Experience and Expression* (Portsmouth, NH: Heinemann, 1994).

5   Pascal Imperato, "Bamana and Maninka Twin Figures," *African Arts* 8 (1975): 52–60, 83–4.

6   Pascal J. Imperato and Gavin H. Imperato, "Twins and Double Beings among the Bamana and Maninka of Mali," in *Twins in African and Diaspora Cultures*, ed. Philip M. Peek (Bloomington, ID: Indiana University Press, 2011), 43–58.

7   Ibid., 58.

8   Ibid., 52.

9   Piontelli, *Twins in the World*, 5.

10 Ibid., 73.

11 Ibid., 72.

12 U.S. Department of State Country Reports on Human Rights Practices for 2012: Madagascar (2013), 25; U.S. Department of State Country Reports on Human Rights Practices for 2012: Benin (2013), 17. See Centre of *Unlawful Killings in Africa: A Study Prepared for the UN Special Rapporteur on Extrajudicial, Summary or Arbitrary Executions*, Thomas Probert (Cambridge: Centre of Governance and Human Rights, University of Cambridge, 2014), 152.

13 Isaac Schapera, "Customs Relating to Twins in South Africa," *Journal of the Royal African Society* 26, no. 102 (1927): 117–37.

14 Ibid., 117.

15 Bosco Kweisei, personal communication, July 12, 2010.

16 SAMBA: The South African Multiple Birth Association, http://www.samultiplebirth.co.za/wabout.php.

17 Raymond Firth, "Twins, Birds and Vegetables: Problems of Identification in Primitive Religious Thought," *Royal Anthropological Institute of Great Britain and Ireland* (1966): 15.

18 Ball and Hill, "Twin Infanticide," 857.

19 Misty L. Bastian, "'The Demon Superstition': Abominable Twins and Mission Culture in Onitsha History," *Ethnology* 40, no. 1 (2001): 5.

20 Misty L. Bastian and Elisha P. Renne, "Reviewing Twinship in Africa," *Ethnology* (2001): 6.

21 Ibid., 7.

22 Bastian, "'The Demon Superstition,'" 8.

23 Jacob Atta Adu Kumi, personal communication, January 15, 2009.

24 Douglas Owusu, "Fifth Annual National Twin Festival in June," *Ghana News Agency*, May 8, 2005.

25 Kofi Asare Opoku, *West African Traditional Religion* (Accra, Ghana: FEP International Private Limited, 1978), 112.

26 Ibid.

27 Piontelli, *Twins in the World*, 5.

28 Kwadwo Kwaa, twin and Akyem, personal communication, August 5, 2009.

29 Marion Kilson, "Twin Beliefs and Ceremony in Ga Culture," *Journal of Religion in Africa* 5, no. 3 (1973): 193.
30 Firth, "Twins, Birds, and Vegetables," cf. E. E. Evans-Prichard, "Customs and Beliefs Relating to Twins among the Nilotic Nuer," 1936.
31 Schapera, "Customs Relating to Twins in South Africa," 15.
32 Kilson, "Twin Beliefs and Ceremony in Ga Culture," 175.
33 Ibid., 194.
34 cf. T. (Tim) J. H. Chappel, "The Yoruba Cult of Twins in Historical Perspective," *Africa* 44, no. 3: 260.
35 Dr. Nii Anum Kpobi, personal communication, November 12, 2007.
36 Imperato and Imperato, "Twins and Double Beings among the Bamana and Maninka of Mali," 43–58.
37 Ellen Moore Suthers, "Perception, Knowledge, and Divination in Djimini Society, Ivory Coast," Ph.D. dissertation (University of Virginia, 1987).
38 Robert Addo-Fening, "The 'Akim' or 'Achim' in the 17th-century and 18th-Century Historical Contexts: Who Were They?" *Institute of African Studies Research Review* 4, no. 2 (1988): 8.
39 Ibid.
40 Richard Rathbone, "Defining Akyemfo: The Construction of Citizenship in Akyem Abuakwa, Ghana, 1700–1939," *Africa: Journal of the International African Institute* 66, no. 4 (1996): 506–25.
41 Ibid., 525.
42 "Ohum Festival at Kyebi, Akyem Abuakwa (Eastern Region)," *Ghana News Agency*, July 22, 2005.
43 Jacob Adu Kumi, personal communication, January 15, 2009.
44 Wolf Bleek, "Did the Akan Resort to Abortion in Pre-Colonial Ghana? Some Conjectures," *Journal of the International African Institute* 60, no. 1 (1990): 129.
45 Ibid.
46 Peek, Introduction, *Twins in African and Diaspora Cultures*, 27–8.
47 Ibid., 27.

Bibliography

Addo-Fening, Robert. "The 'Akim' or 'Achim' in the 17th-century and 18th-Century Historical Contexts: Who Were They?" *Institute of African Studies Research Review* 4, no. 2 (1988): 1–15.
Ball, Helen L., and Catherine Hill. "Twin Infanticide." *Current Anthropology* 37, no. 5 (1996): 856.
Bastian, Misty L. "'The Demon Superstition': Abominable Twins and Mission Culture in Onitsha History." *Ethnology* 40, no. 1 (2001): 13–27.
Blakely, et al. *Religion in Africa: Experience and Expression.* Portsmouth, NH: Heinemann, 1994.
Bleek, Wolf. "Did the Akan Resort to Abortion in Pre-Colonial Ghana? Some Conjectures." *Journal of the International African Institute* 60, no. 1 (1990): 129.
Chappel, T. (Tim) J. H. "The Yoruba Cult of Twins in Historical Perspective." *Africa* 44, no. 3 (1974): 260.
Diduk, Susan. "Twinship and Juvenile Power: The Ordinariness of the Extraordinary (1)." *Ethnology* 40, no. 1 (2001). Web. August 31, 2015.

Douglas, Owusu. "Fifth Annual National Twin Festival in June." *Ghana News Agency*, May 8, 2005.

Firth, Raymond. "Twins, Birds and Vegetables: Problems of Identification in Primitive Religious Thought." *Man*, 1966: 15.

Imperato, Pascal James. "Bamana and Maninka Twin Figures." *African Arts* 8 (1975): 52–60, 83–4.

Imperato, Pascal James, and Gavin H. Imperato. "Twins and Double Beings among the Bamana and Maninka of Mali." In *Twins in African and Diaspora Cultures*, edited by Philip M. Peek, 43–58. Bloomington, IN: Indiana University Press, 2011.

Idowu, E. Bọlaji. *Olódùmarè: God in Yoruba Belief.* New York: Praegar, 1963.

Kilson, Marion. "Twin Beliefs and Ceremony in Ga Culture." *Journal of Religion in Africa* 5, no. 3 (1973): 171–95.

Kpobi, Nii Anum. Personal communication, November 12, 2007.

Kumi, Jacob Atta Adu. Personal communication, January 15, 2009.

Kwaa, Kwadwo. Personal communication, August 5, 2009.

Kweisei, Bosco. Personal communication, July 12, 2010.

Lale Labuko (2013). *National Geographic*. NG Live!: Lale Labuko: Rescuing Children of the Omo (2013). National Geographic.

LaPlante, Matthew. "Is the Tide Turning against the Killing of 'cursed' Infants in Ethiopia? - CNN.com." *CNN*. Cable News Network, November 5, 2011. Web. August 25, 2015.

"Ohum Festival at Kyebi, Akyem Abuakwa (Eastern Region)." *Ghana News Agency*, July 22, 2005.

Opoku, Kofi Asare. *West African Traditional Religion*. Accra, Ghana: FEP International Private Limited, 1978.

Oruene, T. O. "Magical Powers of Twins in the Socio-Religious Beliefs of the Yoruba." *Folklore* 96 (1985): 208–16.

Parrinder, Edward Geoffrey. *African Traditional Religion*. Westport, CT: Greenwood, 1970.

Peek, Philip M., ed. *Twins in African and Diaspora Cultures*, Bloomington, IN: Indiana University Press, 2011.

Petros, Gezahegn. *The Karo of the Lower Omo Valley: Subsistence, Social Organisation, and Relations with Neighboring Groups*. Ababa: Addis Ababa University Dept. of Sociology, Anthropology and Social Administration, 2000.

Piontelli, Alessandra. *Twins in the World: The Legends They Inspire and the Lives They Lead*. New York: Palgrave Macmillan, 2008.

Probert, Thomas. *Unlawful Killings in Africa: A Study Prepared for the UN Special Rapporteur on Extrajudicial, Summary or Arbitrary Executions.* Edited by Thomas Probert. Cambridge: Centre of Governance and Human Rights, University of Cambridge, 2014.

Rathbone, Richard. "Defining Akyemfo: The Construction of Citizenship in Akyem Abuakwa, Ghana, 1700–1939." *Africa: Journal of the International African Institute* 66, no. 4 (1996): 506–25.

Rowe, John. *Drawn from Water*. Documentary. 2012.

Rowe, John. *Omo Child: The River and the Bush*. Documentary. 2015.

SAMBA. "SA Multiple Births." Web. August 20, 2015.

Schapera, Isaac. "Customs Relating to Twins in South Africa." *Journal of the Royal African Society* 26 (1927): 117–37.

Suthers, Ellen Moore. "Perception, Knowledge, and Divination in Djimini Society, Ivory Coast." Ph.D. dissertation, University of Virginia, 1987.

U.S. Department of State Country Reports on Human Rights Practices for 2012: Madagascar, 2013.

U.S. Department of State Country Reports on Human Rights Practices for 2012: Benin, 2013.

4

Marasa Elou

Twins and Uncanny Children in Haitian Vodou

♊

Adam Michael McGee

Marasa elou, mwen kite fanmi lan peyi Gelefwe.
M pa gen fanmi pou pale pou mwen, Marasa elou.
Mwen pa genyen parenn. Sa k ap pale pou mwen?

Marasa *elou*, I left my family in Gelefwe.[1]
I don't have any family to speak for me, Marasa *elou*.
I don't have a godfather. Who will speak for me?

Baptizing the Marasa

"They must be baptized," she said. Manbo Maude, a Vodou priestess and my spiritual mother, had had a dream.[2] In it, children told her that they belonged to me and wished to be baptized. The next day, she called me.

"We must have a baptism for your new *plat Marasa*," she said.[3] A month prior, Maude had accompanied me to purchase a set of the small terracotta one-, two-, and three-chambered pots and jugs that are used in Haitian Vodou to represent the Marasa, the twins who are granted a preeminent place in the pantheon of *lwa*, the holy spirits of the Vodou religion.[4] A few weeks later, Maude and several other Vodouisants came to my apartment. I had cooked food for everyone, because it is important at a Vodou ceremony to be a good host. If people leave hungry, it risks *djòk*, the evil eye—not to mention malicious gossip. While cooking, I had also soaked and washed the *plat Marasa* in a large enamel basin filled with lukewarm water, shredded fresh basil, and a liberal sprinkling of Florida Water.[5]

Vodou ceremonies reliably begin late. Sure enough, hours later than I had planned, everyone finally arrived, everything was ready, and the ceremony started. *Plat Marasa* are always kept on the floor or a low shelf under the altar—one explanation being that young children like to crawl around on the floor. At the time, my altar was simply the top of my dresser. The five or six people in attendance all crowded into my small bedroom. Maude stood closest to the altar and sang a shortened version of the *Priyè Ginen*.[6]

When the *Priyè Ginen* was finished, we began the baptism. Maude explained the purpose of the ceremony in a mixture of Kreyòl and English. She said that we had gathered to baptize my Marasa, to keep them happy and let them know that they were loved and cared for. I then gathered the *plat Marasa* into my arms. I had chosen two of my friends to serve as *parenn* and *marenn* (godfather and godmother) for my Marasa. Together, they held a white candle, and with their free hands, they touched the *plat Marasa*. Maude sang Catholic baptismal songs in French, and with a sprig of basil, she sprinkled each *plat Marasa* with holy water and baptized them in the name of the Father, Son, and Holy Spirit, giving each a name that I had received in a dream.

"Children, behold your father," Maude said, addressing the *plat Marasa* directly. "Obey him, bring him blessings, good health, and riches. Don't cause him any trouble. He will take care of you, and you will take care of him. If you are low, he will uplift you. He will keep you clean. If you are thirsty or hungry, he will feed you. In the name of the Father, the Son, and the Holy Ghost, *ainsi soit-il*."[7]

After this, we sang several songs for the Marasa, and as we did so, I filled the *plat Marasa* with a little bit of each of the food offerings I had purchased for them. The Marasa like sweets and candies, things that children love: cookies, lollipops, gummy candies, cake, peanuts, roasted corn and popcorn, dried fruits, hot chocolate, and the sickly sweet kola champagne soda popular throughout the Caribbean. In each of the

Figure 4.1 Detail of Vodou altar, showing *plat Marasa* and basil. Photo by Patrick Sylvain. By permission of Adam McGee.

bowls, I placed a shiny new penny (the Marasa love money, but are more impressed by the shininess than the cash value). Then I piled in pieces of cakes and candies. I was careful to make sure that I put the same amount of food in each, since the Marasa quickly become jealous if one receives more or less. Finally, I filled the small jugs with water, a bit of kola champagne, and a drizzle of *siwo kann* (sugarcane syrup) to keep them sweet.

This concluded the ceremony, and we squeezed out of my bedroom to gather in the living room. I served the food that I had made, and the event transitioned into a social occasion, a chance to catch up with friends. I now had my own living mystical twins. Although the *plat Marasa* represented some distant ancestral twins, I was now their father. For the rest of my life, they will be my children, bestowing on me spiritual gifts and, in turn, expecting my care and attention.

What Is the Meaning of Two?

Haitian Vodou is a religion created by the descendants of Africans brought as slaves to the French colony of Saint-Domingue. It combines components of multiple West and West Central African religious complexes (notably Fon/Ewe, Kongo, and Yorùbá) with European and Native American cultural and religious elements to create a religion entirely unique to Haiti and her diaspora. Haitian Vodou is the religion of millions of Haitians, though precisely how many is difficult to say. It is equally difficult to say what Haitian Vodou *is*, since it is, in reality, an umbrella term for a variety of Afro-Haitian religious practices that often—though not always—share common assumptions about the world.[8] Vodou is focused on the celebration of ancestral spirits, and all Vodou rituals are, at heart, healing rituals. Through feasting, singing, and ecstatic dance, these rituals mend damaged bodies and restore ruptured social bonds.

Most scholarship about Haitian Vodou has been about the religious practices of the Haitian south. This encompasses, most importantly, the capital city of Port-au-Prince, as well as the southern cities of Léogane, Jacmel, Les Cayes (Okay), and Jérémie. This region broadly represents the dominant style of Vodou, based largely around *peristil* (temples) that utilize the initiation called *kanzo*, which grants the *ason* (sacred beaded rattle) to initiates.[9] This style of Vodou is distinct from the Vodou of the center and north of Haiti, where the *ason* is largely unknown. There, religious practice is centered around *lakou* that honor only one particular "nation" (a pantheon of spirits perceived to share an ethnic origin), as opposed to temples in the south, which honor many nations.[10] This central and northern style of Vodou has often been called *makout* or *tcha-tcha*. Importantly, it is the style practiced by a trinity of three famous *lakou*— Souvenans, Soukri, and Badjo—that are often regarded as the oldest and purest Vodou temples in the country. This style has recently begun to promote the use of the name *Deka* to describe itself.[11] Additionally, neither *ason* nor *Deka* satisfactorily describes the family-centered styles of Vodou that persist in small *lakou* around the country to this day. In these cases, religious practice propitiates a limited number of inherited spirits, and services are directed by an elder member of the family who functions as the family's spiritual leader.[12]

Problematically, scholarship has often treated the southern *ason*-based style of Vodou as though it is the *only* Vodou, contributing to the cultural dominance of Port-au-Prince and its environs, which people from other parts of the country have long resented. Unfortunately, because of the limits of my experience, this chapter also mostly only describes this southern style of Vodou, but I recognize the profound need for similar work to be done about other styles of Vodou. Additionally, my experiences with Vodou are heavily weighted toward the diaspora, where I live and interact with other Vodouisants. In this, I am far from unique: millions of Haitians live in diaspora, particularly in the United States, and Haitian Vodou—both in diaspora and in Haiti—is increasingly shaped by their experiences and needs. As with all religious practice, Vodou is deeply entwined with memory, emotional life, and with the psychic potential not simply to endure, but to flourish through life's vicissitudes.

This was driven home for me one afternoon while visiting Maude. As such afternoons often go, we were sitting in her kitchen while she sang songs for Vodou spirits into my computer. It occurred to me that I should ask her if she knew how to sing the song that opens this paper, since it appears frequently in the scholarly literature about Marasa but I had never heard it used. As Maude looked at the lyrics, she began to hum quietly, but then a look of consternation crossed her face.

"I have the other Marasa *elou* song in my mind, I can't think of this one," she said.[13] The longer she thought, the more frustrated she became. "I have to get up and walk," she declared. Visibly upset, she stood, and with her hands on her hips, she paced from the kitchen into the dining room, returning after a minute.

"We could do some other songs," I suggested, trying to change the subject. "I'm sure it will come to you if you stop thinking about it."

"I'm going to call Mariline," Maude said, already dialing her phone. "She'll know." Manbo Mariline, Maude's most senior initiate living in the United States, is a veritable encyclopedia of praise songs for the spirits. Mariline answered at her hospital job after a few rings. With little preamble, Maude asked her how to sing "the Marasa *elou* song, no, the *other* one."

After a few moments of silence as she listened to Mariline on the other end, Maude began to sing. As she did, her eyes closed. Singing, her arm relaxed, slowly bringing the phone to rest on the table as she pressed the button to end the call. I had expected a song in the stately *yanvalou* rhythm that characterizes most songs for Rada spirits, but instead, it was a *zèpòl* (lit. "shoulders"), the faster rhythm that one dances to enliven and celebrate the Rada nation. The tension that had suffused her body moments before melted as she gave herself to the song.

Marasa elou o, Marasa elou e,
sa k ap pale pou mwen, Marasa elou e?
M pa genyen fanmi. Sa k pou pale pou mwen, Marasa elou e?
M pa genyen marenn, m pa genyen parenn.
Sa k ap pale pou mwen la, Marasa elou?
M pa genyen zanmi. Sa k ap pale pou mwen, Marasa elou?
M pa genyen fanmi, m pa genyen manman,
M pa genyen papa, sa k ap pale pou mwen . . .

Marasa *elou* o, Marasa *elou* e,
who will speak for me, Marasa *elou* e?
I don't have family. Who will speak for me, Marasa *elou* e?
I don't have a godmother, I don't have a godfather.
Who will speak for me here, Marasa *elou*?
I don't have friends. Who will speak for me, Marasa *elou*?
I don't have family, I don't have a mother,
I don't have a father, who will speak for me.[14]

On the last line, Maude's voice cracked as she began to cry. I thought that the sadness of the song had moved her, and that she suddenly felt the closeness of the Marasa. In fact, she was sad that she had forgotten the song, and relieved to have it back. She explained, "I can't believe I forgot. That song is from my people, from Jacmel. My grandmother knew that song, and her mother." In her tears, not only did decades collapse, but also distinctions between joy and sorrow, religious experience and private memory, absence and presence.

In Sosyete Nago, the Vodou community of Manbo Maude (based in Boston, Massachusetts, and Jacmel, Haiti), it is common for members to have significant relationships with the warrior *lwa* Ogou and the Marasa.[15] In the case of the Marasa, to have a relationship with them often means that one is, oneself, a Marasa—since the difference between human, still-living twins, dead twins, and "cosmic" or ancestral twins is one of degree rather than of kind. A number of our members are either Marasa De (what in English would properly be called "twins"), Marasa Dosou or Dosa (children born after Marasa who share and even exceed Marasa De's power)—or else have twins in their families. Marasa, though sometimes referred to as *jimo* (twins), in fact, refers to an entire complex of children who are considered special, unusual, uncanny, and powerful. These include twins, triplets, and the next two children born after doubled or tripled births, as well as the child born before. All of these children, and more, have their role to play in the category of Marasa.

Alongside twins, Vodouisants also believe that an aura of spiritual power adheres to people who have unusual birth circumstances: these include being born breach, with the face covered by a caul, with the umbilical cord wrapped around the neck, with a full head of hair, with webbed fingers or toes, or with a sixth finger.[16] In the last two cases, of webbing and polydactlylism, the child is considered to be Marasa because he or she is said to have devoured the twin in the womb, leaving only the extra finger or the excess webbed skin. Finally, people with physical abnormalities—such as albinos, dwarves, and hydrocephalics—are considered spiritually powerful beings. Although not Marasa, strictly speaking, they are often honored in the same ceremonies that are made to honor Marasa. As such, we must recognize that—while it might be more convenient to discuss Marasa only as twins—the Haitian Vodou concept of Marasa sees twins as inseparable from a much larger category of uncanny children and spirits. As Raoul Altidor writes, "*Marasa gen mil vwa.*"[17] Nonetheless, twinning is used as the controlling and central metaphor for this category of "people" both living and dead—as well as powerful spirits who may or may not have ever been alive—to the extent that as a class, they will often be referred to as *jimo* (twins). Therefore, we must explore why it is that twinning is seen as the appropriate descriptor for this category that far exceeds what would generally be described as "twins," even as we are careful to recognize that, as a label, it disguises as much as it reveals.

In *Prinsip Marasa* [*Marasa Principles*], Max Laroche highlights the complexity of speaking about the Marasa, a concept that encompasses a multiplicity. He begins his reflections on the Marasa by asking a very simple, but easily overlooked, question: What is the meaning of two?[18] At the encouragement of a mathematician friend, Laroche reflects on this as a question of ethnomathematics—that is to say, a question of how people conceptualize the meanings of numbers. As Laroche points out, two is a number intimately tied to concepts of generation and regeneration. Two children are, in a sense, a superabundance of regeneration, and two parents are required to make twins. From two, we can derive all of the other numbers except zero (2 parents = 1 child; 2 parents + 1 child = 3, etc.). Laroche reminds the reader that the concept of zero was not present in all systems of counting, and was introduced to European mathematics by way of the Arab world (thus, why we continue to the present day to call our numbers "Arab numerals").

Modern scientific theories of *ex nihilo* cosmogenesis, notably the Big Bang theory, depend fundamentally on concepts of zero. Physics as we know it would be impossible without zero. However, the Vodou obsession with two—or more—suggests that the most important act of generation is not cosmic but rather human and social. The Marasa are honored at the head of the pantheon, just after Legba.[19] However, given that all prayers and services must be inaugurated with requests to Legba as the gatekeeper (regardless of whether one is starting at the beginning or simply calling one spirit), it might well be that Marasa should be seen as the first in the actual roster of spirits— with Legba, along with Ountò and Gran Chemen, honored beforehand as obligatory opening gestures.[20] In either case, the placement of Marasa at the head of the order of spirits suggests that it is the generative force of the Marasa that gives rise to the other spirits—and to creation more generally. As Odette Mennesson-Rigaud puts it, the Marasa are "the divine principle of life."[21]

Moreover, as two-who-are-one, the Marasa possess a mirror-like quality in the same symbolic vein as the cosmic mirror, which operates in Vodou as the hinge between the human world and the world of the spirits. This mirror serves as a controlling metaphor for the way that the physical world and Ginen are related to one another. The mirror is often said to be a reflective surface of water, and, most iconically, the glimmering surface of the primordial waters in which the dead dwell and through which one must pass to reach Ginen. Through the cosmic mirror, Vodouisants are in constant interplay with the world of the spirits—a world that is linked to ours through relationships of both sameness and obverseness. Much of Vodou aesthetics plays on this, relying on mirrored gestures, backwards movements, and reversed writing to communicate the topsy-turvy ways that we relate to the spirits "as through a glass, darkly." As a divided unity, the Marasa are their own mirror image; thus, they stand on both sides of the cosmic mirror, making them uniquely capable of *sonde miwa* (fathoming the mirror) simultaneously from both directions. This could well explain their psychopompic role in Vodou as the messengers of the spirits: with a foot in each world, they are literally interstitial, and therefore can easily pass information across the barrier. Moreover, their sameness-yet-difference falls naturally into structuralist pairs that exemplify the relationship between the physical world and the world of the spirits. Through the paradoxes of male yet female, identical yet different, plural yet single, alive yet dead, embodied yet cosmic, modern yet ancient, magisterial yet childlike, powerful yet helpless, the Marasa embody in themselves the relationship between our world of limited possibility and the Ginen world of limitless possibilities.

This helps explain as more than mere capriciousness the taboo against treating Marasa unequally, for to do so unbalances the mirror's reflection. Ideally, all major life events for incarnated Marasa should occur simultaneously, including marriage and even death. Should one die before the other, it imperils the life of the still-living twin, who may be pulled to the other side to restore the balance of the pair. For this reason, intensive and ongoing ritual propitiation of the deceased twin is necessary for the remainder of the living twin's life, begging the departed twin's forbearance even as the ritual action creates, in effect, a liturgical "placeholder" for the absent half of their mortally unbalanced equation.[22]

In fact, it is not just the Marasa in Vodou who are viewed as indivisible. The same can be said of *all* of the spirits, who are typically grouped into pairs, or less commonly, into triads. In Vodou's own parlance, one way that this is expressed is as marital units: spirits are said to be married to (or romantically affiliated with) one or more other spirits. Individual *lwa* are considered to have an inherently unbalancing effect upon the life of the devotee, and therefore they must always be paired with another spirit who possesses complementary qualities. For example, one cannot serve the coquettish and luxurious Èzili Freda without also serving her counterbalance, the hardworking and maternal Èzili Dantò. Moreover, all Rada spirits have their counterpart in Petwo, and are in this sense two in one. Understood most sweepingly, one might propose that all *lwa* are twins. This may be another reason that the Marasa are placed so prominently in the pantheon, since they could be seen as prototypical of all of the spirits.

It is important, moreover, that the Marasa are always *children*. After all, there are certainly plenty of twins who live to adulthood (although twins have a considerably higher rate of infant mortality). The Marasa are thoroughly integrated into the Vodou cult of the dead, and excepting living twins, the controlling metaphor of the Marasa is that they are the spirits of dead twins—even though, in many cases, these twins are said to have been born into one's family and died millennia ago. Still, the significant fact that they are *child* spirits may be seen as affirming the multiplicity, natality, and agelessness of the human spirit.[23]

Many classic works on Vodou have treated the Marasa as a category apart from the *lwa*, claiming that there are three distinct groups of spirits honored by Vodouisants, namely the *lwa*, the Marasa, and *lèmò* (the dead). Alfred Métraux and Melville J. Herskovits both say that some of their informants claimed that the Marasa are more powerful than the *lwa*. In my experience, these distinctions do not hold up in practice. Given that Vodouisants believe in apotheosis, it is difficult to make such a rigid distinction between the dead and the *lwa*—since the dead are constantly transforming into *lwa*. In Vodou, death has the capacity to make *anyone* more powerful, under the right circumstances. Because the Marasa are ancestral spirits—that is to say, *dead*—they are not entirely separate from this broader category. The difference is primarily that because twins are already atypically powerful in life, they are also more—and therefore atypically—powerful in death. To make matters more confusing, the Marasa are honored in most ceremonies alongside the rest of the *lwa*, with no indication that they are to be considered distinct from this pantheon. Therefore, while I appreciate the heuristic value of distinguishing these different groups of spirits and their associated practices, I do not find it to be especially true in daily life.

At a sociological level, the importance of the Marasa could be seen as an affirmation of the great significance of children in Haitian culture. Twins, as an abundance of children, represent the ideal of having as many children as possible. Again and again, I have found in my own interactions that the idea of not wanting to have children is unthinkable to most Haitians, regardless of sexual orientation or gender identity. Children are the greatest blessing that *Bondye* (God) can give to a human. Why would someone choose to be excluded from this blessing?

Haitian Vodou is part of a much larger circum-Atlantic complex of religions that honor twins.[24] Such traditions originate in West and West Central Africa, but are now found throughout the Americas. West and West Central Africa have anomalously high rates of fraternal twinning (the rate for identical twinning is fixed around the globe).[25] From a functionalist perspective, then, this high rate of twinning could explain the prevalence of twin cults in these areas, since twins have high infant mortality rates; religious devotion helps to focus much-needed attention upon them, thus ameliorating their vulnerability. The problem with this theory is that, until recent centuries, some West and West Central African twin cults that are seen as progenitors of Haitian Vodou (notably, those of the Fon and Igbo) instructed that twins should be exposed outdoors to die. This is *not* inconsistent with present-day twin cults in Africa and the Americas, if we see that the basis for these beliefs is not per se that twins should receive special care, but rather that they are uncanny and dangerous. Twins in Vodou do not receive extra care simply because they are special; they receive extra care because if they become dissatisfied, they can destroy those who are thought to have wronged them.

While the Marasa have obvious antecedents in West and West Central African twin cults, it remains an unsettled (and mostly unasked) question whether practices relating to the Marasa may owe at least some of their origins to the religion of the Taino, the pre-Columbian people who made Haiti their home. Although their numbers were decimated by disease, famine, war, and enslavement at the hands of Europeans, it is known that some Taino survived into the eighteenth century, hidden in the mountains where they were periodically encountered by maroons.[26] There were certainly material, cultural, and religious exchanges that occurred between these groups. Although little is known about the religious practices of the Taino, Spanish chroniclers indicate that a cult of twins—perhaps twin heroes—was an important element.[27] This is supported by numerous Native American twin-like stone fetishes (*zemi*) and amulets discovered in Haiti, such as the one described in a 1943 issue of the *Bulletin du Bureau d'Ethnologie*. The amulet, carved from manatee bone, shows two figures who have separate faces and torsos, but otherwise share a common body (joined at shoulders and ankles).[28] These sacred twins appear to have been associated with healing and the power to bring rain, as are the Marasa. It is therefore conceivable that Native Americans had an impact on the nascent cult of the Marasa, or at least their primacy within the Vodou *regleman*.[29]

The Family of Twins

The Marasa are a family, complete with a father and a mother. The father of the Marasa is named Papa Marasa or Papa Jimo (Father of Twins), and is also often called by the name of his corresponding saint, Sen Nikola (St. Nicholas). Presaging his eventual merger with Santa Claus, St. Nicholas of Bari has long been associated with children. In the hagiography, he is celebrated as a bishop who saved several children from a deranged butcher who intended to sell their meat. In his lithograph, St. Nicholas is shown giving the benediction while standing over the saved children. The halo of St. Nicholas, rendered in vibrant gold, has led him to be associated with the sun. As Papa Marasa, St. Nicholas is most especially associated with the rising sun and the east. Vodouisants make invocations to Papa Marasa/St. Nicholas by praying at dawn facing east. He is honored as the master of the *quatre partie du monde* (the four parts of the world), as befits the sun. These connections are not merely metaphorical: for Vodouisants, through a mystical coincidence, Papa Marasa *is* St. Nicholas, who *is* the sun.

Manman Marasa, the mother of the Marasa, is usually identified with St. Claire of Assisi.[30] St. Claire is portrayed in her lithograph as holding a monstrance in which hovers a large, perfectly round white consecrated Host. For Vodouisants, this luminous orb is the moon. Again, Manman Marasa *is* St. Claire, who *is* the moon. In other words, the Marasa are the children of the sun and the moon. This has parallels in classical Fon religion, in which the world was created by a divine male-Female pair, Mawu-Lisa, who are the sun and the moon, and who in turn gave birth to multiple sets of twins. Papa Marasa and Manman Marasa—as sun and moon, and progenitors of twins—bear striking resemblances to this pair.

Vodou assigns name and significance to nearly all of the children in a family with twins. The child born before twins is called Choukèt Marasa. The Choukèt does not have any particular mystical powers, although some people say that the Choukèt is weaker because the Marasa who followed sucked his or her life. In other cases, the Choukèt is honored as the child who dragged the Marasa into the world, and who has the power, as older sibling, to excerpt some control over them.

The Marasa themselves come in a number of configurations. Marasa De (Marasa Two) are twins. Notably, Vodou makes no functional distinction between fraternal and identical twins. This often surprises Europeans and Americans, who are fascinated by identical twins and tend to regard fraternal twins as both categorically different and of comparably little interest. By contrast, in Vodou—as in most Afro-Atlantic twin cults—both kinds are considered equally powerful. Identical or not, they are one soul divided between two bodies.[31] Marasa Twa (Marasa Three) are triplets. In this case, the first two children to be born are usually considered to be the Marasa proper, while the third child is the Dosou or Dosa, depending on the gender (Dosou if male, Dosa if female; also Zinsou and Zinsa).[32] The Dosou or the Dosa is the child born *after* Marasa, either as the singleton pregnancy pursuant twins or as the third triplet. This child is also considered to have enormous mystical power—in some cases *more* than Marasa because it is the same amount of power, but in a single child instead of divided between two.[33] The child born after the Dosou is called Dogwe, and is generally considered a restoration to normal births.[34]

Marasa De are identified with Ss. Cosmas and Damian, two of Haiti's most popular saints. Ss. Cosmas and Damian are shown standing next to each other, holding branches. Visually, this connects to their indivisibility, as well as to the belief that the Marasa are born with a perfect knowledge of how to use leaves to heal. Additionally, Ss. Cosmas and Damian are known as powerful healers, like the Marasa.[35] Marasa Twa, on the other hand, are associated with the lithograph known as The Three Egyptians or The Three Virtues. This image shows three young girls from the shoulders up, typically against an abstract background. The hagiography is that they were three girls who were martyred by beheading. However, they have come to be associated with the three Christian virtues—faith, hope, and charity. Choukèt Marasa and the Dogwe have no associated saints.

This seems straightforward enough. However, it becomes more complicated because Vodou contains numerous rites and nations. The two principal rites of Vodou are called Rada and Petwo, Rada being seen as "cooler" and Petwo as "hotter."[36] Within these rites (and in some cases, separate from them) are nations of spirits, many of which are named after African peoples. For example, there are the very important nations of Kongo, Nago, and Ibo. If Marasa De, Marasa Twa, and Marasa Dosou Dosa represent, in essence, meta-Marasa, then the Marasa are divided from there into Rada and Petwo, and then also subdivided into nations.

The main subdivisions of Marasa are as follows: There are Marasa Kay (Marasa of the House), Rada spirits who are considered calm and good-natured. Their counterparts are the Marasa Bwa (Marasa of the Woods), wild spirits who only live outdoors.[37] Their offerings must be taken into the woods, where one calls out "Pi pi pi pi, Marasa Bwa!" to indicate that one is making offerings for them. The offerings are left on the ground, or, in some cases, hung in the trees, where the Marasa Bwa will go to retrieve them after everyone has left.[38] One will also hear reference to Marasa Dan Petwo, who are Petwo Marasa. These Petwo Marasa overlap with the Marasa of many of the nations, most of which are served in the Petwo rite. This would include Marasa Kongo, Marasa Ibo, Marasa Sinigal, and so on. In many Vodou lineages, Marasa De are considered Rada, while Marasa Twa are considered Petwo. However, I was taught by Manbo Maude that all rites and nations have all types of Marasa.

To make matters more confusing, one will hear the Marasa referred to on the basis of where they were born. Marasa Gine (Marasa of Africa) are long-dead ancestral Marasa who were born in Africa. On the other hand, Marasa Kreyòl (Creole Marasa) are those Marasa who were born in Haiti—including still-living Marasa. These are not necessarily assigned to one rite or another (although in our lineage Marasa Gine are, counterintuitively, considered Petwo). Moreover, one will sometimes hear these same terms used to mean completely different things.

Finally, there are the *zanj* (angels), who are the spirits of unbaptized children.[39] *Zanj* are frequently served alongside Marasa, and will typically be fed during a *manje Marasa*. The *zanj* likely came into Vodou through nineteenth-century French Kardecian Spiritism, since similar practices related to *angelitos* ("little angels") are an important part of Latin American Spiritism (*Espiritismo*). While Spiritism did not survive as a separate tradition in Haiti—as it did in many other parts of Latin America, notably Brazil, Cuba, Puerto Rico, and the Dominican Republic—many aspects of Spiritism were absorbed into Haitian Vodou. While the *zanj* are not technically twins, they are (sometimes troublesome) child spirits who have been lumped into the capacious Vodou category of uncanny children—including, as mentioned earlier, many children who are not twins but have unusual physical traits, abnormalities, or atypical births.

It may surprise the reader that, by and large, Vodouisants are untroubled by the complexity that characterizes the Marasa. In part, this is because within individual spiritual lineages, the picture tends to be much simpler. Whatever set of terms one learns from one's spiritual teacher (often a family elder), those are the terms that one continues to use, and in those particular ways. Therefore, while across lineages, terms might become a disordered and unintelligible taxonomy, within lineages, there tends to be relative clarity. As one *oungan* (priest) I used to know—a friend who died too soon—was in the habit of saying, "Where there is no tradition, there is confusion."

However, it is also the case that Vodouisants seem generally unperplexed—and in fact, often derive aesthetic pleasure—from paradoxes. Existential conditions that many outsiders might find irreducible are accepted as essential components of the religious mystery. In this sense, the Marasa—in all of their complexities—are a gestalt, and cannot be parsed into simpler intelligible components. They are all of these things that have been mentioned—living and dead, cosmic principle and real living children, twins and not twins (yet still twins), benevolent and maleficent, divine and human, ancient and yet entirely present and modern. This is perhaps reflected best by their *vèvè*, which shows a number of distinct, smaller circles united by a cruciform and a large letter M: one and many, many and yet one.[40]

Rather than dwell on the irreducibility of the Marasa, Vodouisants tend to focus on the miraculous powers that they possess, and the complications involved in convincing them to share. The Marasa give the gifts of prophetic dreams, clairaudience, divination, and *je*.[41] They are apotropaic, deflecting malevolence, and have so much mystical power that they are able to walk in the crossroads at night.[42] People who are blessed by the Marasa are prosperous, healthy, and always manage to avoid scrapes at the last minute. Additionally, the Marasa have the power to cure intractable illnesses, owing in no small part to their total mastery of the healing power of *fèy* (leaves). Notably, one can make no functional distinction here between living twins and ancestral or "cosmic" twins. Both possess the same range of powers, and one can propitiate spiritual twins for these gifts in the same way that one could ask a twin in one's family to do any of these things.

However, the Marasa are known for being capricious, and so it can be challenging to convince them to be generous. Like children, they often do not like to share. For this reason, when one is serving the Marasa, one must make sure that each is served equally and identically. Otherwise, one or more might become jealous. Additionally, the Marasa have certain dietary taboos unique to them. Most importantly, one must *never* serve Marasa leafy greens. This is seen as a terrible offense and will precipitate disaster. If living Marasa eat leafy greens, they may lose their mystical powers and can even die. This is likely linked to their medicinal mastery of leaves, as it is nearly universal that sources of mystical power are linked with taboos and cannot be casually ingested by those who benefit from their powers.

Marasa in Social Perspective

One of the founders of modern anthropology, Melville J. Herskovits, was fascinated with the Marasa, using them as an example of the unique cultural traits that linked American Black people to Africans and distinguished both from whites. In his landmark 1937 work, *Life in a Haitian Valley*, he argued that the Haitian twin cult was one of the clearest cases for the "survival" of African religious practices in the Americas.[43] Indeed, there are many comparisons that can be drawn between Haitian and African practices, as has already been discussed. However, scholars no longer think in terms of "survival," as that approach leaves little space for the cultural imagination and agency of New World Black people, who endlessly reworked—and continue to rework— African religious practices to respond to their needs.[44]

In 1945, Jean Price-Mars, the father of Haitian ethnography, published a short lecture on the Marasa, in which he suggested that, for Haitians, they encapsulate a poignant nostalgia—for lost ancestors, lost homelands, lost children, and lost childhoods.[45] In his view, the Marasa are ancestral powers capable of staring directly into the face of tragedy, and who do not turn away from their descendants but rather rush to uplift them in times of sorrow. Recounting a *manje Marasa* ceremony, Price-Mars writes,

> something grave and troubling seems to weigh on the gathered. This is the communion of souls—the communion of the dead with the living, the communion with those beings cut from the dawn of life who respond to the entreaties, the prayers, and solicitations of other souls in distress. Then, then, Marasa Bwa, Marasa from long-ago Ginen, Marasa sacrificed during three centuries of servitude—all borrow the voices of the choir to exhale their lamentations, poignant echoes of human anguish. Listen to the song of the Marasa, the sonorous voices heavy with the sadness of man's unending cruelty.[46]

Alfred Métraux, Odette Mennesson-Rigaud, and Milo Marcelin were all captivated, as Herskovits had been, by the fact that religious practices related to the Marasa were often focused upon the care and propitiation of *living* twins who were semi-divinized.[47] In particular, they noted that because Haiti is a gerontocracy (like most of West Africa), it can be a social crisis that the Marasa are uncannily powerful *children*. By right, the most powerful members of society are *granmoun* (older people) because they have the most experience and therefore the most wisdom.[48] To drive home this point, Laroche cites a delightfully odd Haitian aphorism: *Dyol gran moun santi men pawol gran moun pa santi.*[49] Children are supposed to wait on their elders, not the other way around. And yet, as uncannily powerful children—capable of inflicting terrible suffering when unhappy—Marasa represent a serious challenge to normal child-rearing. Métraux, Mennesson-Rigaud, and Marcelin all tell stories of parents who are run ragged trying to satisfy the urges of their twins so as not to incur their wrath.

However, to cater to the every whim of twins also leads to problems, for in time they may become *gate* (spoiled).[50] In the same way that Marasa can be spoiled by breaking their taboos (such as eating forbidden foods), they can equally be spoiled if their parents cave in to their every wishes, giving in to their ever-escalating desires. By doing so, parents can make their Marasa monstrous, causing them to become fearful entities who only inflict suffering and harm—in essence despoiling them of their more miraculous powers to heal, bring rain, and summon bounty.

Marcelin, for example, tells one story of a father who incurred the wrath of his daughter, a Marasa, by refusing to give her some sweets that he was enjoying. When displeased, Marasa will typically afflict the object of their displeasure with a physical ailment, notably toothaches, headaches, and intestinal pain. In particularly dramatic cases, they may kill the victim stone dead. In this case, the daughter gave her father a toothache. The father suffered for some time and eventually went to a dentist. The dentist, himself a Dosou (the powerful child born after twins), took a look at the father's teeth and saw that nothing was physically wrong. Suspecting mystical intervention, he asked the father if he had twins, and when the father confirmed, he said that they had most certainly *mare* (bound) him.[51] It was they alone who could *lage* (release) him. The father returned home in greater pain than before, and eventually learned that, truly, his daughter had inflicted the suffering because he had refused her the sweets. If he would apologize, she would release him. The father was proud and did not think it proper to cede to his child, so he withheld—but eventually the suffering became so extreme that he begged his daughter for forgiveness and promised to give her sweets every day of his life. The daughter then cured him, in typical Marasa fashion, with a *tizann* (herbal tea) made from a leaf of her choosing. The father was almost instantly *lage* (released) from his suffering.

Marcelin notes alarmingly that there is one sure solution for Marasa who have become *gate* (spoiled): every time they request something, they must be vigorously beaten. At the conclusions of the above story, a friend of the afflicted parents relates this advice to them.

> "There is one simple way to rob them of their powers. Don't give in to their caprices. On the contrary, beat them every day with a rope or with a banana-leaf switch." The parents took this advice. Now, for any little thing, they would beat them with a rope or a banana-leaf switch.
> "Mother," they would ask, "give us some sweets."
> Blows from a rope would rain down upon them.
> "Mother, we are going to jump rope."
> They would receive blows from a banana-leaf switch.
> And they could do nothing to get revenge.
> They had lost their power to bind someone."[52]

Bracketing, if we can, the serious humanitarian concerns this raises, I would like to focus on how beating the Marasa is an attempt to restore proper social order. The Marasa's mystical power has been checked in order to resolve the serious disruption of important social norms, such as ageism. The disruption of these norms opens a dangerous mystical and epistemological space where chaotic social forces are unleashed. By restoring age-normal social order, the parents are believed to be protecting their children and their family by returning them to the good graces of society. Moreover, in Vodou, the beating of ritual objects—whether with the bare palms, feet, whips, cutlery, utensils, paddles, sticks, staves, or machetes—is a way of enlivening but also delimiting mystical power, directing and shaping it to manifest powerfully, but only in the desired way and designated space. Therefore, as powerful spirits incarnated as human children, the use of beating to control Marasa—forcing their power to manifest in certain ways and not in others—follows a ritual logic. I hasten to add that the abuse of children is condemned by Vodou, and moreover that this does not represent a common technique for parenting Marasa (we need to bear in mind that Marcelin was researching in the 1930s and 1940s, when striking children was also common in the United States). I include this anecdote only to indicate what a serious intellectual and social problem it is for Haitian parents who are saddled with the task of raising twin children who possess stupefying mystical powers—powers that, on their whims, can be used both for great harm and for great good. Any parent knows how moody young children are. If one can imagine what it would be like if, every time a child threw a tantrum, he or she possessed the power to beset the parent with unspeakable pain and illness, one can perhaps appreciate the desperation of the parents in the story.

More commonly, the Marasa are appeased through regular service. Upon birth, *plat Marasa* like those described at the beginning of this chapter will be baptized in the name of the newborn children. Subsequently, these *plat*—the esoteric doubles of the children themselves—must be kept clean, and regularly refreshed with food and drink. When they reach maturity, the children can request that their *plat Marasa* be given over to them. Should one or all of the Marasa die, then the *plat Marasa* become even more important as the remaining incarnation of them on Earth. If the keeper of the *plat Marasa*—for example, a parent—dies, then the next of kin inherits the *plat* and their concomitant ritual obligations. Naturally, not everyone who inherits his or her family's Marasa considers it to be a privilege. Care of the Marasa involves elaborate and expensive ritual feasting, usually annually. However, the neglect of one's obligations to the Marasa can have serious repercussions—not only for oneself but for the entire extended family—in the form of loss of wealth, misfortune, illness, or even death.

Services for the Marasa

The *manje Marasa* (Marasa Feast), the large ritual feeding of the Marasa, typically takes place annually.[53] It will usually coincide with the feast of St. Nicholas of Bari (December 6), Holy Innocents' Day (December 28), the days surrounding Christmas (December 25), or All Souls (November 2). Though the details vary from region to region and temple to temple, the *manje Marasa* has a number of typical features. The *plat Marasa* are first washed in a bath of *monben* leaves and basil.[54] Afterward, they are usually greased with olive oil. Once they have been cleaned, ritual sacrifices of dappled chickens are made—no fewer than two, but in temple setting where there are many *plat Marasa*, as many as twenty-one. These chickens are prepared simply, along with a dish made from various tubers and root vegetables. Additionally, a platter is prepared with a combination of breads, cassava, cookies, cakes, candies, popcorn, grilled corn, and dried fruits—all broken into pieces that are small enough to be grasped by a child's hands. The ceremony is opened (as is typical for all ceremonies) by the *Priyè Ginen*, followed by ritual salutations to the family and temple society, Ountò, Gran Chemen, and Papa Legba. Songs are then sung for Marasa, and food is distributed evenly into all of the chambers of the *plat Marasa*. Additionally, food is typically deposited into three dug holes, often located in the threshold to the house or temple. Food is also left outside for Marasa Bwa. Finally, portions of the food are piled onto a bed of banana leaves that have been laid upon the ground. All of the children in attendance—all of the uncanny children being honored (twins most especially), but also any other children—are invited to sit on the floor and hungrily scarf down the food, eating with their hands. When they are finished eating, they wipe their hands on the crown of the head of the person hosting the ceremony, and use his or her hair and clothing as a napkin. This final act of smearing the grease of the food into the head of the host bestows the blessing of the Marasa. Any food that remains is distributed to the family or families of those who paid for the service or contributed to its execution.

Because services for the Marasa are costly and involved, temples often host a single *manje Marasa* for all of the Marasa honored in their community. As Métraux notes, large temples often have dozens of *plat Marasa* that are kept in trust for members of the community. In addition to caring for the Marasa of the temple's members, *manje Marasa* must typically be held at the beginning of the *manje lwa* (Spirits Feast) that is held annually, in which all of the spirits recognized by the temple are ritually fed, a process that can easily take weeks to complete. Additionally, a *manje Marasa* is often held prior to the beginning of a *kanzo* (initiation) in order to ensure the blessings of the Marasa—who, among other things, grant communication with the spirits and bestow clairvoyance and clairaudience. These are important both to the initiation itself and to the future success of the new initiates, who will be expected to facilitate spirit communication for their community.

It is rare to hear of someone performing a full *manje Marasa* in the Haitian diaspora. If possible, diaspora Vodouisants will usually arrange to conduct the ceremony while visiting Haiti, where it is felt that major rituals are easier to do "properly." In fact, it is widely believed that many major ceremonies, most especially *kanzo* (initiation), cannot be done anywhere *except* Haiti. There are a number of mystical and practical reasons for this, perhaps most notable being the necessity of the *lakou*. Literally, the *lakou* is the large yard of the family compound, which doubles as a ritual space. However, to say that a ceremony's execution depends upon the *lakou* glosses not only the physical space: by synecdoche, it encompasses the family and fictive kin who utilize the space of the *lakou* as the nexus of their lives, and who function as a mutual aid and pleasure society. For this reason, *lakou* often serves as the emic name for the Haitian system of familial-social organization. In the absence of both a literal and a metaphorical *lakou*, it is difficult to coordinate labor for a large ceremony, which calls for monumental amounts of cooking, cleaning, decorating, singing, dancing, and ritual slaughtering of animals. The *lakou* or temple also makes sure that the expenses incurred by large ceremonies are fairly distributed among members.

Moreover, the *manje Marasa* has the unusual trait of needing neighborhood children to eat the food and smear their hands on the ceremony's patron, the ritual act which seals the blessing. Most Vodouisants in the United States do not advertise their religious practices, and therefore it is difficult to garner the support of neighbors, who moreover likely lack the religious context to understand such a ceremony. Especially in cultures where one or more of the Abrahamic religions are dominant, some Christian, Jewish, or Muslim neighbors might believe *manje Marasa* to be heathenish or morally reprehensible, and would be damned before allowing their children to assist in a Vodou ceremony (even one that ended with a delicious free meal). Moreover, the *manje Marasa* is, in many ways, an extension of a form of charitable spiritual work called *manje pòv* (meal for the poor) that is frequently performed by Vodouisants in Haiti, especially during religious pilgrimage when requesting a boon from—or giving thanks to—the spirits. Just as *manje pòv* is not performed here for lack of a cultural context, so *manje Marasa* is also rarely performed.[55]

Instead, most Vodouisants in the diaspora serve the Marasa in private, smaller ways until they can return to Haiti for more elaborate services. Private services include regular washing and feeding of the *plat Marasa*. In times of need, supplicants can use the *plat Marasa* as lamps, filling them with oil and then floating wicks in them. These lamps summon the Marasa's attention and request that they respond favorably. The water that is used for cleaning the *plat Marasa*—into which medicinal leaves have been shredded and Florida Water added—is kept afterward because it conveys luck and healing. This water will often be used as a mystical bath.

Urban Vodou services in the diaspora are typically conducted in crowded basements that have been converted into ritual space. During services conducted in these spaces, the Marasa are served with a *laye* (winnowing tray) that has been filled with an assortment of bite-sized snacks: peanuts, raisins, prunes, cassava, *bonbon siwo* (gingerbread cake), grilled corn and popcorn, macaroons, dulce de leche, brittle, cookies, and candies. After Papa Legba, the Marasa are saluted with this tray, a white candle, water, and a bottle of kola champagne wrapped in a multicolored *mouchwa* (satin scarf). It is exceedingly rare that the Marasa will possess anyone, even during a *manje Marasa*. In the rare event that they do, they (in the adult bodies of the possessed) behave like children, crawling around on the floor, crying, giggling, and eating with their hands. Songs for the Marasa often tease them about their peculiar habits, ravenousness, and tendency to complain.[56] Through such teasing, the Marasa are jokingly reminded that they have already received the offerings of the community, and should therefore grant their blessings.

Conclusion

During the first half of the twentieth century, the Marasa were the subject of considerable scholarly attention. Bearing obvious connections to African twin cults, devotion to the Marasa was seen as evidence for the "survival" of African practices

Figure 4.2 Wide view of Vodou altar (*plat Marasa* on lower left). Photo by Patrick Sylvain; by permission of Adam McGee.

in the Americas. In subsequent decades, as scholarly interests shifted, the Marasa received less academic attention. Nonetheless, the Marasa remain a central component of the religious lives of Vodouisants, particularly for those who are twins, triplets, or for people in families with multiple or unusual births. The Marasa are a family of spirits—parents, siblings, ancestors, spirits of unbaptized children, and allied unusual people—that in its complexity has often confused outsiders. Examination of the Marasa, their mirror-like qualities and merging of conflicting existential states— living, dead, one, many—provides insight into the ways that Vodouisants believe that the spiritual world interacts with the physical world. The Marasa are renowned for their power as healers. However, their strength as healers is equaled by their power to afflict misery, a source of anxiety and crisis for parents saddled with the task of raising powerful and cantankerous twins. Only through regular ritual action and the careful observance of taboos can this perilous condition be managed. But to those who enjoy their favor, the Marasa bestow good fortune, economic prosperity, spiritual power, and insight into the secret workings of Ginen.

Notes

1　Gelefwe is a name for the place where the dead go. In one variation or another, this song from the oral ceremonial traditions of Vodou has appeared in most scholarly treatments of the Marasa. For the majority of the songs in this open-source corpus, the notion of original author does not apply, as they tend to spread like memes and are endlessly reworked, often on the fly. I learned this version from Manbo

Marie Maude Evans; the translation into English is my own. I will use the spelling "Marasa" throughout this chapter. However, in older scholarship, it is common to see the spelling "Marassa" or "Marassas." These spellings reflect the prevailing fashions of the day for how to spell Haitian Kreyòl. In Kreyòl, the plural is indicated by context and the presence of articles, not by modification to the noun (as in English). Because of this, it looks and sounds strange to Kreyòl speakers to see a Kreyòl word made plural by the addition of an "s"—for example, "Marasas." I have deferred to the Kreyòl convention, rather than the English.

2 Marie Maude Evans, Antiola Bo Manbo, is a *manbo* (priestess) with four decades of experience. She was initiated by the priestess and diviner Mme. Maurice Sixto (Miracia Zephyr), Selide Bo Manbo (d. 2009), of Port-au-Prince. Maude regularly holds services for the *lwa* in her temple in Mattapan, a suburb of Boston. During the summer, before the pandemic, she traveled home each year to Jacmel, Haiti, to conduct services and initiations. I call Maude my mother because she initiated me (rebirthed me) as an *oungan* (priest) and continues to teach me how to be a priest. Moreover, family is the governing metaphor for Vodou congregations.

3 The act of baptizing ritual objects is common in Vodou. However, I would not have baptized my *plat Marasa* at that time had Maude's dream not instructed me to do so. For more on the important role of dreaming as a source of spiritual guidance in Haitian Vodou, see Adam McGee, "Dreaming in Haitian Vodou: Vouchsafe, guide, and source of liturgical novelty," *Dreaming* 22, no. 2 (2012): 231–56.

4 The most common word for a Vodou spirit is *lwa*. Although often translated as "god(s)," this is not correct, since Vodou is monotheistic, honoring a creator divinity called *Bondye* (God). The *lwa* are instead comparable to the saints and angels of Roman Catholicism, with whom their identities are often fused. Vodou practitioners tend, however, to think of the *lwa* as ancestors and therefore intimately enmeshed in their lives. This is different from the connection one has to the saints and angels, which is devotional or even cosmic, but not familial.

5 Basil (*bazilik*) is often used in Haitian Vodou because it is considered astringent, clean, cool, and refreshing. Although sweet basil (*Ocimum basilicum*), Thai basil (*Ocimum basilicum* var. *thyrsiflora*), and holy basil (*Ocimum tenuiflorum* or *Ocimum sanctum*) are used interchangeably, I have heard practitioners express a preference for the smaller-leafed holy basil and Thai basil varieties. Florida Water is an inexpensive cologne used frequently in Vodou for its astringent, cleansing, and grounding properties. Several commercial preparations of Florida Water are available for purchase, the most popular being the one by Lanman and Kemp.

6 The *Priyè Ginen* ("Prayer of Ginen") is the most important piece of Vodou liturgy. Sung as call and response, the *Priyè Ginen* creates sacred space by honoring God, Jesus, the Holy Family, the saints, the angels, the *lwa* (the spirits of Vodou), the blessed dead, and the community of the living. It is also apotropaic, requesting that the spirits use their strength to protect the congregation from evil. The *Priyè Ginen* is in French, Kreyòl, and *langaj* (an untranslatable language spoken by the spirits, with linguistic roots in Africa). A complete ceremony in itself, the *Priyè Ginen* often takes hours—and can take days—to perform. However, for less formal ceremonies, a shortened version of the *Priyè* can be sung that only takes a few minutes. The toponym Ginen (or Gine) can be translated as "ancestral Africa." In the context of Vodou cosmology, this Africa is not the continent presently identified by that name, which Kreyòl speakers instead call *Lafrik* (Africa). Rather, it is the home of the spirits, a forested island residing simultaneously *anba dlo* (at the bottom

of the cosmic waters) and *do miwa* (at the backs of mirrors). At the same time, it cannot be entirely separated from the physical continent of Africa, from which the ancestors came and to which they hoped to return in death. For this reason, one will often hear the compound term *Lafrik Ginen*. As a living and accessible mythic past of ancestors, heroes, and divine spirits, Ginen serves as a vouchsafe for matters of religious authenticity. Ginen is also an eschaton—a place which is longed for, and which one hopes to see someday. In a sense, Ginen is comparable to heaven, the New Jerusalem of John's Apocalypse, Augustine's City of God, and Aztlan of the Aztecs. For more on Ginen, see Adam McGee, "Constructing Africa: Authenticity and Gine in Haitian Vodou," *Journal of Haitian Studies* 14, no. 2 (2009): 30–51. On Aztlan, see Davíd Carrasco, "Aztec Moments and Chicano Cosmovision: Aztlan Recalled to Life," in *Moctezuma's Mexico: Visions of the Aztec World*, rev. ed., eds. Davíd Carrasco and Eduardo Matos Moctezuma (Boulder: University Press of Colorado, 2003), 175–98.

7   The French Catholic liturgical formula *Ainsi soit-il* ("So be it") is used in place of "Amen" to conclude many prayers in Haitian Kreyòl.

8   Even the term *Vodou* is not one that adherents tended until recently to use to describe their religious practices, preferring instead to say simply that they served Ginen. One could argue that the internal name of the religion is *Sèvis Ginen* ("Service to Ginen").

9   In *kanzo*, the initiates are sequestered inside of a *djevo* (a specially prepared Holy of Holies), where they lie down for seven to nine days with the goal of seeking powerful dreams that will grant spiritual power and *konesans* (esoteric knowledge). For this reason, the word *kouche* (to sleep or lie down) is often used as a synonym for *kanzo*. Depending on their grade, initiates of *kanzo* are referred to as *ounsi kanzo* (temple functionaries and chorus members), *manbo* and *oungan sou pwen* (priestesses and priests who are "borrowing" the *ason*), and *manbo* and *oungan asogwe* (priestesses and priests who have been given the *ason* by the spirits and can initiate others). The *ason* is the sacred rattle that is used by *manbo* and *oungan* to summon and control the spirits. It consists of a hollowed gourd onto which a web of porcelain and glass beads is strung; attached to its handle is a small bell at the end of a string. As with most sacred objects, there are strict taboos around how, when, and by whom an *ason* can be handled and wielded. Because the *ason* is absolutely central to this southern style of practice, temples that practice this way are often referred to as *ason* lineages.

10 A *lakou* is the yard around which a family compound is arranged. A *lakou* can also be a temple enclosure. It is this latter meaning that is intended here, although they are often the same because *lakou* serve not only as temples, but also as community centers and residences. This term is discussed at greater length in the penultimate section, "Services for the Marasa."

11 The term *makout* refers to the straw bag that these religious experts use to transport their sacred items. *Tcha-tcha* (or *kwa-kwa*) references the rattle they use when serving the spirits, much as the *ason* is used in the south. For southerners practicing their rigorously formalized style of Vodou, the terms *makout* and *tcha-tcha* can have a slightly derogatory tone to the degree that they gloss a "rustic" or "country bumpkin" quality they believe this style exemplifies. The word *Deka* is of unclear origin and may or may not be antique. Its use has been popularized recently by the organization ZANTRAY (lit. "guts," which stands for *Zanfan Tradisyon Ayisyèn* [Children of Haitian Traditions]) and the leader of ZANTRAY, Reginald Bailly. ZANTRAY was founded in 1987 as an emergency response to the *dechoukaj* by Vodou leaders in the north and central regions. *Dechoukaj* (lit. "uprooting") is the name given to

the murders of Vodou clergy and the destruction of Vodou temples that followed
the ouster of Jean-Claude "Baby Doc" Duvalier. On ZANTRAY and *dechoukaj*;
see Rachel Beauvoir and Didier Dominique, *Savalou E* (Montréal: Les Éditions du
CIDIHCA, 2003).

12 Furthermore, there are numerous secret societies in Haiti that may or may not be part
of Vodou, depending on whom you ask. These secret societies often trace their origins
to maroon and revolutionary groups (as well as West and West Central African secret
societies), and tend to practice more dangerous, morally ambiguous forms of magic.
Many other Vodouisants regard them as outright evil, although they rarely perceive
themselves in this way. Additionally, there are numerous Masonic and pseudo-Masonic
organizations in Haiti that operate under modalities deeply informed by Vodou.

13 The "other" Marasa song is the most popular song for the Marasa, sung in nearly
every Vodou ceremony. It is in *langaj* and thus untranslatable. "*Marasa elou,
Marasa elou elou e* (x 2) / *Ewa ewa, ewa ewa Marasa elou o elou e / Ago ago e, ago
ago.*"

14 This is a traditional song with no ascribed author. I learned this version from Manbo
Maude Evans; the English translation is my own.

15 Ogou is both a spirit and a nation of spirits in Vodou. He is a warrior, and is often
referred to as a general or soldier. However, he is also an excellent politician, a father,
and a renowned lover. He is correlated with Sen Jak Majè (St. James the Greater),
as well as many other saints (including St. George, St. Michael Archangel, and
St. Elias). The pantheon of Ogou spirits is called Nago, probably after the Ànàgó,
a western subgroup of the Yorùbá who were sold into American slavery in large
numbers by the neighboring kingdom of Oyó, with whom they had a protracted war.
As the name would suggest, Sosyete Nago is under the patronage of Ogou.

16 See Marilyn Houlberg, "Magique Marasa: The Ritual Cosmos of Twins and Other
Sacred Children," in *Sacred Arts of Haitian Vodou*, ed. Donald J. Cosentino (Los
Angeles: UCLA Fowler Museum, 1995), 270. The ambiguity between living, dead,
and ancestral twins, as well as the inclusion of other abnormal births within the
category of twins, has parallels with Kongo religion that are likely genealogical.
In classical Kongo religion, all of these children would be considered incarnations
of *simbi*, nature spirits who live in water and ravines. Kongo religion also applies
religious meaning to the mother, as well as the siblings, of twins. For more on
parallels between Kongo and Haitian twin beliefs, see Wyatt MacGaffey, "Twins,
Simbi Spirits, and Lwas in Kongo and Haiti," in *Central Africans and Cultural
Transformation in the American Diaspora*, ed. Linda Heywood (Cambridge:
Cambridge University Press, 2001), 211–26.

17 "The Marasa have a thousand voices." Raoul Altidor, "Marasa," in *Koulè Midi* (Port-
au-Prince: Les Éditions Memoires, 1999), 24.

18 This is a loose translation of Laroche's idiomatic expression, *Ki sa pou m ta di sou
chif 2* ("What could I say about the number *2*"). Max Laroche, *Prinsip Marasa*
(Sillery, Québec: GRELCA, 2004), 65.

19 Legba is an old man carrying a straw bag on his back, smoking a pipe and
accompanied by his faithful dogs. He is the gatekeeper, whose permission must be
obtained to open the world of the spirits.

20 Ountò is the *lwa* of drums and of drumming, who resides inside of the drums
and translates their "speech" into the language of the spirits. Gran Chemen (lit.
"Highway") is the personified road whom the spirits travel to arrive on Earth. In
scholarly literature, Gran Chemen is sometimes confused with Legba.

21 *"Les Marassas sont . . . le principe divin de la vie."* Odette Mennesson-Rigaud, "Étude sur le culte des Marassas en Haïti," *ZAÏRE* 6, no. 6 (1952): 597.

22 Similar proscriptions and ritual requirements exist for the devotees of African and African diaspora religions throughout the Atlantic world. In some cases, these beliefs so suffuse the culture at large that they extend to those who do not otherwise engage in the religious practices from which they spring. For example, Jacob Olúpọ̀nà (of the Yorùbá people of Nigeria) shared in conversation that when his twin died in childhood, he was taken to receive the *Ìbejì* (twin) ritual implements necessary to propitiate his brother's spirit, despite the fact that his family was staunchly Anglican.

23 Michael Jackson beautifully explains Hannah Arendt's idea of natality: "Natality entails the perpetual reconstruction of one's habitus and one's past, *if not in essence then in appearance, in the way one's world is experienced*—as in religious conversion, falling in love, or recovery from tragic loss. This is why the world is surprisingly new in the eyes of the young, who encounter it for the first time, and why it is 'never what it was' in the jaded view of the old, who have seen it all before . . . The world is thus something we do not simply live and reproduce in passivity, but actually produce and transform through praxis, creating a sense that life is worth living." Michael D. Jackson, *Existential Anthropology: Events, Exigencies and Effects* (New York: Berghahn Books, 2008), xxii (italics in original).

24 See Jacob K. Olúpọ̀nà's chapter in this volume for a detailed examination of *Ìbejì* (twins) in Yorùbá religion, as well as the contributions by Babatunde Lawal, Elisha Renne, and Ysamur Flores-Peña in *Twins in African and Diaspora Cultures: Double Trouble, Twice Blessed*, ed. Philip M. Peek (Bloomington: Indiana University Press, 2011). Wyatt MacGaffey's essay "Twins, Simbi Spirits, and Lwas in Kongo and Haiti" is a compelling introduction to how West Central African religion may have influenced twin beliefs in Haiti. Marilyn Houlberg also explores how African twin cults contributed to the cult of the Marasa in Haiti: Houlberg, "Magique Marasa," *Sacred Arts of Haitian Vodou*, 269–70.

25 Houlberg, "Magique Marasa," *Sacred Arts of Haitian Vodou*, 270.

26 The pre-Columbian indigenous people of Haiti are variously referred to as Arawak, Ciboney, Taino, and Caribs—mostly owing to confusion on the part of European chroniclers. Taino is the most correct term. There is no remaining discrete Native American population in Haiti, although recently there have been movements by Haitians to embrace their indigenous (*endijèn*) heritage. The maroons were runaway slaves who formed independent communities and militias in mountainous terrains that were inaccessible to Europeans. These maroon populations were critical to the success of the Haitian Revolution, and also offered formidable resistance to Spanish rule on the island's eastern side. For more on the importance of maroon uprisings in Saint-Domingue and Santo Domingo, see Jane Landers, "A View from the Other Side: The Saint Domingue Revolution through Spanish Sources," parts 1–3 (Nathan I. Huggins Lectures, Hutchins Center for African and African American Research, Harvard University, Cambridge, MA, March 3–5, 2015).

27 Maya Deren, *Divine Horsemen* (1953; repr. New York: McPherson & Company, 2004), 279–80. Deren is one of the few scholars of Haitian Vodou to speculate extensively about the potential Native American sources of Haitian Vodou. Unfortunately, Deren was writing before connections had been established between Haitian Vodou and West Central Africa. Therefore, Deren proposed Native American connections anywhere that there weren't obvious corollaries to West African religion. For this reason, her speculations often go afield. Cf. Hartley Burr Alexander, *Latin-*

American (Boston: Marshall Jones Company, 1920), 15–40. The centrality of twins to the religious practices of the pre-Colombian people of Hispaniola is not surprising, given that they were part of a larger family of Mesoamerican cultures in which twin heroes figured prominently. For more on twins in Native America, see John Grim's and Vincent Stanzione's chapters in this volume.

28 Kurt A. Fisher, "Une amulette jumelée en os de la Section d'Archeologie du Bureau d'Ethnologie de la Republique d'Haiti," *Bulletin du Bureau d'Ethnologie*, 1943, 31–3. *Zemi* are still discovered in Haiti, and are called "eyes of the earth." They are believed to contain spirits, and are venerated by Vodouisants. See Frances Maclean, "The Lost Fort of Columbus," *Smithsonian* 38, no. 10 (2008): 72–6.

29 *Regleman* is the order in which the spirits are honored. It also includes the long series of sung prayers (*Priyè Ginen*) that opens all services. Additionally, it encompasses the dances, offerings, ritual salutations, and songs for the spirits. It is, in short, the liturgical content of Vodou.

30 While St. Nicholas is always Papa Marasa, not all houses use St. Claire for Manman Marasa. For example, our house uses Our Lady of the Assumption for Manman Marasa because she is shown being carried to heaven by a host of cherubim. The use of this image to represent Manman Marasa is also documented in Milo Marcelin, *Mythologie Vodou (Rite Arada)*, vol. 2 (Pétionville, Haiti: Éditions Canapé-Vert, 1950), 124. All future references to Marcelin's *Mythologie Vodou* are to Volume 2.

31 Marilyn Houlberg suggests that the word *Marasa* derives from the Kikongo word *mabassa* (or *mapasa*, according to MacGaffey), meaning "those who come divided." Houlberg, "Magique Marasa," *Sacred Arts of Haitian Vodou*, 269; and MacGaffey, "Twins, Simbi Spirits, and Lwas in Kongo and Haiti," 213.

32 In a conversation with Jacob Olúpọ̀nà, he noted that this word likely derives from the Yorùbá *idowu*, the child born after *ìbejì* (twins). Marasa Twa simply combines Marasa De and Dosou in the same pregnancy, whereas they are generally the product of two separate pregnancies. More rarely, all of the children in Marasa Twa will be considered a true triad, with the next pregnancy being the Dosou or Dosa.

33 There are occasional tantalizing hints that similar beliefs may have been held—and in certain cases, continue to be held—by segments of the African American community in the United States. Evidence for this includes an essay about a hereditary Voodoo priestess with a thriving spiritual healing business in Tucson, Arizona, in the 1970s. Mother D. (a title with clear connections to the Spiritualist Church) claimed that her maternal grandmother had also been a healer, and that she had spiritual power because she had been born after twins. In her own words, "I had two brothers, twins. And I were born behind the twins. Some people believe that twins have the gift, one of 'em. Some people say I have the gift because I were born behind two twins. But I don't know, I always had that *urge* that I cure anything! I've always felt like that. But my grandmother knew it *before* I were born. I cried three time in my mother's womb before I were born. Then she said, 'That's the one. That's the one what's gonna be exactly like me!' I was fortunate, I was born just exactly with the gift." Loudell F. Snow, "'I Was Born Just Exactly with the Gift': An Interview with a Voodoo Practitioner," *The Journal of American Folklore* 86, no. 341 (1973): 277. Unfortunately, Snow's article gives no details about Mother D.'s family; it is unknown whether she may have been of Haitian descent. It is exciting to consider that Mother D.'s beliefs might represent an authentic African American tradition about twins—which was either incorporated through contact with refugees of the Haitian Revolution (late eighteenth and early nineteenth centuries), or else derived

more directly from Africa (suggesting a shared progenitor). Alternately, Mother D. may have read about Haitian Vodou and incorporated its twin beliefs into her own practice.

34 Marcelin claims that the Dogwe has the unusual mystical power of being able to pass long periods of time underwater without needing to surface for air. He writes, "If there are four, the last is the Dogwe. To this one is given the power to stay for long periods of time underwater. An *oungan* or priest from Maïssade (a town in Artibonite) was reputed to have the power to live for a long time underwater. There was also a legend told about a certain eminent politician who would frequently stay for several days and nights underwater, in an enormous basin he had on one of his properties, for the purpose of receiving guidance from a *lwa* regarding his political life. This man, it was said, had the power of the Dogwe." Marcelin, *Mythologie Vodou*, 123 (my translation). I have never read anywhere else that there were special powers attributed to the Dogwe, nor have I heard this from anyone directly.

35 For more on the healing cult of Ss. Cosmas and Damian, see James Skedros's chapter in this volume.

36 The spirits are typically divided into two main categories, Rada and Petwo. Ceremonies typically start with Rada, believed to be the older and more African of the spirits. Rada is associated with the color white, with coolness, and with gentleness. Petwo is associated with the color red, with heat, and with hardness or swiftness. Petwo is often identified as indigenous to Haiti, having its birth in the Haitian Revolution. A genealogical perspective might, on the other hand, classify Rada and Petwo as deriving their aesthetics principally from West and West Central Africa, respectively. Vodou champions things that are cool, slow, relaxed, calm, light, fresh, gentle, sweet, at ease, stoic, and dignified. All of these qualities are glossed as "cool" and as "Ginen." Cool, likened to water, is the ideal *resting* state. Rada is cool and watery. However, Vodou seeks to use and control states that are hot, fast, tense, nervous, obscure, sweaty, hard, salty, overworked, hyper-responsive, and uncouth. These qualities are glossed as "hot." Hot, likened to fire, is the ideal *working* state. Petwo is hot and fiery. See McGee, "Constructing Africa," 41–6.

37 Price-Mars also notes Marasa Satan, served at the very end of the *manje Marasa* ceremony that he observed. Their offerings are placed in a hole that is dug far from the house, and their invocatory language tells them to go away and calm down. This bears strong resemblance to the way that Marasa Bwa are served, and also calls to mind parallels to West African *djinn*, powerful wild spirits who live in the bush and must be propitiated but are not welcomed into civilized spaces. Jean Price-Mars, "Culte des Marassas," *Afroamerica* 1, no. 1–2 (1945): 45, 47.

38 One will sometimes see reference to Marasa Pipi, who presumably are the same as Marasa Bwa. I believe that this may be a confusion (*pipi* means "urine"), and that Pipi is not in fact their name but rather how they are called: "pi pi pi pi!" is what one yells to call chickens when one is spreading feed for them. This emphasizes that the Marasa Bwa are like untamed animals. Manbo Maude also teaches that the Marasa Bwa are homeless children.

39 This is not to be confused with the frequent use of the word *zanj* as a synonym for *lwa*.

40 A *vèvè* is a ritual design traced on the floor in cornmeal either prior to or during a ceremony. It is a two-dimensional representation of the spirit, and invokes the spirit through its creation and presence. In the course of the ceremony, it is effaced by

ritual actions, such as dancing and the pouring of libations. *Vèvè* vary from lineage to lineage; the one I describe is the *vèvè* used for Marasa by Sosyete Nago.

41   Lit. "eyes," *je* is the spiritual power to see the truth about people and events. One might speculate that the Marasa are especially associated with eyes (*je*) and ears (clairaudience) because they have an abundance of each, and thus can hear and see, at once, from all directions.

42   See Houlberg, "Magique Marasa," *Sacred Arts of Haitian Vodou*, 267–8. In Vodou, *kafou a* (the crossroads) is characterized as a place of spiritual power. At night, this intersection is converted into a site of intense spiritual danger, personified by the Petwo *lwa* Kafou, who must be approached cautiously and respectfully because he is a master of fiery, catalytic magic. The nighttime crossroads is also the domain of *lougawou* (witches and sorcerers), *baka* (murderous monsters), *zonbi* (zombies), *djab* (evil spirits), and the much-feared secret societies that work with these dark spiritual powers. Therefore, to boast that one can walk in the crossroads at night is, in essence, to say that one fears nothing.

43   Melville J. Herskovits, *Life in a Haitian Valley* (New York: Alfred A. Knopf, 1937).

44   For an eloquent introduction to this approach, see Sidney W. Mintz and Richard Price, *The Birth of African-American Culture: An Anthropological Perspective* (Boston: Beacon Press Books, 1976).

45   Price-Mars was a Haitian elite who was an extremely influential early figure in global Négritude. His *Ainsi Parla l'Oncle* [*Thus Spoke the Uncle*], published in 1928, was the first monograph devoted exclusively to the serious academic study of Vodou. Jean Price-Mars, *Ainsi Parla L'Oncle* (Port-au-Prince: Imprimerie de Compiègne, 1928).

46   Price-Mars, "Culte des Marassas," 46 (my translation).

47   In 1946 and 1952, Odette Mennesson-Rigaud published essays (the first in English, the second in French) that included vivid, detailed, and lengthy descriptions of the Marasa and their rites. The second essay, "Étude sur le culte des Marassas en Haïti," was exclusively about the Marasa. Odette M. Rigaud, "The Feasting of the Gods in Haitian Vodu," trans. Alfred and Rhoda Métraux, *Primitive Man* 19, no. 1/2 (1946): 1–58. In 1950, Milo Marcelin published the second volume of his *Mythologie Vodou*, which includes a chapter about the Marasa. In 1953, Maya Deren's *Divine Horsemen* included a discussion of the cosmological significance of the Marasa. In 1958, Alfred Métraux published an entire chapter on the Marasa in Alfred Métraux, *Le Vaudou haïtien* (1958; repr. Paris: Gallimard, 1968). In his discussion of twins, Métraux draws on Mennesson-Rigaud's work—particularly her 1946 essay, "The Feasting of the Gods in Haitian Vodu," which he and his wife translated into English for *Primitive Man*. For example, he cites the song that is used as an epigraph for this paper, which appeared in Mennesson-Rigaud's paper (and Price-Mars's lecture before that). Mennesson-Rigaud also took Maya Deren under her wing, contributing an appendix to *Divine Horsemen*. It is likely that some of Deren's ideas about the mystical significance of the Marasa as the source of life derive from conversation with Mennesson-Rigaud, who writes of this "secret" knowledge in her 1952 essay. In recent decades, there has been very little scholarship about the Marasa, with only one work devoted entirely to them. This is Marilyn Houlberg's essay, "Magique Marasa," published in *Sacred Arts of Haitian Vodou* in 1995 (and reprinted twice in other publications with only minimal changes). Houlberg was an art historian and expert on Vodou arts. Her essay provides a number of insights into the material culture associated with the Marasa. She also describes the breadth of children who are considered in Vodou to be uncanny and therefore partaking, to some degree, in the Marasa complex. Marilyn Houlberg, "Magique Marasa," *Sacred*

Arts of Haitian Vodou, 267–83; Houlberg, "Magique Marasa: The Ritual Cosmos of the Twins and Other Sacred Children," in *Fragments of Bone: Neo-African Religions in a New World*, ed. Patrick Bellegarde-Smith (Urbana: University of Illinois Press, 2005), 13–31; and Houlberg, "Two Equals Three: Twins and the Trickster in Haitian Vodou," in *Twins in African and Diaspora Cultures*, ed. Philip M. Peek, 271–89.

48 This is not to say that abuse and neglect of elderly people does not occur in Haiti. It does, just as it does in every culture. However, this is judged by Haitians to be a vile aberration.

49 "The mouths of old people smell, but their words do not smell." Laroche, *Prinsip Marasa*, 74. Another variation on this is *Bouch granmoun santi men s ak ladann se rezon* ("The mouths of old people smell but what is inside is correct"). Examples of this theme abound. For example, a song to the Vodou spirit Bawon, master of cemeteries and terminal justice, complains to him that *timoun grandi k ap joure granmoun* ("growing children are insulting the elderly"), and beseeches him to drag the offenders off to the cemetery (i.e., kill them). Laroche engages in a lengthy discussion of gerontocracy in Haiti vis-à-vis the symbolic significance of the Marasa. Ibid., 73–5.

50 *Gate* does not only mean spoiled in the way that Americans speak of spoiling a child. Often, *gate* is a diagnosis of a psychosocial and spiritual disorder. It means that a person is of no social use—the way food that has spoiled is of no use to anyone and must be thrown away.

51 The verb *kenbe* (to grab, grip, or hold) is often used to mean the same thing.

52 Marcelin, *Mythologie Vodou*, 132 (my translation).

53 The description of the *manje Marasa* draws on my own experiences, as well as the descriptions offered by Houlberg, Herskovits, Mennesson-Rigaud, Price-Mars, Métraux, Marcelin; and Karen McCarthy Brown, *Mama Lola: A Vodou Priestess in Brooklyn* (Berkeley: University of California Press, 1991).

54 *Monben* or *monbenfran* (*Spondias mombin*) is a small tree related to North American sumac. It is used frequently by Vodouisants to perform spiritual cleansings and is also a significant part of the Afro-Haitian pharmacopeia. See François Séverin, *Plant ak pyebwa tè d Ayiti* (Port-au-Prince: Éditions Quitel de Desk Top Advisory, 2002), 95; and Timoleon C. Brutus and Arsene V. Pierre-Noel, *Les plantes et les legumes d'Haiti qui guerissent: Mille et une recettes pratiques*, vol. 2 (Port-au-Prince: Imprimerie de l'État d'Haiti, 1960), 183. Because *monben* does not grow in the northern United States, diaspora Vodouisants will often wash the *plat Marasa* with basil alone.

55 A future subject of research is the question of whether a decreased emphasis on twins in the diaspora—in particular, a decline in open acknowledgment of the miraculous powers of *living* twins—marks a theological shift in response to a cultural landscape that does not offer a readymade space for such beliefs, and may in fact view them as ridiculous.

56 For examples of songs for the Marasa, see Gerdès Fleurant, *Dancing Spirits: Rhythms and Rituals of Haitian Vodun, the Rada Rite* (Westport, CT: Greenwood Press, 1996), 82–4.

Bibliography

Alexander, Hartley Burr. *Latin-American*. Boston: Marshall Jones Company, 1920.
Altidor, Raoul. *Koulè Midi*. Port-au-Prince: Les Éditions Memoires, 1999.

Beauvoir, Rachel, and Didier Dominique. *Savalou E.* Montréal: Les Éditions du CIDIHCA, 2003.

Brown, Karen McCarthy. *Mama Lola: A Vodou Priestess in Brooklyn.* Berkeley, CA: University of California Press, 1991.

Brutus, Timoleon C., and Arsene V. Pierre-Noel. *Les plantes et l.es legumes d'Haiti qui guerissent: Mille et une recettes pratiques.* Vol. 2. Port-au-Prince: Imprimerie de l'État d'Haiti, 1960.

Carrasco, Davíd. "Aztec Moments and Chicano Cosmovision: Aztlan Recalled to Life." In *Moctezuma's Mexico: Visions of the Aztec World*, rev. ed., edited by Davíd Carrasco and Eduardo Matos Moctezuma, 175–98. Boulder: University Press of Colorado, 2003.

Deren, Maya. *Divine Horsemen.* 1953. Reprint, New York: McPherson & Company, 2004.

Fisher, Kurt A. "Une amulette jumelée en os de la Section d'Archeologie du Bureau d'Ethnologie de la Republique d'Haiti." *Bulletin du Bureau d'Ethnologie* (1943): 31–3.

Fleurant, Gerdès. *Dancing Spirits: Rhythms and Rituals of Haitian Vodun, the Rada Rite.* Westport, CT: Greenwood Press, 1996.

Fouchard, Jean. *Langue et Litterature des Aborigenes d'Ayiti.* Port-au-Prince: Editions Henri Deschamps, 1988.

Herskovits, Melville J. *Life in a Haitian Valley.* New York: Alfred A. Knopf, 1937.

Houlberg, Marilyn. "Magique Marasa: The Ritual Cosmos of Twins and Other Sacred Children." In *Sacred Arts of Haitian Vodou*, edited by Donald J. Cosentino, 267–83. Los Angeles: UCLA Fowler Museum, 1995.

Houlberg, Marilyn. "Magique Marasa: The Ritual Cosmos of the Twins and Other Sacred Children." In *Fragments of Bone: Neo-African Religions in a New World*, edited by Patrick Bellegarde-Smith, 13–31. Urbana: University of Illinois Press, 2005.

Houlberg, Marilyn. "Two Equals Three: Twins and the Trickster in Haitian Vodou." In *Twins in African and Diaspora Cultures*, edited by Philip M. Peek, 271–89. Bloomington, IN: Indiana University Press, 2011

Jackson, Michael D. *Existential Anthropology: Events, Exigencies and Effects.* New York: Berghahn Books, 2008.

Landers, Jane. "A View from the Other Side: The Saint Domingue Revolution through Spanish Sources." Parts 1–3. Nathan I. Huggins Lectures, Hutchins Center for African and African American Research, Harvard University, Cambridge, MA, March 3–5, 2015.

Laroche, Max. *Prinsip Marasa.* Sillery, Québec: GRELCA, 2004.

MacGaffey, Wyatt. "Twins, Simbi Spirits, and Lwas in Kongo and Haiti." In *Central Africans and Cultural Transformation in the American Diaspora*, edited by Linda Heywood, 211–26. Cambridge: Cambridge University Press, 2001.

Maclean, Frances. "The Lost Fort of Columbus." *Smithsonian* 38, no. 10 (2008): 72–6.

Marcelin, Milo. *Mythologie Vodou (Rite Arada).* Vol. 2. Pétionville, Haiti: Éditions Canapé-Vert, 1950.

McGee, Adam. "Constructing Africa: Authenticity and Gine in Haitian Vodou." *Journal of Haitian Studies* 14, no. 2 (2009): 30–51.

McGee, Adam. "Dreaming in Haitian Vodou: Vouchsafe, Guide, and Source of Liturgical Novelty." *Dreaming* 22, no. 2 (2012): 231–56.

Mennesson-Rigaud, Odette. "Étude sur le culte des Marassas en Haïti." *ZAÏRE* 6, no. 6 (1952): 597.

Mennesson-Rigaud, Odette [as Odette M. Rigaud]. "The Feasting of the Gods in Haitian Vodu." Translated by Alfred and Rhoda Métraux. *Primitive Man* 19, no. 1/2 (1946): 1–58.

Métraux, Alfred. *Le Vaudou haïtien*. 1958. Reprint, Paris: Gallimard, 1968.

Mintz, Sidney W., and Richard Price. *The Birth of African-American Culture: An Anthropological Perspective*. Boston: Beacon Press Books, 1976.

Peek, Philip M., ed. *Twins in African and Diaspora Cultures: Double Trouble, Twice Blessed*. Bloomington, IN: Indiana University Press, 2011.

Price-Mars, Jean. *Ainsi Parla L'Oncle*. Port-au-Prince: Imprimerie de Compiègne, 1928.

Price-Mars, Jean. "Culte des Marassas." *Afroamerica* 1, no. 1–2 (1945): 41–9.

Séverin, François. *Plant ak pyebwa tè d Ayiti*. Port-au-Prince: Éditions Quitel de Desk Top Advisory, 2002.

Snow, Loudell F. "'I Was Born Just Exactly with the Gift': An Interview with a Voodoo Practitioner." *The Journal of American Folklore* 86, no. 341 (1973): 272–81.

Part Two

Hero Twins in the Americas

5

Twins in Native American Mythologies

Relational Transformation

♊

John Grim

Myths that describe the origins, exploits, and wonders of twins and twinship are abundant among American Indian peoples of North, South, and Meso-America. Yet what has not been overly studied, other than as a kind of rarified mythic theme, are the implications of that doubling to symbolic thought and religious life among Native American cultures into the present. Most well known among these auspicious twins are perhaps Junajpu (Hunahpu) and XB'alamkiej (Xbalanke) described in part II of the *Popul Wuj*.[1] They are actually the sons of twins themselves, so that doubling intensifies the symbolic meanings and values transmitted. It may be that cultural borrowings and narrative influences from the Mesoamerican Mayan and Nahuatl formulations of this mythic theme radiated north especially into the American Southwest. Even if such influences could be substantiated, the particular differences in the twin myths in the Southwest between, for example, Quechan/Yuman peoples of the California-Arizona-Mexico border and Diné /Navajo of the Four Corners region are striking.[2]

The mythic Navajo twins serve humans by heroic activities such as slaying life-threatening monsters. During these fantastic adventures, the Diné twins, as cultural heroes, personify foundational social values similar to those enacted by the Mesoamerican twins. But the motivations and the style of narrations, place references, and specific content that these Diné myths present are unique to this southwestern people. On the other hand, the Quechan peoples located along the Colorado River describe their mythic twins as more primal creative and destructive forces at the beginnings of the world. In this manifestation of twinship, the Quechan are actually more similar to the Northeastern woodland Haudenosaunee/Iroquois than they are to more geographically proximate peoples; in a cosmogonic myth, the latter tell of Good Twin (or Good Mind) and Evil Twin (or Bad Mind), who make the world helpful and harmful for humans.

Several significant observations can be made that ground this study from the outset, namely, the mythic motif of twinship is extremely widespread among indigenous peoples of North America. Yet, in every expression of the theme, cultural particularity is not only evident but also foundational for any interpretation. Cultural radiations that might suggest shared origins of a mythic twins-type are often difficult to verify. For example, the myth cycle of heroic twinship of the Northern Plains Crow/Apsaalooke shares more with their cultural cousins, the Hidatsa, and with southern Shoshoni and Arapaho, as well as with northern Blackfeet and Assiniboine, than it does with the sacred histories of the Lakota, Tsistsistas/Cheyenne, and Gros Ventres, who actually live in closer geographical proximity to the Crow. Moreover, all the twin myths are culturally, geographically, and ecologically nested. That is, they are not isolated artistic or entertainment narrations divorced from the larger lifeworlds of indigenous peoples.[3]

As Seneca scholar Barbara Alice Mann has forcefully argued in *Spirits of Blood, Spirits of Breath: The Twinned Cosmos of Indigenous America*, the Native American cosmos must itself be understood as "a halved and interdependent whole, particularly as expressed in the iconic Twinships of Blood/water/earth Serpents and Breath/air/ sky Thunderbirds. These existed in harmony, not enmity, for the purpose of cosmic balance, in star patterns and earth-bound mirrors of those patterns."[4] Twinship emerges as a root metaphor of Native American cognition, organizing both knowledge and experience: "the Indigenous approach assumes that everything happens by matched sets, and not infrequently, by doubled matched sets."[5]

Often, there are multiple twin myths among a single people, such as those told by the Haudenosaunee who tell not only of the primal cosmogonic twins, Good and Evil Mind, but also of other heroic twins differently named by the confederated tribes of this political alliance. In some of these histories, the boys do not share births as twins, but may instead be related as half-brothers by birth through a parent. They may be boyhood friends, or simply similar mythic forms who undertake the heroic journeys together as multiple expressions of a single enterprise.[6] I would argue that these shared mythic connections between boys who are closely related, but not twins, can still be associated with the theme of twinship. Finally, no major overview study of the cultural radiations or symbolic implications of this mythic theme among North American Indian peoples has been done.

The question arises, then, of how to proceed in laying out an introductory study of the mythic theme of twins among Native North American peoples. In the face of an abundance of material, one way to organize treatments of this mythic theme is simply to present the cultural differences. Yet, there are striking overlaps within many myth cycles with regard to content, personalities, and story plots describing the exploits of the mythic twins. This study proposes four portals for entry into a discussion of the twins' myths that addresses both differentiation and interpretive positions. These are developed in four parts, namely: the story of how twins came to be; heroic activities; doubling and the human condition; and twins as a mythic theme in religious life.

In the first two parts, this study will move from general references to a particular example. This is to suggest the widespread character of twin myths, followed in each case by a closer reading of one particular twin myth: the story-cycle of twins named

Lodge-boy and **Thrown-in-the-Spring** told by the Crow/Apsaalooke peoples of Montana. The third section, "Doubling and the Human Condition," explores a single example of the "Stricken Twins" from the Navajo-Diné peoples. The final section, "The Twins: Mythic Theme and Religious Life," provides an interpretive opportunity. My hope is to generate for the reader a cumulative sense of the widespread character of this mythic theme, but also the depth of symbolic meaning and religious identity transmitted by this imaginative doubling.

The Story of How the Twins Came to Be

Among the Northeastern Haudenosaunee (people of the Longhouse), known in the ethnography as Iroquois, two boy-twins figure prominently in the account of creation. This cosmology opens with a description of the Woman-who-fell-through-the-hole-in-the-sky, or Sky Woman.[7] Her safe landing is assured by herons (or ducks, or geese in some versions). Seeing her fall, they fly up to break her fall, and make a platform of their backs. The herons eventually establish this Sky Woman on the back of a tortoise, or what will become Turtle Island, the Earth. With no attempt at explanation, the myth tells how Sky Woman bears a daughter, and her daughter in turn soon carries twins who quarrel in her womb. The theme of twins who oppose one other in the womb is less common among American Indian peoples, but as I have noted is also found among Quechan peoples of the Southwest.

The five original tribes of the Haudenosaunee confederation, namely, Seneca, Cayuga, Onondaga, Oneida, and Mohawk, all tell versions of this creation story. One source has the Mohawk speak of the twins as Teharonhiawá:kon, Good Mind, and Shawískara, Bad Mind.[8] In most versions, the first twin is born normally through the birth canal. The second, troublesome twin, however, came forth through his mother's side, killing her. Eventually, through deceit and lies the Mohawk twin, Shawískara, tricks their grandmother, Sky Woman, into favoring him. The Good Twin, Teharonhiawá:kon, had to largely raise himself. Another ethnography from the Seneca names the twins, Djuska and Othagwenda.[9] In the Seneca version Sky Woman favors the Good Twin, Djuska and threw Othagwenda into a hollow tree away from their lodge. Eventually, Djuska requests two of everything he receives to share with the boy in the hollow tree. In time Othagwenda is brought back home. In both versions as the two boys grow they initiate their creative and destructive acts that extend the Earth, bring to life beneficial and harmful medicine plants and animals, and form the physical geography in ways that help or harm humans-to-come.

Several points characterize this Haudenosaunee twin-cycle of Good and Bad Mind. First, the twins by birth from the daughter of the celestial woman stand immediately in relation to different realms in the world. That is, there is the sky world from which one could fall, obtain powers, and return. Moreover, there is the realm of the animal beings who break the fall of Sky Woman, provide a foundation for the Earth, and dive into the pervasive waters to bring up soil for the extension of the land. Then, there is the Earth Mother, namely, the daughter who died when the Evil Twin burst from her side. After her burial, her body brings forth the beneficial plants, corns, beans, and squash.

These cosmological characteristics and the movement between realms are central in the many twin mythic cycles of Native North American peoples. Finally, the outright antagonism evident in the Haudenosaunee mythic twins has a deeper interactive logic. This is most evident in later sections of the narrative, in which the healing society of "False Faces" come about through the actions, defeat, and reformation of the Bad Twin. As with all living forms, then, what appears to be fixed in one moral camp may transform into another quite different than one expects. This transformative characteristic has strong cosmological implications, suggesting that movement between realms is at the heart of mythic twinship. The cosmological movements of the twins are potentially sacred, spiritual acts that set in motion ecological and mythic dimensions. This cosmological agency of the twins is evident in the creation of plants that have their own ontological identity, or personhood, such as sweetgrass. Thus, sweetgrass, by virtue of the biocultural understandings of the Haudenosaunee of that plant, can establish right relationships for the people rather than transforming realms or realities themselves. Yet, the fuller ontological identity of the plant importantly connects back to both the good twin, Teharonhiawá:kon, and his creative work in healing and transforming the disruptive work of the Bad Twin, Shawískara.

At a cultural distance from the Haudenosaunee twins myth, but still close in several comparative and symbolic intentions is the Crow/Apsaalooke story of the hero twins, Lodge-boy and **Thrown-in-the-Spring**.[10] In this Northern Plains story, the parents of the twins have moved away from the main camp, engaged in seasonal hunting. That is, they are apart from the security of the communal group, but engaged in culturally affirmed subsistence-gathering activities for their family. With the husband gone hunting, his pregnant wife receives successive visits from a stranger, all of which she forgets to tell her spouse so that the husband is unaware of any impending danger. This mythic theme of the mysterious stranger is, of course, found among so many indigenous peoples, developing in many thematic directions. Here, the stranger from afar stands in opposition to the birth of the twins. As a doubling that intensifies, the twins come to stand in deep relationships with community as opposed to the ominous stranger. Twins, in this sense, stand for community work toward a shared common good.

In time, the wife is killed, by this strange visitor, who is, according to different Crow accounts, either an aged female, Red Woman, Hìsshishtawia, or a sadistic warrior, Long-Arm, Baaáalichke. Both of these strangers visit from heavenly or mythic regions other than the Earth realm. In this account, the twins are forcibly removed from the womb of their murdered mother by the archetypal Crow villain, Red Woman. The sadistic acts of Red Woman are underscored in the myths by her peculiar humor such as burning the dead woman's lips so that she appears smiling. Red Woman then stands the wife's dead body in a welcoming pose for her husband, or in other narrations, props her up seated by the door with that gruesome smile as greeting.

The two twins acquire their names when Red Woman callously throws one behind the tipi lining of the lodge (Bitàalasshiaalitchiasshiituuash), and the other is thrown into a nearby spring (Bahàa Awúuaasshiituuash).[11] The father returns and finds his dead wife, but the children have totally disappeared. Over a stretch of mythic time, the grieving father is preparing a meal in the tipi and hears a voice asking for food.

Because the one requesting uses the correct kinship terms, the father invites him to show himself. Lodge-boy appears and tells what has happened to him, namely, that after being thrown behind the tipi lining of the lodge, he was raised by mice. A sequence of charming exchanges occurs in which the father eventually learns of another twin boy with whom Lodge-boy plays. This child lives in the nearby spring and has sharp teeth and a surly disposition; he has become a fierce water-being.

In order to capture and transform Thrown-into-the spring, the father dresses Lodge-boy in a thick leather outfit so as to protect him from the fierce boy's sharp teeth. The father then advises him to shoot competitive arrows with the boy-in-the-spring and argue over a targeted shot. He does so, and as they argue Lodge-boy catches and holds his double. Then, father and Lodge-boy bring Thrown-into-the spring into a ceremonial sweat lodge with heated rocks in which he eventually cries, "You're burning me father, you're burning me!" With that call of recognition of his kinship to his father, the myth declares how the twin, Thrown-into-the spring, became human. Thus, the spiritual heat and steam-breath of the sacred ceremonial effects the change necessary for the twins to be reunited. Transformation effects the doubling that brings these Crow twins back together.

As both human and spiritual beings, by virtue of their birth, transformation, and miraculous childhoods, these twins undertake heroic adventures. One adventure has comparative reach in this opening discussion regarding origins. That is, at the conclusion of their mythic cycle of heroic activities, these Crow mythic twins kill the villain, whether Red Woman or Long-arm, who cruelly murdered their mother— whom they have miraculously brought back to life. In retaliation they cut off the hand of this murderer. The twins throw it into the sky where it forms the Hand Star constellation. Thus, the Crow twins establish their cosmological capacities and affirm for all ages to come a sign of their victories. It is fitting, then, that at the end of their mythic cycle they also depart into the sky as Morning Star and Evening Star shining forever as guardians for the people.[12] To this day, then, the Crow speak of the shared work of the people and the stars as bringing about the common good evident in the accomplishments of the twins.

In the Crow/Apsalooke twin myth the boys travel through cosmological realms and have extensive adventures. This movement between realms is foreshadowed in the radical transformation of Thrown-into-the spring.[13] The origin of the Crow twins pulled from their mother's womb gives us an indication not only of their extraordinary birth, but also of their inherent spiritual resources that require a quest or journey to achieve. So also their doubling of each other is an achievement because they each initially stand in different realms. For example, Lodge-boy emerges from the social realm of tipis. Raised by liminal animals, namely mice who live in their own realm yet cross into human realms, Lodge-boy is also marked as liminal, and therefore sacred, before coming out into human society.

Thrown-into-the spring, on the other hand, is totally other when he comes to be in the myth. Yet he also stands in relation to fierce animals in the spring—some Crow myths describe his "spring-father" as an alligator, and in other versions fish people with sharp teeth. Before Thrown-into-the spring can undertake his role as a twin he has to be transformed by the creative work of a ceremony, the sweat lodge. This is the oldest known religious ritual among the Apsaalooke. Moreover, the sweat lodge has strong cosmological orientations in its focus on a small domed lodge of bent saplings symbolic of the cosmic womb that births all reality. Having been violently removed from his birth womb, **Thrown-in-the-Spring** is restored to his humanity through the symbolic work of the sweat ritual.

In summary, the coming into being of twins varies among Native North American peoples but they can be distinguished by strong or weak cosmological dimensions at their origin. That is, a strong cosmological dimension has twins creating the primeval Earth along with plants and animals, whereas a weak cosmological dimension describes twins as human born but capable of moving across realms of power. Most importantly, these mythic twins at their appearance undergo some type of transformation that enables them to cross realms of being. These transformations may be a key to the power inherent in their doubling.

Heroic Activities

As I have noted, the mythic twins in Native North American mythology are often heroes who save humans from monsters. Thus, another set of Haudenosaunee twins with a weak cosmological dimension called by the Seneca, Hadentheni (the Speaker) and Hanigongendatha (the Interpreter), kill the mythic bear, Ganiagwaihegowa, who eats people. As with many other twins, these two undertake this heroic act on their journeys to the Sun and to the Land of the Dead.[14] This is paralleled, for example, among the Zuni people who still live in their pueblo and adjacent lands located in northern New Mexico. The Zuni tell of their famous twins, Ahayuta and Matsilema, who lead the people during the cosmogonic time of Emergence from the interior up and onto the surface of the Earth. In addition to this strong cosmological act of bringing the people onto the Earth-surface, their heroic activities involve ridding the world of monsters, establishing landforms from the monsters' body parts, and demonstrating their ritual powers needed to make rain. In the Southwest the native peoples of Acoma Pueblo tell of Masewa and Uyuyewa who also lead the people through the shipapu, or underground opening, at Emergence onto this world. As sons of the Sun, they also journey to their father and acquire powers of rain-making. In asserting their rain powers, these twins manifest another power often related with twin mythology, namely, a warrior's aggression.

The two Acoma twins intentionally stop their ritual dance that assures the rain. Feeling underappreciated, they leave for the underworld. Only after prolonged drought and repeated requests by the Acoma Puebloans will the twins return and with them the rain. This assertive character of the twins coupled with their heroic activities identifies their leadership with a warrior ethos. Interestingly, governance among these puebloan peoples has distinct styles calling for both peace and warrior leaders. In this sense, a distinction can be made between the mythic twins themselves. One twin, often the elder, is particularly militant and often starts off the adventures of killing monsters by breaking a command not to go in a certain direction or interact with a specific monster. This antagonistic, contrary characteristic also distinguishes the elder mythic twin-brother called by the Hopi, Pyukonhoya, and by the Navajo-Diné, Naayéé'neizghání, in English, Monster Slayer; whereas the younger boy among the Hopi is called, Palunhoya, and by the Navajo-Diné, Tóbájíshchíní, Child-of-the-Waters.[15] He is much more passive, less prone to violence, and, in some accounts, more cunning and thoughtful.

We have noted how the Crow/Apsaalooke twins achieve their doubling as twin brothers by means of the transformation of **Thrown-in-the-Spring** in the sweat lodge. Even after his transformation, **Thrown-in-the-Spring** is the more aggressive of the twins. His doubling with Lodge-boy, however, effects a complementary balance so necessary for accomplishing their heroic activities. Thus, after their transformative doubling they begin their heroic adventures subduing and killing the monsters. Like other native mythic twins they overcome such monsters as a human-eating bear, cougar, and elk and, befitting their Plains ecology, a monster buffalo. Unlike their cultural parallels, the Crow twins have a human father, Balàpooshe, and so they do not journey to a father-Sun, nor do they journey to the land of the dead.

However, they do bring their mother back from death by shooting their magical arrows. As they do this, they warn her that the arrows are landing close to her dead body in a tree-scaffold. They also call to her that they have her favorite household implements, namely, her hatchet, her pestle for grinding, and her hair comb. Household items help to bring about this transformation from death back to life. By these means the twins establish again their close relationship with the human community. Grasping her hand, then, the twins pull their mother back from death. Later, she is the one who then tells them of the monsters threatening humans. Typically, as the monsters are killed their bodies and blood become landforms. In this sense, the Crow narration of these heroic activities instills values in the people, and explains the changes and relationships with the land. Thus, the close connections of narratives and landforms in the symbolic consciousness of a people guides and orients them in daily life.

Foremost among the traditional values transmitted to Crow youth in the twins myths are those associated with powers given to revenge attacks on one's clan. Various Crow versions of the twins myth cite either Red Woman or Long-arm as the archetypal, treacherous villain. When the Apsaalooke twins kill this monster, they avenge their mother's death as well as manifest skills of shape-shifting and movement across realms often by climbing upward on the arrows they shoot into the sky. Typically, the twins accomplish their heroic deeds with the assistance of powers and persons from the powerful realms of the spirits.

So it is when the villain, Long-arm, steals Lodge-boy away into the sky. The remaining twin, **Thrown-in-the-Spring**, is initially thrown back onto his own resources to begin the quest to save his brother. Lying down in the place where his brother was kidnapped, he sees a hole in the sky. Shooting his arrows he travels to the sky region where he proceeds through a series of four camps. Disguising himself he shape-shifts into different bird peoples, seeks their advice, and demonstrates his powers. In this way he gains their confidence and they assist him in his efforts to save Lodge-boy. These heavenly camps of little birds, herons, hawks, and eagles all join with **Thrown-in-the-Spring** as he overcomes Long-arm. Having severed Long-arm's hand and creating a new constellation for humans to observe, the twins bring back from the sky world these bird companions. Birds, then, and in other heroic stories, animals all become major power personalities for the Crow. The twins myth of heroic activities affirms the roles of spiritual patrons in the local ecology. In their religious imagination, these powerful persons can assist humans. On two counts, then, the heroic activities of mythic twins make permanent changes: first, in the outer landforms, and, second, in the inner resources of the human person.

Doubling and the Human Condition

As we have seen, doubling in the Native American mythic world of twins can be doubly complex regarding cosmological symbolism. This complexity is also manifest in the realm of strictly human mythic twins, who inherit and echo their legacy on earth [Figure 5.1]. For example, in the Navajo-Diné oral tradition there are "Earth people" twins, that is, human pairs such as the "Stricken Twins." There are also divine pairs, or "Holy People" (*dine'é* and *hashch'e*) such as the twins, Monster Slayer and Child-of-the-Waters, as well as the twins of the Shooting Chant, and the major deity, Talking God, the inner form of significant physical realities such as mountains.[16]

Figure 5.1 A Diné (Navajo) mother with her twins, near a wagon. Gallup area, New Mexico [undated; 1925–30?]. Photo by William Thomas Mullarky (1897–1959). Such images of Native Americans were often taken by white photographers in the nineteenth and twentieth centuries without paying their subjects or receiving their consent. Denver Public Library R7100330121. By permission of the Denver Public Library.

Earlier in this study we have seen how doubling of a supernatural pair can assert strong or weak cosmological dimensions in which twins create the plants and animals as well as landforms and social values. However, in the case of the Stricken Twins the human pair is neither cosmologically strong in creating land or forms of life nor are they wholly cosmologically weak. That is, the Stricken Twins have the capacity to cross realms and communicate with the *yei*/spirits and by this movement effect transformation of themselves. Yet, their situation, rather than their cosmological capacity, calls forth the *yei*/cosmological powers who gradually become sympathetic to their claim.

In this myth, the Stricken Twins are simply human and their doubling seems strikingly different from the warrior style of hero so widespread in the twin myths. That is, the Stricken Twins suffer an unexpected and unexplained transformation that makes one blind and one lame. Going forth on their quest, the blind boy caries the cripple on his back. Their doubling gives rise to empathy, compassion, and thoughtful expediency. Yet the power of this myth is in the doubling of resolve that the boys hold throughout the myth, namely, to be acknowledged as the sons of Talking God, and to find a cure. In this sense, though not even demonstrating weak cosmological powers, they parallel other strong cosmological twin myths. Talking God stands in for the Sun, and the quest for healing stands for the slaying of the monsters and the acquisition of powers.

While the Stricken Twins here are singular pair, the Navajo myth world is filled with duplications and multiple manifestations of divine figures (*yei*).[17] This extraordinary doubling, or multiple selves, is a signal feature of Navajo symbolism exemplified by such divine figures as First Man and First Boy, Pollen boy and Cornbeetle girl, Changing Woman and White Shell Woman. In fact among the Navajo, no supernatural is singular but manifests multiple forms. Among the divine *yei*, Talking God, for example, is considered the inner form of an outwardly manifesting reality especially the sacred mountains. For the Navajo, this inner form is what gives anything its life and sentience. In effect, then, this inner symbolic form duplicates in an external physical reality. For the Navajo, these dimensions can be distinguished but are not separated beings, concepts, or symbols. "Orthodoxy" or the generation of coherent, rational doctrines are not the aim of this narrativity about twins; rather, I would contend that "orthopraxy" is one way of expressing the goal of shared work for the common good that is embodied in the twins.

Deity, then, manifests multiple forms in many places. In the Stricken Twins myth the boys visit specific places that they elaborately and carefully name. These litanies of place-names have both a repetitive prayerful dimension, as well as an oral quality like flowing water wearing away the hardest resistance. In the Navajo symbolic world, humans undertake multiple repetitions, duplications, and multiplications to effect restoration, to heal, and to augment power. Doubling in the Native American twins myths appears to be a means for intensifying these forms of symbolic transformation.

Whether a natural or supernatural doubling, twins often find themselves facing difficulties they did not create. One insight into doubling, then, is the nature of the difficulty faced and the ways in which twinship responds to that difficulty. In the Navajo-Diné story of the Stricken Twins this characteristic is especially poignant as the illness of the two is the vehicle for the powerful healing ceremony of the Night Chant, Klay'jih Hatal'. As one researcher described them:

> The wanderings of the Stricken Twins demonstrate the trial and error, the effort and perseverance necessary to the culmination of the Night Chant. The Stricken Twins put themselves into a position worthy of divine aid; they acceded to requirements no matter how difficult; they emerged from their tribulations to endow their fellow men with the greatest of ceremonies.[18]

Born of a human form of Changing Woman, the Earth, the twins initially have normal bodies until deformed by blindness and paralysis. Abandoned by their father, Talking God, they travel the places associated with him trying to find acceptance and a cure from their handicaps. Unlike the cosmological creativity of many North American Indian twin myths, the Stricken Twins focus on evils that befall humans such as loss of sight and deformed limbs. The blind boy carries the cripple boy on his shoulders so that the two unite to form the capacities of one normal human. As they travel to the holy places they request of the gods that they be accepted as the sons of Talking God and be granted a cure. But in all instances they are met with suspicion, snobbery, and deceit as the gods claim they have no knowledge of such a cure. Each of the *yei*, in truth holds the means that in concert with one another could cure the boys' condition.

When the gods finally decide to help the Stricken Twins, the phenomenon of doubling manifests itself even in the choice of place to hold the ceremony. That is, the first cure at "House-where-they-move-about" fails to work because the twins break a restriction, and a second cure is eventually held at Broad Rock. The reason for the first failure occurs when the twins are led into the sweat house and are told not to make any sound during the ceremony. But as the cure takes effect and the blind boy begins to see light, and the lame boy begins to feel his legs they both cry out with joy. Having broken the command for silence, the ceremony is stopped and the boys are sent packing. As they leave, one ethnographer described their state:

> In despair they walked down the canyon, weeping over their mistakes, knowing not where to turn. Without purpose or direction, they cried; at first they uttered meaningless syllables, but after a while they found words to sing. The Holy Ones, hearing a song, inquired of one another, "Why do they sing?" They sent Talking God to bring the children back. The blind boy resisted, but his brother urged that they return and find out what the gods wanted. Arriving where the gods were, they were asked, "What was that you were singing as you went along?" "We were not singing," they answered. "We were crying." "Why did you cry?" "Because you sent us away and we had no place to go." "What kind of song were you singing?" asked the god. "We certainly heard the words of a song."
>
> Three times the boys insisted that they were merely crying, but when asked the same question the fourth time, the gentler one explained, "We began to cry; we turned our cry into a song. We never knew the song before. My blind brother just made it up as we moved along." Then he sang the song which described their helplessness and despair and included a statement that they would be restored to

health. The song impelled the gods to take counsel once more, and they decided never again to turn their children away with no means of saving themselves.[19]

Just as the Stricken Twins are restored in sight and limb, so also the myth affirms the central symbolic work in Navajo perspective on doubling, namely, restoration through human thought and breath, intention and sound.[20] In Diné religious life and practice these are ways to activate cosmological movement across realms of power. In this regard, the Navajo Stricken Twins story provides an interesting turn within twin myths in Native North America because the twins are so vulnerable. Yet, their creative work by singing transforms the *yei*, the powers of place. Their limitations within the human condition and their eventual restoration point toward embodied transformations through movement which frames the final section.

The Twins: Mythic Theme and Religious Life

Several connections between twin myths and religious life have already been noted. For example, the transformation of **Thrown-in-the-Spring** by means of the sweat lodge in several Crow/Apsaalooke versions of that story makes an overt connection with Crow ritual life. The Navajo-Diné story of Stricken Twins has two major connections. First, the role of the Diné sweat house, differently constructed and performed than the Northern Plains sweat lodge, in curing the twins; and second, the role of this myth in the Night Chant, a major healing ceremonial among these people. Moreover, in virtually all of the twins myths there are meaningful references to specific places in the landscape. Sometimes these references are overt, such as the place-naming in the Diné tradition, or concealed to outsiders but clearly understood by those hearing the narration.

This relationship of twins to sacred places is significant and could certainly be a study of its own. By vision-questing at such a site, or simply visiting and leaving appropriate ceremonial prayer objects, indigenous individuals and communities placed themselves in respectful relationship with the religious values that mythic twins manifested. These powers include doubling the intensity of commitments, warrior endurance, loyalty to comrades, and the opening to spiritual assistance. However, the key to such religious activities is not simply in the sites themselves, neither in the mythic persons of the twins, nor simply in the ceremonies associated with the twin myths. Rather, the central religious feature of the twins' doubling—and re-doubling— is echoed through American Indian life as relational movement.

My focus finally returns to the religious implications of the Northern Plains Crow/ Apsaalooke and their myth of Lodge-boy and **Thrown-in-the-Spring**. In the Crow context of oral transmission, Robert Lowie offers helpful insight into the sacred dimension of this twins myth:

> The Crow divided their tales into two principal groups corresponding roughly to what we should call myths and traditions. The latter are called *baré-tsiwe-tã're* ("something-tell-true") and are supposed to be based on the direct experience of the Crow Indians. Thus the story of Ravenface [an historical story] is classed as

baré-tsiwe-tã're. The mythic tales are designated by a term slightly varying in form but always lacking the evidential suffix and presenting the stem for "to tell" in reduplicated form: *bá+e'tsitsiwá+u, bare'-wa+e'tsitsiwe*. The Old Man Coyote cycle, the Buffalo-wife, Lodge-boy and Thrown-away were cited by natives as illustrations of this category . . .

Stories were told on winter nights when people were sitting by the fire or had stretched out before falling asleep. Old people with a reputation as *raconteurs* were invited for a feast and then expected to narrate their tales. The audience was required to answer "Æ" (yes) after every sentence or two. When no one replied, it was a sign that all had fallen asleep and the story-teller broke off his narrative, possibly to resume it the following night. This response feature figures occasionally in the myths, notably in the Grandchild tale.

People were formerly afraid to tell stories in the summer because, one informant said, the morningstar comes only in the winter time. The reason for restricting the entertainment to the night is that all the stars with names used to live in this world and only come out at night.[21]

The doubling of the term *to tell* is used by the Apsaalooke to indicate an oral transmission that has singular teachings for the people. Such an oral marker orients us not only to the significance of the teachings in the twin myth for religious life, but also to their embodiment in cultural life. That is, there are certain seasons for the telling of certain myths, as well as ways to hear them—and culturally anticipated behaviors that mark both storyteller and audience. These are a kind of dance, or relational movement, that "doubles life." That is, the sacred moves in, around, and in relation to the quotidian. Similarly, just as the myth situates the twins in the broader cultural life of the people, so also it is necessary to locate religious perspectives in the cultural life of a people—in its lifeway.

The doubling of twins in the mythic world occurs in the context of lifeway;[22] the term suggests the close connections between territory and society, religion and politics, cultural and economic life whereby indigenous peoples have maintained their knowledge systems. Indigenous lifeways as ways of knowing the world are presented as both descriptive of enduring modes of sustainable livelihood and prescriptive of what has been termed "ecological imaginaries."[23] These are deep, attractor relationships between place and people that activate the affective, cognitive, and creative forces at the heart of cultural life—relationships that catalyzed the emergence of affect theory. Mythic themes such as that of twins and twinship constitute such an ecological imaginary. When myths are lost or no longer communicated in their original languages, it is the same as when the homelands of indigenous peoples are literally cut down or mined away. The whole possibility of imaging oneself and one's community in place and in words is fragmented and subverted.

In this way Crow religious behavior and ceremonial space are understood as ways of knowing that have interpretive significance. They are responsible movements through nature, space, and the sacred. Rather than separating out religion as a realm apart from the daily life of a people, "lifeway" suggests that religious life and mythic narratives are embedded in the multiple bodies that individuals and communities inhabit. That is, bodies of self, community, land, and cosmos *double* identity. These mythic forms augment the possibility for movement between realms establishing relationships and generating power.

Just as the mythic twins draw on their multiple experiences of bodies, the Crow experience embodied knowing from the perspective of fourfold spaces-in-the-world, namely, personal, social, ecological, and cosmological bodies.[24] These can be understood as sources of multiple selves that are transformed into a unity as with the doubling of twins. In these mythic spaces the complexity of both nature and the sacred becomes lived, moral experiences shaping the bodies and behavior of religious participants. As one interpreter of such symbolic relations in the Navajo-Diné observes:

> By such a method of land claiming for the myth—which has been common in the histories of cultures—an indifferent landscape is transubstantiated, turned into an icon, and the elementary idea is established in a local habitation. Moreover, not alone the landscape: for in this particular mythology of the Pollen Path of Beauty [viz., Navajo Chantways], every water bug and local beast and fowl has been mythologized, so that in the whole known world there is nothing apart from the beauty, since (to make use of another symbolic vocabulary) all are in God, and God is in all.[25]

Figure 5.2 Two dancers with shields, rattles, and raccoon pelts (the Hero Twins?). Quaternity motif on engraved conch shell gorget hanging from leader's necklace. Burial 108, Craig Mound, Spiro Mounds, Oklahoma. Mississippian Culture, 1200–1350 CE. By permission Sam Noble Oklahoma Museum of Natural History.

In a lifeway, one is born into such a fourfold embodiment. This occurs by virtue of individual birth in a culture that inhabits a local ecosystem as well as a cosmological landscape with religious attention; this is represented, for example, in the elegant quaternities of Mississipian and other ancient artifacts [Figure 5.2]. In the Native American worldview we can generally assert that place-naming during rituals is one example among many of the empirical character of this religious attention. Thus, this religio-empirical attention embraces, but should not be understood as reduced to, subsistence needs, and quotidian demands. Thus, Crow lifeway, as evident in the myth of the twins, orients practitioners to a human quest that actualizes these religious relationships through relational movement within community, land, biodiversity, and cosmos. This is a somatic process that reaches toward and through the doubling embodiments recognized as personhood that pervades the world. "Body" is not simply a philosophical trope, then, for an embodied consciousness, but rather also is movement that articulates experiences. Such movement takes the form of creative engagement, such as in the narrations of the symbolic world in which mythic twins become living patterns of relational meaning. For the Crow the reduplication of mythic narratives, namely, "to tell, to tell," suggests this amplified movement.

Intentional movement is evident in the story of the mythic twins as they undergo trials at their origin, in their heroic adventures, and in their doubling to achieve singleness of purpose. Whether cosmological twins that struggle with one another to create the world, or more human twins who make a great effort to search out their deeper identity, these mythic twins undergo trial to come to achievement. As one researcher observed for Northern Plains American Indian peoples:

> . . . religious practice is fundamentally concerned with gaining "power," as well as making supplication and giving thanks. Gaining power means gaining a stronger sense of personal agency, the ability to achieve both in the community and spiritually, but it is also a notion tied to a random "good luck" from uncontrollable spiritual forces.

> Physical being is deeply involved in the attainment of power. Embodied prayer, for example, is found in the form of bodily suffering from the hot steam of the sweat lodge during spiritual and bodily cleansing, during fasting and periods of isolation away from the comforts of human companionship. Such suffering is perhaps felt most intensely by those who participate in the four days of fasting, dancing, and enduring the heat of the sun during the annual sun dance ceremony. Although deeply misunderstood by non-Indians and frequently labeled torture in the historical record by distressed and horrified white observers, the physical suffering endured in the sun dance ceremony is also an important avenue for seeking and gaining power. To view the involvement as only a physical one would be to misinterpret profoundly, because it involves the whole person in the sense of testing fortitude, concentration, commitment, and belief at the same time that it forces reflection upon the individual's past life and present circumstances. Here too, as encoded in both spoken and signed languages, thinking and feeling are inseparable. . . . The only thing a person truly owns is his or her body, and therefore to make a gift

that is a truly meaningful sacrifice in the effort to obtain supernatural help and personal power, it is to the body one must turn. The more pitiful one appears and the more suffering one endures, the greater will be the potential assistance from the grandfather spirits and the creator. There is thus a very real sense in which the act of dancing in the sun dance *is* prayer and not an accompaniment to (spoken) prayer.[26]

In a similar way it can be said that the narration of the twin myths stands as a form of prayer in relation to individual power-gathering, community ritual, empirical observation of ecosystems, and attention to cosmological movement. For the Crow, the mythic twins Lodge-boy and **Thrown-in-the-Spring** continue their quest as individuals of the tribe, in the ongoing struggles of the people to survive, in the recognition of predator-prey relationships, and in those creative acts in which the cosmos radiates forth. Thus, the myth of the twins, Lodge-boy and Thrown-into-the-spring, signals a form of hope through the turmoil of change. A form of hope, less radical than some have ascribed to Crow political leadership, but, interestingly, a form of doubling when considered along with the values enduring in oral narratives, political leadership, star gazing, and land-relating.[27]

Thus, we can say that the myth of twins among Native American and First Nations peoples can have strong cosmological orientations in which the original creation of the world occurs, or weak cosmological orientations in which the human sphere is dominant but the twins become capable of moving across realms of power. Most interesting is the relational dynamic that the twins serve to establish between these realms of power. Even more compelling is that these power configurations are presented in the twin myths as embodied forms that the twins have by birth or acquire by valor. I have used the phrase "fourfold embodiment" to suggest ways of imaging the interplay of those bodies of power. However, in all the particular ways of narrating these myths of twinning, the indicator that measures the success of the twins' accomplishments is their work for the common good of the Earth community.

Notes

1 See *Popol Vuh: The Sacred Book of the Ancient Quiché Maya*, English version by Delia Goetz and Sylvanus Morley from the translation by Adrián Recinos (Norman: University of Oklahoma Press, 1950); also *Popul Vuh: The Definitive Edition of the Mayan Book of the Dawn of Life and the Glories of Gods and Kings*, trans. Dennis Tedlock (New York: Simon & Schuster, 1996); and Mary Miller and Karl Taube, *An Illustrated Dictionary of the Gods and Symbols of Ancient Mexico and the Maya* (London: Thames and Hudson, 1993). In this volume, see the original new study by Vincent Stanzione, "Junajpu and XB'alamkiej: The Maya Hero Twins of the *Popol Wuj*," 176–209.

2 See, for example, the Yuma myth "The Good Twin and the Evil Twin," in *American Indian Myths and Legends, ed.* Richard Erdoes and Alfonso Ortiz (New York: Pantheon Books, 1984), 77–82; and for the Dene/Navajo see Paul Zolbrod, *Diné bahanè: The Navajo Creation Story* (Albuquerque: University of New Mexico Press, 1984), especially the chapter "Slaying of the Monsters," 169–278.

172 *Gemini and the Sacred*

3 For the term *lifeworld*, see Tim Ingold, "Globes and Spheres: The Topology of Environmentalism," Chapter 12 in *The Perception of the Environment: Essays in Livelihood, Dwelling and Skill* (Routledge, 2000), 209–18. "What I hope to have established, at least in outline, is that the lifeworld, imaged from an experiential centre, is spherical in form, whereas a world divorced from life, then, is a matter not of sensory attunement but of cognitive reconstruction.. . . In the global outlook . . . the world does not surround us, it lies beneath our feet . . . [The] world . , . becomes an object of human interest and concern. But it is not a world of which humans themselves are conceived to be a part . . . They [humans] may observe it, reconstruct it, protect it, tamper with it or destroy it, but they do not dwell in it."

4 Barbara Alice Mann, *Spirits of Blood, Spirits of Breath: The Twinned Cosmos of Indigenous America* (New York: Oxford University Press, 2016), 12. See especially Chapter 2, "The Twinned Cosmos of Serpents and Thunderbirds."

5 Mann, *Spirits of Blood, Spirits of Breath*, 45. The result of the cultural misinterpretation of this twinship principle is, as Mann observes, that "only Western observers are baffled to note such things as two creation stories per culture—one of descent from the sky and one of the emergence from the earth" (ibid.).

6 I have in mind the close relations of the Crow/Apsaalooke twins to "Old Woman's Grandson," namely the evening star. But multiple examples of this type of twinship are found in the ethnography. See, e.g., the story of "The Arrow Chain" from the Tlingit peoples of southern Alaska from John R. Swanton, *Tlingit Myths and Texts, recorded by John R. Swanton,* Bureau of American Ethnology, Bulletin 39 (Washington, DC: Smithsonian Institution, 1909), found in *Tales of the North American Indian*, selected and annotated by Stith Thompson (Bloomington: Indiana University Press, 1968), 131–5.

7 See Tom Porter (Sakokweniónkwas), *And Grandma Said: Iroquois Teachings as Passed Down Through the Oral Tradition* (Akwesasne: Xlibris Corp., 2008), 40–53, on "Sky Woman and Turtle Island."

8 See Tom Porter (Sakokweniónkwas), *And Grandma Said: Iroquois Teachings as Passed Down Through the Oral Tradition*, ch. 5, "Mother Earth and Her Twins," 54–68.

9 See ibid.; also *Seneca Indian Myths*, collected by Jeremiah Curtin (New York: E.P. Dutton, 1923), and J. N. B. Hewitt, *Iroquoian Cosmology,* Annual Report of the Bureau of American Ethnology 21 (1899–900) (Washington, DC: Smithsonian Institution, 1903): 127–339; and J. N. B. Hewitt, "Raising and Falling of the Sky in Iroquois Legends," *American Anthropologist*, old series 5 (October 1892): 344.

10 There is a richness of sources on this myth cycle; I have drawn especially from Robert Lowie, *Myths and Traditions of the Crow Indians*. Anthropological Papers of the American Museum of Natural History, vol. 25, part I (1918): 74–98; as well as Timothy McCleary, *The Stars We Know: Crow Indian Astronomy and Lifeways* (Prospect Heights, IL: Waveland Press, 1997), 49–62.

11 McLeary, *The Stars We Know*, 54. The length of Crow/Apsaalooke names comes from a linguistic trait similar to the German language in which descriptive terms are built by compound addition of words.

12 In various Crow accounts of this myth the boys assume positions as different stars, see Lowie, *Myths and Traditions of the Crow Indians* as well as McLeary, *The Stars We Know.*

13 In speaking of the Assiniboine, a people closely located near the Crow/
    Apsaalooke, Brenda Farnell discusses the significance of movement: "It is
    striking that in a language which does not articulate terms for abstract concepts
    such as time and space the term *ska* gives linguistic form to this concept of force-
    for-movement. *Ska* appears not only as a theoretical concept that like the concept
    of gravity cannot in itself be seen, but, according to the myth, is a causal power
    above all others." See Brenda Farnell, *Do You See What I Mean? Plains Indian
    Sign Talk and the Embodiment of Action* (Austin: University of Texas, 1995),
    249–50.
14 *Seneca Fiction, Legends, and Myths,* Annual Report of the Bureau of American
    Ethnology 32 (1910–11), collected by Jeremiah Curtin and J. N. B. Hewitt, ed. J. N.
    B. Hewitt (Washington, DC: Smithsonian Instituent, 1918): 37–819.
15 For the Hopi see Ekkehart Malotki, *Hopitutuwutsi=Hopi Tales: A Bilingual
    Collection of Hopi Indian Stories* (Washington, DC: Smithsonian Institution
    Libraries, 1978); and for the Navajo-Diné see Leland C. Wyman, *Blessingway*
    (Tucson: University of Arizona, 1970).
16 For Monster Slayer and Child-of-the-Waters see the discussion of the Navajo-Diné
    ceremonial called "Shooting Chant" in Paul Zolbrod, *Diné bahanè: The Navajo
    Creation Story*; for the Shooting Chant twins, see Franc Newcomb and Gladys
    Reichard, *Sandpaintings of the Navajo Shooting Chant* (New York: J.J. Augustin,
    1937; Dover reprint, 1968).
17 See *The Night Chant, A Navajo Ceremony*, collected by Washington Matthews,
    Memoirs of the American Museum of Natural History 6 (1902): 215–67.
18 Gladys A. Reichard, *Navaho Religion: A Study of Symbolism*, Bollingen Series XVIII
    (Princeton, NJ: Princeton University Press, 1974), 150.
19 *The Night Chant, A Navajo Ceremony*, 244–5.
20 See the insightful study of Gary Witherspoon, *Language and Art in the Navajo
    Universe* (Ann Arbor: The University of Michigan Press, 1977).
21 Lowie, *Myths and Traditions of the Crow Indians*, 13.
22 I note the parallel to lifeworld, see n. 3 above.
23 For "ecological imaginaries," see Richard Peet and Michael Watts, *Liberation
    Ecologies: Environment, Development, Social Movements* (London and New York:
    Routledge, 1996).
24 An inquiry using the fourfold embodiment posits an obvious reference to a body in
    space. But there is as well an inner, or implicate, reference in which the relational
    character of the embodiments are seen as embedded in one another. They intimately
    illuminate one another. That is, each embodiment may or may not find distinct or
    explicate articulation in any religious expression. Yet, they are deeply implicated in
    one another. Questions arise in relation to religious activities from the perspectives
    of each embodiment even if they are not accentuated by the religion itself. For
    an intensive treatment of the philosophical and ritual implications of fourfold
    embodiment in Native American thought, see Mann, *Spirits of Blood, Spirits of
    Breath,* especially Chapter 2.
25 Joseph Campbell, *The Way of the Animal Powers*, Historical Atlas of World
    Mythology, vol. 1 (San Francisco: Harper & Row, 1983), 248.
26 Farnell, *Do You See What I Mean?*, 250–1.
27 See the insightful study on the leadership of the last Apsaalooke chief, Plenty
    Coups, by Jonathan Lear, *Radical Hope: Ethics in the Face of Cultural Devastation*
    (Cambridge, MA: Harvard University Press, 2006), esp. 103–8 and 113–17.

Bibliography

Campbell, Joseph. *The Way of the Animal Powers*. Historical Atlas of World Mythology, vol. 1. San Francisco: Harper & Row, 1983.

Erdoes, Richard, and Alfonso Ortiz, eds. *American Indian Myths and Legends*. New York: Pantheon Books, 1984.

Farnell, Brenda. *Do You See What I Mean? Plains Indian Sign Talk and the Embodiment of Action*. Austin, TX: University of Texas, 1995.

Hewitt, John Napoleon Brinton (J. N. B.). "Raising and Falling of the Sky in Iroquois Legends." *American Anthropologist*, old series 5 (October 1892): 344.

Hewitt, John Napoleon Brinton (J. N. B.). "Iroquoian Cosmology." Annual Report of the Bureau of American Ethnology 21 (1899–900) (Washington, DC: Smithsonian Institution, 1903): 127–339.

Ingold, Tim. *The Perception of the Environment: Essays in Livelihood, Dwelling and Skill*. New York: Routledge, 2000.

Introduction to Seneca Fiction, Legends, and Myths. Annual Report of the Bureau of American Ethnology, 32 (1910–11). Collected by Jeremiah Curtin and J. N. B. Hewitt. Ed. J. N. B. Hewitt. Washington, DC: Smithsonian Institute, [repr.] 1918.

Lear, Jonathan. *Radical Hope: Ethics in the Face of Cultural Devastation*. Cambridge, MA: Harvard University Press, 2006.

Lowie, Robert. *Myths and Traditions of the Crow Indians*. Anthropological Papers of the American Museum of Natural History v. 25, pt 1. New York: AMNH, 1918.

Malotki, Ekkehart. *Hopitutuwutsi=Hopi Tales: A Bilingual Collection of Hopi Indian Stories*. Washington, DC: Smithsonian Institution Libraries, 1978.

Mann, Barbara Alice. *Spirits of Blood, Spirits of Breath: The Twinned Cosmos of Indigenous America*. New York: Oxford University Press, 2016.

McCleary, Timothy. *The Stars We Know: Crow Indian Astronomy and Lifeways*. Prospect Heights, IL: Waveland Press, 1997.

Miller, Mary, and Karl Taube. *An Illustrated Dictionary of the Gods and Symbols of Ancient Mexico and the Maya*. London: Thames and Hudson, 1993.

Newcomb, Franc, and Gladys Reichard. *Sandpaintings of the Navajo Shooting Chant*. New York: J.J. Augustin, 1937; Dover reprint, 1968.

The Night Chant, A Navajo Ceremony. Collected by Washington Matthews. Memoirs of the American Museum of Natural History Vol. 6, 1902: 215–67.

Peet, Richard and Michael Watts. *Liberation Ecologies: Environment, Development, Social Movements*. London and New York: Routledge, 1996.

Popol Vuh: The Sacred Book of the Ancient Quiché Maya. English version by Delia Goetz and Sylvanus Morley, from the translation by Adrián Recinos. Norman: University of Oklahoma Press, 1950.

Popul Vuh: The Definitive Edition of the Mayan Book of the Dawn of Life and the Glories of Gods and Kings, revised ed. Translated by Dennis Tedlock. New York: Simon & Schuster, 1996.

Porter, Tom (Sakokweniónkwas). *And Grandma Said: Iroquois Teachings as Passed Down Through the Oral Tradition*. Akwesasne: Xlibris Corp., 2008.

Reichard, Gladys A. *Navaho Religion: A Study of Symbolism*. Bollingen Series XVIII. Princeton, NJ: Princeton University Press, 1974.

Seneca Indian Myths. Collected by Jeremiah Curtin. New York: E.P. Dutton, 1923.

Swanton, John R. *Tlingit Myths and Texts*, recorded by John R. Swanton. Bureau of American Ethnology, Bulletin 39. Washington, DC: Smithsonian Institution, 1909.

In *Tales of the North American Indian*, selected and annotated by Stith Thompson, 131–5. Bloomington, IN: Indiana University Press, 1968.

Tales of the North American Indian. Selected and annotated by Stith Thompson. Bloomington, IN: Indiana University Press, 1968.

Witherspoon, Gary. *Language and Art in the Navajo Universe*. Ann Arbor, MI: The University of Michigan Press, 1977.

Wyman, Leland C. *Blessingway*. Tucson: University of Arizona, 1970.

Zolbrod, Paul. *Diné bahanè: The Navajo Creation Story*. Albuquerque: University of New Mexico Press, 1984.

6

Junajpu and XB'alamkiej

The Maya Hero Twins of the *Popol Wuj*

♊

Vincent James Stanzione

Dedicated to Alfredo López Austin 3.12.1936–10.15.2021

This chapter seeks to illuminate religious ideas, expressed to this day, in myth and ritual among the K'iche' Maya, in which twins, doubles, and couples embody the cosmos and its actors.[1,2] These persistent ideas range from the "twinning" ways of Junajpu (Hunapu) and XB'alamkiej (Xbalanque), hero twins of the Mayan epic *Popol Wuj* to the ways in which contemporary Maya often meet life's challenges by "twinning" with one another, as in the case of two brothers I knew who lived as one by mirroring these primordial mythic patterns and archetypal ways of being in the world. Life's dual nature is thus brought into balance by Traditional Maya, who seek to follow in the footsteps of their ancestors the hero twins. By harmonizing the collaborative powers of twins, the Maya believe that all aspects of life can be brought to fruition. It is my belief that the balanced and complimentary ways of the hero twins create the deep structure—the root metaphor—of traditional Maya religion, as well as a kind of universal spirituality among Traditional Maya, who, no matter how individualistic each of whose conscious self-understanding might be, still live out their interior lives as twins. The myth of the hero twins once guided male initiates through rites of initiation that sought, among other things, to find the spirit guide or "twin" of the initiate. This idea of being "a twin to oneself" is the most productive way of understanding the hero twins of the Maya, whereby one is the person who lives in the world, and the other is that person's interior guide who lives as the intimate "other" or *nawal*. By knowing intimately the ways of one's "spirit guide," also understood as one's "animal transform," one is enabled to walk through life well accompanied by an inner ally who helps overcome life's challenges in a dangerous and often hostile world.

It is twinning that constitutes the Maya cosmos and the Maya who live within it. For thousands of years the Maya have recognized the two ears of maize-growing on a single cane as the heads and faces of the hero twins come back to life in their *milpas* (cyclically cultivated corn fields), making their presence a ubiquitous fact of nature encountered on earth. These plant-twins, who are both the Lords of Maize—and the replacements of those lords by the "heads" of maize—make the hero twins a vital rather than a remote myth. Through them, the ancestors inhabit the sacred landscape that still feeds and gives meaning to Maya lives. For the Traditional Maya, the hero twins and their sacred histories—doubling and duplicating the past, present, and future—are the very center of their ancient religion. Twinship appears everywhere in the Maya world, creating the balanced, complementary relationships that ensure survival.

I will tell an abbreviated version of the story of the hero twins Junajpu and XB'alamkiej as it is found in the *Popol Wuj*, which, among other things, means not telling it in chronological order. I have done this for both didactic and interpretive purposes, especially for those who are not already familiar with this sacred book of the Maya. I have also allowed the twins to speak for themselves, "one" coming out and just saying it while letting the "other" comes around to fill in where necessary. The use of "one" and the "other" is how the twins might be conceived: "one" is Junajpu, while the "other" is his brother XB'alamkiej. These two often physically act as one, even when spiritually acting as two, in a story where Junajpu acts out his will as the "one" while his twin, XB'alamkiej, shadows his actions as the "other."[3] Junajpu is the agent of mischievous heroics, while XB'alamkiej is the agent of rescue and salvation. The two work together ordering the world while at the same time striving to transform themselves into the guardians of their ancestor's world by both day and night as the sun and moon.

Junajpu and XB'alamkiej always work in a collaborative way: there is the "one" with the exteriorized voice and the "other" with the internalized reflective mind to temper the voice; there is the daring and adventurous "one" and the protective "other" who defends before renegotiating their way; there is the "one" who acts without thinking and the "other" who thinks without acting; there is the "one" that is playful and the "other" that is guarded and circumspect; "one" who is the radiant persona and the "other," the misty shadow; "one" who is the overzealous trickster, hungry for all that life offers and the "other," that trickster's animal transform who suffers because of his twin's insatiable appetite; "one" who is the spirit of the diurnal sun and the "other," the essence of the nocturnal moon; "one" who is likened to fire and the "other" to water; "one" who is the sacrificed and the "other" who is he who sacrifices; "one" is the hunter and the "other" the hunted; "one" who is "civilized" (Tolteca) and the "other" who is "wild" (Chichimeca). *The two together nevertheless create the one.* This is what forms and shapes the perfected "replacements" or *k'exel* of ancestors and their sacred lineage in which "civilized" is balanced by "wild," creating a perfectly integrated being known as a *Tolteca-Chichimeca*, a cultural entity of the Post-Classic world. It is from this integration that our present-day version of the *Popol Wuj* originates. The twins come together to cooperate with one another, bringing equilibrium through their contradictory nature. The resulting integration of opposites transforms a world or "sky-earth" that yearns to be put in order by the heroic actions of Junajpu and XB'alamkiej. The story of the *Popol Wuj* is one of continual balancing and harmonizing of the twin powers, primordial and complementary natures existing in the world as twin brothers who act as one to order their world.

The doubling or twinning of the hero manifests the Mesoamerican idea that individuals are created from a duality, two beings in one person: the self and the "other" or *nahual*, best thought of as a "spirit or soul guide." According to Traditional Maya and most Mesoamericans, human beings have an inner guide or *cuate* that manifests as a "double" or "twin." This "twin" or *cuate* is able to transform in order to help or protect a person throughout life in a world fraught with challenge and danger. The *coatl nahualli* or "twin transform"[4] is the manifestation of the "other" who acts in the archetypal ways of the ancestral animal transforms. These *cuates* act as the hero twins once acted, ensuring an ordered world within the surrounding chaos of wild nature reigned over by the Great Mother, in the form of highly predatory animals like the ever-hungry macaw, puma, jaguar, or caiman. Traditionally, a person's *cuate* or *nahual* transformed according to the situation in which one found oneself. The more powerful the shaman or transforming being, the more powerful and diverse were his or her manifestations. These transforming beings or *nahuales* took on animal or plant forms, as well as aspects of nature like the night-wind or whirlwind; rain and mist; lightning and thunder; or even the heavy sky that puts the watchman asleep at one's passing through some impenetrable gate. Sometimes it was a bee or butterfly, at other times a hummingbird or yellowjacket, a bunch of grass or a bridge over a river. Simply put, the *nahual* could transform into whatever was needed to get the job done.

The Classic Maya also had a term for this transforming spirit: *way*. Today this refers to the transformation of grains of maize into sustenance or *way*, which can take the form of either *tortillas* or *tamalitos*. The words *nagual*, *nahual*, and *nawal* have been used in the Maya area perhaps ever since the Northern Mesoamericans from Central Mexico came down to build their own temples and cities on the South Coast of Guatemala, greatly influencing the Maya who lived all around them. These people from the Teotihuacan culture were nobles or *pipiles* who continued to live in Guatemala in various periods, forms, and phases all the way up to the Spanish invasion. The language they spoke was Nahuat, from which the word *nahual* may originate. What scholars call "the Maya area" was highly influenced by Northern Mesoamerican cultures whose emissaries lived among the Maya and spoke either Nahuat or Nahuatl among themselves. In the Post-Classic period Nahuatl was the common language of the court, temple, and marketplace, thus influencing the Maya language with words and concepts like the ubiquitous term *nahual*, used to define a twinned spirit that guides and protects its human counterpart as both an inner intuitive voice and an outer transformative guide. The hero twins of *Popol Wuj* are great transformers; they use their transformative magic to change the world forever. As the hero twins say to the two seers Xulu and Pacam, thereby tricking the Lords of Xibalba into killing and thereby resurrecting them,

> This is a good death for them, and it would also be good to grind their bones on a stone, just as corn is refined to flour, and refine them separately, and then:
>   *"Spill them into the river,*
>   *sprinkle them on the water's way,*
>   *among the mountains, small and great,"*
> you will say, and then you will have carried out the instructions we've named for you,
>   said little Hunahpú and Xbalanqué.
> When they gave these instructions they already knew they would die.[5]

Coatl nahualli or "Twinned Double"

The psychospiritual phenomenon of the *coatl nahualli* or "twinned double" among Mesoamericans created a need for myths in which both the heroes and their rival were twinned. This grew out of their chronic use of a "double" or "other" to overcome and destroy their enemies. This undoubtedly originates from a world of hunter-gatherers who survived by deceiving both prey and predator in their shared landscape. In a hungry world of "eat or be eaten," it was imperative that one's "twin" was there to protect one's back while in quest for one's sustenance. In a world where human beings were shadowed or mirrored by their "twin," it was inevitable that the Maya should create sacred histories that reified the idea of the "twin" or *nahualli* on whom one could always count, especially in life-threatening danger. Thus it seems clear that the concept of the "double" or "twin" in Maya myth and religion is as much about an individual having an "other" as it is about two supernatural brothers who collaborate with one another in order to create a world of their own making and liking.

Tricksters make the world. The twins Junajpu and XB'alamkiej are tricksters who make a world ready made for the maize-growing people known in this story as the Maya K'iche'. They will offer their ancestors, the hero twins, worship and sacrifice for the heroic deeds they performed *in illo tempore* in order to prepare the way. The hero twins walked the path of their ancestors and improved on their efforts—until they themselves walked into the sky as brother sun and sister moon. The complementary powers of male and female inherent to the twins enabled them to defeat the Lords of Death in the underworld known as Xibalba. The story of the hero twins forms the central pillar of the sacred history of the Maya known as the *Popol Wuj*. That pillar might be thought of as two trees perfectly entwined around one another, an ancestral tree whose roots reach into the underworld and whose limbs branch out into the heavens.[6] The *Popol Wuj* is not just a story of the K'iche' Maya. It is an ancient story they used to substantiate their claim of being an original and ancient people who are the rightful lords of the K'iche kingdom.

The hero twins' story is the oldest Mesoamerican narrative that exists that is completely intact. It was likely told even before the people we know as the Maya existed as a people; we find what appear to be aspects of it on the Itzapan stela in Chiapas that predate the formative Maya period. The Mayan sacred cycle of maize pairs the hero twins' life and death struggle for survival with the ordeal of their mirroring enemies, the twins known as "One" and "Seven Death," also called "the Lords of Death."

The *Popol Wuj* as a Sacred History of Twinned Divinity

The *Popol Wuj*, the sacred history of the K'iche Maya, articulates the religious deep structure of the Traditional Maya. It is told in sometimes rhyming, and always complementary couplets, where duality seeks out complementary unity. It manifests the nature of opposites found in life and death, fire and water, male and female, above and below, dry and wet, sky and earth—pairs that are in constant flux as they move in and out of equilibrium. Not all the couplets rhyme, but similar to parallelism in the Hebrew Bible, they fill one another out as two "takes" on a given idea, creating a deeper or more complete reflection of the sentiment or idea being expressed: "So this is why monkeys look like people: they are a sign of a previous human work, human design—mere manikins, mere woodcarvings."[7]

In other words, the Maya used twinned words or phrases to elaborate on concepts and feelings that could not easily be expressed by a single word or phrase. This twinning of sacred speech, emblematic of the poetic style of ancient America, manifests the *Popol Wuj*'s importance as a sacred history of the ancient world. Contemplation of the *Popol Wuj*'s twinned poetics invokes an ancient American world that was itself twinned from its inception with the separation of the sky and earth. The knowledge and wisdom expressed in and through the complementary couplets manifest the twinned way the Maya still think and act. The goal is to attain perfection in a world that seeks balance through mirrored reflection. The archetypal ways in which the hero twins speak and act teach the way human beings should speak and act as did their divine ancestors, thereby becoming their replacements and experiencing divinity itself.

It is in the stories of the twins that the ancestors are remembered; by doing this, one enters the world that formed and shaped Maya lives. The essential goal of the *Popol Wuj* is to teach how a human being must reflect and even repeat both the speech and the action of the ancestors, *in order to become their living replacements.* The sacred speech that forms the complementary verses of the *Popol Wuj* is the perfected speech of the twinned, paired ancestors. For the K'iche' Maya, the paradigmatic actions of its characters demonstrate both the way to be and the way not to be.

And here their father is put back together by them.

They put Seven Hunahpu back together;
they went to the Place of Ball Game Sacrifice to put him together.[8]

Careful reading of the sacred history's plot makes clear that the hero twins never make assumptions about the speech or actions of others. They respond to the world just as it is, with nothing added. They never complain or wish their circumstances were different: it is as it is. Instead of reacting to others, they act and speak according to the revelations and insights that come to them as reflections from the dual-named supreme deity, Heart of the Sky, Heart of the Earth. They remain attentive to all that happens around them, while acting as though everything that befalls them is for some divine reason, one that always has the potential to catalyze their achievement of divine destiny.

Junajpu and XB'alamkiej always speak their truth, even if they are forced to lie to conquer others. They always do their best and are honest with one another. The twins do not judge others, even while cunningly eliminating those who make themselves obstacles on the path of their divine calling. They never blame a single soul for their difficult predicament in life, instead working ceaselessly to overcome the obstacles that bar them from their goal. Furthermore, they never take the suffering caused them by others personally. Instead, from their difficult birth on earth until their apotheosis in the sky, the twins use their enemies' ill-will and cruel ways to make themselves ever stronger. *They reverse their enemies' malevolence and use it in contradictory ways* as the path to their own perfection, and eventually, to the transformation of the whole world. This ironic way of the twins is played out beautifully throughout the text of the *Popol Wuj*.

The hearer of this sacred tale, annually enacted, was thus reflexively included in the twins' arduous journey. As is usually the case in ritual performance of a core cultural history, the actors had the benefit of their audience knowing the story well, thus enabling them to play up the suffering of the twins. The ironies of the heroic life and its great reversals come through with wit, intelligence, and parody. The twins are the victors in the end—but that isn't the way they start out in a world that seems, at first, completely against them. The Maya loved paradox, contradiction, and irony, just as they venerated those who came from nothing to rise up to glory. This, ultimately, is what the story of the Maya hero twins is all about.

The end is the beginning and the beginning the end, or so it seems in the life of the Maya who lived life as a never-ending cycle that eternally returns to life from death, as do the first set of twins One Junajpu and Seven Junajpu. The names of the First Fathers, One and Seven Junajpu, suggest the beginning and ending of a calendar cycle—these represent the "day-names" that begin and end a 260-day life cycle of maize. These primordial twins are the embodiment of the ancestors of the maize-growing people. It is their seed-like essence, contained in their bones, that their sons bring back to life on the face of the earth after rescuing these precious bones from the Lords of Death. Thus the hero twins renew the world and regenerate life. These reanimated bones will be the spiritual and physical sustenance of their people.[9]

Junajpu and XB'alamkiej are born into the world to attain the perfection that will enable them to renew the world. By liberating the souls of their fathers, held captive in the underworld, the hero twins liberate themselves from their human forms to become the Sun and the Moon (or in some versions, the Sun and Venus). The journey of the First Fathers is the ordeal of the life cycle of maize. Their sons are the protectors and nurturers of that sacred seed and its hallowed cycle of life, death, and rebirth. As descendants of their two sets of twinned heroes, the Maya re-enact this myth in its performance, and through their sacred work of cultivation when they plant the seed-skulls of the ancestors in their *milpas* at the end of the dry season. Through humanity's archetypal actions, time is regenerated and the world renewed. When all is done just right, the first rains fall and the green mantle returns. In this way life's eternal return is revitalized by human custom, ritual performance, and nature's cycles.

The *Popol Wuj* was more than likely performed in the warm clear nights at the end of the dry season when maize was planted during the day; the sacred histories that informed these plantings may have been played out at night. It was at this time of year that young Mayan men were initiated into the rites of passage that separated them from their mother's and grandmother's world, binding and knotting them to their father's and grandfather's world. Through the story of the hero twins, young men died to their mothers in order to be reborn to their fathers, re-creating in them the mind of the ancients. The hero twins' story was the reflective mirror, *lemo*, "The Light that Came from Beside the Sea," in which the Maya contemplated their existence on earth;

reflecting the starry nighttime sky that told the story of the *Popol Wuj* throughout the clear dry season nights. Dew dripped from the sky throughout the night at the threshold of time between the dry and wet seasons of the year. The transforming face of the renewed earth was complemented and informed by the hero twin's sacred history, as the maize sprouted forth from the "turtle carapace earth" as the Maya called it.

This "world" or "Sky-Earth" is a twinned creation formed from a primal duality in which the above is reflected by the below; the face of the earth being a reflection of both the sky and the underworld. It is this mirrored reflection that creates a unified "Sky-Earth" or "Kajulew" in constant flux and transformation in which the hero twins Junajpu and XB'alamkiej are at the very center of creation, destruction, and recreation. For the Maya, the sky reflects what happened on earth both night and day. The hero twins became the sun and the moon. To know their story enables those of knowledge to divine the future of the Sky-Earth.[10] To know the movements of the sky was and remains the key to knowing what had to happen on earth. To know the cycles of the sun, moon, and stars was and is the key to outmaneuvering the Lords of the Death who reigned over the underworld: Xibalba, Place of Fear, Place of Ordeal.[11] The primordial twinning, pairing, and coupling of the Sky-Earth, shadowed by the deities of the underworld, was the foundation upon which all forms of twinning, pairing, and coupling were rooted in the Maya cosmos. The sacred count of days that makes up the divinatory calendar was simply the twin of the sacred history told in the *Popol Wuj*.[12] Each day told part of the ancestors' story.

The actions of the *Popol Wuj*'s heroes are always performed in twos, as if the twins were united in a world where it takes two to defeat the forces of the enemy who wish to control both sky and earth through self-inflation, ill-will, and trickery. As do other culture heroes, the twins of the *Popol Wuj* must conquer the natural forces that come to life as personified "supranatural giants" before their descendants are able to take their place on the stage of the human drama played out on the face of the earth.[13] In the Mayan tradition, the destruction and dismemberment of these malevolent forces of nature prepare the way for the dawning of the present "age" or "sun." Among other things, *The Popol Wuj* is a sacred history that tells of the progressive transformations of life on earth through the "suns" that lead up to the time of humanity when the "People of Maize," *Ixim Winaq*, reign over the "Sky-Earth" and its "Mountain-Plain." The hero twins order the world and open the road for the maize-cultivating people known as the Maya K'iche.'[14]

Origins: The Hero Twins are the "Boys" of Mothers and Grandmothers

In the beginning there was just the great water of the great sea mirrored in the great sky. There was no movement, no wind, no inspiration, and then the "Heart of the Sky, Heart of the Earth" (*RK'ux Kaj*, *RK'ux Ulew*) thought and reflected before realizing it would be good to create beings who could give their "Former" and "Shaper" (*Tz'aqol*, *Bitol*) praise by remembering them through prayer, worshipping them through ritual, and nurturing them through sacrifice. The Sky-Water separated and the Earth appeared as the four-sided and four-cornered world rose and stood up sustained by the four pillars at the four corners of the sky and earth. This creation was called *Kajulew* or "Sky-Earth." The Former and Shaper were invoked by the one supreme being known as "Heart of the Earth, Heart of the Sky" who called out to them to create all that was to inhabit the world. And so it was that the Former and Shaper invoked and enchanted the creation of the Sky-Earth and all that lived upon it. The names of all things were called out, and just like that the world was covered with the "Mountain-Plain," *Juyub'-Taq'aaj'* with all the many beings that existed upon it.

The Former and Shaper created the rocks, trees, plants, and animals, but none could give them praise; none could remember the sacred names of their creator. So the Creator Couple formed and shaped human beings from wet clay, but those beings of earth just fell apart in the rain. And so their creators destroyed them before transforming them into the animals of the forest. Then the creators carved and sculpted human beings from the soft wood of the talking tree, Tz'ite by name, but those beings could only squawk and grunt like the animals which was no good for those who wished to be praised, worshipped, and offered sacrifice. So the Former and Shaper called out to the dogs and turkeys, cooking pots and utensils as well as the wooden people's tools to rise up against the failed wooden beings destroying them one and all. The creator couple reflected on their human creation and its destruction before returning to their creative work with the divine desire to create a perfect human being and the divine will to get it right. Aspects and remnants of their previous creations would remain on the face of the earth in a story where creative acts always result in something being destroyed and discarded, only ironically to return to power in contradictory ways.[15]

Before long there was an Ancestral Couple by the name of Grandmother and Grandfather, Xmukane and Xpiayakok, who divined and prayed for the next inspired idea and divine inspiration to enter their minds from the "Heart of the Sky, Heart of the Earth." And before they knew it the creator couple begot and bore into this world the First Fathers, One Junajpu and Seven Junajpu. This primordial couple created the pattern for all subsequent pairs, couples, and twins that run throughout the sacred history of the *Popol Wuj*: they collaborate with one another to create a better world. It will be their grandsons Junajpu and XB'alamkiej who will bring the divine will of "Heart of the Sky, Heart of the Earth's" to fruition with each of their creative thoughts and inspired actions on the earth and in the underworld. It will be by cooperating with one other that they will bring their lives to fruition before ascending into the Heart of the Sky as the sun and moon. It is by bringing the contradiction of opposites together to complement one another that the past is destroyed in order that the world be made anew.

The Ancient Couple are invoked by paired names throughout the *Popol Wuj* like Junajpu Coyote and Junajpu Opossum, Bearer and Begetter, White Coatimundi and White Peccary.[16] These are the names of trickster's animal familiar, their *coatl nahualli*. Their names identify them as tricksters as well as the root lineage of the K'iche people, a trickster people capable of endless transformations. Xpiayakok and Xmukane are deities who manifest the primordial separation of unity into a male-female duality in constant flux for they transform according to their needs as tricksters with changing skins.[17] They are known till this very day as Mother-Fathers or Chuch-Qajaw who are Maya diviners and day-keepers, calendar priests and priestesses. These Mother-Fathers are called by the ancestors to the sacred work of finding their people's way back to health and happiness as well as to their calling and its success. Chuch-Qajaw are formed themselves from the opposite gender that complements their physical gender from within in a balanced and harmonious way. Maya K'iche' spiritual guides, healers, and diviners know themselves as being made up of twinned male and female aspects from the inside out: spiritually powerful women have a pronounced male side, just as spiritually powerful men are guided by a strong female voice and intuition from within. These Mother-Fathers follow the exemplary pattern of the Ancient Couple.[18] This ancient couple Xmukane and Xpiayakok[19] remain the primordial archetypes of diviners and day-keepers, healers and soul guides, and mid-wives and matchmakers who are bound to the world and twinned from within like the ancestors whose path they follow. Those who are called to the sacred arts of healing and divination must bring their own "twin" into balance with their "persona," just as this ancestral couple exemplify by their archetypal way of coupling themselves as opposites with the goal of achieving equanimity that brings wisdom and strength, transformation and abundance to life.[20]

The Ancient Couple, Xpiayakok and Xmukane, begot and bore the First Fathers of the Maize People, and it is they who begin the sacred lineage of the hero twins. These First Fathers, One and Seven Junajpu, or One and Seven Blowgun Man were flawed in that they were unable to listen to their inner voice. They can't reflect on themselves or the past. They don't have the quality of the moon and night where reflection and introspection take place. They are influenced by the sun and its movement across the earth. Like the sun, they repeat what they know even if it kills them. They do not awaken to the divine intuition that is sent to guide them as revelation from the "Heart of the Sky" known as "One Foot One," *Jun Raqan*, or Hurricane. These First Fathers are sound asleep in the womb of the Great Mother. They pay for their inability to detach and differentiate themselves from the Uroboros by being caught off guard in the underworld before having the seed of their spirit imprisoned in the form of a gourd-skull on the fork of a calabash tree at the center and pivot of the underworld. The story of the hero twins is all about waking up to one's inner voice and "spirit guide" or *nahual* twin, before taking control of destiny by following one's calling. It is the hero twins who break away from their "Grandmother" and "Mother's" world to create a world of the male hero for the good of the budding patriarchy whose free will take them wandering through the world before finding a nice place to call their own in order to make a life of their own.[21]

Three Sets of Twins

The concept of "hero twins" found in the *Popol Wuj* arises from three different sets of twins that stem from one single sacred lineage, which in turn unfolds from the very first invocations of the *Popol Wuj* and actions of the "Former" and "Shaper" (*Tz'aqol,*

Bitol) with the primordial separation of Sky and Water from which rises the Earth. Ancestral Grandfather and Grandmother come into existence and from them are born the First Fathers: Jun Junajpu and Wuqub' Junajpu, "One Blowgun Man" and "Seven Blowgun Man." This set of twins lives as happy as can be in the preconscious and unreflective world of their Grandmother Xmukane. Mostly they play the rubber ball game whenever they get the chance.[22] It is on the ball court that these joyful earth-dwellers evoke the wrath of the Lords of the Underworld, who are irritated by the ball playing of One Junajpu and Seven Junajpu. They are the first set of twins whose life essence remains only in their bones, buried in the Underworld of Xibalba. These First Fathers fail the trials visited upon them by the Lords of Xibalba with their mirroring names, "One Death" and "Seven Death," and must be saved from eternal oblivion—the awful negation of being forgotten upon the earth—by their heroic offspring, the hero twins, Junajpu and XB'alamkiej.[23]

The people of maize live a carefree existence on the face of the earth creating their destinies as artists and musicians, singers and dancers, painters and writers, hunters and birds, planters and nurturers of their sacred *milpas*. These blissful beings who live as contented families are symbolized by the second set of twins, One Monkey and One Artisan, sons of Jun Junajpu and the first mother White Egret Woman is of the waterside. They are taught by their father and uncle to be scribes, singers, flautists, and workers of jade and metal.

The third set of twins are the children of the second mother Blood Maiden, of the underworld. She gave birth to Junajpu and XB'alamkiej by the spittle spat into her palm by the skull of Jun Junajpu, growing as a calabash fruit in the fork of the tree at the Place of Ball Game Sacrifice in Xibalba. Yet even that inseminating head is said by the *Popol Wuj* to be "the head of [Jun] and Seven [Junajpu]—they were of one mind when they did it."[24]

It is the third pair of twins, Junajpu and XB'alamkiej, who are the "real" hero twins in this Maya epic of creation and destruction, order and chaos, domination and reversal, life, death and rebirth.[25] The enemy twins, One Death and Seven Death, along with six other paired—"twinned"—Lords of the Underworld, humiliate and subjugate humanity through death and disease, accidents and contingencies of the road. Xibalba is a place of deathly extremes, populated by evil-minded beings who live like hungry ghosts off the warm-blooded people of maize. Living on the face of the earth, they are the natural prey of the Xibalba and its hungry beings, all of which is a mirrored image of the transforming nighttime sky. These death-dealing Lords annihilate their enemies, then enslave their captive souls in order parasitically to nourish themselves. It takes all the cunning and trickery the hero twins possess to overcome these malevolent beings and their wicked ways.

Junajpu and XB'alamkiej conquer the Lords of Death by making their way through the trials and ordeals of the underworld before emerging victoriously on the face of the earth with their father's bones [Figure 6.1]. The hero twins conquer death and disease and revive their lineage by regenerating the life spirit of their fathers. The *Popol Wuj*, the sacred history of K'iche' Maya, has served as an inspired guide for many generations of Maya in their struggle to survive as an autonomous people. It is a story in which nomadic hunter-warriors from the north the dry and barren north

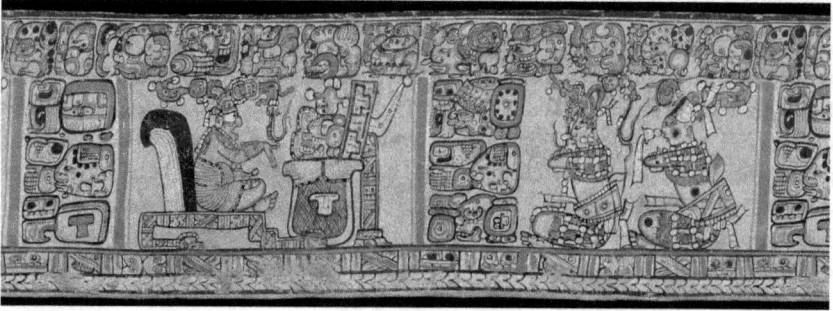

Figure 6.1 "Junajpu (Hun Ahaw) and XB'alamkiej (Yax Balam), the Hero Twins of the Popul Wuj, request Its'amnaj, a primary lord of the Underworld, to return the bones of their father, the Maize god. His bones reside in the basket in front of Its'amnaj." Late Classic Period Mayan cylinder earthenware vase, 600–750 CE. Campeche, Mexico. Museum of Fine Arts, Boston 1988.1169. Caption and image courtesy of the Museum of Fine Arts.

descended upon the Maya to live off their sedentary ways as predators and parasites since time immemorial.[26] The *Popol Wuj* can undoubtedly be read as a people's struggle to endure the dominance of an enemy people who seek to subjugate them and their sedentary maize-growing ways.[27] For thousands of years the hero twins have shown the Maya how to overcome their enemy without that enemy ever knowing they are being conquered. The K'iche' Maya have often been forced to feign being defeated as the twins do, as the opossum does, only to rise up and take back their lives and their destiny. The bones of the defeated ancestors must be gathered before placing them at the center of the altar in order to ritually bring them back to life.

Junajpu and XB'alamkiej improve on their fathers' effort to beat the lords of the underworld at their game. The heroes succeed at fulfilling their destiny for many reasons, one of which is that their mother is a moon goddess from the underworld. *By integrating the knowledge of their mother's underworld lineage, the twins come to know the underworld in ways their fathers never could.* It will be the combination of the underworld blood of their mother and that of their earthly father that will endow the twins with the mirrored powers of above and below. Through their mother Blood Maiden, who emerges like the moon from the underworld to give birth to Junajpu and XB'alamkiej, the twins are enabled to cross the threshold between two worlds, making both worlds their own.[28]

They also learn from the mistakes of their ancestors and thus improve their lot in a world informed by archetype and repetition. "As above, so below": the sun walks across the sky as the people walk across the face of the earth; the moon moves across the night sky as the animals step out of the shadows and into the moonlight. The celestial inspiration manifest in the light of the sun and shadows of the moon generate the diurnal inspiration and nocturnal intuition of the divinely inspired hero twins who become the sun and the moon at the end of their tale. It is the tears of the moon and the sweat of the sun that flow as blood through the bodies of the hero twins. The blood of their mother Xkik, Blood Maiden, mixes with the spittle of their father, Jun Junajpu, creating the supernatural heroes who live out their lives in twinship: this symbiosis is translated into the movements of the ever-transforming sun and moon, also twins unto themselves.

According to the Maya, humanity is fated to follow the movement of the celestial spheres toward preordained destiny. One must know one's calling, however, before one can be guided from above in order to bear it to fruition. And one must know the past to move knowingly in the present toward the future. It is by knowing the past that one can temper the influence it has on the present, and then move cautiously ahead in order to not repeat the mistakes of those that came before. In perhaps the inverse of modern Western views, the Maya believe that by learning from the actions and speech of the ancestors, one will succeed in a constantly changing world.

According to the *Popol Wuj*, humanity improves with the passing of the various "ages" or "suns." These ages may be "failed," but through those failures, humanity acquires valuable experiential knowledge through suffering and sacrifice. It is experience that teaches, and it is from experience that humans are able to meet life's challenges by transforming themselves and the world. The first set of twins, One Junajpu and Seven Junajpu, can't read the signs of the road, the signs of life. They can't interpret their way successfully and thus they die due to their mistaken choice of roads—leading not to rebirth and regeneration but to their own death and destruction. They venture into the underworld only to be beaten and humiliated, sacrificed, and dismembered on the ball court altar of dust and ashes at the hands of the Lords of Death. But their trickster "sons," who learn from their mistakes, bring their father's ancestral souls back to life as the sprouting maize that shoots forth from the ancestral seed buried in the fertile and fecund earth.

Twinned from Within

For Traditionalist Maya who practice and live by the Old Ways of their ancestors, the story of the hero twins, Junajpu and XB'alamkiej, informs the deep structure of their interpretive inner world. The life ways and heroic deeds of the twins provide meaning and understanding to the signs that the Traditionalist Maya receive from the natural world—signs that must be interpreted from within the person. In Mayan cosmology, the lived human world is a mirrored image, reflecting what one experiences from the inside out as well as from the outside in. The ancestors reveal themselves in nocturnal dreams and diurnal insights, as well as in the signs they give through nature: a hovering butterfly, a mischievous hummingbird, a strange leaf floating in the wind, the sudden shake and quake of a tremor, or a just an unusual wind. This outer revelation of inner knowing creates a very lively existence for those spiritual workers who are chosen to follow the path of the ancients in the footsteps of the hero twins. These ways are as much about learning from the past as they are being ingenious and inventive in the present.

Traditional Maya believe each individual is a "twin" unto themselves. They know that they live in a world of imperfection; but by acting and speaking as the ancestors once did, one can live a life of perfection. *It takes being aware of the two sides of one's being to live as a twin of one's self.* One of the two sides is the persona of masked appearances who must be willing to deceive in a world of deception; lie in a world of liars; take in a world of takers; and change face in a world of constant change.[29] The second side is the intuitive and feeling "other" that lives within as a *nahual* twin, a transforming "other." The *nahual* acts as one's "soul guide," leading one through this world and the Santo Mundo, or Spirit World, a world that mirrors the phenomenal world. Like the Platonic *daimon* or the Manichaean *syzygos*, the *nahual* guides, protects, and nurtures as an inner voice that shows one the way on the path of life both night and day, in waking conscious and in the dream world. For the Traditional Maya these twin worlds intersect at sacred places in sacred moments when the "wholly other" of the sacred world crosses the threshold to enter the world of natural phenomena.[30] In and out of these worlds the hero twins, Junajpu and XB'alamkiej, move like fish at home in the water, like birds at home in the sky, like animals at home in the mountains, like magicians at home in the world. In their extremity, tricksters cross these boundaries at will as they seek to redefine the limits of human existence. Many of humanity's transformations began with people getting themselves seriously injured or killed trying to do what their ancestors would have never attempted—but which, once achieved by those who survived, all of their descendants would learn to do in time. No normal person wants to do something that has never been done before. This is exactly why tricksters are not normal at all, as many of my readers must know very well themselves.

Let us turn to the story of the *Popol Wuj* and enter upon the road of the twins and their quest to prepare the world for the coming of the maize-growing people. To know the story of the hero twins is to know the ways of the Traditional Maya, to follow their ways is to learn how to be a divine being, a Nawal, born to transform the world through repeating the words and deeds of the ancestral twins, Junajpu and XB'alamkiej. It is my prayer that the Maya will see beyond the demonizing ways that foreigners have taught them, so that they might return to their ancestors' spiritual path where twins showed one the way.

Junajpu and XB'alamkiej

The literal translation of Junajpub' or Junajpu is "One Man of the Blowgun." The verb *pubaj* means to "blowgun" that is to say hunt with a blowgun. *Jun* means "One." A person who uses a blowgun is an AjPub' or AjPu, a person who uses a blowgun. It is the blowgun and the blow-gunning that gives this ancestor his identity. Both names, Junajpu and Junajpub', are found in different translations of the *Popol Wuj*.[31] It is Junajpu's use of the blowgun that makes him a magician who becomes a trickster that ends up a hero of his people. XB'alamkiej as the *nahualli* twin of his brother Junajpub' is the "Lord of the Animals." It is XB'alamkiej as "Lord of the Animals" that walks alongside his brother Junajpu the "Hunter." The two of them shoulder their blowguns before wandering off into world of endless challenges and opportunities, all of which are faced by the twins with their blowguns. The hero twins are blowgun boys who become blowgun men that use their blowguns to survive in a world replete with predator and prey.[32] Sometimes Junajpu is the hunter and XB'alamkiej is the hunted; at other times Junajpu is the prey and XB'alamkiej the predator. The hunter must know the hunted, and the hunted must know the hunter in a world informed by nature's struggle for dominance and survival.

The name Ixbalamkiej-XB'alamkiej means "she-he" of the Jaguar-Deer. XB'alamkiej balances Junajpu's maleness with a feline feminine energy. The use of the prefix "X" indicates that this being is at essence female in nature. The *Popol Wuj* is a study of Maya gender, teaching us there was no clear gender boundary in a world filled with beings in constant transformation between male and female aspects of self. XB'alamkiej is a transforming being that balances the energy of his or her twin Junajpu, who acts in an almost hyper-masculine way. This complementing of opposites also manifests itself on an individual level when and where men and women must balance themselves through the knowledge of their "other side," or their "twin," that brings the soul and spirit, body and mind into balance, giving them the powers of healing and divination, knowledge and wisdom, sacrifice and survival in an eternal return of the never-ending cycle of life, death, and rebirth.

XB'alamkiej is the Lord of the Animals, symbolized by a combination-type name formed out of Jaguar-Balam and Deer-Kiej. XB'alamkiej is the animal guide of Junajpu the exemplary hunter. XB'alamkiej is the "Lord of the Animals," just as Junajpu is the "Lord of the Hunters." XB'alamkiej is the paradigmatic "animal transform" or *nahual* of his brother the hunter who must be intimately tied to the hunted. The jaguar's hunger/love for the deer balances the deer's hunger/love for maize. Man's hunger/love for maize necessitates the control of nature through feeding the jaguar-sun and the deer-earth with the hearts and blood of human sacrifice. It is XB'alamkiej who will originate both human and animal sacrifice by creating ritual sacrifice through his exemplary actions on the face of the earth and in the underworld. Thus the natural cycles of the Sky-Earth will be fed in an ordered way so that human beings created from maize can multiply and prosper on the fertile moist earth under the nurturing wet sun. It is the dance of the Jaguar-Deer that controls the movement of the wind, sun, breeze, pollination, and rain on earth. XB'alamkiej embodies this movement just as the jaguar and deer create it through their hunger and love for that which sustains them.

Junajpu's twin brother XB'alamkiej is the opposite of his elder brother, which makes them complements of one another. If they were identical to one another, they would be rivals but they are not, nor are they equals. It is their complementary ways that lead to the collaboration that comes to fruition in their victory over their enemy, the redemption of their fathers and the transformation of themselves into celestial beings that return to the Heart of the Sky. By reflecting on these two Maya heroes' names and their births, one is able to understand a great deal about sacred twinning in the Maya world, where hunger and sustenance are the reasons for the progressive transformations of life on the ever-changing face of the earth.[33]

The Transformation of Junajpu and XB'alamkiej

Junajpu and XB'alamkiej face the Lords of Death with the knowledge of their father's experience in the underworld. Remember the First Fathers, One Junajpu and Seven

Junajpu, were summoned on the face of the earth by the owl messengers to play ball in the underworld by the Lords of Death. It seems they disturb the dead with all the noise they make in both worlds. It doesn't go well for the First Fathers who were sacrificed by the Lords of Death on the underworld ball court known as the *puqub'al chaaj*, "the dusty place of ashes" in Xibalba.[34] These first blowgun men, One and Seven Junajpu by name, make the mistake of taking the Black Road when they enter Xibalba. This road leads to darkness and death. They should have taken the center road, the Green Road that leads to rebirth, as is in the green sprout of maize that shoots forth from its burial place in the underworld. After making the mistake of stepping into the underworld on to the Black Road the First Fathers, One Junajpu and Seven Junajpu, continue on their way making mistake after mistake until they end up with their decapitated heads placed in the fork of the calabash tree. Their mistakes are instructive as they teach the way not to be.[35]

The magical skulls of One Junajpu and Seven Junajpu radiate a mysterious life force. This is the same latent essence of life that resides in seeds that only come to life once they've come in contact with the ground. It is this spark of life that emanate from the twins' skulls that come to life on the calabash tree. The Lords of Xibalba forbid all those of the underworld to go near these mysterious skull-like fruit. The beautiful maiden, Xkik', "Blood Maiden," the young moon goddess, cannot resist the temptation to "know the face of this beautiful fruit" of this mystifying tree. So she approaches the tree, and the skull tells her to come closer so he can show her his essence. This speaking skull convinces Blood Maiden to reach out her hand into which he spits his spittle. Without realizing what's happened, Blood Maiden is pregnant with the replacements of the First Fathers. The ancestor's essence has found a way to return to the world. Blood Maiden bears the fruit of this most miraculous conception in her womb, the sons of the First Fathers, the hero twins Junajpu and XB'alamkiej.

The birth of the hero twins Junajpu and XB'alamkiej is perfectly magical. They are said to just appear in the mountains. Xkik', Blood Maiden, is an underworld woman; there is nothing that she cannot endure and her twin boys will be just like her: tough and ingenious, enduring and self-reliant. The twins are grateful for what little they receive in a life in which they have plenty to complain about but never do. They follow closely in their mother's footsteps, enduring all kinds of suffering and humiliation. It is from the experience of suffering and sacrifice that they learn the most important lessons of life.

It is through their quest to know the face of their father that they become great "knowers" and "magicians" just like their elder brothers the monkey twins, with whom they share the home of their father.[36] The moment Junajpu and XB'alamkiej enter the house of their father, they face the envy and resentment of the twin boys who are already living there contentedly with their Grandmother, Xmukane. These twins, One Monkey and One Artisan, are not happy that their father has engendered two more sons, twins like themselves, and the "monkey twins" cause their rival siblings to suffer for the annoyance that they are what for them is a perfect life. The monkey twins are spoiled by their grandmother and free from the strictures and corrections of their fathers whose souls are imprisoned in the underworld as gourds on the calabash tree. The hero twins escape from life in grandmother's house and find freedom in the mountain and forest places of their fathers.[37]

Junajpu and XB'alamkiej grow up like wild boys, born out of the womb-cave of the underworld, to wander through their father's mountains, hunting with their blowguns and living in wilderness surrounded by the perfection of nature.[38] The cultured and artistic world of Grandmother's household is an unfriendly place, tarnished with the iniquitous hierarchy of the "courtyard" that always seem to lead to social and cultural decay. The wild world of the young hunters, on the other hand, is filled with the vibrant potential of a new order in a world transformed by the genius and longing of the hungry young newcomers. The hero twins will bring a naturally pure sense of justice home from the wilderness when they come of age; it will be the hierarchy of the young hunters that will replace that of their envious elder brothers, ruined by their overprotective and overpowering grandmother. The elder monkey and artisan twins lack the guidance of their fathers. They are uneducated in the sense that they don't take care of their younger brothers. They are ignorant of what it takes to be men who bear the burden of their lineage. Their lack of human education creates a type of ignorance that will cost them dearly. But their ways of being is powerful way of teaching those who come after them how to treat those who are in need of a protective and nurturing hand. The *Popol Wuj* teaches one what it takes to be a "human being" and those who don't have what it takes are quickly transformed into animals.

When Junajpu and XB'alamkiej are brought into their grandmother's house, it is the last time we hear of their mother, Xkik. Her boys, the hero twins, grow up as if they were "orphans, outcasts or slaves."[39] The artisan twins and their grandmother can't be bothered by the "boys" who cry out for care and attention. Grandmother tells the monkey twin to "just take them out of here; they really are loud-mouthed these two." One Monkey and One Artisan take their little twin brothers outside and set them on an ant pile hoping for their sibling's death. The text says that the elder brothers wished only that the twins would die right there, but they don't. So when it comes time to take them outside again the elder twins place their rivals on the spines of the wild blackberry brambles. But Junajpu and XB'alamkiej don't die there either. As they say, what doesn't kill you will only make you stronger. And with that in mind Junajpu and XB'alamkiej become stronger and stronger.[40]

It had cost One Monkey and One Artisan great suffering to become great knowers and they didn't want to give up their prized position in their father's house to their newly arrived younger twin brothers, Junajpu and XB'alamkiej. The elder twins use the younger twins as deceptively as they can, but Junajpu and XB'alamkiej see through the deception. The elder twins create rivalry with their younger twin brothers that will give cause for the artisans to lose their humanity and their grandmother's contentment. The older boys could have been nicer, but they weren't and for that mistake they lost everything, just another lesson of how *not* to act as the failed ancestors did.

It wasn't long before Junajpu and XB'alamkiej were doing all the work around the house and hunting all the meat their Grandmother and elder brothers could eat. Junajpu and XB'alamkiej happily provided for their grandmother and her favorite grandsons with the birds they hunted with their blowguns. The twins never protest.

They never took their suffering personally and always did their best no matter what it costs them. They endure their suffering and their endurance empowers them. Junajpu and XB'alamkiej just do as they are told without ever questioning the life they have been given. They accept their destiny while praying to the Heart of the Sky, Heart of the Earth for guidance. They bide their time, hoping others will change, but when they don't, they act decisively, transforming, in order not to kill, those who become obstacles to their divine calling.

Junajpu and XB'alamkiej didn't seem to mind being treated poorly by their elder brothers, even though they go hungry because the elder twins eat up all the meat that they bring into the house.[41] The hero twins are taught the sacred arts of the Maya by their rivals right up to the day they turn those rivals into monkeys. The younger twins learn to dance and sing, play music and perform, sculpt and paint, all of which they will put to good use down the road in the underworld as they face and defeat the Lords of Death in Xibalba.

Now it was the younger twins who through great suffering had become great knowers in a world where experience taught one everything about the struggle of life on earth. In the K'iche' Maya world it is the poor and abused who become spiritually powerful. It takes living in poverty to hone one's spiritual and supernatural powers, powers that will bring about the "great reversal" when the reckoning comes. It is the hunting of the younger twins and the hunger of the elder twins that teaches one how to share life's sustenance and get along with others. According to the Maya, humans mustn't let their appetite for fame and fortune stop one from treating others with respect. It is up to those in power to show mercy for others by pitying those in need by helping them as best they can.

The destiny of the hero twins showed itself in a calling all their own. Life experience taught the growing boys that the life they were living was not for them. As the inheritance of their mixed lineages pulsed through their veins, they realized their destiny was to be found not only in the sky and earth, but in the underworld as well. They came into their own as their physical and psychological suffering brought them spiritual strength that quickly became focused on a longing to know the face of their father. They realized the path through life they were walking had been forced upon them by their dire circumstance of being boys without a father. That was not their destiny, not their calling, and it was time they did something about it.

They had tried to make their grandmother and elder brother's content without fulfilling their own calling: it was they who were born to redeem their father's "face" by recovering their bones from the underworld. The act of gathering the remains of their father as the seed of their people that would transform the world. It was the hero twins who would save their father's memory from "dying dead" by following their life's calling that led them to the underworld and their own sacrificial death and rebirth. Their destiny to reclaim the bones of Lords of Maize from which would be formed and shaped the creation of the next age of the world.[42] It is the maize seed of the Maya that continues to evoke the idea of the ancestral fathers whose twinning ways duplicates the doubling and redoubling of maize from seed to sustenance. The First Fathers are the Lords of Maize while their twin sons are the lords of every other destiny possible for humanity. Both the elder and younger set of twins offer ways of being human for the Maya, and it is they who the Traditional Maya turn to in their quest of a destiny that leads to a very specific identity.

The Destiny of the Hero Twins

Eventually Junajpu and XB'alamkiej are forced by destiny to transform their rival brothers into monkeys and send them back to the past to live as the ancestors in the trees. There is nothing their grandmother Xmukane can do but laugh at the monkey twins every time they are called in by the hero twins. It is grandmother's laughter that bars the elder twins from ever returning home again as men. With the elder brothers up in the trees and out of the way, the hero twins only need to follow the calling they so longed for. They know it is a special destiny, but they can't quite figure it out. They know their destiny will lead to the renewal and regeneration of the world so they try growing milpa as they believe they should. Since maize is their sacred sustenance they think they should become *milperos*, but they find tilling the soil is not their way. The boys suffer from self-doubt and anguish over their inability to magically control the natural world, even though they are able to get their tools to work all by themselves while they head off into the mountains doing what they do best, which is hunting with their magical blowguns.

After a few good attempts at growing maize they give up because the work they do by day is undone by the animals at night. They do their best to catch one of the culprits but fail, until finally they are able to catch the rat who tells them that growing maize is not their destiny. The twins ask the rat what their destiny is, at which point the rat tells them that they are ball players, like their fathers. They must descend into the underworld to take up the struggle of their fathers in Xibalba on the ball court of dust and ashes. It dawns on them that they must find the bones of their fathers before returning from Xibalba to the land of the living.[43] They don't know all the details, but they intuit the importance of their calling that leads them down into the underworld to fight against death for the life of their ancestors and those who descend from their sacred lineage.

With that on their minds and in their hearts the boys descend into the underworld in search of the bones of their fathers: One Junajpu and Seven Junajpu. And so it was that they took the road to Xibalba, the Place of Fear, with their blowguns balanced over their shoulders, dressed for "battle" wearing their gaming equipment with their neck guards, arm guards, and knee pads in place. This taking up the struggle of their ancestors is the essence of this sacred history as the twins teach the proper way of remembering the ancestors and their exemplary ways. At the crossroads the hero twins choose the Green Road upon which they will find a way to resurrect their father's face and thus restore to life the ancient ways of the men of maize on earth.

Once the twins enter the underworld landscape of Xibalba, the Lords of Death begin testing them in an attempt to humiliate these young heroes, who have apparently ventured onto the path of their fathers' own death and destruction. It is Junajpu and XB'alamkiej who now enter their mother's world, where their father's "essence" is held captive. The underworld blood of their mother Xkik', "Blood Women," runs through their veins as a magical transformative substance, empowering them with the ways and knowledge of the underworld. Junajpu and XB'alamkiej are blessed by a mixed lineage: half of their character comes from the land of the dead and the other half comes from the land of the living. This supernatural pair of twins is a cross of earthly maize lords and underworld lords of death, giving them the power of life over death. The twins' special nature mirrors the two different worlds they come from by reflecting the authority of both realms. They will use both the power of life and the power of death to transform first themselves and then the world.[44]

The twins know the destructive forces of rivalry, and they know the creative forces of collaboration. The hero twins demonstrate that, although rivalry might be natural, it is not the way to act if one is to create something new and lasting in this world. Junajpu and XB'alamkiej show the superior ways of those twins who work together by joining forces in order to create a more empowered whole. The collaboration of the twins is best exemplified by their heroic actions in the underworld and the cunning way they defeat the Lords of Death. It is only through collaboration that the twins succeed in bringing their lineage out of the shadows and into the light, just as it was only through collaboration that initiates survived rites of initiation that transformed them through rituals of sacrifice that ended in their own deaths and rebirth.

In the first test the twins are able to gain access to ancestral memory, magically tapped from the blood sucking spike of the mosquito, through which they are able to name the lords of the underworld, one after the other in perfect succession until they identify all six sets of the Lords of Xibalba. This is something their fathers simply could not do. It is an act of knowledge borne through esoteric information that both baffles and terrifies the lords of the underworld. To know the names of the lords of diseases was the first step in defeating those diseases. To be able to identify an illness through proper diagnosis is the most assured way of curing that illness. The twins then survive the different "houses" of ordeal to the amazement and humiliation of the Lords of Death, who suddenly intuit the beginning of their own end. The house of darkness doesn't destroy the twins; the house cold doesn't freeze them; they aren't cut to pieces in the house of obsidian blades; they aren't eaten in the house of jaguars; and, the house of fire doesn't consume them either. It isn't until at dawn of the fifth night that Junajpu is decapitated by a "killer bat," *Kamatzotz,* when he sticks his head out of the neck of his blowgun to see if the dawn has come.[45]

This is the way of the twins: Junajpu loses a limb and XB'alamkiej helps him get it back. Earlier on, Junajpu loses his arm to the Great Bird Deity, Seven Macaw, and Xbalamke helps him get it back in place with the assistance of two old white-haired tricksters. These elderly magicians and healers, Pakam and Xulu, will show up again just when they are needed to help XB'alamkiej and Junajpu transform themselves at their sacrificial death on the funeral pyre. The idea is that the hero twins need the help of the elderly ancestors or *nahuales* when they can't get the job done themselves. The Maya have a strong sense of calling on the help of the elderly guides, whose material poverty is an indication of their spiritual wealth and whose age exudes the sense of ancestral wisdom and knowledge gained through experience.

The Lords of Xibalba are utterly devastated by the ways of the hero twins who pass one test after the next. This is the Lords of Xibalba's defeat but not their destruction. The hero twins deceptively give themselves up to the Lords of Death before jumping into a great bonfire in which they burn until only their ashes and bones are left. The Lords of Xibalba are tricked by the Old Curanderos, Pakam and Xulu, into grinding up the twins' bones and then having them throw the ground bones into the transformative waters of a crystalline river. This is just the genius of the boys who bring into play the skills of the ancient one's in the form of Pakam and Xulu who embody the powers of ancestral transformation. It is in the waters of life that Junajpu and XB'alamkiej transform into beautiful catfish that in turn transform back into beautiful young men in five days' time [Figure 6.2].[46]

> After that they summoned Xulu and Pacan, who kept their word: the bones went just where the boys had wanted them. Once the Xibalbans had done the divination, the bones were ground and spilled in the river, but they didn't go far—they just sank to the bottom of the water.
>
> . . . AND ON THE FIFTH DAY THEY REAPPEARED. They were seen in the water by the people. The two of them looked like [channel] catfish when their faces were seen by Xibalba.[47]

The hero twins return dancing down the road of Xibalba, disguised now as performers and dancers who act out the ancient ways by dancing the animal dances. XB'alamkiej, as Lord of Wild Animals, and Junajpu, as the Lord of the Hunt, know all the dances of their animal allies who embody the remnants beings of past ages as well as their childhood companions of the wild. Between the two of them there is not a living soul in the forest that does not fall under their dominion of knowledge. The knowledge of their "dances" is a way of showing the twins are empowered with the ways of each and every animal that live on the mountain-plain. The animals are the *nahualli* twins of human beings, to know their dance is to know their way and thus have them as an animal familiar or nahual twin who can guide and protect them. This is the true imitative magic of the hero twins, who command the world by dancing and enchanting it into what they will with their incantations and life transforming movements of

Figure 6.2 The hero twins as catfish in Xibalba. Polychrome Mayan ceramic vase, classical period. From Petén Lowlands. Princeton Art Museum 1987.65 (rollout). Kerr 5225. Courtesy Justin Kerr and the Kerr Archives.

dance. It is now their divine will that comes into full flower as they recreate the world by dancing it into being.

As the boys come down the road toward the Lords of Xibalba, performing one miraculous and astounding trick after the next, they are stopped by the Lords One and Seven Death in order that they perform their magic for them. First the twins burn a house with the Lords of Death inside without the lords being burnt and after which the house is magically put back together. Next, the twins sacrifice a dog before bringing him back to life. It is then that XB'alamkiej as the Lord of Sacrifice binds Junajpu's legs and arms behind him before cutting open his chest and ripping out his beating heart before lopping off his head. XB'alamkiej then puts his twin brother back together before bringing him back to life. This simply astounds the lords of the underworld. One and Seven Death want nothing more than to know what it is like to be sacrificed and to know death before being brought back to life. The Lords of Death ask to be sacrificed, and so they are by XB'alamkiej, but he does not bring them back to life. Thus the Lords One Death and Seven Death are destroyed once and for all by the hero twins Junajpu and XB'alamkiej.

With the formative work of the twins brought to completion, Junajpu and XB'alamkiej can ascend into the heavens. But before they do so they take dominion over the world while showing mercy toward their vanquished enemies who are given their places to live along with their water and sustenance. Now the people of the land are forced to give tribute to the K'iche lords while giving worship and providing sacrifice to the sacred K'iche' lineage, all of which is due to the heroic deeds of the hero twins, Junajpu and XB'alamkiej. Jun Junajpu's divine bones are gathered and put back together, and he rises out of Sustenance Mountain as the Maize Lord, emerging out of the back of the turtle-like earthen carapace.[48]

Sustenance Mountain is a cleft mountain known as Paxil, Broken Mountain, where the maize broke through the hardened earth to sustain the K'iche' people with the essence of life embodied by the maize seed. It is this life essence that runs through the body and blood of his sacred lineage of maize-growing people. His heart was left in the middle of the ball court of the underworld as a sign of his death that calls out for an eternal return of the sacred maize ancestor at the heart of the Maya cosmos symbolized by the ball court. Seven Junajpu is remembered as the lord of the calendar and the way to be a perfectly civilized and educated lord of the splendid city. Grandmother burned copal incense as an offering in the Middle of the House, Middle of the Ball Court, giving thanks and praise to her sons and grandsons, who fought against the enemy to open the way for the people of maize, her descendants whom she shaped and formed from ground maize with her own hands.

The Lords of Xibalba were conquered and no longer were given sacrifice or remembered in prayer by the people as the lords who reigned over the Sky-Earth. Junajpu and XB'alamkiej walked off into the sky as the Sun and Moon, and it is they who watch over the Mountain-Plain as protectors and providers, guardians and nurturers of the maize growing people know today as the Maya K'iche. [Figure 6.3]

Then they rose up in the midst of the light, and instantly they were lifted into the sky. One was given the name of the sun, the other, the moon. Then the arch of heaven and the face of the earth were lighted. And they dwelt in heaven.

Figure 6.3 The reborn Sun; same band decorations as the catfish: the three dots that identify the Hero Twins in life and in death (the *kimi* sign). Polychrome Mayan vase, classical period. Photo by Justin Kerr (K4871). Courtesy Justin Kerr and the Kerr Archives.

Two Brothers Who Lived as One

We are able to approach the mythically informed psychology of the Traditionalist Maya found in the ways of the sacred twins, Junajpu and XB'alamkiej. For it is they who teach us how the Traditionalist Maya think and act, sing and dance, speak and pray, hunt and plant as they walk the path of the ancestors in search of a life worth living. The Maya, whenever possible, work in pairs—and not just because two people working together can produce better results in less time. When one works alone it is hard to find a balance of work and enjoyment. According to the Maya, it takes two to get the job done and be contented: just as it is written in the *Popol Wuj*.

In the close to forty years I have lived among the Maya of Western Highlands of Guatemala, I have only known one set of men who "lived as twins." These men, who lived, worked, and practiced religion together, were not biological twins, but brothers who acted like twins. Their parents died when they were quite young, leaving them abandoned in this world as *meeb'a* or "orphans" to suffer fortune's slings and arrows. The unbearable experience of losing their parents as young boys created an unbreakable bond of brotherly love between them. That bond was founded on their will to survive through unquestioned collaboration with one another in a world that seemed to be against them. They complimented one another in ways that transformed their differences into advantages as they rounded out each other's rather unusual way of acting and speaking as one.

People close to them believed that their suffering and poverty empowered them spiritually, while enriching them in the *Santo Mundo* or Holy World. They had an appearance so similar it was hard to tell them apart until one came to know them better. They acted alike and unlike one another in ways that made one feel as if they each had become the mirror image of the other. They quarreled with each other almost all the time, while at the same time being bound to one another with the kind of fraternal love unique to twins. The sacred life ways of these extraordinary brothers would end with the modernizing of Maya through radical religious change and violent social and cultural upheaval.[49]

These two men were different from others and they knew it. They were destined to live extraordinary spiritual lives by being born as poor as any human on earth could be. Just as other powerful "nature priests" before them, they used their material poverty to gain spiritual wealth and empowerment. They were born with a vocation that made them the nature priests and dancers of animal skins in order to provide their people and village with "water" while protecting their "sustenance." When they were allowed to manifest their destiny and perform their vocation they entered the realm of the ancestors by performing their rituals just as the divine twins once did in the ancient past. They had no children of their own making them the perfect priests for their villages water (*ya*) and sustenance (*way*). Jesus was interpreted by the Traditionalist Maya as taking up this religious duty and it was He who had the power to multiply the bread of life as tortilla and transform water into mind-bending corn liquor. Humanity has always had priests and priestesses responsible for their people's well-being at this most fundamental level of human survival. These men I knew embodied this reality in the most fundamental way.

Men who performed their sacred duties as twins in the past were treated with great respect, because it was they who played out the Maya archetypes of elder and younger "brothers" so important to the sacred structures of Maya myth and religion, wherein twins and twinship were at the center of Mayan cosmo-magical thinking. In the case of the twins I knew, the eldest twin or Nabeysil ("First Mover" or "First Born") was the incarnation of a long lineage of Tz'utujil Maya rain-, cloud- and mist-men, while the younger was his animal companion.[50] The Nabeysil danced a very sacred Sky-Earth bundle that was revered for its power to transform the sky and thereby to control wind and rain, cloud and mist, mountain breeze and tempestuous storm. The earth reflects the transformations of the sky, and so it was with this extremely sacred bundle of Water (*Ya*) and Sustenance (*Way*) that balanced the needs of the earth with the movements of the sky and its celestial waters. The Nabeysil's brother, Salvador, nicknamed "Salvador del Mundo," was one of the principal Deer-Jaguar dancers, also known as XB'alamkiej. As the lead dancer of the town's sacred deer skins and stuffed ocelot pelts, he would run and dance through the streets leading others in a ritual that controlled the wild animals of the forest and the wind that transformed the earth. It was his movements as Lord of the Wild enchanted the animal spirits while coaxing them to leave the *milpas* for the humans and to take what was theirs on the high slopes of the volcanoes. It was his dancing the deer skins that persuaded the sun to rise and the wind to blow so the maize would grow tall, flower and fertilize itself with its golden pollen. To listen to their praying and to watch their dancing transformed one's soul, just as it changed my life. The Nabeysil and his brother, the Deer-Jaguar, were able to instantaneously transport one to another time and space, when and where humans acted as the divine twin ancestors by performing ritual, just as their Nawal ancestors once did. These two brothers were from another age and when that age came to an end, so did their reason to live.

It was in a world antagonistic to them, a town of evangelical Christians, that the brothers struggled to live out the Old Ways. They continued along the path of the ancestors by performing rituals of rain and wind, by bearing the sun across the sky, by evoking the perfect movements of the Sky-Earth with their ritual dancing and praying that invoked the ancient ones and enchanted of the lords of the Sky-Earth to provide the people with heavenly waters or life-sustaining winds and nurturing breezes. They weren't demons at all, but were demonized nevertheless. Before long they started acting in extremely demonic ways.

It still seems like a nightmare to me, the way that the people these two were destined to protect and nurture should turn against them with such hatred and heartlessness, but that is exactly what happened. Christian neighbors mocked their ancient ways and calling them witches. Before long they turned from creative sustenance to destruction, taking vengeance on people who no longer believed they needed their sacred services of ordering the fertile elements of the sky with the fecund powers of earth. The two brothers fought this war side by side until one of them finally died.

In retrospect it seems almost impossible that I came to be their companions just when the world turned violently and vindictively against them and their ancient ritual. In the past men of their position were treated as semi-divine beings or "man-gods"[51] who were supported by the town's people, just as they in turn nurtured those same people with their ritual invocation of wind and rain, sun and breeze, clouds and mist, water and sustenance. With the coming of the Pentecostals these men, and those who performed ritual with them, were demonized and treated as if they were evil incarnate. There was nothing more that the brothers could do in their minds than to drink themselves into a profoundly disturbing sense of isolation and abandonment, as if they sought to repeat their orphaned childhood once again.

Conclusion

The *Popol Wuj* affirms the lifeways of the twins as extraordinary beings who enter the category of the humanly divine. Human male twins among the Maya must have assumed positions of ritual importance, in accord with the idea that human beings replace their divine ancestors. Like the hero twins of the *Popol Wuj*, the twins I knew lived together in both the world of work and the world of ritual. In this way, they replicated the ways of the twins found in the *Popol Wuj*.

It is a blessing to be an identical twin who knows what one's twin longs for in life and can, together with her or him, follow a twinned calling. Twins who live and work together create a special bond that takes them farther down the road of life than single individuals that must go it alone. Twins have a great advantage over the rest of humanity, since their identical nature, emerging from a shared womb, enables them to double up their efforts so as to bring their lives to fruition. According to Maya myth, it is a great gift to be born a twin—and if lacking that gift, one must listen to one's inner voice as if one had an inborn twin.

The myth of the Maya hero twins teaches one to follow the divine path of the ancestors. By acting as they acted, one learns how to control one's passions, conquering the anger or hunger that could otherwise lead to humiliation and defeat. Through the *Popol Wuj* the Maya learn strength, and how to endure the suffering placed upon them by their rivals and enemies. By reflecting on the speech and actions of the ancestors and mirroring their lives—following the divine footprints of the hero twins—one is better able to find one's way through the ordeals and challenges of life.

Those who seek the knowledge and wisdom of the ancestors need to be strong enough to face their fears of the unknown, to endure the road of trial and tribulation that leads to transformation through death and rebirth. The unknown naturally causes fear; yet by following the ways of Junajpu and XB'alamkiej and imitating their twinned nature, one is able to find the path that leads to one's unique destiny and calling. For the K'iche' Maya there remains an ancient, yet self-renewing, way to be in the world: the way of the hero twins as they continue to transform themselves and the world.

Notes

1   I wish to thank Professor Kimberley Patton for inviting me to participate in this study of twins and twinship in myth and religion. I thank Professor Davíd Carrasco for his teachings on irony, contradiction, and paradox in the field of Mesoamerica studies. Paul Goepfert read and corrected my writing for which I am very thankful. The orthography for Maya K'iche' names and words follow the current 2022 orthography of Maya linguists at the Academia de Lenguas Mayas Guatamaltecas (A.L.M.G.).

2   I use "Traditional Maya" to talk about those Maya who practice a creative religious syncretism that has adopted and adapted the Catholic saints and ritual calendar into their Maya-Mesoamerican religious beliefs revolving around the maize plant, the 260-day divinatory calendar, and Maya sense of cosmos whereby the four corners sustain the sky above the earth. Today many Maya call themselves Catholics, while maintaining much of the Mesoamerican worldview of their ancestors: twinship and twinning balance the powers of the Lords of the Earth and Sky.

3   In the terms of depth psychology, as the development of the human ego took place, a "shadow" figure was created in the human psyche; hence were created myths that took into consideration this twinning of human consciousness with the "ego" and its "shadow." From this perspective, the Mayan hero twins are a doubling of the hero from the inside out in an attempt to bring the twinning of the human psyche to life through the articulation of myth. See Eric Neumann, *The Origins and History of Consciousness*, trans. R. F. C. Hull (New York: Harper & Brothers, 1954).

4   See *Diccionario de Mitología y Religión de Mesoamerica* by Yolotl González Torres (Mexico, DF: Ediciones Larousse, 1991), for a succinct discussion of the twins, *los gemelos*, and their many manifestations in Mesoamerican myth and religion. For a simplified discussion of Mesoamerican souls see Jill Leslie Mckeever Furst, *The Natural History of the Soul in Ancient Mexico* (New Haven, CT: Yale University Press, 1995). For a more definitive discussion of Mesoamerican concepts of the soul and the *nahual* see Alfredo López Austin, *The Human Body and Ideology: Concepts of the Ancient Nahuas* (2 vols.), trans. Thelma Ortiz de Montellano and Bernard Ortiz de Montellano (Salt Lake City: University of Utah Press, 1988).

5   Dennis Tedlock, trans. *Popol Vuh: The Definitive Edition of the Mayan Book of the Dawn of Life and the Glories of Gods and Kings* (New York: Simon & Schuster, 1985; 1996), Part Three, 130. I recommend the Munro Edmonson edition (1971) for its side-by-side English-K'iche' translations; the Dennis Tedlock edition (1985; 1996) for its readability and detailed translation notes; and Sam Colop's K'iche'-Spanish

edition for its authenticity. I have also recently completed a translation of the *Popul Wuj*, the result of a decade of work.

6 There is an image of a twinned calabash tree, braided together, on the mural of the West Wall of San Bartolo, manifesting the idea that the twins and their twin fathers were perceived as the pillar-like tree made up of two trees entwined with one another. At the top of the this "braided" tree are the two skull gourds of One and Seven Junajpu, clutched by the claws of the Principal Bird Deity known as Seven Macaw, whose clawlike talons cross over one another in such a way as to manifest the numbers "one" and "seven," the calendar names of the twins One and Seven Junajpu, fathers of the hero twins Junajpu and XB'alamkiej. This is the oldest known mural in the Maya area dating back to 150 BCE; this takes the Twins' story back to the origins of the Maya as a people and a culture. Seven Macaw is the seven stars that make up the constellation Ursa Major, reigning over the dry season's nighttime sky. Seven Macaw is a nighttime underworld deity whose daytime *nawal* is the predatory Macaw and destroyer of the maize lords; these lords live in peril in the *milpas* of Maya and need the protection of the hero twins who must hunt these voracious birds that come to feed off their ancestors in the form of maize.

7 The fate of the third (wooden) generation of human beings created at the beginning of time; *Popul Vuh*, trans. Tedlock, Part Two, 78.

8 *Popul Vuh*, trans. Tedlock, Part Three, 141.

9 The twins become one with their father through the act of recovering their father's seed-bones held captive in the maw of the underworld. The "father" of the hero twins is actually doubled in the form of twinned fathers, One (Jun) Junajpu and Seven Junajpu, as in other hero myths of the ancient world. *Jun* means "one" and the hero Junajpu becomes "one" with his father Jun Junajpu or "One-One Blowgun Man" by redeeming his ancestral spirit seed found in his bones. Jun Junajpu is the earth father of the twins; his twin brother Seven Junajpu is their celestial father. Seven Junajpu is never seen or heard, thus performing the role of the "invisible god behind everything." Although Seven Junajpu does not show himself, he is ever present, a perfect reflection of the idea of the *nahualli* or *cuate* as the "other" twin. It is the number "one" that calls to mind the twins becoming one with their father through their sacred journey to redeem their ancestor's spirit, seed essence, or ancestral soul held captive in the underworld by the Lords of Death. When the hero twins rise from the underworld, they are reborn as divine beings unto themselves—just as after their trials of initiation, young Mayan male initiates would be reborn into the mature men who replaced their ancestors, to continue their work on the face of the earth under an ever-watchful sky.

10 To know the sacred history of the Maya K'iche' found in the *Popol Wuj*, in correlation with the divinatory calendar was and is the way of becoming a divinely inspired human being here on earth, under the mirrored reflection of a transforming sky as well as the underworld reflected in the night sky.

11 The idea of Xibalba as underworld might be best understood as those nether worlds of the unknown experienced as either the shadowy unconscious of the human mind or the cave-like entrails of the earth. The Maya sense of the underworld was specifically a certain house of initiation, as well as an unspecific unknown that caused fear.

12 There is strong evidence that the Divinatory Calendar of 260 days (twenty day-names combined with thirteen divine numbers) was used as a mimetic device to remember the *Popol Wuj*. This is to say the paradigmatic actions of the hero twins in the *Popol*

Wuj can be correlated to the permutations of the sacred calendar of which the hero twins are the lords.

13 See Jerome H. Long's entry on "Culture Heroes," in *The Encyclopedia of Religion*, 2nd ed., vol. 3, ed. Lindsay Jones (Detroit: Macmillan Reference USA, 2005), 2090–3.

14 See Raphael Girard's classic *Esoterismo del Popol-Vuh* (*Esotericism of the Popol Wuj*) (México: Editores Mexicanos Unidos, 1948), and Nahum Megged's *Los Héroes Gemelos del Popol Vuh* (Guatemala: Ed. Pineda Ibarra, 1979) for stunning interpretive insights into the deeper meanings of the *Popol Wuj*.

15 See Linda Brown's work on found objects in the forests and fields of the Maya that become powerful conduits of communication to the past and the ancestors who dwell there. While out working in "the world," Maya pick up old pieces of ceramic, obsidian points, bones, stones, beads, clay figurines and anything else peculiar that are perceived as being the remnants of past ages. Once placed on a person's home altar they become *sacra*, creating avenues of communications and sacred connections to the ancestors and their powerful ways.

16 Every Maya I have ever known has various names by which they are called. The name given them at birth is only used when dealing with the state; otherwise, the Maya go by the names that fit their character and its way. It is only natural that humans have various names denoting the multiplicities inherent to all human beings; it causes one to wonder whether monotheistic thinking has limited humanity in untold ways.

17 The ancestors are *versipellis*; like other Tricksters, they often find themselves in need of a change of skins. This ancestral couple is divine in their ways but susceptible to transgressions characteristic of humanity also just like other Tricksters who make their world. See Lewis Hyde's *Trickster Makes This World* (New York: North Point Press, 1998) for everything you ever wanted to know about *versipellis* beings.

18 These ancestral forms of being and acting are twinned by hero twins Junajpu and XB'alamkiej who then go beyond the ancestral style of being by creating an exemplary style of their own: the twins transcend this world leaving it all behind to ascend into the heavens.

19 Xpiayakok is the god behind it all who never does anything other than existing as a supranatural creator force behind the scenes just as Seven Junajpu does. IxMuqane's world is that of the matriarchy of the Great Mother. The hero twins go beyond her world by bringing into the light of conscious their divine will of the male hunter-warrior who endures the injustices of Grandmother before taking over her world.

20 The work of Mircea Eliade is still very useful for understanding archetype and repetition in both history and religion. The hero twins might be ingenious and enterprising, but their grandparents are not. The hero twins are not about repetition; they are about being different by remembering and rethinking the past to create something new in the present. This is what leads them to a luminescent future.

21 The *Popol Wuj* may be seen as the text that informs the transformations and changes young male initiates must go through to become men in the world of the Maya. It is they who must wake up to the inner voice, find their animal guide, *nahual* protector and break away from their mother and grandmother's hearth, to become heroes in their world of their father and grandfather's sacrificial fire.

22 The Mesoamericans had a strong idea of paradise, edited out of the European colonial texts that describe their world. When taking the entire corpus of Mesoamerican art and architecture into consideration, one quickly realizes theirs was a civilization that

was more about being content with the abundance of a naturally abundant flowering world than it was about anything else. See Alfredo López Austin's *Tamoanchan, Tlalocan: Place of Mist* for a deep understanding of this pivotal aspect of paradise in the Mesoamerican world.

23 The numbers One and Seven have a relationship to calendar numbers and names too esoteric to expand upon here. Suffice it to say the Lords of Life and Death reflect one another both above and below the earthly plane through One and Seven Junajpu on earth and One and Seven Death in the underworld respectively. As fathers of the hero twins One and Seven are "doubled fathers" who reflect the birth and rebirth of the hero twins. It is in the doubling that lays the power of regeneration as in the doubling and redoubling of the maize seed that demonstrates the power of multiplication of one into many: as with maize plants in which one seed becomes many seeds.

24 *Popul Vuh*, trans. Tedlock, Part Three, 99.

25 See Lawrence Sullivan's "Tricksters: Mesoamerican and South American Tricksters," in *The Encyclopedia of Religion*, 2nd ed., vol. 14, ed. Lindsay Jones (Detroit: Macmillan Reference USA, 2005), 9357–9.

26 The story of the Tolteca-Chichimeca may well reach back 2,000 years to the time when princes and nobles of the Central Mexican city of Teotihuacan moved south to create satellite settlements on the fertile piedmont above the Pacific littoral known as the paradisiacal place of Flower Mountain: Suchitepequez. It was the lords of the north, the white land of the dead, that moved south to the yellow land of the golden abundance. The invaders and the invaded become one people in both Mesoamerican epics: *The History of the Tolteca-Chichimeca* and the *Popol Wuj*.

27 See the contemporary written work of Maya voices: Rigoberta Menchu, Victor Montejo, Gaspar Pedro Gonzalez, Demetrio Cojti, Sam Colop, and many others for an understanding of how the Maya present continues to mirror the Maya past in an attempt to order and balance an abundant future.

28 The story of the *Popol Wuj* with its various levels and modes of transforming consciousness seems to beg for a psychological analysis of the Jungian sort in the vein of James Hillman and others. There is much one could unearth by implementing said analysis of this potent myth of young men seeking to rise above their grandmother's intentions by following their own calling. See James Hillman's rich work, especially *The Soul's Code* (London: Thames and Hudson Ltd., 1993) and *A Blue Fire*, ed. Thomas Moore (New York: HarperPerennial, 1997), for a deeper understanding of the calling and the re-visioning of archetypal psychology.

29 See Hyde's *Trickster Makes This World* for a cross-cultural understanding of trickster's mischievous ways. See William Hynes and William Doty, eds., *Mythical Trickster Figures: Contours, Contexts, and Criticisms* to round out the perspective of the trickster from around the globe.

30 See Mircea Eliade's classic *The Sacred and Profane* for continual insight into the religious world of *homo religiosus*. No writer has surpassed Eliade's humanistic description of the sacred and only a poet could hope to.

31 It is a miracle of myth and history that the *Popol Wuj* survived the fires of the Spanish Inquisition and the subsequent terrors of history in both Europe and the Americas. There is no other document quite like it in the Americas as it is *the* sacred history of the Maya through which various generations of scholars have come to understand and interpret the Maya. Remnants of its sacred narrative our found in the stone carving at Itzapa that date back to the very beginning of the Classic period of Maya Civilization around 250 BCE.

32 Like the ejected semen-spittle from the mouth of the One Junajpu that magically
    impregnates IxKik' so do the hero twins "blow from their mouths" the magical spirit
    force with which they come to control the world. The twins' blowguns increase
    their strength by "elongating" the virility of the hunting instrument. Maya medicine
    men continue to blow tobacco smoke and alcohol over the sick enveloping them
    in the mist of transformative renewal in a primordial act of curing through a return
    to origins. The blowguns of the twins are instruments of magical powers like the
    wizard's magical wand. It is with their blowguns that the twins survive the tests of
    the underworld to be reborn and transformed into celestial beings that literally walk
    into the sky as the complementary twins known as the sun and moon.

33 See Rafael Girard's classic *Esotericism of the Popol Vuh* for an insightful discussion
    of the transformation of the ages in the Maya cosmo-magical thinking. Girard
    outlines the evolutionary concepts of the Ancient Maya by following the sequence
    of sustenance in the *Popol Wuj*: from fruit to crabs to birds to maize. It is hunger
    and appetite that identify the different ages as well as the rulers and beings that lived
    and found sustenance through the ages. It is the sustenance of an "age" or "sun" that
    is the core of the stories that tell of the epic in Maya world and it various ages. It is
    all about either being controlled by our appetite or us taking power over the world
    by controlling appetite. As Lewis Hyde explains in *Trickster Makes This World*,
    the trickster's power comes from his ability to forgo the pleasure of his loins and
    the hunger of his belly. If he succumbs to either he is done for, just as humans are
    when they want more of what they can't get enough of, until they end up getting
    themselves dismembered.

34 This "Dust Place of Ashes" ball court may have been where the sacrificed and dead
    received the rights of immolation, leaving only ash and fragments of bone on the
    bodies. The rite of immolation was the preferred way of the gods to transform the
    world as in the story of Quetzalcoatl as well as those who became the sun and moon
    at the beginning of time on the sacrificial pyre at Teotihuacan. The ball court is best
    thought of as the transformation place of sacrificial death and rebirth, so it is well
    symbolized by dust and ash. Also known as Pusb'al Chaaj-Sacrificial Ballcourt.

35 The errors of the ancestors are one of the principal ways of teaching in the *Popol
    Wuj*. For example, "You wouldn't want to do as the failed ancestors did and end up
    with your head sprouting out of a calabash tree in the underworld." The improvement
    of humanity is always founded on the mistakes of those who came before, something
    which the second set of twins take to heart and put into practice.

36 One Junajpu and Seven Junajpu through the White Egret Woman, Xbaqiyalo, father
    One Monkey and One Artisan who stay behind with their Grandmother, IxMuqane.
    It is the monkey-artisan twins who become the men of the house once the First
    Fathers descend into the underworld to play ball with the Lords One and Seven
    Death. When the First Fathers, One and Seven Junajpu, don't return to the face of the
    earth, their mother, IxMuqane, is consoled by One Monkey and One Artisan, who
    bring laughter into her lonely life. The First Fathers then father a second set of twins,
    the hero twins Junajpu and XB'alamkiej through IxKik', Blood Maiden. It is they
    who are not loved by their envious elder brothers, One Monkey and One Artisan.
    IxMuqane isn't happy that the youngest set of twins are part of her home until they
    begin hunting and become the providers for this broken, yet contented, family.
    Many Mayan homes have been made up of grandmothers raising the boys because
    of warfare, just as is the case today where so many men died in the violence of the
    1980s.

37   The Nabeysil (the "First Mover" whose calling is to "dance the Martín bundle [life-giving essence of rain]" for the community; see Stanzione, *Rituals of Sacrifice*, 280–1) and his brother Salvador whom I knew well told stories of their childhood that were almost exactly like this childhood saga of the hero twins who also lived out their boyhood as forest-dwellers.

38   See the Mesoamerican studies masterpiece *City, Cave and Eagle's Nest*, edited by David Carrasco and Scott Sessions, for a detailed look at the History of the Tolteca-Chichimeca in which the sacred history of the *Popol Wuj* is complemented with the sacred history of the Tolteca-Chichimeca peoples from which the K'iche Maya see themselves originating. The last section of the *Popol Wuj* makes direct reference to their emergence out of the place of origin Seven Caves or Chichimoztoc, Wuqub' Peq, of the Tolteca-Chichimeca. In Mesoamerica it is the younger and hungrier outsiders who sneak into places of power and rule and then through superior magic, cunning and sacrifice take over the kingdom from the older lineages of nobles, artisans, and singers who no longer are sharp or astute enough to maintain their control over their house or rule over their kingdom. The story of Junajpu and XB'alamkiej is just another take on this very important Mesoamerican theme of the new arrivals sacrificing everything and giving their all for a place in the sun.

39   The hero twins of the *Popol Wuj* are the perfect archetype of heroes in that they are the manifestation of twinned or doubled divinity raised by none other than themselves while suffering as strangers the oppression of an unjust world ruled by a tough old crone and her evil favorites. Like all heroes the twins have two mothers: one, the spiritually open maiden of pure delight, IxKik'; and two, the castrating chthonic old crone, IxMuqane. The divine twins are twinned by their fathers without receiving their love and attention. Their longing to be one with their father drives them on in their quest to redeem the "treasure hard to attain" from the maw of the underworld before being reborn as the sun and moon. In many ways the *Popol Wuj* is the perfect hero twin myth, begging more attention in the history of religions. Joseph Campbell, Ken Wilber, and Eric Neumann have all treated the myth of the hero.

40   The Maya live by the metaphor that life is a struggle. Without struggle one cannot attain experience and life experience is what the Maya most value in a world where education is found in the school of a life replete with suffering and sacrifice. Needless to say, not all metaphors of the ancient world are easy to live by, thus the recent desire of the Maya to change from the inside out, by changing the metaphors that inform and guide their lives.

41   For the Maya, to not share one's food with others is one of the greatest transgressions one can commit. If there is food to eat—and "food—can take many forms, then it must be shared no matter what the circumstance. The text is saying, "Now this is a bad style of being, don't be like these bad twins who eat up all the food without sharing it, even with those who brought it in from the forest." In a similar story from Santiago Atitlan, the younger twins cut off the penis of their spoiled tattle-tail brother, leaving him castrated before serving his tasty little "bird" to their hungry grandmother. She eats the "bird" and becomes mortally ill. They cook her up in the sweat bath and from her body comes the squash that is the sustenance of the first people. For the Ancient Maya, life is all about sharing the surplus abundance, instead of hoarding it for oneself. It is no wonder that the world we live in today seems to them to be a lost cause, completely void of human ethics.

42   See James Hillman's insightful work on *The Soul's Code* and the understanding of one's destiny and calling in life. Hillman uses the case of twins and calling to

discuss the unique quality of our individual callings. The K'iche' make very specific reference to the hero twins wish to find what is theirs in the world and then do their very best to follow their calling to its resplendent fruition. The K'iche' Maya are still very concerned about the destiny and calling of their children and will often hire a divining priest known as a "day-keeper" to help find the way of their children. And by extension, the K'iche Maya allow their children to like and dislike what they wish according to their intuition and inner desire, their twin, that tells them what is and isn't right for them. This makes activities such as going to elementary school an option rather than an obligation, children since not all children are expected to like going off to school every morning and sitting in class all day long.

43 This is the core idea of many Mesoamerican hero myth in which the essence of maize found in the bones of the ancestors must be carried out of the underworld and emerge from the darkness and into the light as replacements of the original seeds of maize. The First Fathers who die in the underworld are the Lords of Maize who are kept captive in the underworld by the Lords of Death. It is just the sacred work of the hero twins that brings life to the face of the earth. The rebirth of the First Fathers takes the form of maize plants growing out of the "little skulls" of the maize seed symbolized by the bones of their fathers. This treasure hard to attain is the gift they give to humanity for which they are given ascendancy into the sky or heavens as the sun and the moon.

44 This sacred history of the K'iche' Maya was the mental map that initiates followed in their rites of initiation that took them on the path of trial and ordeal through the underworld upon which they died to their mothers to be born unto their fathers. Initiates found their "twin" guide in these initiations that helped and protected them throughout life. The initiates rose reborn as the son of the celestial father, the sun, filled with cosmic lore, ancestral knowledge and secret doctrines all earned through endurance of suffering that gave them power and insight. It was all a matter of "waking up" and "staying awake" to become a son of the Sun King at the Heart of the Sky, Heart of the Heavens. The initiate had to die to grandmother and mother to be born again to the totem and titular lord of the tribe, in this case maize and the maize lord that rise up out of the deathly underworld maw. The entire section of the hero twins in the underworld reads like a manual for initiating young men through the ritual of nightly ordeal and transformation.

45 To this day Traditional Maya put themselves through rituals that primarily consist of an ordeal of staying up all night long while praying to the ancestors and their gods throughout the night until dawn returns. It is this staying up under the stars or rain that strengthens the Maya ritualists, giving them insights and direction in their life's calling. See Vincent James Stanzione, *Rituals of Sacrifice: Walking the Face of the Earth on the Sacred Path of the Sun* (Albuquerque, NM: University of New Mexico Press, 2003).

46 *Popul Vuh*, trans. Tedlock, Part Three, 131–2. I have always believed the hero twins transform into fish because fish once were placed underneath the maize plants as fertilizer, thus creating the idea that fish became maize through their transformation beneath the maize plant, in the underworld. It is just the ground bones of the hero twins that are thrown like maize into the river to transform into beautiful fish that in another transformation will become the twins again, protectors and guardians of the Lord of Maize, their father Jun Junajpu.

47 *Popul Vuh*, trans. Tedlock, Part Three, 131–2.

48 Jun Junajpu is remembered and worshipped by the K'iche' Maya as the Lord of Maize, whose essence renews and revitalizes everything that it enters. This is why

maize is a sacred plant, because its seed never dies and does not sprout back to life until it is buried under the earth in the underworld. Jun Junajpu's skull is replaced by the skull-like seed of maize that comes back to life and feeds the people, so they themselves can multiply and prosper just like their sacred maize. It is Jun Junajpu's life essence that lives as the sacred spark of life in the sustenance of his people, just as it entered the calabash tree and brought it to life.

49 La Violencia and "great death" experienced by the Maya that transformed Guatemala during the decade of the 1980s would mark the end of the Old Ways of the Maya while initiating the New Ways of the Pentecostal Christians. This new age of the Maya brought tremendous changes and an odd kind of rebirth to the Maya in a new creation that is as Maya as it is a strange twist on foreign ideas and images. It was the older people who acted out ancestral ways like these "twins," scorned by their own people for being who they were raised to be: the replacements of the ancestors, men born to act out the ancient ways of the *Nawales* who once walked the face of the earth on the path of the sun.

50 See my *Rituals of Sacrifice: Walking the Face of the Earth on the Sacred Path of the Sun*, 280–1, for a description of the Nabeysil's dancing the Sky-Earth bundle known as Martín or Atin, "the Bather" or supreme rain deity and Lord of the Earth.

51 Alfredo Lopez Austin's work details the concept of "Man-Gods" in Mesoamerica, see especially his treatment of Quetzalcoatl as a "man-god." I would experience Lopez Austin's work brought to life by the Nabeysil who became the Earth Lord known as Martín or Atin, "the Bather," which he danced into life. I danced with the Nabeysil from the summer of 1987 until the year 2000. He drank because the world was coming to an end, and the town's people hounded him out of existence. I came to know god as man through performing ritual with him, and for that I will always be forever grateful.

Bibliography

Ajpacaja Tum, Pedro F. *Diccionario K'iche'*. Iximulew [i.e., Guatemala]: Proyecto Linguistico Francisco Marroquín, 2005.

Bianchi, Ugo. "Twins." In *Encyclopedia of Religion*, 2nd ed., edited by Lindsay Jones, vol. 14, 9411–19. Detroit: Macmillan Reference USA, 2005.

Byland, Bruce E. *The Codex Borgia*. New York: Dover Publications, Inc., 1993.

Campbell, Joseph. *The Hero with a Thousand Faces*. Princeton, NJ: Princeton University Press, 1949.

Carlsen, Robert S. *The War for the Heart and Soul of a Highland Maya Town*. Austin, TX: University of Texas Press, 1997.

Carmack, Robert M. *The Quiche Mayas of Utatlán*. Norman: University of Oklahoma Press, 1981.

Carrasco, Davíd. *The Oxford Encyclopedia of Mesoamerican Cultures*. Oxford: Oxford University Press, 2001.

Carrasco, Davíd, and Scott Sessions, eds. *Cave, City and Eagle's Nest: An Interpretive Journey through the Mapa de Cuauhtinchan No. 2*. Albuquerque, NM: University of New Mexico Press, 2007.

Caso, Alfonso. *El Pueblo del Sol*. México: Fondo de Cultura Económica, 1986.

Clendinnen, Inga. *Ambivalent Conquests*. Cambridge: Cambridge University Press, 1987.

Coe, Michael D. *The Maya*, 5th ed. London: Thames and Hudson, 1993.

Colop, Sam. *Popol Wuj: Versión Poética K'iche'*. Guatemala: Cholsamaj, 1999.

Dayley, Juan Felipe. *Diccionario Tz'utujil*. Antigua, Guatemala: P.L.F.M., 1996.

Durán, Diego. *Book of the Gods and the Rites and Ancient Calendar*. Translated. F. Horcasitas and Doris Heyden. Norman: University of Oklahoma Press, 1970.

Edmonson, Munro. *The Book of Counsel: The Popol Vuh*. MARI Publ. 35. New Orleans: Tulane, 1971.

Ehrenrich, Barbara. *Blood Rites*. New York: Holt and Company, 1997.

Eliade, Mircea. *Patterns in Comparative Religion*. Translated by Rosemary Sheed. New York: Sheed & Ward, 1958.

Eliade, Mircea. *Rites and Symbols of Initiation*. Woodstock, CT: Spring Publications, 1958.

Eliade, Mircea. *The Sacred and the Profane: The Nature of Religion*. Translated by Willard R. Trask. New York: Harcourt Brace Jovanovich, 1959.

Eliade, Mircea. *The Quest*. Chicago, IL and London: University of Chicago Press, 1984.

Eliade, Mircea. *The Myth of the Eternal Return*. Princeton, NJ: Princeton University Press, 1991.

Furst, Jill Leslie McKeever. *The Natural History of the Soul in Ancient Mexico*. New Haven, CT: Yale University Press, 1995.

Girard, Rafael. *Esoterismo del Popol-Vuh*. México: Editores Mexicanos Unidos, 1948.

Gonález Torres, Yolotl. *Diccionario de Mitología y Religión de Mesoamérica*. Mexico, DF: Ediciones Larousse, 1991.

Graulich, Michel. *Myths of Ancient Mexico*. Norman: University of Oklahoma Press, 1997.

Hillman, James. *A Blue Fire: Selected Writings by James Hillman*. edited by Thomas Moore, New York: HarperPerennial, 1997.

Hillman, James. *The Soul's Code*. New York: Warner Books, 1997.

Hyde, Lewis. *Trickster Makes This World*. New York: North Point Press, 1998.

Katz, Freidrich. *Ancient American Civilizations*. London: Weidfeld and Nicolson, 1989.

Lash, John. *Twins and Doubles*. London: Thames and Hudson Ltd., 1993.

León-Portillo, Miguel. *Time and Reality in the Thought of the Maya*. Norman: University of Oklahoma Press, 1988.

Long, Jerome H. "Culture Heroes." In *The Encyclopedia of Religion*, 2nd ed., edited by Lindsay Jones, vol. 3, 2090–93. Detroit: Macmillan Reference USA, 2005.

López Austin, Alfredo. *The Human Body and Ideology: Concepts of the Ancient Nahuas*, 2 vol. Translated by Thelma Ortiz de Montellano and Bernard Ortiz de Montellano. Salt Lake City: University of Utah Press, 1988.

López Austin, Alfredo. *Tamoanchan, Tlalocan: Places of Mist*. Translated by Bernard R. Ortiz de Montellano and Thelma Ortiz de Montellano. Niwot, CO: University Press of Colorado, 1997.

Markman, Roberta and Peter. *The Flayed God*. New York: Harper Collins, 1994.

Megged, Nahum. *Los Héroes gemelos del Popol Vuh: anatomía de un mito indígena*. Guatemala: José de Pineda Ibarra, 1979.

Miller, Mary, and Karl Taube. *The Gods and Symbols of Ancient Mexico and the Maya*. London: Thames and Hudson, 1993.

Neumann, Erich. *The Origins and History of Consciousness*. Translated by R. F. C. Hull. New York: Harper & Brothers, 1954.

O'Brien, Linda. "Songs of the Face of the Earth: Ancestor Songs of the Tzutuhil Maya of Santiago Atitlán, Guatemala." Ph.D. thesis. Los Angeles: The University of California at Los Angeles, 1975.

Piontelli, Alessandra M. D. *Twins in the World: The Legends They Inspire and the Lives They Lead*. New York: Palgrave Macmillan, 2008.

Sahagún, Bernardo. *Florentine Codex; General History of the Things of New Spain*. Salt Lake City: University of Utah Press, 1981.

Sharer, Robert J. *The Ancient Maya*. Stanford, CA: Stanford University Press, 1994.

Stanzione, Vincent James. *Rituals of Sacrifice: Walking the Face of the Earth on the Sacred Path of the Sun*. Albuquerque, NM: University of New Mexico Press, 2003.

Stanzione, Vincent James. "Walking is Knowing." In *Cave, City and Eagle's Nest: An Interpretive Journey Through the Mapa de Cuauhtinchan No. 2*, edited by Davíd Carrasco and Scott Sessions. Albuquerque, NM: University of New Mexico Press, 2007.

Sullivan, Lawrence E. "Tricksters: Mesoamerican and South American Tricksters." In *Encyclopedia of Religion*, 2nd ed., edited by Lindsay Jones, vol. 14, 9357–59. Detroit: Macmillan Reference USA, 2005.

Tedlock, Dennis, trans. *Popol Vuh: The Definitive Edition of the Mayan Book of the Dawn of Life and the Glories of Gods and Kings*. New York: Simon & Schuster, 1985; 1996.

Thompson, Eric J. *Maya History and Religion*. Norman: University of Oklahoma Press, 1970.

Vico, Domingo de. *Vocabulario de la lengua cakchiquel y quiche*. Manuscript in Princeton University Library, 1555. Princeton, NJ.

Wilber, Ken. *Up from Eden*. Boulder, CO: Shambala Publications, Inc., 1981.

Part Three

South Asian Legacies

7

Wars within the Womb

♊

Wendy Doniger

Introduction

Hindu mythology, as recorded in the ancient Sanskrit texts, regards the embryo as sentient within the womb.

What happens when there is less than one embryo in the womb? The fractured embryo is magically restored. This is illustrated by the stories of Bhagīratha and Jarāsandha.

What happens when one embryo lives in two wombs? The embryo maintains its personality even when transferred to another womb or another mother (the story of Kṛṣṇa). Each twin has its own *karma*, and therefore its own agenda, which often results in antagonism or at the very least competition within the womb (the story of Dīrghatamas).

What happens when there are more than two embryos? Again, there is violence and antagonism. Sometimes the mother must choose between one great child and the multiple births that we associate with fertility drugs (Gandhārī's children, Sāgara's children). Even without a choice, the division of the embryo into multiple viable pieces gives rise to brothers who are at least in competition and often at war (Rāma and his brothers, the sons of Diti and Aditi, Skanda).

What happens when the fragmentation is sexual, when the embryo becomes male and female? (The Origin of the Licchavis of Vesālī).

How are we to reconcile these generally positive mythologies of fractional embryos with the strict Hindu sanction against abortion—a very serious crime in ancient India, one of the defining mortal sins, along with Brahminicide? Or, to put it differently, why are none of these mutilated mythological embryos killed? And, finally, what is the relationship between human twins and divine twinship?

Let's unpack this cluster of myths and try to answer some of these questions.

1 Hindu Mythology, as Recorded in the Ancient Sanskrit Texts, Regards the Embryo as Sentient within the Womb

Hindu texts imagine the reincarnating soul meditating on its next life in the womb of the soul's future mother, where it (not yet he or she) not only remains fully conscious but remembers its previous lives, in agonizing detail:

> Then it begins to remember its many previous existences in the wheel of rebirth, and that depresses it, and it tosses from side to side, thinking, "I won't ever do *that* again. As soon as I get out of this womb I will do everything I can, so that I won't become an embryo again." It thinks in this way as it remembers the hundreds of miseries of birth that it experienced before, in the power of fate. Then, as time goes by, the embryo turns around, head down, and in the ninth or tenth month it is born. As it comes out, it is hurt by the wind of procreation; it comes out crying, because it is pained by the misery in its heart. When it has come out of the womb, it falls into an unbearable swoon, but it regains consciousness when it is touched by the air. Then Viṣṇu's deluding power of illusion assails him, and when his soul has been deluded by it, he loses his knowledge. As soon as the living creature has lost his knowledge, he becomes a baby. After that he becomes a young boy, then an adolescent, and then an old man. And then he dies and then he is born again as a human. Thus he wanders on the wheel of rebirth like the bucket on the wheel of a well.[1]

Life in the womb is physically ghastly, as the embryo is squashed into a most uncomfortable position and is disgusted by the pus, feces, urine, and blood that fill the womb. But it is even more uncomfortable mentally: chagrin at the memory of previous mistakes, and despair at the realization that one will make them all again in this life, too, is what makes the baby cry as it enters the world.[2] Mae West once said that if she had her life to live over again she would make all the same mistakes, but she would make them sooner. The embryo fears that it, too, will make them again, sooner or later.

1.1 What Happens When There Is Less than One Embryo in the Womb?

This happens often, when an embryo becomes fragmented and partial.

1.1.1 *Bhagīratha*

King Dilīpa died without an heir, and one of his two widowed queens ate a special bowl of rice consecrated to make her pregnant; the other had intercourse with her "in the manner of a man"; the elder queen became pregnant, and after the usual time brought forth a son, but since the boy had been born without any semen of a man, which provides the hard, white parts of a child, bones and cartilage (while the mother provides the soft, red parts, flesh, and blood), he had no bones, and was just like a ball of flesh. Eventually, a special boon from a sage gave the child bones, and named him Bhagīratha, since he had been born from a mere portion (*bhaga*) of the usual parents.[3]

This is a kind of counter case: not a double embryo but a half an embryo, an Un-twin. Yet it shows that the individual child is, in a way, always a twin, regarded as compounded of the substance of the two parents. If either is neglected, the consequences for the embryo are disastrous. (A parallel case, outside the womb, this time neglecting the female rather than the male half of the embryo, is the case of Bhṛngin, who wanted to honor his father, Śiva, but not his mother, Pārvatī; she cursed him to be nothing but a skeleton, lacking the flesh that she would have given him.)

1.1.2 Jarāsandha

Another famous instance of a fragmented/composite embryo is the tale of Jarāsandha, told in the *Mahābhārata* [2.16]:

> A childless king with twin wives was given a mango consecrated to ensure the birth of a son. He had promised never to favor either wife, and so he gave it to them both; they split it in half, and each gave birth to half a child, each with one eye, arm, leg, and buttock, with half a face and half a belly. The wives, horrified, exposed the two halves, but a demoness (*rākṣasī*) who was not a demoness, and who was named Jarā ("old age"), found them and tied them together. They became a whole child; she returned him to the king, who named him Jarāsandha ("Joined Together by Old Age").[4]

A fruit divided between several wives produces multiple fragments of a single son. Each wife apparently would rather have half a loaf than no bread at all. The mother who joins him is a demoness by birth and diet and is said to live upon flesh and blood, but she has a divine beauty and saves the deformed child instead of devouring him as demonesses usually do. She is Old Age, who will eventually break him back down into fragments again. Jarā appears near the end of the *Mahābhārata* with a change of sex and a mission more appropriate to her name, that is, death rather than birth: Jarā is the name of the hunter who kills Kṛṣṇa (16.5.19–21).

1.2 What Happens When One Embryo Lives in Two Wombs?

1.2.1 The Embryo Maintains Its Personality Even When Transferred to Another Womb or Another Mother

1.2.1.1 Kṛṣṇa

Queen Devakī conceived Kṛṣṇa, and the cowherd woman Yaśodā conceived Kālī.

When the babies were born, the fathers switched them, so that Yaśodā raised Kṛṣṇa while Devakī handed Kālī over to the wicked Kaṃsa to destroy.[5] There was another child, too: before she bore Kṛṣṇa, Devakī conceived Balarāma and was said to miscarry in the eighth month; but Balarāma was actually transferred to the womb of Rohiṇī, who brought him forth a month later. These are regarded as three separate births, but emotionally, Rohiṇī has one child, Yaśodā has two, and Devakī has three. The Hindu tradition regards all three children as siblings, despite their different mothers. Kṛṣṇa and Balarāma, of noble birth, grew up incognito as the children of simple cowherds. This is what Freud called the Family Romance, and the *Mahābhārata* calls the story of Karṇa: the widespread story of an apparently low-born child who has a noble alter ego, a kind of twin, from whom he is separated at birth and with whom he seeks to reunite, through the hero's quest.[6]

1.2.2 Each Twin Has Its Own karma, and Therefore Its Own Agenda, Which Often Results in Antagonism or at the Very Least Competition within the Womb

1.2.2.1 Dīrghatamas

When a sage tried to rape his brother's pregnant wife, the unborn embryo protected his mother by kicking out the intruding penis, shouting, "Get out, uncle! There's only room for one in here, and I was here first!" That is, knowing that the sage's semen must invariably father a child, the unborn embryo did not want to share the womb with that future embryo, who would have been his younger twin. The infuriated rapist cursed the embryo to be blind; the child was born as Dīrghatamas ("Long Darkness").[7]

1.3 What Happens When There Are More than Two Embryos? Again, There Is Violence and Antagonism

1.3.1 Sometimes the Mother Must Choose between One Great Child or the Multiple Births That We Associate with Fertility Drugs

1.3.1.1 Gāndhārī's Children

In the *Mahābhārata*[1.107.7–24], when a sage offers two queens boons that will give them children, Gāndhārī chooses a hundred children, while her rival Kuntī chooses just one.

Gāndhārī, impatient when her pregnancy goes on for two years, gives birth to a great ball of flesh that the sage Vyāsa shatters into a hundred pieces of flesh, which become the hundred evil sons of Dhṛtarāṣṭra. But before this happens, Kuntī gives birth to Yudhiṣṭhira, the good king (and, later, to two other sons of *Pāṇḍu*). The sons of *Pāṇḍu* and Dhṛtarāṣṭra fight to the death.

1.3.1.2 Sagara's Children

The *Rāmāyaṇa* and the *Mahābhārata* tell the story of King Sagara, who had two wives, the elder virtuous, the younger beautiful. He won the boon that one wife would have one son to carry on the family line, and the other would have 60,000 sons of great strength. Guess who chose the one son, named Asamañja? The second wife gave birth to a ball of flesh, which split into 60,000 sons.[8] The ocean was first formed when the 60,000 sons dug into the earth to find the lost sacrificial horse of Sagara, who was performing a horse sacrifice.[9] (Some versions say that Indra, the king of the gods, stole the horse.[10]) A sage burned the princes to ashes, and years later, Bhagīratha, the great-grandson of Sagara, persuaded the Ganges, which existed at that time only in the form of the Milky Way in heaven, to descend to earth in order to flow over the ashes of his grandfathers and thus purify them so that they could enter heaven.[11] (Bhagīratha, you may recall, was the very son born, posthumously, of King Dilīpa and the two queens who gave birth to a piece of formless flesh, in the very first story we considered.) Again we have the basic fragmentation of the wife into co-wives, always a situation of rivalry, magnified into the grotesque fragmentation of the sons; both generations are fragmented on moral grounds.

1.3.2 Even without a Choice, the Division of the Embryo into Multiple Viable Pieces Gives Rise to Brothers Who Are at Least in Competition and Often at War

1.3.2.1 Rāma and His Brothers

Viṣṇu divides himself into four unequal pieces, distributed among three queens, to produce Rāma and his three brothers. Rāma's brothers are in fact fractional brothers, not even half-brothers. The childless king Daśaratha had obtained a magic porridge of rice and milk, infused with the essence of Viṣṇu, to share among his queens; he gave half to his first wife Kausalyā, who gave birth to Rāma; 3/8 to Sumitrā, who bore Lakṣmaṇa and Śatrughna (each made of 3/16 of Viṣṇu), and 1/8 to Kaikeyī, who bore Bharata. (Other versions of the story divide the fractions slightly differently, but Kausalyā always gets half.) The rivalry of the mothers at the time of birth is muted, though we must note the unequal distribution of the fragments; that rivalry, however, breaks out later, when the younger, prettier wife (the greedy type who chooses multiple sons, as in the Sāgara myth) prevails over the older wife, and the throne fails to go to the eldest son, Rāma. Then strife (though not among the brothers) and tragedy result. This story begins, like the tale of Jarāsandha, with a fruit divided between several wives; but where that fruit produced multiple fragments of a single son, this one produces multiple sons.

1.3.2.2 The Sons of Diti and Aditi

The birth of Rāma and his brothers is foreshadowed, in the *Mahābhārata*, by the narration of the myth in which Indra learns that the goddess Diti is carrying a child who will kill him. Waiting for a moment when Diti becomes careless about purity rules, Indra enters her womb and chops the embryo into seven pieces, which become the Maruts, gods of the winds.[12] Diti's sister, Aditi, also has embryo problems involving sevens: Like the incarnate Ganges, who bears seven sons who die before she has the great Bhīṣma, and like the mother of Kṛṣṇa, who bears seven children who are murdered before she manages to save Kṛṣṇa's life,[13] Aditi (the Ṛg Veda tells us) bore eight sons: "With seven she went forth among the gods, but she threw Mārtāṇḍa, the sun, aside. . . so that he would in turn beget offspring and then die."[14] Other Vedic texts, the Brāhmaṇas, tell us that, even in the womb, the Sun was inadvertently mutilated and consciously rejected by his own mother, who miscarried him and pushed him away, still unformed: "[The Sun] was an unshaped lump, as broad as it was high, the size of a man. His brothers, however, shaped him so that he was not lost; they cut the flesh away from him and threw it into a lump."[15] Like Gāndhārī, Aditi is so impatient with her long pregnancy that she gives birth to a shapeless mass, and only the intervention of male figures saves him, as the sage Vyāsa saved Gandhārī's children.

1.3.2.3 Skanda

The fragmentation of the embryonic Skanda leads to conflict not between his various parts but between his many mothers. Engendered when Pārvatī and Śiva made love, but carried first by the god Agni and then by the river Ganges, the semen that is to become Skanda is split into six pieces in six out of the seven wives of the Seven Sages, and then reunited to become Skanda.[16] But he has six heads, so that each of the six wives of the Sages can suckle him at the same time.[17] Again we find the pattern of seven out of eight [or here, constrained by the given number of Sages, six out of seven], a fragmentation of parents that parallels the fragmentation of the child.

1.4 What Happens When the Fragmentation Is Sexual, When the Embryo Becomes Male and Female?

Let me close with a story that is probably less familiar to you, as it was to me, than the *Māhabhārata* and *Rāmāyaṇa* and *Purāṇa* stories I've reviewed until now. This is a fairly late text that purports to tell the origin of the Licchavis of Vesālī:

1.4.1 A Story about the Origin of the Licchavis

A child, it seems, was conceived in the womb of the chief queen of a king of Varanasi.

She gave birth to a piece of flesh like a lump of lac or like hibiscus flowers. As a consequence she thought, "They might criticize me before the king, saying that the other queens give birth to children like golden statues, but the chief queen has given birth to a piece of flesh." Thinking to escape such criticism, she put the piece of flesh in a vase, had it covered and sealed with the royal seal and then set it afloat on the Ganges. Deities arranged for the guarding of what human beings had rejected, and after inscribing in vermilion on a gold label the words "Offspring of the chief queen of the king of Varanasi," they tied it on [the vase]. After that the vase floated on the current of the Ganges untroubled by danger of waves and so on.

On that occasion a certain ascetic was living in dependence on a cowherd's family by the banks of the Ganges. Early one morning he went down to the Ganges, and seeing the vase coming by, he picked it up, regarding it as flotsam. Then he saw the written label and the royal seal on it. He opened it and found the piece of flesh. When he saw that, [he thought] "It might be a living fetus, and that is why there is no bad smell of decay about it," and so he brought it to his hermitage and put it in a clean place. Then at the end of a fortnight there were two pieces of flesh. When the ascetic saw that, he put them in a better place. At the end of another fortnight five swellings for the hands, feet and head appeared on each piece. Then at the end of another fortnight one piece of flesh became a boy like a golden statue and the other a girl. Child-love sprang up in the ascetic then, and milk was produced from his thumb. After that, when he obtained milk-rice he ate the rice and sprinkled the milk on the children's mouths. Whatever entered their stomachs was visible as if it were inside a crystal jug, so skinless (*nicchavi*) were they—some others have said, however, that their skins adhered (*līnā chavi*) to each other as if stitched together. At any rate they became known by the name of Licchavi either because of their skinlessness (*nicchavitā*) or because of their skins' adherence (*līnāchavitā*).

With his nursing of the children the ascetic was late in going to the village for alms and when he returned the day was already advanced. When the cowherds came to know about his interest [in the children], they said, "Venerable sir, nursing children is an impediment to those gone forth [from the householder life]. Give us the children. We will nurse them. You do your own work." The ascetic agreed. When the boy was sixteen years old, they anointed him king, and they married him to the girl. From their first cohabitation two children were born, a daughter and a son. Sixteen times there were two born in this way. The [town] came to be called Vesālī. This is the story of Vesālī.[18]

The shapeless ball of flesh follows the pattern of the many Hindu myths we have considered in which an inchoate mass becomes divided into several living creatures. But in this text, unlike the others, the queen who gives birth to this abnormal infant is ashamed of the abnormality, and that is a part of another familiar theme into which the story then segues, the Family Romance: the child is abandoned on the river, picked up by a foster parent, and raised among lower class people. (There are many variants of this tale, in addition to the tale of Kṛṣṇa that we have already considered, such as the story of Moses in the Hebrew Bible and of Oedipus in Sophocles' play.) This text then appends a new ending, also familiar from other mythologies: the brother and sister produce a new lineage.

2 How Are We to Reconcile These Generally Positive Mythologies of Fractional Embryos with the Strict Hindu Sanction against Abortion—a Very Serious Crime in Ancient India, One of the Defining Mortal Sins, along with Brahminicide? Or, to Put It Differently, Why Are None of These Mutilated Mythological Embryos Killed?

Apparently twins in the womb already have individually differentiated souls.

Hindu mythology, as we have seen, regards the embryo as not only sentient within the womb but already in possession of its own *karma*. But the bodies in which the karmically charged souls are lodged have not yet been brought to life at the moment of exit from the womb, so they cannot be killed yet; they are in limbo. This belief is expressed through the recurrent myth of a woman giving birth to a lump of flesh, not yet separated into the elements of a living child—or, more often, into multiple children; Aditi gives birth to such a lump, as do Gāndhārī and the younger wives of

Sagara and of Dilīpa. The difference between a live, though still shapeless, embryo and a murdered fetus is precisely referenced in the musings of the ascetic in the story of the Licchavis: "It might be a living fetus, and that is why there is no bad smell of decay about it."

Hindu texts, therefore, conceive of abortion in entirely different terms from these mutilations of embryos. A miscarriage is called "the falling of the embryo," that is, the removal of the embryo from the womb where it was safe, before it has become a viable child capable of living on the outside of the womb. The moment of embryo-killing in an abortion is the moment when, after the embryo leaves the womb, it fails to be brought to life, as the balls of flesh were revived by the sprinkling of holy water or some other device. The aborted embryo is like a person in cardiac arrest who does *not* revive under the efforts of the emergency room doctors. The body of the aborted child is never activated, like a cell phone before you sign on to the billing cycle; or, to change the metaphor yet again, the soul moves on to find another home, never having really moved in to the aborted home at all.

Many of these stories project the possibility of the death of the fractional embryo onto another recurrent theme: the death of some fraction of the total offspring of the woman in question, the death of the first seven of eight, or the first six of seven. In this context, I think it is interesting to note that the fraction (*aṃśa*) of Viṣṇu that produces Rāma and his brothers is divided into eight parts.

To chop up an embryo, to wage war inside the womb, is therefore not to kill an unborn child. One might fruitfully compare these myths with the stories of the vying of twins, such as Jacob and Esau, or the twin sons of Tamar, within the wombs of their mothers in the Hebrew Bible. Within the womb is where the most profound sibling rivalries take place; the wars on the outside, afterward, are merely anticlimactic.

3   What Is the Relationship between Human Twins and Divine Twinship?

The violence and antagonism that hedge so many myths of human twinship stand in stark contrast with the Hindu metaphysics of divine doubling. From the earliest Vedic myths, the mother of the human race, Saṃjñā (also called Saraṇyū—even her name is doubled) leaves a double in her place when she abandons her husband and her twin children, causing all the human domestic tragedies that we know so well.[19] There is conflict here, between the wife and her husband, between the wife and her double, and between the male twins (Yama, the god of the dead—whose name actually means "twin"—and Manu, the ancestor of the human race). But there is also creativity, coming from Saraṇyū and her son Manu, who creates the human race; and, in other versions of the story, coming from Yama and his twin sister Yamī, who become the ancestors of the human race in Avestan mythology, though they do not mate in the Vedic myth.

The Vedas also speak of another, deeper sort of doubling, the belief that there are bonds (*bandhus*) between earthly and celestial phenomena, between your eye and the sun, your breath and the wind; in that sense, the sun is the twin of your eye. The Upaniṣads developed this idea into a major metaphysical doctrine of Hinduism, the belief that every human soul (*ātman*) is a part of the world-soul (*Ātman*), with whom the individual seeks not so much to unite as to realize the already existing unity. In another Upaniṣadic text, the creator divides himself into male and female, who become man and wife and procreate.[20] This concept (which follows the line of the Avestan version of the myth of Yama and Yamī) is echoed in the tale of the Licchavis and is in fact a widespread theme; it appears in Plato's *Symposium* in the myth of the primeval androgyne, the two halves of which are split apart and become all the couples who strive constantly to get back together again through sexual union. Here again we have the theme of the soul searching for its twin, in this case not the divine twin, the *Ātman*, but merely the human soul-mate. (Plato, unlike the Upaniṣadic text, imagines, in addition to the heterosexual couple, two sets of same-sex couples, male/male and female/female, who are more literally twins.)

The wars of the twins, in this context, are a symptom of the basic human mistake of dualism, the false belief that there is a radical disjunction between humans and the divine, or between male and female, or between the illusion of matter (*māyā*) and the reality of God.

Notes

1   *Mārkaṇḍeya Purāṇa* (with commentary. Bombay: Venkateshvara Steam Press, 1890), 10.1–7, 11.1–21; Wendy Doniger O'Flaherty, *Textual Sources for the Study of Hinduism* (Chicago: University of Chicago Press, 1990), 97–8.
2   The idea that the reincarnating soul remembers its former lives but is nevertheless constrained to make the same efforts over and over again is expressed in the myth of Er in Plato's *Republic* and in numerous Indian texts. See Wendy Doniger, *The Woman Who Pretended to Be Who She Was* (New York: Oxford University Press, 2005), 112–36.
3   *Padma Purāṇa, Svarga Khaṇḍa* 16.6–24; O'Flaherty, *Textual Sources for the Study of Hinduism*, 98.
4   *Mahābhārata* 2.16–17. Wendy Doniger, *Splitting the Difference: Gender and Myth in Ancient Greece and India* (Chicago and London: The University of Chicago Press, 1999), 233–4.
5   *Harivaṃśa* 47–8. Wendy Doniger O'Flaherty, *Hindu Myths: A Sourcebook, translated from the Sanskrit* (Harmondsworth: Penguin Classics, 1975), 206–13.
6   Otto Rank, *The Myth of the Birth of the Hero* (New York, 1914). Republished in *In Quest of the Hero*, ed. Otto Rank et al. (Princeton, NJ: Princeton University Press, 1990).
7   *Mahābhārata* 1.98.7–33; cf. the telling in the *Bṛhaddevatā* 4.11–15. Wendy Doniger, *The Bedtrick: Tales of Sex and Masquerade* (Chicago: University of Chicago Press, 2000), 250.
8   *Rāmāyaṇa* 1.108.
9   *Rāmāyaṇa* 1.37–43; see Wendy Doniger O'Flaherty, *Asceticism and Eroticism in the Mythology of Siva* (Oxford: Oxford University Press, 1973; retitled: *Śiva: The Erotic Ascetic*, 1981), 230, and fn 88: *Śiva Purāṇa* 5.38; *Liṅga Purāṇa* 1.66; *Vāyu Purāṇa* 88; *Brahmāṇa Purāṇa* 3.46–53; *Viṣṇu Purāṇa* 4.4; Doniger O'Flaherty, *Śiva*, 230, and fn. 88.

10 Wendy Doniger O'Flaherty, *The Origins of Evil in Hindu Mythology* (Berkeley: University of California, 1976), 88, 100 on Indra as performer of horse sacrifices and obstructer of horse sacrifices. For the many variants of the story of Indra's theft of the sacrificial horse of King Sagara, see *Mahābhārata* 3.104–8; *Rāmāyaṇa*1.38–44; *Viṣṇu Purāṇa* 4.4.1–33, etc. For a discussion of these stories, see Wendy Doniger O'Flaherty, *Women, Androgynes, and Other Mythical Beasts* (Chicago: University of Chicago Press, 1980), 220–2.

11 *Mahābhārata* 3.105–8.

12 *Mahābhārata* 9.37.28–31; *Vāmana Purāṇa* 46.

13 *Harivaṃśa* 47–8.

14 *Ṛg Veda* 10.72.8–9; Wendy Doniger O'Flaherty, *The Rig Veda: An Anthology, 108 Hymns Translated from the Sanskrit* (Harmondsworth: Penguin Classics, 1981), 37–9.

15 *Śatapatha Brāhmaṇa* 3.1.3.3; see Doniger O'Flaherty, *Women, Androgynes, and Other Mythical Beasts*, 174–6.

16 *Śiva Purāṇa* 2.4.1–2; Doniger O'Flaherty, *The Origins of Evil in Hindu Mythology*, 161–8.

17 *Rāmāyaṇa*1.37.

18 This is an abridgement of a story that appears in two commentaries, both of which are attributed to the fifth century CE Sri Lankan commentator Buddhaghoṣa. These occur in the discussion of the *Ratana Sutta* in the *Paramathajotikā* commentary on the *Khuddaka-Pāṭha*, and in the commentary on the *Mahā-Sīhanādasutta* in the *Papañcasūdanī* commentary of the *Majjhima-Nikāya*. The tale is also told in the *Shan-Chien-P'i-P'o-Sha*, the Chinese translation of the *Samantapāsādikā* (which original Pali text is also attributed to Buddhaghosa), although the Pali version only mentions the name of the city. The story also appears later in the as yet untranslated Sinhalese *Pūjavali* from the thirteenth century. I am indebted to Charles Preston for this source.

19 Doniger, Splitting the Difference, 43–55.

20 *Bṛhadāraṇyaka Upaniṣad* 1.4.

Bibliography

Primary Texts

Brahmāṇḍa Purāṇa. Bombay: Venkateshvara Steam Press, 1857.

Bṛhadāraṇyaka Upaniṣad. In One Hundred and Eight Upanishads. Bombay: Nirnaya Sagara Press, 1913.

Bṛhaddevatā of Śaunaka. Text, with a translation by A. A. Macdonell. Harvard Oriental Series no. 5. Cambridge, MA: Harvard University Press, 1904.

Harivaṃśa. Poona (Pune): Bhandarkar Oriental Research Institute, 1969.

Liṅga Purāṇa. Calcutta: Sri Arunodaraya, 1812.

Mahābhārata. Critical ed. Poona (Pune): Bhandarkar Oriental Research Institute, 1933–69.

Mārkaṇḍeya Purāṇa. Bombay: Venkateshvara Steam Press, 1890.

Padma Purāṇa, Svarga Khaṇḍa. (The Svarga Khanda of the Skanda Purana). Edited by
  A. C. Shastri. Benares: All-India Kashiraj Trust, 1972.
Rāmāyaṇa of Vālmīki. Critical ed. Baroda: Oriental Institute, 1960–75.
Ṛg Veda, with the commentary of Sāyana. 6 vols. London: Oxford University Press,
  1890–2.
Śatapatha Brāhmaṇa. Benares: Chowkhamba Sanskrit Series, no. 96, 1964.
Śiva Purāṇa. Benares: Pandita Pustakalaya, 1964.
Vāmana Purāṇa. Benares: All-India Kashiraj Trust, 1972.
Vāyu Purāṇa. Poona: Anandashrama Sanskrit Series, 1860.
Viṣṇu Purāṇa, with the commentary of Śrīdhara. Calcutta: Sanatana Sastra, 1972.

Secondary Sources

Doniger, Wendy. *Splitting the Difference: Gender and Myth in Ancient Greece and India*.
  Chicago, IL and London: University of London Press and University of Chicago
  Press, 1999.
Doniger, Wendy. *The Bedtrick: Tales of Sex and Masquerade*. Chicago, IL: University of
  Chicago Press, 2000.
Doniger, Wendy. *The Woman Who Pretended to Be Who She Was*. New York: Oxford
  University Press, 2005.
Doniger O'Flaherty, Wendy. *Asceticism and Eroticism in the Mythology of Siva*. Oxford
  University Press, 1973; retitled: *Siva: The Erotic Ascetic*, 1981.
Doniger O'Flaherty, Wendy. *Hindu Myths: A Sourcebook, Translated from the Sanskrit*.
  Harmondsworth: Penguin Classics, 1975.
Doniger O'Flaherty, Wendy. *The Origins of Evil in Hindu Mythology*. Berkeley, CA:
  University of California, 1976.
Doniger O'Flaherty, Wendy. *Women, Androgynes, and Other Mythical Beasts*. Chicago,
  IL: University of Chicago Press, 1980.
Doniger O'Flaherty, Wendy. *The Rig Veda: An Anthology, 108 Hymns*. Translated from
  the Sanskrit. Harmondsworth: Penguin Classics, 1981.
Doniger O'Flaherty, Wendy. *Textual Sources for the Study of Hinduism*. Chicago, IL:
  University of Chicago Press, 1990.
Rank, Otto. *The Myth of the Birth of the Hero*. New York, 1914. Republished in *In Quest
  of the Hero*, by Otto Rank et al. Princeton, NJ: Princeton University Press, 1990.

8

Twins in Hindu Mythology and Everyday Life in the California Diaspora

♊

Vijaya Nagarajan

Three Navarathris

Navarathri Festival—2000

On September 27, 2000, after eighteen long years of desiring children and encountering only obstacles, including five intense and despairing years of infertility, and after undergoing medically required bed rest for nearly six months of a high-risk pregnancy with a poor prognosis, I gave birth to twins—non-identical, sororal[1] children: Jaya Lakshmi and Uma Maheswari. They were born during the Hindu festival of the nine nights of the Goddess—Navarathri—a festival celebrated throughout India honoring the three major forms of the Hindu goddess: Lakshmi, the calm, serene goddess of wealth, health, radiance, and alertness, whose iconography typically includes a showering of gold coins; Durga, the fierce martial goddess of Shakti, female energy and power among whose other forms are the arcadian manifestations of Parvathi and Uma; Saraswathi, the goddess of wisdom and learning, of music and the arts. Quite coincidentally, I had named our children after two of the goddesses that were celebrated at the time of their birth—Jaya Lakshmi is another name for the goddess Lakshmi, who represents victory, and Uma Maheswari is another name for the goddess Durga, who represents ultimate female force and strength. A sense of the miraculous pervaded their time in the womb and their subsequent births as twins. Even the five years of severe infertility prior to their birth gave their sudden appearance into our lives a sense of incredulity, marvel, and abundance. The best part of their births was the very idea of two-ness, as I knew it would have been impossible for me to have two separate births, given my difficulties in achieving even one successful pregnancy. So I felt a sense of deep pleasure and gratitude at their birth. As they grew older, witnessing my children's side-by-side parity of equivalent forces of will, desire, and intelligence in operation was both surprising and mysterious, though at times, and often at the same time, daunting and overwhelming. My experience of motherhood is deeply inflected by twin-ness. I began to wonder what it was like for other mothers of twins.[2]

Navarathri Festival—2006

A long shimmering moment of time unfolds as we enter the vast, boxy, factory-like space of the Sunnyvale Hindu temple in Northern California. It was September 2006, and Uma, Jaya, and I had traveled to attend the Navarathri festival there. I arrived with my twin children, Uma and Jaya, dressed in their beautiful new clothes, a multicolored bright Gujarathi long skirt with top set and a light scarf wrapped crosswise on their torsos that we had bought in India the winter before. They pranced around me, as five-year-olds often do, oblivious in some ways to the multi-sited commotion around them. I think they were aching to do the cartwheels and handstands that they had learned in gymnastics over the years; they loved that big, open space. There were several deities lined against one of the walls and lines of people offering fruits, flowers and sweets and praying, bowing down on their hands and knees, touching the flame as it went around after it had done the oval circles around the images of the gods and goddesses. I felt as if I was entering with two embodiments of the goddess and apparently, so did many others. We made our offerings, prayed, and then, slowly, to our immense surprise, one family after another came toward us and asked my permission to present gifts of cloth, sweets, and small toys to Jaya and Uma. Uma and Jaya both looked surprised, amazed, and startled as each family presented the gifts and bowed down to them. They took the gifts and each child soon had a small hillock of gifts at her/their side. They grinned, happy with the pleasure of being treated so well. Periodically, they would look at me quizzically, asking "Why are people treating us like this?" I remembered, all of a sudden, scenes such as this one in my own childhood, whether in New Delhi or Maryland, when adults, especially women, would bestow my sisters and me with gifts and honor us during this Goddess festival. There was a traditional belief of a temporary investiture of the goddess in the physical body of the young pre-pubescent girl that was being mapped onto us. I wondered if there seemed a more intense focus on Jaya and Uma because they were twins: There was an aura around them of balance, harmony, ease, and laughter. I would never know the answer, but the question stayed with me for a long time.

Was it the effect of this magical aura of "the twins" that attracted the templegoers' focus toward Uma and Jaya that day? Was it seeing the double-ness side-by-side of two siblings equivalent in power and presence, who were both individuals and simultaneously together as one category, that made them suddenly think and feel the awe-inspiring duality of the enormous fertility of life that twins represent visually and categorically? What was going on in their minds? How do Hindus think of twins?

Navarathri Festival—2010

A few weeks before the festival, we had an unusual invitation. The Brahma Kumaris, a spiritual group which has many overlapping vocabularies with Hinduism in its mission and practices, invited Uma and Jaya, then age ten, to be dressed up as goddesses for their Navarathri Festival. I felt ambivalent but flattered that they had been asked; the twins were excited about the dressing up part and said, in response, "Sure! That sounds like fun!"

When we came into the dressing room area, we saw seven girls and women of varying ages getting ready. It was determined by the organizers that Uma would be Gayathri, another form of Parvathi, and Jaya would be Saraswathi, the goddess of creativity. They were dressed up in heavy silk saris, jewels, and makeup, and then installed inside of paper mache ensembles with different backgrounds and curtains in front of each of the nine goddesses [Figure 8.1]. Once the girls and women were installed as goddesses, there was one requirement and that was—to be very still. The mostly Indian crowd gathered, sang, chanted, performed ārathi (circling of lamps before the goddesses), prayed, offered flowers and fruit, and bowed. Little girls would walk below the tableau of living goddesses and express with astonishment: "Mom, are the goddesses real?" I could see Jaya and Uma fighting their urge to giggle. They mostly kept still. I was intrigued by the physical essence of the feminine as embodied in actual human forms and enacted during a goddess festival, and then actively worshipped by the community.

The very timing of Jaya and Uma's birth in September 2000 during Navarathri was itself remarkable. In September 2006, although all the women and girls present were treated with honor, I could see that there was a special intensity with which the community treated Uma and Jaya as goddesses and as I wrote earlier, I was convinced that that was because they were twins. Now in 2010 I could see how this ritual was a personification of how I had imagined them before as miraculous because they were twins, and as divinities because they were born during the Navarathri festival.

Figure 8.1 Uma Nagarajan-Swenson as the Goddess Gayatri on the left; Jaya Nagarajan-Swenson as the Goddess Saraswathi on the right. Navarathri Festival 2010, Anubhuti Meditation and Retreat Center, Novato, California. Photo by Vijaya Nagarajan.

Hindu Twinship, Earthly and Divine: Some Questions

These three experiences inspired me to explore questions I have been contemplating, almost unconsciously, for nearly a dozen years: Are there any major Hindu goddesses and gods who are twins? What insights about doubled identity and power do their myths reflect? How do actual Indian-American twins and their families narrate these sacred stories? What common themes can be found in their experiences?

In order to approach these questions, I will explore, first, the presence of divine twins and their significance in Hindu mythology. Second, I will report on ethnographic research conducted among Indian-American families of twins in northern California. I will then explore how the first two themes relate to each other. In other words: Do Hindu mythological narratives and ideas frame the experiences of actual Indian-American families with twins? And if so, how? If not, why not?[3]

In other words, how do Indian-Americans speak about the contemporary phenomenon of twins in relation to twins in Hindu mythology? How do they speak about the normally exceptional biological phenomena of twins in the context of the rapid contemporary increase in twins? An increasing use of scientifically advanced technology often has the potential to solve the problem of infertility, with not one but two children or sometimes even more. The infertility of the family often creates a religious crisis, and, in turn, in solving the biological and religious crisis, creates an increase in twins? How do the families deal with the additional impact of identity issues regarding twins on top of the already loaded impact of immigrant identity issues? Can we sense any personal or transpersonal interactions between the mythic narratives and the narrative experience of twins in actual families?

This chapter traces the presence of twins in Hindu cultural traditions and sets them against a broader South Asian cultural framework and even broader global presence. From the distant past of the Vedas, featuring the twin horsemen, the Ashwins, and many divine doubles, to the contemporary literary present of a Man Booker prize–winning novel; from traditional fertility metaphors and invocations to today's startling increase in twins due to the biotechnology of IVF, I seek to locate the multiple meanings and metaphors of twins in the Indian-American context, especially indicating to the ways in which these semiotics are changing. My goal is to deepen our understanding of the presence and absence of religious and cultural categories of "twin," and particularly the Hindu-American diaspora—once an exceptional category and now nearly commonplace.

Twins in Hindu Mythology

At first glance, the presence of twins in Hindu mythology seems minimal. Yet when we look closer, there are more and more layers of twins. I will highlight two families from Hindu mythology where twins appear in significant ways; these first appear in the Vedas and later in the epic literature. Although these two families by no means exhaust the list, they are among the most well known in the popular Hindu imagination.

Vedic Mythology

The figure of twins first appears in ancient Vedic mythology in the *Rig Veda* (*c*. 1500 BCE–900 BCE), a text of hymns of praise to various gods and goddesses. The figure of Saranyu is a divine mother who has two sets of twins—Yama, the god of death, and Yami (who later becomes Yamuna, the river goddess); and the Aśvin brothers, who are often referred to as a single unit of two individuals without names. As the mother of two sets of twins, Saranyu is one of the key figures in interpreting the expressed role of twins in Hindu mythology.[4]

Saranyu's husband is Surya, the sun god. Saranyu, after she births the first set of twins, Yama and Yamuna, interestingly, does not want to stay married to Surya or to continue as a mother. She wants to leave because she is unsatisfied and uncomfortable with Surya's excessive fieriness and darkness. Before her secret departure, she creates a "shadow double," Chaya (her name reflecting her source—"Shadow"), an identical twin who looks and acts like her—to literally substitute for her, both as a wife for Surya and as a mother to her twins. Saranyu then runs away from Surya, first to her father, who does not welcome her and in fact urges her to return to her husband. Leaving her father, she assumes the form of a mare, wandering in a hidden forest for many years. Meanwhile the Shadow double has her own children and begins to subtly treat Saranyu's twins as second-class citizens. After the Shadow double curses Yama, costing him his foot when he raised it to her in anger because of her maltreatment of him, Yama turned to his father, complaining of the Shadow double's excessive curse for a minor infraction.

Surya discovers Saranyu's deception and begins searching for her. Discovering her in a hidden forest, he goes to her in the form of a male horse, a stallion, chases her, and impregnates her. She then bears the second set of twins, the Ashwins, who are half-horse and half-human centaurs. They are bright, agile, and fast, serving as charioteers to help move the sun across the sky. They are also considered remarkable healers and restorers of youth, and achieve immortality. In some later versions, these second set of twins serve as a way for Saranyu to return back to the family household and again manage the household as a co-wife with her Shadow double and her children. Interestingly, the other wife, the double whom she had left behind to manage her household, also has a child—Manu, the first human being. Perhaps Saranyu's story, as a doubled mother of two sets of twins, may be, at a certain level, a wish-fulfilling fantasy of many mothers of twins; they may ache for a double, shadow, or copy-mother to cope with all the simultaneous double work of first birthing and then raising twins, especially in the early years.

In some versions of the myth, as Wendy Doniger eloquently traces its historical development through multiple Hindu texts over time, Saranyu and the shadow wife are considered twins. In her *Splitting the Difference: Gender and Myth in Ancient Greece and India*, Doniger offers a profound analysis of the act of doubling and twinning.[5] She traces Saranyu's movement from the *Rig Veda* to the Puranas. She finds that in certain ways Saranyu over time becomes a figure that has more and more agency. For instance, she herself creates the double and leaves her to take care of her children and husband. But there is a deep ambivalence to this agency. In certain other ways, she has become less of an individual. For example, when she returns back to her husband and her children, she seems to become more and more domesticated as a Hindu female. She lives in a co-wife situation with the Shadow double she had left behind to substitute for her; she becomes less her individual self and becomes more identified as the double of her shadow. In fact we can see this in the ultimate twinning of her self in the twin goddesses, Chotila and Chamunda, the personifications of the Devi mentioned earlier [Figure 8.2]. The very identical identity makes it a challenge to distinguish between the two figures. Doniger elaborates: "In the course of her long history in India, Saranyu not only loses her own intrinsic power (if not her agency) but accumulates more and more co-wives, who implicitly further limit both her individuality and her power."[6] So the act of this doubling, though enabling her agency, initially, also acts as a brake to her intrinsic powers. Here, we also notice from the beginning that there is an overlap between the categories of twin-ness and doubling, or even a kind of *shadowing of the main individual identity that is created by the very existence of the doubled version of the self.* This is an important feature of twin-ness that we need to keep in mind throughout this chapter.

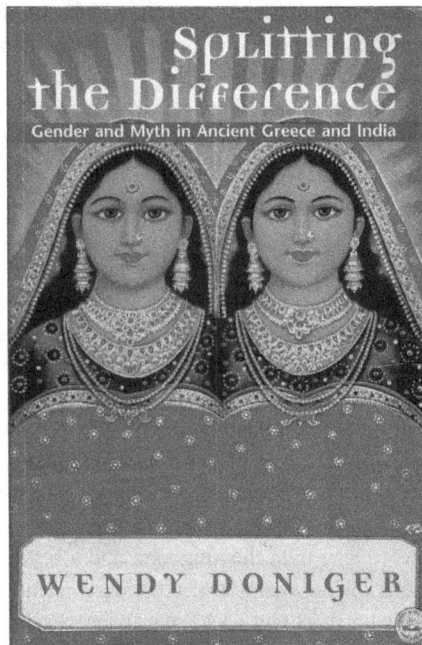

Figure 8.2 Chamunda and Chotila, twin goddesses from Gujarat. Cover image of Wendy Doniger, *Splitting the Difference: Gender and Myth in Ancient Greece and India* (The University of Chicago Press, 1999). By permission of the University of Chicago Press.

Twins in the *Ramayana*

In the major ancient epic, the *Ramayana*, twins appear as well. There are Dasharatha's twin sons, Lakshmana and Shatrughan, who are two of the four sons born to his third wife after a long drought of infertility, Rama being the eldest son of the four and the major hero of the story. Lakshmana serves as the ideal male companion to Rama, whereas Shatrughan plays a minor role. It is not clear whether they are identical or fraternal twins, but they lead very different lives and are rarely together except at their birth.

The *Ramayana* is usually finished with the lively and auspicious coronation of Rama as the ultimate good king of Ayodhya. But in some versions of the *Ramayana*, there is another additional book, called the Uttarakandam, which acts as a kind of epilogue to the *Ramayana*. It is not clear whether this was a part of the original *Ramayana* or not. This is a sad part of the story of the *Ramayana*, when Rama rejects Sita. Following a townsman's criticism of Sita's purity as she had been kidnapped by Ravana, the rakshasaic evil demonic king, and trapped for a long time in Ravana's palace, Rama, not wanting to favor his wife or behave unethically, asks Lakshmanan, to take Sita out of Ayodhya and leave her in the forest, alone. Sita, once arriving there, is helped by the great sage, Valmiki, who assists her in setting up a household in the forest. In most versions, she is abandoned, pregnant with twins, though Rama does not know that she is pregnant. During her banishment, she bears identical twins, Lava and Kusa (Kusha), in the forest and raises them.

In some versions, according to an elderly seventy-three-year-old Tamil immigrant grandmother, Richa, who is a grandmother of twin daughters, Sita is said to have only one child. In these versions, one day when Sita had left the child with Valmiki, Valmiki opened his eyes after meditating and saw that the baby had disappeared. He called out to the baby and there was no response. Afraid of Sita's wrath when she returns to find her child gone, he immediately meditated to create another baby of the exact image of the original lost infant child. When Sita returns back from her errand, with the original lost infant child in tow, Valmiki confesses what he had done. This oral version reveals one version how Sita ended up having twins. In any case, as they get older, Lava and Kusa are portrayed as close siblings and are idealized as siblings who get along and have an ideal amount of *orrumai*, a deep harmony, between them. They are trained by Valmiki to learn and sing the song of the *Ramayana,* and end up being reunited with Rama. At the same time, Sita decides to enter back into the womb of the earth; she disappears into the earth that opens up and receives her as her daughter. Rama then trains his twin sons to take over the kingdom, and after some years, disappears himself. In some versions of the *Ramayana*, the elderly Tamil grandmother, Richa, adds, Rama and all of his brothers end up having twins. So, in some versions of the *Ramayana*, there were four sets of twin children, one for each brother, an abundance of fertility and twins.

What is interesting to note in this story of Lava and Kusa is the theme of the loss or break up of the family once the twins are born. Somehow the husband is separated from the wife; and even when reunited, then *she* disappears. They are never together as a family again: Rama, Sita, Lava, and Kusa.

Yet, interestingly, these mythological twins, Lava and Kusa, symbolize a certain archetypal harmoniousness often associated with twin-ness itself. There is a sense that they never fought; they had a certain deep understanding between each other; they were very well behaved. There is little mention of sibling rivalry mentioned in this story, as is atypical of real life twins, who, as Kimberley Patton quotes her brother's identical twin children identical twin relatives in the Introduction to this volume, fight "because we *have to*."

Twins in Indian-American Families in Northern California

Parents of twins are increasingly present in various Indian-American organizations throughout the United States, reflecting the increase in IVF use and the greater likelihood of multiple births among many ethnic groups, apart from those that religiously prohibit it. I was interested in how Indian-Americans speak about the contemporary phenomena of twins in relation to twins in Hindu mythology, and additionally as to whether there were mythologies and stories that anchor these Indian-American families and affect their religious beliefs regarding twins. How do they refer to the normally previously exceptional biological phenomena of twins in the context of the rapid contemporary increase in twins? To answer these questions, I will now turn to my research conducted in the San Francisco Bay Area during the fall of 2008.

I conducted ten in-depth interviews of Tamil twin families, both by phone and in person from a sample of families in the California Tamil Academy, a weekly Sunday program for teaching Tamil to children in the San Francisco Bay Area. Founded in 1998, this organization currently has six branches: Cupertino, Fremont-Irvington, Fremont-Washington, Pleasanton, Evergreen, and San Ramon,[7] enrolling over 2,200 students between the ages of three and eighteen, studying Tamil from pre-school to high school age. These interviews are gathered from families of various backgrounds: Hindu and Christian, Tamil, Telugu, among others. I sent my twin children to one of the Fremont branches of the California Tamil Academy for four years and the Pleasanton branch for one year. Over these five years, I observed that there were at least a dozen sets of twins enrolled. I was able to interview ten sets of twins and their families, either directly or indirectly through their parents and grandparents.[8]

Initially I had imagined that I needed only to interview the mother of the twins to address the research questions I posed. But, I found it necessary to interview not only the mothers, but also the fathers and even the grandparents. Ever more frequently, I find myself interviewing the twins themselves, as they clamored to be included as a part of the process.

Four themes emerged from these interviews: (1) a sense of miraculousness surrounding the birth of twins; (2) the inherent, continual difficulties of the twins' mother; (3) the twins' constant oscillation between harmony and rivalry, and (4) the struggle of each twin for a self—an individual identity—versus a dual, twinned identity.

The Miraculousness of Twins and the Everyday Ordinary

The increasing use of scientifically advanced technology often has the potential to solve the problem of infertility, with not one but two children or sometimes even more. The infertility of the Indian-American family, whether Hindu, Muslim, Christian, Sikh, or Buddhist, creates a biological and social crisis; it also usually creates a religious crisis, just as it would in the native Indian family. However, in the United States, medical interventions that are more readily available to solve the biological, social, and religious crisis—IVF, IVI, GIFF, and various other procedural technologies—create an increase in twins beyond what would normally be the case in a given non-diasporic community. There has been a marked increased presence of twins among Indian-Americans, due to these procedures but also perhaps due to the delay of childbearing, as more and more women in this group have careers first before they become mothers.

Here I begin to map out some critical questions one might pose in a contemporary ethnography in California among diasporic Indians who have twins. To understand the presence and absence of religious and cultural categories bearing on twinship, I conducted some qualitative interviews to measure the ways in which the mythological twins in Hinduism operate in diasporic life. The results suggest that what was once an exceptional characteristic of families has become nearly commonplace. Yet the "specialness" of twins persists as a collective perception, and hence, as my young children experienced while representing goddesses for six hours, as a reality.

The questioning of traditional religious faith occasioned by the cruel, unrelenting experience of infertility, plunging the entire family into an experience of emptiness, is suddenly transformed from nothingness to a deep sense of double fulfillment.[9] The idea of two-ness (or *retta*, in Tamil) invokes the lived miracle of twin births, radiating a sense of supernatural "abundance" that these families carry within them. One father of twins, a computer programmer in the Silicon Valley named Raghavan, had told a story about his nearly seven-year-old non-identical, sororal twins. He said they first discovered they were going to have twins when the doctor heard two heartbeats in the ultrasound images. At first they did not know if it was one child with two heartbeats and their hearts were filled with fear and foreboding; they thought if it were not twins, it could be a child with special needs, for which they felt unprepared. A few minutes of silence passed, while the doctor continued to explore the ultrasound, and finally, to their relief, she said, "Ah, there are two heartbeats and they are, in fact, twins." His wife was so joyous and ecstatic that she was laughing out loud the entire time from the doctor's office to their car. When people asked her why she was laughing so much, his wife replied, still laughing, "We are going to have twins." The father continued, "She was so happy. Every time she has seen twins she had always wanted to have twins herself."

As an eleven-year-old set of sororal Tamil-American twins (although at first they looked identical, and also dressed nearly identically) said to me, "We are each other's best friends. We do fight, though. But it is more like bickering." When I first saw these twin girls, even though I am myself a mother of twins, I was stunned. There was a certain magical quality to them, as they moved with a certain grace-in-two-ness. They had an unusual rhythm with each other as if tied to each other by invisible strings. Though I had seen numerous twins in my life, because these particular twins seemed identical, they had an extraordinary atmosphere around them. A chill went through my body. I saw them, and wondered, for a moment, am I seeing double? Who are these two? Oh, yes, they are twins, my mind immediately answered. Rarely have I reacted in this way to twins, because most of the twins I encounter are non-identical. For the first time, I understood why people stopped us in the streets, and asked us, are they twins? I myself felt a certain awe at seeing a biological rarity. "There is a wow effect," as a Tamil-American father, Murthy, put it. "There is a wow effect that you never quite get over."

The elderly seventy-two-year-old Tamil grandmother, Richa, who had played an intimate and significant role in her Tamil-American twin granddaughter's lives, puts it this way: "The twins when they were born were so beautiful. I cannot even say how beautiful they looked. To have two girls, side by side from the same exact womb; to see two children of the same size, side by side in real life, whether identical or non-identical, was an extraordinary sight. It was a kind of magic." She reflects on her memories of twins in her rural village childhood in Tamil Nadu in southern India:

> Twins were so unusual in the old times. I remember twins in my childhood growing up in a village in Thanjavur district. There were rare sets of twins; and nearly every time, only one of the twins survived. It was extremely rare for both twins to survive childhood, let alone adulthood. It was rare for the mother to even survive, even with a normal one-child delivery; with two, there was nearly a guarantee of death. Now twin births are so common, *Sarva satharnana* (everyday ordinary). Everywhere you go now, everywhere you see twins all over the place. Here are women who delay childbearing, and then, cry over fertility programs that won't work and they do all their medical stuff, and now, here are twins all over the place![10]

Because of the exceptional nature of twins in earlier times, and their more commonplace nature now, they are *sarva sadharnam*, "everyday ordinary," and thus there is a huge shift of perception toward a lack of extraordinariness. Their appearance has become ordinary, common, though still tinged with the "magical," especially if they are identical twins. One might say that there is therefore an abundance of the extraordinary: magic abounds, rather than being fully diluted or negated as one might expect.

Mothers' Difficulties

One Tamil-American twin mother, a Christian, Maria, who works in the high-tech industry as a computer programmer, was very moving, forthright, and honest about her difficult experience in having twins. Her twins, fraternal, one boy and one girl, were ten years old at the time we spoke. She expressed her harrowing time, looking at me with deep sadness in her eyes.

> It was so hard to have twins. For me the pregnancy was a real challenge. I was on bed rest for a couple of months during the last part. I was so tired all the time. I am still tired all the time. It is an impossible situation, to have to tend to two

same-age children's needs at the same time, without prejudice or distinction. I am barely surviving myself. I can barely hold on being a mother of twins; it is too difficult.

Wearily, she continued,

It is an impossible task, and I nearly did not make it through myself as it was always too hard. I felt I could not bear the burden of carrying two. There is no rest for such a mother. You are either working, or you are taking care of the intensive needs of two children of the same age. To be honest with you, there is a kind of dread in me about the idea of twins. I still have that in me. Even though they are now ten, I have not gotten used to the idea of mothering twins.. . . .

As a mother, I am still angry at God about having twins. I did not want twins, and it has been too difficult in my life. In previous times, there were so many cases where the mother would not survive, or at least one of the twins would not survive birth, or the twins would have to be separated from each other or from their mother and fend for themselves. That is a common plot among some famous Tamil movies. So, I felt a dread when I was told that I was going to have twins.

In other words, Maria felt dread *not* because one or more members of the triad (of mother and twin infants) might perish, or because the triad would be separated in some way, as in the past, and reflected in the recurrent plot line of famous Tamil movies she knew. Rather, hauntingly, she felt dread because in twenty-first-century California, she knew that *the entire triad would probably survive*. In some ways, Maria's dread is echoed by the ancient Vedic story of Saranyu mentioned in the earlier section on Hindu Mythology. It occurred to me that Maria might welcome a substitute mother to care for her twins. Her sadness, perhaps biological depression, bespoke the way that the normal physical burden of caring for one infant is compounded by the overwhelming energy needed to take care of twin infants. This is perhaps what is highlighted in the story of Saranyu. Although I cannot speak for Maria's inner state, the interview conveyed to me at some level her Saranyu-like desire to somehow escape the situation.[11]

This dread of having and raising twins because of the overwhelming work involved is also paralleled in Arundhati Roy's highly nuanced Indian novel, *The God of Small Things*, where a set of fraternal twins, a boy and a girl, are separated at the age of seven years old. Their single mother falls apart after a tragedy occurs to her, and is no longer able to take care of them and dies in a state of penury. The twins do not meet again until they are in their thirties. This kind of narrative in films and literature seems to echo this woman's antipathy to the idea of twins, and her ongoing negative emotions about the reality of mothering them.

In my view, Maria implied a conscious or unconscious desire to leave the situation. She pointed out that in many old Tamil films, when there is a motif of a set of twins, inevitably the family breaks up. Usually the mother dies. The twins are separated. And then later reunited. The father disappears. They are orphaned, either together or alone. This feeling of being overwhelmed that Maria expresses is echoed by the mythic narratives of Saranyu's and Sita's split families, where the children in Saranyu's case are raised by an identical "shadow" twin whereas in Sita's, she is raising them alone as a single mother (though that does not really have anything directly to do with her having twins).[12]

At the first level of understanding these interviews with Hindu families of twins, my mention of Hindu mythology often seemed to elicit some connection to their sense of family life. Furthermore, questions about fertility and the relationship between the concept of fertility and twins in Hinduism frequently elicited a stated perception of the mother of twins in superlative, even quasi-supernatural terms. Raghavan, the father of seven-year-old non-identical sororal twins mentioned earlier, told me,

> Yes, the relationship between how we see fertility and the appearance of twins is direct. When a woman bears twins, she is considered to be a kind of super-mother. In fact, among other Tamil women, my wife, because she has born twins successfully, has a high status among other mothers. I see that all the time.

Here it is interesting to note that the twin mother is seen as a kind of "magical" mother, the magic of mothering doubled in her, primarily, I would argue, in her having survived the extra peril of the double birth herself, and secondarily, in the survival of her twin children. This may reflect a kind of vestigal mystification and mythologization of twins that has persisted for millennia and is globally distributed.

Sibling Rivalry vs. Harmony

As the elderly grandmother Richa stated, "While they are growing, when I see them, they are able to have an intimacy of friendship, rare among siblings. Because of their same age, [they have] a similar life experience." One set of eleven-year-old sororal twins, strikingly similar in appearance, said that they are each other's best friends. "Do you ever fight?" I asked them. They giggled and lost their smooth interview composure. "All the time!" they replied. The most common Hindu mythological twin frequently referenced in the interviews I conducted were not Saranyu or Yama and Yami; in fact, people were not really aware of these twins as such; the most commonly mentioned were Lava and Kusa, Sita's twins in the tail end of the epic *Ramayana*. In most of my interviews, the reference seems to have originated in popular cinema. This story has had many film renditions. In 2010, an animated film, Lava and Kusa: The Warrior Twins, was a major hit.[13] As in other versions of Lava and Kusa, their relationship was framed as always harmonious, without any sibling rivalry.

In fact, in my interviews, the Lava and Kusa myth was invoked to express the parents' surprise and disappointment over the intense, ongoing sibling rivalry manifested in their own, very real and non-epic twins. As Raghavan said,

> We had the image of Lava and Kusa as our original image of how our twins would be—that they would be harmoniousnessly incarnated. And it was a shock for us to realize once our twins were born, they were not at all like Lava and Kusa. In fact the rule was more of disharmony and frequent sibling rivalry.

Raghavan laughed. The mythological story of Lava and Kusa was often used as the transcendent corollary to what they expected from their own twins' behavior. Many parents expressed intense disappointment at the stark disparity between the myth and reality.

Among first-generation Indian-Americans who have come from India in the last two or three decades, in their thirties at the time of my research, there was little direct reference to the Vedic twin gods and goddesses in their narratives of their own actual twins. In-depth interviews of ten Indian-American families revealed a lack of direct influence of Vedic or Hindu mythology on the experience of parenting Indian-heritage twins in America. The exceptions are Rama's twins from the *Ramayana*, and that is, as I noted earlier, primarily through the vehicle of their popularization in film. However, Hindu mythology, or, at least, culturally internalized notions of superabundance and auspiciousness do seem to influence the multiple ways in which infertility, fertility, and twins are perceived in the community.

All of these families are intimately tied to the highly modern and contemporary world of high technology; their parents focused them as children on math and science while they were being raised in India. Among most of the families, there was a general disinterest in mythological traditions. Many of these families are also associated with the California Tamil Academy and so have chosen to put a significant amount of resources into the passing on of the Tamil language to their children, leaving less time and energy for exposure to Vedic-Hindu mythology. Another factor could be that the presence of twins in sacred literature is obscure enough to be difficult to have access to. Therefore, though the presence of Saranyu, Yama, and Yami is not echoed explicitly in the narratives of the families I spoke with, Lava and Kusa in the *Ramayana* in the Hindu religious traditions are found explicitly in the narratives of the families with whom I spoke. This popularity is referenced in the interviews to several popular Indian film renditions of the Lava-Kusa story, thus becoming the primary Hindu mythological reference point for twinship for these diasporic families, socially embedded in the California social landscape as highly skilled, upwardly mobile immigrants in very particular ways.

Twins and Self-Identity

It does make a difference on your sense of identity what type of twin you are, whether you are identical or non-identical (fraternal/sororal). Being an identical twin has an enormous impact on your perception of self and others' perception of you as a self and as a duality. According to Lawrence Wright, "Fraternal, or dizygotic, twins are caused by the fertilization of two separate eggs, and they are no more alike than ordinary siblings."[14] Although this is technically true, fraternal twins still have some of the common perceptions of twins foisted onto them in everyday life. The questions that have intrigued me most, both in the trope of twins in Hindu mythology and in Tamil-Indian-American family narratives about twinship, are those that trouble "the self" as a referent of identity. Between living twins, from birth onward, as I have myself observed in my own children, there are expressions of deep emotional intimacy, friendship and rivalry, of a sense of sibling-ness that is of two equal and opposite forces, facing each other sometimes and at other times facing away from each other, inexorably of each other and yet determinedly not of each other as well. What is this dynamic, even oscillating sense of self in an individual who is a part of a dyadic twin pair and how does it evolve over time? Is it static or fluid? Is individual self-representation in the individual responsive to the particular family construction of twinship? If so, how does that evolution of identity relate to the wider cultural context of having been born a twin? Are there any parallels between these psychological processes and Hindu mythological narratives and ideas?

The condition of being identical versus non-identical (or fraternal/sororal) makes a clear difference in identity formation. Yet even non-identical twins, though they do not have the experience of "interchangeable" identities that identical twins do, undergo many similar experiences of identification and mutuality that shape their personality and character. Individuation begins at an early age for each person, but fundamental notions of self, identity, and personhood that may be assumed for single children almost always become much more accentuated and fraught for biological twins. The very notion of twins has a built-in singularity that is in opposition to the duality of the individuals composing the singular category of twins.

In her novel *The God of Small Things*, Arundhati Roy speaks of the struggle, often bordering on inability, of twins to distinguish themselves from each other as independent entities:

> They never did look much like each other, Estha and Rahel, and even when they were thin-armed children, flat-chested, wormridden and Elvis Presley-puffed, there was none of the usual "Who is who?" and "Which is which?" from oversmiling relatives or the Syrian Orthodox bishops who frequently visited the Ayemenem House for donations. The confusion lay in a deeper, more secret place. In those early amorphous years when memory had only just begun, when life was full of Beginnings and no Ends, and Everything was Forever, Esthappen and Rahel thought of themselves together as Me, and separately, individually, as We or Us. As though they were a rare breed of Siamese twins, physically separate, but with joint identities. Now, these years later, Rahel has a memory of waking up one night giggling at Estha's funny dream. She has other memories too that she has no right to have. She remembers, for instance (though she hadn't been there), what the Orangedrink Lemondrink Man did to Estha in Abhilash Talkies. She remembers the taste of the tomato sandwiches—*Estha's* sandwiches, that *Estha* ate—on the Madras Mail to Madras. And these are only the small things. Anyway, now she thinks of Estha and Rahel as *Them*, because, separately, the two of them are no longer what *They* were or ever thought *They'd* be. Ever. Their lives have a size and shape now. Estha has his and Rahel hers.[15]

Identifying the self as a part of "them" or "they" is common for twins whether in fiction or in everyday life. As Roy describes them: "Esthappen and Rahel thought of themselves together as Me, and separately, individually, as We or Us. As though they were a rare breed of Siamese twins, physically separate, but with joint identities." In many ways, this "together as me" and "individually, as We" is the summation of the struggle for the separate, identifiable self in the context of being always seen in the context of two-ness that twins have to struggle under, another layer of becoming for the individual autonomous self in a twin set. We shall see this as one of the major themes in the following interviews with Jaya and Uma, my own twin children.

Interview with Jaya and Uma

Jaya and Uma clamored to be interviewed while I was working on this chapter. So I include a partial transcript of their interviews here, conducted in our home just prior to their eleventh birthday.[16] The caveat accompanying this particular snapshot is just that—as with any set of two siblings in a family, the relationship between twins, is necessarily evolving and kaleidoscopic, where the shift of balance of energies, competition, harmony all change, it seems, sometimes depending on the day, month, year. A few months after the initial interview while I was revising this chapter, they seemed much more harmonious than they had been in September when I spoke to them, and they were turning eleven that very month.

Excerpt of Interview of Jaya[17]

> **V:** *What are the things you most like about being a twin?*
> **J:** *It can be nice . . . sometimes. One of the most annoying things is that when I want to do something that she's doing, and we only have one of it, then I have to wait. But it can be nice because what if I don't have any other kids to play with, then I can always talk to her. And annoy her.*
> **V:** *And what are the things you most dislike about being a twin?*
> **J:** *We argue a lot, over like who does what first and who does what second. And if we both want to do the same thing, then we argue over who gets to do it first, and if one of us is doing one thing, and we both want to do it, we have to wait until the other person is done doing it. And then by that time we might have found another thing to do.*
> **V:** *Then how is that different from having a sibling where you have to share?*
> **J:** *If you have a sibling and you have to share, they might like different things than you. If they are younger than you, if you are maybe eight and they are maybe three, then they might be into choo choo trains or princesses, and you probably won't be into them because you are eight or nine. But if you have a twin, then you are both mainly into the same things.*
> **V:** *What do you two compete the most about?*
> **J:** *I don't know. We compete basically about everything.*
> **V:** *Oh okay! Why is it that you compete? What do you want or need from winning?*

J: *I don't know. We just want to feel good.*

V: *And what does that involve?*

J: *Competing and winning.*

V: *Do you consciously do things differently from your twin or consciously do things the same?*

J: *We consciously do things different but then sometimes we unconsciously do things the same. If we are consciously doing it different, for example, for our birthday parties just yesterday, she asked me what I was doing, a beach party or a slumber party, because she wanted to do the different one. So when I said beach, she said, "I'm doing slumber." Then when I said slumber, she said, "I'm doing beach."*

V: *What do you think about the word or concept of twins? Do you like or not like being called twins?*

J: *OK, I really dislike intensely being called "the twins" and I'm a little bit more okay with being called "the girls" but I'd rather be called by our names.*

V: *So what is it about the word "twin" that makes you feel like . . .*

J: *I don't know, I guess because we could be any gender, like a boy and a girl, or two boys, or two girls, and so it's not giving very much information, just saying "the twins," but "the girls" is a bit more specific then you know that they're both girls.*

V: *So how do you define the "I" of you and the "we" of you? When you are a twin, you're part of an "I" like an individual Jaya, but then you are also part of Jaya and Uma as a twin. So how would you think about those two different ideas?*

J: *I think of myself as just myself, not as "we." I think of me as "I."*

Excerpt of Interview with Uma[18]

V: *What are a few key things you would tell the world about being a twin from your own experience? Because most people aren't twins.*

U: *OK . . . people think it's like having a friend by your side all the time, but it's not like that. In this twin book, written by a twin, which I think is impossible* [in other words, Uma does not believe that an actual twin would have described the experience of twinship in this entirely positive way], *she says to have a twin is to have a best friend all the time!! That is not true!*

V: *What are the things you most like about being a twin?*

U: *Hmmm . . . hard to say. Oh you're never alone, but that can be a bad thing, too.*

Q: *In what way?*

U: *Sometimes you want to have some privacy. And you feel your twin says, "Ooh let me see what you're doing, oooh let me see what you're doing, ooooh let me see what you're doing!" And you're thinking, I don't want to show you, and then they grab the book from you that you are writing in or something and then say, "Ooh amazing! Dun dun dun." Then you say, "That's not funny," and walk out. And then you are sad. . ."*

V: *So what do you want or need from winning over them?*

U: *I want them to not be able to gloat!*

V: *Oh but then what about when you gloat?*

U: *I don't gloat!! (laughs)*

V: *(laughs) Okay let's just say you don't believe that you gloat. OK, somehow you feel them gloating more than you feel your gloating.*

U: *Umm, I'm always sure not to say, "I won and you didn't oh yeah oh yeah!"*

V: *Do you consciously do things differently from your twin or consciously do things the same?*

U: *We unconsciously do things the same but we consciously do things differently.*

V: *Can you give me an example?*

U: *So we always talk at the same time.*

V: *Why is that? Because that's really hard for a mother to hear!*

U: *Yeah, but sometimes we say the same thing at the same time! If someone asks us, what is your favorite thing about being a twin, we will both say "nothing" at the same time. That's an annoying question!*

V: *Why?*

U: *Because it's so normal for us! We'd either say "nothing" or "normal."*

V: *So when you compare yourselves to friends of yours who have siblings, what are the differences and the similarities?*

U: *I don't know. But for the most part, I can see that we argue more. Because if you have an older sibling they are usually doing homework or something, and if you have a little sibling, they can be really annoying but they're usually so cute you can let them off. But if it's the same age, then it is harder.*

I want to remind the reader of the ways in which Saranyu created an identical "shadow" twin who ends up taking up her primary place in the household, and who, when Saranyu returns, must share the household with her. This is true, I think, of actual twins as well. Jaya and Uma's desire to not be a shadow of each other in each of their own perceptions of themselves and each other as well as in other people's minds and imaginations is a constant theme, I think, in their relationship to each other as well as to me. It is a challenge to everyone to not elide one into the other, even from the usual mixing up of names that every parent with multiple children often do, but it has an extra effect with twins, I believe. Even though non-identical twins are considerably different than identical twins, there is still a proportionality of sameness and difference as they have shared deeply the same primary and secondary life experiences.[19] Yet they struggle constantly to escape from being thought of as the same from their very biological two-ness. Recently, a new classmate in a new school they were attending relentlessly teased them by calling them "clones," and they were very upset and felt it was utterly demeaning to them. They still talk of this put-down as the worst kind of insult, because it erased their very individualities by collapsing them into twin-ness: by seeming to assert that the very nature of twinship annihilated the possibility of separate selves.

Maternal Challenges

When a twin is experiencing herself or himself, is the twin concerned that the outsider looking at them is considering them as a copy or double of the other twin? Do they therefore feel less special, singular, unique? At the same moment that there is a doubling in the perception of the outsider, is there a halving of the self? As a mother of twins, I often feel as if I can give each of them only half of my attention, so that may be true for every person who encounters them. You cannot focus on one without ignoring the other, without making the other disappear from your view temporarily. *Is that what the other twin actually feels?*

It is true that when one twin is being attended to, the other may feel a kind of existential non-existence, invisible to the maternal "eye," or worse, to the mother's heart, even though for a moment. Is this radically different from the experience of singleton siblings, or any other relationship based on duality, such as a romantic couple? It may or may not be. Our eyes, despite their symmetrical duality, neurologically merge two perspectives to focus on only one thing. For one who "sees" as a mother or father, the ability to only focus on one of two equally valued "objects," one's own doubled children, occupying the same kinship niche (as Victor Turner observed), and often speaking at the same time or competing for parental attention, must necessarily create a kind of agitation or fundamental stress. As Jaya and Uma said in their interview, siblings of different ages would most likely have different interests, different household "niches." It is much harder for twins as they develop to create their own interests because they are constantly steeped in a shared cauldron with the same life experiences. It is clearly necessary for twins and their parents to work hard at creating space for individualized interests, dispositions, and understandings.

Conclusion

What we have seen so far is that the relationship between Hinduism and twinship is multivalent and inherently provocative. The themes of magical births, mothers' difficulties, twins' peaceful harmony alternating with intense competition, and constant challenge to negotiate identity and constitute a self all intertwine in both Hindu mythology and everyday Indian-American twin family lives. Saranyu, the original Vedic mother of a double set of twins, the one who escapes her burden by copying herself into a "shadow twin" to mother her children, does not seem to appear in contemporary Indian-American family narratives. Might this partially have to do with the myth's unflinching representation of (literal) maternal ambivalence? On the other hand, Lava and Kusa, the Hindu *Ramayana's* hero twins, appear often in contemporary diasporic awareness. They frame the actual experience of raising twins, even in faraway northern California: because the relationship of Lava and Kusa is idealized in the epic; they are, at least for some of my informants, the source of disillusion with their own twins' (very normal) friction and bickering. The simultaneous fusion and splitting of identity in twins remains a thorny fascination, both for those within the sphere of twinship and for those observing twins from the outside.

Notes

1   Though *sororal* is not a recognized word in some dictionaries, its prevailing use
    among non-identical twins born female has made this a compelling word. There is
    a general unease and resistance about using the word *fraternal* as it seems to erase
    their gender identity. As I walked around our small northern California town with a
    double stroller filled to the brim with Jaya and Uma when they were infants, I was
    corrected dozens of times by twin girls of varying ages: "We are not fraternal twins,
    we are sororal twins." After a while I began using the term as well and find that it
    is a more appropriate term than "fraternal," which eclipses the gender of the pair of
    twins. However, honoring the self-knowledge and determination of gender, I note that
    one of my twins, Jaya, identifies as gender non-binary over the past many years and
    now uses "they/them" pronouns. In this chapter I have therefore avoided words like
    "girls" and "daughters" in referring to my own twins, and I have since stopped using
    the term *sororal*, since this would misgender one of them.
2   I want to thank Uma and Jaya for helping me with this research paper, for providing
    me the inspiration and love fueling my curiosity and sustaining me with their good
    humor and creative insights throughout our intertwined lives. The seed of this
    chapter was planted with my paper "Twins in Hindu Mythology and everyday life
    in the California diaspora," as part of a panel on twins that Prof. Kimberley Patton
    pulled together among leading scholars. I want to especially thank Prof. Kimberley
    Patton for organizing this panel on twins at the American Academy of Religion
    (2009) in Chicago and inviting me to develop more fully the ideas I presented in
    that paper. Her encouragement and wise editorial assistance was crucial in shaping
    this chapter; Bethany Schmid, my research assistant, was so helpful in so many
    ways in making this chapter a reality. I wish to thank Professors Wendy Doniger,
    Kirin Narayan, Robert Goldman, and Shana Sippy for their help throughout our
    conversations over the past many years. Finally, and most importantly thank you
    to the California Tamil Academy and the many families and their twin children
    for supporting this research work by sharing their stories and, most of all, their
    enthusiasm and delight.
3   My ethnographic research stems from a selection of Tamil twins from a group of
    families who attend a weekend language acquisition of Tamil as organized by the
    California Tamil Academy and this, in fact, affects my findings.
4   See Wendy Doniger, *Splitting the Difference: Gender and Myth in Ancient Greece
    and India* (Chicago: University of Chicago Press, 1999), 43–55, for "The Shadow
    Sita and the Phantom Helen," enormously helpful to me in understanding the story of
    Saranyu and her role as a mother of twins.
5   Doniger argues persuasively that Saranyu is a liminal figure that acts as the bridge
    between the time of "abstract goddesses who have children and anthropomorphic
    goddesses who do not" (Doniger, *Splitting the Difference*, 155–6). Later on, human
    women marry or have sexual relationships with divine gods in order to have progeny,
    such as the wife of Pandu in the Mahabharatha. Goddesses no longer bore children
    (except for Parvathi, who conceived through parthenogenetic means, that is, from
    her own body). See also [Doniger] O'Flaherty, *Women, Androgynes, and Other
    Mythical Beasts* (Chicago: University of Chicago Press, 1980), 174–85) for a more
    detailed explication of various Saranyu myths in relation to Irish myths involving
    mares. Reflecting this theme of the mother as a twin, there is a set of twin goddesses
    in hill temples in the Saurashtra area of the state of Gujarat. Their names are Chotila,

who wears a green sari and Chamunda Devi, who wears a red sari; they both carry tridents and ride a lion as their animal vehicle or *vahana* and are considered to be personifications of Devi, a more ubiquitous name for the main goddess figure in Hinduism.

6 Doniger, *Splitting the Difference*, 50–1.
7 https://www.catamilacademy.org/branches.html, accessed July 25, 2017.
8 Names have been changed to protect the participants' identities.
9 For an excellent study on how modern reproductive technology is perceived through the lens of Hindu myths, see Swasti Bhattacharyya, *Magical Progeny, Modern Technology: A Hindu Bioethics of Assisted Reproductive Technology* (Albany: SUNY Press, 2006).
10 Many interviews over four years, 2009–2012.
11 Despite its frequent cultural insensitivity (see the note below), one of the rare books that unsparingly addresses the universal maternal ordeal and burden of bearing and raising twins is obstetrician Alessandra Piontelli's *Twins in the World: The Legends They Inspire and the Lives They Lead* (New York: Palgrave Macmillan, 2008).
12 For a range of cross-cultural perceptions of twins, Piontelli's views are based on many years of field experience of providing direct obstetrical care to underserved mothers in Italy, Northern and West Africa, and China. As a cultural anthropologist, I found her lack of empathy and compassion disturbing in her reports of twins' experiences around the world, especially in appreciating the powerful roles both of religion and of exigency. What I found missing from her book were twins' own accounts of their experiences from within the cultures she worked as a physician. This is arguably partly due to her own uncontextualized position in these cultures as a foreign, "First World" physician in obstetric care in conditions of dire poverty, including disease, socially sanctioned domestic and community abuse, and starvation. Piontelli often delivered twins and then tried to treat the consequences of maternal ambivalence and hardship, including extreme situations such as social stigmatization, child abuse or abandonment, including shockingly persistent traditions of twin infanticide. That her reports as a physician, trained first and foremost to ameliorate human suffering, may be accurate does not make them valid, especially when she appears to be passing judgment unfairly with an inadequate cultural depth of understanding. In particular she fails to appreciate the pressures of economic and other forms of distress on maternal and wider community treatment of twins, especially as infants. Unfortunately, Piontelli's is one of the few cross-cultural studies of twinship, a lacuna the present volume tries to begin to help fill. For benchmark behavioral research on twins, though not cross-cultural, see Nancy L. Segal, *Entwined Lives: Twins and What They Tell Us About Human Behavior* (New York: Penguin Group, 1999). For an excellent study on how twins appear in Western films and literature, see Juliana de Nooy, *Twins in Contemporary Literature and Culture: Look Twice* (New York: Palgrave Macmillan, 2005).
13 *Lava and Kusa: The Warrior Twins* film was directed by Dhavala Satyam (Kanipakam Creations with RVML Animation, 2010).
14 Lawrence Wright, *Twins and What They Tell Us About Ourselves* (New York: John Wiley and Sons, 1997), 11.
15 Arundhati Roy, *The God of Small Things* (New York: Random House, 1996), 4–5.
16 I interviewed my twin children, Uma and Jaya, in September 2011.
17 [Ed.]: This interview with Jaya Nagarajan-Swenson conducted by their mother when they were nearly eleven years old by their mother, the author Prof. Vijaya Nagarajan, is published with their express written permission. As mentioned above, Jaya

identifies as gender non-binary; therefore throughout the transcript of this interview, gendered language and pronouns referring to Jaya reflect that reality.

18 This interview with Uma Nagarajan-Swenson by her mother, the author Prof. Vijaya Nagarajan, is published with her express written permission.

19 For a fascinating exploration of the cultural modern notion of the "copy," whether person or thing, see Hillel Schwartz, *The Culture of the Copy: Striking Likenesses, Unreasonable Fascimiles* (New York: Zone Books, 1998). For an understanding of the ways in which different siblings may experience the same reality, see Judy Dunn and Robert Plomin, *Separate Lives: Why Siblings Are So Different* (New York: Basic Books, 1992).

Bibliography

Bhattacharyya, Swasti. *Magical Progeny, Modern Technology: A Hindu Bioethics of Assisted Reproductive Technology*. Albany: SUNY Press, 2006.

de Nooy, Juliana. *Twins in Contemporary Literature and Culture: Look Twice*. New York: Palgrave Macmillan, 2005.

Doniger, Wendy. *Splitting the Difference: Gender and Myth in Ancient Greece and India*. Chicago, IL: University of Chicago Press, 1999.

Dunn, Judy, and Robert Plomin. *Separate Lives: Why Siblings Are So Different*. New York: Basic Books, 1992.

Nagarajan, Vijaya. "Twins in Hindu Mythology and Everyday Life in the California Diaspora." Paper presentation in panel, "Twins and Twinship: Ongoing Comparative Development of a Theme," Kimberley Patton, convener and chair. Comparative Studies in Religion Section, American Academy of Religion, Chicago, IL, November 2009.

Narayan, Kirin. *My Family and Other Saints*. Chicago, IL: University of Chicago Press, 1997.

O'Flaherty, Wendy Doniger. *Women, Androgynes, and Other Mythical Beasts*. Chicago, IL: University of Chicago Press, 1980.

Patton, Kimberley, ed. *Gemini and the Sacred: Twins and Twinship in Religion and Myth*. London: Bloomsbury Academic, 2022.

Piontelli, Alessandra. *Twins in the World: The Legends They Inspire and the Lives They Lead*. New York: Palgrave Macmillan, 2008.

Roy, Arundhati. *The God of Small Things*. New York: Random House, 1996.

Satyam, Dhavala. *Lava and Kusa: The Warrior Twins* (film). Directed by Dhavala Satyam. Kanipakam Creations with RVML Animation, 2010.

Schwartz, Hillel. *The Culture of the Copy: Striking Likenesses, Unreasonable Fascimiles*. New York: Zone Books, 1998.

Segal, Nancy L. *Entwined Lives: Twins and What They Tell Us About Human Behavior*. New York: Penguin Group, 1999.

Ward, Daniel. *The Divine Twins: An Indo-European Myth in Germanic Tradition*. In University of California Publications: Folklore Studies, 19. Berkeley, CA: University of California Press, 1968.

Wright, Lawrence. *Twins and What They Tell Us About Ourselves*. New York: John Wiley and Sons, 1997.

Part Four

Twins in the Ancient Mediterranean

9

Entangled Bodies

Rethinking Twins and Double Images in the Prehistoric Mediterranean

♊

Lauren Talalay

Introduction

Prehistoric figurines in the shape of the human form—which first appear in the archaeological record approximately 40,000 years ago—have long captured both public and scholarly imagination. Initially interpreted as fertility items and Mother Goddesses, these images have now become the focus of more theoretical discourses, with recent discussions exploring the roles figurines played in shaping an early anthropology of the body, rather than their possible functions in religion and ritual.[1] Among the numerous collections interrogated as part of these ongoing discussions are several thousand Neolithic and Bronze Age figurines from the eastern Mediterranean. For the most part, these depict *single* images of standing or seated figures. What has largely eluded analysis within this group is a handful of items representing two identical portrayals, conjoined, merged, or encapsulated in some way.[2]

The concepts of twins and twinship provide a valuable optic through which to view these unusual images.[3] Cast as metaphors for unity and balance or, alternately, duality and conflict (e.g., see Aldhouse-Green in this volume), twins and the notion of a "second self" are well documented in the social lexicon and written sources of many ancient cultures (e.g., see Nagy, Frame, Skedros, Riley, Stang, and Patton in this volume; and the work of Dasen[4] and Price[5] on twins and multiples in the ancient Mediterranean world, including early Christian thought). We know, however, almost nothing about twins and the concept of human doubles in early societies where we are solely dependent on mute remains. Did the arrival of twins in prehistoric periods, for example, leave imprints, however faint, in the archaeological record?[6] Are the striking, twin-like images, which form the focus of this paper, a referent or visual rhetoric for such complex concepts as individuality, shared identities, and sameness (and by association the notion of difference) in these remote periods?

In an attempt to begin answering these questions, the ensuing pages gather together evidence of twin and double human images from the Neolithic through Middle Bronze Age periods (approximately 6500 to 1700 BCE, uncalibrated radiocarbon dates) in regions extending from the ancient Near East and Turkey to Greece and the Balkans. Such large swaths through time and space preclude precisely gauged insights into how each society might have shaped the production, use, and meanings of these representations. Studies since 2000 have shown that the symbolic significance of twins and doubles is culturally contingent, complex, and unstable (e.g., work by Renne and Bastian;[7] de Nooy;[8] Stewart;[9] and Peek;[10] Viney's recent book[11] asserts the same). Twinning and doubling, however, are also global phenomena that embrace comparable themes in the mirror-worlds of nature and culture. This chapter, therefore, poses not a particular question about what each figure may have meant, but a broader, more basic query, embedded in an overarching approach: why did many early cultures choose to represent identical dyads, materializing ideas of "sameness" and "the double," particularly in their repertoire of human figurines? Although the precise definition of "twins" and "doubles" are not identical, they are closely related; it has even been suggested that twins express "the most ancient and pervasive version of the double."[12] Exploring the contours of that observation may help us locate an early, pan-Mediterranean discourse on human doubles in this part of the ancient world.

Twins and Doubles in Mediterranean Prehistory

Given current data, there is no way to determine if the figurines discussed here were construed by the users and makers as actual twins, be they mortal, mythical, or divine. It is reasonable to posit, however, that these figures were intentionally crafted to give the impression of twins (rather than opposite sexed couples). All the examples are designed as composite entities, entailing identical double images conjoined at several points (rather like Siamese twins), shared or merged bodies with twin heads, or two matching images incorporated into one another in some fashion. Variations on these basic types notwithstanding, the visual vocabulary seems to materialize the idea of twinship, and, as I will argue in this chapter, foreground questions about compound identities, or what Hillel Schwartz has labeled "indivi/duality."[13]

Twins have occurred in the history of every society of the world, and the ethnographic record is rife with reports of double births: the occurrence of a double delivery, in place of the more expected single-birth, is cause for notice. Responses are notably variable: twins may be hailed with joy and ceremony or greeted with anxiety and caution. Regardless of the particulars, anthropological studies indicate that twins are usually assigned a category that sets them apart, cast as possessing special powers, and often seen as creating social disruptions that require "strategies of normalization."[14] Whether comparable ideas characterized thinking in the prehistoric Mediterranean is not yet knowable, but the universality (both past and present) of these attitudes, the rarity and difficulty of twin births,[15] and the hardships of raising twins suggest that these early societies also may have viewed twins as a distinct class with attendant needs and unusual powers.[16]

Although the prehistoric record in the eastern Mediterranean has left virtually no evidence of twin births or burials, the twin-like figurines provide a good starting point for exploring the significance of human doubles in this region.[17] Before proposing an analysis of the conjoined images, I briefly review the data, moving geographically from east to west.

Near East

The most dramatic examples of double figures come from 'Ain Ghazal, Jordan, a large "egalitarian" Neolithic community that was occupied for over 2,000 years (*c.* 7200 to 5000 BCE), probably housing thousands of individuals over the millennia. Excavations in the 1980s unearthed remarkable examples of large human statues, small figurines, and specially treated skulls, all of which hint at complex and sophisticated social rituals.[18] Among these objects are more than thirty statues constructed of limestone plaster on an armature of twigs, reeds, and cordage and measuring 35 to 100 cm tall, appreciably larger than most contemporary human images.[19] Three definite and two possible examples depict a schematized body (often referred to as busts in publications) out of which spring two identical heads [Figure 9.1a].[20] Although the makers opted for no bodily details, the faces are modeled with mouths and noses, and large, staring eyes outlined in black. It has been suggested that these unusual figures were once clothed and adorned with wigs and headgear, creating a slightly different appearance than the one depicted here.[21] While such additions may have helped differentiate the conjoined images, such adornments also could have rendered them more identical. In either case, they could certainly have been perceived as melded images conveying the notion of a "double self."

All of the statues were recovered from two separate caches dating to 6700 and 6500 BCE respectively, with the twin-headed examples confined to the later cache. Both deposits were located beneath the floors of long-abandoned houses, thus segregating them from the living, yet still associating them with the domestic sphere. As some archaeologists have imagined, the statues originally stood in shrines or structures, associated with public enactments linked to important social events reinforcing community identity and values.[22]

Both the twin- and single-headed versions have been variously interpreted: as elements in ancestor cults;[23] as ghost images employed in expulsion rituals (an interpretation based on later Babylonian texts);[24] or as representations of specific gods. Schmandt-Besserat, for example, proposes that the twin-headed types portray the Babylonian god Marduk, who is described in later Near Eastern texts as having two heads, four ears, and four eyes, all of which, according to the verses, express the ideas of infinite beauty, omnipresence, and wisdom.[25] Their particular symbolic intents notwithstanding, what is most striking for our purposes is that they broadcast ideas of a compound or merged identity in which a single body supports twin heads.

Later and quite different Near Eastern images of twin-like figurines come from the site of Tell Brak in northeastern Syria, one of the largest tells in northern Mesopotamia. Occupied for several millennia (roughly 6000–1360 BCE), the site is well known for

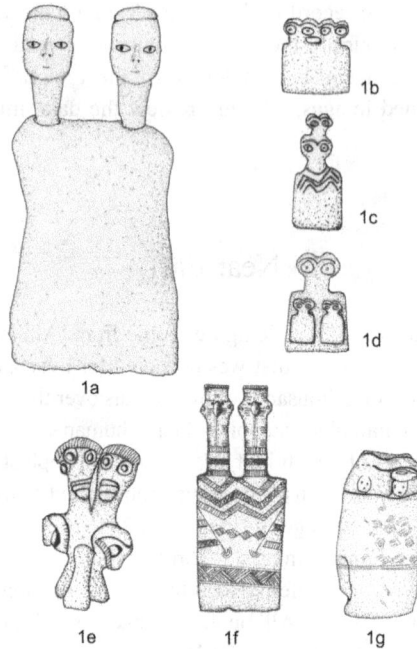

Figure 9.1 a–g. All drawings in this chapter (Figures 9.1–4) are the work of the author and are published with her express permission. 1a. Double-headed statue, 'Ain Ghazal, Jordan. Ht. 83 cm (one head mostly restored). After http://www.asia.si.edu/jordan/html/views2.htm. 1b-d. Eye Idols, Tell Brak, Syria. Hts. *c.* 3–6 cm. After Mallowan 1965, Ill. 40. 1e. Double-headed seated male figure, unknown provenance, Syria. Ht. *c.* 9 cm. After Badre 1980, pl. LXVI, 68. 1f. Double-headed plank figure, Dhenia, Cyprus. Ht. 28.5 cm. After Morris 1985, fig. 218. 1g. Double cradle figure, Lapithos, Cyprus. Ht. 19.9 cm. After Karageorghis 2003, fig. 50.

its so-called Eye Temple. Originally excavated in 1937–8 by Max Mallowan, the Eye Temple is actually a series of successive platforms and temples, built one atop the other.[26] The second temple, which has recently been re-dated to the earlier part of the fourth millennium,[27] yielded thousands of "eye idols," found together with thousands of beads and amulets.[28] Ranging from roughly 3 to 6 cm in height and 3 to 7 mm in thickness, the eye idols are carved mostly from limestone or alabaster. They are noted for their short necks topped by two pronounced eyes, some of which were originally colored with black, red, or green paint, enhancing their intent gaze.[29] Despite the mass-produced look of these idols, there are distinct variations; of most interest to us are those, like the 'Ain Ghazal images, that show a single body with twin heads. Also like the substantially larger 'Ain Ghazal examples, the bodies of the eye idols are highly schematic and virtually devoid of anatomical detail, suggesting (at least to our modern eye) that they were either sexless or sexually ambiguous. The twin heads are most often represented side-by-side, emerging out of the blockish body [Figure 9.1b] or sometimes perched one set of eyes atop the other [Figure 9.1c]. In addition, the repertoire includes twin-headed eye idols with two or sometimes three smaller, identical figures carved onto the abdomen of the idol, or single-headed eye idols also with smaller, twin images etched into the belly of the figure [Figure 9.1d].

All of the eye idols, along with the beads and amulets, were buried and sealed within a 60 cm thick stratum of gray bricks that constituted part of an early temple. Although Mallowan could identify the stratum from which these idols derived, he could not ascertain their exact position, partially because later plunder's tunnels substantially disturbed the area.[30] Some of the figures were apparently part of the brick's matrix (a common practice in the ancient Near East), but it is difficult to know if other idols served as foundation offerings, functioned as votive gifts made throughout the life of the temple, or found their way into the stratum through other means.

The precise meaning of these eye-idols remains enigmatic. Mallowan suggested that all eye idols, regardless of their differences, represented abstract symbols of a divinity, perhaps an all-seeing goddess associated with childbirth or protection. He envisioned these items produced by the thousands, sold at a temple workshop, and dedicated by pilgrims or by members of the local population to the presiding deity of the temple.[31] As to the double images, Mallowan proposed that the pairs might reflect either a joint dedication by a man and wife or the representation of the divinity as an indivisible pair, incorporating both the male and female counterparts essential to reproduction.[32] Given Mallowan's ideas, the "twins in the belly" type would have been in keeping with a focus on fertility, possibly expressing a wish for twin births.[33] Other archaeologists have suggested that the eye idols represented the individuals of Brak who dedicated these objects during the building of the temple foundation as symbols of their devotion.[34]

Finally, there is a very different and unprovenanced twin-headed example [Figure 9.1e], probably dating between 1900 and 1450 BCE, from the Aleppo Archaeological Museum, Syria. Fashioned from clay, it depicts a seated, two-headed, bearded image with a possible axe on each shoulder. Unlike the other Near Eastern images discussed earlier, the Aleppo piece is male, aligned with a known type of seated males providing offerings.[35]

In sum, the twin images from these early periods of the ancient Near East present three different, but perhaps related, types: (1) figures with single bodies out of which emerge two identical heads ('Ain Ghazal; Tell Brak; Aleppo Museum); (2) single-headed anthropomorphs with blockish bodies onto which are depicted twin portrayals (Tell Brak); and (3) double-headed figurines with twins (or triplets) etched into the belly (Tell Brak).

Cyprus

Prehistoric Cyprus is relatively rich in the production of double anthropomorphs, in keeping with a long tradition among early Cypriote artisans for playful and inventive pottery with duplicating motifs.[36] Most relevant to our concerns are the so-called plank figures, which are primarily confined to the final phase of the Early Cypriot through Middle Cypriot periods (*c.* 2000–1700 BCE), and have been the focus of debate among scholars for many decades.[37] Although most plank figures are single-headed clay images, nearly twenty-five examples portray twin heads emerging out of a single body [Figure 9.1f].[38] Not as large as the 'Ain Ghazal images, they are still substantial, some measuring up to 26 cm in height. Flat and simplified in their overall outline of the human form, the twin-headed images differ from both the 'Ain Ghazal and Tell Brak examples in having their fronts and backs covered with incised designs (perhaps depicting facial features, dress, tattoos, or scarification). Those examples that have good archaeological contexts were excavated from Early Bronze Age collective graves on the northern part of the island, suggesting mortuary intentions.[39]

There are, in addition, other doubles found on Cyprus in prehistoric contexts, each quite different from one another, but all linked to the notion of creating twin-like human images to be used, handled, or somehow incorporated into the lives of the people who inhabited these early settlements. The first is a variant of the "classic" cruciform figurine, dating to the Chalcolithic (roughly 3800–2400 BCE). Classic cruciforms, which are usually carved from picrolite (a stone with distinctive green and blue hues), depict seated or squatting figures with extended, widespread arms, often with no details of hands, wrists, or fingers, lending a cross-like aspect to the image. Many are quite small and pierced near the top, apparently to be worn as pendants. In the twin-like variations the arms have been transformed into a second, virtually identical body that may be slightly smaller in size [Figure 9.2a].

Four such figures are currently published and in each case both of the cross-like figures are almost identical, imparting a degree of visual playfulness, with "arms becom[ing] bodies and bodies becom[ing] arms, as the object is turned in the hand."[40] Equally intriguing is a unique and beautifully crafted classic cruciform image that has become emblematic of prehistoric Cyprus, sold in tourist shops as a necklace, pendant, or reproduction [Figure 9.2b]. Excavated from a Chalcolithic tomb[41] and standing nearly 16 cm tall, this unusual piece is adorned with a necklace portraying a miniature version or double of itself (perhaps the world's first selfie).

Finally, two examples of possible twin "cradle figures"[42] were excavated from Middle Bronze Age tombs dating between 1950 and 1700 BCE in the northern part of the island. Single cradle figures are categorized as a type of plank figure in which the plank has become the board of a baby's cradle, with the baby "snugly tucked in [its] swaddling clothes"[43] and safely secured to a cradle. The rare double examples [e.g., Figure 9.1g] show two nearly identical figures laying side-by-side in their cradle, and have been variously interpreted as twin babies with the board personifying a female figure,[44] or as a heterosexual couple lying in a bed.[45]

All of the examples from Cyprus—the two-headed plank figures, the cruciform images, the figure wearing itself as a pendant, and the twin cradle figures—have elicited a range of interpretations. Most figures are seen as charms or fertility items having magical or apotropaic powers. Cypriote plank figures, for example, have been traditionally interpreted as fertility charms, Mother Goddesses, hybrid monsters, or even marriage contracts.[46] Some assessments have suggested that they represent certain kinds of personal identities[47] or were purposely multifunctional and sexually ambiguous, allowing for flexible uses within mortuary and ritual contexts.[48] The twin-like cruciform figures, which are apparently unique to the island of Cyprus, have also

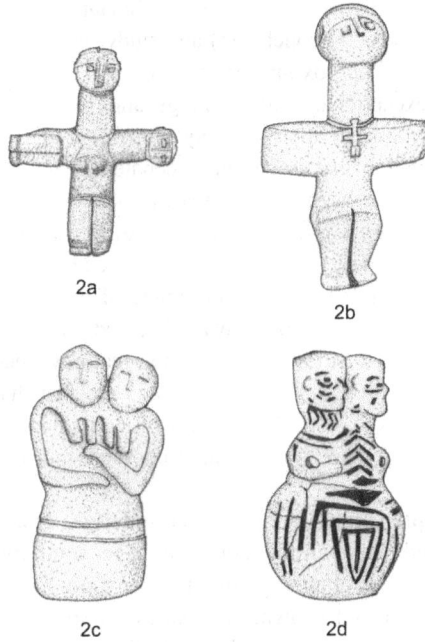

Figure 9.2 a–d. 2a. Cruciform figurine, Paphos district, Cyprus. Ht. 9.3 cm. After Morris 1985, fig. 169. 2b. Cruciform figurine, Yiala, Cyprus. Ht. 15.6 cm. After Morris 1985, fig. 150. 2c. Double-headed figurine, Çatalhöyük, Anatolia. Ht. 16.4 cm. After Mellaart 1967, fig. 70. 2d. Double-headed clay vessel, Hacilar (?), Anatolia. Ht. 32 cm. After Aitken et al. 1971, pl. 4.

been interpreted as fertility images, focusing on a wish for twin births; as "double-strength" charms; as mating figures or depictions associated with ideas about birth and death; and as items related to the idea of the island's kinship system.[49] The figurine wearing itself has been classified as yet another example of a fertility charm,[50] with particular focus on the pendant as a kind of fetish that would be worn on the body or held during the birthing ritual.[51] Interestingly, the more metaphorical considerations entertained in this chapter are less investigated; indeed, surprising little has been said about these figures and their possible connections to the philosophy of the double.

Anatolia

The Anatolian doubles fall within similar paradigms, including the single body supporting two identical heads (Çatalhöyük, Hacilar, and Kültepe), the "twins in the belly" type (Kültepe), and identical, frontal images attached at one hand and the hip (Alaca Höyük).

The earliest example [Figure 9.2c], dating to approximately 5900–5800 BCE, comes from the site of Çatalhöyük, a well-known Neolithic settlement in south central

Turkey initially excavated in the 1960s by James Mellaart[52] and for 25 years, the focus of renewed fieldwork (recently concluded) and study under Ian Hodder.[53] Occupied during the Neolithic from approximately 7500 to 5700 BCE, the site is famous for its substantial size, exceptional wall paintings and plaster reliefs, and figurines. The original excavator labeled approximately 30 percent of the rooms as shrines or sanctuaries,[54] a designation that is currently debated. Vocabulary notwithstanding, these rooms appear to have been special areas, possibly for some kind of public or private gathering. One "shrine" yielded a number of figurines, including an unusual example of a conjoined female figure depicting a shared body, four breasts, two arms and two heads. Measuring 16.4 cm tall and made of marble, it was seen as a cult statue of a "twin goddess" by Mellaart, who observed that "[T]win goddess figures are by no means rare" at the site,[55] an observation that now seems overstated, given some dubious reconstructions, misattributions, and the fact that recent excavations are casting doubt on the goddess status of many of the figurines. Twinning of various motifs does, however, occur on some wall decorations but their meanings remain elusive.[56]

The second example [Figure 9.2d] allegedly derives from the site of Hacilar, another Neolithic and Chalcolithic community in southern Turkey excavated by Mellaart (1957–60). Probably dating to the sixth millennium, the precise provenance of the piece is not known.[57] Measuring approximately 30 cm in height, it is a well-made, decorated clay vessel with hollow, twin heads emerging out of a shared body.

There are, in addition, a series of later figurines from Kültepe in southern Anatolia, reminiscent of examples from Tell Brak, Cyprus, and 'Ain Ghazal, as well as several unusual figures from the Early Bronze Age tombs at Alaca Höyük.

Kültepe (ancient Kaneš), an important trading center of the third millennium, was the focus of both official and clandestine excavations during the first decades of the twentieth century. Those excavations unearthed at least twenty examples of striking stone figurines, all of which are circular, have no arms or legs, and show long necks topped by triangular heads. Sex is usually indeterminate, although a few may indicate a pubic triangle. Of the twenty published examples,[58] six have double heads [e.g., Figure 9.3a], seven triple heads, and possibly two are carved with "twins in the belly" [e.g., Figure 9.3b]. Reports are skimpy, but these pieces, when complete, range in height from 10 to 27 cm. Although many of them are unprovenanced, they probably date to the first half of the third millennium.

The examples from Alaca Höyük are quite different. The figures were recovered from Tomb H, one of the so-called Royal Tombs of the settlement; these tombs consist of approximately a dozen graves dug within the confines of the site, and containing a number of flexed individuals. Although the precise chronology is still debated, the tombs can be attributed to the middle of the third millennium. Part of the lavish assortment of gold, silver, electrum, and ceramic grave gifts buried with the deceased, these small, violin-shaped figures of repoussé gold measure around 4 cm in height and depict twin images attached at one hand [Figure 9.3c]. Although their sex is debatable, they could be seen as female. At least five are reported, found near the chin of one of the deceased.[59]

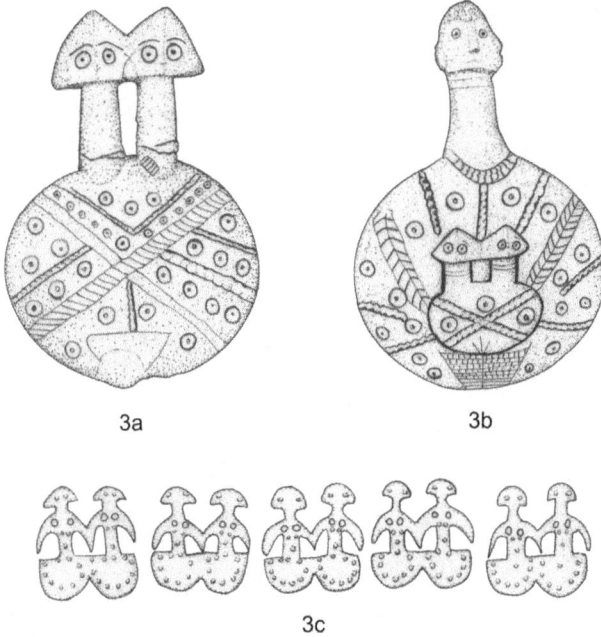

3a   3b

3c

Figure 9.3 a–c. 3a. Two-headed figure, Kültepe, Anatolia. After http://commons
.wikimedia.org/wiki/File:Two-headed_goddess_kultepe.jpg. 3b. "Twins in the belly" type
figure, Kültepe, Anatolia. Ht. 20.2 cm. After Karamete 1935, pl. 11. 3c. Series of double
figures, Alaca Höyük, Anatolia. Hts. *c.* 4 cm. After Koşay 1951, pl. CXXIX, 2.

Greece

Only one definite example of a twin image has been reported from prehistoric
Greece [Figure 9.4a], probably dating to the Early Neolithic, sometime between
6000 and 5000 BCE. Said to be from Thessaly[60] it represents a well-made and
carefully fashioned clay figurine, measuring approximately 6 cm tall. Two
identical figures stand side by side, attached at the buttocks and upper thigh, with
a possible depiction of their respective arms on the connected side draped across
each other's back and shoulder. They show no sexual attributes, but have slightly
swollen bellies.

A second image, perhaps half of an originally conjoined figure, is also reportedly
from Thessaly.[61] It also comes from a private collection, thus offering no details
of context. Finally, it is worth mentioning that twin images are also found in the
prehistory of the Balkans. In the case of Eastern Europe, the figures are primarily
Neolithic, restricted to single bodies with two heads [e.g., Figure 9.4b].[62]

Although it is impossible to estimate how many twin or double figures were produced
during the time period discussed (perhaps as many as fifty, excluding the twin eye
idols from Tell Brak), they clearly form a distinct component of the overall figurine

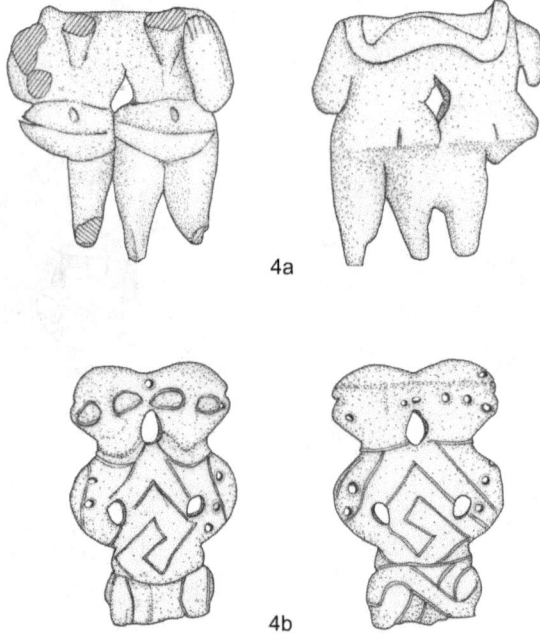

Figure 9.4 a-b. 4a. Double figurine, Larissa, Greece. Ht. 5.9 cm. After Papathanassopoulos 1996, fig. 234. 4b. Double-headed figure, Gomolova, Serbia. Ht. *c.* 7 cm. After Gimbutas 1974, figs. 100, 101.

repertoire. Widely scattered in time and space, the corpus reveals instructive patterns. Twin-like doubles are expressed in several forms and, as noted above, can be loosely classified into a few basic types. Whether the symbolic intention of each type was similar is not known; what is clear, however, is that these images surprise the viewer by either substituting an individual body where two would be expected (or, depending on one's viewpoint, two identical heads where one would be anticipated), or by conjoining two bodies in various fashions. In most cases, the boundaries of individual identity are effectively blurred, replaced with a visual code suggesting shared or double identities. Equally noteworthy is the fact that designation of sex is often submerged. Although a few examples are arguably female, and the 'Ain Ghazal statues may have worn clothes and wigs signaling their sex, many of the images seem to be sexless, perhaps intentionally ambiguous. Age is also a seemingly unimportant parameter: the larger figures might be interpreted as "adults," and the "twins in the belly" and cradle types could be seen as infants. The materials selected for many of the images—gold for the Alaca examples, alabaster for the Tell Brak eye idols, marble or calcite for the figures from Kültepe and Çatalhöyük—are not common for figurines of these time periods. In some instances, the original source of the raw material appears to have been located some distance from the site, indicating the object's value as a metric of distance and labor. When the more common material, namely clay, is employed, the figures are carefully formed and sometimes decorated with intricate details. These objects, therefore, are not dispensable items destined for the rubbish heap, as appears to be the norm for cruder, contemporaneous, anthropomorphic figurines usually fabricated from clay. Although contexts vary, most twin figures derive from burials, "shrines," or caches, pointing to a status outside the domestic sphere, and possibly to attendant activities or enactments associated with their deposition in these contexts. Finally, with the exception of the 'Ain Ghazal examples, all of the figures are small to mid-sized, indicating that they were easily manipulated, perhaps part of a miniature world created by the users. In sum, these fairly rare types represent specialized, high-quality, often sexually ambiguous, and mostly portable images that required a degree of intimacy, tactility, and close contact when used. Equally important, they are often deposited in singular contexts, frequently outside the domestic realm of a site.

Discussion

It is impossible in this limited space to do justice to the symbolic complexity of these images, to the myriad possibilities they raise about the double in prehistoric contexts, or to parse the variety of meanings across types. As suggested already by several scholars, these objects probably broadcast different meanings, depending on their cultural contexts: the 'Ain Ghazal images may have indeed represented deities, and the Cypriot cruciforms possibly served as fetishes connected to birthing rituals. The distinctive forms certainly evoke deities or the supernatural, and the notion of multiplicity suggests fertility.

Symbols, however, are notoriously layered and pluralistic, often characterized by a network of stronger and weaker meanings. While the more traditional proposals seem plausible, it is instructive to step back and think about these objects from a more expansive perspective. My concern is not whether these pieces represent particular deities, twin-headed monsters, fertility items, or the like. I explore, instead, a realm of thought behind those specifics. In particular, I am interested in the philosophy of the double, and ideas inspired by twin studies, which repeatedly note that double births and twinship provide ideal vehicles for exploring the notion of the "self."[63] Unlike singletons, twins demand a "looking twice" in order to sort out their confusing status as "two as one" or "one as two," calling into question how societies define the concept of individual identity.

Rather than the polarity of singularity and reduplication, these ancient Mediterranean images appear to present a *continuum of the double*, running the gamut from two identical depictions attached at various points of the body, to two bodies seemingly merged into one, out of which spring twin heads, to bodies that wear tiny replicas of themselves, to two identical images that are not attached or melded into a single body but rather conjoined in some other fashion. Despite these differences, all focus on visually duplicating some part or all of the human form, thus questioning what governs our thinking about identity, human resemblances, and the self/other opposition.[64] From our Western vantage point, for example, even a casual study of the twin-headed and conjoined images engenders pointed questions: What does it mean to strongly resemble someone else? What if one possessed not a single and bounded body but a double and entangled one? How do we understand the notion of divided unity in human identity? Do all societies possess a sense of individual uniqueness and how is that mediated? These questions problematize, among other things, the notion of the self as bound to a single bodily entity. Although such reflections might seem more at home in a post-modern world of analysis, we should not discount that some semblance of them existed in these early societies. Members of early Mediterranean societies surely dealt with definitions of "personhood" and how one's identity played out through the body.

Gaining any real purchase on ideas about identity in prehistoric contexts, however, is a vexed enterprise. Marilyn Strathern's frequently referenced *dividual* self may be helpful as a theoretical starting point.[65] The concept of dividuals—as distinct from the western idea of individuals—refers to the idea that persons and bodies are not irreducibly unique and bounded units, but composite and divisible entities that interact throughout their lifetimes, creating and defining a variety of shifting relationships. While we cannot prove that some segments of the prehistoric Mediterranean population held similar ideas, the archaeological record provides some tantalizing data in keeping with such notions. For example, human skeletons are often fragmented, with heads and other parts of the body apparently removed prior, during, or after burial. Anthropomorphic figurines are also often intentionally fractured for various and still poorly understood reasons. Whether such divisions reflect a dividual or partible self is open to debate, but the evidence suggests that the body and, perhaps by extension, "the person" were conceived in parts, subject to division, dispersement, and re-assemblage. It is possible, therefore, that at least some of the twin-headed and conjoined examples cited in this study were part of this continuum of partible bodies, possibly even a "special edition" of the dividual.

Going a step further, I suggest that these double images were used in special circumstances to reference the idea that some identities were seen as divided into twin-like components, with each part capable of being joined or merged into a new entity. Comparable ideas surface in other cultures and are instructive: the ethnographic literature, for example, frequently notes the existence of a second self or "double spirit,"[66] as do some ancient societies.[67] In these contexts, persons appear to be defined not as a single entity, but composed of two parts whose double or twin can act as a stand-in, ghost, or mirror image that may be particularly effective in accessing the divine or the deceased. Persons are seen as "indivi/duals"; two entities that are the same, but different, fused as one but still somehow distinct. Like "real twins" studied by ethnographers across the globe, they represent a special category that possesses unusual powers.

If the early Mediterranean images do indeed materialize a comparable concept, they would remind the users that, in some instances likely linked to ritual, persons and their bodies are connected to the idea of "two as one" or "one as two," thus effectively questioning when, where, and how the boundaries of the "self" are expressed as a single, physical entity. While such ideas may not have been transmitted by all of the examples, the double-headed, singled-bodied pieces from the Near East, Cyprus, Anatolia, and the Balkans might well have foregrounded such ideas. Whether such concepts were at one time rooted in the appearance of actual twins, particularly the rare birth of Siamese twins, cannot be determined, but it is possible that the oddity of double births would have remained in the long-term or institutional memory of a group, ultimately serving as an effective tool for expressing the complexity of human identity in these early societies.

The basic idea proposed in this chapter—that these early, twin-like images were linked to notions of partible dividuals, probably surfacing only in select ritual contexts—admittedly raises many questions, especially about how overarching concepts of doubleness might have intersected with the more specific intentions of these images. Even if we can't currently answer these questions, the approach suggested here underscores the need to move beyond the more traditional interpretations already offered, to contemplate the untidy world of prehistoric figurines and the body, and to explore what has been termed the early "corporeal politics of being."[68] In deconstructing these images, we need to begin thinking more creatively but judiciously about the double and identical images as a unique, albeit unstable category, to ponder what was involved in the production of that category in these particular cultures, and to sort out how the ideas expressed by reiterative human forms become an important portal for expressing various identities, be they sacred or profane. Doubles, or more precisely twins, are indeed ideal forms for bringing into sharp relief questions about the complex—and potentially fractured—nature of the self. Twin figurines provide a flexible symbol for expressing shared and multiple identities, which were certainly issues that arose in prehistoric Mediterranean communities. Such images also embody—at least to our eyes—a degree of mystification and ambiguity, in keeping with the ritual contexts in which many have been found. Although we do not know who designed and produced these images, it may well be that the artists recognized and intentionally stressed the ambiguity of their creations. We should not imagine that, once created, these images sat unattended throughout their lifetime; they probably participated in an active life, possessing a degree of agency when held, employed, touched, passed around, and finally laid to rest.

Although we may never completely understand these striking images of twinship, who produced and consumed them, and to what ends, I have attempted to demonstrate the scholarly need to start collecting this kind of data within wider conceptual categories. This enables us to look beyond their precise meanings, where the current discussion sometimes ends, and to consider their wider horizon. These depictions may have reflected a larger, implicit narrative about the notions of individuality and the philosophies of doubleness and reduplication throughout the eastern Mediterranean during the Neolithic through Middle Bronze Ages. As symbols, these double images likely broadcast multiple meanings, with some meanings more dominant or stronger than others. At least one level of symbolic importance may have evoked questions about the definitions of the self, stories of resemblances, and the place of twinship, broadly defined, in these early societies. As Juliana de Nooy argues in her book on twins in contemporary literature, twins raise all sorts of intriguing questions, especially ideas about identity, sameness and difference, and the problems of not telling twins apart, but "telling them together."[69] Twin identity is complex and illusive, and as one reviewer of de Nooy's book aptly observes, "sameness can never sustain itself:

even identical twins are never absolutely the same [thus giving] rise to a critique of sameness and a philosophy of difference."[70]

As distant and culturally biased viewers, who can only glimpse the meanings embodied and broadcast by the miniature worlds these double images created millennia ago, we face significant challenges trying to decipher how these dyads were understood by the early cultures of the Mediterranean. It seems clear, however, that any legitimate interpretive attempt at disentangling these merged, melded, and seemingly identical bodies must, paradoxically, honor their entanglement as an *a priori*. Like twins, whom they both do and do not resemble, these ancient figures visually insist on both duality and unity—both reduplication and uniqueness. This complex marriage of ideas could not be expressed by a single-bodied, normative image. Rather, some other kind of depiction was required, or perhaps invented, to construct a narrative about the notion of the double, the definition of the self, its constituent parts, and its boundaries in these early cultures.

Notes

1 E.g., Rosemary A. Joyce, "Archaeology of the Body," *Annual Review of Anthropology* 34 (2005): 139–58; Douglass W. Bailey, *Prehistoric Figurines* (London: Routledge, 2005); Douglass W. Bailey, Andrew Cochrane, and Jean Zambelli, *Unearthed: A Comparative Study of Jomon Dogu and Neolithic Figurines* (Norwich: Sainsbury Centre for the Visual Arts, 2010).

2 See however, Vicki Noble, *The Double Goddess: Women Sharing Power* (Rochester, VT: Bear & Company, 2003); Denise Schmandt-Besserat, "'Ain Ghazal 'Monumental' Figures," *Bulletin of the American Schools of Oriental Research* 310 (1998): 11–12.

3 This chapter is based on a paper delivered at the European Association of Archaeologists annual meetings held on Malta in 2008 (Talalay and Cullen 2008). That paper was co-authored with Tracey Cullen, to whom I owe an enormous debt. I would also like to thank my twin sister, Kathryn Talalay, my husband, Steve Bank, and Kimberley Patton for their invaluable suggestions. I dedicate this chapter to my mother, Marjorie Talalay (1921–2008) and my father, Anselm Talalay (1912–94), who were all too familiar with the complexities of identical twins.

4 Véronique Dasen, *Jumeaux, Jumelles dans l'antiquité Grecque et Romaine* (Zurich: Akanthus, 2005).

5 Theodora H. Price, "Double and Multiple Representations in Greek Art and Religious Thought," *Journal of Hellenic Studies* 91 (1971): 48–69.

6 It is generally acknowledged that twin births, both identical and fraternal, are rare, although there is some inconsistency among reports on the precise rates worldwide. According to a study annually updated by the researchers, the rate of monozygotic twins remains constant globally at approximately four in every 1,000 births (Garth E. Fletcher and Terence L. Zach, "Multiple Births," *Medscape* 12.20.2019. https://emedicine.medscape.com/article/977234-overview, last accessed 3.12.22). Birth rates of dizygotic twins are more variable, with the highest occurrence among African nations, especially the Yoruba, who have a birth rate of 45 twins per 1,000 live births, 90 percent of which are dizygotic. Since the 1970s, the frequency of dizygotic

twinning has increased, attributable, among other things, to the use of fertility drugs (John Collins, "Global Epidemiology of Multiple Birth," *Reprod Biomed Online* 15 Suppl. 3 (2007): 45–52, doi: 10.1016/s1472-6483(10)62251-1), and the overall twinning rate has also continued to increase. See the study published in mid-2021 by Christiaan Monden et al., "Twin Peaks: More Twinning in Humans Than Ever Before," *Human Reproduction* 36, no. 6 (June 2021): 1666–73, https://doi.org/10.1093/humrep/deab029. The authors write that "since the 1980s, the global twinning rate has increased by a third, from 9.1 to 12.0 twin deliveries per 1000 deliveries, to about 1.6 million twin pairs each year. . . . The absolute and relative number of twins for the world as a whole is peaking at an unprecedented level. An important reason for this is the tremendous increase in medically assisted reproduction in recent decades. This is highly relevant, as twin deliveries are associated with higher infant and child mortality rates and increased complications for mother and child during pregnancy and during and after delivery" (1666). Despite variability among the reports I consulted, the fact remains that, until recently, twin births have been rare, with twins representing approximately 1.9 percent of the world's population. It is likely that the occurrence of twin births was equally exceptional in prehistory—especially before the era of medical intervention, and when both natural and cultural factors would often have imperiled twin survival.

7   Elisha P. Renne and Misty L. Bastian, "Reviewing Twinship in Africa," *Ethnology* 40, no.1 (2001): 1–11.

8   Juliana de Nooy, *Twins in Contemporary Literature and Culture: Look Twice* (Basingstoke: Palgrave Macmillan, 2000).

9   Elizabeth A. Stewart, *Exploring Twins: Towards a Social Analysis of Twinship* (Basingstoke: Palgrave Macmillan, 2000), 17–19.

10 Philip M. Peek, "Couples or Doubles? Representations of Twins in the Arts of Africa," *African Arts* 41, no.1 (2008): 14–23.

11 William Viney, *Twins: Superstitions and Marvels, Fantasies and Experiments* (London: Reaktion Books, 2021).

12 Gordon E. Slethaug, *The Play of the Double in Postmodern American Fiction* (Carbondale: Southern Illinois University Press, 1993), 8.

13 Hillel Schwartz, *The Culture of the Copy: Striking Likenesses, Unreasonable Facsimiles* (New York: Zone Books, 1996), 45. The composite nature and questionable purposes of these images raise problems with vocabulary. Which words best describe the figures: are they "twin," "twin-like," or "double"? I have chosen to use these words interchangeably and not to parse them too narrowly.

14 Stewart, *Exploring Twins*, 13–15.

15 Although we have no statistics on the difficulties of twin birthing in the past, current data are instructive. Even today with good medical care and facilities in developed countries, twin gestations are a risk for both the mother and the twins: maternal mortality and complications are frequent, and prenatal mortality is three to ten times higher for twins than in singleton births. Postnatal mortality is estimated at six to seven times more likely than in the neonatal period. See Alessandra Piontelli, an Italian obstetrician who works globally, in *Twins in the World: Legends They Inspire and the Lives They Lead* (New York: Palgrave Macmillan, 2008), 53–5.

16 Raising twins, especially as infants, generates hardships and "double trouble" for parents, the offspring, and even the whole community. As one specialist on twins writes, "Twins as toddlers are especially taxing, suggesting the relative unfitness

of the human species to care for two children simultaneously" (Piontelli, *Twins in the World*, 14). Categorized as "lowered-viability infants"—meaning that they are constitutionally weaker than single-birth babies—they have been subjected to what some anthropologists call "twin infanticide" (a concept that has been challenged; see Helen L. Ball and Catherine M. Hill, "Reevaluating 'Twin Infanticide,'" *Current Anthropology* 37, no. 5 [1996]: 856–63; but *contra* this the remarks of African anthropologists Jacob Olúpọ̀nà and Pashington Obeng in this volume, verifying the reality of this historical practice in Nigeria, Ghana, and the Omo peoples of contemporary Ethiopia, among other African contexts). There is also the added social and psychological complexity that communities face in trying to deal with twins as two people who seem the same, and often share the same social position.

17   To my knowledge, there is only one reference to twin interments in the region under discussion: in 2005, excavators from Shahr-e Sukhteh in the Iranian province of Sistan va Baluchestan reported a twin burial, side-by-side in fetal positions, dated to some point in the third millennium BCE ("5000-year-old twin grave unearthed in Burnt City," *Stone Pages*: "Archaeo News," December 19, 2005, from Cultural Heritage News Agency December15, 2005, http://www.stonepages.com/news /archives/001643.html, accessed December12, 2021). Geographically further afield, but worth mentioning, is the fieldwork at Krems-Watchber in Austria where excavators unearthed an unusual double infant burial dating to the Gravettian period, approximately 27,000 years ago; see Thomas Einwögerer et al., "Upper Palaeolithic Infant Burials," *Nature* 444, no. 7117 (November 16, 2006): 285. Two well-preserved skeletons were found at that site embedded in red ochre, with both covered by a mammoth scapula and one decorated with more than 30 ivory beads. Analysis indicates that these perinates were the same age at death (ninth to tenth lunar month), and the excavators propose that their simultaneous burial suggests the likelihood that they were twins. Child burials are rare for this time period and the special treatment of these perinates is noteworthy, perhaps indicating that they held a degree of importance in this community of hunter-gathers. Whether that status was linked to their twinship cannot be determined, but it should be entertained.

18   Gary O. Rollefson, "Ritual and Ceremony at Neolithic 'Ain Ghazal (Jordan)," *Paleorient* 9 (1983): 29–38; idem, "Neolithic 'Ain Ghazal (Jordan)—Ritual and Ceremony II," *Paleorient* 12 (1986): 45–51.

19   Carol A. Grissom, "Neolithic Statues from 'Ain Ghazal: Construction and Form," *American Journal of Archaeology* 104 (2000): 27.

20   Ibid., 43.

21   Ibid.

22   E.g., Peter M. M. G. Akkermans and Glen M. Schwartz, *The Archaeology of Syria* (Cambridge: Cambridge University Press, 2003), 86, 98.

23   Alan H. Simmons, Ann Boulton, Carol Roetzel Butler, Zeidan Kafafi, and Gary O. Rollefson, "A Plastered Human Skull from Neolithic 'Ain Ghazal, Jordan," *Journal of Field Archaeology* 17 (1990): 109.

24   See Angela M. H. Schuster, "Ghosts of 'Ain Ghazal," *Archaeology* 49, no. 4 (1996): 65–6.

25   See the work of Schmandt-Besserat for references to the Babylonian texts, the use of substitute figures in ghost rituals, and her arguments against this interpretation in "'Ain Ghazal 'Monumental' Figures," 10–11.

26   Max E. L. Mallowan, "Excavations at Brak and Chagar Bazar," *Iraq* 9 (1947): 1–266.

27 Joan Oates and David Oates, "The Reattribution of Middle Uruk Materials at Brak," in *Leaving No Stones Unturned*, ed. E. Ehrenberg (Winona Lake, IN: Eisenbrauns, 2002), 145–54.

28 Mallowan, "Excavations at Brak and Chagar Bazar," 33, 150 ff. No comprehensive catalogue of eye idols has been published, but 4,000 examples from Mallowan's original excavations brought back to England were studied in the 1980s (Timothy Matney, *A Technical Study of the Eye-Idols from Tell Brak, North Syria*, unpublished BA thesis [University of London, 1986]). Given the usual practice of *partage* in the early days of Near Eastern excavations, it is possible that the entire sample of eye idols might have been as large as 8,000. The percentage of twin idols is not known, but Matney gives a very rough estimate of perhaps 5 percent (personal communication with Tim Matney, to whom I am very grateful for providing me with unpublished material on these images).

29 Mallowan, "Excavations at Brak and Chagar Bazar," 150.

30 Ibid., 35.

31 Ibid., 151–9; idem, *Twenty-Five Years of Mesopotamian Discovery* (London: British School of Archaeology in Iraq, 1956), 25, 27; idem, *Early Mesopotamia and Iran* (London: Thames and Hudson, 1965), 48.

32 Mallowan, "Excavations at Brak and Chagar Bazar," 156, 158.

33 Alternatively, the "twins in the belly" type may not reference a desire for twins; rather, given what we know from the ethnographic record where the powers of twins are frequently viewed as dangerous and disruptive, this type could have functioned as amulets protecting *against* the birth of twins.

34 E.g., Matney, *A Technical Study of the Eye-Idols from Tell Brak*, 16.

35 Leila Badre, *Les Figurines Anthropomorphes en Terre Cuite à l'Age du Bronze en Syrie* (Paris: Librairie Orientaliste Paul Geuthner, 1980), 61–2; pl. LXVI, 68.

36 For examples of double or multicomponent jugs as well as twin-necked vessels, see Desmond Morris, *The Art of Ancient Cyprus* (Oxford: Phaidon Press, 1985), 85–92.

37 For bibliography see Lauren E. Talalay and Tracey Cullen, "Sexual Ambiguity in Plank Figures from Bronze Age Cyprus," in *Engendering Aphrodite: Women and Society in Ancient Cyprus*, ed. Diane Bolger and Nancy Serwint, ASOR Archaeological Reports 7/CAARI Monographs 3 (Boston: American Schools of Oriental Research, 2002), 181–95.

38 See Morris, *The Art of Ancient Cyprus*; Maria R. Belgiorno, "Le statuette antropomorfe cipriote dell'età del Bronzo I: Gli idoli del Bronzo Antico III–Bronzo Medio I," *Studi Micenei ed Egeo-Anatolici* 25 (1984): 9–63; and Anna L. a Campo, *Anthropomorphic Representations in Prehistoric Cyprus: A Formal and Symbolic Analysis of Figurines, c. 3500–1800 B.C.*, Studies in Mediterranean Archaeology, Pocket-book 109 (Jonsered: Åström, 1994).

39 The occurrence of a few, fragmentary, single-headed pieces in settlements, as well as mend-holes and wear patterns on some planks, indicate that at least some were probably used prior to burial (see Talalay and Cullen, "Sexual Ambiguity in Plank Figures from Bronze Age Cyprus," 184, for a fuller discussion).

40 Morris, *The Art of Ancient Cyprus*, 130; for a recent discussion on the tactile and multivalent nature of figurines from Çatalhöyük, see Carolyn Nakamura and Lynn Meskell, "Articulate Bodies: Forms and Figures at Çatalhöyük," *Journal of Archaeological Method and Theory* (2009): 205–30.

41 Porphyrios Dikaios, "Two Neolithic Steatite Idols," *Report of the Department of Antiquities, Cyprus* (1934): 16; pl. 6:1.

42 Vassos Karageorghis, *The Cyprus Collections in the Medelhavsmuseet* (Nicosia: A.G. Leventis Foundation, 2003), 61; fig. 59; Belgiorno, *Le statuette antropomorfe cipriote*, figs. 21, 3 & 22; pl. XIX.

43 Morris, *The Art of Ancient Cyprus*, 152.

44 Karageorghis, *The Cyprus Collections in the Medelhavsmuseet*, 61.

45 Nancy Serwint, "Aphrodite and Her Near Eastern Sisters: Spheres of Influence," in *Engendering Aphrodite: Women and Society in Ancient Cyprus,* ed. D. Bolger and N. Serwint, ASOR Archaeological Reports 7/CAARI Monographs 3 (Boston: American Schools of Oriental Research, 2002), 329.

46 See Talalay and Cullen, "Sexual Ambiguity in Plank Figures from Bronze Age Cyprus," 185–6.

47 A. Bernard Knapp and Lynn Meskell, "Bodies of Evidence on Prehistoric Cyprus," *Cambridge Archaeological Journal* 7 (1997): 183–204.

48 Talalay and Cullen, "Sexual Ambiguity in Plank Figures from Bronze Age Cyprus."

49 See Morris, *The Art of Ancient Cyprus*, 131–2, for a brief discussion and references.

50 Ibid., 126–7.

51 Diane Bolger, "Figurines, Fertility, and the Emergence of Complex Society in Prehistoric Cyprus," *Current Anthropology* 37, no. 2 (1996): 365–73.

52 James Mellaart, *Çatal Höyük: A Neolithic Town in Anatolia* (New York: McGraw-Hill Book Co., 1967).

53 www.catalhoyuk.com.

54 See the table in Mellaart, *Çatal Höyük*, 70.

55 Ibid., 110–11.

56 Lynn Meskell, "Twin Peaks," in *Ancient Goddesses*, ed. Lucy Goodison and Christine Morris (Madison: University of Wisconsin Press, 1998), 50.

57 See Martin J. Aitken, Peter R. S. Moorey, and Peter J. Ucko, "The Authenticity of Vessels and Figurines in the Hacilar Style," *Archaeometry* 13, no. 2 (1971): 89–142, for authentication testing.

58 See Kemaleddin Karamete, "Idoles du Kültepe au Lycée et au Musée de Kayseri," *Revue Hittite et Asianique* 3 (1935): 63–6; idem, "Nouvelle Idoles du Kültepe au Musée de Kayseri," *Revue Hittite et Asianique* 3 (1936): 245–7; idem, "Idoles Récemment Decouvertes au Kültepe," *Revue Hittite et Asianique* 4 (1938): 205–7; and Helmuth Bossert, *Altanatolien* (Berlin: E. Wasmuth G.M.B.H., 1942), figs. 334; 338; 340–5.

59 Hamit Z. Koşay, *Les Fouilles d'Alaca Höyük. Rapport préliminaire sur les travaux en 1937–1939* (Ankara, 1951), 156; pl. CXXIX, 2.

60 George A. Papathanassopoulos, *Neolithic Culture in Greece* (Athens: Nicholas P. Goulandris Foundation Museum of Cycladic Art, 1996), fig. 234.

61 Kostas Gallis and Lala Orphanidis, *Figurines of Neolithic Thessaly*, vol. 1 (Athens: Academy of Athens, Research Center for Antiquity, 1996), fig. 221.

62 Interestingly, the production of twin-headed images in Neolithic Greece and the Balkans is not confined to anthropomorphic figurines. A number of twin-headed zoomorphic images, often with the heads at either end of the figure, have been reported.

63 E.g., de Nooy, *Twins in Contemporary Literature and Culture*; Piontelli, *Twins in the World*; Schwartz, *The Culture of the Copy*.

64 de Nooy, *Twins in Contemporary Literature and Culture*, 93.

65 Marilyn Strathern, *The Gender of the Gift* (Berkeley and Los Angeles: University of California Press, 1988).

66 E.g., Peek, "Couples or Doubles?"
67 Maarten van de Guchte posits similar ideas among the Maya in "Sculpture and the Concept of the Double among the Inca Kings," *RES: Anthropology and Aesthetics* 29/30 (1996): 256–68; see also the discussion in Vincent Stanzione's chapter in this volume.
68 Bailey, *Prehistoric Figurines*, 197.
69 de Nooy, *Twins in Contemporary Literature and Culture*, 22.
70 Dimitris Vardoulakis, review of Juliana de Nooy, "Twins in Contemporary Literature and Culture," *COLLOQUY Text Theory Critique* 11 (2006): 271. www.arts.monash .edu.au/others/colloquy/issue11/vardoulakis.pdf.

Bibliography

a Campo, Anna L. *Anthropomorphic Representations in Prehistoric Cyprus: A Formal and Symbolic Analysis of Figurines, c. 3500–1800 B.C.* Studies in Mediterranean Archaeology, Pocket-book 109. Jonsered: Åström, 1994.

Aitken, Martin J., Peter R. S. Moorey, and Peter J. Ucko. "The Authenticity of Vessels and Figurines in the Hacilar Style." *Archaeometry* 13, no. 2 (1971): 89–142.

Akkermans, Peter M. M. G., and Glen M. Schwartz. *The Archaeology of Syria.* Cambridge: Cambridge University Press, 2003.

Badre, Leila. *Les Figurines Anthropomorphes en Terre Cuite à l'Age du Bronze en Syrie.* Paris: Librairie Orientaliste Paul Geuthner, 1980.

Bailey, Douglass W. *Prehistoric Figurines.* London: Routledge, 2005.

Bailey, Douglass W., Andrew Cochrane, and Jean Zambelli. *Unearthed: A Comparative Study of Jomon Dogu and Neolithic Figurines.* Norwich: Sainsbury Centre for the Visual Arts, 2010.

Ball, Helen L., and Catherine M. Hill. "Reevaluating 'Twin Infanticide.'" *Current Anthropology* 37, no. 5 (1996): 856–63.

Belgiorno, Maria R. "Le statuette antropomorfe cipriote dell'età del Bronzo I: Gli idoli del Bronzo Antico III–Bronzo Medio I." *Studi Micenei ed Egeo-Anatolici* 25 (1984): 9–63.

Bolger, Diane. "Figurines, Fertility, and the Emergence of Complex Society in Prehistoric Cyprus." *Current Anthropology* 37, no. 2 (1996): 365–73.

Bossert, Helmuth. *Altanatolien.* Berlin: E. Wasmuth G.M.B.H., 1942.

Collins, John. "Global Epidemiology of Multiple Birth." *Reprod Biomed Online* 15, Suppl. 3 (2007): 45–52. doi:10.1016/s1472-6483(10)62251-1.

Dasen, Véronique. *Jumeaux, Jumelles dans l'antiquité Grecque et Romaine.* Zurich: Akanthus, 2005.

de Nooy, Juliana. *Twins in Contemporary Literature and Culture: Look Twice.* Basingstoke: Palgrave Macmillan, 2005.

Dikaios, Porphyrios. "Two Neolithic Steatite Idols." *Report of the Department of Antiquities, Cyprus* (1934): 16.

Einwögerer, Thomas, Herwig Friesinger, Marc Händel, Christine Neugebauer-Maresch, Ulrich Simon, and Maria Teschler-Nicola. "Upper Palaeolithic Infant Burials." *Nature* 444, no. 7117 (November 16, 2006): 285.

Fletcher, Garth E., and Terence L. Zach. "Multiple Births." *Medscape*, December 20, 2019. https://emedicine.medscape.com/article/977234-overview (accessed March 12, 22).

Gallis, Kostas, and Lala Orphanidis. *Figurines of Neolithic Thessaly*, vol. 1. Athens: Academy of Athens, Research Center for Antiquity, 1996.

Gimbutas, Marija. *The Gods and Goddesses of Old Europe*. Berkeley and Los Angeles: University of California Press, 1974.

Grissom, Carol A. "Neolithic Statues from 'Ain Ghazal: Construction and Form." *American Journal of Archaeology* 104 (2000): 25–45.

Joyce, Rosemary A. "Archaeology of the Body." *Annual Review of Anthropology* 34 (2005): 139–58.

Karageorghis, Vassos. *The Cyprus Collections in the Medelhavsmuseet*. Nicosia: A.G. Leventis Foundation, 2003.

Karamete, Kemaleddin. "Idoles du Kültepe au Lycée et au Musée de Kayseri." *Revue Hittite et Asianique* 3 (1935): 63–6.

Karamete, Kemaleddin. "Nouvelle Idoles du Kültepe au Musée de Kayseri." *Revue Hittite et Asianique* 3 (1936): 245–7.

Karamete, Kemaleddin. "Idoles Récemment Decouvertes au Kültepe." *Revue Hittite et Asianique* 4 (1938): 205–7.

Knapp, A. Bernard, and Lynn Meskell. "Bodies of Evidence on Prehistoric Cyprus." *Cambridge Archaeological Journal* 7 (1997): 183–204.

Koşay, Hamit Z. *Les Fouilles d'Alaca Höyük. Rapport préliminaire sur les travaux en 1937–39*. Ankara: Türk Tarih Kurumu Basımevi, 1951.

Mallowan, Max E. L. "Excavations at Brak and Chagar Bazar." *Iraq* 9 (1947): 1–266.

Mallowan, Max E. L. *Twenty-Five Years of Mesopotamian Discovery*. London: British School of Archaeology in Iraq, 1956.

Mallowan, Max E. L. *Early Mesopotamia and Iran*. London: Thames and Hudson, 1965.

Matney, Timothy. *A Technical Study of the Eye-Idols from Tell Brak, North Syria*. Unpublished BA thesis, University of London, 1986.

Mellaart, James. *Çatal Höyük: A Neolithic Town in Anatolia*. New York: McGraw-Hill Book Co., 1967.

Meskell, Lynn. "Twin Peaks." In *Ancient Goddesses*, edited by Lucy Goodison and Christine Morris, 46–62. Madison: University of Wisconsin Press, 1998.

Monden, Christiaan, Gilles Pison, and Jeroen Smits. "Twin Peaks: More Twinning in Humans Than Ever Before." *Human Reproduction* 36, no. 6 (June 2021): 1666–73. https://doi.org/10.1093/humrep/deab029.

Morris, Desmond. *The Art of Ancient Cyprus*. Oxford: Phaidon Press, 1985.

Nakamura, Carolyn, and Lynn Meskell. "Articulate Bodies: Forms and Figures at Çatalhöyük." *Journal of Archaeological Method and Theory* 16, no. 3 (2009): 205–30.

Noble, Vicki. *The Double Goddess: Women Sharing Power*. Rochester, VT: Bear & Company, 2003.

Oates, Joan, and David Oates. "The Reattribution of Middle Uruk Materials at Brak." In *Leaving No Stones Unturned*, edited by Erica Ehrenberg, 145–54. Winona Lake, IN: Eisenbrauns, 2002.

Papathanassopoulos, George A. *Neolithic Culture in Greece*. Athens: Nicholas P. Goulandris Foundation Museum of Cycladic Art, 1996.

Peek, Philip M. "Couples or Doubles? Representations of Twins in the Arts of Africa." *African Arts* 41, no. 1 (2008): 14–23.

Piontelli, Alessandra. *Twins in the World: Legends They Inspire and the Lives They Lead*. New York: Palgrave Macmillan, 2008.

Price, Theodora H. "Double and Multiple Representations in Greek Art and Religious Thought." *Journal of Hellenic Studies* 91 (1971): 48–69.

Renne, Elisha P., and Misty L. Bastian. "Reviewing Twinship in Africa." *Ethnology* 40, no. 1 (2001): 1–11.

Rollefson, Gary O. "Ritual and Ceremony at Neolithic 'Ain Ghazal (Jordan)." *Paleorient* 9 (1983): 29–38.

Rollefson, Gary O. "Neolithic 'Ain Ghazal (Jordan)—Ritual and Ceremony II." *Paleorient* 12 (1986): 45–51.

Schmandt-Besserat, Denise. "'Ain Ghazal 'Monumental' Figures." *Bulletin of the American Schools of Oriental Research* 310 (1998): 1–17.

Schuster, Angela M. H. "Ghosts of 'Ain Ghazal." *Archaeology* 49, no. 4 (1996): 65–6.

Schwartz, Hillel. *The Culture of the Copy: Striking Likenesses, Unreasonable Facsimiles.* New York: Zone Books, 1996.

Serwint, Nancy. "Aphrodite and Her Near Eastern Sisters: Spheres of Influence." In *Engendering Aphrodite: Women and Society in Ancient Cyprus*, edited by Diane Bolger and Nancy Serwint, 325–50. ASOR Archaeological Reports 7/CAARI Monographs 3. Boston: American Schools of Oriental Research, 2002.

Simmons, Alan H., Ann Boulton, Carol Roetzel Butler, Zeidan Kafafi, and Gary O. Rollefson. "A Plastered Human Skull from Neolithic 'Ain Ghazal, Jordan." *Journal of Field Archaeology* 17 (1990): 107–10.

Slethaug, Gordon E. *The Play of the Double in Postmodern American Fiction.* Carbondale: Southern Illinois University Press, 1993.

Stewart, Elizabeth A. *Exploring Twins: Towards a Social Analysis of Twinship.* Basingstoke: Palgrave Macmillan, 2000.

Stone Pages. "5000-Year-Old Twin Grave Unearthed in Burnt City." "Archaeo News," December 19, 2005, from Cultural Heritage News Agency December 15, 2005. Accessed December 12, 2021.http://www.stonepages.com/news/archives/001643 .html.

Strathern, Marilyn. *The Gender of the Gift.* Berkeley and Los Angeles: University of California Press, 1988.

Talalay, Lauren E., and Tracey Cullen. "Sexual Ambiguity in Plank Figures from Bronze Age Cyprus." In *Engendering Aphrodite: Women and Society in Ancient Cyprus*, edited by Diane Bolger and Nancy Serwint, 181–95. ASOR Archaeological Reports 7/CAARI Monographs 3. Boston: American Schools of Oriental Research, 2002.

Talalay, Lauren E., and Tracey Cullen. "Rethinking Double Images in the Prehistoric Mediterranean." Paper delivered at the 14th annual meeting of the European Association of Archaeologists, Malta, 2008.

Turner, Terence. "Social Body and Embodied Subject: Bodiliness, Subjectivity, and Sociality among the Kayapo." *Cultural Anthropology* 10, no. 2 (1995): 143–70.

Van de Guchte, Maarten. "Sculpture and the Concept of the Double among the Inca Kings." *RES: Anthropology and Aesthetics* 29/30 (1996): 256–68.

Vardoulakis, Dimitris. Review of Juliana de Nooy, "Twins in Contemporary Literature and Culture." *COLLOQUY Text Theory Critique* 11 (2006): 271–4. www.arts.monash .edu.au/others/colloquy/issue11/vardoulakis.pdf.

Viney, William. *Twins: Superstitions and Marvels, Fantasies and Experiments.* London: Reaktion Books, 2021.

Achilles and Patroklos

As Models for the Twinning of Identity

♊

Gregory Nagy

Twinning in myth is a way to think about identity. As Douglas Frame shows in his chapter, "Achilles and Patroklos as Indo-European Twins: Homer's Take," which is a twin to this one, mythical twins share one identity, but this identity is differentiated.[1] That is, the fused identity of mythical twins is at the same time a split personality. In this chapter, I will argue that the epic heroes Achilles and Patroklos are paired off in the Homeric *Iliad* in such a way as to resemble and even to duplicate such a model of twinning in myth.

Two ancient Greek words that will figure prominently in my argument are *therapōn*, conventionally translated as "attendant," and *philos*, meaning "friend" as a noun, and "near and dear" or "belonging to the self" as an adjective. The uses of these two words, as we will see later, are interconnected in shaping the plot of the *Iliad*, since Achilles and Patroklos care for and about each other, and they care more for each other than for anyone else. Such caring, as we will also see, is at the root of the meaning of both words, *therapōn* as well as *philos*. To say it another way, such mutual caring determines the identification of Patroklos as the virtual twin or body double of Achilles in Homeric mythmaking [Figure 10.1].

Both the fusion and the differentiation of twins can be expressed in myth by way of picturing their conception as a dyadic affair, where the mother of the twins is impregnated by two different fathers, one of whom is divine while the other is human. A classic example is the mythical dyad of Herakles and Iphikles. Here I offer a most abbreviated paraphrase of the standard version of the myth, as reported in the *Library* of "Apollodorus" (2.4.8):

> *These twins Herakles and Iphikles share the same mother, Alkmene, but their fathers are different. The first twin of the dyad, Herakles, is fathered by the immortal god Zeus himself, who impregnates Alkmene by assuming the appearance of her husband, Amphitryon the mortal. Only the second twin, Iphikles, is fathered by that mortal. This way, one twin can be immortal while the other twin must be mortal.*

Figure 10.1 Achilles tending the wound of Patroklos. Inscribed names in Greek. The Sosias Painter (name vase; signed). Vulci, Etruria, 500 BCE. Attic red-figure kylix, Berlin, Antikenmuseen F2278. Photo credit: bpk Bildagentur/Berlin, Antikenmuseen/Johannes Laurentius.

In the myth of Herakles, his immortality happens only after he experiences death. We see him die a most spectacular death before he ever becomes immortalized (a classic account is given by Diodorus of Sicily 4.38.4–5; the immortalization is narrated in 4.39.2–3). Still, once he is immortal, Herakles stops acting like a twin; and his mortal twin brother, once dead, is no longer of any consequence.[2]

As Frame shows, however, immortality can be shared by twins. The most prominent example is the dyad known as the Dioskouroi, whose name means "sons of Zeus." Despite this apparently coequal meaning, however, only one of these twins, Polydeukes, is the son of the immortal god Zeus, while his twin brother Kastor is fathered by the mortal man Tyndareos. In contrast to the twins Herakles and Iphikles, who are separated from each other after the mortal Iphikles dies, these twins Polydeukes and Kastor must stay together forever, since the immortal twin shares his immortality with his mortal twin, while the mortal twin shares his death with his immortal twin; at any given moment, they can be either both dead or both alive (a classic account can be found in "Apollodorus" *Library* 3.11.2).

In the myth of Herakles, by contrast, the twins are not only separated from each other after the mortal Iphikles dies. More than that, Herakles takes the place of Iphikles after the death of his mortal twin. This aspect of the myth is most relevant to my overall argument: just as appearances are deceiving at the moment when Herakles is conceived, since his immortal father appears to be a mortal at the moment of conception, so also the deceptiveness of appearances persists throughout the heroic life of Herakles, since he is known as either "son of Amphitryon" or "son of Zeus" after his twin Iphikles dies. Once Iphikles is out of the picture, then Herakles can take his place. As a monad who lives on without his twin, Herakles can now develop a split personality, sometimes appearing to be human while at other times appearing to be divine.[3]

There is a striking parallel to be found in the case of the hero Nestor. I follow here the seminal book of Frame, *Hippota Nestor*, in which he reconstructs the relevant myth all the way back to its Indo-European origins. He shows that there was a pastoral aspect of Nestor, linked with cattle, to be distinguished from the warlike aspect of this hero's brother Periklymenos, linked with horses.[4] In terms of the myth, this distinction between the two brothers is fused after Periklymenos is killed. His killer, I must add, is none other than the hero Herakles (Hesiod F 33 MW; see also "Apollodorus" *Library* 1.9.9). Once Nestor's brother Periklymenos is out of the picture, as Frame shows, Nestor can develop a split personality of his own, sometimes linked with cattle while at other times linked with horses.

That said, I am ready to show that myth has even further ways of fusing identities and then differentiating them into a split personality. A case in point is the myth of Achilles and Patroklos as narrated in the Homeric *Iliad*. As we will see, there are patterns of fusion in myths about their identities, but there are also corresponding patterns of differentiation.

To experience a fusion of identity, you don't have to be born of the same mother. Certainly in the case of Achilles and Patroklos, they have different mothers as well as different fathers. Still, as we will see, Achilles and Patroklos can behave as twins behave in myth—and they can even look alike, just as twins are expected to look alike.[5] Like mythical twins, they can undergo the same experience at given moments of epic narration and, at such moments, they will look the same, as when Patroklos wears the armor of Achilles in *Iliad* XVI. Here Patroklos is leading an attack against the Trojans and, at this moment, the warriors who are being attacked actually mistake him for Achilles. More than that, as we will see later, Patroklos in such moments of fused identity can even wear, as it were, the same epithets that are worn by Achilles. Appearances really *are* deceiving in this case, and consequentially they are lethal. Patroklos is no Achilles. In the Homeric *Iliad*, Patroklos succeeds in saving the Achaeans for the moment; but he fails to kill Hektor. Instead, Hektor kills Patroklos in *Iliad* XVI. Later on, in *Iliad* XXII, Achilles will succeed in killing Hektor.

Thus this is how the two halves of this dyad are differentiated in the *Iliad*: one hero succeeds where the other fails. But the two halves are also fused in the *Iliad*. We can see the fusion clearly when we take a second look at the killing of Patroklos by Hektor in *Iliad* XVI, since the ultimate killer here is not Hektor but the god Apollo. In the same way, beyond the *Iliad*, the ultimate killer of Achilles himself is not Paris but the same god Apollo, as we know directly from the plot outline of the *Aithiopis*, which is part of the Epic Cycle. What fuses the dyad of Patroklos and Achilles is the twinning experience of death induced by the same one god, Apollo. And this death by Apollo, as we will soon see, is defined by the Homeric use of the words *therapōn*, usually translated as "attendant," and *philos*, meaning "friend" as a noun, and "near and dear" or "belonging to the self" as an adjective.

I start with *therapōn*. Here is a particularly revealing passage, where the narrative quotes the words of Achilles praying to Zeus:

> Ζεῦ ἄνα Δωδωναῖε Πελασγικὲ τηλόθι ναίων
> Δωδώνης μεδέων δυσχειμέρου, ἀμφὶ δὲ Σελλοὶ
> 235 σοὶ ναίουσ' ὑποφῆται ἀνιπτόποδες χαμαιεῦναι,
> ἠμὲν δή ποτ' ἐμὸν ἔπος ἔκλυες εὐξαμένοιο,
> τίμησας μὲν ἐμέ, μέγα δ' ἴψαο λαὸν Ἀχαιῶν,
> ἠδ' ἔτι καὶ νῦν μοι τόδ' ἐπικρήηνον ἐέλδωρ·
> αὐτὸς μὲν γὰρ ἐγὼ μενέω νηῶν ἐν ἀγῶνι,
> 240 ἀλλ' ἕταρον πέμπω πολέσιν μετὰ Μυρμιδόνεσσι
> μάρνασθαι· τῷ κῦδος ἅμα πρόες εὐρύοπα Ζεῦ,
> θάρσυνον δέ οἱ ἦτορ ἐνὶ φρεσίν, ὄφρα καὶ Ἕκτωρ
> εἴσεται ἦ ῥα καὶ οἷος ἐπίστηται πολεμίζειν
> ἡμέτερος θεράπων, ἦ οἱ τότε χεῖρες ἄαπτοι
> 245 μαίνονθ', ὁππότ' ἐγώ περ ἴω μετὰ μῶλον Ἄρηος.
> αὐτὰρ ἐπεί κ' ἀπὸ ναῦφι μάχην ἐνοπήν τε δίηται,
> ἀσκηθής μοι ἔπειτα θοὰς ἐπὶ νῆας ἵκοιτο
> τεύχεσί τε ξὺν πᾶσι καὶ ἀγχεμάχοις ἑτάροισιν.
> Ὣς ἔφατ' εὐχόμενος, τοῦ δ' ἔκλυε μητίετα Ζεύς.
> 250 τῷ δ' ἕτερον μὲν ἔδωκε πατήρ, ἕτερον δ' ἀνένευσε·
> νηῶν μέν οἱ ἀπώσασθαι πόλεμόν τε μάχην τε
> δῶκε, σόον δ' ἀνένευσε μάχης ἐξαπονέεσθαι.

"King Zeus," he cried, "lord of Dodona, god of the Pelasgoi, who dwells afar,
  you who hold stormy Dodona in your sway, where the Selloi,
235 your seers, dwell around you with their feet unwashed and their beds made upon the ground—
  just as you heard me when I prayed to you before,
  and did me honor by sending disaster on the Achaeans,
  so also now grant me the fulfillment of yet a further prayer, and it is this:
  I shall stay here at my assembly [*agōn*] of ships,
240 but I shall send my companion into battle at the head of many Myrmidons,
  sending him to fight. Grant, O all-seeing Zeus, that victory may go with him;
  put boldness into his heart so that Hektor
  may find out whether he [Patroklos] knows how to fight alone,

[Patroklos,] my <u>attendant</u> [*therapōn*], or whether his hands can only then
    be so invincible
245   with their fury when I myself enter the war struggle of Ares.
Afterwards when he has chased away from the ships the attack and the cry
    of battle,
grant that he may return unharmed to the ships,
with his armor and his companions, fighters in close combat."
Thus did he [Achilles] pray, and Zeus the Planner heard his prayer.
250   Part of it he did indeed grant him—but the other part he refused.
He granted that Patroklos should thrust back war and battle from the ships,
yes, he granted that. But he refused to let him come safely out of the fight.
                                 —*Iliad* XVI 233–48

As we see at verse 244 of *Iliad* XVI here, Achilles himself refers to his nearest and
dearest friend Patroklos as his own personal *therapōn*. What does the context of this
word here tell us about Patroklos and his relationship with Achilles? What we see is
an affirmation about the meaning of the word *therapōn* in the narrative, and the future
events of the epic will prove this affirmation to be true. As the narrative affirms, the
wording of Achilles is mistaken when he expresses his own fond hopes for Patroklos.
As the future events of the epic will show, Patroklos cannot fight alone, cannot defeat
Hektor alone, and can succeed only if he fights as a pair, together with Achilles. Once
Patroklos fights alone, he will die. And it is in this telling context, at *Iliad* XVI 244,
that the wording of Achilles refers to Patroklos as his personal *therapōn*.

In general, what does it mean for Patroklos to be the personal *therapōn* of Achilles?
As I will now argue, it means that Patroklos is doomed to die as the other self of Achilles.
As we notice in other contexts as well, Patroklos is the personal *therapōn* of Achilles
(for example, at *Iliad* XVI 165, 653; XVII 164, 388; XVIII 152). In each one of these
contexts, *therapōn* is conventionally translated as "attendant." So what does it mean in
particular, that the hero Patroklos serves as the "attendant" of the hero Achilles? As we
know from a variety of additional contexts where the relationship of these two heroes is
described, Patroklos is the nearest and dearest companion of Achilles. Also, Patroklos
is subservient to Achilles and to no one else. For example, Achilles orders Patroklos to
mix and to pour wine (IX 202–04), and Patroklos complies (IX 205 ἐπεπείθετο); also,
Patroklos serves the hero Achilles by preparing a meal for that hero and his guests,
performing most of the tasks required for the preparation, especially the task of cooking
the meat that will be served (IX 206–15). Helping Patroklos perform these tasks is
another companion of Achilles, named Automedon (IX 209). This Automedon, as we
will see, is an understudy of Patroklos: at a later point in the narrative, after Patroklos
is already dead, Automedon will be described as a *therapōn* of Achilles (XXIV 573).

More needs to be said about the occasion when Patroklos helps prepare a meal for
Achilles and his guests. As the host on this occasion, Achilles assumes a primary role
by actually slicing the meat before it is cooked (*Iliad* IX 209) and then distributing the
sliced portions, after they are cooked, for his guests (IX 217), while Patroklos is left
with the secondary role of distributing portions of bread that are placed into baskets
(IX 216–17). After Patroklos is dead, Automedon takes his place in the secondary role

of distributing bread in baskets on another occasion when Achilles acts as host (XXIV 625–6), while Achilles retains his primary role of distributing the meat (XXIV 626). As we will see later, this role of Automedon is relevant to his service as a *therapōn* of Achilles (XXIV 573).

In brief, then, Patroklos as *therapōn* of Achilles is the nearest and dearest companion of that primary hero in the *Iliad*. As the personal *therapōn* of Achilles, Patroklos is a secondary hero, and he attends Achilles just as other *therapontes* who are secondary heroes will attend Achilles after Patroklos dies. A simpler way of saying it, as we will soon see, is that Patroklos takes care of Achilles. For the moment, though, I continue to use the conventional translation for *therapōn* as "attendant." But there is more to it—much more.

I now turn to the prehistory of the word *therapōn*, seeking to show that this word had once meant "ritual substitute" and that it had been borrowed into the Greek language from Anatolian languages of Indo-European origin. The borrowing must have happened sometime in the later part of the second century BCE, during which period the two major Indo-European languages of Anatolia were Hittite and Luvian. The major political power in Anatolia at that time was the Hittite Empire. Accordingly, I will use the term *Hittite* as a shorthand way of referring to the relevant linguistic evidence.

In Hittite ritual texts dating from roughly 1350 to 1250 BCE, we find these two relevant words: *tarpanalli-* (or *tarpalli-*) and *tarpašša-*.[6] As Nadia van Brock has shown, these words were used as synonyms, and both meant "ritual substitute."[7] Such a meaning, "ritual substitute," must be understood in the context of a Hittite ritual of purification that expels pollution from the person to be purified and transfers it into a person or an animal or an object that serves as a ritual substitute; the act of transferring pollution into the victim serving as ritual substitute may be accomplished either by destroying or by expelling the victim, who or which is identified as another self, *un autre soi-même*.[8] According to the logic of this Hittite ritual of substitution, the identification of the self with the victim serving as the other self can take on a wide variety of forms: the victims range from humans to animals to figurines to ceramic vessels.[9]

The mentality of identifying with your victim operates on homological principles. In the case of animal victims designated by the word *tarpalli-*, for example, one ritual text specifies that bulls are to be killed as ritual substitutes for men, while cows are to be killed as substitutes for women.[10] There are other examples of homologies based primarily on gender. In another ritual text involving the word *tarpalli-*, bulls and rams and other male animals are killed as ritual substitutes for the king, while corresponding female animals are killed for the queen.[11] There are cases of tighter homologies. In yet another ritual text involving the word *tarpalli-*, for example, it is specified that the victims who are designated as ritual substitutes for the king include men as well as bulls and rams.[12] Further, there are other cases as well where humans are being designated as ritual substitutes.[13]

The range of victims that are designated as ritual substitutes, extending all the way to humans, indicates that the victim of the ritual substitution, as the other self, can be identified as closely as possible with the human self—even if the ritual substitute and the human self may not be all that close to each other when they are viewed from outside the world of ritual.[14] What makes the substitute in ritual seem so intimately close to you is that he or she or it must die for you. Here I find it relevant to quote from a text of royal ritual substitution a most explicit formulation, expressed in dialogic format:

> *nu-wa-at-ta ku-u-uš [tar-pa]-al-li-uš [*
> *. . . nu-wa ku-u-uš ak-kán-du am-mu-uk-ma-w[a le]-e ak-mi*

> And for you, here are these ritual substitutes [*tarpalliuš*]
> . . . And may they die, but I will not die.
> —*Keilschrifturkunden aus Boghazköi* XXIV 5 I 15–16[15]

I draw special attention to these and other cases of ritual substitution where the person to be purified is a king. In such cases, as van Brock argues, the ritual of substitution is "périodique," ideally annual; and it is a common idea, as we can see from a survey of myths and rituals around the world, that the king is an incarnation of the body politic, of society itself, which needs to be renewed periodically by being purified of pollution.[16]

As we consider the relevant evidence from the Near East, a well-known model of periodic renewal is the Babylonian New Year festival, centering on the sacrificial killing of a goat, and it is nowadays generally agreed that the Hittite rituals of substitution derive at least in part from the Babylonian rituals that marked this festival;[17] a related practice, attested in texts stemming from the neo-Assyrian empire of the first millennium BCE, is the periodic appointing and subsequent killing of substitute kings. Especially relevant are the correspondences of the kings Asarhaddon (680–669 BCE) and Assurbanipal (668–627 BCE).[18] Still another related practice is the ritual of the scapegoat described in the Hebrew Bible, Leviticus 16:8, where a designated goat (who is the *tragos pempomenos* of the Greek Septuagint and the *caper emissarius* of the Latin Vulgate) is not killed but expelled into the wasteland—hence the word *scapegoat*; this periodic expulsion, as is well known, figures as a climactic moment in the rituals and sacred narratives of the Jewish Day of Atonement.

Since Hittite is an Indo-European language, no matter how deeply it is influenced by Near Eastern civilizations, we may also compare the relevant evidence of Hittite ritual formulations that are cognate with wording that we find in other Indo-European languages. A case in point is Latin *sōns / sontis*, meaning "guilty," which is cognate with the Greek participle *ōn / ontos* (ὤν / ὄντος) of the verb meaning "to be" as in *esti* (ἐστι) "is" and with the corresponding Hittite participle *ašān* that likewise means "to be," as in *ešzi* ("is"). In the Plague Prayers of King Muršilis II, dating from the second half of the fourteenth century BCE, it is prescribed that the king is to utter a "confessional" formula, *ašān-at, iyanun-at* "it is true, I did it" (*Keilschrifturkunden aus Boghazköi* XIV 8, in the second prayer); this formula is cognate with the formula implicit in Latin *sōns*, where the meaning "guilty" is to be understood in the legal sense of "declared guilty" or, to say it even more legalistically, "found guilty."[19] So also in the "confessional" formula of the Hittite king, the guilty party must declare that he really "is" the guilty one, that he really is "it."[20] Similarly in the children's game of tag, the formula "you're it" indicates by way of the verb "to be" the identity of who will be "it."

A moment ago, I said that the ritual substitute can seem intimately close to you because he or she or it must die for you, and I gave the example of the formula used by the Hittite king for saying that the *tarpalli-* or ritual substitute will die for him so that he may live. But there are two sides to this formula. The intimate closeness is matched by an alienating distance, marked by pollution, separating the king from his substitute. I draw attention here to a most telling example. In one particular ritual text (*Keilschrifturkunden aus Boghazköi* XXIV 5 + IX 13 I lines 19–26), where the word *tarpalli-* applies to a prisoner, this ritual substitute is anointed with royal oil, crowned with a diadem, and dressed in the regalia of the king; then this *tarpalli-* is expelled from the king's territory and sent back home to his own territory, so that he takes home with him the pollution that had been intimately associated with the king.[21] I stress here the intimacy of the actual transfer of pollution, even if the pollution itself is alienating. In another ritual text (*Keilschrifttexte aus Boghazköi* XVI 1 I line 10), it is specified that the king is to take off the royal clothing that he wears so that the prisoner who serves as his ritual substitute may now put on this same clothing.[22]

In the two examples we have just seen, the ritual substitute is expelled and does not die for the king, but the basic fact remains: the king and the body politic get rid of the pollution by getting rid of the ritual substitute. Let me restate the fact by using the English word *eliminate*, derived from a most telling Latin word, *ē-līmin-āre* "take outside the boundary [*līmen*]." So the king and the body politic <u>eliminate</u> the pollution by <u>eliminating</u> the ritual substitute. A remarkable parallel is the case of the goat that gets expelled into the wasteland on the Jewish Day of Atonement, instead of getting killed like the sacrificial goat of the Babylonian New Year.

Rituals of elimination, that is, of expelling a polluted person or animal or thing, are in fact homologous with rituals of killing. For example, when an animal is designated as a ritual substitute for the king in Hittite texts, we may expect two alternative outcomes: in some rituals, the animal victim is killed and its body is burned,[23] but in other rituals the victim is instead expelled.[24] And I think that there existed a parallel set of two alternative outcomes when a human was designated as a ritual substitute. That is, I think we may expect that human substitutes could be not only expelled but also killed in rituals dating from the Hittite era, just as substitute kings could be killed in rituals dating from a later era represented by neo-Assyrian texts. Granted, the testimony of the existing Hittite ritual texts is opaque concerning the actual killing of humans in contexts of ritual substitution, but the fact remains that there are clear examples of killings of humans in other Hittite ritual contexts.[25]

Throughout this analysis I have refrained from using the term *human sacrifice*, since some readers will view the word *sacrifice* too narrowly by thinking only of the killing and subsequent dismembering and cooking and eating of animal victims. If we allowed, however, for a broadening of this word "sacrifice" to include the killing and subsequent burning of animal victims, which, as we have seen, is an option in the case of animal victims of ritual substitution, then the term *human sacrifice* could still apply in the case of human victims of ritual substitution.

That said, I bring to a close my analysis of the relevant Hittite evidence by offering this summary, following the earlier formulation by van Brock: <u>the mentality of substitution rituals requires that someone who is notionally close to the king must die or be in some other way eliminated so as to preserve the king</u>.[26]

I now turn to the corresponding evidence in Greek. The Hittite words *tarpanalli-/tarpalli-* and *tarpašša-*, as van Brock has argued, were borrowed by the Greek language sometime in the second millennium BCE, and the corresponding Greek words were *therapōn* (θεράπων) and *theraps* (θέραψ), both of which can be translated as "attendant."[27] Like the two Hittite words *tarpanalli-/tarpalli-* and *tarpašša-*, the two Greek words *therapōn* and *theraps* were once synonyms, as is evident from the fact that the verb *therapeuein* is attested as a functional derivative of the noun *therapōn* in Homeric diction. We can see this functional derivation at work when we look at the context of *Odyssey* xiii 265, where this verb *therapeuein* means "be a *therapōn*," even though it is formally derived not from the noun *therapōn* but from the noun *theraps*, which is absent from Homeric diction.[28] We find attestations of *theraps* only rarely, as in Ion of Chios F 27 ed. West; or in Euripides *Ion* 94 and *Suppliants* 762. In the fragment from Ion of Chios, the plural form *therapes* refers to attendants who serve wine at a symposium; in the *Ion* of Euripides, the same plural form refers to the priests of Apollo at Delphi who serve as attendants of the god as they approach the streams of the spring Kastalia; and in the *Suppliants* of Euripides, *therapes* again refers to attendants—in this case, the hero Adrastus is asking the Messenger whether *therapes* have removed the corpses of the fallen dead.

How then do we explain the meaning of the Hittite words *tarpanalli-* and *tarpašša-* as "ritual substitute" when we compare the meaning of the borrowed Greek words *therapōn* (θεράπων) and *theraps* (θέραψ) as "attendant"? Here I return to my formulation summarizing the role of Patroklos as the personal attendant of Achilles:

> *Patroklos as* therapōn *of Achilles is the nearest and dearest companion of that primary hero in the* Iliad. *As the personal* therapōn *of Achilles, Patroklos is a secondary hero, and he attends Achilles just as other* therapontes *who are secondary heroes will attend Achilles after Patroklos dies.*

Building on this formulation, I will now explore another aspect of the service of Patroklos as the personal *therapōn* of Achilles in the *Iliad*: Patroklos serves as the personal charioteer or *hēniokhos* of Achilles (*Iliad* XXIII 280 ἡνίοχος). The role of Patroklos as the charioteer of Achilles is specially highlighted in *Iliad* XVII (475–8), where Automedon describes Patroklos as the best of all charioteers by virtue of driving the chariot of Achilles. Automedon, as we have already seen, is another near and dear companion of Achilles. And he too, as we will now see, is a chariot driver.

The wording used by Automedon in *Iliad* XVII (475–8) in describing Patroklos as the best of all charioteers is most relevant to his own role as a charioteer. Here in *Iliad* XVII, Patroklos is, of course, already dead. He died in *Iliad* XVI, getting killed in place of Achilles. Back then in *Iliad* XVI, it was Automedon who had served as the charioteer of Patroklos. To appreciate this role of Automedon as charioteer of

Patroklos, I now review what happened in *Iliad* XVI when Patroklos had died fighting Hektor.

The setting for the death of Patroklos in *Iliad* XVI is a classic chariot fight. The fight starts when Patroklos leaps out of his chariot:

Πάτροκλος δ' ἑτέρωθεν ἀφ' ἵππων ἆλτο χαμᾶζε

Patroklos, from one side, leapt from his chariot, hitting the ground.

Iliad XVI 733

In a moment, Hector will leap out from his own chariot. Before that happens, however, Patroklos picks up a rock and throws it at Kebriones, the charioteer of Hector, hitting Kebriones on the forehead and smashing his skull (*Iliad* XVI 734–54). And then, just as Patroklos had leapt out of his chariot, Hector too leaps out of his own chariot:

Ἕκτωρ δ' αὖθ' ἑτέρωθεν ἀφ' ἵππων ἆλτο χαμᾶζε.

Then Hector, from the other side, leapt from his chariot, hitting the ground.

Iliad XVI 755

Patroklos and Hector proceed to fight one-on-one in mortal combat on foot—a combat that is won by Hector (XVI 756–863). In this chariot fight that happened in *Iliad* XVI, I highlight the fact that it is Automedon who serves as chariot driver for Patroklos. And, at this moment, it is Patroklos, and not Achilles, who is the chariot fighter, since it is Automedon, and not Patroklos, who was the chariot driver. In preparation for this chariot fight between Patroklos and Hektor, it is Automedon, serving as chariot driver for Patroklos, who yokes the horses of Achilles to the chariot (XVI 145–54).

Like Patroklos, as we have already noted, Automedon is described in the *Iliad* as a *therapōn* of Achilles (XVI 865). Also, in another Iliadic passage, Automedon and a companion named Alkimos are described as *therapontes* of Achilles (XXIV 573). That passage goes on to say that Achilles honors these two companions, Automedon and Alkimos, more than anyone else —now that Patroklos is dead (XXIV 575). And, in still further Iliadic passages, we see that one of the functions of these two honored *therapontes* of Achilles is the unyoking of horses or mules (at XXIV 576) as well as the yoking of horses (at XIX 392–3, where Automedon and Alkimos are yoking Achilles's horses for him). So also, as we have just seen, Automedon yokes for Patroklos the horses of Achilles (at XVI 145–54).

After the death of Patroklos, when Achilles finally rejoins the Achaeans in battle, his chariot is now driven by Automedon (XIX 395–9). As we have seen, however, Automedon had at an earlier point served as chariot driver for the hero Patroklos when that hero took the place of Achilles in war (XVI 145–54). And here I note a most telling detail about that earlier point in the narrative of the *Iliad*: after Patroklos is killed by Hektor, the chariot driver Automedon says that he now wants to become a chariot fighter, but he cannot fight the Trojans while he is still driving the chariot (XVII 463–5). So he asks another companion, Alkimedon, to take his place as a chariot driver in order that he, Automedon, may now become a chariot fighter:

ἀλλὰ σὺ μὲν μάστιγα καὶ ἡνία σιγαλόεντα
δέξαι, ἐγὼ δ' ἵππων ἀποβήσομαι, ὄφρα μάχωμαι

But you [= Alkimedon], take this whip and these splendid reins,
take them, while I [= Automedon] step off [*apobainein*] from the chariot, so that
I may fight.

—*Iliad* XVII 479–80

And, sure enough, Alkimedon quickly leaps into the chariot, landing on the chariot-platform (XVII 481 ἐπορούσας) and taking hold of the whip and the reins (XVII 482), while Automedon leaps out of the chariot; that is, he leaps off the chariot platform (XVII 483 ἀπόρουσε) and lands on the ground, where he can then start fighting.[29] So we see here a functioning dyadic relationship between Automedon as a chariot fighter and Alkimedon as a chariot driver, both of whom are secondary substitutes for the primary substitute Patroklos, the premier chariot driver who became a chariot fighter for Achilles and who thus died for him as his *therapōn*, as his personal ritual substitute.[30]

I conclude, then, that the relationship of the chariot fighter to the chariot driver who substitutes for him is parallel to the relationship of a hero like Achilles to a hero like Patroklos, who is his *therapōn*. By now we see, on the basis of evidence from the narrative traditions of Homeric poetry, that Patroklos as the *therapōn* of Achilles does in fact serve as his substitute. In the end, the chariot driver in this case dies in place of the chariot fighter: that is, the chariot driver takes the hit, as it were, for the chariot fighter. But now that we see how Patroklos is a substitute for Achilles, the question remains: how is he not only a substitute but also a <u>ritual</u> substitute? We must now examine more closely how the actual concept of a <u>ritual substitute</u>, as attested in Hittite ritual texts, was translated into the ancient Greek song culture.

For analyzing the concept of <u>ritual substitute</u> as attested in the Greek evidence, an ideal starting point is a climactic passage in *Iliad* XVI where the warrior hero Patroklos is killed in battle: at this moment, the hero is visualized as *atalantos Arēi* "equal to Ares" (line 784). Now we will see that Patroklos in such a context is a stand-in for Achilles, or, in other words, Patroklos is a <u>ritual substitute</u> for the main hero of the *Iliad*. And just as Patroklos as ritual substitute of Achilles qualifies as "equal to Ares," we can expect Achilles himself to qualify for epithets meaning "equal to Ares."

Here I find it most relevant to consider some basic facts about the use of the word *therapōn*, the plural form of which is *therapontes*. In the *Iliad*, warriors are conventionally called the *therapontes* of Ares as the god of war (II 110, VI 67, XV 733, XIX 78).[31] With this fact in mind, I now make an argument that can be formulated in this way:

> *When a warrior is killed in war, he becomes a* therapōn *or "ritual substitute" who dies for Ares by becoming identical to the war god at the moment of death; then, after death, the warrior is eligible to become a cult hero who serves as a sacralized "attendant" of the war god.*[32]

As an epic warrior, Achilles is a *therapōn* or "ritual substitute" of Ares by virtue of becoming identical to the war god at the moment of death. In the *Iliad*, however, this relationship between Achilles and Ares is expressed only by way of an intermediary, who is Patroklos. This warrior is described not as the *therapōn* of Ares but rather as the *therapōn* of Achilles, and, as such, Patroklos is not only that hero's "attendant" but also his "ritual substitute," since he actually dies for Achilles. So Achilles in the *Iliad* dies only indirectly as the *therapōn* of Ares through the intermediacy of Patroklos, who dies in this epic as the *therapōn* of Achilles.

Here I come back to *Iliad* XVI 233–48, which was the first passage that we considered in this essay: there we saw that Patroklos qualifies as *therapōn* of Achilles only so long as he stays within his limits as the recessive equivalent of the dominant hero; once he is on his own, however, he becomes a *therapōn* of Ares and dies in place of Achilles.[33]

As an epic warrior, Achilles qualifies as *īsos Arēi* "equal to Ares," just like Patroklos. This description suits Achilles in the *Iliad*—though it applies to him only vicariously by way of Patroklos, who takes upon himself the role of a ritual substitute for Achilles.[34] In *Iliad* XVI 784, as we have already seen, Patroklos is called *atalantos Arēi* "equal to Ares" at the exact moment when he is killed. And, as we will soon see, Patroklos is actually called *īsos Arēi* "equal to Ares" at the exact moment when the story of his fatal impersonation of Achilles begins.

Besides being equated with Ares, however, Patroklos is also being equated with Apollo. It happens in *Iliad* XVI 705 and 786, when Patroklos is called *daimoni īsos* "equal to a *daimōn*." As we know from the contexts of these passages, the *daimōn* or "otherworldly force" here is the god Apollo himself.[35] So in these contexts Patroklos is "equal" to Apollo, though his identification with this god is not fully spelled out, since the word *daimōn* partly masks the identity of the god.

As one who is equal to Apollo at the moment of his death, Patroklos participates in a specialized god-hero relationship.[36] By being equal to Ares at the moment of his death, Patroklos participates in a generic god-hero relationship that is typical of heroes who are warriors.[37] In identifying with both Ares and Apollo, however, Patroklos is experiencing something more special—something that will later be experienced by Achilles himself, who will also be identifying with both Ares and Apollo at the moment of his own heroic death, though his death scene is not directly pictured in the *Iliad*.

In this way, Patroklos is a perfect stand-in for the main hero of the narrative, Achilles, whose specialized ritual antagonist is Apollo. Although Achilles, just like other warriors, can have as his generalized ritual antagonist the god Ares, he also has as his specialized ritual antagonist the god Apollo.

Patroklos is drawn into the specialized relationship of Achilles with Apollo at the precise moment when he is equated with Ares and thus marked for doom:

> τὸν δὲ ἰδὼν ἐνόησε ποδάρκης δῖος Ἀχιλλεύς·
> 600 ἑστήκει γὰρ ἐπὶ πρυμνῇ μεγακήτεϊ νηῒ
> εἰσορόων πόνον αἰπὺν ἰῶκά τε δακρυόεσσαν.
> αἶψα δ᾽ ἑταῖρον ἐὸν Πατροκλῆα προσέειπε
> φθεγξάμενος παρὰ νηός· ὃ δὲ κλισίηθεν ἀκούσας
> ἔκμολεν ἶσος Ἄρηϊ, κακοῦ δ᾽ ἄρα οἱ πέλεν ἀρχή.

605   τὸν πρότερος προσέειπε Μενοιτίου ἄλκιμος υἱός·
       τίπτέ με κικλήσκεις Ἀχιλεῦ; τί δέ σε χρεὼ ἐμεῖο;

He [Nestor] was seen and noted by swift-footed radiant Achilles,
600   who was standing on the spacious stern of his ship,
       watching the hard stress [*ponos*] and tearful struggle of the fight.
       He called to his companion Patroklos,
       calling from the ship, and he [Patroklos] from inside the tent heard him
         [Achilles],
       and he [Patroklos] came out, equal [*īsos*] to Ares, and here indeed was the
         beginning of the doom that presently befell him.
605   He [Patroklos], powerful son of Menoitios, was the first to speak, and he
         said [to Achilles]:
       "Why, Achilles, do you call me? what need do you have for me?"

Iliad XI 599–606

Here at verse 604 Homeric poetry declares explicitly that the application of the epithet "equal to Ares" will doom Patroklos to death.[38]

A generic warrior, as we have noted, is called a *therapōn* of Ares. Generically, then, heroes as warriors die for Ares. More specifically, however, a special hero will die for his special divine antagonist.

Generically, Achilles would be a *therapōn* of Ares; specifically, however, we can say that he is a *therapōn* of Apollo, because it is Apollo who will directly kill him, as we know from the plot summary of the *Aithiopis*. And, while the *therapōn* of Apollo must be Achilles, the *therapōn* of Achilles must be, as we have seen, Patroklos.

Patroklos must die for Achilles, who must die for Apollo. The death of Patroklos is caused by Ares generically; but it is brought to fulfillment by Apollo personally.

I return here to the moment when Patroklos dies. At that moment, as we saw, he is called *daimoni īsos*, "equal to a *daimōn*" (XVI 705 and 786). And, at that precise moment, he is in sacred space. Since war is ritual, the battleground is for the warrior a sacred space. Patroklos is doomed, selected for death, and that is why he is "equal to a *daimōn*." But this sacred space is not only sacred: it is also violent and even sinister. When you are a warrior fighting in the sacred space of Ares, being "equal to a *daimōn*" is to have martial fury. Ares is not only the god of war, he is the god of martial fury in war.[39]

I return here to the ritual background of the word *therapōn*: it was borrowed into the Greek language, as we have seen, from Anatolian languages, sometime in the second millennium BCE. The corresponding word in those Anatolian languages meant "ritual substitute." Someone who is notionally close to the king, as we have also seen, may have to die in place of the king. Such a death, I argue, has the effect of healing society by way of healing the king, who is viewed as the embodiment of society, of the body politic. What I describe here for the first time as a <u>healing</u> is an act of purifying the king and his people from impurities, from pollution. If the king is polluted, then society is polluted. That is why the pollution of the king has to be transferred to a ritual substitute who will be eliminated in place of the king and will thus remove the royal pollution while also removing the pollution of society. This principle of purification has been described by van Brock as the transfer of evil, "le transfert du mal."[40] Evil must be passed on, to a sacrificial victim.

In Greek visual art, I must now add, the dead hero Patroklos can be represented as a sacrificial ram, who is shown with his throat slit open and with blood streaming from the gaping wound: such a picture is painted on an Attic vase executed by the Triptolemos Painter, *c*. 480 BCE.[41] Similarly in Hittite rituals of substitution, as we have seen, rams can be sacrificed in place of kings.

The meaning of the Greek word *therapōn* as ritual substitute and the function of such a *therapōn* as a healer helps explain why the related Greek word *therapeuein* means not only "be a *therapōn*," as we have seen at *Odyssey* xiii 265, but also "heal, cure"; we still see such a meaning embedded in the English-language borrowings *therapy* and *therapeutic*. But before I cite some contexts where the ancient Greek word *therapeuein* means "heal, cure," I must return once again to that passage at *Odyssey* xiii 265 where *therapeuein* means "be a *therapōn*," since I have yet to explain the context.

There are in fact three attestations of *therapeuein* where the word does not overtly mean "heal, cure." The first attestation is at *Odyssey* xiii 265, the passage we are considering right now. Here the first-person narrator of a "Cretan tale" says that he was unwilling to "be a *therapōn*," *therapeuein*, for the Cretan king Idomeneus, preferring instead to be the leader of his own companions. The second attestation is at *Homeric Hymn to Apollo* 390, where the god Apollo selects a group of Cretans to serve as his attendants, *therapeuein*, at his shrine in Delphi. Finally, the third attestation is at Hesiod *Works and Days* 135, where the prototypical humans who represent the second generation of humankind are said to be unwilling to serve as attendants, *therapeuein*, to the gods; and, as we read in the next verse, these sacrilegious proto-humans are likewise unwilling to sacrifice to the gods at their altars (*Works and Days* 136).[42]

As we consider these three early attestations, the first one of the three is not decisive in establishing the overall meaning of *therapeuein*, since the story of the upstart Cretan who refused to serve as *therapōn* to the king of Crete has no attested parallels. Still, it is safe to say that the social position of the *therapōn* in this story cannot be too different from the social position of Patroklos himself, who is subservient to Achilles by virtue of serving as that hero's *therapōn*.[43] But the second and the third attestations are, in fact, decisive: in these two cases, *therapeuein* refers to the service that needs to be rendered to gods by humans who are designated as the gods' attendants. As we are about to see, the contexts of *therapeuein* in these two cases can help explain later attestations of the verb *therapeuein* in the sense of "heal, cure."

In speaking of later attestations, I have in mind evidence dating from the fifth century and thereafter. In this later era, *therapeuein* in the sense of "take care of" can refer to the procedure of healing a body by removing some form of sickness or, more basically, to the procedure of maintaining the well-being of the body. To maintain the well-being of the body is to keep it healthy—that is, keeping it sound and immune from any sickness.[44]

But there are also more specialized contexts of *therapeuein* in the sense of "take care of," some of which are explicitly sacred. And, in such sacred contexts, the body that is being cared for and kept sound by those who are attending it is either (1) the notional body of a god or (2) the actual body of a cult hero. Such a sacred body can lend its sacredness to anything that makes contact with it, such as a temple or shrine or any other kind of sacred enclosure. In the case of gods, the sacred power of the sacred body can extend to a sacred simulacrum of the body, such as a sacred statue or picture or any other object that stands for the body of the god. There are many different attestations of *therapeuein* where the object of the verb is whatever such sacred thing or place is attended by the attendants who care for it. Here are three shining examples:

1) An Attic inscription dating from the fifth century BCE (*Inscriptiones Graecae* I³ 1–2 138.17) speaks of the need for *therapeuein* "taking care of" the *temenos* "sacred precinct" of the god Apollo "in the most beautiful way possible" ([τõ τε]-μένõς τõ Ἀπόλλõνο[ς ἐπιμελέσθõν, ὅπõς ἂν κάλλισ]τα θεραπεύ̃εται).

2) A Cretan inscription dating from the second century BCE (*Inscriptiones Creticae* III:2 1.5) speaks of the need for *therapeuein* "taking care of" archaic statues of divinities (τὰ ἀρχαῖα [ἀ]γάλματα θαραπεύσαντες).⁴⁵

3) In the *Ion* of Euripides (110–11), dating from the late fifth century BCE, the young hero Ion speaks of his service of *therapeuein* "taking care of" the temple of Apollo at Delphi (τοὺς θρέψαντας | Φοίβου ναοὺς θεραπεύω).

It is in the light of such relatively later attestations of the verb *therapeuein* that we can understand the earlier attestations of the noun *therapōn* in combination with the genitive case of names of gods like Apollo, the Muses, Ares, and so on.⁴⁶ Also, of special relevance to my ongoing argumentation about twinning is the attestation of the dual form *theraponte* with reference to the twin sons of Poseidon, who are Pelias and Neleus, described as attendants of the god Zeus himself (θεράποντε *Odyssey* xi 255).

By now we have seen that *therapeuein* in the basic sense of "maintain the well-being" and in the derivative sense of "heal, cure" is in fact related to the idea of a ritual substitute who maintains the well-being of someone superior whom he serves by standing ready to die for that special someone. That is the therapeutic function, as it were, of the *therapōn*. Earlier on, I noted the English-language borrowings *therapy* and *therapeutic*. Now I note a semantic parallel in the use of the Greek word *pharmakon*, which means "drug used for healing" or, more generally, "drug used for medication or for poisoning," and we see the more specific meaning "drug used for healing" embedded in the English-language borrowings *pharmacy* and *pharmaceutical*. The meaning of this word *pharmakon* as "drug used for healing" helps explain the related meaning of a related Greek word, *pharmakos*, which designates a person who serves a very special ritual function. That person is what we call a "scapegoat," that is, someone who takes the blame for a pollution that afflicts a whole society.⁴⁷ Here again we see at work the principle of a _transfer of evil_, comparable to what we saw in the case of the Hittite ritual substitutes.

Having said this much about *therapōn*, I turn to the other of the two words that I intended to analyze in this essay. That word, as I noted at the beginning, is *philos*, meaning "friend" as a noun and "near and dear" or "belonging to the self" as an adjective. By contrast with my lengthy analysis of *therapōn*, however, I can confine myself here to the shortest of summaries, since I have already analyzed this word *philos* at some length in my earlier work.[48] Here I attempt to summarize all that work in a single nested paragraph:

> *Patroklos as the personal* therapōn *of Achilles is thereby also the nearest and dearest of all the companions of Achilles. This closeness is measured in terms of the word* philos *in the sense of being "near and dear" to someone. Achilles considers Patroklos to be the most* philos *"near and dear" of them all. Or, if we were to express this idea in terms of the noun* philos, *meaning "friend," instead of using the adjective* philos, *meaning "near and dear," we would say that Patroklos is the very best friend of Achilles. This word* philos *defines identity by way of measuring how much you can identify with someone else: the more you love someone, the more you identify with this special someone—and the closer you get to your own self. That is why Patroklos is truly the alter ego of Achilles. In his essays on morality, Aristotle defined a true friend as an* allos egō, *"another I." This terminology helps explain the use of the pseudo-scientific Latin term* alter ego *in translations of the works of Freud into English.*

Such an idea of Patroklos as the other self of Achilles is surely parallel to the idea of twinning, and this parallelism helps explain other features of Achilles and Patroklos that they share with the Dioskouroi, such as the power to heal. The therapeutic powers of Achilles and Patroklos are analyzed in this light by Douglas Frame in his twin chapter.

I might add that the therapeutic function of caring for someone as a patient in mythical contexts of healing can be linked with the emotional function of caring for someone who is *philos* in these same contexts. That is because *therapeuein* in the sense of "care for" is linked with *philos* in the sense of "near and dear";[49] and, further, *therapōn* in the sense of "ritual substitute" is linked with philos in the sense of "belonging to the self."[50]

As the other self who is ready to die for the self that is Achilles, Patroklos achieves an unsurpassed level of intimacy with the greatest hero of the Homeric *Iliad*. This intimacy is sacral, thus transcending even sexual intimacy. But this sacred intimacy has an uncanny other side to it, which is a kind of sacred alienation. As we saw in the case of the Hittite prisoner, about to be expelled into an alien realm, he must wear the clothing of the king, thus becoming ritually intimate with the body of the king. So too Patroklos wears the armor of Achilles when he dies; and he wears something else that is even more intimately connected with his best friend. Patroklos wears also the epic identity of Achilles, as expressed by the epithets they share. These heroic epithets, such as the one that makes them both "equal to Ares," will predestine both of them to live and die the same way. And the sameness of their shared life and death can be seen as an uncanny mix of intimacy and alienation that only twins will ever truly understand.

Notes

1 Frame's chapter is best read in conjunction with his book on myths about twinning, with special emphasis on myths about Nestor: see Douglas Frame, *Hippota Nestor*, Hellenic Studies 37 (Washington, DC: Center for Hellenic Studies, Trustees of Harvard University; Cambridge, MA: Distributed by Harvard University Press, 2009).

2 Frame, *Hippota Nestor,* 239, 305.

3 See again ibid.

4 Ibid., chapter 4.

5 There are also striking exceptions to the idea of twins as lookalikes. For example, the hero Meleager has as his twin a smoldering log: in this case, the other twin may not look like Meleager on the surface but, deep down inside, the two are fatally homeopathic with one other (the classic account can be found in Diodorus of Sicily 4.34.6–7).

6 For more on the dating of these Hittite ritual texts, see Hans M. Kümmel, *Ersatzrituale für den hethitischen König* (Wiesbaden: Otto Harrassowitz, 1967), 188.

7 Nadia Van Brock, "Substitution rituelle," *Revue Hittite et Asianique* 65 (1959): 117–46. with special reference to the Hittite ritual text *Keilschrifttexte aus Boghazköi* IV 6 (*tarpašša-* at Recto line 11, *tarpalli-* at Recto line 28; see also Verso line 14); Gregory Nagy, *Greek: An Updating of a Survey of Recent Work* (Cambridge, MA and Washington, DC: Center for Hellenic Studies, 2008), 55.

8 Van Brock, "Substitution rituelle," 119; Nagy, *Greek,* 55.

9 Kümmel, *Ersatzrituale für den hethitischen König,* 131, 150.

10 Van Brock, "Substitution rituelle," 121, with reference to *Keilschrifttexte aus Boghazköi* IX 129 I lines 5–9. For the principle of analogical substitution in general, see Kümmel, *Ersatzrituale für den hethitischen König,* 22.

11 Van Brock, "Substitution rituelle," 120–1, with reference to *Keilschrifturkunden aus Boghazköi* VII 10.

12 Van Brock, "Substitution rituelle," 123–5, with reference to *Keilschrifturkunden aus Boghazköi* XXIV 5 + IX 13.

13 Van Brock, "Substitution rituelle," 123; see also especially Kümmel, *Ersatzrituale für den hethitischen König,* 20 and 121–2, with reference to the mention of a female *tarpašša-* in *Keilschrifttexte aus Boghazköi* IV 6 I line 11.

14 For a variety of further examples taken from Hittite ritual texts, see Steven Lowenstam, *The Death of Patroklos: A Study in Typology*, Beiträge zur Klassischen Philologie 133 (Königstein/Ts: Hain, 1981), 127–30.

15 Commentary by van Brock, "Substitution rituelle," 123; also Kümmel, *Ersatzrituale für den hethitischen König,* 25. At lines 10–16 of this same ritual text, *Keilschrifturkunden aus Boghazköi* XXIV 5 I, we see that a bull is to be driven to a place where it is killed and its body is burned, while the moon god is invoked to witness with his own divine eyes the smoke that rises up to the heavens from the burning body; see also Kümmel, *Ersatzrituale für den hethitischen König,* 37.

16 Van Brock, "Substitution rituelle," 125. Kümmel (*Ersatzrituale für den hethitischen König,* 194–5) cautions against anachronistic formulations, but there is no doubt that the ritual purification of the Hittite king extends to a homologous purification of his royal subjects. In the ritual text *Keilschrifttexte aus Boghazköi* XV 1 I lines 19–20

and 39, for example, it is made clear that the removal of pollution extends from the king to the whole army and to the whole land of Ḫatti; commentary by Kümmel, *Ersatzrituale für den hethitischen König,* 120.

17 Kümmel, *Ersatzrituale für den hethitischen König,* 189, 193–4, 196–7.

18 Kümmel, *Ersatzrituale für den hethitischen König,* 169–87. He emphasizes how little textual evidence has been preserved, considering the pervasiveness of the custom of ritual substitution in Near Eastern civilizations (191). The period of the substitute king's tenure can be measured in units of time, such as 100 days (176–7, 179). See also in general Simo Parpola, *Letters from Assyrian Scholars to the Kings Esarhaddon and Assurbanipal* I-II (Kevelaer: Butzon & Bercker, 1970–83).

19 Calvert Watkins, *How to Kill a Dragon: Aspects of Indo-European Poetics* (New York and Oxford: Oxford University Press, 1995), 167–8.

20 Calvert Watkins, "Latin *sōns*," in *Studies in Historical Linguistics in honor of George Sherman Lane*, ed. W. W. Arndt et al. (Chapel Hill, NC: The University of North Carolina Press, 1967), 186–94. Reprinted in Calvert Watkins, *Selected Writings* II, ed. Lisi Oliver (Innsbruck: Innsbrucker Beiträge zur Sprachwissenschaft 80, 1994), 405–13.

21 Text and commentary by Van Brock, "Substitution rituelle," 123; see also Kümmel, *Ersatzrituale für den hethitischen König,* 27–32.

22 Commentary by Kümmel, *Ersatzrituale für den hethitischen König,* 118.

23 *Keilschrifturkunden aus Boghazköi* VII 10 II; see Kümmel, *Ersatzrituale für den hethitischen König*, 131.

24 *Keilschrifttexte aus Boghazköi* XV 1 I; see Kümmel, *Ersatzrituale für den hethitischen König*, 115.

25 Kümmel, *Ersatzrituale für den hethitischen König,* 150–68; at 147, he leaves the door ajar for the possibility that a human *tarpanalli-* could in fact be ritually killed.

26 Van Brock, "Substitution rituelle," 125–6.

27 Ibid.

28 Nadia Van Brock, *Recherches sur le vocabulaire médical du grec ancien* (Paris: Klincksieck, 1961), 118n1, 120n3. We would have expected the denominative verb of *therapōn* to be *theraponeuein*, just as the denominative verb of, say *hēgemōn* is *hēgemoneuein*. So the fact that *therapeuein* in the sense of "be a *therapōn*" functions as the denominative verb of *therapōn* proves that this noun *therapōn* was once a synonym of *theraps*.

29 The wording that expresses here the complementary of the chariot fighter and the chariot driver can be found elsewhere as well in the *Iliad*, as at V 218–38. Here we see Aeneas urging Pandaros to leap into the chariot of Aeneas (V 221) so that Pandaros may act as the chariot driver while Aeneas acts as the chariot fighter by leaping out of his chariot and fighting on the ground (226–7). Pandaros refuses, saying that he prefers to fight on the ground (V 238) and telling Aeneas to continue driving his own horses, since they would not get used to a new charioteer (V 230–7). As the narrative proceeds, it becomes clear that the choice made by Pandaros proves to be fatal.

30 For more on the multiformity of the figures Alkimedon (/Alkimos) and Automedon as *therapontes*, see Dale S. Sinos, "Achilles, Patroklos, and the Meaning of Philos," *Innsbrucker Beiträge zur Sprachwissenschaft* 29 (1980): 38n6.

31 Gregory Nagy, *The Best of the Achaeans: Concepts of the Hero in Archaic Greek Poetry*, revised ed. with new introduction (Baltimore: Johns Hopkins Press, 1999), 17§5, especially 295.

32 A longer version of this formulation is presented in Nagy, *The Best of the Achaeans*, 17§§5–6 = 293–5. I have already noted that the charioteer Alkimos is described as a *therapōn* of Achilles (*Iliad* XXIV 573); now I add that Alkimos is also described as an *ozos Arēos* "attendant of Ares" (XXIV 474 ὄζος Ἄρηος); see Nagy, *The Best of the Achaeans*, 17§5, n. 8 = 295 on *ozos* as a synonym of *therapōn*.

33 Sinos, "Achilles, Patroklos, and the Meaning of Philos," 46–54; Nagy, *The Best of the Achaeans*, 17§4 = 292–3.

34 Nagy, *The Best of the Achaeans*, 2§8 = 33, also with reference to the hero Leonteus as *īsos Arēi* "equal to Ares" at *Iliad* XII 130; more in 17§§4–5 = 292–5.

35 Nagy, *The Best of the Achaeans*, 17§5, especially 293.

36 Gregory Nagy, "The Epic Hero," in *A Companion to Ancient Epic*, ed. J. M. Foley (Oxford: Oxford University Press, 2005), 71–89. Online, expanded version, with notes (2006): Nagy.The_Epic_Hero.2005, §§105, 110, 115.

37 Nagy, *The Best of the Achaeans*, 18§9 = 307.

38 Ibid., 2§8 = 32–4, 17§5 = 293–5.

39 Nagy, "The Epic Hero," §110.

40 Van Brock, "Substitution rituelle," 129.

41 This painting, along with another related painting, is analyzed by Victoria Tarenzi, "Patroclo ΘΕΡΑΠΩΝ," *Quaderni Urbinati di Cultura Classica* 80 (2005): 25–38, who makes major improvements on the earlier interpretations of Alan Griffiths, "Patroklos the Ram," *Bulletin of the Institute for Classical Studies* 32 (1985): 49–50 and idem, "Patroklos the Ram (Again)," *Bulletin of the Institute for Classical Studies* 36 (1989): 139.

42 Commentary in Nagy, *The Best of the Achaeans*, 9§§2–3 = 151–2.

43 Lowenstam, in *The Death of Patroklos*, 136–40, has argued persuasively that the upstart Cretan in this story is a narrative stand-in for the Cretan hero Meriones, who refuses to "take the hit," as it were, for the over-king of the Cretans, Idomeneus.

44 Van Brock, *Recherches*, 123–7, collects examples.

45 This example and the previous one are cited by van Brock, *Recherches,* 122–3.

46 Nagy, *The Best of the Achaeans*, 17§6 = 295; van Brock, *Recherches*, 115–17, surveys the various attested combinations of *therapōn* with the name of a god in the genitive case.

47 I refer here again to the analysis of Kümmel, *Ersatzrituale für den hethitischen König*, 193.

48 Nagy, *The Best of the Achaeans*, 5§27 = 82–3, 6§§12–22 = 102–11; see also the work of Dale S. Sinos, "The Entry of Achilles into Greek Epic," Dissertation (Baltimore: Johns Hopkins University, 1975).

49 On the meaning of philos as "near and dear," derived from *phi* in the sense of "near," see Gregory Nagy, *Greek Mythology and Poetics* (Ithaca, NY, 1990), 203n7, http://nrs .harvard.edu/urn-3:hul.ebook:CHS_Nagy.Greek_Mythology_and_Poetics.1990, with further references.

50 Nagy, *The Best of the Achaeans*, 6§§13–16 = 103–6.

Bibliography

Allen, Thomas W., ed. *Homeri Opera V* (Hymns, Cycle, Fragments). Oxford, 1912.

Chantraine, Pierre. *Dictionnaire étymologique de la langue grecque: histoire des mots*. Edited by Jean Taillardat, Olivier Masson, and Jean-Louis Perpillou, with a supplement Chroniques d'étymologie grecque, 1–10, edited by Alain Blanc, Charles de Lamberterie, and Jean-Louis Perpillou. Paris: Klincksieck, 2009. Abbreviated *DELG*.

Davidson, Olga M. "Indo-European Dimensions of Herakles in *Iliad* 19.95–133." *Arethusa* 13 (1980): 197–202.

Frame, Douglas. *Hippota Nestor*. Hellenic Studies 37. Washington, DC: Center for Hellenic Studies, Trustees of Harvard University; Cambridge, MA: Distributed by Harvard University Press, 2009. http://nrs.harvard.edu/urn-3:hul.ebook:CHS_Frame .Hippota_Nestor.2009.

Griffiths, Alan. "Patroklos the Ram." *Bulletin of the Institute for Classical Studies* 32 (1985): 49–50.

Griffiths, Alan. "Patroklos the Ram (Again)." *Bulletin of the Institute for Classical Studies* (1989): 36: 139.

Janko, Richard. *The Iliad: A Commentary: Vol. 4, Books 13–16. In G.S. Kirk, The Iliad: A Commentary*. Cambridge and New York: Cambridge University Press, 1985–93.

Kümmel, Hans M. *Ersatzrituale für den hethitischen König*. Wiesbaden: Otto Harrassowitz, 1967.

Lowenstam, Steven. *The Death of Patroklos: A Study in Typology*. Beiträge zur Klassischen Philologie 133. Königstein/Ts: Hain, 1981.

Nagy, Gregory. "Introduction, Parts I and II, and Conclusions." *In Greek: A Survey of Recent Work*, edited by F. W. Householder and G. Nagy, 15–72. Janua Linguarum Series Practica 211. The Hague: Mouton, 1972.

Nagy, Gregory. *The Best of the Achaeans: Concepts of the Hero in Archaic Greek Poetry*. Baltimore: Johns Hopkins University Press, 1979. Revised ed. with new introduction, 1999. http://nrs.harvard.edu/urn-3:hul.ebook:CHS_Nagy.Best_of_the_Achaeans.1999.

Nagy, Gregory. *Greek Mythology and Poetics*. Ithaca, NY, 1990. http://nrs.harvard.edu/ urn-3:hul.ebook:CHS_Nagy.Greek_Mythology_and_Poetics.1990.

Nagy, Gregory. *Pindar's Homer: The Lyric Possession of an Epic Past*. Baltimore: Johns Hopkins University Press, 1990. http://nrs.harvard.edu/urn-3:hul.ebook:CHS_Nagy .Pindars_Homer.1990.

Nagy, G. "The Epic Hero." In *A Companion to Ancient Epic*, edited by J. M. Foley, 71–89. Oxford: Oxford University Press, 2005. Online, expanded version, with notes (2006): http://nrs.harvard.edu/urn-3:hlnc.essay:Nagy.The_Epic_Hero.2005.

Nagy, Gregory. "An Apobatic Moment for Achilles as Athlete at the Festival of the Panathenaia." *Imeros* 5 (2005): 311–17. Online, expanded version (2009): http://chs .harvard.edu/publications/.

Nagy, Gregory. "'Lyric and Greek Myth' and 'Homer and Greek Myth'." In *The Cambridge Companion to Greek Mythology*, edited by R. D. Woodard, 19–51; 52–82. Cambridge: Cambridge University Press, online editions: http://nrs.harvard.edu/urn-3 :hlnc.essay:Nagy.Lyric_and_Greek_Myth.2007.

Nagy, Gregory. *Greek: An Updating of a Survey of Recent Work*. Cambridge, MA and Washington, DC: The Center for Hellenic Studies, Harvard University, 2008. http://nrs .harvard.edu/urn-3:hul.ebook:CHS_Nagy.Greek_an_Updating.2008.

Nagy, G.. *Homer the Classic*. Hellenic Studies 36. Cambridge, MA and Washington, DC: Center for Hellenic Studies, Harvard University, 2008 (online) and 2009 (print). http://nrs.harvard.edu/urn-3:hul.ebook:CHS_Nagy.Homer_the_Classic .2008.

Nagy, Gregory. *Homer the Preclassic*. Berkeley, CA: University of California Press, 2009 (online) and 2010 (print). http://nrs.harvard.edu/urn-3:hul.ebook:CHS_Nagy.Homer _the_Preclassic.2009.

Parpola, Simo. *Letters from Assyrian Scholars to the Kings Esarhaddon and Assurbanipal I-II*. Kevelaer: Butzon & Bercker, 1970–83.

Sinos, Dale S. "The Entry of Achilles into Greek Epic." Dissertation. Baltimore: Johns Hopkins University, 1975.

Sinos, Dale S. *Achilles, Patroklos, and the Meaning of Philos*. Innsbruck: Innsbrucker Beiträge zur Sprachwissenschaft 29, 1980.

Stähler, Klaus P. *Grab und Psyche des Patroklos: Ein schwartzfiguriges Vasenbild*. Münster i. W., Bonn, Habelt in Kommission, 1967.

Tarenzi, Victoria. "Patroclo ΘΕΡΑΠΩΝ." *Quaderni Urbinati di Cultura Classica* 80 (2005): 25–38.

Van Brock, Nadia. "Substitution rituelle." *Revue Hittite et Asianique* 65 (1959): 117–46.

Van Brock, Nadia. *Recherches sur le vocabulaire médical du grec ancien*. Paris: Klincksieck, 1961.

Watkins, Calvert. "Latin *sōns*." In *Studies in Historical Linguistics in Honor of George Sherman Lane*, edited by Walter W. Arndt et al., 186–94. Chapel Hill: The University of North Carolina Press, 1967. Reprinted in Calvert Watkins, *Selected Writings II*, edited by Lisi Oliver, 405–13. Innsbruck: Innsbrucker Beiträge zur Sprachwissenschaft 80, 1994.

Watkins, Calvert. *How to Kill a Dragon: Aspects of Indo-European Poetics*. New York and Oxford: Oxford University Press, 1995.

11

Achilles and Patroclus as Indo-European Twins

Homer's Take

♊

Douglas Frame

There are two forms of the Indo-European twin myth relevant to the story of Patroclus and Achilles in the *Iliad*. In one, the twins remain together; in the other, they separate. The Greek Dioscuri remain together, and the dynamic between them is the following: Castor, who is mortal, dies in battle, and Polydeuces, who is immortal, brings him back to life, and ever after they alternate daily between life and death together. (See Figure 11.1 for a representation of the Greek twin gods.) In the second form of the myth one twin again dies, but his brother, instead of bringing him back

Figure 11.1 Apparition of the Dioskouroi (Dioscuri) at a banquet and sacrifice: Theoxenia relief. Hellenistic, second century BCE. Larissa, Thessalia. Inscription: "To the Great Gods [dedicated by] Danaa, daughter of Aphtonetos (Atthoneiteia)." Louvre Ma746. Marble, 63.5 X 40.5 X 15 cm. Photo: Hervé Lewandowski. Musée de Louvre. ©RMN-Grand Palais/Art Resource, NY.

to life, takes his place as a warrior. When Patroclus takes Achilles's place in battle Achilles is, of course, not dead, but only out of action. Patroclus's deed is nevertheless viewed in the *Iliad* through the prism of this second form of the twin myth.[1]

The aged counselor Nestor instigates Patroclus to take Achilles's place. He tells Patroclus a story of his own youthful heroism and then urges Patroclus either to rouse his companion or to take his place. These are the alternatives of the Indo-European twin myth transferred to an analogous relationship, that of a warrior and his *therapōn*.[2] Nestor himself, although his myth is well disguised in Homer, is the chief exponent of the twin who takes his brother's place, and the story that he tells Patroclus is at bottom this.[3]

In his story Nestor tells how he first became a warrior. He had eleven brothers and Heracles killed all of them when he sacked Pylos. This left Pylos prey to hostile neighbors until Nestor went out to meet these neighbors in battle and defeated them. Left unsaid in Nestor's account is the name of his brother Periclymenus, who alone had been more than a match for Heracles until Heracles finally undid him (the *Odyssey* names Periclymenus, and Hesiodic fragments tell of his fight with Heracles). This was the mighty warrior whose place Nestor took.[4]

When Indo-European twins are viewed as a pair they are both saviors of distressed mortals and they are both horsemen. Again the Dioscuri. In a Homeric hymn addressed to the Dioscuri, sailors caught in a storm call on the divine twins and they come at once through the air in their horse-drawn chariot. The Vedic divine twins provide a close comparison. Cognate with the *Dios kouroi*, "sons of Zeus," the Vedic twins, whose epithet *divo napātā*, "off-spring of Dyaus," makes them sons of the same Indo-European sky-god, are saviors and healers on the one hand (they too save mortals at sea) and, on the other hand, their chariot is a fixed feature in their hymns. Their two names, both in the dual, relate to their two attributes: *Aśvinā*, meaning "horsemen," occurs most frequently; *Nāsatyā*, meaning "saviors," occurs less frequently, but is demonstrably old. The meaning of *Nāsatyā*, which was probably no longer understood in Vedic, emerges from a widely accepted comparison with Germanic cognates, in particular the Gothic verb *nasjan*, "to save."[5]

Characteristics shared by the twins when they are viewed as a pair become characteristics of one of them in contrast to the other when they are viewed as distinct. As a pair both Greek twins are *Dios kouroi*, "sons of Zeus," but individually only Polydeuces is Zeus's son, and Castor is the son of the mortal Tyndareus. The Vedic twins are viewed almost exclusively as a pair (in their ritual they are invoked to come to their sacrifice as a pair, and in their rescue myths they are likewise seen acting as a pair), but an exceptional verse of the *Rig Veda* says that only one of the twins was called the "son of Dyaus," and that the other was called the son of Sumakha, an otherwise unknown figure, but presumably a mortal like Tyndareus. Dual paternity, a widespread feature in twin myths, often contrasts a god with a mortal, and in the Indo-European myth this was evidently the case. In the Greek myth the twins themselves are contrasted as immortal to mortal, and this contrast underlies yet further contrasts. The twins' characterization as "horsemen" becomes the characteristic of the mortal Castor alone, who is represented as a warrior in contrast to his brother, and who has the distinctive epithet in epic "breaker of horses." On the other hand, the twins' characterization as "saviors" becomes the attribute of Polydeuces alone when the mortal Castor dies in battle and the immortal Polydeuces brings him back to life.

This is the central myth of the Dioscuri, and it is likely to have been Indo-European as well. The myth is not directly attested in Vedic, given the Vedic constraint against representing the twins individually, but it can be inferred from a patterned use of their two names in their hymns. Sanskrit epic, which, as we know it, postdates the Vedic hymns, preserves distinctions between the twins which are ignored in Vedic, and here we find the equivalent of Castor, the warrior "horseman." In the epic *Mahābhārata*, the twin gods are fathers of two of the heroes of the poem, the twins Nakula and Sahadeva, and Nakula is differentially characterized as a warrior and a horseman. The divine twins themselves must have been similarly differentiated, and in the Vedic verse mentioned above, in which one twin is called the son of Sumakha, there is a clear sign of this: this twin is also called "conquering," and his father's name, Sumakha, means something like "good warrior." In epic the warrior twin's brother, Sahadeva, is characterized by "intelligence" and associated with "cattle."

The contrast between horses and cattle that characterizes the epic twins Nakula and Sahadeva is also found in the hymns of the Vedic twins, and is paired there with a contrast between their two dual names: the name *Aśvinā*, "the horsemen," is naturally paired with the idea of "horses," and the name *Nāsatyā* is paired with the idea of "cattle." This means that the twins, who are both "saviors/healers" (i.e., *Nāsatyā*) when viewed as a pair, must have had the same myth as the Dioscuri when viewed as distinct: one twin must have been mortal, and the other twin, the immortal son of the sky-god Dyaus, must have brought his mortal brother back to life when he died in battle. This correspondence with the Dioscuri establishes the Greek myth as also the Indo-European myth in all likelihood.

The epic twin Sahadeva, who is associated with "cattle" and is characterized by "intelligence," preserves basic features of the immortal twin in the Indo-European stage of the myth. In Vedic cattle are associated with the name *Nāsatyā*, and Sahadeva's father is thus to be seen as a singular *Nāsatya* ("savior"), who brings a singular *Aśvin* ("horseman") back to life. The "intelligence" of this twin is connected with the miraculous cure of his brother if we draw an inference from the divine twins as a pair. As "saviors" and "healers" of mortals they are called *dasrā bhiṣajau*, "miracle-working physicians" in their hymns, and the epithet *dasrā*, "miracle-working," actually means "skillful, clever" in terms of its Iranian cognate and Indo-European root. The epithet *dasrā*, which combines the notions of "intelligence" and "miraculous cures," functions just like the name *Nāsatyā* in oppositions between cattle and horses in the twins' hymns. The upshot of this functional equivalence between the epithet *dasrā* and name *Nāsatyā* is that a singular *Nāsatya* must have had both "intelligence" and a "miraculous cure" to his credit. The immortal twin's "intelligence," which in Indic is evidenced by the epic hero Sahadeva and in the Vedic twins' epithet *dasrā* (both the hero and the epithet are associated with cattle), also belonged to the Indo-European myth. In Greek Polydeuces is characterized by "intelligence." He is called "good with his fists" in Homer, and his skill as a boxer is presented as a matter of "intelligence" in his bout with the giant Amykos, a well-attested myth in later tradition. Polydeuces's son's name, *Mnāsinoos*, "he who remembers mind (*noos*)," occurred on two archaic sculptures in the Peloponnesus according to Pausanias, and like the names of other sons of famous fathers (Astyanax, Telemachus) it is the father's attribute that is expressed in this son's name.

In the Indo-European myth, the immortal twin brought the mortal twin back to life, and, if the Vedic twins' paired epithets *dasrā bhiṣajau*, "skillful healers," are a guide, this was a matter of "intelligence." In both the Greek immortal twin Polydeuces and the Sanskrit epic hero Sahadeva, "intelligence" manifests itself as a generalized attribute, but the origin of this attribute in the central myth of the Indo-European twins can be inferred. Cattle are differentially associated with the non-horseman twin in Indic on the evidence of both epic (the cattleman Sahadeva in contrast to the horseman Nakula) and Vedic (the twins' name *Nāsatyā* and epithet *dasrā*, both contrasted with the name *Aśvinā* in oppositions between cattle and horses). In Greek the central myth of the Dioscuri has two episodes: a cattle-raid and a battle. The cattle-raid is a success, but the ensuing battle causes the death of the mortal warrior Castor. While Castor, "breaker of horses," is explicitly associated with horses, Polydeuces is not explicitly associated with cattle, but the two episodes of their central myth can be traced to an opposition between the twins themselves in the original Indo-European myth.

The Dioscuri are the best guide to the primary form of the Indo-European twin myth. The secondary form of this myth, to which Nestor is the guide,[6] presupposes the myth's primary form and plays against it. This was well appreciated by the Homeric poets, as Book 11 of the *Odyssey* shows.[7] Here Odysseus meets a group of dead heroines in the underworld who tell him of their offspring, and it is not an accident that Nestor and the Dioscuri are found side by side in the passages devoted to their mothers. The two heroines in question come exactly halfway through this "catalog of heroines," and their respective passages relate to each other in significant ways. Leda, who comes next after Nestor's mother Chloris in the catalog, gave birth "under Tyndareus" to "horse-breaking" Castor and to Polydeuces, "good with his fists"; both twins are said to be alive though held fast by the earth; even under the earth they receive honor from Zeus, living and dying on alternate days, and having a share in sacrifices like gods. This is the essential résumé of the Indo-European twins in the primary form of their myth: dual paternity (alluded to, if not spelled out in this passage); an opposition between mortality, including burial, on the one hand, and immortality, including divine worship, on the other hand; the mortal twin's association with horses, and thereby with war; the immortal twin's distinctive pursuit, a matter of brains over brawn, requiring skill with the two hands. Whereas attention is focused squarely on the Dioscuri in the passage devoted to Leda (nothing about Leda herself is said apart from her being Tyndareus's wife), the passage directed at Nestor and his myth gives only what is necessary and sufficient for the purpose, the name of his warrior brother Periclymenus together with Nestor's own name, and the name of a third brother as well (the third brother, a cipher, is a nod to the tradition found in *Iliad* 11 that Nestor had eleven brothers—Nestor's twin myth, I repeat, is always disguised). This is the only time in Homer that Periclymenus is named, and his name is sufficient to evoke Nestor's variant of the twin myth, which is in stark contrast to the Dioscuri (Periclymenus, unlike the Dioscuri, did not go on living once he was beneath the earth). Attention in this passage is diverted from its main point, Nestor and his myth, to Chloris herself, about whom (in contrast to Leda) we hear a good deal (father, place of birth, rank as youngest daughter, marriage, subsequent rule in a new city). This lore about Chloris precedes the birth of Nestor and his brothers in the text, and what follows their birth in the text makes a climactic connection with Leda and the Dioscuri, who come next. Like Leda, who had a daughter Helen besides the two Dioscuri, Chloris had a daughter Pero besides her sons; and like Helen, whom the whole heroic world wooed, Pero was wooed by all her neighbors. Again like Helen, who was successfully wooed by a pair of brothers, Agamemnon wooing for Menelaus, Pero was successfully wooed by a pair of brothers, Melampus wooing for Bias. Pero and the myth of her wooing end the passage about Chloris, and when Leda is named in the following line of the catalog one is immediately reminded of her daughter as well. The fact that her daughter, Helen, is passed over in silence, whereas Pero's story is explicitly evoked, is what binds the two passages together. Pero is the only daughter mentioned in the catalog of heroines, which otherwise features sons, and her presence has a meaning.

There is more to say about this female figure in relation to twins.[8] The Indo-European twin myth entailed a triad: the two brothers had a sister who was also their common wife. In Baltic tradition, where "sons of the sky-god" still persist in the Latvian *dieva deli* and Lithuanian *dievo suneliai*, the sister of the twins is the "daughter of the sun": Latvian *saules meita* and Lithuanian *saules dukterys*. In Vedic this female figure is the common wife of the twins (they are called her "wooers") and here too she is called the "daughter of the sun," *duhitā sūryasya*. In Greek the twins' double relationship to the female figure as both sister and wife is split into two different relationships: Helen is sister to one pair of brothers, and is wooed by another pair of brothers. Nestor and his sister follow the Greek pattern. There is more to say about what binds Nestor and the Dioscuri in the catalog of heroines in *Odyssey* 11, beginning with the fact that twins are found in four other passages of the catalog (Neleus and Pelias, Amphion and Zethos, Heracles,[9] Otos and Ephialtes), but to address this fact account must be taken of a second fact, namely that the original Ionian version of the catalog has undergone an extensive Athenian overlay. The Ionian catalog, without the Athenian overlay, points directly at Nestor and his myth by its structure, which is double in form.[10]

The key point in Nestor's myth is his characterization as a "horseman." In the aftermath of Heracles's sack of Pylos there was no Pylian champion to keep marauding neighbors at bay. As Nestor tells the story to Patroclus in *Iliad* 11, cattle-raids had nearly drained the life from his city before he came on the scene. His story features two episodes, and in both he is the central figure. The first is a cattle-raid, in which the Pylians won back their livelihood, indeed their life, and the second is a battle between horsemen, in which the Pylians routed their neighbors when the neighbors came in force soon after. This twofold structure, featuring cattle and horses in distinct episodes, is the same as in the central myth of the Dioscuri, but here the secondary form of the myth is at play. Nestor carries out the cattle-raid single-handedly, no brother having survived at his side, and then, when his cattle-raid provokes a war, he becomes a warrior as well, taking his brother's place and in effect becoming two twins in one.

Nestor's story emphasizes that he became a "horseman" for the first time in this battle. When Nestor wants to join the Pylians rushing from their city to confront the enemy horsemen, his father hides his horses. Nestor goes anyway, on foot, and keeps pace with the Pylian horsemen until the armies clash, when Nestor at once kills the leader of the enemy horsemen and seizes his chariot. Sweeping ahead like a whirlwind in his newly won chariot Nestor proves that he is the equal of two twins at once by single-handedly capturing fifty chariots and slaying the double occupants of each chariot. The champions on the enemy's side, the twins known as the Aktorione Molione, would also have met their end under Nestor's spear if their father Poseidon had not saved them. In this virtual encounter with twins Nestor's own twin myth becomes all but overt. By taking his brother's place he has in effect become two twins in one.

In Homer, Nestor is called "the Gerenian horseman Nestor." The epithet "Gerenian" is obscure, but it seems to relate to the Homeric figure's old age and to the honor that old age has brought him [Figure 11.2]. Behind the aged Nestor of relatively recent epic tradition is the young Nestor of older epic tradition, and that figure was simply "horseman Nestor," *hippota Nestōr*. This epithet and noun combination is cognate with the two names of the Vedic twin gods, *Aśvinā* and *Nāsatyā*. While corresponding names and epithet are differently formed, they match each other in terms of roots: the word for "horse" (Sanskrit *aśvas* and Greek *hippos* from Indo-European **ekwos*) on the one hand, and an Indo-European verbal root (**nes-*) on the other hand. Greek "Nestor" is "he who brings home," his name containing the verbal root of Greek *nostos*, "return home."[11] One can see the salvific function of the Homeric Nestor in the *Odyssey*, the *nostos* poem as opposed to the war poem of the two paired Homeric epics. Here Nestor himself tells the story of the Greeks' *nostoi*, "returns," from Troy, and in his story he reveals himself as "savior" of the hero Diomedes, and as pointedly "not savior" of the hero Odysseus.[12] Behind the notion of "homecoming" in the Greek *nostos* tradition lies the notion of "returning to life," and in terms of the Indo-European

Figure 11.2 Nestor. Attic red-figure, detail. Fifth century BCE. Paris, Bibliothèque Nationale (Collection Luynes, CM) AKG262720. Photo: Erich Lessing/Art Resource, NY.

twin myth, "Nestor" means "he who brings back to life," corresponding to the Vedic name *Nāsatyā*, and to the myth in which a singular *Nāsatya* once brought his mortal brother back to life. As the equivalent of this *Nāsatya* in the secondary form of the twin myth, Nestor both does and does not act out his name in relation to the heroes Diomedes and Odysseus, but in his own basic myth he cannot act out his name: his myth is not to bring his brother back to life, but to take his brother's place. Odysseus experiences this negative side to Nestor in his own failed relationship with him after Troy.

In the comparison between *hippota Nestōr* and the *Aśvinā Nāsatyā*, one point remains unaddressed, namely, the "intelligence" of the Vedic twin properly called *Nāsatya*. The idea that the "intelligence" of this twin is bound up with his bringing his brother back to life, as is implied by the combined epithets *dasrā bhiṣajau*, "skilled physicians," characterizing both twins as a pair, gains more precise definition in Greek, where the noun *noos*, "mind," is seen to be a close equivalent of the name *Nestōr* in terms of its etymology and semantics: if *Nestōr* is originally "he who brings back to life," the noun *noos* (reconstructed as **nos-os*, with the same verbal root as *nos-tos*, "return," but in the active sense seen in *Nestōr*) means a "bringing back to life," and originally probably designated "consciousness." The Homeric Nestor, as counselor of the Greeks, has not only "intelligence," but also an affinity with the word *noos* itself, and it is in his story about his own homecoming in the *Odyssey* that the connection is played out at the most significant level.[13]

When Nestor in *Iliad* 11 tells Patroclus to rouse his warrior companion Achilles, or, failing that, to take his warrior companion's place in battle, he has already given Patroclus the paradigm to follow in his own story, which is the story of how "Nestor" became "horseman Nestor" by taking the place of his fallen warrior brother. Patroclus does not put Nestor's exhortation into effect until *Iliad* 16, when he finally returns to Achilles. When he does so he repeats Nestor's exhortation, but only the second part of it, to send Patroclus into battle in Achilles's place. Introducing this dramatic speech the poet addresses Patroclus directly with an epithet which occurs here for the first time of Patroclus in the poem, and which, together with a closely equivalent epithet, occurs six more times of him before he is finally slain, and not again after that. Both epithets mean "horseman," and the vocative phrase "Patroclus horseman," spoken by the poet five times, by Achilles once, and by a mocking Hector impersonating Achilles a final time, clearly evokes the phrase "horseman Nestor" in spite of differences between Nestor's epithet, *hippota*, and the two vocatives in question, *hippeu* and *hippokeleuthe*. The meaning of Nestor's story in *Iliad* 11 leads directly to the use of these two epithets of Patroclus in *Iliad* 16.

Parallels between Nestor and Patroclus are deliberately constructed throughout their encounter in *Iliad* 11, and in the wider context of their encounter, which culminates in *Iliad* 16. The episode that sets the stage for their encounter begins on the battlefield when Nestor is called on to rescue the hero Makhaon, struck in the shoulder by Paris's arrow, on his chariot. This is one of two episodes in the *Iliad* in which "horseman Nestor" takes part in the action as a still active "horseman," driving his chariot from the battlefield back to the ships. Achilles sends Patroclus to find out who the wounded hero on Nestor's chariot is, and the stage is set for the encounter between Nestor and

Patroclus to ensue. Nestor in this prelude to his meeting with Patroclus is not only a "horseman" but also a "savior, healer." He treats Makhaon in his tent with an all but magical elixir, such that when Patroclus arrives, doctor and patient are already enjoying a pleasant conversation together.

Despite the separation in time and place we are here in the domain of the "miracle-working doctors" of the Vedic pantheon. Makhaon and his brother Podaleirios, who is also with the Greek army at Troy, are themselves twins, and they are also both doctors, Podaleirios (as the Epic Cycle attests) a specialist in mental diseases, and Makhaon a surgeon who treats wounded bodies. Nestor has here rescued a "mortal" twin cast straight from the Indo-European mold. Even his name Makhaon, "fighter," bears this out. Nestor as the "savior" and "healer" of Makhaon (they form a Dioscuric pair for the limited time of this episode) sets the pattern for Patroclus, who immediately after his encounter with Nestor becomes the "savior" and "healer" of a second victim of Paris's arrows, the hero Eurypylos. Incited by what Nestor has told him to do, Patroclus hastens to return to Achilles, but he stops out of pity to treat Eurypylos, who has dragged himself from the battlefield with a grave wound to his thigh. Like Nestor, Patroclus has the necessary medical knowledge, and in tending to Eurypylos he is kept immobilized for the time. Further losses to the Achaeans bring the battle closer to the ships as the narrative continues, and both Nestor and Patroclus must leave their patients to the care of others and return to the war. Again Nestor and Patroclus are presented in parallel, Nestor leaving Makhaon in *Iliad* 14 to join the retreating Achaean leaders in council, Patroclus leaving Eurypylos in *Iliad* 15 to persuade Achilles to send him into battle and save the Achaeans from disaster.

Patroclus and Achilles are not twins, however much their story is viewed through the prism of Nestor's twin myth. The category of "intelligence" illustrates the limits of the twin myth as a paradigm for this pair of Iliadic comrades. On the one hand, something like the distinction between the "intelligence" of the immortal twin and the "warlike" nature of the mortal twin of the Indo-European myth is found in Nestor's speech to Patroclus when he reminds Patroclus of the time before the war. Nestor and Odysseus went then together to Phthia to recruit Achilles and Patroclus for the war, and Nestor repeats what the father of each one said, Peleus telling Achilles always to excel in war, Menoitios telling Patroclus, as the older of the two, to advise Achilles for the good. However, the essential difference here is not "intelligence," but age. Patroclus's medical skill likewise seems to line up with the immortal twin in contrast to the mortal twin of the Indo-European myth, but in fact it does not. As we learn in the episode with Eurypylos, it was Achilles who taught Patroclus his medical skill, and Achilles himself learned it from the centaur Chiron. Achilles's education at the feet of the wise centaur Chiron is testimony to Achilles's own intelligence. An even more important difference from the twin myth, as exemplified by Nestor and his brother Periclymenus, is that Achilles has not died when Patroclus takes his place, but only removed himself from action. The most important difference of all, however, is on Patroclus's side, for unlike Nestor, who survived the battle in which he took his brother's place, Patroclus does not survive the battle in which he takes Achilles's place. This difference gives to the carefully balanced parallels between Patroclus and Nestor in the *Iliad* an underlying sense of disequilibrium. It is not too much to say that Nestor, in giving Patroclus a paradigm to follow, is responsible for his death. Since everything of significance in the relationship between Nestor and Patroclus is implied rather than stated in the *Iliad* (I have yet to point out that Nestor tells how he first became a horseman as if the story pertained to Achilles rather than to Patroclus, its real object), Nestor does not bear responsibility for Patroclus's death on the surface of the poem. But at Patroclus's funeral games it is not an accident that the main contest is the chariot race and that Nestor is again on hand, in both the foreground and the background, throughout this race.[14] At the very end of the contest, when every contestant has received a prize, Achilles awards an unexpectedly vacant prize to Nestor, saying that it is a memorial of Patroclus, whom the old man will not see again. Nestor accepts the prize gladly and thanks Achilles warmly, saying that he is too old to compete as he once did at funeral games for a long-dead king near home. He says that on that distant day he won all the contests except one, the chariot race. (See Figure 11.3 for a later classical representation.) The "horseman Nestor" lost only the chariot race on that day—this should get our attention—and he lost it to the same twins whom he met on the battlefield—or rather did not meet on the battlefield—on a different day, when he became *hippota* Nestor for the first time. The reason for Nestor's loss in that chariot race is not stated, except that he was outnumbered by the twins, who each had a different function in the race: while one twin held the reins, the other twin used the whip. This is just enough to work out what Nestor's race must have been, and what its relevance to Patroclus and his fate is, but the story is a complex one, and is best left to one side.[15]

Figure 11.3 Chariot race. Attic black-figure hydria, *c.* 510 BCE. Attributed to the Priam Painter. New York, Metropolitan Museum of Art L.1999.10.12. Marie-Lan Nguyen (2011), CC BY 2.5, https://commons.wikimedia.org/w/index.php?curid=13879854.

The main point is already clear: Nestor's loss came about because he had lost his brother, a warrior and a horseman, and had not yet learned to take his place; he was therefore outmatched as one against two in the race. Patroclus's death came about because he too, at Nestor's instigation, became separated from his warrior companion, but in Patroclus's case, unlike Nestor's, there was to be no day of redemption.

Notes

1 I developed this argument in a study called *Hippota Nestor*, Hellenic Studies 37 (Washington, DC: Center for Hellenic Studies, Trustees of Harvard University; Cambridge, MA: Distributed by Harvard University Press, 2009). http://nrs.harvard .edu/urn-3:hul.ebook:CHS_Frame.Hippota_Nestor.2009.
2 In the companion chapter to this one, Gregory Nagy investigates the nature of this relationship in its own right. The Anatolian borrowing that lies behind Greek *therapōn*, "attendant," belongs to the second millennium BC. The Indo-European twin myth can be thought of as belonging, at latest, to the second half of the third millennium BC.
3 Nestor's myth is the chief object of *Hippota Nestor*, Parts 1 and 2 (Chapters 1–7).
4 Nestor's story in *Iliad* 11 is discussed in *Hippota Nestor*, Chapters 1 and 4.
5 The Vedic twins are discussed in *Hippota Nestor*, Chapter 3; for the Indo-European twin myth the basic comparison is between the Vedic twins and the Greek Dioscuri, but there is also important Baltic evidence, discussed with the Vedic and Greek evidence in Chapter 3.
6 This is the basic thesis of *Hippota Nestor*; cf. n. 3 above.
7 See *Hippota Nestor*, Chapters 1 and 7.
8 She is discussed in *Hippota Nestor*, Chapter 3.
9 Heracles's brother is not named in the passage, but his brother's father is: Amphitryon is father of the mortal Iphicles, whereas Zeus is the father of the immortal Heracles.
10 The difference between the Ionian and Athenian versions of the catalog of heroines in *Odyssey* 11 is crucial for an understanding of the history of the Homeric text from the eighth to the sixth centuries BCE, and is argued in detail in *Hippota Nestor*, Chapter 7.
11 The derivation and semantics of the name *Nestōr* are considered fully in *Hippota Nestor*, Chapter 2. The name, which lost all significance in the post-Homeric period, is deeply meaningful in Homer (see *Hippota Nestor*, Chapter 6). It is Homeric formulaic diction, properly understood, that clinches the force of the verbal root in Nestor's name, a point not sufficiently appreciated by those unversed in historical linguistic methods.
12 Discussed in *Hippota Nestor*, Chapter 6.
13 See note 12.
14 The chariot race in the funeral games for Patroclus in *Iliad* 23 is discussed in detail in *Hippota Nestor*, Chapter 6.
15 See n. 14; Nestor's long-ago loss to the twins must have involved a crash at the turn.

Bibliography

Frame, Douglas. *Hippota Nestor*. Hellenic Studies 37. Washington, DC: Center for Hellenic Studies, Trustees of Harvard University; Cambridge, MA: Distributed by

Harvard University Press, 2009. http://nrs.harvard.edu/urn-3:hul.ebook:CHS_Frame .Hippota_Nestor.2009.

Nagy, Gregory. "Achilles and Patroklos as Models for the Twinning of Identity." In *Gemini and the Sacred: Twins and Twinship in Religion and Mythology*, edited by Kimberley C. Patton, 269–88. London: Bloomsbury Academic, 2022.

12

Ss. Cosmas and Damian

Synergistic Brother Healers

♊

James C. Skedros

Introduction

A holy pair of brother healers from Late Antiquity, Ss. (Saints) Cosmas and Damian, figures prominently in the collage of saints that decorates the Eastern Christian tradition. Remembered as medical practitioners who refused to accept payment for their treatment of the afflicted, their posthumous veneration was centered at their shrine located just outside the walls of Constantinople, the capital of the Byzantine Empire. By the sixth century CE, this monastic complex had become a major pilgrimage center where crowds flocked to benefit from their healing powers. In the East, other shrines and churches were dedicated to the saints both prior to and following the sixth century, but their shrine at Constantinople continued to receive pilgrims up to the fall of Constantinople [modern Istanbul] to the Ottoman Turks in the mid-fifteenth century.

Iconographic images of Cosmas and Damian are also attested in both the East and the West by this time, including their famous basilica built in 527 CE in the Roman Forum.[1] The work of this brotherly pair inspired the creation of a separate category of saints in the Eastern Orthodox Church known as "unmercenaries"—in Greek, *anargyroi* literally meaning "the silverless ones"—holy physicians who treated their patients without pay. That such selflessness is reduplicated, and thereby amplified, in their symbolic twinship, is no accident, as will be discussed. Ss. Cosmas and Damian continue to be venerated to this day throughout the Orthodox world, and at many shrines still sought out for miraculous healing. (See Pl. 11 and Figure 12.1; note the complementary colors of the saints' robes and cloaks, reiterating familiar twinship themes of complicated symmetry, identity, and differentiation.) As Adam McGee discusses earlier, they also continue to have a sanctified and powerful presence as healing twins through the historical assimilation of Catholic saints with West African *orisha*s in Afro-Caribbean traditions (Cuban Santería and Haitian Vodou) and the Afro-Brazilian religion of Candomblé.[2]

The cult of the duo flourished during the Late Antique and medieval periods in both the eastern and western halves of the Mediterranean. The paucity of reliable evidence regarding the identity of the saints has led to a diversity of opinions about their origins.[3] Their popularity during the medieval period was most likely the catalyst for their reduplication into two additional pairs of medical saints in the Eastern Christian tradition, also brothers, also bearing the same names.[4] All three pairs were medical practitioners who treated not only suffering human beings but also ailing animals. Furthermore, all three sets of brothers were noted for their refusal to accept payment for their services. Each pair hailed from a different region: one from Asia Minor, one from Rome; and a third one from Arabia.[5] All three pairs are said to have lived prior to the peace of the Church inaugurated by the emperor Constantine: the brothers from

Figure 12.1 Ss. (Saints) Cosmas and Damian, painted icon on wood, Greek, seventeenth century. By permission of Fine Art Icons.

Asia Minor dying peacefully at some unspecified time and buried in Pherema; the brothers from Rome having been martyred by beheading at the order of the Emperor Carinus (283–285 CE); and the brothers from Arabia martyred in Cilicia during the great persecution of the early fourth century. The double multiplication of the already "twinned" brother physicians suggests that Cosmas and Damian came to be a kind of ideal type, perhaps the most significant pair of heavenly intercessors within the Orthodox Christian tradition.[6]

In this chapter I will focus on the pair from Asia Minor, the only ones not remembered as martyrs, yet by far the most popular among the Byzantine faithful. In particular, I will examine the ways in which the duality of the brothers Cosmas and Damian powerfully affected the religious and clinical dimensions, and perhaps also the human experience of their cult. Focusing on the textual evidence for the healing cult of this duo in the Greek East at their major shrine in Constantinople, I will seek to evaluate the influence and importance of their identity as a saintly pair, and in a certain sense, as interchangeable and mutually affective twins. I will also interrogate the religious value of their dual nature to their shared hagiography, particularly with respect to their divine healing powers.

The Kosmidion

By the fifth century CE, the cult of Ss. Cosmas and Damian was firmly established in both Western and Eastern Christendom. In Rome, Bishop Felix IV (526–530) reconstructed the temple of Romulus located next to the Forum into a church in their honor. A magnificent apse mosaic dating from the conversion of the temple into a church depicts the Apostles Peter and Paul offering the two brothers to Christ.[7] In Constantinople, during the late fifth century (*c.* 480 CE), a church dedicated to them was built outside the city walls, probably by Paulina, the mother of the general Leontius. By the beginning of the sixth century, the church had a monastic community attached to it.[8] Known in the Byzantine sources as the Kosmidion, this extramural ecclesial complex became the focal point of the veneration of Ss. Cosmas and Damian in the imperial capital, and a place of cultural and political importance, lending its name to that surrounding sector of the polis, and to the site of a famous battle during the Ottoman Interregnum, interestingly between two brothers.[9] A major cult and pilgrimage center, the Kosmidion functioned much like other healing shrines in antiquity. At the entrance of the church was a large atrium with covered porticos. It was in the porticos that the faithful sought refuge from and assistance for their ailments. The emperor Justinian I visited this church and was healed from sickness.[10] The seventh ecumenical council, held in Nicaea in 787 CE, mentions in its official *acta* the existence of an icon of the virgin flanked by Cosmas and Damian that was located on the wall of one of the porticoes attached to the outside of the church of the Kosmidion.[11] The eleventh-century Byzantine emperor Michael IV Paphlagon provided several significant improvements to the church complex, including bathhouses, gardens, fountains, and additional mosaic decorations.[12] The saints were venerated outside Rome and Constantinople as well. Churches and pilgrimage sites dedicated to the brother-physicians are known to have existed in Asia Minor, Mesopotamia, Syria, Egypt, southern Italy, and Spain.[13]

In addition to the artistic and archaeological records, the single most significant source for our knowledge of the Byzantine-era cult of Ss. Cosmas and Damian is a collection of miracle stories associated with their shrine at Constantinople. The majority of these miracles date from an anonymous sixth-century collection, although a handful of them were penned *c.* 1300 CE by Maximos the Deacon.[14] The miracles recount healings or hierophantic appearances of the two brother saints at the Kosmidion. Aside from a handful of other minor texts (sermons, *synaxaria* notices, etc.), the miracles constitute the main literary evidence of the cult of the twin saints in the Byzantine period. This collection has an extensive manuscript tradition, attesting to the popularity of the saints in the medieval period.[15] The forty-eight stories, all composed in Greek, are organized into six collections or series. The first five series, which include Miracles 1–38, describe miraculous healings performed by Cosmas and Damian at their sanctuary, refurbished by the emperor Justinian in the sixth century. The testimonies span the 100-year period from approximately 527 to 626 CE; the church was pillaged in that year during the Avar siege of Constantinople, and subsequently burned in 629.[16] It was restored in the eighth century. The sixth collection, produced by Maximos the Deacon, of whom nothing is known, was written at the beginning of the fourteenth century.[17] Although the *miracula* imply a lacuna in the cult of Ss. Cosmas and Damian from the seventh through twelfth centuries, other evidence suggests that the Kosmidion functioned more or less continuously as a shrine sought out by the desperately ill and suffering from the fifth century to the fall of Constantinople in 1453.[18]

The Saints

The physician-brothers Cosmas and Damian shared several of the traits characteristic of many of the saints who made up the kaleidoscope of hagiographic figures in Late Antiquity and the medieval world, such as intercessors for those in need, protectors, and heavenly communicants. However, as mentioned, they offered a few unique traits. First and foremost was their medical knowledge and skill. In the miracle stories, the brothers administer *pharmaka* (reflected in the medical chests they each hold in their traditional icon) and perform actual surgeries. In their *vita* not only are they called "doctors," but they are said to have been taught the art of medicine by the Holy Spirit.[19] The Byzantines venerated them as brothers who learned the medical arts in order to fulfill the evangelical command to heal "every disease and every infirmity."[20] Their healing abilities extended beyond the human realm, as they are consistently identified as healers of both human beings and animals. Related to their prowess is their aforementioned zeal to offer their medical services for free. This characteristic, too, has its biblical justification. In several places in the various hagiographic texts the command given by Jesus to his disciples, "Heal the sick, raise the dead, cleanse lepers, cast out demons. You received without pay; [therefore] give without pay," is often repeated in their hagiographies.[21] The last part of the Lord's command, which could also be translated, "freely you received, so freely shall you give," become a sort of textual marker, identifying the two saints in their ancient healing accounts. Cosmas and Damian belong thereby to a wider Byzantine category of *anargyroi*, all of whom are healing saints.[22]

A second characteristic of this pair, which is by contrast virtually unique to them, is their chronic personification as twins.[23] Although the tradition does not specifically name as "twins" the brothers Cosmas and Damian from Asia Minor, they who so magnetically drew the attention of the Byzantines, this latent idea remains deeply formative in their hagiography. One particular miracle story from the Kosmidion seems directly to invoke twinship, at least by extension from pre-Christian prototypes. An unnamed pagan who visits the shrine of Ss. Cosmas and Damian in Constantinople in search of a cure for an unspecified ailment is miraculously healed. Significantly, we read that local pagans identified the Christian healing pair with the ancient Greek gods Castor and Pollux (Poludeukes), the two Dioskoroi or twin sons of Leda (Castor the mortal son of Tyndareus, and Poludeukes the divine son of Zeus in the form of a swan). Like their Vedic counterparts the Ashwins, the Dioskoroi were most often associated with horses and interceded at moments of personal or collective crisis.[24] One of the pagans becomes sick; his friends, thinking that they are taking him to a shrine dedicated to Castor and Pollux, mistakenly bring him to the church of Ss. Cosmas and Damian. Once laid in the shrine, the ill pagan sees the saints ministering to the sick and cries out to the brothers for healing. After Cosmas and Damian upbraid the man for thinking that they are to be identified with the ancient pagan pair, the man is healed and then receives Christian baptism.[25]

Among the several compelling elements within this story, of particular significance is the evidence for the continuation of pagan beliefs in sixth-century Constantinople and the clear identification by some inquirers of Cosmas and Damian with Castor and Pollux. Certainly, one of the main purposes of the story is to refute any association of the Christian brothers with the popular pagan twins, even though they may share some common characteristics. The miracle story offers the reader (or listener) little explanation regarding what these pagans—referred to simply as "Hellenes" ("Ελληνες)—understood about the cult of Castor and Pollux.[26] However, the anonymous author of the miracle notes that the friends of the sick man brought him to the shrine of Ss. Cosmas and Damian because "they had in view the names Castor and Pollux taken from accounts of them found in those empty and harmful mythical readings."[27] Though Cosmos and Damian are not specifically identified as twins in this or in any of the other miracle stories, the association of the pair with the twin sons of Zeus suggests that the twinning of the Christian brothers was never far from the surface of their identity, and perhaps of their numinous powers.

The cult of Sts. Cosmas and Damian was, above all, a healing cult. Though not having exclusive ownership of the healing market among saints in the Byzantine Church, Cosmas and Damian certainly occupied a major place in the sector of miraculous healings within Byzantine society. As medical doctors who performed their services without remuneration, their earthly careers anticipated and legitimized their heavenly roles as healers and intercessors. Healing came to their human devotees in many forms, but most commonly through dream incubation or a waking, physical appearance of the saints to those seeking aid. As miracle-working saints operating (in both senses) within a medieval society with rudimentary medical knowledge and skills, a society where precious money and resources were often squandered on ineffective medical treatments,[28] the saints, not surprisingly, were known by two primary epithets: *thaumatourgoi* ("miracle workers") and, as already mentioned, *anargyroi* ("unmercenary [silverless] ones"). How the dual identity of these brothers and companions influenced their role as *thaumatourgoi* working side by side, offering their services for free, remains now to be considered.

The Saintly Pair at Work in Their Clinic

Procopius, the sixth-century historian of the reign of Justinian, tells us that the emperor, out of gratitude to the saints for being healed at their shrine, remodeled the earlier Kosmidion which, he writes, was "unsightly . . . and not worthy to be dedicated to such powerful saints." Justinian beautified and enlarged the church and, as Procopius notes, "when anyone finds themselves assailed by illnesses which are beyond the control of physicians, in despair of human assistance they take refuge in the one hope left to them."[29] From the description of the shrine found in the miracle stories, we can piece together a fairly accurate depiction of the healing sanctuary after it had been altered by Justinian.[30] I have mentioned the large course of porticoes, under which the infirm were laid.[31] Those unable to walk were brought to the shrine on litters and were placed in the porticoes. Beds were also available at the shrine for those who needed them. There was an area within the portico nearest to the entrance to the church where curtains could be drawn to create an isolated area for private incubation. As was true in ancient Greek Asklepieia, there seems to have been no organized manner in which the infirm were arranged—women next to men, rich next to the poor. Those who could would walk to the church to offer prayers daily; others would spend the night sleeping in the church, the atrium, or the adjoining hostel. Beyond the porticoes, several other buildings are attested. Procopius refers to a hostel or hospice (ξενών) along with an infirmary and an operating room where one could find pallets and a pharmacy containing several remedies. It was here where on occasion the saints would perform surgery and then transport their patients back to the porticoes of the atrium for postoperative recovery.

That there exists a collection of miracles of Ss. Cosmas and Damian associated with their shrine at Constantinople is not unique within the Byzantine religious tradition. Miracle collections of other saints circulated throughout the Byzantine period, a good number of them surviving. What is notable about the collection associated with Cosmas and Damian is that *every* miracle reported is a healing miracle; the main purpose of the miracles, therefore, seems to have been the legitimation and thus the popularization of the saintly brothers as highly effective healers. Those who seek aid at the shrine are said in this collection to come from various religious and cultural backgrounds: clerics associated with the Great Church of Hagia Sophia, a Jew, an Arian heretic, pagans, a promiscuous woman, a horseracing fan, and important Byzantine bureaucrats. In this regard, it is most curious that, unlike most of the pre-Christian *iamata* testifying to

miraculous healings by Asklepios at his great sanctuary at Epidauros—some of which
are preserved—or Amphiaraios at Oropos, the majority of the miracle stories from
the Kosmidion do not give the *personal* names of those who were healed, nor their
specific homelands. More often than not, the stories tell of the healing of a certain
man (τις ἀνήρ) or a certain woman (τις γυνή), omitting any geographical information
about their origins. The apparent pattern of deliberate rhetorical choice for pilgrim
anonymity and generic healings, in contrast to many of the Epidaurean and other
Asklepieian votive texts which give the name of the grateful patient and her homeland,
suggests that the *Miracles* were intended to sidestep or even quietly suppress local or
ethnic affinities, thus imbuing themselves with a more universal appeal in order to
enhance the prestige of the shrine.

Another curious aspect of the cult of Ss. Cosmas and Damian is the relative
lack of importance given to the relics of the saints. This, in part, can be explained
by the fact that relics of the saints were known to have existed elsewhere, that is,
in the city of Cyrrhus, which was located some 21 kilometers northeast of Aleppo
in Syria. Theodoret, bishop of Cyrrhus from 423 to 457, speaks of a basilica of the
two saints in his episcopal city.[32] Indeed, only one of the forty-eight miracle stories
references the saints' relics: an ill man incubates next to a casket containing the holy
relics of the saints.[33] The text's simultaneous lack of interest in the relics and the
singular attestation to their existence suggest a minimal role for them in the cult.[34] It is
significant, however, that the existence or non-existence of relics plays no role in the
actual healing of the saints. This allows for the saintly pair to remain active in their
healing through appearances and actual surgeries and not be hindered by the location
of or encumbered by the physicality of their own bodily remains.

In the Byzantine iconographic tradition Ss. Cosmas and Damian, to my knowledge,
are never depicted separately. The same holds true for the textual witness to their cult
where the saints work in tandem in their roles as heavenly intercessors and powerful
healers. In the overwhelming majority of miracles, it is the two brothers together who
bring about the healing. A Jewish woman with cancer is healed through "the prayer"
of the saints, that is, one prayer that is offered by both saints together (2.33–34). It
is "the goodwill" (2.40–42) of the saints that heals her body, and not surprisingly
in the framework of conversion that was the goal of Christian healing sanctuaries,
her soul as well, since the work of the saints led her to baptism.[35] An unnamed man
has an abscess in his midsection and after several unsuccessful attempts by doctors
to remove it the man visits the shrine of the saints, who successfully excise it. This
miracle story ends with an exhortation noting that those who are in need are visited
by the watchful hand of the saints (5.29). It should be noted that "hand" (χείρ) in the
singular, signifying the combined, unified work of the saints. Elsewhere the *power*
of the saints is described in the singular—*dynamis* (δύναμις) in 11.93 and *energia*
(ἐνεργία) in 11.98—even though their *activities*, expressed in verbs, are presented in
the plural. In other words, they speak, heal, appear, and so on in the third-person plural,
while the nouns used to express their activity are predominately singular. The authors
of the miracle stories depict the saints as a unit or as a pair and understand their actions
as a unified, collective activity. Cosmas and Damian speak collectively ("The saints
answered him . . ." [Miracle 9.37]). In only one miracle do the saints speak individually

and that because they are speaking to each other (30.38–39), interestingly, to debate the appropriate course of treatment in a difficult case. In many of the miracles, the saints address the supplicant, but it is always as a pair. The saints conduct their healing ministry jointly, working so closely as a team that their individual identities become superfluous.

Two of the forty-eight miracle stories, however, tell of healings performed by only one of the saints. Yet, even in these two examples, the saint who executes the healing is not named. Rather, he is referred to as simply "one of the saints," as if the two brothers are interchangeable. One story concerns a paralyzed priest from the Church of the Holy Wisdom (Hagia Sophia) in Constantinople. "One of the saints" assists the priest in bathing in the baths in the city of Constantinople, resulting in a cure. It is curious that throughout this miracle, even though clearly only one of the saints is present, even whispering in the paralyzed priest's ear in order to inform him that he will be cured, his identity is not given. This serves to reinforce the shared identity of the two saints.[36]

The tag-team, dynamic nature of the therapy provided by Ss. Cosmas and Damian is vividly shown in a miracle story about an unnamed man who suffers from a fistula at his hip joint (Miracle 30). The account tells the hearer that the man has spent fifteen years in extreme pain, undergoing several surgeries and other remedies all to no avail. The encouragement of his friends and a nocturnal visit in a dream by Cosmas and Damian at his home leads the man to the saints' healing sanctuary. Once there, he is taken by the saints to the operating room located in the hostel where visitors to the shrine lodged. Seeing yet another operating room, the man tries to convince the saints not to operate. St. Damian agrees, and tries to prevent St. Cosmas from making an incision. Cosmas argues back to Damian, who then relents, allowing the surgery to proceed. After the operation, the man instructs the saints to put a honey-soaked cloth on the incision to aid its healing, claiming that this is the practice he has learned from having undergone so many operations.[37] The saints indignantly respond, "You will teach us how to practice medicine?" and then go on to bandage the wound without honey. A few days later, the saints appear to the man, who is now recovering in the atrium of the shrine, and anoint the wound with the healing salve associated with their cult, the *kērotē* (κηρωτή), apparently a poultice of beeswax or honeycomb (κηρός), which was available to visitors to the shrine.[38] The fistula and the wound from the surgery are healed, and the man offers praises and thanksgiving to the Lord and to his saintly healers Cosmas and Damian.

Conclusion

Evidence abounds from the Late Antique and Byzantine periods of the healing activities of the powerful Cosmas and Damian, largely anchored at their shrines, yet radiating throughout Eastern Christendom. The miracle stories bolstered the renown of the pair—amplified because of their dual nature—and illumined the reputation of the Kosmidion as a place of healing. Such accounts also safely confined the miraculous abilities of the saints within the Christian tradition, suppressing earlier Greco-Roman traditions, equally localized to particular places, of the physician-gods and celestial twin demigods they replaced.

Curiously, the miracle stories tell us very little about the relationship between the two brother saints. The miracles are content to present the saints in unison: they speak with one voice, as identical twins sometimes do, participate together in healings, and appear simultaneously to suffering pilgrims. Further, the stories reveal little regarding the dress, the facial features, or the personality of the saints. In iconography, they are depicted wearing tunics, each holding a small medicine chest, which is often shown open, holding phials and surgical instruments. At most, Cosmas and Damian are medical wonder-workers who appear to the many pilgrims at their shrine, usually at night, and frequently in dreams or visions, just as their pagan predecessors did. They can sometimes also appear in disguise, but these appearances reveal little more than that the saints are capable of costume changes.

Who, then, were Ss. Cosmas and Damian? For the Byzantines, and especially those living in or oriented toward the imperial capital, Constantinople, they were a pair of brotherly saints who met one of the fundamental needs of any human society, from the individual to the family to the polis—the need for physical healing. Trained as physicians, their earthly medical careers were infused by their Christian faith, and made transcendent. They are said to have refused pay for their medical services. In death, released from their earthly bodies, the twinned saints animated one of the most significant and active healing shrines in Late Antique and medieval Byzantium. Though not considered to be identical twins by the Byzantines as they were in the West, the two brothers functioned as such—as a pair of healing saints united in purpose and cult. The importance of their duality is reflected in the multiplication of the pair: as we have seen, the Byzantine ecclesiastical calendar commemorated three pairs of brothers of the same names, though the most important pair, the one celebrated by the faithful in Constantinople, was the pair remembered each year on first day of November. The exact location of their great church outside the city walls of Constantinople, carrying on the extramural tradition of Asklepieia, also usually built outside the harried, quotidian life of the polis, continues to elude us. We can be certain, however, that it was an important center for healing, combining ancient shared Mediterranean practices of prayer, incubation, the medical arts, and the dedication of sacred space found in other healing cults. Unlike its counterparts among the other Christian healing centers of the medieval period, the Kosmidion offered not one but two physician saints, a pair of pious Christian brothers, joined for life in their shared medical vocation, yet also able after their earthly deaths to ply their heavenly, healing arts for the benefit of living, suffering bodies: their powers doubled on behalf of all those who sought their aid in the hope of God's mercy.

Notes

1   The Basilica of Santi Cosma e Damiano incorporated two earlier imperial buildings,
    an early-fourth-century CE temple thought to have been dedicated to the deified
    Valerius Romulus, son of Maxentius, and what might have been a library.

2 Adam Michael McGee, "Marasa Elou: Twins and Uncanny Children in Haitian Vodou," in *Gemini and the Sacred: Twins and Twinship in Religion and Mythology*, ed. Kimberley C. Patton (London: Bloomsbury Academic, 2022), 136.

3 See Alexander Kazhdan and Nancy Patterson Ševčenko, "Kosmas and Damianos," in *The Oxford Dictionary of Byzantium*, II, ed. Alexander Kazhdan (Oxford: Oxford University Press, 1991), 1151. The classic study of these saints in the Byzantine Church is that of Ludwig Deubner, *Kosmas und Damian: Text und Einleitung* (Berlin: B. G. Teubner, Leipzig, 1907). The numbering of miracles used in this chapter are those of the Deubner edition. For a French translation see André Jean Festugière, trans. and ed., *Sainte Thècle, saints Côme et Damien, saints Cyr et Jean (extraits), saint Georges* (Paris: A. et J. Picard, 1971), 97–213. For more recent studies, see Cyril Mango, "On the Cult of Saints Kosmas and Damian at Constantinople," in *Θυμίαμα Στη Μνήμν Της Λασκαρίνας Μπούρα* (Athens: Benaki Museum, 1994), 189–92; Nuray Özaslan, "From the Shrine of Cosmidion to the Shrine of Eyûp Ensari," *Greek, Roman and Byzantine Studies* 40 (1999): 379–400; Alice-Mary Talbot, "Metaphrasis in the Early Palaiologan Period: The *Miracula* of Kosmas and Damian by Maximos the Deacon," in Eleōnora Kountoura-Galake, ed., *The Heroes of the Orthodox Church: The New Saints, 8th–16th c.* (Athens: National Hellenic Research Foundation, 2004), 227–37.

4 Although given the tendency in the traditional Christian Church, especially in the East, for the devout to adopt the reputational and wonder-working mantle of previous holy figures, it is not impossible that two later pairs of brother physicians did exist after the original Sts. Cosmas and Damian.

5 The *Synaxarion of Constantinople*, a liturgical calendar of fixed feasts and produced *c.* 1000 CE, gives the liturgical commemoration of the three pairs of saints at Constantinople: the brothers from Arabia on October 17, the Asia Minor pair on November 1, and the Roman brothers on July 1. *Synaxarium ecclesiae Constantinopolitanae. Propylaeum ad AASS Novembris*, ed. Hippolyte Delehaye (Brussels: Apud Socios Bollandianos, 1902).

6 The origin of, and relationship among, the three pairs of saints remain unclear. In the early twentieth century, it was argued that Ss. Cosmas and Damian were unhistorical figures who were purposely created by the Christian Church to replace the role of the Dioscuri; see J. R. Harris, *The Cult of Heavenly Twins* (Cambridge: Cambridge University Press, 1906), 96–100. Ernst Lucius, in his *Die Anfänge des Heiligenkultes in der christlichen Kirche* (Tübigen: J.C.B. Mohr [P. Siebeck], 1904), 259–61, argued, rather, that Cosmas and Damian replaced the role of Asklepios. For the Byzantine Church, the Asia Minor pair of saints was the most popular, and Deubner (*Kosmas und Damian*, 82) dates their *vita* to the fourth century CE, although a sixth-century date is more likely; see Mango, "On the Cult of Saints Kosmas and Damian at Constantinople," 190.

7 The mosaic depicts Cosmas and Damian holding crowns of martyrdom accompanied by the martyr Theodore. In the Byzantine tradition, this set of brothers were commemorated on July 1 in the liturgical calendar. For an image and discussion of this apse see Herbert L. Kesler, "Bright Gardens of Paradise," in *Picturing the Bible: The Earliest Christian Art*, ed. Jeffrey Spier (New Haven, CT: Yale Univerisity Press, 2007), 136–8; see also detailed pictures at http://www.sacred-destinations.com/italy/rome-santi-cosma-e-damiano-photos. redirects to comprehensive overview of other websites depicting mosaics. In the Roman Catholic Missal, Sts. Cosmas and Damian are commemorated on September 27.

8   Andreas Külzer, (Vienna: Österreichische Akademie der Wissenschaften, 2008), 471–2.
9   The Battle of Kosmidion, *Eyüp Muharebesi*, fought between Musa and Süleyman Çelebi in 1410. Five other churches or monasteries dedicated to Ss. Cosmas and Damian at Constantinople can be identified in the historical sources. See Raymond Janin, *La géographie ecclésiastique de l'Empire byzantin. Première partie, Le siège de Constantinople et le patriarcat œcuménique*, Tome III, Les églises et les monastères, 2nd ed. (Paris, 1969), 284–9.
10 Procopius, *On Buildings* I.iii.5–8, trans. Henry Bronson Dewing. Procopius vol. VII. Loeb Classical Library 343 (Cambridge: Harvard University Press, 1940).
11 Giovanni Domenico Mansi, *Sacrorum conciliorum nova et amplissima collectio*, vol. 13 (Paris: H. Welter, 1901–27), 64–5, 68. The council relates in detail three miracle stories associated with Ss. Cosmas and Damian, published by Deubner in *Kosmas und Damian* as Miracles 13, 15, and 30.
12 Deubner, *Kosmas und Damian*, 30–1, citing Michael Psellos, *Chronographia*, 4.31, in *Bibliotheca graeca medii aevi*, ed. Konstantinos N. Sathas, vol. 4 (Paris: 1874).
13 Deubner, *Kosmas und Damian*, 81.
14 Talbot ("Metaphrasis in the Early Palaiologan Period," 229) gives the date of composition of the miracles by Maximos as "sometime after 1305/6."
15 The details of the manuscript tradition were worked out admirably by Deubner (*Kosmas und Damian*, 3–37) in his critical edition of the miracle stories. More recently, Alice-Mary Talbot has argued that miracle 39, which Deubner attributed to Maximos, is a reworking of an original sixth-century miracle ("Metaphrasis in the Early Palaiologan Period," 250, n.17).
16 Procopius, *Buildings*, I.vi. For the dating of the first four collections see Festugière, *Sainte Thècle, saints Côme et Damien*, 87–9 and 165, n.1, and Mango, "On the Cult of Saints Kosmas and Damian at Constantinople," 189–92.
17 Deubner (*Kosmas und Damian*, 97–208) has edited the six collections accordingly: series I (Miracles 1–10); series II (11–20); series III (21–6); series IV (27–32); series V (33–8); and series VI (39–47); miracle 48.
18 Talbot, "Metaphrasis in the Early Palaiologan Period," 228–9. The *Synaxarion of Constantinople* and Theophanes, *Chronicle*, AM 6064, make reference to the veneration of Ss. Cosmas and Damian on November 1 at a church "*en tois Dareiou*," a district of Constantinople.
19 "ἐδιδάχθησαν δὲ ὑπὸ τοῦ ἁγίου πνεύματος τὴν ἰατρικὴν ἐπιστήμην," *Life of Ss. Cosmas and Damian*, 1.9. The healing pair is also referred to as "doctors" in the phrase οἱ τῶν ἰατρῶν παῖδες ("the servants of the doctors"; Miracle 34.14). Deubner edited the *vita* of the Asia Minor pair (87–96), and the martyrdom accounts of the Roman (208–17) and Arabian pairs (218–25). In the martyrdom accounts of the Arabian and Roman pairs also called Cosmas and Damian, they are referred to as medical doctors as well. The supernatural origin of the ability to heal is an ancient and recurrent theme in many traditions (compare, for example, the powers, especially herbal healing, of the Greek physician-god Asklepios, imparted to him by his foster-father the centaur Chiron).
20 Cf. Matt. 4:23, 9:35, and esp. 10:1.
21 *Life of Ss. Cosmas and Damian*, 1.19; Matt. 10:8.
22 In addition to Cosmas and Damian, other saints known as *anargyroi* include Cyrus and John (commemorated together, although not as brothers), Sampson, and Panteleimon.

23 In the West, Gregory of Tours identifies Cosmas and Damian as "the two twins, [who] were skilled doctors," see Gregory of Tours, *Glory of the Martyrs*, 97, trans. with an introduction by Raymond van Dam (Liverpool: Liverpool University Press, 1988), 122. For a fuller discussion of the veneration of Ss. Cosmas and Damian in the Latin Church see Anneliese Wittmann, *Kosmas und Damian. Kultausbreitung und Volksdevotion* (Berlin: Erich Schmidt, 1967).

24 Most recently see Henry John Walker's *The Twin Horse Gods: The Dioskouroi in the Mythologies of Ancient Greece and Vedic India* (London, I.B. Tauris, 2015).

25 Miracle 9.14–22: "τόυτῳ πάντες οἱ φίλοι ὡς ἐκ μιᾶς συμφωνίας συνεβουεύσαν ἐν τῷ οἴκῳ τούτῳ τῶν ἁγίων Κοσμᾶ καὶ Δαμιανοῦ ἐλθεῖν, οὐ πρὸς αὐτοὺς τοὺς ἁγίους τοῦτον ἀποστείλαντες . . ., ἀλλὰ πρὸς τὴν προσηγορίαν ἀφορῶντες τῶν ἐν τοῖς ματαίοις καὶ ἐπιβλαβέσιν ἀναγνώσμασιν ἐμφερομένων μύθων Κάστορος καὶ Πολυδεύκος." "His friends together of one accord advised him [the ill man] to go to the house of the holy saints Cosmas and Damian, not sending him to the saints themselves . . . , they had in view the names Castor and Pollux taken from accounts of them found in those empty and harmful mythical readings."

26 The Miracle simply remarks of these anonymous pagans that "knowing the power and diversity of their (Ss. Cosmas's and Damian's) remedies and activities, and the variety of their miracles, . . . used to call these esteemed servants of Christ Cosmas and Damian, Kastor and Polydeukes, according to the defilement of their impious religion." Miracle 9.7–11.

27 Miracle 9.20–22.

28 See the admirable observations of John Duffy on the place of the medical profession in Byzantine miracle collections of the sixth and seventh centuries, "Byzantine Medicine in the Sixth and Seventh Centuries: Aspects of Teaching and Practice," *Dumbarton Oaks Papers* 18 (1984): 24.

29 Procopius, *Buildings*, I.vi (Loeb Classical Library, Procopius, vol. 7, 63). Parallels to the language used to describe Asklepios as the last refuge of the desperate in the classical and Hellenistic period are striking.

30 The following description is based, in part, on that found in Festugière, *Sainte Thècle, saints Côme et Damien*, 89–90.

31 Timothy Gregory, in his "The Survival of Paganism in Greece: A Critical Essay" (*American Journal of Philology* 107 (1986): 38–9), notes that this arrangement parallels the archaeological remains of the late-fifth-century church built on the site of the famous Asklepieion on the south slope of the acropolis in Athens.

32 On the church at Cyrrhus see Paul Peeters, *Le tréfonds oriental de l'hagiographie byzantine*, Subsidia hagiographica no. 26 (Brussels, 1950): 65–7. Miracle 12.11–12 specifically notes that the holy relics are kept at Cyrrhus.

33 Miracle 34.20 and 34.30.

34 According to accounts of Russian pilgrims to Constantinople during the second half of the fourteenth century, pilgrims venerated the gold-covered skulls of Ss. Cosmas and Damian kept at the Kosmidion; see George Majeska, *Russian Travelers to Constantinople in the Fourteenth and Fifteenth Centuries* (Washington, DC: Dumbarton Oaks Research Library and Collection, 1984), 331–3.

35 Although it would not be historically accurate to speak of religious "conversion" as a goal or even a byproduct of healing at an ancient Asklepieion, preceding the Christian healing shrines of Cosmas and Damian, Nock's 1933 work *Conversion* argued for a recognition of legitimate religious conversion outside of Christianity in the mystery cults and certain of the philosophical schools of the Hellenistic, Roman,

and Late Antique periods. The fervid and intensely personal devotion to Asklepios of the orator Aelius Aristides occasioned by the god's healing activity at his sanctuary, the second century CE Asklepieion at Pergamon, may be part of the wider continuum of personal conversion, that is, spiritual as well as physical transformation, that characterized Mediterranean religiosity in the centuries of early Christianity.

36 The notion of collectivity among the saints in Byzantium is not unique to the brother *anargyroi*. There are a series of collective saints (usually martyrs) within Byzantine hagiography; an examination of the lives of these "cohort" saints yields an awareness of the collective nature of the power and frequent autosacrificial martyrdom of the group.

37 Honey was a known bactericidal remedy for the dressing of wounds in the ancient world; see Robert Sallares, "Honey," in *The Oxford Classical Dictionary*, 5th ed., ed. (Sander Goldberg, December 2015), doi:10.1093/acrefore/9780199381135.013.3145.

38 Miracle 30.54ff. The *kerote* figures prominently in many of the miracles and seems to have been made available to the faithful on Saturday evenings. As is still the practice at Eastern Orthodox tomb-shrines of the saints, it was most likely a mixture of oils taken from oil-burning lamps at the shrine.

Bibliography

Delehaye, Hippolyte, ed. *Synaxarium ecclesiae Constantinopolitanae. Propylaeum ad AASS Novembris*. Brussels: Apud Socios Bollandianos, 1902.

Deubner, Ludwig. *Kosmas und Damian*. Text und Einleitung. Leipzig: B.G. Teubner, 1907.

Duffy, John. "Byzantine Medicine in the Sixth and Seventh Centuries: Aspects of Teaching and Practice." *Dumbarton Oaks Papers* 38 (1984): 21–7.

Festugière, André-Jean, trans. and ed. *Sainte Thècle, saints Côme et Damien, saints Cyr et Jean (extraits), saint Georges*. Paris: A. et J. Picard, 1971.

Gregory of Tours. *Glory of the Martyrs*. Translated by Raymond van Dam. Liverpool: Liverpool University Press, 1988.

Gregory, Timothy. "The Survival of Paganism in Greece: A Critical Essay." *American Journal of Philology* 107 (1986): 38–9.

Harris, James Rendel. *The Cult of Heavenly Twins*. Cambridge: Cambridge University Press, 1906.

Janin, Raymond. *La géographie ecclésiastique de l'Empire byzantin. Première partie, Le siège de Constantinople et le patriarcat œcuménique, Tome III, Les églises et les monastères*, 2nd ed. Paris: Institut français d'études byzantines, 1969.

Kazhdan, Alexander, and Nancy Patterson Ševčenko. "Kosmas and Damianos." In *The Oxford Dictionary of Byzantium, II*, edited by Alexander Kazhdan, 1151. Oxford: Oxford University Press, 1991.

Kesler, Herbert L. "Bright Gardens of Paradise." In *Picturing the Bible: The Earliest Christian Art*, edited by Jeffrey Spier, 136–8. New Haven, CT: Yale University Press, 2007.

Külzer, Andreas. *Tabula Imperii Byzantini: Band 12, Ostthrakien (Eurōpē)*. Vienna: Österreichische Akademie der Wissenschaften, 2008.

Lucius, Ernst. *Die Anfänge des Heiligenkultes in der christlichen Kirche*. Tübigen: J.C.B. Mohr (P. Siebeck), 1904.

Majeska, George. *Russian Travelers to Constantinople in the Fourteenth and Fifteenth Centuries*. Washington, DC: Dumbarton Oaks Studies 19. Cambridge, MA: Harvard University Press, 1984.

Mango, Cyril. "On the Cult of Saints Kosmas and Damian at Constantinople." In *Θυμίαμα Στη Μνήμν Της Λασκαρίνας Μπούρα*, 189–92. Athens: Benaki Museum, 1994.

Mansi, Giovan Domenico. *Sacrorum conciliorum nova et amplissima collectio*. Paris: H. Welter, 1901–27.

Özaslan, Nuray. "From the Shrine of Cosmidion to the Shrine of Eyûp Ensari." *Greek, Roman and Byzantine Studies* 40 (1999): 379–400.

Peeters, Paul. *Le tréfonds oriental de l'hagiographie byzantine, Subsidia Hagiographica no. 26*. Brussels: Société des Bollandistes, 1950.

Procopius. *On Buildings*. Translated by Henry Bronson Dewing. Procopius vol. VII, Loeb Classical Library 343. Cambridge, MA: Harvard University Press, 1940.

Sacred Destinations: Church of St. Cosmas and Damian. Rome, Italy. http://www.sacred -destinations.com/italy/rome-santi-cosma-e-damiano-photos.

Sallares, Robert. "Honey." In *Oxford Classical Dictionary*, 5th ed., edited by Sander Goldberg. Subfield: Greek Material Culture: Classical and Hellenistic, Science and Technology. doi:10.1093/acrefore/9780199381135.013.3145. December 2015.

Talbot, Alice-Mary. "Metaphrasis in the Early Palaiologan Period: The *Miracula* of Kosmas and Damian by Maximos the Deacon." In *The Heroes of the Orthodox Church: The New Saints, 8th–16th c.*, edited by Eleonora Kountoura-Galake, 227–37. Athens: National Hellenic Research Foundation, 2004.

Walker, Henry John. *The Twin Horse Gods: The Dioskouroi in the Mythologies of Ancient Greece and Vedic India*. London: I.B. Tauris, 2015.

Wittmann, Anneliese. *Kosmas und Damian. Kultausbreitung und Volksdevotion*. Berlin: Erich Schmidt, 1967.

Part Five

Divine Twinship in the Ancient Near East and Eastern Christianity

13

Primordial Twins in Ancient Iranian Myth

♊

Prods Oktor Skjærvø

The Zoroastrian belief system is perhaps best known for its "(radical) dualistic" solution to the Problem of Evil by positing two original "principles," one good and one evil.[1] In this contribution, we shall take a look at how these two principles, the "twin spirits," one good and one evil, are represented in the older and younger Avestan texts and in the later literature. I shall discuss their roles, from the oldest texts on, in the cosmogonic myth and the mythical-ritual (re)creation of the world and, especially, the relationship between the good spirit and the supreme god Ahura Mazdā. I shall then examine the effects of the merger of these two and the related "Zurvanite" myth, in which Ahura Mazdā himself and the Evil Spirit are the twins, sired in the womb of Zurwān, god of Time. Finally, I shall suggest that the oldest form of the cosmogonic myth is a complete birth myth, which may, in turn, explain the origin of the Zoroastrian dualistic myth.

The Texts

The Old Iranian texts that make up the *Avesta* are in two forms of an old Iranian language: Old Avestan and Young Avestan.[2] Both text corpora survive, like the *Vedas*, in "crystalized" form, that is, preserved in a form of the language spoken at a specific, but unknown, time in their history and no longer updated linguistically as the language evolved. Old Avestan may reflect the language spoken during the last centuries of the second millennium (like Rigvedic), while Young Avestan probably reflects the language spoken during the mid-first millennium. Orally transmitted for millennia, the Avestan texts may have been written down for the first time about 600 CE, but the oldest manuscripts date only to the thirteenth century CE.

The *Old Avesta* is part of the Young Avestan *Yasna* and is recited halfway through the (original) morning sacrifice, the *yasna*.[3] It includes the five *Gāθās*, "songs," said to have been recited for the first time in the other world by the divine Sraoša (*Yasna* 57.8) and in this world by Zarathustra (implied in 1.29.7 and *Yašt* 13.88). In this chapter, references to the *Gāθās* are in the form "1.31.7" = first *Gāθā*, *Yasna* 31, strophe 7. The

Old Avesta also contains a liturgical text, the *Yasna haptanghāiti*, recited during the animal sacrifice, between the first and second *Gāθā*.

The main Young Avestan texts quoted in this chapter are the *Yasna*; the *Yašt*s, hymns to individual deities; and the *Videvdad*, a text accompanying a lengthy purification ritual, with a mythological/etiological introduction and conclusion.[4]

The writings of the later, Sasanian, Zoroastrian tradition include a few third-century inscriptions and a large corpus of written texts from the ninth century onward based on oral traditions, the "Pahlavi books," written in Pahlavi, or Middle Persian, the immediate ancestor of modern Persian.[5] It should be noted that the lateness of these texts does not necessarily imply lateness of contents and ideas.

All translations are mine and based on the manuscripts and standard editions. Especially uncertain translations are marked with an asterisk.

Some Terminology

The earliest references to the myth of the primordial twin spirits (*maniiu*) are found in the *Gāθā*s, while more elaborate forms are found in the *Young Avesta* and the later Zoroastrian texts.

The translation of *maniiu* as "spirit" is traditional (in the west) and *ad sensum*. The term is linguistically related to *maniia-* "think" and must refer to some thought process or product (not "breathing, wind," as in English from Latin *spiritus*, Hebrew *rū*ᵃ*h*). In the context of the poet, it may also refer to the "in-spir-ation." Note also that the verb "think" (*maniia-*) can take a direct object to signify "produce by one's thought" (not "think *about*" as sometimes assumed).

The epithet of the Life-giving Spirit, *spənta*, implies endowed with "swelling" (cf. Old Indic *śvā-/śū-* "swell"), that is, producing fecundity and growth. This is also how the Pahlavi tradition understood it, rendering it as "producing increase" (*abzōnīg*). The rendering as "holy" (and "holy spirit") is quite misleading. From the same root is *saošiiant* "he who shall make swell," that is, the *ahu* (see below), a term denoting the successful sacrificer (the rendering as "savior" is misleading).[6]

The epithet of the Evil Spirit, *angra* (for *ahra* from **as-ra*) may be related to Old Indic *as-ita* "black," and its meaning may be similar, hence my rendering as "Dark Spirit." In Young Avestan, the original meaning of the epithet was probably no longer known, hence my generic "Evil Spirit." The Pahlavi tradition, however, understood *angra* as "smiter, destroyer." In Pahlavi, the term *angra maniiu* became Ahrimen (in which the original meaning was lost), interpreted as Gannāg Mēnōy, presumably the "Foul Spirit," from the verb *gand-* "smell foul" (the past participle of which, *gasta*, was used in Old Persian as a generic term for evil). The form *spen-āg* is probably a learned adaptation of Avestan *spənta* modeled after *gann-āg* "smell-ing."

In the post-Gathic literature, the Life-giving Spirit and the Evil Spirit are presented as adversaries and creators, but, already in the *Young Avesta*, the Life-giving Spirit tends to be identified with Ahura Mazdā and is less often mentioned. In the Pahlavi texts, the original good twin, Spenāg Mēnōy, plays a minor role,[7] and the two adversaries are Ohrmazd and Ahrimen.

In the *Gāθās*, the supreme deity is referred to by his two epithets, *ahura* and *mazdā*, "(ruling) lord" (Pahlavi *xwadāy*) and "all-knowing" (Pahlavi *wisp-āgāh*). In the *Young Avesta* the terms usually go together, and their original meaning may no longer have been understood. In the Achaemenid inscriptions, we have univerbated Ahuramazdā, which gave Pahlavi Ohrmazd, which by itself has no meaning, but his epithets are still "all-knowing" and "ruler."

Ahura Mazdā's six offspring are the "Life-giving Immortals" (*aməša spəṇta*),[8] which became Pahlavi *amšāspand* or *amahrspand* (seven including Ohrmazd himself), in which the original meaning was, of course, no longer recognized. In the *Young Avesta* they are Good Thought, Best Order, Well-deserved Command, Ārmaiti/ Humility (the Earth),[9] Wholeness, and Not-dyingness (not dying before one's time, rather than Immortality). They were sired by Ahura Mazdā, presumably during his primeval sacrifice.[10] Ahura Mazdā and Ārmaiti, his daughter and spouse, probably also represent the ancient couple Heaven and Earth.[11]

The verb for "sacrifice" is *yaza-* (Old Indic *yaja-*), often rendered as "worship," which is too vague. The verb implies "sacrificing to (sb.)" and "offering up in sacrifice (sth./with sth.) to (sb.)."

The Creator and the Life-giving Spirit

From the *Old Avesta* on, Ahura Mazdā is the principal "creator." As the supreme deity, he was the first to arrange the ordered cosmos, presumably out of chaos, by his "thinking" (not "speaking"!) "Order" and the heavenly lights suffusing space. The cosmic/ritual Order (*aša*, Old Indic *ṛtá*)[12] was the ordering principle, and the (Life-giving) "Spirit" assisted and was instrumental in Ahura Mazdā's growth:

1.31.7
He who was the first to think those (thoughts): "The free spaces are blending with the lights"—(it was) by (this/his) guiding thought (*xratu*) that he, the *dāmi* [see below] (thought) Order, by which he upholds Best Thought. By that spirit you grow, O All-knowing one, who still here and now are the same, O Lord.

1.31.19
He who (first) thought Order has now listened (to my words?, namely, you?), the knowing one, the healer of the *ahu*, O Lord . . .

2.44.7
I am asking you this: tell me straight, O Lord! Who fashions Humility, the *esteemed one, together with (royal) command? Who first made in the *covering (*viiānā*: of the womb?) a vigorous son for the father? Knowing beforehand (the answers to the questions?), O All-knowing one, *I* am offering *you* (my) help with

these (things), (who) through the Life-giving Spirit (are) the establisher of them all.

4.51.7
Give me now, you who fashioned the cow, the waters, and the plants, Not-dyingness and Wholeness through (your) most Life-giving Spirit, O All-knowing one, (as) "tissue strength" and "tissue connectedness"[13] for (me) to announce (them) with (my) good thought.

The opposite principle was *drug/druj* (Old Persian *drauga*, cf. Old Indic *drúh*) commonly translated as "the Lie," that is, the cosmic deception.[14]

Ahura Mazdā sired and/or fashioned all elements in the ordered part of the cosmos[15]—although at times he had helpers, such as carpenters (e.g., the Fashioner of the Cow)—and set them in their places, being himself the master artisan:

Yasna haptanghāiti 37.1–2
In this way, then, we sacrifice to the All-knowing Lord, who set in place (*dā-*) the cow and Order, who set in place the waters and the good plants, and set in place the (heavenly) lights and the earth and all good things by his power, greatness, and artisanship (*hauuapaŋha*). So, to *him* we sacrifice with the *first fruits* of the sacrifices of those who dwell with the cow.

The principal creative activity is thus the ordering of the cosmos, for which the verb used is *dā-* = Old Indic *dhā-* "set in place," and the "creator" is the *dātar*, apparently, "the one who sets in place" or the *daduuah* "the one who has (always) set in place."[16] In the *Young Avesta*, the "creations" are the *dāman*s, presumably derived from the same verb. The term is notoriously ambiguous, however: although it corresponds etymologically to Old Indic *dhā́man* "things set in place" by the cosmic ordering process, it also reflects Old Indic *dā́man* "tether," and, in the Old Avesta, we may well have both meanings. The *dāman*s "creations" I suspect are Ahura Mazdā's and the sacrificer's woven fabrics (cf. Middle Persian *dām* "net"), but I shall assume here that they are simply artistic creations, those of the successful sacrificers being preserved in Ahura Mazdā's house (2.45.8, 3.48.7).

The new existence produced by these processes is referred to as *ahu*, which is the cyclical (new) existence that needs to be regenerated daily. The good *ahu* has as its counterpart the bad *ahu*, which needs to be healed every morning. The last three chapters of the *Vīdevdad* are devoted to the myth of the healing of the *ahu* and Ahura Mazdā (see below).

The two new-born *ahu*s are described as "that which has bones" and that "which is of thought," that is, the world of living beings and that of the gods and other entities beyond human touch:

1.28.2
I who want to circumambulate you all, O Mazdā Ahura, with my good thought, for you to give to me the spoils of the two *ahu*s, the one with bones and the one of thought.

The ordered cosmos thus fashioned goes through a gestation period (according to the Pahlavi texts, see *Bundahišn* 1.58 below) and is then born:

2.43.5
Thus, I (now) "think" *you* (as) life-giving, O All-knowing one, O Lord, when I (now) see you at the birth (*zqθa*) of the *ahu*, when you set in place, for the first (time), actions, as well as (the words) that are to be uttered, as fee-earning (and established) a bad (fee?) for the bad (but) a good reward for the good—by your artistry (*hunara*)—at the final turn of (= about ?) the *dāmi* [see below].

The Two Spirits in the *Gāθā*s

The myth of the two spirits is referred to in several places in the *Gāθā*s, although briefly. The most famous reference is in the first *Gāθā*, where they are described as follows:

1.30.3
Thus, those two spirits in the beginning,[17] which have been renowned as the twin "sleeps" (*yə̄mā xᵛafnā*) . . .

A long time ago, I proposed that "sleep" in the dual in this strophe is used metonymically for two sleeping fetuses (or embryos), comparing the description of the origins in the Old Indic *Laws of Manu*:[18]

Manusmṛti 1.5
This (thing) *was*, *risen from darkness, unknown, with no distinguishing marks, inconceivable, incomprehensible, like asleep (*prasuptam*) all over.

No other satisfactory explanation of *xᵛafna* (Old Indic *svápna*), taken at face value as "sleep," has to my mind yet been offered.[19]

The text then goes on to emphasize the irreconcilable differences between the two and then describes how it is by the antagonism of the two spirits that life and lack of living are "established":

1.30.3
. . . two thoughts and two speeches; they (are) two actions, a better and an evil. And between those two, those giving good gifts choose straight, not those giving evil gifts.

1.30.4
And also: whenever the two spirits come together one *determines (*dazdē*) for the first (time) both life (*gaiia*: for the good) and lack of living (*a-jiiāti*: for the wicked) and how (their) *ahu* shall be at last: The worst *ahu* (will be that) of those possessed by the Lie, (but) for the sustainer of Order (there will be) best thought.

Here, the verb "come together" (*hə̄m . . . jasa-*) probably implies competition or fight (like Old Indic *saṃ-gam-*), as in 2.44.15 "when two armies come together"; see also *Videvdad* 7.52, below).

The exact meaning of *dazdē* (< *dhā-*; middle, but transitive, lit., "one sets in place for oneself," here rendered as "one *determines," is problematic. I shall propose another possible interpretation at the end of this chapter.

Of these two options the two spirits must choose one:

1.30.5
Of these two spirits, the one possessed by the Lie chose to perform the worst (thoughts, etc., but) the most Life-giving Spirit, who wears the hardest stones, (chose) Order, (as do) those, too, who wish to win the favor of the Lord, turning by their true (*haiθiia*) actions to the All-knowing one.

Here, the reference is perhaps to the (divine, human) poetic inspiration, which may have to be smashed out of the rock, or to the sun, which must rise out of the rock in which it is held (*Videvdad* 21.5).

In the second *Gāθā*, we are given further details of the two spirits, who are now introduced as conversing together:

2.45.2
So now I shall proclaim the two spirits in the first (*ahu*?) [or: "the two first spirits (of the *ahu*)"], of which two the Life-giving one shall tell (him) whom (we/you know to be) the Dark one:

"Neither our thoughts, nor announcements (*sə̄ngha*), nor guiding thoughts, nor preferences (*varəna*), nor utterances, nor actions, nor vision-souls (*daēnā*), nor breath-souls (*uruuan*) go together."

This somewhat innocent-looking list summarizes the entire Old Avestan ritual myth. Thoughts, utterances, and actions obviously make up the entire ritual; there is nothing in the ritual that is not one of the three. In addition, the two "triads" of good/evil thoughts, etc., form the basis of Zoroastrian ethics still today, and are made manifest in a person's *daēnā*, "materialized" as a female that meets the (breath-)soul (*uruuan*) on its journey after death into the beyond to be judged and whose form is according as the soul's good thoughts, etc., weigh more than its evil thoughts, etc. The abodes of the departed are in the houses of good and evil thought (1.32.15, 1.32.13), the houses of Ahura Mazdā and the Dark Spirit, respectively (cf. 1.30.4, above).

On the level of the cosmological myth, "good thought" also represents the sun-lit sky that is woven and stretched out every morning, whereas "evil thought" and Wrath, the embodiment of the dark night sky, are cut back and removed from the cosmic loom (see on 3.48.7, below).

The "guiding thoughts" (*xratu*) of the successful poet-sacrificers (*saošiiaṇt*) are said to be the draught animals that pull the sun wagon up the sky:

2.46.3
When, O All-knowing one, will those who are the bulls of the days move forth for the upholding (*dar-*) of the Order of the *ahu* by (our) announcements (now) grown (more powerful, they,) the guiding thoughts of the revitalizers?

The "announcements" (*sə̄ngha*) are solemn utterances that, besides helping to uphold Order, by themselves, permit the speaker to overcome evil:

2.44.14
How might I deliver the Lie into the hands of Order for it to be wiped out by the Words (*maθra*)[20] of *your* announcement?

The *daēnā*s are also the guides and protectors of the sacrificial chariot, which conveys the breath-soul to the gods for it to perform the hymns of praise and present the sacrificial offerings. Together with the other forces of good, along the way, they successfully fight and chase the forces of evil lingering in the late-night sky:[21]

Yasna haptanghāiti 39.2
Thus, we are offering up in sacrifice the breath-souls of the sustainers of Order . . . , whose vision-souls, better (than those of the rivals) are winning, shall win, or have won (*van-*).

Yasna 12.9
I present with praise the Daēnā Māzdaiiasni (lit., "*daēnā* of those who sacrifice to Ahura Mazdā"), throwing off (her) harness, laying down (her) weapons.

There is not much in these fragments of a narrative to identify the two spirits, although 1.30.5 (above) suggests a connection between the Life-giving Spirit and the sun, as does the following passage from the *Yasna haptanghāiti*:

Yasna haptanghāiti 36.3
You are definitely "the fire of Mazdā Ahura." You are definitely "*his* most Life-giving Spirit," or whichever of your names is the most invigorating, O fire of the All-knowing Lord, with that we are now circumambulating *you*.

The simplest identification of the twins might then be with light and darkness (day and night) themselves. This would also fit 1.31.7 to the effect that Ahura Mazdā grows with light, diminishes with darkness. In the Pahlavi texts, Ohrmazd is said to be all light, Ahrimen all darkness.

The reference in the *Yasna haptanghāiti* passage, however, could also be to the rebirth of the good *ahu*, whose embryo is the Life-giving Spirit and whose visible sign is the newborn sun. This is in any case not, however, the whole story, as we shall see.

The Life-giving Spirit

Other references to the Spirit, the Life-giving Spirit, or the most Life-giving Spirit are frequent throughout the *Old Avesta*, but less straightforward, and it is likely that *maniiu*, like *manah* "thought" and *xratu* "guiding thought," had ritual-mythical references that still escape us. Also, the notorious lack of pronouns (*my, your*, etc.) makes it difficult to determine to whom the spirit is to be assigned. In some cases poetic "inspiration" may be the easier interpretation:

2.45.5
Thus, I shall proclaim the word that the most "life-giving" one tells *me*, which (is) the best for mortals for (it) to be heard: Those whosoever shall give readiness-to-listen (*sraoša*)[22] to this one of mine, shall come to Wholeness and Not-dyingness. By the actions of (my/his) good inspiration/spirit the Lord (is) All-knowing.

2.45.6
Thus, I shall proclaim the greatest one of all, praising (him) with Order who (is) generous (to all those) who are, through (his) Life-giving Spirit/ (my) inspiration. Let the All-knowing one, the Lord, listen, in whose hymn I converse with (my) good thought. Let him teach me the best (thoughts, etc.) by *his* guiding thought.

The first section (six strophes) of the third *Gāθā* is in its entirety devoted to the assertion that the good workings of the cosmos is in accordance with the Life-giving Spirit.

Additional references in the *Gāθā*s to cosmological (stellar?) functions may be found in contexts that also involves the term *dāmi*, the exact meaning of which is also unclear. It may be derived from *dāman* "tether" and mean "the one in charge of the tethers." This may be supported by the expression *dāmōiš uruuaēsē apǝmē* "at the last turn(ing) of the *dāmi*," which may refer to the stellar entity that holds the reins of the heavenly horses. These run their race in a circle around the Firmament, measuring out the time to the final turn of life, as in the Young Avestan *Hādōxt nask* (1.15) "at life's final turn" (*ustǝme uruuaēse gaiiehe*); of the world (cf. 2.43.5, above); and, perhaps, of the ritual chariot race, as in the following strophe:

2.43.6
The turn at which you come with your Life-giving Spirit, O All-knowing one, and (your) command, at that (turn *he* is) on account of (his) good thought, (he) by whose actions the herds are being furthered through Order. For *these* (actions) Humility is announcing the models (*ratu*) of *your* guiding thought, whom/which no one can cause to lie.

The Two Spirits in the Young Avestan Texts

The Young Avestan references to the spirits' creative activities, although more explicit than in the *Gāθā*s, are also only fragments of a narrative. Here, the Life-giving and Evil Spirits have both produced their own creations:

Yašt 13.76 (to the fravashis) = *Yasna* 57.17 (to Sraoša)
. . . when the two spirits set in place the creations, the Life-giving Spirit and the Evil one.

Yašt 15.43 (to Vaiiu)
. . . because I pursue (*vaiiemi*) both creations, both the one the Life-giving Spirit set in place and the one the Evil Spirit set in place.

Both spirits apparently also performed cosmogonic sacrifices, which are imitated by the current sacrificer during the *yasna* ritual, as implied in the following text:

Yasna 13.4
I place all around for you, the Life-giving Immortals, who bestow good command and good gifts, "even the life breath of my own body," as well as "all good gains" [from 1.33.14 and 1.33.10]. Thus the two Spirits have ever thought, thus they have ever spoken, thus they have ever wrought/acted.

Elsewhere in the *Young Avesta*, the creations of the Life-giving Spirit include the stars (*Yasna* 1.11, etc.) and good animals (*Videvdad* 3.20: corpse-eating birds), while evil animals (*xrafstra*) are the creations of the Evil Spirit (*Videvdad* 16.12). In *Videvdad* 13.1–2, Zarathustra asks Ahura Mazdā which are the creations among the creations of the Life-giving and Evil Spirits that come at dawn to smite the other with a thousand blows, to which Ahura Mazdā responds "the hedgehog" (and an unidentified animal). In all these descriptions, the Life-giving Spirit appears to be separate from Ahura Mazdā, as are their creative activities.

One remarkable passage even suggests that the two spirits antedated Ahura Mazdā himself or, at least, that their creative activities were separate from his own:

Yašt 15.2–3 (to Vaiiu)
Ahura Mazdā, who has set all in place, sacrificed to him . . . He implored him:

Give me that prize, Vaiiu, whose work is above, that I may strike down (all) of the creations of the Evil Spirit, but not at all those of the Life-giving one.

Finally, there is a fascinating little story told in *Yašt* 19, but nowhere else, about Kərəsāspa, the youthful dragon-slayer:

Yašt 19.43–44
(Kərəsāspa), who killed Snāuuidka . . . who deliberated thus:
"I am but a child. If ever I come of age, I shall make the earth into a wheel and the sky into a chariot. I shall bring down the Life-giving Spirit from the luminous House of Song. I shall make the Evil Spirit fly up from the horrid Hell. They shall pull my chariot, the Life-giving and the Evil Spirit, unless, that is, manly-minded Kərəsāspa kills me first."

Manly-minded Kərəsāspa did kill him, before the end of his life, depriving him of life breath.

The Young Avestan adjective *spəṇtō.maniiauua* "belonging to/made by the Life-giving Spirit" gives us further clues to the nature of the spirits. The adjective is applied to their "creations" (see below), but also to some cosmic entities, among them the divine Vaiiu (Old Indic Vāyu), the space between this and yonder world, through which the souls of the departed must pass on the way to their final resting place, good or bad. Because of this position, Vaiiu has both a good and a frightening side, and sacrifices to him are made sure to be addressed to the good Vaiiu:

Yasna 0.9 et al.
Vaiiu, whose work is above, set in place beyond the other creations; this of yours, O Vaiiu, that belongs to the Life-giving Spirit.

Yašt 15.42
We invoke him as none other than Vaiiu . . . We sacrifice to (him as) the best one worthy of sacrifice. We sacrifice to (him), wealthy (and) munificent, as belonging to the Life-giving Spirit.

The epithet here clearly limits the address to the part of Vaiiu that is in the upper hemisphere of the cosmos, the embryo of which was the Life-giving Spirit. This cannot be the whole story, however, because Vaiiu is one of several entities that, apparently, were not created (see below), and it is therefore possible that the cosmos was thought of as established around and inside Vaiiu.

In the Pahlavi tradition, the adjective *maniiauua* became the origin of the term *mēnōy*, which denotes the world of (belonging to, made by) the (two) spirits, the other world, separate from the *gētīy* (from Avestan *gaēθiia* "pertaining to living beings"), the world of living beings, this world. Note that the traditional renderings of these two terms as "spiritual" and "material" are likely to produce completely misleading associations.[23] Note, too, that the Pahlavi term also represents Avestan *maniiu*, for example, Spenāg Mēnōy for *spəṇta maniiu*.

The Two Spirits and the Fravashis

Further details about the two spirits are found in *Yašt* 13 to the fravashis, the preexisting souls of all living beings,[24] where we are told how the fravashis assisted Ahura Mazdā in his creative activities, when he "spread out and held up" (*vīδāraiia-*) the sky, the heavenly river, the earth, and the sons in the amnions (*Yašt* 13.2–11). We are also told how it was by the assistance of the fravashis that it was possible to resist the attack of the Evil one, so that Ahura Mazdā, and not the other one, was able to become lord of the ordered cosmos:

Yašt 13.12–13
For if the strong fravashis of the Orderly had not given me assistance, then beasts and men here would not have been mine, (they) who are the best of species. The strength would have belonged to the Lie, the command would have belonged to

the Lie, the world with bones would have belonged to the Lie. Of the two spirits the lying one would have been sitting between heaven and earth; of the two spirits the lying one would have conquered between heaven and earth. Thereafter the conqueror, he would no longer be surrendered with the conquered, the Evil Spirit to the Life-giving Spirit!

The Evil Spirit's unsuccessful attempt to insert himself into Ahura Mazdā's ordered cosmos is described as follows:

Yašt 13.77
When the Evil Spirit was about to pass the "foundation band" (*dāhi*) of the good Order, Good Thought and the Fire came down between (and held him) at bay.

The *dāhi*, as far as I can see from a review of all the Rigvedic instances of Old Indic *dhāsí*, may originally have referred to the "foundation band," that is, the beginning of the web (here the web of the day sky), which is woven in a particularly firm and elaborate way, although the meaning gradually developed into any kind of "beginning, foundation."[25]

Finally, in the *yašt* to Best Order, we have a description of the Evil Spirit's fall, caused by Ahura Mazdā uttering a sacred formula, the *Ašəm vohu* "Order (is the best) good":

Yašt 3.13
He fell (headlong) from in front of heaven (*diiaoš*), the most lying of *daēuua*s, the Evil Spirit full of destruction.

Remarkably, this fragment is the only time in the *Avesta* that the old word for "heaven" is used (Old Indic *dyau-*, Greek Zeus, etc.).

In yet another (poorly understood) text, however, we are told that it was the *Ahuna vairiia* (first strophe of the first *Gāθā*) that Ohrmazd recited to exclude the other, which is also what we see in the Pahlavi texts:

Yasna 19.15
Ahura Mazdā the best . . . said forth the *Ahuna Vairiia* . . . He interdicted the one possessed by the Lie by this interdiction: "Neither our thoughts . . . go together" [from 2.45.2].

In this tantalizing fragment of the myth, it would seem that Ahura Mazdā as the Life-giving Spirit uttered the sacred formula first to produce an effect we do not understand and then "inter-dic-ted" him (*aṇtarə . . . āmrūta: aṇtarə* = inter-; *mrū-* = *dic-* "say").

Still later, the Zoroastrian priest Zādspram (fl. 900) has Ohrmazd come forth himself to wrestle with Ahrimen:[26]

Zādspram 1.4
When he came forth to the border, Ohrmazd came forth to compete "leg-to-leg" (*ham-rānīh*) in order to hold Ahrimen back from his realm.

This detail also appears to be ancient, as it reflects an Avestan formula found in a slightly different context:

Videvdad 7.52
For over this man the two Spirits shall not set down their legs (*rəna*; i.e., to fight).

The Pahlavi translation has:

Pahlavi Videvdad 7.52
For over that man the two Spirits do not stand in contest (*pahikār*).

Ahura Mazdā as the Life-giving Spirit

As we have seen already, by the time of the *Young Avesta*, Ahura Mazdā tended to become identified with the Life-giving Spirit, and the first chapter of the *Videvdad* contains the description of how Ahura Mazdā and the Evil Spirit established the areas of the inhabitable earth: once Ahura Mazdā had expertly crafted a place, the Evil Spirit "whittled forth" adversaries (illnesses, natural calamities, etc.) to it. Here the Life-giving Spirit is no longer mentioned as the creator opposite the Evil Spirit, but rather is Ahura Mazdā himself. At the other end of the *Videvdad*, Ahura Mazdā recounts how the "villain" = the Evil Spirit fashioned illnesses and how he asked the Life-giving Word (*maθrō spəṇtō*; see below) to heal him:

Videvdad 22.1–2
Ahura Mazdā said to Zarathustra: I, Ahura Mazdā, I, who set in place (all) good things, when I made that house, beautiful, bright, luminous, then the Villain looked at me, then the Villain, the Evil Spirit full of destruction, made 99,999 illnesses. So now you must heal me, you my Life-giving Word.

In the Pahlavi creation narratives, Ahrimen is Ohrmazd's primary adversary. Here, Spenāg Mēnōy is not usually identified explicitly as Ohrmazd, although he sometimes is, as in the writings of Zādspram (1.5), where Ahrimen addresses Ohrmazd as "you who are Spenāg Mēnōy" (*tō kē spenāg menōy hē*), when he promises to destroy his creations.

The Two Spirits Conversing

Let us return to the Gathic strophe 2.45.2 cited earlier. The most remarkable feature of this strophe is the way it presents the two spirits as conversing, presumably already in the womb. The assumption that it is the womb is strengthened by two non-Zoroastrian texts, one Manichean, which appears to be describing the Zoroastrian myth, the other a late Vedic text.

The Manichean version of the myth is found in a fragmentary Manichean Middle Persian text (third to fourth centuries CE?):

Berliner Turfantexte IV, text no. 23 (M 8101)[27]
... and] mixture. And, in this manner, they reckon that they were from one egg (*xāyag*) and from one seed. And it is shown in their book concerning all the gods and *mārāspand*s [see below] that the gods (are/were ...) with the gods and ...

[*long gap in the text*]
" ... when] we have come out from (*be uzīd hom*) ... "

Then that egg was divided (*baxt*) into two parts. From the one part of that egg that was upward, which was split (off; *gugāft*) and divided (from the lower part), heaven [was set up?]

[*long gap in the text*]
... and all creatures that move about on it (= the earth) came from that. And they, because they are deceived, mix together good and evil, light and darkness in this manner.

The statement "we have come out" (*uzīd hom*) can hardly be other than a fragment of direct speech and refer to the two spirits discussing how to assign the parts of the cosmos between them once they "have come out." The verb can also be rendered as "we came out," but that would imply that the two spirits had by then come out of the womb/egg and perhaps were recounting their former experiences, which seems less likely.

The Old Indic text, a passage from the Mārtāṇḍa myth found in the *Kāṭhaka-saṃhitā*, has far-reaching consequences for our interpretation of the Zoroastrian cosmogonic myth, which I shall discuss in the remainder of this contribution. Here too we are in the presence of a speaking embryo, which provokes the rivalry of its brothers:

Kāṭhaka-saṃhitā XI.6[28]
(Aditi) became pregnant (*gárbham adhatta*). The embryo, (still) within (her), spoke. The Ādityas [= his brothers] thought, "If this one will be born, he will thrive (*bhaviṣyati*) here." They smashed (*níraghnan*) him out [= "aborted him"]. Expelled/aborted [*nírasto*, lit. "thrown out"][29] he lay there.

There can be little doubt that this is part of an ancient Indo-Iranian myth.[30]

The later, Pahlavi, texts also have Ohrmazd and Ahrimen converse, but the setting of the womb is absent (see discussion on Zurwān).[31]

Cosmic Eggs

Let us now return to the notion of a cosmic egg from which the two spirits were born as seen in the Manichean fragment. This scenario is found in several versions of the creation myth in Zoroastrian literature, as well, and a similar myth was cited by Plutarch (first to second centuries CE):

Of Isis and Osiris 370A-B[32]

Then, Horomazes having increased himself threefold, moved as far away from the sun as the sun is away from the earth and decorated the heaven with stars . . .

Having made (ποιήσας) twenty-four other gods, he placed (ἔθηκεν) them in an egg (ᾠὸν). But the gods who came (γενόμενοι) from Areimanios, who were equal in number, bored a hole in the egg [*missing text*] whence evil things have become mingled with good things.

In this version of the cosmogony, Ohrmazd and Ahrimen are already outside their own egg (not mentioned) and are now in the process of creating additional gods. Ohrmazd creates his gods, whom he places in another egg, but Ahrimen's gods bore a hole in the egg and so enter Ohrmazd's ordered world and contaminate it.

The *Bundahišn* contains an indigenous version of the myth, in which we are told that Ohrmazd first established the sky in the shape of an egg, inside which he established (*bē dād*) the entire creation (*Bundahišn* 1A.7), but, when the Foul Spirit attacked, he bored (*suft*) a hole in the center of the earth and came inside (*Bundahišn* 4.10).[33] Note that, according to these texts, the sky is spherical, going all the way around the earth.

Yet another version of the creation narrative is found in the *Pahlavi Rivāyat Accompanying the Dādestān ī dēnīg*, one which recalls the Rigvedic description of how the world was made out of the sacrificed giant, Man (*Rigveda* 10.90). Here, the identity of its maker is not revealed, but it *contains both* Ohrmazd *and* his creations.[34]

Pahlavi rivāyat 46

About this matter: how and from what was the sky made (*kerd*)?

The tool was something like a cinder of fire of pure light, fashioned (*brēhēnīd*) from the Endless Light. And he made the entire creation (*dām-dahišn*) from it. And when he had made it, then he brought it into (his) body. And he kept it for 3000 years in the body, making it grow and making it better. And then he kept fashioning one thing after the other from his own body.

And first he fashioned the sky from the head . . . And Ohrmazd sits inside it with his entire creation.[35]

After his attack, Ahrimen too was contained *inside* the creation, for, after he had penetrated into Ohrmazd's still motionless creation, the sky was made into a fortress guarded by the fravashis to keep him inside (that is, below) and not let him get out of and up above the sky into the good realm of Ohrmazd (*Bundahišn* 4.10–12, 6A.1–4, *Zādspram* 1.33, 3.2–3).[36]

The Twin Brothers

All these versions of the myth make no explicit reference to a progenitor of the two spirits. Indeed, in the *Gāθās*, where Ahura Mazdā is said to have sired/given birth to a variety of entities, the spirits do not seem to be included. It is true that it has been assumed that 3.47.3 refers to Ahura Mazdā as father of the Life-giving Spirit, taking *tā* in 3.47.3 to be the same as *ptā* seen in 3.47.2, but this interpretation is based on a presumption of the meaning and is not imperative:

3.47.2

He produces (*vərəziia-*)[37] the best of this most Life-giving Spirit by the utterances of (his) good thought (to be sped) along by (his) tongue and the actions of Humility by (his) hands, by this insight: He there is the father (*ptā*) of Order, the All-knowing one.

3.47.3

You are of (= belong to) this Spirit. Through it (*tā*) (you are?) the Life-giving one, who fashioned together the pleasure-giving cow for this one (= me?).

It is possible that *ptā* is gapped in 3.47.3, however, being already explicit in 3.47.2, which would give "you are (the father) of this inspiration," but it is always safer to take the transmitted text at face value before making assumptions that may or may not be true.

It is, however, implied in 2.43.5 (above) and 3.48.6 (below) that Ahura Mazdā is the father of the *ahu*, which, if my interpretation of this concept is correct, implicates Ahura Mazdā in the birth of the two spirits.

In the Pahlavi versions of the myth, we find a much more explicit birth scenario. Thus, in the *Bundahišn* narrative, Ohrmazd is said to have been both father and mother of the creation:[38]

Bundahišn 1.58

Ohrmazd has motherhood and fatherhood of the creation by setting the creation in place (*pad dām-dahišnīh*). For, when he nurtured the creatures in the other world (*mēnōy*), that was being its mother; when he placed them in this world (*gētīy*), that was being its father.

Below, I shall propose a slightly different interpretation of this event.

In some versions of the myth, after the two spirits had merged with Ohrmazd and Ahrimen, since both Ohrmazd and Ahrimen were contained inside the creation, this was finally understood as Ohrmazd and Ahrimen being brothers born from the same womb. This view was cited as extremely sinful by both Zoroastrians and Manicheans, as in the Manichean polemical hymn M 28:[39]

M 28 I r ii1–4

And they say that Ohrmezd and Ahrimen are brothers. And on account of such speech they will come to destruction.

On Ohrmazd in Manicheism, see below.

The same statement was polemicized against in the *Warštmānsr nask* in the *Dēnkard*, precisely in the exegesis of 1.30.4:[40]

Dēnkard 9.30.4

And from the saying of Zardušt about the demon Arš, how he howled to people: "Ohrmazd and Ahrimen were brothers from one womb!

The Single Creator

It seems reasonable to assume that the myth of the twin spirits born from the same womb was bound to provoke the question: "Whose womb?" An explicit answer to this question is given in the so-called Zurvanite myth, in which the womb belongs to Zurwān, Time, which we shall look at below.

The *Young Avesta* knows four primordial entities that were probably not originally part of Ahura Mazdā's ordering process, but preceded it. Differently from all the other entities listed in the *Yasna*, these four are not *ratus*; that is, they are not blueprints for cosmic constituents to be reordered during the ritual.[41] They must therefore be entities that stand beyond the created universe, as said specifically in the case of Vaiiu (above).

In the *Young Avesta*, these entities, which are invoked at the end of the smaller and toward the end of the greater regeneration rituals (*Yasna* 72.10, *Videvdad* 19.13), are the following:

Vaiiu, whose work is above, set in place beyond the other creations (*dāman*),
Θβāša (the Firmament), which obeys its own laws (*x^{v}aδāta*),
Time without borders (*akarana*),
Time which long obeys its own laws (*darəyō.x^{v}aδāta*), that is, for the duration of the creation and the battle between good and evil.

In the *Bundhišn* (1.42), we are told that "Time is stronger than both creations, the creation of Ohrmazd and that of the Foul Spirit," and, according to Zādspram (1.27), Ohrmazd fashioned the creation in this world with the help of Spahr (Θβāša) and Zurwān, which again shows they antedated the creation.

We also find in the *Gāθās* the notion, however, that, apparently, the same artisan had established both light and darkness:

2.44.5

Which artisan (*hu-apah*) set in place both the lights and the darknesses? Who set in place sleep (*x^{v}afna*) and wakefulness?

The answer to this question can hardly be Ahura Mazdā. In the context of sleep and wakefulness, such an idea might have been harmless enough (similarly, Rigvedic Dawn and Night are sisters), seeing how Ohrmazd fashioned sleep:

Bundahišn 1A.15
And to help him (i.e., Gayōmard [see below]), he fashioned sleep, the rest of the creator, for Ohrmazd fashioned forth that sleep in the shape of a luminous tall young man of fifteen.[42]

Once Ahura Mazdā became the single creator, however, it would ascribe to him both light and darkness, that is, in the Old Iranian myth, both good and evil. It is therefore just possible that one of the primordial entities, Time or the Firmament, was the one maker of both light and darkness.

Zurwān as Progenitor of the Two Spirits

In the post-Avestan so-called Zurvanite narrative, Zurwān, Time, is father and mother of both Ohrmazd and Ahrimen. This narrative is known from a variety of sources, including Theodore (bishop of Mopsuestia, 392–428?) cited by Photius (ninth century), the fifth-century Syriac martyr stories, Armenian historians, early Muslim authors, and others.[43]

According to a late version of the myth told by Shahrastani (b. 1086) and other authors about the Zurwāniyya, before the world existed, there was Zurwān. He sacrificed for 1,000 years to have a son who would create heaven and earth. Seeing his sacrifice had no effect, he doubted its value, and, from his doubt, Ohrmazd and Ahrimen were conceived. Then, seeing that he would bear two sons, he decided that the first-born would be king. Ohrmazd knew what his father was thinking and told his brother, who tore open his progenitor's womb and emerged. Ahrimen, insisting upon his rights, was grudgingly accorded 9,000 years of rule, after which Ohrmazd would rule. They both then began creating.[44]

In addition, in his description of the beliefs of the Kayūmarθiyya, a sect that entertained beliefs centered around Gayōmard (see below), Persian Gayūmarθ, Shahrastani tells us that, according to this sect, Ahrimen originated from a thought by god (*yazdān*) wondering how his adversary would be.[45] Here, as in the *Gāθās*, the very act of thinking on the part of the divinity brought what was thought into being.

There is no direct evidence for how early Zurwān was involved in the creation myth as primordial progenitor, but it would seem that he must have been connected with the origin of the cosmos in some capacity before the third century, when his name (Zurwān) was given to the Father of Greatness in the Persian (and later Sogdian) versions of Manicheism, while the name of Ohrmazd was reserved for the First Man, emanated from the Father via the Mother of Life and whose Sons were called *(a)mahrāspandān*, *mārāspandān* from the Pahlavi form of the "Life-giving Immortals" (*amahrspandān*).[46]

With the ambiguous function of Ahura Mazdā/Ohrmazd in the myth, we need not wonder that some may have wanted to exonerate the supreme god from the possibility of having produced evil himself, by substituting a god of Time as the ultimate cause, alternatively, adopted an already existing myth, which the *Avesta* just does not mention explicitly. It then followed naturally, as it were, that Zurwān-Time became identified with the cosmic egg or womb that had contained the two spirits and that the parthenogenesis myth and the myth of the "Caesarean" delivery (from inside) were associated with it. The presence of such a myth, which is found throughout Indo-Iranian mythology, from the birth of Indra to that of Rostam, both of whom were too big for their mothers to give birth to them naturally,[47] may well have played a role in developing the Zurvanite myth.

Gayōmard

Let us now return to 1.30.4, which I translated as "whenever the two spirits come together, one *determines for the first (time) both life and lack of living." Here, it must be pointed out that we do not know the exact connotations of *gaēmcā ajiiātīmcā* "life and lack of living/non-living" from *gaiia-* and *a-jiiāti-*, but elsewhere *gaiia* is "life" in the usual sense, while *a-jiiāti* is not found elsewhere (*jiiāti* only in *fra-jiiāti* "subsistence, survival"?).

We have already seen that the exegesis in the *Dēnkard* interpreted the statement as a reference to the Zurvanite myth, but, in another part of the tradition, it was regarded as a reference to the cosmic giant, the first living being, Gayōmard, Avestan *Gaiia Marətān*:

> *Pahlavi Yasna* 1.30.4
> And in that way those two spirits came together to that first creation (*dahišn*), that is, both spirits came to Gayōmard.

Since the exact references of the Gathic strophe are unclear, this interpretation is not to be rejected off-hand.

Hoffmann, in his comparative study of Gaiia Marətān and the Old Indic Mārtāṇḍa, rendered the Iranian name as "sterbliches, menschliches Leben," but *marətān* can hardly simply mean "mortal, human," a synonym of Old Indic *márta*.[48] Rather, the precise meaning of *marətān* from *marta-Han[49] appears to be "what contains (*–Han-*) what is dead (*marəta*)," although *marəta* is probably not quite the same as *mərəta* "died, dead," Old Indic *mṛtá*. Such a meaning makes the name nearly synonymous with "life and lack of living/non-living," and it is not impossible that we may have here an Old Avestan allusion to the first quasi-human creation, father of mankind, produced by the two spirits coming together. If so, we must assume that the good spirit was responsible for the "life" part and the evil one for the "death" part. Below, I shall propose a different interpretation of *marətān*.

Such an interpretation of *marətān* would now also give an acceptable meaning to another Gathic passage, in which the (wrong) choice of the old, now evil, gods, the *daēuua*s (Old Indic *deva*) is described:

> 1.30.6
> Between those two (spirits), the *daēuua*s in particular did not choose right, because deception came upon them so that they chose the worst thought. And so they run together to Wrath, by which those who are *marətān* sicken the new *ahu*.

Here, Wrath is the embodiment of the night sky and the evil contained in it, and the worst thought the opposite of good thought, which also represents the day sky (see on 3.48.7, below). Those who are *marətān* will then be the creatures of the Evil Spirit (in Pahlavi called "abortions"), who ipso facto support Wrath and, by bringing back the night sky, *do* sicken Ahura Mazdā's good *ahu*.

It is also possible that we have a secondary allusion to the sickening of Gaiia Marətān himself, as told in the later tradition, for instance, by Zādspram:[50]

Zādspram 2.18
I (= Ahrimen) have polluted the water, I have pierced the earth and soiled it with darkness, I have dried out the plant, I have brought death to the kine and sickness to Gayōmard.

The Pahlavi tradition understood "Gayōmard" as "dying (mortal) life" (he lived for thirty years before dying), as Zādspram's brother Mānuščihr tells us:

Dādestān ī dēnīg 63.5[51]
Then that battle-making Lie came, and it soiled him; the life/living thing (*zīndagīh*) became severe mortality (*margōmandīh*). It is called Gayōmard, which is explained as "living and dying" (*zīndag ī mīrāg*).

Zādspram himself, on the other hand, in his description of the battle of heaven and the fravashis against Ahrimen, quotes the Pahlavi version of 1.30.4 and adds yet another tradition:

Zādspram 3.5
That is, both spirits came to the body of Gayōmard, both the one (coming) with life, Ohrmazd, for the reason that they might keep him alive; and the one (coming) with non-life (*a-zīndagīh*), the Foul Spirit, so that they might kill him.

Gayōmard, like the universe, was probably in spherical form:[52]

Bundahišn 1A.15
Sixth he fashioned Gayōmard, luminous like the sun. And he measured 4 reeds (ca. 40 feet) in height. His width was equal to his height.

In Manicheism, too, we find the notion of the making of man as a microcosm in the image of the spherical macrocosm. It is stated in a fragment of the Latin "catechism" of the North-African Manicheans in the description of the creation of Adam from the abortions of the powers of evil, but here the creation involves weaving:[53]

Epistula fundamenti, fragment 9
. . . whose (= the demiurge's) partner received these things like a well-cultivated earth usually receives the seed. And, in her, the images of all the heavenly and earthly powers were put together and woven together (*construebantur et*

contexebantur), so that that which was being shaped (Adam) came to look like the full sphere (*orbis*).

We see that Adam was made by weaving, and that is probably how Gayōmard was made, too, as we shall now see. Although the prototype of man, he remained in the spherical form he had been woven into. It is noteworthy that the Persian Manicheans borrow his name for Adam, calling him Gēhmurd, changing it slightly to make the second part explicitly "dead" (*murd*), as opposed to Pahlavi *mard* "man."

Ancient Iranian Cosmogony as Birth and Weaving of Birth Tissues

The Ancient Iranian cosmogonic narrative involves birth and rebirth, as well as a fashioning and ordering. The cosmogonic birth myth applies to both the macrocosm (the world) and the microcosm (the human body). The cosmic birth is explicitly mentioned in the *Gāθā*s:

> 2.43.5
> Thus, I (now) "think" *you* (as) life-giving, O All-knowing one, O Lord, when I (now) see you at the birth (*zqθa*) of the *ahu* . . .

> 3.48.6
> Thus, for *her* (= Ārmaiti/Humility, the Earth) the All-knowing one, by (his new) Order, shall now make plants grow, he, the Lord, at the (re)birth of the first *ahu*.

But there is also a less explicit and much less clear, but important, reference to the rebirth of the *ahu*:

> 3.48.7
> Let Wrath be tied down! Cut back obstruction! you who wish to stretch out hither through Order and hold firmly (*ā . . . dīdrayža- < ā-drang-*) the tissue (*viiąm*) of Good Thought, whose *tier (*hiθao*) is the Life-giving Man, while its fabrics/ tethers (*dāman*) are there in your dwelling, O Ahura.

Here, Wrath is again the embodiment of the night sky, a demon who, in the later Avestan tradition bathes the creation in blood with his "bloody club" at sunset and who is fought by the divine Sraoša and his helpers all through the night until he is finally overcome. The replacement for the night sky is Good Thought, which therefore stands for the sunlit day sky, which, perhaps woven by Ārmaiti, is woven upward (from the *dāhi*, the first appearance of dawn) and stretched out through the luminous spaces of Order. This identification of the day sky and Good Thought (Pahlavi Wahman) is stated repeatedly in the Pahlavi texts.[54]

The important word here, however, is *viiā*, which denotes a plaited or woven fabric, a tissue, from the verb seen in Old Indic as *vyā-/vī-*. What makes it important is the fact that it is used in a Young Avestan description of the assembling of the fetus:

Yašt 13.11
By their (= the fravashis') wealth and munificence I (= Ahura Mazdā) held out (*vīδāraiia-*), O Zarathustra, the sons in the wombs (*baraθrī*, lit. "she who carries"), enclosed and not dying beforehand, (and) until the destined delivery, I assembled in the tissues (*viiā*) in the right order the bones and the hairs (or: guts), the *muscles and the intestines, the sinews and the limbs.

Here, "in the tissues" (*viiās*) presumably refers to the amnion or caul, conceived of as plaited or woven tissues, the membrane enveloping the human fetus. In modern languages, biological weaving is a frequent metaphor, and implied in the term *tissue* (cf. French *tisser* "weave," German *Gewebe*) itself.
The related Old Indic verb *vyā-/vī-* is also used in the context of the womb:[55]

Rigveda 1.164.32 (riddle hymn)
Enveloped (*pári-vīto*, lit., "plaited all about") in the womb (*yónā*) of the mother, (while) having much offspring, he (himself) has entered disarticulation (*nírṛtim*; "unraveling").

The verbs used in 3.48.7, *ā-drang-* "stretch hither and hold firmly" and *vīδāraiia-* "hold up and out" used in *Yašt* 13, correspond to Old Indic *draṃh-* and *dhāraya-* "uphold," as well as *ā-tan-* "stretch hither" used in similar contexts, e.g.:

Rigveda 6.67.6 (Mitra, Varuṇa)
For you two, there, uphold (*dhāraya-*) the (royal) command day after day; you two hold firmly (*draṃh-*) the back of heaven as if from above. (Thus) held firmly (*draṃh-*), the *nákṣatra*, too, belonging to all the gods, has stretched out hither (*ā-tan-*) earth (and) heaven (*dyām*) by means of *their dhāsí* [= Avestan *dāhi*, see below].

We see that the Gathic *ā-drang-* may be regarded as a telescoped version, as it were, of *ā-tan-* and *draṃh-*.[56]
Examples of cosmic and ritual weaving are common in the Vedic literature.[57] Here, let me cite the *Maitrāyaṇī saṃhitā*, according to which Sarasvatī wove a new body (*vápus*) and she and other poet-gods a new form (*rūpá*) for Indra:

Maitrāyaṇī saṃhitā 3.11.9 [304.3][58]
In exchange for lead(en weights) and wool yarn, the imaginative poets weave by their thought a fabric (*tántra*): the sacrifice—the Aśvins, Savitar, Sarasvatī, and Varuṇa—healing Indra's form.

Maitrāyaṇī saṃhitā 3.11.9 [304.9]
With thought, Sarasvatī weaves a spectacular body (for Indra).

The myth of weaving the day and night skies is explicit in the *Rigveda*:[59]

> *Rigveda* 2.3.6 (Dawn and Night)
> (May) dawn and night, who grew for us of old, (make their/our?) works (*ápas*) succeed, like two speedy weavers, the two of them together weaving (their) stretched thread into (?) the adorned (fabric?) of the sacrifice.

> *Rigveda* 2.38.4 (Savitar)
> The weaveress (Night) has again rolled up (*sám avyad* < *vyā-*) that which was stretched out (*vítata*) (by her) . . . Gathering (his limbs), he has stood up.

In the *Gāθā*s, we have an explicit statement as to Ahura Mazdā's involvement in the weaving:

> 1.34.10
> . . . (as someone) who knows life-giving Humility, the *dāmi*, and the *tier (*hiθao*) of Order and (who knows) all those weaving gears (*vōiiaθra*s), O Ahura Mazdā, (to be) there in your command!

Here, the term *vōiiaθra*, taken here for the first time at face value, is derived from the same verb (probably not attested in the *Avesta*) as Old Indic *vaya-* "weave."

The involvement of Ārmaiti is probably similar to or the same as that of Arámati:

> 2.43.6
> For these (actions) Humility is announcing the models (*ratu*s) of your guiding thought, whom/which no one can cause to lie.

> *Rigveda* 2.38.4 (continued)
> Arámati has (spread?) out (and) holds firmly (*adardhar*) the models (*r̥tú*s).

Here, I suspect that the *r̥tú*s that Arámati has taken hold of and the *ratu*s that Ārmaiti announces are to be understood as the other worldly "models" or "blueprint" for the cosmic web. Such a meaning makes perfect sense in the contexts of the *Yasna*, where the priest "announces [like an usher] and assembles" the "models of Order" to recreate the new ordered cosmos.

Let us return to the cosmogony of the hymn to the fravashis, where the cosmogonic verb is "hold up and out, stretch out" (*vi-dāraya-*), which we can now tentatively assume not only refers to the actual "stretching out," which makes less sense with the "fetuses" as direct object, but to the act of weaving and stretching out the macro- and microcosmic amnions.[60]

In *Yašt* 13.11, we first have Ahura Mazdā himself performing the "holding out" of the sky, the heavenly waters, and the earth. This is then followed in *Yašt* 13.22 by a description of the fravashis themselves "holding out" the sky, the heavenly waters, the earth, the cow/bull, and the human fetuses. And, finally, in *Yašt* 13.28–29, we see the Life-giving Spirit "holding out" the sky, the heavenly waters, the earth, the cow/bull, and the human fetuses, but also the fravashis themselves.

This brings us to the function of the fravashis in the weaving, on which I cannot elaborate here. Suffice it to say that their descriptions strongly suggest they are the warp threads of the macro- and microcosmic webs, and the weft is likely to be the breath-soul (*uruuan*). This would also explain why Ahura Mazdā asked his Life-giving Word (*mąθra spənta*), to heal him; according to *Yašt* 13.81, the Life-giving Word is precisely Ahura Mazdā's breath-soul,[61] and Ahura Mazdā appears to be asking it to weave him a new "body," as the deities did for Indra.

In fact, the later tradition knew of a myth in which the soul was the "artisan" who made the body, presumably (originally) by weaving it:

Book of advice of Wehzād son of Farrox-Pērōz 22[62]
For, when the body has been dissolved and the bodily frame (*kālbod*) has been broken, then the soul (*gyān*), too, having forgotten the body leaves it. The artisan has risen from his work and the bodily frame has become fruit-less (*abē-bar*). The artisan has left, having become weary of the bodily frame it made.

And the body as the garment of the soul (*ruwān*) is seen in:

Dēnkard 3.401[63]
The battle of the Lie is against man's selfdom, which is the soul (*ruwān*), and against his weapon, which is the body, the garment of the soul.

That the myth is of Indo-European date is suggested by its presence in Plato's *Phaedo* (87b–88b) (unless he borrowed it from Iran), where Cebes likens the soul (ψυχή) to a weaver who wears out all his cloaks except the last. Similarly, he represents the soul as weaving its own body:[64]

Phaedo 87d
For if the body is constantly changing and being destroyed while the man still lives, and the soul is always weaving anew (ἀνυφαίνοι) that which wears out, then when the soul perishes it must necessarily have on its last garment (ὕφασμα), and this only will survive it.[65]

The meaning of the threefold repetition in *Yašt* 13 now appears to be as follows.

1. Ahura Mazdā's ordering sacrifice, in which he was assisted by the fravashis and whereby the Evil Spirit was barred from becoming the ruler of the material world. This would be Ahura Mazdā's original weaving, when he was alone to weave the first fabric, presumably using, first, his own fravashi (*Yašt* 13.80) as warp thread and his "breath-soul" as weft and, then, those of the Life-giving Immortals.[66]
2. The model for ritual recitation spoken by Ahura Mazdā to Zarathustra: by the poet-sacrificer praising, invoking, and weaving (*ufiia-*) the fravashis, they "hold out" the sky, and so on.

3. The Life-giving Spirit weaves *his* own amnion containing his creations. The Evil Spirit then also makes his own, since, in str. 76, we are told that both spirits established their creations (*dāman*), after which the Evil Spirit tried to pass from his own chaotic fabric, past the "foundation band (*dāhi*) of Order," into the upper part of the new *ahu*, that is, the ordered fabric woven by the Life-giving Spirit.

Thus, it would seem that, in this version of the myth, Ahura Mazdā must have woven the tissue of his new cosmos in the form of a sphere that contained the twin spirits, placed above and below, respectively, whether he was identical with the sphere, as seems likely, or separate from it.

The Evil Spirit, as we saw, was contained by the divine Fire and Good Thought and was confined to weaving his fabric of darkness beneath the (upper) sky, from which Ahura Mazdā and his supporter must remove it daily.

The cosmic weaving myth thus explains the link between the macrocosmic *viiā*, which is the tissue/covering of the sky, and the microcosmic *viiā*, the amnion.[67] In the same way that the fabric of the sky envelops the new cosmic Life (*ahu*) that is about to be born, the biological tissue also envelops the new human Life that is about to be born.

An Embryological Explanation of the Iranian Cosmology

The element of birth that pervades the Iranian creation myth and the notion of two fetuses, a good and a bad, combined with the ancient Indo-Iranian myths of Gaiia Marətān and Mārtāṇḍa, finally permits us to take yet one step further. That Mārtāṇḍa, whose shape matched that of Gayōmard, whose width "was equal to his height," is sometimes represented as the *afterbirth* of the birth of the Ādityas from Aditi is well known, although it may also be an aborted fetus.[68] In the *Śatapatha-brāhmaṇa*, the description of Mārtāṇḍa closely resembles that of a placenta:[69]

Śatapatha-brāhmaṇa III.1.3.3–4
She bore an eighth, unshaped (*ávikṛta*): Mārtāṇḍa.
He was a lump (*saṃdeghá*), as broad as he was tall.

Taking all the evidence presented earlier, as well as much not included here, but especially the name of Gaiia Marətān, I want to propose that the ancient Iranians viewed creation as a complete birth myth and that the "radical dualistic" element in it originated in the observation of the dual birth: of the new living being and of the afterbirth, which, although it was what kept the fetus alive, was now dead (and disposed of).[70] We may also note that, in Persian, the afterbirth is called *joft* "twin."[71] The form of the placenta is that of a thick lump, somewhat disk-shaped, from which the navel string goes out, which might explain the intriguing comment in *Yašt* 13.87 that Ahura Mazdā made the navel strings (or families, *nāf–*) out of Gaiia Marətān.

A second notable correspondence between the Old Avestan and Old Indic texts here is the use in *Kāṭhaka-saṃhitā* XI.6 (cited above) of *dhā* "place" in the middle voice + *gárbham* to express "become pregnant." If we apply this meaning to *dazdē* in the Old Avestan passage, we obtain a remarkable sense:

1.30.4
. . . and when those two spirits come together (in someone), then one becomes pregnant (*dazdē*) for the first time with life and non-life.

Such a meaning of the Pahlavi verb *dā-*, present *dah-* is, in fact, also attested. The clearest examples are the following:[72]

Dēnkard 7.8.56
. . . and she conceives (*dahēd*) that son inside, whose name is "He who makes Order grow" (Uxšiiaṯ.ərəta, the first of Zarathustra's three eschatological sons).[73]

The Supplementary Texts to the Šāyist nē šāyist 19.10
Ten (*Ahunwar*s should be recited by) him who goes to seek a wife, in order that (the chance of) conception (*dahišn*) during the "action" be better.

Pahlavi yasna 13.1
"This earth, which I say (is) our conception (*dahišn*) and carrier (= womb), her I say (is) the *rad* of females."

Such a meaning would also explain the use of *dahišn* in *Dēnkard* 7 apparently to refer to the (proto-)embryo of Zarathustra, which Ohrmazd has "fashioned" (like a carpenter):

Dēnkard 7.2.37
Then, when Ohrmazd had fashioned forth Zarathustra's *dahišn*, (i.e.) the body substance (*gōhr*), Zarathustra's *dahišn* *slid down from before Ohrmazd . . . onto a cloud.

We can now also return to the meaning of Avestan Gaiia Martān from *gaiia marta-Han*, which I suggested earlier seems to mean "life with a dead thing," the perfect description of the products of the birth process: the living new human followed by the lifeless afterbirth, the (circular) placenta.

Moreover, the otherwise unattested Avestan **marəta*- may survive in Pahlavi *mardag*, which possibly means "placenta." It is found in two passages in Zādspram's description of the fate of the wicked at the Činwad bridge. The first example is fairly straightforward:

Zādspram 31.3–4
On the fourth day, the form of young woman (i.e., the *dēn*) receives the Soul and makes it pass the Činwad bridge, the frightening passage of wails, in the same manner as a mother during the birth of her children: the wicked one, like the

placenta (*mardag*) which is "thrown" (i.e., "aborted") from the body, falls down into hell.

The second example is less straightforward, but appears to contain a classification of births as those of a healthy child, an aborted child (which seems to be thought of as the product of the placenta), and an impaired child:

Zādspram 31.1
Sometimes (a child) comes out from the body of the mothers through a narrow passage, sometimes it falls forth from the placentas (*mardagān*), (and) sometimes it is born as *čihr*, not sensing, not speaking, not walking and is in need of a mother to nurture it.

In both these instances, the word is spelled *mardag*, not *murdag*, which means "having died, dead." It would seem to be different from "dead fetus," which is usually *nisēy*. Scribal confusion must have been common, however, and it is likely that some of the *murdag*s in other texts should be emended to *mardag*, as, fairly explicitly, in the following text from *Dēnkard* book V:[74]

Dēnkard 5.24.19b
Here we begin to talk about the pollution of the various parts that come apart from the body also in life, but especially from a dead body. Not only flesh, but also semen, blood, and all the other things that are called *hixr*. And the most severe of them is menstrual discharge and the *placenta (*murdag*, spelled <YMYTNtk'> = *murdag*), a part of what is attached to (*niwast*) to the child's *texture (*hambandagīh* or *hambandišnīh*, lit. "what is bound together").

Such an interpretation is strengthened by the fact that, in Persian, the afterbirth is called *joft* "twin."[75] Note also James G. Frazer's description of the treatment of the afterbirth in a large variety of societies, where it is commonly referred to as "brother," "sister," or "double" and is saved for various purposes and various lengths of time, and sometimes ritually buried in a significant spot that "anchors" the newborn to her lineage and home.[76] The name of Gaiia Marətān may then refer to the fact that he was the first human fetus, but never developed into human form; instead, he remained in the spherical form he would have had in the womb, containing both the living fetus and the dead placenta.[77]

Introductions to Old Iranian religion rarely, if ever, consider in any depth the creation processes. For instance, Mary Boyce, in her section on Avestan creation terminology mentions "shape by cutting, carve, fashion": "employed for animate things," as well as "spread out": "used for the act of establishing the sky, waters and earth,"[78] but she does not mention spreading out "the sons in the wombs" (see *Yašt* 13.22, above). Nor does she include there *zqθa* "birth" and the verb *dā-* "set in place," although they feature prominently in the cosmogony. In modern translations of the *Gāθā*s, the birth scenario is also left undiscussed. For instance, Stanley Insler translates "birth" as "creation" and "birth," but without comment,[79] and Jean Kellens and Eric Pirart have "engendrement," also without comment.[80]

Once the word "birth" is given its full meaning, however, we have seen above that creation as a birth scenario, well known from the Pahlavi literature, imposes itself also for the *Gāθā*s. Applying this scenario to the two primordial twin *maniiu*s, however, is not completely unproblematic since we seem to have two successive (pro)creations: first the birth of the Life-giving Spirit and the Dark/Evil Spirit and then *their* (pro) creations, as described in *Yasht* 13, and in the Pahlavi tradition, but this problem cannot be further discussed here.

Dualism versus Monotheism

After the fall of the Sasanian Empire, in face of the increasingly influential monotheistic cultures, Zoroastrians thought of various ways to defend themselves against criticism of the dualist position. The problem of the origin of evil was commonly utilized to show the untenability of monotheism: Why was there evil in the world if God was an all-powerful good and compassionate god? In *Dēnkard* III, the criticism takes the following form:[81]

> *Dēnkard* 3.122.8
> Those holding (other) beliefs, whose belief is that there is only one beginning and that all things that have a beginning are from that same beginning, including evil *dēn*s,[82] and from him whom they regard as god, and ascribe to that beginning also the quality of the Foul Spirit, they deny him the quality of Spenāg Mēnōy . . .

> *Dēnkard* 3.383.6
> Those holding (other) beliefs, whose belief is that there is only one beginning, ascribe to it the origin and cause of evil actions, wickedness, harm, damage, and people's evil behavior and the antagonism against the creations and deny its being god and creator and a friend of the creations.

The Zoroastrian priests, however, like the monotheists, had a hard time explaining why the omnipotent creator allowed evil to enter his own perfect creation or why he let it persist without immediately doing something to get rid of it. A defense of the Creator is found in the *Bundahishn*:

> *Bundahishn* 1.56
> Ohrmazd did not think something that he could not do, while the Foul Spirit thought what he could not do and even brought it about violently.

Among the issues frequently brought up was that of the ontological nature of Ahrimen. In the Pahlavi texts, Ohrmazd and Ahrimen have both always been and are, but only Ohrmazd will be, that is, after the original existence is permanently renewed at the end of time, but Ahrimen is also said to have no existence in the world of the living, only in the other world.[83] The idea may go back to the *Avesta*, where divinities (*yazata*) are said to be of both this and the other world, but demons (*daēuua*) only of that world.[84]

After the Muslim conquest of Persia and the exodus of many Zoroastrians to India and after having been exposed to both Muslim and Christian propaganda, some Zoroastrians, especially among the Parsis in India, went so far as to deny dualism and to view themselves as outright monotheists, and the dualist aspect of the religion is today often downplayed or explained away.[85] Its origin in a myth of the primordial conception, gestation, and birth of cosmic twins and their struggle until the end of time was forgotten long ago.

Notes

1 On Zoroastrian dualism, see, e.g., Prods Oktor Skjærvø, "Zoroastrian Dualism,"
   in *Light Against Darkness: Dualism in Ancient Mediterranean Religion and the
   Contemporary* World, ed. Armin Lange et al. (Göttingen: Vandenhoeck & Ruprecht,
   2011), 55–91, and "Zarathustra: A Revolutionary Monotheist?," in *Reconsidering
   the Concept of Revolutionary Monotheism*, ed. Beate Pongratz-Leisten (Winona
   Lake: Eisenbrauns, 2011), 325–58. General introductions to Zoroastrianism: Jenny
   Rose, *Zoroastrianism: An Introduction* (London and New York: I.B. Tauris, 2011);
   Mary Boyce, *A History of Zoroastrianism*, vol. 1, *The Early Period* (Leiden: Brill,
   1975); vol. 2, *Under the Achaemenians* (1982). There is a large secondary literature,
   especially on the *Gāθās*, which cannot be considered here.
2 See Prods Oktor Skjærvø, "Iran iv. Iranian Languages and Scripts," in *Encyclopædia
   Iranica* 13, no. 3 (2006): 344–77; "The *Avesta* and the Avestan languages," in *The
   Oxford Handbook of Iranian History*, ed. Touraj Daryaee (Oxford: Oxford University
   Press, 2012), 57–119.
3 See Prods Oktor Skjærvø, "The Avestan *yasna*: Ritual and Myth," in *Religious
   Texts in Iranian Languages: Symposium Held in Copenhagen May 2002*, ed.
   Claus V. Pedersen and Fereydun Vahman (Copenhagen: Det Kongelige Danske
   Videnskabernes Selskab, 2006a), 57–84.
4 See Prods Oktor Skjærvø, "The *Videvdad*: Its Ritual-Mythical Significance," in Vesta
   S. Curtis and Sarah Stewart, ed. *The Age of the Parthians* (London and New York:
   I.B. Tauris, 2007), 105–41.
5 See, e.g., Prods Oktor Skjærvø, *The Spirit of Zoroastrianism* (New Haven and
   London: Yale University Press, 2011) for translations.
6 See ibid., 29–30.
7 For an example, see ibid., 78–9.
8 See ibid., 14–15, 92–5.
9 "Humility" is a translation based on her function as Ahura Mazdā's daughter and wife
   and her identification with the Earth, Latin *humus*.
10 See Skjærvø, *The Spirit of Zoroastrianism*, 14–15, 95. On sacrificing gods, see also
   Kimberley C. Patton, *Religion of the Gods: Ritual, Paradox, and Reflexivity* (Oxford
   and New York: Oxford University Press, 2009).
11 James Darmesteter, *Ormazd et Ahriman: leurs origines et leur histoire* (Paris: F.
   Vieweg, 1877), 256; Prods Oktor Skjærvo, "Ahura Mazdā and Ārmaiti, Heaven and

Earth, in the Old Avesta," in *Indic and Iranian Studies in Honor of Stanley Insler on His Sixty-Fifth Birthday*, ed. Joel P. Brereton and Stephanie W. Jamison, *Journal of the American Oriental Society* 122, no. 2 (2002): 399–410.

12 The word *aṣa*, although often translated as Truth, nowhere means "truth" in any usual sense of the word, as in "speak the truth"; see Prods Oktor Skjærvø, "Truth and Deception in Ancient Iran," in *Jamshid Soroush Soroushian Commemorative Volume*, vol. 2, *Ātaš-e dorun: The Fire Within*, ed. Carlo G. Cereti and Farrokh Vajifdar (Bloomington: 1st Books Library, 2003), 383–434.

13 See Skjærvø, *The Spirit of Zoroastrianism*, 30–1.

14 Like *aṣa*, *drug/druj* is not used in the usual sense of "lie," as in "speak a lie."

15 See, e.g., Jean Varenne, *Cosmogonies védiques* (Paris: Société d'édition "Les Belles lettres," 1982), 62–8, on the similar Old Indic terminology.

16 See Jean Kellens, "Ahura Mazdā n'est pas un dieu créateur," in *Études irano-aryennes offertes à Gilbert Lazard*, ed. Ch.-H. de Fouchécour and Ph. Gignoux (Paris: Association pour l'avancement des études irannienes, 1989), 217–28.

17 The form *pauruiiē* can be from locative **parwiyai* "at first, in the beginning" or **parwiyā* adjective "first" agreeing with *maniiu* (nominative dual). Similarly in 2.45.2.

18 After Patrick Olivelle's translation in *The Law Code of Manu: A New Translation Based on the Critical Edition* (Oxford and New York: Oxford University Press, 2004), 13, with some differences.

19 Henrik S. Nyberg, *Irans forntida religioner, Olaus-Petri-föreläsningar vid Uppsala universitet* (Stockholm: Svenska kyrkans diakonistyrelses bokförlag, 1937), 113, 117–20 suggested that *x^vafnā* was an elliptic dual meaning "sleep (and death)," translating "Sleep [and his brother]" and interpreted this as "sleep and wakefulness" as a reference to day cult characterized by trance versus night cult and wakefulness. There are several explanations that do not take *x^vafnā* at face value; see Jean Kellens and Eric Pirart, "La strophe des jumeaux: stagnation, extravagance et autres méthodes d'approche," *Journal Asiatique* 285 (1997): 58–60. See Eric Pirart, *Maṇiiu et la mythologie protozoroastrienne: Étude de textes vieil-avestiques*. Acta Iranica 59 (Leuven: Peeters, 2020), 32 renders the first line of 1.30.3 as "Deux sentiments fondamentaux sont alors connus comme songes jumeaux." He does not comment on songes ("dreams.").

20 I think the *mąθra* is Ahura Mazdā's thought expressed in words or similar.

21 See Skjærvø, *The Spirit of Zoroastrianism*, 19.

22 See ibid., 15–16.

23 The common transcription of these words as *mēnōg* and *gētīg* is baseless.

24 See, e.g., Skjærvø, *The Spirit of Zoroastrianism*, 31.

25 See also Klaus L. Janert, *Sinn und Bedeutung des Wortes "dhāsi" und seiner Belegstellen im Rigveda und Awesta* (Wiesbaden: O. Harrasowitz, 1956).

26 Most recent edition and translation: Philippe Gignoux and Ahmad Tafazzoli, *Anthologie de Zādspram* (Paris: Association pour l'avancement des études iraniennes, 1993).

27 Werner Sundermann, *Mittelpersische und parthische kosmogonische und Parabeltexte der Manichäer* (Berlin: Akademie-Verlag, 1973), 79–80.

28 Text and translations after Stephanie Jamison, *The Ravenous Hyenas and the Wounded Sun: Myth and Ritual in Ancient India* (Cornell, 1991), 116.

29 The verb "throw" is commonly used of spontaneous abortion, for instance, in Persian (*andāxtan*), English (*throw*), Norwegian (*kaste*). Pahlavi has *abgandan: kōdak bē abganēd* "she throws = aborts the child" in *Rivāyat of Ādur-farrōbay* 51.1, ed. and (not so reliably) trans. Behramgore Tahmuras Anklesaria, *The Pahlavi Rivāyat of Āturfarnbag and Farnbag-srōs* (Bombay: P.K. Anklesaria at M.F. Cama Athornan Institute, 1969).

30 On Vedic analogues, in this volume, see Wendy Doniger, "Wars within the Womb."
    In fact, the theme may be more common, cf. *Genesis* 25:22–3 about Jacob and Esau:
    "The children struggled together within her [Rebekah's womb]; and she said, 'If it is
    to be this way, why do I live?' So she went to inquire of the Lord. And the Lord said
    to her, 'Two nations are in your womb, and two peoples born of you shall be divided;
    the one shall be stronger than the other, the elder shall serve the younger'"; NRSV
    translation.
31 See, e.g., Skjærvø, *The Spirit of Zoroastrianism*, 84–5.
32 Carolus Clemen, *Fontes historiae religionis Persicae* (Bonn: Marcus & E. Weber,
    1920), 48–9; W. Sherwood Fox and R. E. K. Pemberton, "Passages in Greek and
    Latin Literature Relating to Zoroaster and Zoroastrianism Translated into English,"
    Journal of the K. R. Cama Oriental Institute 14 (1929): 51–3.
33 See, e.g., Skjærvø, *The Spirit of Zoroastrianism*, 90–1. The lexical correspondences
    are remarkable: *xāyag* ~ ᾠὸν "egg" (both from < **ōyo-*); *bē dād* ~ ἔθηκεν
    "established, placed" (both from < **dhē-*), *suft* ~ διατρήσαντες "bored."
34 Most recent edition: Allan V. Williams, *The Pahlavi Rivāyat Accompanying the
    Dādestān ī Dēnīg* (Copenhagen: Det Kongelige Danske Videnskabernes Selskab,
    1990), vol. 1, 160–1; vol. 2, 72, 202–6; cf. Skjærvø, *The Spirit of Zoroastrianism*,
    81–2.
35 This is similar to chapter 28 of the *Bundahišn* on the human body reflecting the
    macrocosm.
36 See also Skjærvø, *The Spirit of Zoroastrianism*, 97, 99–100.
37 This verb is used as "work, make" generically, but especially poetry and babies.
38 Most recent translation: Domenico Agostini and Samuel Thrope. *The Bundahišn:
    The Zoroastrian Book of Creation* (New York, NY: Oxford University Press, 2020);
    see also Fazlollah Pakzad, *Bundahišn: Zoroastrische Kosmogonie und Kosmologie,
    Band I, Kritische Edition* (Tehran: Centre for the Great Islamic Encyclopaedia,
    2005); the paragraph numbering is after this edition. See also Skjærvø, *The Spirit of
    Zoroastrianism*, 89.
39 Skjærvø, Prods Oktor, "The Manichean Polemical Hymns in M 28 I," *Bulletin of the
    Asia Institute* 9 (1995, pub. 1997): 245. Note that Ohrmezd here is the name of the
    First Man, not the ruler of the world of light, who is Zurwān (and other names); see
    below.
40 *Bonyād-e Farhang-e Īrān, The Codex DH, Being a Facsimile Edition of Bondahesh,
    Zand-e Vohuman Yasht, and Parts of Denkard* (Tehran, n.d. [1970]), 202–3.
41 See Skjærvø, "The Avestan *yasna*," 72–4.
42 See also Skjærvø, *The Spirit of Zoroastrianism*, 91–2.
43 See Robert C. Zaehner, *Zurvan: A Zoroastrian Dilemma* (Oxford: Clarendon, 1955;
    repr. New York: Biblo and Tannen, 1972), 60–1 and elsewhere.
44 Shahrastani, *Livre des religions et des sectes*, trans. with intro. and notes by D.
    Gimaret and G. Monnot, vol. 1 (Paris: Peeters, 1986), 638; Zaehner, *Zurvan*,
    419–29.
45 Shahrastani, *Livre des religions et des sectes*, 636. See also Zaehner, *Zurvan*, 367.
46 From this to assuming the Sasanian kings were "Zurvanites" is a long and unlikely
    leap, see, e.g., Mary Boyce, *A History of Zoroastrianism*, vol. 2, 392–41. See
    also Zaehner, *Zurvan*, 30, 37–8; and Prods Oktor Skjærvø, "Iranian Elements in
    Manicheism: A Comparative Contrastive Approach. Irano-Manichaica I," in *Au
    carrefour des religions: Hommages à Philippe Gignoux,* ed. Rika Gyselen (Bures-
    sur-Yvette: Groupe pour l'étude de la civilisation du Moyen-Orient, 1995), 271–2.

47 *Rigveda* 4.18.2 "I will not go out from there. These (places) are hard to squeeze through. I shall go out cross-wise from the side." When Rudābe was unable to deliver Rostam, her husband, Zāl, called upon the Simorγ bird for help, who instructed him in how to perform a caesarian delivery: "without pain he split (*be-kāfīd*) the side of the moon (-faced Rudābe)." See Abu 'l-Qāsem Ferdousi, *Šāhnāma*, ed. Djalal Khaleghi-Motlagh (New York: Bibliotheca Persica, 1988–2008), vol. 1, 267, line 1473; Jules Mohl, trans., *Le livre des rois* (Paris: Imprimerie impériale, 1838–68), vol. 1, 352, line 1695. Note that the verb used (*kāf-*) is the same as that used in the Manichean text about the two spirits cited above, which has *gugāft* (< *vi-kāft-*) "split" (the egg).

48 Karl Hoffmann, "Mārtāṇḍa und Gayōmart," *Münchener Studien zur Sprachwissenschaft* 11 (1957): 100 = idem, *Aufsätze zur Indoiranistik*, vol. 2 (Wiesbaden: L. Reichert, 1975), 435.

49 See Karl Hoffmann, "Ein grundsprachliches Possessivsuffix," *Münchener Studien zur Sprachwissenschaft* 6 (1955): 36 = *Aufsätze*, vol. 1, 378–83.

50 See Skjærvø, *The Spirit of Zoroastrianism*, 97–8, 108.

51 Only in manuscripts.

52 See Skjærvø, *The Spirit of Zoroastrianism*, 91–2.

53 See Erich Feldmann, *Die "Epistula Fundamenti" der nordafrikanischen Manichäer: Versuch einer Rekonstruktion* (Altenberge: Akademische Bibliothek,1987), 18–21. On cosmic weaving in Zoroastrianism and Manicheism, see also Antonio Panaino, *Tessere il cielo: Considerazioni sulle Tavole astronomiche, gli Oroscopi e la Dottrina dei Legamenti tra Induismo, Zoroastrismo, Manicheismo, e Mandeismo* (Rome: Istituto Italiano per l'Africa e l'Oriente, 1998).

54 See, e.g., Skjærvø, *The Spirit of Zoroastrianism*, 208–9, 213.

55 The translations from the *Rigveda* are my own, based mainly on the text and the translations in Karl Friedrich Geldner, *Der Rig-Veda aus dem Sanskrit ins Deutsche übersetzt und mit einem laufenden Kommentar versehen*, vols. 1–3 (Cambridge, MA: Harvard University Press, 1951); repr. 3 vols. in 1, Harvard Oriental Series 33–5 (Cambridge, MA and London: Harvard University Press, 2003); Louis Renou, *Études védiques et pāṇinéennes* (Paris: Collège de France. Institut de civilisation indienne, 1955–69); vols. 1–3, 2nd ed. (1980–6). They diverge to a slight extent from those in Joel P. Brereton and Stephanie W. Jamison, *The Rigveda: The Earliest Religious Poetry of India*, 3 vols. (Oxford and New York: Oxford University Press, 2014).

56 See also Alain Christol, "De ΦΟΩΣ ἘΡΕΩΝ à *ā dyām tanoṣi*: Note de phraséologie," *Bulletin de la société linguistique* 81 (1986): 181–204.

57 On poetic weaving in the *Rigveda* and the *Avesta*, see Prods Oktor Skjærvø, "Poetic and Cosmic Weaving in Ancient Iran: Reflections on Avestan *vahma* and Yasna 34.2," in *Haptačahaptāitiš: Festschrift for Fridrik Thordarson*, ed. Daug Haug and Eirik Welo (Oslo, 2005), 267–79; idem, "The *Gāθās* and the *kusti*," in *One for the Earth: Prof. Dr. Y. Mahyar Nawabi Memorial Volume*, ed. Mahmoud Jaafari-Dehaghi (Tehran, 2008), 117–21. See also John Scheid and Jesper Svenbro, *Le métier de Zeus: Mythe du tissage et du tissu dans le monde gréco-romain* (Paris: La Découverte, 1994); trans. Carol Volk, *The Craft of Zeus: Myths of Weaving and Fabrics* (Cambridge, MA and London: Harvard University, 1996). This work inspired much of my own thinking on cosmic and ritual weaving.

58 Cited and translated by Wilhelm Rau, *Weben und Flechten im Vedischen Indien* (Mainz: Verlag der Akademie der Wissenschaften und der Literatur, 1971), 23–4.

59 Cf. Rau, *Weben und Flechten im Vedischen Indien*, 25.

60 See Skjærvø, *The Spirit of Zoroastrianism*, 64–6.
61 See Skjærvø, *The Spirit of Zoroastrianism*, 19, 68–9. It is also the chariot of the sun; see Karl Hoffmann, "Zur awestischen Textkritik: Der Akk. Pl. mask. der *a*-Stämme," in *W. B. Henning Memorial Volume*, ed. Mary Boyce and Ilya Gershevitch (London, 1970), 197–9 = *Aufsätze*, vol. 1, 285–7, on *Yasna* 9.26.
62 Jamaspji M. Jamasp-Asana, *The Pahlavi Texts Contained in the Codex MK Copied in 1322*, vol. 2. (Bombay, 1913), 76.
63 Mark J. Dresden, ed., *Dēnkart: A Pahlavi Text: Facsimile Edition of the Manuscript B of the K. R. Cama Oriental Institute Bombay* (Wiesbaden: O. Harrassowitz, 1966), [298]; Jean de Menasce, Le troisième livre du Dēnkart (Paris: Klincksieck, 1973), 360.
64 Plato, *Plato with an English translation by Harold North Fowler* (Cambridge, MA: Harvard University Press, 1990), 303–5. See also Scheid and Svenbro, *Le métier de Zeus*, 129; *The Craft of Zeus*, trans. Volk, 161–2.
65 Note also Psalm 139:13: "For it was you who formed my inward parts. You wove (*təsukkēnī*) me together in my mother's womb." At a much later date, Proclus of Constantinople (b. 390 CE) envisaged the Virgin as a "textile-loom (ἱστός). In this image, the Virgin's womb (γαστήρ) is depicted as a workshop (ἐργαστήριον) containing the textile-loom on which the flesh of God is knit, woven together, and, upon its completion, wrapped around the bodiless divinity, giving it form and texture" (Nicholas P. Constas, "Weaving the Body of God: Proclus of Constantinople, the Theotokos, and the Loom of the Flesh," *Journal of Early Christian Studies* 3 [1995]: 180).
66 According to *Bundahišn* 26.38 (cf. *Yašt* 13.83), Ohrmazd fashioned all the seven Life-giving Immortals including himself.
67 Note that the similarity between *dyām* and *vyām* is probably only apparent, as we must read *d(i)yām* and *vya'am*.
68 See Jamison, *The Ravenous Hyenas and the Wounded Sun*, 200, 204–8.
69 Ibid., 206. On the Indo-Iranian myth, see also Hoffmann, "Mārtāṇḍa und Gayōmart."
70 According to *Bundahišn* 1.58, the cosmic fetus developed exactly like a human fetus, but the text does not mention the placenta; see Skjærvø, *The Spirit of Zoroastrianism*, 89. On various interesting aspects of creation and birth in Zoroastrianism, see also Ela Filippone, "The Mazdean Notions of Creation and Birth: Some Reflexes in the Iranian Languages," in *Religious Themes and Texts of Pre-Islamic Iran and Central Asia: Studies in Honour of Professor Gherardo Gnoli on the Occasion of His 65th Birthday on 6 December 2002*, ed. Carlo Cereti, Mauro Maggi, and Elio Provasi (Wiesbaden, 2002), 91–109.
71 See Marten Stol, *Birth in Babylonia and the Bible: Its Mediterranean Setting* (Groningen: Styx, 2000), 144–5; Fereydun Vahman and Garnik Asatrian, *Notes on the Language and Ethnography of the Zoroastrians of Yazd* (Copenhagen: Det Kongelige Danske Videnskabernes Selskab, 2002), 72. See also James G. Frazer, *The Golden Bough: A Study in Magic and Religion*, 1 vol., abridged ed. (London and New York: Touchstone Books/Simon and Schuster, 1996), 45–7: description of the treatment of the afterbirth in a large variety of societies, where it is commonly referred to as "brother," "sister," or "double," and is saved for various purposes and various lengths of time, and sometimes ritually buried in a significant spot that "anchors" the newborn to her lineage and home.
72 Most recent edition of *Dēnkard* book VII: Marijan Molé, *La légende de Zoroastre selon les textes pehlevis* (Paris: Klincksiek 1967); and of *The Supplementary Texts to the Šāyist nē šāyist*: Firoze M. P. Kotwal, *The Supplementary Texts to the Šāyest nē-šāyest* (Copenhagen: Det Kongelige Danske Videnskabernes Selskab, 1969).

73 Here, Marijan Molé (*La légende de Zoroastre selon les textes pehlevis* [Paris: Klincksiek 1967], 91), remarkably, already translated *dahēd* as "*concevra*," but without comment.

74 Most recent edition: Jaleh Amouzgar and Ahmad Tafazzoli, *Le cinquième livre du Dēnkard: Transcription, traduction et commentaire* (Paris: Association pour l'avancement des études iraniennes, 2000).

75 See Stol, *Birth in Babylonia and the Bible*, 144–5; Vahman and Asatrian, *Notes on the Language*, 72.

76 Frazer, *The Golden Bough*, 45–7.

77 The Zoroastrian myth of the twins is strongly reminiscent of several Greek myths, for instance: existence from eternity of Chronos and Zâs (Pherecydes of Syros); the twin brothers Sleep and Death (Homer, *Iliad* 16.682, Hesiod, *Theogony* 756); and the two kinds of strife (Hesiod, *Works and Days* 11–21), see, e.g., Timothy Gantz, *Early Greek Myth: A Guide to Literary and Artistic Sources* (Baltimore and London: Johns Hopkins Press, 1993), 5–6, 9–10, 739. That the myth of the two spirits also recalls myths about male/light ~ female/dark principles goes without saying, and 1.30.4 in our new interpretation does suggest that the two spirits represent the male and female semen. There is, however, no indication, as far as I can see, that the two are male and female in Old Iranian religion (although Ahrimen performs anal intercourse on himself to produce his creations), and I shall not pursue this aspect of cosmic myths here.

78 Boyce, *A History of Zoroastrianism*, vol. 1, 131.

79 Stanley Insler, *The Gāthās of Zarathustra* (Tehran and Liège, 1975), 61, 66, 91.

80 Jean Kellens and Eric Pirart, *Les textes vieil-avestiques*, 3 vols. (Wiesbaden: L. Reichert, 1988, 1990, 1991).

81 Cf. de Menasce. *Le troisième livre*, 124, 341–2.

82 Pahlavi *dēn* (Avestan *daēnā*, see above) is often lightly translated as "religion," but, more precisely, refers to the oral tradition of the Zoroastrians and is often invoked by "as it says in the *dēn*." But see now BeDuhn, Jason D., "The Co-formation of the Manichaean and Zoroastrian Religions in Third-Century Iran." In *Entangled Religions: Interdisciplinary Journal for the Study of Religious Contact and Transfer* 11.2, 2020

83 See other texts in Shaul Shaked, "Some Notes on Ahreman, the Dark Spirit, and His Creation," in *Studies in Mysticism and Religion, Presented to Gershom G. Scholem on His Seventieth Birthday by Pupils, Colleagues and Friends*, ed. Ephraim E. Urbach, R. J. Zwi Werblowsky, and Chaim Wirszubski (Jerusalem: Magnes, 1967), 227–34; Hanns-Peter Schmidt, "The Non-Existence of Ahreman and the Mixture (*gumēzišn*) of Good and Evil," in *Second International Congress Proceedings* (Bombay: K. R. Cama Oriental Institute, 1996), 79–95.

84 Schmidt, "The Non-Existence of Ahreman," 83.

85 See, for instance, John R. Hinnells, "Contemporary Zoroastrian Philosophy," in *Companion Encyclopedia of Asian Philosophy*, ed. Brian Carr and Indira Mahalingam (London and New York: Routledge, 1997), 64–91; Philip G. Kreyenbroek and Shehnaz Neville Munshi, *Living Zoroastrianism: Urban Parsis Speak about their Religion* (Richmond, Surrey: Cruzon, 2001), 298–9.

Bibliography

Agostini, Domenico, and Samuel Thrope. *The Bundahišn: The Zoroastrian Book of Creation*. New York, NY: Oxford University Press, 2020.

Amouzgar, Jaleh, and Ahmad Tafazzoli. *Le cinquième livre du Dēnkard: Transcription, traduction et commentaire, Studia Iranica. Cahier 23*. Paris: Association pour l'avancement des études iraniennes, 2000.

Anklesaria, Behramgore Tahmuras. *The Pahlavi Rivāyat of Āturfarnbag and Farnbag-srōš*, vol. 1, Text and Transcription, Vol. 2, Introduction and Translation. Bombay: P. K. Anklesaria at M. F. Cama Athornan Institute, 1969.

BeDuhn, Jason D. "The Co-formation of the Manichaean and Zoroastrian Religions in Third-Century Iran." In *Entangled Religions: Interdisciplinary Journal for the Study of Religious Contact and Transfer* 11.2. Bochum, Germany: Ruhr-Universität Bochum, 2020.

Bonyād-e Farhang-e Irān. *The Codex DH, Being a Facsimile Edition of Bondahesh, Zand-e Vohuman Yasht, and Parts of Denkard*. Tehran: Bonyād-e Farhang-e Irān, [1970].

Boyce, Mary. *A History of Zoroastrianism, Handbuch der Orientalistik I, viii: Religion 1, 2, 2A; I. The Early Period; II. Under the Achaemenians*. Leiden and Cologne: Brill, 1975 and 1982.

Brereton, Joel P., and Stephanie W. Jamison. *The Rigveda: The Earliest Religious Poetry of India*, 3 vols. Oxford and New York: Oxford University Press, 2014.

Christol, Alain. "De fows Δerewn à *ā dyām tanoṣi*: Note de phraséologie." *Bulletin de la société linguistique* 81 (1986): 181–204.

Clemen, Carolus (Carl Christian). *Fontes Historiae Religionis Persicae*. Bonn: Marcus & E. Weber, 1920.

Constas, Nicholas P. "Weaving the Body of God: Proclus of Constantinople, the Theotokos, and the Loom of the Flesh." *Journal of Early Christian Studies* 3 (1995): 169–94.

Darmesteter, James. *Ormazd et Ahriman: leurs origines et leur histoire*. Paris: F. Vieweg, 1877.

Dresden, Mark J., ed. *Dēnkart: A Pahlavi Text: Facsimile Edition of the Manuscript B of the K. R.* Cama Oriental Institute Bombay. Wiesbaden: O. Harrassowitz, 1966.

Feldmann, Erich. *Die "Epistula Fundamenti" der nordafrikanischen Manichäer: Versuch einer Rekonstruktion*. Altenberge: Akademische Bibliothek, 1987.

Ferdousi, Abu 'l-Qāsem. *Šāhnāma*. Edited by Djalal Khaleghi-Motlagh. New York: Bibliotheca Persica, 1988; trans. Jules Mohl, *Le livre des rois*. Paris: Imprimerie impériale, 1838–68.

Filippone, Ela. "The Mazdean Notions of Creation and Birth: Some Reflexes in the Iranian Languages." In *Religious Themes and Texts of Pre-Islamic Iran and Central Asia: Studies in Honour of Professor Gherardo Gnoli on the Occasion of His 65th Birthday on 6 December 2002*, edited by Carlo Cereti, Mauro Maggi, and Elio Provasi, Beiträge zur Iranistik 24, 91–109. Wiesbaden: L. Reichert, 2002.

Fox, W. Sherwood, and R. E. K. Pemberton. *Passages in Greek and Latin Literature Relating to Zoroaster and Zoroastrianism Translated into English*. Journal of the K. R. Cama Oriental Institute 14, 1929.

Frazer, James G. *The Golden Bough: A Study in Magic and Religion*, 1 vol., abridged ed. London and New York: Touchstone Books/Simon and Schuster, 1996.

Gantz, Timothy. *Early Greek Myth: A Guide to Literary and Artistic Sources*. Baltimore and London: Johns Hopkins Press, 1993.

Geldner, Karl Friedrich. *Avesta. The Sacred Book of the Parsis*, 3 vols. in one. Stuttgart, 1896.

Geldner, Karl Friedrich. *Der Rig-Veda aus dem Sanskrit ins Deutsche übersetzt und mit einem laufenden Kommentar versehen*, 3 vols. Cambridge, MA: Harvard University Press, 1951; repr. 3 vols. in 1. Cambridge, MA and London: Harvard University Press, 2003.

Gignoux, Philippe, and Ahmad Tafazzoli, eds. *Anthologie de Zādspram. Edition critique du texte pehlevi traduit et commenté.* Studia Iranica. Cahier 13. Paris: Association pour l'avancement des études iraniennes, 1993.

Hinnells, John R. "Contemporary Zoroastrian Philosophy." In *Companion Encyclopedia of Asian Philosophy*, edited by Brian Carr and Indira Mahalingam, 64–91. London and New York: Routledge, 1997.

Hoffmann, Karl. "Ein grundsprachliches Possessivsuffix." *Münchener Studien zur Sprachwissenschaft* 6 (1955): 35–40. = idem, *Aufsätze zur Indoiranistik* vol. 2, 378–83. Wiesbaden, 1975.

Hoffmann, Karl. "Mārtāṇḍa und Gayōmart." *Münchener Studien zur Sprachwissenschaft* 11 (1957): 85–103. = *Aufsätze zur Indoiranistik* vol. 2, 422–38.

Hoffmann, Karl. "Zur awestischen Textkritik: Der Akk. Pl. mask. der *a*-Stämme." In *W. B. Henning Memorial Volume*, edited by M. Boyce and I. Gershevitch, 187–200. London, 1970 = *Aufsätze zur Indoiranistik*, vol. 1, 274–87.

Hoffmann, Karl. *Aufsätze zur Indoiranistik*, 2 vols. Wiesbaden: L. Reichert, 1975.

Insler, Stanley. *The Gāthās of Zarathustra, Acta Iranica 8.* Tehran and Liège: Brill, 1975.

Jamasp-Asana, Jamaspji M. *The Pahlavi Texts Contained in the Codex MK Copied in 1322*, Vol. 2. Bombay, 1897–913.

Jamison, Stephanie. *The Ravenous Hyenas and the Wounded Sun: Myth and Ritual in Ancient India.* Cornell: Cornell University Press, 1991.

Janert, Klaus L. *Sinn und Bedeutung des Wortes "dhāsi" und seiner Belegstellen im Rigveda und Awesta.* Wiesbaden: O. Harrasowitz, 1956.

Kellens, Jean. "Ahura Mazdā n'est pas un dieu créateur." In *Études irano-aryennes offertes à Gilbert Lazard*, edited by Ch.-H. de Fouchécour and Ph. Gignoux. Studia Iranica Cahier 7, 217–28 Paris: Association pour l'avancement des études irannienes, 1989.

Kellens, Jean, and Eric Pirart. *Les textes vieil-avestiques*, 3 vols. Wiesbaden: L. Reichert, 1988, 1990, 1991.

Kellens, Jean, and Eric Pirart. "La strophe des jumeaux: Stagnation, extravagance et autres méthodes d'approche." *Journal Asiatique* 285 (1997): 31–72.

Kotwal, Firoze M. P. *The Supplementary Texts to the Šāyest nē-šāyest, Historisk-filosofiske Meddelelser* 44, 2. Copenhagen: Det Kongelige Danske Videnskabernes Selskab, 1969.

Kreyenbroek, Philip G., and Neville Munshi, *Shehnaz. Living Zoroastrianism: Urban Parsis Speak About their Religion.* Richmond, Surrey: Cruzon, 2001.

de Menasce, Jean. *Le troisième livre du Dēnkart.* Paris: Klincksieck, 1945.

Moazami, Mahnaz. *Wrestling with the Demons of the Pahlavi Widēwdād: Transcription, Translation, and Commentary.* Leiden and Boston: Brill, 2014.

Nyberg, Henrik S. *Irans forntida religioner: Olaus-Petri-föreläsningar vid Uppsala universitet .* Stockholm: Svenska kyrkans diakonistyrelses bokförlag, 1937.

Molé, Marijan. *La légende de Zoroastre selon les textes pehlevis.* Paris: Klincksiek 1967.

Olivelle, Patrick, ed. and trans. *The Law Code of Manu: A New Translation Based on the Critical Edition.* Oxford and New York: Oxford University Press, 2004.

Pakzad, Fazlollah. *Bundahišn: Zoroastrische Kosmogonie und Kosmologie, Band I, Kritische Edition.* Tehran: Centre for the Great Islamic Encyclopaedia, 2005.

Panaino, Antonio. *Tessere il cielo: Considerazioni sulle Tavole astronomiche, gli Oroscopi e la Dottrina dei Legamenti tra Induismo, Zoroastrismo, Manicheismo, e Mandeismo.* Rome: Istituto Italiano per l'Africa e l'Oriente, 1998.

Pirart, Eric. *Mańiiu et la mythologie protozoroastrienne: Étude de textes vieil-avestiques.* Acta Iranica 59. Leuven: Leuven, 2020.

Patton, Kimberley C. *Religion of the Gods: Ritual, Paradox, and Reflexivity*. Oxford and New York: Oxford University Press, 2009.

Plato. *Plato with an English Translation by Harold North Fowler*. Cambridge, MA: Harvard University Press, 1990.

Rau, Wilhelm. *Weben und Flechten im Vedischen Indien*. Mainz: Verlag der Akademie der Wissenschaften und der Literatur, 1971.

Renou, Louis. *Études védiques et pāṇinéennes, Publications de l'Institut de civilisation indienne, sér. in-8°, fasc. 1*. Paris: Collège de France, 1980–86. Institut de civilisation indienne [distribution E. de Boccard], 1955–69; vols. 1–3, 2nd ed.

Rose, Jenny. *Zoroastrianism: An Introduction*. London and New York: I.B. Tauris, 2011.

Scheid, John, and Jesper Svenbro. *Le métier de Zeus: Mythe du tissage et du tissu dans le monde gréco-romain*. Paris: La Découverte, 1994; *The Craft of Zeus: Myths of Weaving and Fabrics*, trans. Carol Volk. Cambridge, MA and London: Harvard University Press, 1996.

Schmidt, Hanns-Peter. "The Non-Existence of Ahreman and the Mixture (*gumēzišn*) of Good and Evil." In *Second International Congress Proceedings*, 79–95. Bombay: K. R. Cama Oriental Institute, 1996.

Shahrastani. *Livre des religions et des sectes*. Translated with intro. and notes by Daniel Gimaret and Guy Monnot, vol. 1. Paris: Peeters, 1986.

Shaked, Shaul. "Some Notes on Ahreman, the Dark Spirit, and His Creation." In *Studies in Mysticism and Religion, Presented to Gershom G. Scholem on His Seventieth Birthday by Pupils, Colleagues and Friends*, edited by Ephraim E. Urbach, R. J. Zwi Werblowsky, and Chaim Wirszubski, 227–34. Jerusalem: Magnes, 1967.

Skjærvø, Prods Oktor. "Iranian Elements in Manicheism: A Comparative Contrastive Approach. Irano-Manichaica I." In *Au carrefour des religions: mélanges offerts à Philippe Gignoux*, edited by Rika Gyselen, Res Orientales 7, 263–84. Bures-sur-Yvette: Groupe pour l'étude de la civilisation du Moyen-Orient, 1995.

Skjærvø, Prods Oktor. "The Manichean polemical hymns in M 28 I." *Bulletin of the Asia Institute* 9 (1995, pub. 1997): 239–55.

Skjærvø, Prods Oktor. "Ahura Mazdā and Ārmaiti, Heaven and Earth, in the Old Avesta." In *Indic and Iranian Studies in Honor of Stanley Insler on His Sixty-Fifth Birthday*, edited by Joel P. Brereton and Stephanie W. Jamison, *Journal of the American Oriental Society* 122, no. 2 (2002): 399–410.

Skjærvø, Prods Oktor. "Truth and Deception in Ancient Iran." In *Atash-e Dorun—The Fire Within: Jamshid Soroush Soroushian Memorial Volumes*, vol. 2, edited by Carlo G. Cereti and Farrokh J. Vajifdar, 383–434. Bloomington: 1st Books Library, 2003.

Skjærvø, Prods Oktor. "Poetic and Cosmic Weaving in Ancient Iran: Reflections on Avestan *vahma* and Yasna 34.2." In *Haptačahaptāitiš: Festschrift for Fridrik Thordarson*, edited by Daug Haug and Eirik Welo. Instituttet for Sammenlignende Kulturforskning: Serie B: Skrifter 116, 267–79. Oslo: Novus, 2005.

Skjærvø, Prods Oktor. "The Avestan *yasna*: Ritual and Myth." In *Religious Texts in Iranian Languages: Symposium Held in Copenhagen May 2002*, edited by Fereydun Vahman and Claus V. Pedersen, 57–84. Copenhagen: Det Kongelige Danske Videnskabernes Selskab, 2006.

Skjærvø, Prods Oktor. "Iran iv. Iranian Languages and Scripts." *Encyclopædia Iranica* 13, no. 3 (2006): 344–77.

Skjærvø, Prods Oktor. "The *Videvdad*: Its Ritual-Mythical Significance." In *The Age of the Parthians*, edited by Vesta S. Curtis and Sarah Stewart, The Idea of Iran 2, 105–41. London and New York: I.B. Tauris in association with The London Middle East Institute at SOAS and the British Museum, 2007.

Skjærvø, Prods Oktor. "The *Gāθās* and the *kusti*." In *One for the Earth: Prof. Dr. Y. Mahyar Nawabi Memorial Volume*, edited by Mahmoud Jaafari-Dehaghi, 117–33. Tehran: Centre for the Great Islamic Encyclopaedia, 2008.

Skjærvø, Prods Oktor. "Zoroastrian Dualism." In *Light Against Darkness: Dualism in Ancient Mediterranean Religion and the Contemporary World*, edited by Armin Lange et al., 55–91. Göttingen: Vandenhoeck & Ruprecht, 2011.

Skjærvø, Prods Oktor. "Zarathustra: A Revolutionary Monotheist?" In *Reconsidering the Concept of Revolutionary Monotheism*, edited by Beate Pongratz-Leisten, 325–58. Winona Lake, Ind.: Eisenbrauns, 2011.

Skjærvø, Prods Oktor. *The Spirit of Zoroastrianism*. New Haven, CT and London: Yale University Press, 2011.

Skjærvø, Prods Oktor. "Avestan Society." In *The Oxford Handbook of Iranian History*, edited by Touraj Daryaee, 57–119. Oxford: Oxford University Press, 2012.

Stol, Marten. *Birth in Babylonia and the Bible: Its Mediterranean Setting*. Groningen: Styx, 2000.

Sundermann, Werner. *Mittelpersische und parthische kosmogonische und Parabeltexte der Manichäer*. Berlin: Akademie-Verlag, 1973.

Vahman, Fereydun, and Garnik Asatrian. *Notes on the Language and Ethnography of the Zoroastrians of Yazd*, Historisk-filosofiske Meddelelser 85. Copenhagen: Det Kongelige Danske Videnskabernes Selskab, 2002.

Varenne, Jean. *Cosmogonies védiques*. Paris: Société d'édition "Les Belles lettres," 1982.

Williams, Allan V. *The Pahlavi Rivāyat Accompanying the Dādestān ī Dēnīg. Part I: Transliteration, Transcription and Glossary; Part II: Translation, Commentary and Pahlavi Text*, Historisk-filosofiske Meddelelser 60: 1–2. Copenhagen: Det Kongelige Danske Videnskabernes Selskab, 1990.

Zaehner, Robert C. *Zurvan: A Zoroastrian Dilemma*. Oxford: Clarendon, 1955; repr. New York: Biblo and Tannen, 1972.

14

Didymos Judas Thomas

The Twin Brother of Jesus

♊

Gregory J. Riley

Early in his public ministry, Jesus called twelve disciples to be his followers, one of whom was Thomas. We learn nothing explicit about Thomas in the New Testament except in the Gospel of John, where he appears as one of John's several important characters, like John the Baptist or Nicodemus or the Samaritan Woman at the Well. Unlike these others, however, the portrayal of Thomas is negative in nearly every respect. He spends his career in the Gospel of John contradicting, misunderstanding, or doubting Jesus. No other disciple but Judas Iscariot is so negatively portrayed. This may be because, as we also learn, he is called "twin," the very meaning of the Hellenized name "Thomas" in its original Aramaic. But whose twin? In other literature that bears his name, we find that Thomas was considered by those who looked to him for apostolic inspiration to be the twin brother of Jesus. That unique relationship to Jesus had profound spiritual implications for subsequent Christianity, both within and outside of more traditional theologies.

The Names of the Twelve Disciples

The names of Jesus' disciples, soon to be known simply as "the Twelve," are listed four times in the Synoptic Gospels and Acts. The lists provide some intriguing information and present an interesting, though spare, picture of relationships between Jesus and his disciples. Some of the disciples, unfortunately, are mere names on the lists, with no further information given: Philip, Bartholomew, Thaddeus. Family relationships are mentioned for others: "James son of Alphaeus," or "James son of Zebedee and John the brother of James," or "Simon . . . and his brother Andrew." Matthew is said to have been "the tax gatherer"; Judas Iscariot, "the one who betrayed [Jesus]." Jesus himself seems to have given nicknames to some of his close disciples: we read of "Simon, to whom he gave the name Peter"; or James and John, "to whom he gave the name Boanerges, that is, Sons of Thunder." There were two disciples named Simon, so perhaps the lesser Simon was given his epithet to differentiate him from Simon Peter: "Simon, who was called the Zealot." One disciple remains, whose actual name was not even preserved on the lists, but is designated only by his epithet: Thomas.

The Real Name of Thomas

The name "Thomas" was originally a Semitic word given a Greek ending "-s," like the Hellenized "Judas" from an original Semitic "Judah," or "Jonas" from an original "Jonah." So "Thomas" is a Hellenized form of the originally Semitic root "thom/ thoma," meaning "twin." The name "Thomas" is a nickname, an epithet, not Thomas's real name.[1]

No explanation or translation of the epithet is given in the texts of the Synoptic Gospels or Acts. No one in the Greco-Roman world who was not versed in Semitic languages would know what "Thomas" meant. It would have sounded like a foreign name, unfamiliar, perhaps like "Na'ima," or "Byong Soo" might sound to English speakers. Greek readers would know, of course, that "Philip" meant "lover of horses" and that "Andrew" meant "brave," but since the meaning of the name of Philip or Andrew does not matter in the story of these texts, no translation is necessary. Only in the case of Peter (= "rock" in Greek) does the meaning of his name carry another significance: Jesus says to him, "You are Peter, and on this rock I will build my Church" (Matt 16:18).

The Gospel of John, however, does give a translation of the epithet: "Thomas, who is called 'Twin'" (John 11:16; 20:24; 21:2). The Gospel of John translates the Semitic epithet, as it had earlier for two other titles: we are told that "Rabbi" means "teacher" and "Messias" means "Christ" (John 1:38, 41). In like manner, Thomas's name means "twin."

The Gospel of John is translating the Semitic term "Thomas" into Greek: *Didymos* is the Greek word here for "twin." "Didymos," however, was sometimes used as a name. The Vulgate, for example, in its translation into Latin of the same passages of the Gospel of John, does not translate the name "Thomas" as *Geminus* (= "twin" in Latin), but reads: *Thomas qui dicitur Didymus*, "Thomas who is called Didymus." For readers of the Vulgate, for Christians in the Latin West, the whole idea that Thomas is a twin is lost. Latin Christians would just hear two foreign-sounding names: Thomas Didymus. One with facility in Hebrew/Aramaic and Greek, however, would know that both of the terms are merely epithets: the man is being called "Twin Twin." The reader is still no closer to his real name.

One must move outside of the New Testament, however, to other texts related to the Thomas tradition of eastern Syria to discover his real name. Christians of the East had more information, more options. The Gospel of Thomas (GTh) begins: "These are the secret words that the Living Jesus spoke and Didymos Judas Thomas wrote."[2] The Book of Thomas (BTh) begins similarly: "The secret words that the Savior spoke to Judas Thomas. . ."[3] In the opening lines of The Acts of Thomas (ATh), we find, "Judas Thomas who is also Didymos." Eusebius includes in his *History of the Church* the

Abgar legend, in which one finds, "Judas who is also Thomas" (1.13.11). In addition, the Old Syriac version of the Gospel of John in 14:22 replaces the name "Judas, not Iscariot" with "Thomas." Here we see that the Twin, "Thomas who was called Didymos," had a real name: Judas.[4]

Judas, Brother of Jesus, in the New Testament

There is a tradition preserved in the New Testament about the several children of Mary, that is, Jesus and his siblings. In the Gospel of Mark, one reads, "Is not this the carpenter, the son of Mary and brother of James and Joses and Judas and Simon, and are not his sisters here with us?" (6:3; cf. Mt 13:55). One of Jesus' brothers is Judas. The Syrian Thomas tradition understood this Judas to be Judas Thomas, the twin brother of Jesus.

But in the New Testament, this cannot be so. Note that the order of the names of the brothers of Jesus in Mark 6:3 are "James and Joses and Judas and Simon." Matthew 13:55 reads: "And are not his brothers James and Joseph and Simon and Judas?" Of the four brothers of Jesus, Judas is the second-to-last name on the list in Mark and the last name on the list in Matthew. Jesus by tradition is the eldest child, the first-born. So, if the sons of Mary were listed, Jesus would be first on the list. Judas, one would assume, if he were Jesus' twin, would certainly be mentioned next, not next-to-last or last. The writers of the New Testament lists of Jesus' brothers did not find Judas to be especially important. The impression is that he is the fourth or fifth male child of Mary, after Jesus as first-born. That would mean that he is at least four or five years younger than Jesus, and not his twin. And nothing at all is said about this Judas being called "Thomas" or being a twin of anyone.

The tradition that Jesus had a twin brother Judas Thomas cannot have been dependent on anything in the New Testament. The New Testament never says that Thomas was Jesus' twin or that his name was really Judas. No one could possibly have read the New Testament lists of Jesus' siblings and the lists of Jesus' disciples, and deduced that Thomas was Jesus' twin. Jesus' brother Judas is at least four years younger than Jesus, and he is never said to be a twin, or also called Thomas. The claim that Thomas and Jesus were twins requires information not found in the New Testament.

Judas Thomas as Twin of Jesus

How then did it happen that Jesus and Judas were understood to be twins?[5] Outside the New Testament, in the eastern Syrian tradition of Thomas Christianity, Thomas was known to be Judas, the twin brother of Jesus. In the Book of Thomas, Jesus speaks with Thomas and refers to an oral tradition already current: "It has been said that you are my twin" (138:7–8). In the Acts of Thomas, a serpent says to Thomas, "I know that you are the twin brother of Christ" (31). Later, a donkey's colt addresses him as "Twin brother of Christ" (39). In fact, Jesus is so like Thomas in appearance that he is mistaken for him; he must say, "I am not Judas, who is also Thomas; I am his brother" (11). At some time in early eastern Christianity an oral tradition arose that knew that "Thomas" meant "twin," knew that his real name was Judas, and knew that Jesus had a brother named "Judas the twin." Before and in parallel with the writing of the New Testament and completely independent of it, Thomas became, in the understanding of these Christians, the twin brother of Jesus. Thomas Christians were operating on their own oral and in their minds historical traditions, independent and apart from any New Testament texts. The motivation for developing such a tradition was fundamental to the spirituality of Thomas Christianity.[6]

Thomas Christianity as a Way to Be Christian

What did it mean to be a Thomas Christian, a follower of Jesus who had a twin brother Judas? In the New Testament, one finds different, but recognizable, ways to be Christian in Paul's epistles, in the Gospel of Matthew, in Luke-Acts, in the Gospel and epistles of John, among others, much like different Christian denominations today. There is no information at all, however, about a way to be Christian that looks to or is inspired by Thomas. For that, one must look elsewhere, to the non-canonical Thomas literature.

Image of the Twin in the Gospel of Thomas

The Gospel of Thomas begins with the statement, "These are the secret words that the Living Jesus spoke and Didymos Judas Thomas wrote." The very next sentence proclaims that "Whoever finds the interpretation of these words will not taste death." We, however, are left in the dark: the "secret words" that Jesus spoke are not explained, and the "interpretation" of his words is lost to us.

In antiquity, the secret words would have been explained orally by a teacher to an inner group of disciples who were on their way to initiation into the mysteries. For example, Jesus proclaims the enigmatic Parable of the Sower to the multitudes. Later he is asked by his inner circle of disciples in private what this puzzling story meant. He replies, "To you has been given the secret of the kingdom of God, but for those outside, everything comes in parables" (Mark 4:11). He then explains the parable to them. Yet in the Gospel of Thomas, we are left with the sayings only, like the outsiders who heard only the parable. We are without the oral instruction that would have explained the secret words and given us their proper interpretation.

The Gospel of Thomas does, nevertheless, provide a number of clues about these sayings and what they may have meant to a follower of one who was the twin of Christ. We read of the familiar concept of "knowing oneself" (GTh 3), although we are not told what it is about ourselves we are to know. Next we find becoming a "single one" (GTh 4),[7] or "making the male with the female into a single one . . . neither male nor female" and "making the two one" (GTh 22), and of being a "solitary one"

(GTh 49). Later we read of the "bridal chamber" (GTh 75) and of our "images" (GTh 84), and, again with no explanation at all, of "making Mary male" (GTh 114). None of these phrases and concepts are common in the New Testament or the associated literature that was deemed "orthodox" by the later Church. Some of these ideas seem completely absent and foreign.

Taken together, however, these ideas form a recognizable way of being Christian that had its beginnings in the first century, but flowered especially in the second Christian century and later. They were most at home outside of the New Testament in the Thomas tradition, a denomination of early Christianity found especially in Syria. These ideas had profound influence on the development of Christian spirituality, Christian Gnosticism, asceticism, and eventual monasticism.

One important metaphor, one way to understand these ideas is in the incipit: the relationship between the Living Jesus and Didymos Judas Thomas, between Jesus and his twin brother. According to Layton,

> This relationship provided a profound theological model for reciprocal relationship between the individual Christian and the inner divine light or "living Jesus": to know oneself was to know one's divine double and thence to know god.[8]

To know oneself according to the Delphic oracle was to know one's limits, to know that all are subject to fate determined by the gods, to know that one is mortal. In contrast, to know oneself in the Thomas community was to know that one is immortal, that one is superior to fate and limited only by one's drunken blindness to one's actual divine origin and destiny.[9] In one of the most famous statements of this type of self-knowledge, of the knowledge that saves the initiate, Clement of Alexandria quotes the Christian gnostic teacher Theodotus:

> Fate, they say, is true until baptism. But after this, the astrologers no longer speak the truth. For it is not the washing alone that sets one free, but also knowledge [*gnosis*]: who we were; what we have become; where we were, or where we were thrown; where we hasten, from what we are redeemed; what is birth, what is rebirth. (Clement of Alexandria, *Excerpta ex Theodoto* 78)

Before initiation into the mysteries of the faith, according to Theodotus, all human beings are subject to the fate that is written in the stars. At baptism, the individual is set free by the special knowledge of one's origin, present circumstances, and future destiny.

This excerpt describes what has been often termed "the Journey of the Soul." The human being is viewed as a duality of a material body that contains a spiritual soul. The soul originated in the divine, became incarnate in the body on the earth, and at death will separate from the body and return to its divine origin. What is described in the passage just quoted was the viewpoint of many enlightened souls in the ancient world. Thomas Christianity melded that viewpoint with further ideas drawn from biblical and Jewish sources.

The Image

A number of cultures thought that there was first a pattern in heaven for everything that was made on earth. The gods designed the plans, and from the plans the world as we know it came to be. Plato, for example, imagines that the Craftsman who created the universe was working from predesigned plans (Plato, *Timaeus* 28c). Moses is shown the heavenly plans of the Tabernacle so that he might know how to construct the shrine on earth (Ex 25:40; cf. Heb 8:5). In rabbinic tradition, this idea could extend even to the individual. In a discussion of the biblical passage about Jacob's ladder on which angels are ascending and descending between heaven and earth (Gen 28:12), the conclusion of the discussion reads: The angels "ascended and saw [Jacob's] image; and they descended and saw him asleep" (*Bereshith Rabbah* 68.12). Likewise in the Thomas community: each person is made from a pattern. So we read:

> When you see your likeness, you rejoice. But when you see your images that came into existence before you, (that) neither die nor are manifested, how much will you bear! (GTh 84)

There are two stages of action in view here. The first is to look at oneself perhaps in a mirror and be pleased at seeing one's likeness. The second is somehow to see the heavenly image from which one was patterned at birth and be overwhelmed by the vision.

The idea that all things are made after patterns became a Christian mode of thinking about God and Christ and the individual person. The goal of the spiritual life, in fact, was to join in the perfection of the pattern, to rejoin one's image and again become one with the ideal form that God had originally planned for each person. God is in a sense the pattern of all else. To bring all things into being, God emanated an image through which and according to which all things are made. That image is Christ, the "image of the invisible God, the first-born of all creation, for in him all things were created" (Col 1:15–16). So Christ is the image of God, and we are the image of Christ. We are destined to return to our image, the very image of God, "that God may be all in all" (1 Cor 15:28).

This goes all the way back to Adam and Eve. Adam was created in the image of God as an earthly copy of heavenly reality. So the first human image of God was of the earth, "the first Adam"; the heavenly image of God is Christ, "the last Adam." There are two kinds of humans: the earthy after the pattern of Adam, and the heavenly after the pattern of Christ. "The first (type of) human is of the earth, earthy; the second (type of) human is from heaven." We incarnated humans are copies in our bodies of the original earthy copy, Adam. But we have a higher destiny available to us in our heavenly souls. "Just as we have borne the image of the earthy, so shall we bear the image of the heavenly" (1 Cor 15:45–49). Those who are chosen are destined "to be conformed to the image of [God's] Son" (Rom 8:29).

But what is that image? Here the Thomas tradition made a surprising turn, assimilating and building on ideas found in Jewish interpretations of the biblical story of Adam and Eve.

There are in fact two stories of the creation of Adam and Eve in the book of Genesis. In the first God created Adam "in the image of God, . . . male and female he created them" (Gen 1:27). Later the same event is described:

> When God created Adam, he made him in the likeness of God. Male and female he created them, and he blessed then and named them "Adam." (Gen 5:1–2)

No mention of Eve per se is made, only the curious "male and female he created them . . . and named them Adam." In the second creation story, God made Adam sleep, took one of his ribs, and made Eve from it (Gen. 2:21–2). This was interpreted as a two-stage creation: a spiritual Adam was created as an androgyne, "male and female."[10] Later he was divided into two persons, Adam and Eve, of opposite genders.

The Apocryphon of John describes the first meeting of Adam and Eve as follows: "Adam saw the woman beside him. . . . And he recognized his counter-image" (II 23.10). This text is preserved in four Coptic manuscripts.[11] In two of the four manuscripts, the words translated as "counter-image" are the transliterated Greek words *ousia* and *synousia*, "essence" and "fellow-essence." The other two translate the Greek with the Coptic word meaning "image, likeness." Eve is soon after called his "consort, companion." The first two manuscripts here have the transliterated Greek word *synzygos*[12] in the Coptic text, likely preserving the original Greek text (23.18). In the other two manuscripts *synzygos* is translated by the Coptic word *shber*. This is the Coptic term that Jesus uses to describe Thomas in the Book of Thomas: "You are my twin and true companion" ("companion" = *shber*, NHC II.7.138.8). One may conjecture that the original Greek of this sentence in the Book of Thomas read: "You are my *didymos* and my true *synzygos*." *Synzygos* is also the term used by Mani to describe his "companion" and heavenly counterpart in the Cologne Mani Codex (often translated as "Twin": 18.15; 23.5; 32.8; 69.15 *et al.*), whom he also calls his "mirror-image" (*katoptron* 17.14–15).[13]

Several important observations may be drawn from this material. Human beings are created according to a pattern or image that still exists in heaven. Individuals may have individual images, as in GTh 84, or a single image may stand for all individuals, as in the biblical view of Adam and later Christ as patterns for all humans. A human is a replica in flesh of the heavenly image. Thus we are able to understand that Jesus and Thomas are twins, Jesus the heavenly Thomas and Thomas the earthly Jesus. In like manner one would naturally understand Jacob sleeping on the ground while his image is visible to the angels in heaven. In the case of Mani, his *synzygos* actually visits him and grants him divine guidance and revelation.

The single image for the entire human race, however, presents another possibility. If Adam or Jesus is the image for everyone, then the single male image has to work for people of both genders. The counter-image of Adam in the garden is Eve his female *synzygos*. The task for Adam is somehow to reincorporate Eve back into himself so that "the two may become one" and Adam may be as God had first created him, "male and female" united. The separation was cataclysmic and reintegration essential. We learn from the Gospel of Philip that:

When Eve was still in Adam death did not exist. When she was separated from him death came into being. If he enters again and attains his former self, death will be no more. (NHC II,3.68.24–26)[14]

Death is a consequence of the separation of the original androgyne into two beings, not the result of eating an apple.

The Genesis text emphasizes the bodily union of man and wife in the marriage relationship: "the man shall leave his father and mother and cleave to his wife, and the two shall become one flesh" (Gen 2:24). For those in the Thomas tradition, the clause "the two shall become one" is lifted from this text and elevated to the spiritual plane, to describe spiritual union: "the two shall become one" in spirit. So in the Gospel of Thomas, the goal is to "make the two one."

Paul describes a similar contrast of fleshly union and spiritual union in a rebuke of some libertines in Corinth who are sleeping with prostitutes. He writes:

Do you not know that whoever is united to a prostitute becomes one body with her? For it is said, "The two shall be one flesh." But anyone united to the Lord becomes one spirit with him. (1 Cor 6:16–17)

Here Paul uses the same text from Genesis, transferring the image of human marriage and human sexuality to the realm of the spirit. But for Paul, one spirit with the Lord means much more than it seems on the surface.

In Galatians 3:28 we find a version of an early Christian saying that was current in the early Church and inherited by Paul. It reads:

There is no longer Jew or Greek, there is no longer slave or free, there is no longer male and female; for all of you are one in Christ Jesus.

Here union in Christ eliminates distinctions based on the body entirely, an idea that led to some notable social innovations among Christian communities. Most remarkable is the removal of the gender distinctions of Genesis: the saying actually quotes the LXX of Genesis 1:27 and 5:2, "male and female," returning the initiate to the unity that existed before the division of the original human pair.

Versions of this saying are found in three other sources outside the canon.[15] From early in the second century, 2 Clement preserves a very similar saying.[16] Asked when the kingdom would come, the Lord replied:

When the two are one and the outside as the inside, and the male with the female neither male nor female. When you have done these things the kingdom of my Father will come. (2 Clement 12.2)

Clement of Alexandria quotes a passage from the Gospel of the Egyptians:

When Salome asked when the events about which she asked would take place, the Lord said: ". . . when the two are one and the male with the female are neither male nor female." (Clement of Alexandria, *Strom.* 3.13.92)

These two texts help us understand the difficult saying in Gospel of Thomas 22:

When you make the two one, and when you make the inner as the outer and the outer as the inner and the above as the below, and when you make the male and the female into a single one, so that the male will not be male and the female (not) be female, when you make eyes in the place of an eye, and a hand in the place of a hand, and a foot in the place of a foot, (and) an image in the place of an image, then you will enter [the Kingdom].

The four texts taken together demonstrate a rather widespread understanding among Christians of an essential unity to be attained by spiritual unity with the original image of God. That image was Christ, and unity with Christ repaired the ruptures of racial division, social class, and gender. Here is the essential meaning of the idea that Thomas was the twin of Jesus. Jesus was the image not only of Thomas himself, but of all who were able to "make the two one."

We may now be able to understand the rather enigmatic collection of ideas that are presented by the Gospel of Thomas. The "images" of GTh 84 are the models according to which we were created. Becoming a "single one" (GTh 4), "making the two one" (GTh 22), and being a "solitary one" (GTh 49) are clearly based in the return to the unity of the original Adam. This also helps one understand "making Mary male" (GTh 114). Spiritual union with Christ eliminates the male-female distinction and brings Mary back to the original androgynous Adam, male in name and appearance.[17]

The Bridal Chamber: *Askesis* and Unification

How is one to accomplish this spiritual rejoining of image with image? The ritual means by which "the two became one" was conceived of as a bridal chamber. Gospel of Thomas 75 tells us: "Many are standing at the door, but the solitary are the ones who will [enter] the bridal chamber." Like so many things in the Gospel of Thomas, what the "bridal chamber" signifies is not explained. Yet we are able to discern much about this idea by comparison with the other Thomas documents and related literature.

The solitary enter the bridal chamber. The word "solitary" in GTh 75 is a translation of the Greek word *monachos*, which in Classical Greek meant "individual, only, solitary" and in later times became the term used to designate the "monk" of asceticism and monasticism. Chief among the ascetic practices of the *monachos* in the Thomas tradition is sexual abstinence.

Polemic against the body and denigration of the fleshly envelope of the soul is an important feature of the Gospel of Thomas. For example, Jesus declares: "I marvel at how this great wealth has made its home in this poverty" (GTh 29). The context is a contrast of flesh and spirit, that it is a marvel that these two dwell together at all in the "home" of the human being. The marvelous wealth of the spirit dwells in the poverty that is the flesh. This helps us understand the enigmatic ending of GTh 3:

> If you know yourselves, then you will be known and you will know that you are the children of the Living Father. But if you do not know yourselves, then you are in poverty and you are poverty.

If one does not know one's divine origin and destiny, then not only does one's soul dwell in the poverty of the body, but one's soul itself is empty of its value and shares that poverty. So, "woe to the soul that depends upon the flesh" (GTh 112).

The Book of Thomas may be said to be almost entirely devoted to the promotion of celibacy and the denigration of the body and those who "indulge" its normal appetite for sexuality.[18] Thomas questions Jesus directly concerning those who defend themselves and blame their "iniquity," their sexuality, on the fact of their incarnation. He asks:

> What teaching should we say to these pitiable mortals who say, "We came to do good, not for a curse . . . If we had not been begotten in the flesh, we would not have known iniquity." (141.22–25)

Jesus disregards their self-defense and tells Thomas: "Do not consider them as humans, but count them as beasts" (141.26). He later continues his condemnation, addressing them directly:

> Woe to you who love intercourse with women, and polluted association with them! And woe to you in the grip of the powers of your body, for those will afflict you! Woe to you in the grip of the workings of evil demons! (BTh 144.8–14)

The Acts of Thomas brings together the themes of self-knowledge, the divine destiny of the soul, ascetic practice, the denigration of sexuality, and the bridal chamber.[19] In the opening scenes, Jesus sends his apostle Thomas to India to preach the word there. On the way the apostle arrives at the city of Andrapolis on the eve of the wedding of the king's daughter. The king asks Thomas, "Pray for my daughter. For she is my only child, and today I give her in marriage." Thomas is led into the bridal chamber of the young couple, makes a beautiful prayer, asking Jesus "to do for them the things that help and are useful and profitable," and then departs (ATh 9–10).[20]

As the groom lifts the veil of the bridal chamber to join his new bride, he finds Jesus sitting and conversing with her. Jesus instructs them to "abandon this filthy intercourse . . . waiting to receive that incorruptible and true marriage, . . . entering into that bridal chamber which is full of immortality and light." They "believed the Lord and gave themselves entirely to him, and refrained from the filthy passion" (ATh 12–13).

On the following morning, when met by her father, the bride declares: "I have set at naught this man and this marriage which passes away . . . because I am bound in another marriage. I have had no intercourse with a short-lived husband . . . because I am yoked with the true man" (ATh 14). The groom in turn responds with a prayer:

> I thank you Lord, who has removed me from corruption and sown in me life . . . and implanted in me sober health; . . . you united me with yourself; . . . you showed me to seek myself and to recognize who I was and who and how I now am, that I may become what I once was. (ATh 15)

Here the two young people decide to remain celibate rather than enter into normal human marriage. They each unite in a spiritual and eternal union with Jesus in the bridal chamber. The bride is "yoked with" the true man, a verb from the same root and with exactly the same meaning as the term *syzygos*, literally "yoked with." So Jesus is her *syzygos*, just as is Thomas. The groom not only is united with Jesus, but learns in the process to know himself, that is, to know his divine origin and destiny.

Conclusion

Both Jewish and Greek tradition, among other cultures, included the understanding that God had provided a heavenly plan from which all things came into being. That plan was the pattern behind the entire universe for Plato, the tabernacle in the desert for Moses, or the patriarch Jacob for the Rabbis; each had its prior heavenly model. For the Thomas Christians, every individual had been patterned after an individual heavenly image. The idea that Jesus had a twin brother Thomas expressed just this spiritual reality. The image, the twin according to which we all were created, proved that each of us was in the divine plan from the beginning, that each had a divine origin, and that each had the potential for a divine destiny.

Notes

1 See the interesting survey of double names by Gregory H. R. Horsley, "Names, Double," in *The Anchor Bible Dictionary*, ed. David Noel Friedman (New York: Doubleday, 1992), 4.1011–17.

2 Antoine Guillaumont, et al., *The Gospel according to Thomas: Coptic Text Established and Translated* (New York: Harper and Row, 1959). All translation of The Gospel of Thomas are taken from this edition, with adjustments.

3 John D. Turner, *The Book of Thomas the Contender*, SBL Dissertation Series 23 (Missoula: Scholars Press, 1975). All quotations of The Book of Thomas are taken from this edition, with adjustments.

4 Cf. John J. Gunther, "The Meaning and Origin of the Name 'Judas Thomas,'" *Muséon* 93 (1980): 118–19.

5 On the theme of Thomas as twin, see Raymond Kunztmann, "Le symbolisme des jumeaux au Proche-Orient ancien. Naissance, fonction et évolution d'un symbole," *Beauchesne Religions 12* (Paris: Beauchesne, 1983), 164–82.

6   On the relationships among the three Thomas texts, see John D. Turner, "A New Link in the Syrian Judas Thomas Tradition," in *Essays on the Nag Hammadi Texts in Honor of Alexander Böhlig*, Nag Hammadi Studies 3, ed. Martin Krause (Leiden: E. J. Brill, 1972), 109–19; and Paul-Hubert Poirer, "*Évangile de Thomas*, Actes de Thomas, Livre de Thomas: Une tradition et ses tranformations," *Apocrypha* 7 (1996): 9–26.

7   Albertus F. J. Klijn, "The 'Single One' in the Gospel of Thomas," *Journal of Biblical Literature* 81 (1962): 271–8.

8   Bentley Layton, *The Gnostic Scriptures* (Garden City, NY: Doubleday, 1987), 359.

9   On self-knowledge in the Thomas tradition, see Patrick J. Hartin, "The Search for the True Self in the Gospel of Thomas, the Book of Thomas, and the Hymn of the Pearl," *Hervormde Teologiese Studies* 55 (1999): 1001–21; Raymond Kuntzmann, *Le livre de Thomas (NH II,7)* (Quebec, Canada: Laval, 1986), 59–61.

10 Cf. Wayne A. Meeks, "The Image of the Androgyne: Some Uses of a Symbol in Earliest Christianity," *History of Religions* 13 (1973–4): 165–208.

11 Michael Waldstein and Frederik Wisse, eds., *The Apocryphon of John: Synopsis of Nag Hammadi Codices II,1; III,1; and IV,1 with BG 8502,2* (Leiden, New York and Cologne: E.J. Brill, 1995), 132–3.

12 *Synzygos* or *syzygos* is a compound of two words: *syn* meaning "with, together," and *zygos* meaning "yoke" (of a plough or carriage). The word means "yoked together, paired, united," and was a normal word for "comrade, companion, spouse." The "n" of *syn* is normally assimilated in writing and pronunciation to the following "*z*" but was sometimes still written out in full, as here.

13 Ron Cameron and Arthur J. Dewey, eds. and trans., *The Cologne Mani Codex: Concerning the Origins of His Body*, Texts and Translations 15, Society of Biblical Literature (Missoula: Scholars Press, 1979).

14 Wesley W. Isenberg, trans., "The Gospel According to Philip," in *Nag Hammadi Codex II, 2–7*, ed. Bentley Layton (Leiden: E. J. Brill, 1989), 1.179.

15 The texts of 2 Clement and the Gospel of the Egyptians are quoted from Dennis Ronald MacDonald, *There is No Male and Female: The Fate of a Dominical Saying in Paul and Gnosticism*, Harvard Dissertations in Religion 20 (Philadelphia: Fortress Press, 1987), 18.

16 Cf. Tjitze Baarda, "2 Clement 12 and the Sayings of Jesus," in *Logia: Les paroles de Jésus – The Sayings of Jesus*, ed. Joel Delobel (Leuven: Leuven University Press, 1982): 529–56; Terrance Callan, "The Saying of Jesus in Gos. Thom. 22 /2 Clem. 12 /Gos. Eg. 5," *Journal of Roman Studies* 16 (1990): 46–64.

17 Cf. Jorunn Jacobsen Buckley, "An Interpretation of Logion 114 in *the Gospel of Thomas*," *Novum Testamentum* 27 (1985): 245–72; Marvin Meyer, "Making Mary Male: The Categories 'Male' and 'Female' in the Gospel of Thomas," *New Testament Studies* 31 (1985): 554–70.

18 "Hans-Martin Schenke, "Radikale sexuelle Enthaltsamkeit als hellenistisch-jüdisches Vollkommenheitsideal im Thomas-Buch (NHC II,7)," in *La Tradizione dell'Enkrateia*, ed. Ugo Bianchi (Roma: Edizione dell' Ateneo, 1985), 263–91.

19 Yves Tissot, "L'encratisme des Actes de Thomas," *Aufstieg und Niedergang der Romischen Welt* 25, no. 6: 4415–30.

20 "The Acts of Thomas," 2.425–531, ed. and trans. Gunther Bornkamm, in *New Testament Apocrypha*, ed. Edgar Hennecke and Wilhelm Schneemelcher, trans. Robert McLachlan Wilson (Philadelphia: Westminster Press, 1963), 343–5.

Bibliography

Baarda, Tjitze. "2 Clement 12 and the Sayings of Jesus." In *Logia: Les paroles de Jésus— The Sayings of Jesus*, edited by Joel Delobel, 529–56. Leuven: Leuven University Press, 1982.

Bornkamm, Gunther, ed. and trans. "The Acts of Thomas." In *New Testament Apocrypha*, edited by Edgar Hennecke and Wilhelm Schneemelcher, translated by Robert McLachlan (R. McL.) Wilson, 2.425–531. Philadelphia: Westminster Press, 1963.

Buckley, Jorunn Jacobsen. "An Interpretation of Logion 114 in *the Gospel of Thomas*." *Novum Testamentum* 27 (1985): 245–72.

Callan, Terrance. "The Saying of Jesus in Gos. Thom. 22 /2 Clem. 12 / Gos. Eg. 5." *Journal of Roman Studies* 16 (1990): 46–64.

Cameron, Ron, and Arthur J. Dewey, eds. and trans. *The Cologne Mani Codex: Concerning the Origins of His Body*. Texts and Translations 15, Society of Biblical Literature. Missoula: Scholars Press, 1979.

Guillaumont, Antoine, et al. *The Gospel According to Thomas: Coptic Text Established and Translated*. New York: Harper and Row, 1959.

Gunther, John J. "The Meaning and Origin of the Name 'Judas Thomas.'" *Muséon* 93 (1980): 118–19.

Horsley, Gregory H. R. "Names, Double." In *The Anchor Bible Dictionary*, edited by David Noel Friedman, 4.1011–17. New York: Doubleday, 1992.

Isenberg, Wesley W., trans. "The Gospel According to Philip." In *Nag Hammadi Codex II*, edited by Bentley Layton, 2–7. Leiden: E.J. Brill, 1989.

Klijn, Albertus F. J. "The 'Single One' in the Gospel of Thomas." *Journal of Biblical Literature* 81 (1962): 271–8.

Kunztmann, Raymond. "Le symbolisme des jumeaux au Proche-Orient Ancient. Naissance, fonction et évolution d'un symbole." In *Beauchesne Religions 12*, 164–82. Paris: Beauchesne, 1983.

Layton, Bentley. *The Gnostic Scriptures*. Garden City, NY: Doubleday, 1987.

MacDonald, Dennis Ronald. *There is No Male and Female: The Fate of a Dominical Saying in Paul and Gnosticism*. Harvard Dissertations in Religion 20. Philadelphia: Fortress Press, 1987.

Meeks, Wayne A. "The Image of the Androgyne: Some Uses of a Symbol in Earliest Christianity." *History of Religions* 13 (1973–4): 165–208.

Meyer, Marvin. "Making Mary Male: The Categories 'Male' and 'Female' in the Gospel of Thomas." *New Testament Studies* 31(1985): 554–70.

Poirer, Paul Hubert. "*Évangile de Thomas*, Actes de Thomas, Livre de Thomas: Une Tradition et ses Tranformations." *Apocrypha* 7 (1996): 9–26.

Schenke, Hans-Martin. "Radikale Sexuelle Enthaltsamkeit als hellenistisch-jüdisches Vollkommenheitsideal im Thomas-Buch (NHC II,7)." In *La Tradizione dell' Enkrateia*, edited by Ugo Bianchi, 263–91. Roma: Edizione dell' Ateneo, 1985.

Tissot, Yves. "L'encratisme des Actes de Thomas." In *Aufstieg und Niedergang der Romischen Welt Band 25/6. Teilband Religion (Vorkonstantinisches Christentum: Leben und Umwelt Jesu; Neues Testament; Kanonische Schriften und Apokryphen [Schluss])*, edited by Wolfgang Haase, 4415–30. Berlin and Boston: De Gruyter, 2016.

Turner, John D. "A New Link in the Syrian Judas Thomas Tradition." In *Essays on the Nag Hammadi Texts in Honor of Alexander Böhlig*. Nag Hammadi Studies 3, edited by Martin Krause, 109–19. Leiden: E. J. Brill, 1972.

Turner, John D. *The Book of Thomas the Contender*. SBL Dissertation Series 23. Missoula: Scholars Press, 1975.

Waldstein, Michael, and Frederik Wisse, eds. *The Apocryphon of John: Synopsis of Nag Hammadi Codices II,1; III,1; and IV,1 with BG 8502,2*. Leiden, New York and Cologne: E. J. Brill, 1995.

15

The Divine Double in Late Antiquity[1]

♊

Charles M. Stang

The second and third centuries CE witnessed the sudden appearance of a peculiar figure in the imagination of the Eastern Mediterranean: the divine double. We do not know the exact origin of this figure, but like ink that bleeds through the page, we find him seeping through the literature of Late Antiquity in all its diversity. Through an array of ancient sources—Christian and Manichaean, philosophical and religious, surviving often in fragments and in several languages—runs this single thread: the notion that each individual has a divine twin, counterpart, or alter ego whom he or she may actually meet. This encounter is imagined and narrated very differently in the various sources, but in all cases it marks the beginning of self-knowledge: not the knowledge of the self one thought one was (because, after all, one thought one was *one*self), but the knowledge of a new and more divine self, for which these ancient sources struggle to give an adequate name and description.

In this chapter I will introduce the divine double by focusing on representative texts from three traditions of Late Antiquity: (1) early Christianity, which in the second and third centuries witnessed a vast diversity of thought and practice before the narrowing work of an emerging orthodoxy gained momentum (and imperial support) in the fourth and fifth centuries; (2) Manichaeism, a wildly successful missionary religion that emerged in southern Mesopotamia and spread westward to the Mediterranean and eastward past the Iranian plateau within a century of its founder's death; (3) Neoplatonism, a name given to the renaissance of Platonism associated with the third-century philosopher Plotinus. Our first text, the *Gospel of Thomas*, is a collection of Jesus' sayings attributed to the apostle Judas Thomas "the twin." Our second is the *Cologne Mani Codex*, a fifth-century anthology that narrates how Mani, the "apostle of light," was awakened to his mission by the arrival of his heavenly twin-companion. Our third and final text is Plotinus's *Enneads*, which describes how we are each a "pair," a doubled intellect, one half residing in the intelligible realm of the Forms and the other half descending into a body. I will conclude by considering the interest of the scholar Henry Corbin in this figure, then reflect briefly on the significance of the history of thought presented in the chapter for the theme of twinship.

The Gospel of Thomas

We have long known that there was circulating in Egypt, at least as early as the third century, a gospel attributed not to one of the four canonical evangelists—Matthew, Mark, Luke, and John—but to another apostle, Thomas. A number of early Christian writers—whom we now, retrospectively, label as more or less "orthodox"—took an active interest in it. The authors interested in the *Gospel of Thomas* were motivated less by intellectual curiosity and more by an anxiety that this gospel, and others like it, posed a threat to a proper (that is to say, their own) understanding and practice of Christianity. Apart from a stray quotation preserved in another, extant text, however, this gospel was lost to us. Only in the late nineteenth and early twentieth centuries did fragmentary evidence for the *Gospel of Thomas* begin to emerge; and only in the mid-twentieth century, with the discovery of the Nag Hammadi library in Egypt, did we have a complete version of this gospel, albeit in Coptic translation from the original Greek.[2] I use "gospel" because that is what the text calls itself. But the *Gospel of Thomas* differs considerably from the four canonical gospels, first and foremost in that it is a collection of sayings of Jesus and *not* (as the canonical gospels are) a narrative of his life, ministry, death, and resurrection. The *Gospel of Thomas* does not call Jesus by the title *christos*, "anointed" (in Hebrew, messiah). Strictly speaking, then, the text does not have a "Christology." Rather, it is "the living Jesus" who speaks these "secret sayings," and only to one of his apostles, Judas Thomas the Twin, who is said to have written them down.

Who is this apostle, Judas Thomas the Twin? All three of the synoptic gospels (Matthew, Mark, and Luke) provide lists of "the twelve," those disciples closest to Jesus who were "sent out (*apostellēi*) to preach" (Mark 3:14) and therefore called "apostles." All three lists include someone named Thomas (Math 10:3, Mark 3:18, Luke 6:15), although nothing more is said of him. The name "Thomas" is a Hellenized form of the Aramaic word *tāwmā*, meaning "twin." It is not so much a name as an epithet in Aramaic, but none of the synoptic gospels pauses to explain why the apostle bears this particular epithet. Only in the Fourth Gospel (John's), do we learn anything more. When he is introduced in 11:16, this Thomas is "called the Twin (*didymos*)." We are told the same in 20:24 and 21:2, but not *why* this apostle is called "the Twin" or whose twin he is supposed to be. To a reader familiar with Aramaic and Greek, these verses would sound as if the disciple were being called "Twin Twin."[3] Although Jesus gave nicknames to others among the twelve (Mark 3:16–17: "Simon, whom he surnamed Peter; James the son of Zebedee and John the brother of James, whom he surnamed Boanerges, that is, sons of thunder"), the apostle Thomas is alone in having *only* an epithet and no proper name. Given that his epithet is "twin," however, it is no surprise that some early Christians looked to Jesus' own family for an explanation. In Mark 6:3, members of the synagogue, upon hearing Jesus teach, ask each other incredulously, "Is not this the carpenter, the son of Mary and brother of James and Joses and Judas and Simon, and are not his sisters here with us?" A similar list of Jesus' brothers is found in Matthew 13:55, with Judas listed fourth rather than third. Both lists names James first, suggesting that he is, after Jesus, the eldest. This is reflected in the traditions around James "the brother of our lord" (Gal 1:19), who is remembered as a leader in the early community of Jesus' followers in Jerusalem. Judas, by contrast, would appear to be a younger brother. Strange, then, that it is Judas who was regarded, at least by some early Christians, as the twin brother of Jesus, and so identified with the apostle Thomas the Twin.[4]

Another distinguishing feature of the *Gospel of Thomas* is what I call its *theology of twinning*—perhaps our very earliest witness to a Christian tradition of the divine double. Many of the sayings speak of the relationship of the one and the two, and what it means to become a "solitary" or "a single one." I will attempt to isolate this thread and reconstruct the gospel's distinctive account of the divine double, its theology of the twin.

The first four sayings of the *Gospel of Thomas* serve as a sort of interpretive key for the others, that these four sayings begin to teach the reader how to read, that is, how to interpret its secret sayings. They frame our inquiry into its theology of the twin and the question of the one and the two. The most important saying of the *Gospel of Thomas* is the first: "And [Jesus] said, 'Whoever finds the interpretation of these sayings will not experience death.'" We might not know yet what exactly it means not to experience death, but we do know that the means to this end is interpretation. We are called to interpret these sayings—secret sayings—suggesting that the practice consists in finding the esoteric meaning of Jesus' words. From the start, then, this gospel announces to its reader both the proper end or goal of reading this gospel—not experiencing death—and the means to achieve that end: interpretation, that is, reading and pondering the sayings of the living Jesus.

The second saying expands on the first, offering a litany of stages along the interpretive path: (§2) "Jesus said, 'Let him who seeks continue until he finds. When he finds, he will become troubled. When he becomes troubled, he will be astonished, and he will rule over the all.'" Interpretation culminates in our "rul[ing] over the all"—we will come to learn more about both this reign and "the all" as we move through these sayings. This reign, however, is not placid or static: the interpreter will be "troubled" and "astonished." The Greek fragment P. Oxy. 654 concludes with an additional phrase, "And [once having ruled], he will attain rest." Even this rest (*anapausis*) is humming with a kind of energy, as we learn in a much later saying where Jesus tells his disciples that "the sign of your father in you . . . is movement and repose" (§50).

So far, the end on offer—not experiencing death, ruling over the all, an energetic rest—remains somewhat mysterious, drawing the reader in. But already the fact that these sayings are attributed to "the living Jesus" suggests that our not experiencing death is somehow equivalent to our becoming like this living Jesus, that is, to our being alive in whatever distinctive way he is. We should not immediately think that this refers to some resurrection following death, because nothing in this gospel indicates that "the living Jesus" is a resurrected Jesus. Instead, this living Jesus is he who lives and speaks with his disciples, and who offers some life-giving teaching.

The link between "living" and "ruling" carries the reader directly into the third saying:

> (§3) Jesus said, "If those who lead you say to you, 'See, the kingdom is in the sky,' then the birds of the sky will precede you. If they say, 'It is in the sea,' then the fish will precede you. Rather, the kingdom is inside you, and it is outside of you.

When you come to know yourselves, then you will become known, and you will realize that it is you who are the sons of the living father. But if you do not know yourselves, you dwell in poverty and it is you who are that poverty."

The link is clear: "he will rule" (§2)—literally "he will become king"—and the "kingdom" (§3) have the same root. Notice that while §2 encourages seeking, §3 warns against "those who lead"; thus the reader is encouraged to pursue the interpretive enterprise apart from leading authorities. This suggests in turn that "ruling over the all" and finding the "kingdom" happen only to those who refuse to subject themselves to misled or misleading leaders. Rather than look for the kingdom in the sky or the sea, Jesus says that "it is inside you, and it is outside you." This is first of many opposed pairs that will confront the reader of the *Gospel of Thomas*. Already it suggests that finding the kingdom by way of interpretation will have something to do with opposed pairs, with wrestling with and overcoming perceived contraries such as inside and outside (and, later, the one and the two).

This suggestion is strengthened by what immediately follows: "When you come to know yourselves, then you will become known." First of all, this remark suggests that finding the kingdom will consist in simultaneously knowing oneself and having oneself known, in overcoming the disjunction between what we might call an interior and an exterior perspective on oneself.[5] Second, the fact that interpretation of written sayings yields self-knowledge suggests an analogy between self and text. In other words, it suggests that the reading and interpretation is not strictly about these secret sayings, but also is about our so-to-speak secret selves—that we, like these sayings, are in need of reading and interpretation. Thus, by the third saying, an astute reader is prompted to begin questioning any sharp distinction between himself and the text in his hands, and as a result any sharp distinction between what we might call "anthropology" and "textuality."

The fourth saying narrows our gaze and focuses our attention on perceived contraries and their overcoming: (§4) "Jesus said, 'The man old in days will not hesitate to ask a small child seven days old about the place of life, and he will live. For many who are first will become last, and they will become one and the same.'" For many scholars, what catches their eye in §4 is a detail about the small child, namely, that he is seven days old. They wonder about the secret significance of this detail. But for an uninitiated reader the most significant feature of this saying is surely the inversion, namely, that an old man is asking a small child about "the place of life." This phrase recalls the only other "place" to which the reader has yet been introduced, namely the "kingdom" (§3)—where we will live, rule over the all, and realize that we are sons of the living father. In other words, the old man asks the small child about the kingdom. The unsettling image of an old man asking an infant about matters of life and death sets up the next line, "for many who are first will become last." This suggests another inversion: the old man and the small child will exchange places.[6] The final line transforms the force of the saying—"and they will become one and the same." This suggests not just the exchange of the two positions, an exchange that would keep each distinct and intact, but the combination of the two into "one and the same" (*oua ouōt*).

With this phrase—"one and the same" in Coptic (*oua ouōt*), which translates "a single one" in Greek (*heis monos*)—we land upon a fundamental tension in the gospel. On the one hand, there is a clear endorsement of unity, of our becoming one—though in exactly what sense "one" requires further investigation. On the other hand, there is a clear understanding that unity is forged from duality, and that duality that does not disappear in the unity, that the one preserves the two. In order to follow the thread of the gospel's theology of the twin and its meditation on the one and the two, we will have to jump from saying to saying, and often double back.

Perhaps the best place to begin is §11:

> Jesus said, "This heaven will pass away, and the one above it will pass away. The dead are not alive, and the living will not die. In the days when you consumed what is dead, you made it what is alive. When you come to dwell in the light, what will you do? On the day when you were one you became two. But when you become two, what will you do?"

In the interests of keeping on the trail of the one and the two, we will have to skip over the first half of this saying and what it has to teach the reader about life, death, resurrection, and the passing away of the heavens. For our purposes, the crucial detail is the parallel between the two temporal clauses: "When you come to dwell in the light" and "when you become two." The parallel is confirmed by the repetition of the question "what will you do?" The parallel suggests that dwelling in the light is somehow the equivalent of becoming two. What would it mean if the day when you become two is the same as the day when you come to dwell in the light?

This is the first mention of light in the *Gospel of Thomas,* but a more robust discussion comes much later, in §77:

> Jesus said, "It is I who am the light which is above them all. It is I who am the all. From me did the all come forth, and unto me did the all extend. Split a piece of wood and I am there. Lift up the stone, and you will find me there."

We learn that it is Jesus who is the light in which we might come to dwell, and so become two (§11). He simultaneously *is* and is *above* "the all." This echoes §2, where the end on offer is "ruling over the all," suggesting again that the goal is to take up the position of Jesus *above* the all, ruling rather than being ruled. Jesus is figured here as the comprehending source of everything, a beacon of light that both is and exceeds that which "comes forth" from him and "extends" back to him. If we take the parallel in §11 seriously, then to dwell in the light, to stand in the place of Jesus, the comprehending source of all, is to become two.

If §77 figures the light as a transcendent, comprehending source, then §24 brings the light into the most immanent and intimate realm:

> (§24) His disciples said, "Show us the place where you are, since it is necessary for us to seek it." He said to them, "Whoever has ears, let him hear. There is light within a man of light, and he lights up the whole world. If he does not shine, he is darkness."

Here is that "place" again—the kingdom, the place of life. Just as in §3, the disciples seem to expect that the place "where you are" is some determinate place, *here* rather than *there*. But when asked where to seek him, Jesus does not answer directly, but tells his disciples that there is light "within a man of light." Of course this light is none other than Jesus himself: the transcendent, comprehending source of all is now said to be within us. And the disciples are directed to seek him by finding this interior light, and letting it shine. There could be no clearer restatement of §3: "the kingdom is inside of you, and it is outside of you."

More importantly, however, this is the key to understanding how dwelling in the light is equivalent to becoming two. The light within the man of light is Jesus the transcendent, comprehending source of all. When one finds this light, one realizes that one is not entirely oneself, not entirely *one*, but has *another*, namely, Jesus, already inside. This is the splitting, the doubling, the becoming two that marks the entry into the kingdom, the place of life, from which vantage point one rules over the all—not from a place of distance from the all, but from a place of intimacy within the all, paradoxically embedded in a world that issues forth from a source within you.

In §16 Jesus hints that his hearers will not be attuned to his (quite literally) divisive message:

(§16) Jesus said, "Men think, perhaps, that it is peace which I have come to cast upon the world. They do not know that it is dissension which I have come to cast upon the earth: fire, sword, war. For there will be five in a house: three will be against two, and two against three, the father against the son, and the son against the father. And they will stand solitary *(monachos)*."

Some scholars regard this saying as an especially early one, attesting to the historical Jesus' vibrant apocalyptic imagination. On this reading, Jesus' mention of fire, sword, and war is equivalent to his issuing a threat (or promise) of trial and tribulation prior to the advent of a new age. But this eschatological interpretation overlooks how this saying functions within the *Gospel of Thomas*, where fire, sword, and even war carry a very different set of connotations. Consider fire, for example. At first §10 would seem to endorse the eschatological interpretation: "Jesus said, 'I have cast fire upon the world, and see, I am guarding it until it blazes'." But if we allow the *Gospel of Thomas* to tell us what it means by its own words, we come to see that far from being a threat of an eschatological burn, fire is another name for Jesus himself, the light that is above the all and yet in humans of light: "Jesus said, 'He who is near me is near the fire, and he who is far from me is far from the kingdom'" (§82). Simply put, fire = Jesus = kingdom. So when Jesus says in §10 that he is casting fire upon the world and fanning the flames, he is setting souls ablaze with the divine light that is already within them. Fire is not a purifying punishment, but a deifying reward.

Even though the sword may be an instrument of war, here at least it is more precisely an instrument of division, of cutting in two. Five will be divided, three against two and vice versa, father against son and vice versa. And so divided, they will all "stand as solitary ones" *(ᵉm-monachos)*. The Coptic translator has used a Greek word *monachos* here, meaning "solitary" or "single one."[7] It is the word that will come to be applied to Christian ascetics starting in the fourth century, namely, "monk."[8] It is not clear, however, what the *Gospel of Thomas* means by "solitary." It is best, I think, to leave it as Lambdin translates it, "solitary," because the reader is then free to ponder how someone who is "solitary" or "single" is also "one" or "two" (or both at once). §49 offers its own beatitude for the "solitary": "Blessed are the solitary *(monachos)* and elect, for you will find the kingdom. For you are from it, and to it you will return." We know from our discussion earlier, however, that to enter the kingdom—to "rule the all" as Jesus does—is first to recognize that one is not strictly speaking *one*, but one has *another*, namely, Jesus, inside and outside of one, just as the kingdom is both inside and outside. Jesus the transcendent light is also the intimate light, the fully interior divine double. And if this is what it means to be *monachos* or "solitary," then it is a strange kind of solitude, becoming solitary only with the recognition of one's inner double.

It is important to underscore, however, that the unity imagined here is not one that fully overcomes or annihilates duality. In other words, "when you make the two one *(snau oua)*," the resulting "one and the same" *(oua ouōt)* is a tense unity-in-duality, humming with possibility, much as the energetic rest that marks our rule in the kingdom: recall that "the sign of your father in you" is precisely "movement and repose." In §23 Jesus says, "I will choose you, one *(oua)* out of a thousand, and two *(snau)* out of ten thousand, and they shall stand as a single one *(oua ouōt)*." This phrase is not merely some "common expectation in apocalyptic literature," namely, "the eschatological selection of the few."[9] The phrase may function that way in other contexts, but here in the *Gospel of Thomas* the message is quite clear: Jesus will choose one *(oua)* and two *(snau)* and they—the one and the two—will be "one and the same" *(oua ouōt)*. The unity that is captured by the phrase *oua ouōt* is one that preserves the two.

This unity-in-duality is in fact the theme on which a short sequence of sayings (§§47–50) meditates. §47 begins with a wariness of duality: "It is impossible for a man to mount two *(snau)* horses or to stretch two *(s^ente)* bows. And it is impossible for a servant to serve two *(snau)* masters; otherwise, he will honor the one *(oua)* and treat the other one *(pkeoua)* contemptuously." This serves as a warning: a certain kind of duality can ruin you by rendering you divided. But the warning about duality leads to a vision of unity-in-duality. In the very next saying Jesus encourages us, "If two *(snau)* make peace with each other in this one house, they will say to the mountain, 'Move away,' and it will move away" (§48). Moving mountains would be familiar to the reader from §106, where Jesus says, "When you make the two one *(snau oua)*, you will become the sons of man, when you say, 'Mountain, move away,' it will move away." It is crucial to understand, then, that making the two one *(snau oua)* is the equivalent of "two *(snau)* mak[ing] peace with each other in this one *(ouōt)* house." The unity imagined here is one in which two "make peace with each other" and so become one, or more precisely, "one and the same" *(oua ouōt)*. The "solitary one" *(monachos)* or "one and the same" *(oua ouōt)* are the names given, not to celibates, but to those in whom the one and two coincide, or coexist in peace. They are from the kingdom, and to it they will return (§49). The meditation series concludes with the saying we have already discussed, but I will now quote in full:

(§50) Jesus said, "If they say to you, 'Where did you come from?,' say to them, 'We came from the light, the place where the light came into being on its own accord and established [itself] and became manifest through their image.' If they say to you, 'Is it you?,' say, 'We are its children, and we are the elect of the living father.' If they ask you, 'What is the sign of your father in you?,' say to them, 'It is movement and repose.'"

With this saying we return to some of the themes raised by the first four sayings of the gospel: Jesus the light, who rules over the all, whose "place" is the kingdom. The blessed, elect, solitary ones are those in whom the one and the two coincide, those in whom contraries like movement and rest can coincide.

The practice of interpreting the secret sayings of Jesus invites the astute reader into the play between the one and the two, but a play that takes place simultaneously on the page and in his or her own self. Thus, the practice of interpreting the gnomic sayings regarding the one and the two, the "single one" and the "one and the same," serves to transform the reader into what Henry Corbin calls a *unus-ambo,* a one-yet-two. The kingdom is the place of light, our whence and our whither, and the sign of paternity is the coincidence of movement and repose. We also know that Jesus is that light, both the transcendent source of the all and the intimate light illuminating us, the children of the living father. Thus Jesus, like the kingdom, is inside and outside of us. All this helps us get further clarity on what "the one and the two" mean. On the one hand, to make the one two is to realize that this light within oneself is Jesus, and thereby to realize that one is no longer strictly speaking *one*self, but somehow also two. On the other hand, to make the two one is to hold this duality together in peace, to be a one that is also two, a unity-in-duality, and so to bear the name "solitary" and "single one." The categories of the one and the two are not simply abstractions that the reader is supposed only to ponder, but instead refer precisely to the indwelling of Jesus in oneself (the one self becoming now two) and the self's negotiated identity as a unity containing but not annihilating that duality (the two becoming one). Interpreting these secret sayings not only discloses the truth of who we are, but realizes that truth in us. The gospel imagines its readers not only learning that Jesus is the light in them, but in fact awakening Jesus in them.

But what has any of this to do with the apostle Judas Thomas the twin (*tāwmā/didymos*)? How does the indwelling of Jesus that renders oneself a unity-in-duality relate to the apostle to whom Jesus spoke these secret sayings, the apostle who is said to be the very twin of Jesus? Are they distinct discourses, the meditation on the one and the two and the theology of twinning? To answer these questions, we will have to look closely at another handful of sayings.

(§13) Jesus said to his disciples, "Compare me to someone and tell me whom I am like."

Simon Peter said to him, "You are like a righteous angel."

Matthew said to him, "You are like a wise philosopher."

Thomas said to him, "Master, my mouth is wholly incapable of saying whom you are like."

Jesus will go on to praise Thomas for his confession of impotence and ineffability. Perhaps the key to understanding Thomas's confession is to be found in another saying: "Jesus said, 'I shall give you what no eye has seen and what no ear has heard and what no hand has touched and what has never occurred to the human mind'" (§17). What does Jesus give except his own light and life, the knowledge of our whence and whither (the kingdom) as children of light. This gift can be specified only by a series of negations of sight, hearing, touch, and thinking. If Jesus is the transcendent light—ruling the all, shining inside the children of light—it should come as no surprise that Thomas "is wholly incapable of saying whom [he] is like," for he is beyond any simile. In response to his confession, Jesus praises Thomas:

> (§13) Jesus said, "I am not your master. Because you have drunk, you have become intoxicated from the bubbling spring which I have measured out."
> And he took him and withdrew and told him three things. When Thomas returned to his companions, they asked him, "What did Jesus say to you?"
> Thomas said to them, "If I tell you one of the things which he told me, you will pick up stones and throw them at me; a fire will come out of the stones and burn you up."

The reader is never told what Jesus said to Thomas as they withdrew in private. Some might think that the gospel suggests that this dangerous secret is itself ineffable, or that the author of the gospel did not wish to put this esoteric revelation on the page, preferring to have it delivered orally to a ready adept. I am inclined to think, rather, that the careful reader of the gospel can infer what three things Jesus told Thomas.

The first hint is Thomas's claim that the other disciples would stone him if he were to divulge the secret. Stoning was a punishment reserved by Jews for severe crimes, with none more severe than blasphemy. Following Nicola Denzey Lewis, I suggest that a reader of the *Gospel of Thomas* would infer from this saying that Jesus told Thomas, "I am God."[10] The second hint is Jesus' immediate reaction to Thomas's confession. "I am not your master"—what could this mean except that Thomas is Jesus's equal: both of them "rule over the all" (§2)? Jesus goes on to say that "because you have drunk, you have become intoxicated from the bubbling spring which I have measured out." Again, the careful reader will straightaway recall §108, where Jesus says, "He who will drink from my mouth will become like me. I myself shall become he, and the things that are hidden will be revealed to him." More than merely equals, Jesus and Thomas begin to merge into a single entity—on my reading a unity-in-duality, a "single" or "solitary" one (*oua ouōt* or *monachos*) that makes the two (*snau* = Jesus and Thomas) one (*oua*). Again, following Denzey Lewis, I suggest that a reader of the gospel would infer that the second thing Jesus told Thomas was "I am you." Notice that when Jesus speaks from the first-person singular—"I myself"—he suggests a future identity between Thomas and himself: "I shall become he." But when he speaks from the third-person singular—"He who"—he suggests not a future identity but a likeness: "he will become *like* me." This is not a fully reciprocal relationship, not an identity that can be rendered 1 = 1.[11] For one who has drunk from the ecstatic cup of self-knowledge, Jesus *is* his innermost self such that Jesus can say, "I am he" or "I am she." But the same one—whom Jesus can claim to be—can only say "I am *like* Jesus." The one who comes to realize that he is two—himself and Jesus—does not therefore entirely annihilate the difference between the two. The gap between identity and likeness persists, and it is the persistence of this gap or difference that ensures that the resulting one carries always the trace of the two. I have already suggested that the name for the one that carries the trace of the two is precisely and paradoxically the "single" or "solitary" one (*oua ouōt, monachos*). I wish now to suggest that "twin" (*didymus/tāwma*) is another name for this same one, namely, he who is drunk from the ecstatic cup of self-knowledge, who knows that Jesus is his innermost self who can claim identity with him, but with whom he can claim only progressive likeness. Here is where the discourse of the one and the two and the theology of twinship meet and merge.

There remains the third and final thing that Jesus told Thomas in secret—what might it have been? The answer brings us back to the very first saying, and what is on offer to the reader, the interpreter: "And [Jesus] said, 'Whoever finds the interpretation of these sayings will not experience death.'" According to Denzey Lewis, "Thomas is twins with Jesus, but he is also twins with someone else: whoever reads and understands the words of the living Jesus. One who understands these words, in the end, is returned to the primordial light. In effect, she, or he, understands that they too, become Christs."[12]

The third saying would, on this reading, suggest to Thomas that not only he but also all who hear (and later read) these secret sayings, and find their proper interpretation, are twins of Jesus. The third saying extends the gift of twinship to the community of readers, of interpreters. The ever-expanding community of twins, of those in whom the primordial light of Jesus shines, of those who have made the one two and the two one, is the realization of the kingdom. Hence Denzey Lewis opines that the third saying might have been, "We are the Kingdom of God." The "radical" question posed by the Gospel of Thomas, then, is simply, "Can we all become Thomases? Can we, too, all become Christs?"

On my reading, the *Gospel of Thomas* is perhaps our first, but more importantly our most profound, Christian witness to the divine double. The reader is invited to interpret these secret sayings, and to realize that Jesus the transcendent light is his innermost self. Thus rendered two, he must now make those two one: he and his divine double must make peace in a single house. The self who succeeds in finding the identity or union of the two is named a "single one" (*oua ouōt*) or a "solitary" (*monachos*). And that self thereby takes up the position of Judas Thomas, Jesus' twin (*didymos*) or equal.

The Cologne Mani Codex

The prophet Mani was born in Mesopotamia in the year 216 CE to a father named Pattek and a mother probably named Maryam.[13] Although he was descended from royal blood of the Arsacid dynasty that ruled over the Parthian kingdom (247 BCE– 224 CE), he grew up in the shadow of the Arsacids' successors, the Sasanians, several of whose kings he was destined to know and advise. His mother cared for him in his first four years. According to legend, his father was told by a divine voice in a temple in the capital city, Seleucia-Ctesiphon, that he should abstain from meat, wine, and women. In response he abandoned his wife and joined a community of "baptists" living in southern Mesopotamia, taking with him his young son, who would spend the next twenty years of his life with them.[14] According to the ancient sources, Mani was visited at least twice by a heavenly messenger, his "twin" or "companion." This divine double became for Mani a kind of alter ego, the other half of his whole self, protecting and guiding him throughout the rest of his life. It was this heavenly twin-companion who persuaded Mani to break with the baptists, strike out on his own, and preach his own enlightening gospel.

When he did so, his father joined him as his first disciple. Mani himself wrote a canon of scriptures, as well as extracanonical commentaries;[15] established a two-tiered community structure or catechumens ("hearers") and elect, each with its own incumbent rights and responsibilities;[16] preached far and wide, and in different idioms to diverse audiences; and reached out to political powers to help ensure that his fledgling faith could survive in the Persian empire with its newly reascendant Zoroastrian ideology. Indeed, "he may be said to have combined the charisma of Jesus, the missionary purpose of Paul, and the doctrinal stringency of an Augustine."[17]

Underlying all his efforts was a conviction, seconded by his twin-companion, that his message was a universal one, the culmination of previous prophecies, practices, and teachings—in other words, the universal truth. Mani seems to have regarded himself as the final incarnation of a heavenly figure, the Apostle of Light, sent to successive generations to reveal the truth, which was veiled according to need and circumstance. Previous incarnations included Zoroaster, Buddha, and Jesus (among others). Mani's good news spread throughout the Persian empire, and well beyond, eventually stretching the full latitude of the known world, east to west. His success won his share of friends at the Sasanian court, as well as enemies. When Bahram I ascended to the throne in 274 (r. until 276 or 277), he rescinded the support that his brother Hormizd (r. 272–3) and his father Shapur I (r. 240–73) had lent Mani, and, with the help of the chief Magian or *mobad* named Karder, arranged to have the prophet imprisoned. After a month in chains, during which time he was able to receive visitors and arrange for the survival of his communities after his departure, Mani died in the year 276 or 277. Mani probably understood himself as a Christian, and his universal message as the truth of Christianity, restored after successive generations of corruption. "Manichaeism"—derived from the Syriac title "Mani the living" (*Mani hayya*) or in Greek, *Manichaios*— is a name used first by Christian heresiologists and then by modern scholars to distinguish it sharply from forms of Christianity more familiar to us from the early centuries of the Common Era.

In 1969 a tiny Greek codex, no larger than a matchbox, was discovered somewhere in the area of Asyut (Lycopolis) in Egypt. While the text provides its own title, "On the Origin of His Body" (*peri tēs gennēs tou sōmatou autou*), it has come to be known as the *Cologne Mani Codex* (hereafter *CMC*) because the papyrus codex resides at the Institut für Altertumskunde at the University of Cologne. The *CMC* is often called Mani's biography, but in fact it is more properly an anthology: a collection of excerpts from the writings of Mani's earliest disciples, which an anonymous editor has arranged into chronological order.[18] The codex itself has been dated to the fifth century, although scholars agree that the anthology was probably compiled much earlier, perhaps soon after Mani's death, and furthermore, that the anthology is a Greek translation of a Syriac original. The *CMC* offers a wealth of information on Mani and early Manichaeism, but my interest in it has to do specifically with questions about Mani's twin or companion, here named the *syzygos*.

In the *CMC* we read:

> Then, at the time when my body reached its full growth, immediately there flew down and appeared before me that most beautiful and greatest mirror-image of [myself] (*katoptron tou prosōpou mou*). (17, 1–16)[19]

And again on the following page,

> [When] I was twenty[-five] years old [. . .] the most blessed Lord was greatly moved with compassion for me, called me into his grace, and immediately sent to me [from there my] *syzygos*, [appearing in] great [glory]. (18,1,10–16)

This would seem to suggest two discrete visits from the *syzygos*: one at age twelve (17,8–10) and another at age twenty-four (18,1) or twenty-five (73,5–6). Formed from the prefix "together" (*syn-*) and the word "yoke" (*zygos*), a *syzygia* is, at its most literal, a conjunction of two cattle "yoked together," forming a pair or a couple.[20] The adjectival form, *syzygos* (often used as a noun), refers to one half of the conjoined pair, and can mean "spouse," "comrade," or "companion." I have refrained from translating *syzygos* as "twin" largely because this seems to confuse matters. As François de Blois points out, the Manichaean tradition remembers this visitor under two distinct, but related, clusters of titles: those having to do with twinning and those having to do with companionship or partnership.[21] *Syzygos* falls squarely into the latter category.

The *syzygos* is given other titles, including "my ever-vigilant *syzygos*" (22,16–17), "that all-glorious and all-blessed one" (29,9–10), "a good counselor of all counsels" (32,14–16), "ally and protector" (33,4), and "my most unfailing *syzygos*" (69,14–15), among others. But more important than any title is what the *syzygos* does for Mani and, moreover, teaches him. His most important intervention, of course, is his having separated Mani from the baptists: "drawing [me to the divine] side" (20,1–17). Having brought him face-to-face, and arm in arm, with his mirror image, the *syzygos* teaches him, in Mani's words,

> who I am, what my body is, in what way I have come, how my arrival into this world took place, who I am of the ones most renowned for their eminence, how I was begotten into this fleshly body, by what woman I was delivered and born according to the flesh, and by whose [passion] I was engendered. (21,2–16)

This instruction in Mani's cosmic "whence and whither" centers on his sojourn in the body—recall that the title of the *CMC* is "On the Origin of His Body" (*peri tēs gennēs tou sōmatou autou*). But the more precise constitution of this "I" is also a central piece of the curriculum: "concerning me, who I am, and who my inseparable *syzygos* is; moreover, concerning my soul, which exists as the soul of all the worlds, both what it itself is and how it came to be" (23,4–11).

This lesson in the nature of Mani's "I" is hardly systematic, but a good deal can be gleaned from the following:

> I acquired [the *syzygos*] as my own possession. I believed that he belongs to me and is (mine) and is a good and excellent counselor. I recognized him (*epegnōn*) and understood that I am that one from whom I was separated. I testified that I myself am that one who is unshakeable. (24,3–15)

On the one hand, Mani's relationship to his *syzygos* is one of possession: the *syzygos* belongs to him. The *syzygos*'s relationship to Mani, on the other hand, is one of counseling. The relationship is not entirely symmetric, despite the *syzygos* being Mani's mirror image. Furthermore, the *syzygos* is someone whom Mani must recognize, and recognition (*epignōsis*) consists in Mani's understanding that he, Mani, is identical with that one, his *syzygos*, from whom he was separated. The identity is made clear in the closing testimony: "I myself am that one" (*egō ekeinos autos eimi*).

We have from Mani (whether it be the historical Mani or the hagiographical character) no clearer an "I" statement than this.[22] Albert Henrichs judges the constitution of Mani's "I" as "far from . . . original, [but rather] well known as the classical Gnostic expression of *Selbstfindung*"—*Selbstfindung* or "self-discovery."[23] The revelation of Mani's *syzygos* is a moment of *Selbstfindung* (self-discovery); but precisely the moment of *Selbstfindung* is simultaneously a moment of *Selbst-spaltung* (self-division) and of *Selbst-einigung* (self-unification). In other words, it is precisely the coincidence of division and unification that constitutes Mani's distinctive selfhood.

I take this coincidence of division and unification to be the backdrop to Mani's further first-person declarations in the *CMC*: "I am solitary (*monērēs d'egō*) . . . I, alone against all (*monos ōn para pantas*)" (31,1–9). In its immediate context, these "I" statements contrast Mani with "the multitude," the errant crowd of baptists and "the ordinances of that teaching in which I was reared" (44,4–6). Mani "became like a stranger (*othneiōi*) and a solitary (*monērei*) in their midst" (44,6–8), but his estrangement and solitary selfhood are made possible only by his union with his double, his *syzygos*. Much later in the *CMC* Mani worries, "I am alone (*egō de monogenēs*)" (104,8–9), in contrast to the many "kings and dynasts of the world and the founders of the sects" (103,21–104,3). But then "the splendid one" reassures him, making clear that because he (Mani) has his (the *syzygos*'s) help, he "alone" (that is, with his companion) will triumph over these many powers. The contrast between Mani and the multitude, then, is not between the one and the many, but between the "solitary"—understood as Mani's being one and yet two—and the many. In other words, the only way to contend against the many is not to be merely one, but to be one *and* two, to be the Mani whose singularity includes himself and his double. The three

Greek terms that Mani used to describe his singular or solitary selfhood here (*monos, monēros, monogenēs*) probably translate three of Mani's own terms from Syriac (*had, mshāwhad, īhīdāyā*).[24] In another Manichaen source, the *Kephalaia of the Teacher*, all three terms are rendered in Coptic with *ouōt*, and with an indefinite article as *oua ouōt*. The phrase should be familiar: *oua ouōt* or "one and the same" is a phrase that appears often (along with *monachos* or "solitary") in the *Gospel of Thomas*. Earlier I argued that the *Gospel of Thomas* forwards a particular understanding of selfhood, according to which one first discovers that one is in fact two because Jesus the light dwells within oneself, whereupon the urgent enterprise is living into the reality of this unity-in-duality—and that the Gospel's consistent name for this new selfhood is both *monachos*, "solitary," and *oua ouōt*, "a single one." This is not a unity that annihilates duality, but rather one that depends on and preserves it.

Scholars have long debated whether Mani or his followers were familiar with the *Gospel of Thomas*. Cyril of Jerusalem (*c.* 313–386) insisted that the *Gospel of Thomas* was authored by "one of the three wicked disciples of Mani."[25] Because the *Gospel of Thomas* almost certainly predates Mani, the more relevant question is whether Mani or his followers made use of the gospel. Henrichs is skeptical, deeming it "rash to assume that the *Gospel of Thomas* was known to Mani."[26] More recently Wolf-Peter Funk has asked the question anew, and argued that three *logia* from the *Gospel of Thomas* influenced Manichaeism.[27] Although I recognize that the evidence suggests that influence was "a possibility, but only that," I suspect that Funk is correct that the *Gospel of Thomas* did influence Manichaeism, perhaps even Mani himself.[28] If my suspicion is correct, then Mani's "I" statements from the *CMC*—confessions of his being "one," "alone," "singular" (Coptic: *oua ouōt*; Greek: *monos, monēros, monogenēs*; Syriac: *had, mshāwhad, īhīdāyā*) should be understood as appropriating and developing the *Gospel of Thomas*'s peculiar understanding of selfhood as *monachos* and *oua ouōt*. According to this logic, Mani, an Apostle of Light at first ignorant of his apostolate, is visited by his own image, his own counterpart and companion, then discovers that he is not merely one, but has a double. This recognition inaugurates his becoming a new self: in his own words a single one, but words we should read in light of the *Gospel of Thomas*'s meditation on the one and the two. If this is right, then Mani and his followers regard him as the exemplary "solitary" or "single one," as described in the *Gospel of Thomas*, precisely because he is doubled.

Plotinus

In the year 243 the young emperor Gordian III, barely eighteen years old, marched against the Sasanians and their king, Shapur I. The campaign ended badly for Gordian, who was killed (perhaps by his own troops), and his successor, Philip the Arab, was forced to sue for an unfavorable peace. Somewhere in the Roman force was a thirty-nine-year-old philosopher from Alexandria by the name of Plotinus (cs. 204/205–270). At this same time Mani, the Apostle of Light (together with his twin-companion), was in the royal entourage of King Shapur. It is tempting to imagine these two, the philosopher and the apostle, meeting amid the cacophony of that campaign, facing off as rivals, or perhaps as a pair, as counterparts. Certainly it was what Plotinus was hoping for: his student Porphyry tells us that he was "eager to make acquaintance with the Persian philosophical discipline and that prevailing among the Indians."[29] Alas, such a meeting was not to be, and Plotinus was lucky to escape with his life to Antioch. He then quit the Roman East, and at the age of forty made a new home for himself in Rome.

He spent the following nineteen years in the capital, forming around himself a "school" of philosophy—more of an extended circle of students and supporters than a proper school with a set curriculum. He died in 270 of a painful and hideous illness; in his last moments he was visited by his longtime friend and physician, Eustochius, to whom he is reported to have said, "I have been waiting a long time for you. Try to bring back the god in us to the divine in the All."[30] After his death, Porphyry, whom Plotinus had sent away to Sicily to recover from his suicidal depression, took up the task of editing and arranging Plotinus's writings—a task to which he was entrusted, so he says, by Plotinus himself. Porphyry arranged the fifty-four treatises of uneven length into a neat scheme of six sets of nine—hence the title *Enneads* or "nines."

My challenge in this section is to try to isolate Plotinus's understanding of the self as doubled.[31] Isolating Plotinus's understanding of selfhood, however, cannot be done with surgical precision. The doubled self is not strictly an issue of anthropology, but reaches up, so to speak, the great chain of being all the way to the three hypostases: the One, Intellect, and Soul. In other words, anthropology is tied up with metaphysics, specifically with protology and soteriology—Intellect's emergence from the One and the possibility of our return thereto.

Plotinus's simplest and clearest definition of selfhood is this: "For every human is double (*dittos*), one of him is the sort of compound being (*to synamphoteron*) and one of him is himself (*autos*)" (2.3.9.31–2). The compound being is an individual soul in a particular body. While this itself is a kind of dualism, "a crude dualism of body and soul," it is not the dualism Plotinus thinks is most important.[32] The individual soul is *itself* double, and this is the crucial dualism for Plotinus. As he writes in 3.8,

> The first part of the soul, then, that which is above and always filled and illuminated by the reality above, remains There; but another part, participating by the first participation of the participant goes forth, for the soul goes forth always, life from life; for actuality reaches everywhere, and there is no point where it fails. But in going forth it lets its prior part remain where it left it, for if it abandoned what is before it, it would no longer be everywhere, but only at the last point it reached. But what goes forth is not equal to what remains. (3.8.5.10–18)

Plotinus, then, regards every individual soul or intellect as already divided, or at least bi-located: one part of it is here, having descended into the composite body, and another part of it is there, eternally fed on the vision of intelligible beauty.

This doctrine of the undescended intellect appears throughout the *Enneads*; here are two further examples:

> Our soul does not altogether come down, but there is always something of it in the intelligible. (4.8.8.2–4)

> The human, and especially the good human is not the composite (*to synamphoteron*) of soul and body; separation from the body and despising its so-called goods make this plain. (1.4.14.1–4)

There are therefore two dualisms in Plotinian anthropology: the "apparent" dualism of body and soul, and the "real" dualism of lower and higher, descended and undescended, intellect.[33] Our descended intellect is an image of our undescended intellect, and thus we are in a position of conforming the image ever more to its archetype.

Plotinus appeals to an Orphic myth about how the Titans lured the child Dionysus away with a mirror (*katoptron*): distracted by his own image, Dionysus was helpless as they slew him and then ate him (4.3.12.1–3). We are like the god Dionysus, Plotinus says. Our intellects see their images (*eidōla*) and plunge down to the level of that reflection, that is, they descend: "But even these are not cut off from their own principle and from intellect. For they did not come down with intellect, but went on ahead of it down to earth, but their heads are firmly set in heaven" (4.3.12.2–6). The critical point here is that the undescended intellect erred: it saw its own image and descended in pursuit of that image, into embodiment. But part of that intellect remains "firmly set in heaven," and thus we are doubled. To overcome our constitutive division, we have to reverse the Titans' mirror trick. Here Plotinus figures matter as a kind of mirror that threatens to capture the intellect's attention by showing it its own image.

But how do we ascend, how do we incline upward to our undescended intellect? To answer this question we have to look at one of Plotinus's descriptions of the descent of the soul or intellect. In the myth of the mirror of Dionysius, it is the image of the intellect that beguiles the intellect such that it plunges downward. In this next account of descent, something seems to reach up to the intellect and pull it down:

> But we—who are we? Are we that which draws near and comes to be in time? No, even before this coming to be came to be we were there, humans who were different (*alloi*), and some of us even gods, pure souls and intellects united with the whole of reality; we were parts of the intelligible, not marked off or cut off but belonging to the whole; and we are not cut off even now. But another human (*anthrōpos allos*), wishing to exist (*einai thelōn*), approached that man; and when he found us—for we were not outside the All—he wound himself round us and attached himself to that man who was then each of us . . . and we have come to be the pair (*synampho*) of them, not the one which we were before—and sometimes just the other which we added on afterwards, when that prior one is inactive and in another way not present. (6.4.14.17–32)

This description should be familiar to us by now: pure souls or intellects feasting on the intelligible—that is who we really are. But somehow "another human," whose distinguishing mark as an outsider is his wishing (for there is no distinction between desire and fulfillment at the level of the Intellect), finds us there. He penetrates into the intelligible realm and wraps himself around each of us—like a lamprey on a host or a tumor around an organ. He makes of us a pair, and his wishing weighs us down. Yes, "we are not cut off even now," at least not entirely, but we now wax and wane between him and our true self. What is perhaps most surprising in this description is that the lower self initiates the descent of the higher: it reaches upward and pulls it down.

What is even more important in the description of the descent, however, is that the union or identity of the two—the higher and lower human, the undescended and descended intellect—is named a "pair" (*synampho*). Any individual self—insofar as the self is the soul or intellect—is an individual insofar as he is a "dividual," divided between higher and lower halves.[34] The *synampho* is thus the Plotinian equivalent of Mani's *oua ouōt*: a singularity preserving, indeed pulsing with, duality. Leo Sweeney says of Mani's and Plotinus's parallel accounts of selfhood that "each formulated a monism which is dynamic rather than static"—we might call it "dynamonism."[35] If the power of *dynamis* of this monism consists in the two halves held together, we might further specify it as "dyadic" dynamonism.

Despite the striking parallel, however, there is still a crucial difference between Mani and Plotinus on how the lower half ascends. The reader may recall that in Manichaeism the Apostle of Light sojourns on earth in different bodies at different times in order to free the light of souls trapped in bodies. It is the twin-companion who descends to awaken the apostle to his divine mission. In other words, the initiative is on the part of the divine double, not the earthly sojourner. In Plotinus, however, the undescended intellect cannot show such initiative or interest in what is beneath it. Of our undescended intellect Plotinus says that "it is separate because it itself does not incline towards us, but rather we look up towards it" (5.3.3.43–5). The undescended intellect cannot descend so as to save us, as Mani's twin-companion does for him. One "half" of our intellect is enjoying the intelligible realm. The other, lower "half" suffers the misfortune of descent into embodiment. Our salvation consists not in our rescue by our higher power per se, but by our struggling to see the archetype of which we are the sad image: "The more [the soul] is directed to that contemplation [of that which is before it, that is, its higher half], the fairer and more powerful it is. It receives from there and gives to what comes after it, and is always illuminated as it illuminates" (2.9.2.17–19).

The doubled structure of the self finds expression in another discussion in the *Enneads*: whether each individual embodied intellect has its own Form. The question has an important genealogy in Plato and his own changing theory of Forms. Plato is generally thought to have posited Forms as "one over many," that is, a causative principle of many particular instantiations: the Form of horse, for example, is the causative principle of all horses. In other words, "there is a Form, according to the *Republic* (596a5-7), corresponding to every set of things that have a common name."[36] After the *Republic*, however, Plato's theory of Forms underwent many changes and challenges, principally in such dialogues as the *Parmenides*, *Sophist*, *Timaeus*, and *Philebus*. Nowhere in Plato, however, nor in any of the early Platonists, do we find a version of the theory that suggests that there are Forms for every individual or instantiated particular.[37] In fact, one of Aristotle's many objections to the theory of Forms is that it leads to this view—but it is a view no Platonist accepts (*Metaphysics* 990b14).[38] No Platonist, it seems, except Plotinus.

Why might Plotinus hold the peculiar view that *each* individual intellect had an eternal archetype in the intelligible realm? Wouldn't it be more elegant if there were a finite number of more general Forms that caused all particular intellects? After all, weren't Forms introduced by Plato precisely to explain the specificity of the world by appeal to a set of more general, intelligible principles? Furthermore, in what sense can we really say that the individual intellect-Forms are *individuals*? What differentiates one intellect-Form from another?

Answers to these questions are hard to come by. Perhaps Plotinus's "radical innovation" was his conviction that individuality so to speak *mattered*, mattered so much in fact that individuation must be native to the intelligible realm rather than result of some successive stage in its instantiation.[39] But why might individuation matter so much? I suggest that Plotinus takes this peculiar stand on the Forms of individuals because he is concerned ultimately about our return to the realm of Intellect and, beyond even that, to the One. I am not alone is this regard. Paul Kalligas writes, "it is the ability of each individual human being to return to his intelligible origin by making use of the essential features that makes it necessary to postulate a *different* form for each human being."[40] Evidence for this can be found in the very opening of treatise 5.7: "Is there an idea of a particular thing? Yes, if I and each one of us have a way of ascent and return (*anagōgēn*) to the intelligible, the principle of each of us is there" (5.7.1.1–3). Our return to our "whence" depends on, and so demands, that some version of ourselves, namely, the Form of our individual intellect, be already there.

Plotinus describes a cyclical universe, in which each cycle sees a finite number of Forms cause a finite number of individuals.[41] We individual intellects each have an eternal archetype in the realm of the intelligible, and in the universe's next cycle that eternal archetype will generate a new image, a new individual intellect. Our connection to that subsequent individual intellect in the next age is not horizontal but vertical: we are connected only by virtue of the fact that we are two images of a single archetype. The two images could (but need not) differ radically from one another across two cycles, much as Plato describes changes in a soul's embodiment through reincarnation.

A passage we have already cited sheds further light on his view:

> But we—who are we? Are we that which draws near and comes to be in time? No, even before this coming to be came to be we were there, humans who were different (*alloi*), and some of us even gods, pure souls and intellects united with the whole of reality; we were parts of the intelligible, not marked off or cut off but belonging to the whole; and we are not cut off even now. (6.4.14.17–22)

Notice that this description of our prior, pre-embodied life as intellects insists that we were in the plural even there. There we were *tines*, that is, distinct intellects. There is not a single Form from which we are derived; rather, we are "parts of the intelligible" but "belonging to the whole." When Plotinus says that we were different (*alloi*), he means that we were different from what we are now, after our "coming to be" and descent into bodies. But the fact that we are called "different" raises the question of whether and how intellect-Forms can be said to be individual. In other words, in what ways, if any, do the intellect-Forms differ from one another?

The short answer is that they do not: intellect-Forms are identical to one another. Yet, although identical, they are still distinct. Plotinus speaks of this unity-in-distinction in a rather riddling way: "The soul when it is altogether apart [from the body] is particular without being particular . . . it is part, not the whole, though even so it is in another way the whole" (6.4.16.32–4). What does it mean that the soul is particular without being particular? It seems that the intellects' distinctiveness consists only in their numerical, rather than qualitative, difference. In other words, individual intellect-Forms differ from each other only insofar as there are many of them. The individuality of an undescended intellect consists in this and only this. What we typically regard as individuality is a matter of qualitative difference (a particular), which according to Plotinus begins to adhere to the individual intellects only as they begin their descent as souls into bodies.

With this, however, we return to the pressing question of why Plotinus held to this view, and the suggestion that it is necessary to account for our return to the intelligible realm and beyond. Most importantly, this view ensures that there is an unbroken line between the undescended and descended intellect, that our doubled self is lashed together. We can be confident of our return to our whence precisely because our essential selves, our souls distilled into intellects, are already there, numerically individuated intellect-Forms. As we have noted earlier in contrast to Mani, however, the placement of our higher half "there" does not imply that the intellect-Form can descend to elevate or "save" us from the burden of embodiment. The initiative for our return, so it seems, must be our own. But the fact that there are Forms of our individual intellects also means that for Plotinus Plato's famous descriptions of our ascent to the contemplation of the Forms, in the *Symposium* and *Phaedrus*, for example, or the allegory of the cave in *Republic* (514a–520a), can be understood as our ascent to ourselves.

Conclusion

More than any other scholar, the twentieth-century French philosopher Henry Corbin has enlightened the ancient tradition of the divine double, notably in his book *L'homme de lumière dans le soufisme iranien*.[42] He begins that short work with an exploration of "an innovation in philosophical anthropology" from antiquity, a notion that "the individual person as such . . . has a transcendent dimension at his disposal," "a counterpart, a heavenly 'partner,' and that [the person's] total structure is that of a bi-unity, a *unus-ambo*."[43] Corbin rather hurriedly traces this innovation through some of the same traditions as I will because he is principally interested to show the ancient witnesses' relevance for understanding medieval Persian mysticism (which is his particular expertise). However abbreviated his discussion, Corbin's interest in these sources centers squarely on how they imagine the self as a *unus-ambo* or "bi-unity." This new identity

> does not correspond to a relationship of 1 = 1, but if 1 x 1: the identity of an essence raised to its total power by being multiplied by itself and thus put in a condition to

constitute a biunity, a dialogic whole whose members share alternately the roles of first and second person. Or again the state described by our mystics: when, at the climax, the lover has become the very substance of love, he is then both the lover *and* the beloved. But *himself* will not be *that* without the second person, without the *thou*, that is to say without the Figure who makes him able to see himself because it is through his very own eyes that the Figure looks at him.

It would therefore be as wrong to reduce the two-dimensionality of this dialogic unity to a solipsism as to divide it into two essences, each of which could be itself with the other.[44]

To my mind, Corbin has put his finger on what is most interesting and significant in the texts and traditions of the divine double, namely a model of selfhood as, in his words, a *unus-ambo* or "bi-unity." The significance of this model of selfhood has at least two dimensions. First of all, most obviously, it resists a certain monism of the self, that is, the notion that the self is meant to be wholly one. On this model, to assume that one is a single self is a form of false consciousness. Rather than overcoming division, the self must first be initiated into its constitutive division, the difference between the "I" and its double. The self is not one half of the pair—*either* the "I" or its double—but is rather the pair itself, somehow preserving that constitutive difference or division in a new self, a new "I." Second, this model of selfhood constitutes a chapter in the history of mysticism, more specifically an early version of the doctrine of deification. Corbin flags this when he describes "bi-unity" as a "state described by our mystics."[45] We think we are one, but when we are initiated into the mystery of the divine, we come to realize that we are in fact two (and yet somehow also one). To be ushered into this new selfhood is to be put on an itinerary of increasing conformity to the divine. Thus, this model of selfhood is not a static description but an urgent prescription: the self is an enterprise or project of becoming divine.

Corbin's rhetoric raises a final question, namely whether any treatment of this alternative anthropology is strictly descriptive or also inevitably prescriptive. Corbin also colors his enterprise with a certain urgency: "These few remarks throw light on the way by which the present research *must* be pursued. The attempt *must* be made to establish the identity of the Figure under the various names that are given to its apparitions."[46] Such a project is urgent because this "Figure" challenges what Corbin takes to be a predominant anthropology, according to which "Self designates an impersonal or depersonalized absolute, a pure act of existing which obviously could not act as a second person, the second term of a dialogic relationship."[47] As his enterprise proscribes one anthropology, it prescribes an alternative, the *unus-ambo* option. And so Corbin turns to the ancient sources in an attempt to recover the voices of this *unus-ambo* option, in order to contravene a predominant model of selfhood that refuses any internal dialogue of first and second person in favor of a mythology of a singular and monological self. Far from faulting Corbin for eliding the difference between description and prescription, however, I would suggest that we commend this dual enterprise and carry it further. What is needed, in my mind, is not only a close and careful consideration of the ancient sources and their ambiguities, which will yield a nuanced description of this anthropological option, but also the courage to acknowledge the prescriptive edge of this enterprise, to explain why the *unus-ambo* option should be forwarded as a contemporary philosophical and theological anthropology of twinning.

Notes

1   For a fuller discussion of these texts and the tradition of which they are a part, see Charles M. Stang, *Our Divine Double* (Cambridge, MA: Harvard University Press, 2016); the book significantly develops ideas from an earlier version of this chapter, on which the following readers provided helpful comments, and to whom I am grateful: Giovanni Bazzanna, Ryan Coyne, Sarabinh Levy-Brightman, Kimberley Patton, and Richard Valantasis. The current version of the chapter has been revised for *Gemini and the Sacred* in light of *Our Divine Double.*

2   All citations from Thomas Lambdin's translation of the Gospel of Thomas in Bentley Layton, ed., Nag Hammadi II, 2–7: Together with XIII, 2*, Brit. Lib. Or. 4926(1), and P.Oxy. 1, 654, 655: with Contributions by Many Scholars (Leiden: Brill, 1989), which includes a critical edition of the Coptic (§ refers to a single numbered saying, §§ to more than one). This also includes an appendix with the Testimonia to the Gospel of Thomas and the Greek Oxyrhynchus fragments, edited and translated by Harold Attridge. I have also consulted Michael Grondin's Coptic-English interlinear edition, last modified 2015, ; other useful online resources, including extensive bibliography, can be found at "Gospel of Thomas: Bibliography, Coptic & Greek Texts," Syzte Van der Laan, ; "The Gospel of Thomas Homepage," Stevan Davies,. Accessed August 22, 2016; last accessed March 15, 2022.

3   Gregory J. Riley, "Didymos Judas Thomas, the Twin Brother of Jesus," in *Gemini and the Sacred: Twins in Religion and Myth*, ed. Kimberley Patton (London: I.B. Tauris, 2016), in this volume 354–67.

4   Jesus' brother Judas must be distinguished from three other figures from the New Testament who share this very common proper name: (1) Judas Iscariot; (2) Judas, the son of James (Luke 6:16, Acts 1:13); and (3) Judas Barsabbas (Acts 15:22).

5   P. Oxy. 654.16–18 makes no mention of being known: "And, the [kingdom of God] is inside of you, [and it is outside of you. Whoever] knows [himself] will discover this."

6   This exchange is made fully reciprocal in P. Oxy. 654.26, which adds, "and the last will be first."

7   Risto Uro, "Is *Thomas* an Encratite Gospel?," in *Thomas at the Crossroads,* ed. Risto Uro (Edinburgh: T&T Clark, 1998), 157: "*Monachos,* although a Greek loan-word, has not been preserved in the Greek fragments of the gospel, and it has sometimes been suggested that it derives from a fourth-century Coptic editor and not from (the) earlier Greek author(s)."

8   Edwin A. Judge, "The Earliest Use of Monachos for 'Monk' (P. Coll. Youtie 77) and the Origins of Monasticism," *Jahrbuch für Antike und Christentum* 20 (1977): 72–89; Françoise E. Morard, "Monachos: Une importation sémitique en Égypte?," *Studia Patristica* 12 (1975): 242–6; Morard, "Encore quelques reflexions sur Monachos," *Vigiliae Christianae* 34 (1980): 395–401.

9   April DeConick, *The Original Gospel of Thomas in Translation* (London: T&T Clark, 2007), 119.

10 Nicola Denzey Lewis, *Introduction to "Gnosticism": Ancient Voices, Christian Worlds* (New York: Oxford University Press, 2013), 115.

11 Henry Corbin, *L'homme de lumière dans le soufisme iranien* (Paris: Éditions Présence, 1971): 1 x 1 = 1. But here if 1_1 is Jesus, and 1_2 is Thomas, then $1_1 = 1_2$ (although $1_2 \neq 1_1$), but $1_2 \leq 1_1$.

12 Denzey Lewis, *Introduction to "Gnosticism,"* 115. As she points out, the *Gospel of Thomas* never uses the term "Christ."

13 Much of what follows depends on the excellent introduction by Iain Gardner and Samuel N. C. Lieu to their compilation, *Manichaean Texts from the Roman Empire* (Cambridge: Cambridge University Press, 2004), 1–25.

14 On the identity of these "baptists," see Albert Henrichs, "Mani and the Babylonian Baptists: A Historical Confrontation," *Harvard Studies in Classical Philology* 77 (1973): 23–59.

15 Mani's canon consisted of seven works: (1) The Living (or Great) Gospel; (2) The Treasure of Life; (3) The Pragmateia (or Treatise or Essay); (4) The Book of Mysteries; (5) The Book of the Giants; (6) Letters; (7) Psalms and Prayers. We also know of a canonical *The Book of Pictures*, with images painted by Mani, which might be reconstructed from tenth-century manuscripts as well as Uigur and Tang-Ming Chinese murals and mortuary banners. See *Mani's Pictures: The Didactic Images of the Manichaeans from Sasanian Mesopotmani to Uygur Central Asia and Tang-Ming China* by Zsuzsanna Gulácsi (Leiden: Brill, 2015).

16 The structure of the church is in fact more elaborate than this. The church was headed by Mani; below him was his deputy (*archēgos* or *princeps*). Below the deputy were 12 apostles, followed by 72 bishops, and 360 presbyters. At the lower levels of this ecclesiastical hierarchy were the ranks of the elect and the catechumens (*auditores*).

17 Gardner and Lieu, Manichaean Texts from the Roman Empire, 9–10.

18 The disciples include: Salmaios the Ascetic, Baraies the Teacher, Timotheos, Abiesus the Teacher, Innaios the brother of Zabed, a certain Za[cheas?], Koustaios the Son of the Treasure of Life, and Ana the brother of Zabed the Disciple.

19 Here [. . .] marks my ellipsis, not the *CMC*'s.

20 See, for example, Plato's famous analogy of the soul as a charioteer with two horses. At *Phaedrus* 254a5 the obedient horse is described as the *syzygos* or "yokemate" of its violent, disobedient counterpart. For a further discussion of the zygos (ζύγος) in Homeric and later ancient Greek usage, and its relationship to the concept of "compelled companionship," such as an oxen-yoke or chariot-team provide, see Kimberley C. Patton, in this volume, "Yoking the Winds: The Tears of Xanthos and Balios," 441–3.

21 François de Blois, "Manes' 'Twin' in Iranian and non-Iranian Texts," in Religious Themes and Texts of Pre-Islamic Iran and Central Asia: Studies in honour of Professor Gherardo Gnoli on the occasion of his 65th birthday on 6th December 2002, ed. Carlo G. Cereti, Mauro Maggi, and Elio Provasi, 12–13 (Wiesbaden: Reichert, 2003).

22 Here may be the clue as to Mani's silence on Gal 2:20. Perhaps he was wary of saying, as Paul does, *"no longer* I, but Christ who lives in me," wary of the suggestion that his "I" might be not just symbiotically paired, but replaced entirely by the *syzygos*. Paul himself hedges against the extinction of his "I" with the addition of *in me,* thus preserving an "I" in whom Christ may dwell. But Mani's self-conception seems to be clearly centered on his "I" as doubled. In effect, Mani is saying: "I, Mani, am only I myself *(egō autos)* when I am also that one *(ekeinos)* from whom I was once but am no longer separated."

23 Henrichs, "Mani and the Babylonian Baptists," 24.

24 Ibid., 39.

25 Cyril, *Catechesis* 6.31 (PG col. 593A); cited in J. Kevin Coyle, "The *Gospel of Thomas* in Manichaeism?," in *Colloque international "L'Évangile selon Thomas et les texts de Nag Hammadi," Québec, 29–31 mai 2003,* ed. Louis Painchaud and Paul-Hubert Poirier (Quebec: Presses de l'Université Laval, 2007), 80, n34.

26 Henrichs, "Mani and the Babylonian Baptists," 38. He cites some of the relevant earlier bibliography on the question.

27 Wolf-Peter Funk, "'Einer aus tausend, zwei aus zehntausend': Zitate aus dem Thomas-Evangelium in den koptischen Manichaica," in *For the Children, Perfect Instruction: Studies in Honor of Hans-Martin Schenke on the Occasion of the Berliner Arbeitskreis für kotisch-gnostische Schriften's Thirtieth Year,* ed. Hans-Gebhard Bethge, *Nag Hammadi and Manichaean Studies* 54 (Leiden: Brill, 2002): 67–94.

28 Coyle remains skeptical: "Thus there is no doubt about the expression's popularity among Manichaeans. That it also circulated beyond Manichaeism precludes a definite conclusion as to its influence upon or by the Gos. Thom" ("The *Gospel of Thomas* in Manichaeism?," 85).

29 *Vita Plotini* 3.16–17, trans. A. H. Armstrong, *Plotinus: Enneads,* 7 vols. (Cambridge, MA: Harvard University Press, 1966–88), vol. 1.

30 Ibid., 2.25–27. On the last words of Plotinus, see Paul Henry, "La dernière parole de Plotin," *Studi classici e orientali* 11 (Pisa, 1953): 113–20; and more recently Glenn W. Most, "Plotinus' Last Words," *Classical Quarterly* 53, no. 2 (2003): 576–87.

31 See also Leo Sweeney, "Mani's Twin and Plotinus: Questions on 'Self,'" in *Neoplatonism and Gnosticism,* ed. Richard T. Wallis (Albany: SUNY Press, 1992), 381–424; Henry Blumenthal, *Plotinus' Psychology: His Doctrine of the Embodied Soul* (The Hague: Martinus Nijhoff, 1971); Gerard O'Daly, *Plotinus' Philosophy of the Self* (Shannon: Irish University Press, 1973), which engages earlier scholarship, including Emile Bréhier, E. R. Dodds, Pierre Hadot, W. Himmerich, Willy Theiler, and Jean Trouillard; Carlos Steel, *The Changing Self: A Study on the Soul in Later Neoplatonism; Iamblichus, Damascius and Priscianus* (Brussel: Paleis der Academiën, 1978); Robert Bolton, *Person, Soul, and Identity: A Neoplatonic Account of the Principle of Personality* (London: Minerva, 1994); Gary Gurtler, *Plotinus: The Experience of Unity* (New York: Peter Lang, 1984); Lloyd Gerson, *Plotinus* (London: Routledge, 1994); Manfred Krüger, *Ichgeburt: Origenes und die Entstehung der christlichen Idee der Wiederverkörperung in der Denkbewegung von Pythagoras bis Lessing* (Hildesheim: Olms, 1996); Werner Beierwaltes, *Das wahre Selbst: Studien zu Plotins Begriff des Geistes und das Einen* (Frankfurt am Main: Vittorio Klostermann, 2001); Pauliina Remes, *Plotinus on Self: The Philosophy of the 'We'* (Cambridge: Cambridge University Press, 2007).

32 Frederic M. Schroeder, "Plotinus and Language," in *The Cambridge Companion to Plotinus,* ed. Lloyd Gerson (Cambridge: Cambridge University Press, 1996), 136.

33 Stephen R. L. Clark, "Plotinus: Body and Soul," in Gerson, *The Cambridge Companion to Plotinus*, 276.

34 "On the concept of the "dividual," building on Dumont, Strathern, and Deleuze, among others, see Simon Critchley, *The Faith of the Faithless: Experiments in Political Theology* (Brooklyn: Verso, 2012), 6–7."

35 Sweeney, "Mani's Twin and Plotinus," 398.

36 John M. Rist, "Forms of Individuals in Plotinus," *Classical Quarterly* 13, no. 2 (1963): 223.

37 In his handbook, Albinus remarks that "most Platonists do not accept that there are Forms . . . of individuals, like Socrates and Plato" (*Didaskalikos* 9.2, 163, 23–8).
38 For a reassessment of Aristotle's own view of Forms of individuals, see Paul Kalligas, "Forms of Individuals in Plotinus: A Re-examination," *Phronesis* 42 (1997): 207–8.
39 Rist, "Forms of Individuals in Plotinus," 223.
40 Kalligas, "Forms of Individuals in Plotinus," 212.
41 See also John Bussanich, "Rebirth Eschatology in Plato and Plotinus," in *Philosophy and Salvation in Greek Religion,* ed. Vishwa Adluri (Berlin: De Gruyter, 2013), 243–88.
42 Henri Corbin, *L'homme de lumière dans le soufisme iranien* (Paris: Éditions Présence, 1971). English translation by Nancy Pearson, *The Man of Light in Iranian Sufism* (Boulder, CO: Shambhala, 1978). All citations are from Pearson's translation.
43 Ibid., 4, 6, 7.
44 Ibid., 9.
45 Ibid.
46 Ibid., 11 (my emphasis).
47 Ibid., 9.

Bibliography

Beierwaltes, Werner. *Das Wahre Selbst: Studien zu Plotins Begriff des Geistes und das Einen.* Frankfurt am Main: Vittorio Klostermann, 2001.

de Blois, François. "'Manes' 'Twin' in Iranian and non-Iranian Sources." In *Religious Themes and Texts of Pre-Islamic Iran and Central Asia: Studies in Honour of Professor Gherardo Gnoli on the Occasion of his 65th Birthday on 6th December 2002,* edited by Carlo G. Cereti, Mauro Maggi, and Elio Provasi, 7–16. Wiesbaden: Reichert, 2003.

Blumenthal, Henry. *Plotinus' Psychology: His Doctrine of the Embodied Soul.* The Hague: Martinus Nijhoff, 1971.

Bolton, Robert. *Person, Soul, and Identity: A Neoplatonic Account of the Principle of Personality.* London: Minerva, 1994.

Bussanich, John. "Rebirth Eschatology in Plato and Plotinus." In *Philosophy and Salvation in Greek Religion,* edited by Vishwa Adluri, 243–88. Berlin: De Gruyter, 2013.

Clark, Stephen R. L. "Plotinus: Body and Soul." In *The Cambridge Companion to Plotinus,* edited by Lloyd Gerson, 275–91. Cambridge: Cambridge University Press, 1996.

Corbin, Henry. *L'homme de lumière dans le soufisme iranien.* Paris: Éditions Présence, 1971. English translation by Nancy Pearson: *The Man of Light in Iranian Sufism.* Boulder, CO: Shambhala, 1978.

Coyle, J. Kevin. "The *Gospel of Thomas* in Manichaeism?" In *Colloque International "L'Évangile selon Thomas et les texts de Nag Hammadi," Québec,* 29–31 mai 2003, edited by Louis Painchaud and Paul-Hubert Poirier. Quebec: Presses de l'Université Laval, 2007.

Critchley, Simon. *The Faith of the Faithless: Experiments in Political Theology.* Brooklyn: Verso, 2012.

Davies, Stevan. "The Gospel of Thomas Homepage." http://users.misericordia.edu/davies
/thomas/Thomas.html. Last accessed March 15, 2022.

DeConick, April. *The Original Gospel of Thomas in Translation*. London: T&T Clark,
2007.

Denzey Lewis, Nicola. *Introduction to 'Gnosticism': Ancient Voices, Christian Worlds*.
New York: Oxford University Press, 2013.

Funk, Wolf-Peter. "'Einer aus tausend, zwei aus zehntausend': Zitate aus dem Thomas-
Evangelium in den koptischen Manichaica." In *For the Children, Perfect Instruction:
Studies in Honor of Hans-Martin Schenke on the Occasion of the Berliner Arbeitskreis
für kotisch-gnostische Schriften's Thirtieth Year*, edited by Hans-Gebhard Bethge. Nag
Hammadi and Manichaean Studies 54, 67–94. Leiden: Brill, 2002.

Gardner, Iain, and Samuel N. C. Lieu, eds. *Manichaean Texts from the Roman Empire*.
Cambridge: Cambridge University Press, 2004.

Gerson, Lloyd. *Plotinus*. London: Routledge, 1994.

Grondin, Michael. "An Interlinear Coptic-English Translation of The Gospel of Thomas."
http://gospel-thomas.net/x_transl.htm. Last accessed March 15, 2022.

Gulácsi, Zsuzsanna. *Mani's Pictures: The Didactic Images of the Manichaeans from
Sasanian Mesopotmani to Uygur Central Asia and Tang-Ming China*. Leiden: Brill,
2015.

Gurtler, Gary. *Plotinus: The Experience of Unity*. New York: Peter Lang, 1984.

Henrichs, Albert. "Mani and the Babylonian Baptists: A Historical Confrontation."
Harvard Studies in Classical Philology 77 (1973): 23–59.

Henry, Paul. "La dernière parole de Plotin," *Studi classici e orientali* 11 (Pisa, 1953):
113–20.

Judge, Edwin A. "The Earliest Use of Monachos for 'Monk' (P. Coll. Youtie 77) and the
Origins of Monasticism." *Jahrbuch für Antike und Christentum* 20 (1977): 72–89.

Kalligas, Paul. "Forms of Individuals in Plotinus: A Re-examination," *Phronesis* 42
(1997): 207–8.

Krüger, Manfred. *Ichgeburt: Origenes und die Entstehung der christlichen Idee der
Wiederverkörperung in der Denkbewegung von Pythagoras bis Lessing*. Hildesheim:
Olms, 1996.

Layton, Bentley, ed. *Nag Hammadi II, 2–7: Together with XIII, 2*, Brit. Lib. Or. 4926(1),
and P.Oxy. 1, 654, 655: With Contributions by Many Scholars*. Leiden: Brill, 1989.

Morard, Françoise E. "Monachos: Une importation sémitique en Égypte?" *Studia
Patristica* 12 (1975): 242–6.

Morard, Françoise E.. "Encore quelques reflexions sur Monachos." *Vigiliae Christianae*
34 (1980): 395–401.

Most, Glenn W. "Plotinus' Last Words." *Classical Quarterly* 53, no. 2 (2003): 576–87.

O'Daly, Gerard. *Plotinus' Philosophy of the Self*. Shannon: Irish University Press, 1973.

Patton, Kimberley C. "Yoking the Winds: The Tears of Xanthos and Balios." In *Gemini
and the Sacred: Twins in Religion and Myth*, edited by Kimberley C. Patton, 435–80.
London: Bloomsbury Academic, 2022.

Plotinus. *Vita Plotini. Plotinus: Enneads*, vol. 1. Cambridge, MA: Harvard University
Press, 1966.

Remes, Pauliina. *Plotinus on Self: The Philosophy of the 'We'*. Cambridge: Cambridge
University Press, 2007.

Riley, Gregory J. "Didymos Judas Thomas, the Twin Brother of Jesus." In *Gemini and the
Sacred: Twins in Religion and Myth*, edited by Kimberley C. Patton, 354–67. London:
Bloomsbury Academic, 2022.

Rist, John M. "Forms of Individuals in Plotinus." *Classical Quarterly* 13, no. 2 (1963): 223–31.

Schroeder, Frederic M. "Plotinus and Language." In *The Cambridge Companion to Plotinus*, edited by Lloyd Gerson, 336–55. Cambridge: Cambridge University Press, 1996.

Stang, Charles M. *Our Divine Double*. Cambridge, MA: Harvard University Press, 2016.

Steel, Carlos. *The Changing Self: A Study on the Soul in Later Neoplatonism; Iamblichus, Damascius and Priscianus*. Brussels: Paleis der Academiën, 1978.

Sweeney, Leo. "Mani's Twin and Plotinus: Questions on 'Self.'" In *Neoplatonism and Gnosticism*, edited by Richard T. Wallis, 381–424. Albany: SUNY Press, 1992.

Uro, Risto. "Is *Thomas* an Encratite Gospel?" In *Thomas at the Crossroads*, edited by Risto Uro, 140–62. Edinburgh: T&T Clark, 1998.

Van der Laan, Syzte. "Gospel of Thomas: Bibliography, Coptic & Greek Texts." http://www.agraphos.com/thomas/about/. 1995–2022.

Part Six

Powerful Twins in the
Archaeology of Myth

16

Óðinn's Twin Ravens, Huginn and Muninn

♊

Stephen A. Mitchell

Introduction

In the summer of 2016 in a field in Nybølle on Lolland, Denmark, an important discovery was made: it was a small silver object, no larger than a fingernail according to Torben Christjansen, the amateur archaeologist who found the item through metal detecting. What has made this miniscule Viking Age find especially intriguing is that the amulet, as it seems to be, features the same tantalizing grouping of figures (*inter alia*, a chair and two birds) as are found on two similar South Scandinavian objects— one from the key trade town of Hedeby and the other from the ancient manorial estate at Lejre. As Peter Pentz, curator at the Danish National Museum, noted at the time of the Nybølle discovery, "The three amulets have in common that they have two ravens sitting on the back of a chair, and that quickly leads one's thoughts to Odin and his two ravens."[1]

Indeed, this Odinic interpretation of the three amulets would seem to be nearly inescapable, given the dominant exegetical background we possess, that is, the later medieval textual presentations of pre-Christian Nordic mythology. Thus when in September of 2009 one of the other small Viking Age silver objects, this one with niello inlay—approximately 1.75 cm in height and weighing just 9 grams—was discovered at Gammel Lejre, it was quickly dubbed "Odin from Lejre" [Pl. 12b; Figure 16.1].[2] That this discovery was made at Lejre has played its role too, one suspects, in the interpretation, for Lejre was a key "central place" in Denmark both in the Viking Age and before it, a location often portrayed in medieval literature as an ancient royal residence, an image considerably bolstered by the archaeological research of the past decades.[3]

Dated to the first half of the tenth century, this tiny amulet from Lejre has ignited much debate as to how it fits into the pagan world of the ancient Scandinavians, at least as that world has been reported to us by later Christian descendants. Discussion among archaeologists, students of religion, and others has thus far mainly focused on the gender of the individual seated on the elaborate high settle that dominates the object, and its possible identity within the reconstructed Nordic Pantheon: Is

Figure 16.1 "Odin fra Lejre." Miniature silver figurine identified as Óðinn on the throne Hliðskjálf, with twin ravens Huginn and Muninn. 1.75 cm. From Gammel Lejre, Denmark, tenth century CE. Photo by Ole Malling. Courtesy of Roskilde Museum.

the figure male or female?[4] Does it perhaps portray the goddess Freyja wearing her famous necklace, the Brísingamen? Or is it perhaps Óðinn's wife, Frigg? Or does it represent a seeress, or possibly a cross-dressed seer, seated on a raised dais, performing a so-called *seiðr* ceremony? Or is it indeed Óðinn, possibly a cross-dressed Óðinn, seated on Hliðskjálf, the throne from which the god can look into all the worlds?[5]

Or is it *none* of these storied characters from later literary sources? Perhaps the little Lejre silver figure is nothing more (or less) than the image of some nameless, lost-to-history, tenth-century human. Or conceivably it is not even meant to represent any specific individual, and is simply an idealized, anthropomorphous being. If we take seriously the demands for absolute certainty about what we can say of the figure, we are reduced to little more than its "vital statistics," namely, its weight, height, date of discovery, and so on.[6] Absent an inscription or other written confirmation on the object itself, an empirically absolute determination about the meaning of any material object is virtually impossible—in that pinched view of cultural history, even the centaurs from the Parthenon's metopes could never be more than wondrously torsoed men showing seemingly inexplicable equine attributes!

That would be thin gruel, indeed, and I am inclined to probe the issue beyond such rudimentary facts. So, *pace* the objections of, for example, Martin Rundkvist and Lasse Sonne, and absent more compelling factors than have hitherto been offered,

I find it difficult not to accept Christensen's conclusion that what is portrayed in the item is likely to be some variation of what later sources identify as Óðinn, seated on Hliðskjálf. In addition to the human figure, several animal forms ornament this tiny yet important object, two birds and two other creatures of some sort, all posed in heraldic opposition. The artist, it has been argued, has apparently been at some pains to demonstrate that the birds are ravens, while the nature of the other creatures is much less easily identified.[7] The interpretation of these two creatures necessarily varies according to how one resolves the identity question, but if, in fact, it is meant to be Óðinn, then it stands to reason that the birds are intended to be those specifically associated with him in later sources, the ravens, Huginn and Muninn, whose names touch on aspects of our mental faculties, roughly "thought" and "mind," a point even critics are inclined to accept.[8]

The Lejre ravens, and indeed, possibly the ravens on all three objects, are perched on the arms of the throne, positioned such that they could easily, in the case of the Lejre amulet, for example, be speaking into the ears of the seated figure, very reminiscent of the way the thirteenth-century Icelander Snorri Sturluson describes Óðinn's feathered assistants: "Two ravens sit on his [i.e., Óðinn's] shoulders and speak into his ear all the news they see or hear. Their names are Huginn and Muninn. He sends them out to fly over the whole world at daybreak and they return at the morning-meal. From this he becomes wise about many things. For this [reason] he is called the Raven God."[9] It is easy to see why the ancient Scandinavians would have favored the raven in such zoomorphic contexts: opportunistic, gregarious, omnivorous, quarrelsome, thieving, intelligent, and adaptable as these birds are, there is much about the raven that must have appealed to the mentality of the Viking Age, as well as the cultures that preceded it. That this common but remarkable bird is also capable of vocalizations, even imitating the human voice, made the raven a perfect choice for its role in Óðinn's obsessive attempts to be informed about events.

Yet beyond the zoomorphic use of the raven, something the Nordic peoples shared with many other cultures, how are we to understand the metonymy of the twinning of Huginn and Muninn? That is, why should this deity need to have two such birds, rather than just a single one? Is the very existence of two such assistants itself of importance? Not only do the three amulets—and Old Icelandic literature—present the ravens in pairs, but it has even been suggested that something similar—that is, wearing two figurative ravens, one adorning each shoulder—may have been a style among Norse warriors.[10] And beyond their obvious roles as the god's eyes and ears, what larger practices and significance do the ravens indicate? Interpretations to date of Óðinn's news-gatherers tend either toward the pragmatic or the philosophical, that is, scholars generally view these ornithic assistants in the context of Óðinn's magical healing functions, or in terms of the corvids' own many connections to battle and slaughter, or as the hypostasis of the gods' all-knowing and wise qualities, or as echoes of possible shamanistic practices.[11] But whatever the plausibility of any one of these approaches, or, indeed, a combination of any, or even all, of them, what is the usefulness, perhaps even necessity, of pairing the ravens' etymons, *hugr* and *munr* (alt. *muna*)?[12]

Twins in Old Norse

Actual twins (Old Norse *tvíburar*),[13] that is, of the mono- and dizygotic sort, surely existed in Viking Age Scandinavia, and we occasionally see references to them in later literature. Thus, one of the legendary settlers of Iceland, Geirmundr heljarskinn ("hell-skin"), has a twin, Hámundr heljarskinn (also "hell-skin"), and their early adventures, told along very traditional narrative lines, form a status-enhancing predicate for this famous family progenitor's subsequent move to Iceland.[14] Indeed, writers in the Nordic tradition were quick to take advantage of the narrative possibilities of twins, or in any event, of similar pairings that offered character and plot foils of the most intimate sort. So, for example, we encounter with some frequency suggestive sibling dyads like Freyr-Freyja in the mythological texts,[15] Sigmund-Signý in *Völsunga saga*, and the two Haddings (*Haddingjar tveir*) of *Hervarar saga* and elsewhere. Troublesome sets of men, always, it seems, with paired names, are wont to show up in the sagas and create mischief, as, for example, do Gautan ("Babbling") and Ógautan ("Not Babbling") in *Þorsteins saga Víkingssonar,* and Olíus and Alíus in *Ásmundar saga kappabana*. Even though we are not always explicitly told that they are twins in the biological sense, there can be little doubt but that we are to interpret them as paired in a way similar to twins. A female parallel occurs in the poem *Gróttasöngr* when the giantess slaves, Fenja and Menja, grind out on their quern an army to destroy King Fróði.

The preserved mythological materials delight in such meaningful pairings: in addition to those cases already enumerated, the horse Skínfaxi ("shining mane") pulls Day across the sky, while it is Hrímfaxi ("rime mane") that pulls Night. Óðinn sires the avenging brother deities Váli ("little warrior") and Víðarr ("widely separated"), who will be among the six deities to live on after Ragnarök, the Scandinavian apocalypse.[16] A similar sort of "twinning" may be at work in the evolution of the Fjörgyn-Fjörgynn pair: with the first of these Óðinn fathers the god, Þórr, while the second of them is the father of Óðinn's wife, Frigg. Of course, it is possible that some of the names are predicated more or less entirely on such practical matters as the metrical needs of the native alliterative poetry, but when we encounter a dyad pregnant with meaning, like Þórr's sons, Móði ("angry one") and Magni ("the strong"), even the most ardent skeptic is likely to admit that these members of the Nordic Pantheon should be understood as reflecting, and reflecting on, the nature of the deity with whom they are most closely associated.

Twinned "Thoughts" at Gammel Lejre

Coming back then full circle to the three amulets with their twinned, information-bearing specimens of *Corvus corax,* what meaning does the pairing of the ravens, with their seemingly transparent names, offer?[17] Writing in the mid-nineteenth century, Jacob Grimm noted the raven's parallel role already in Greek tradition as Apollo's messenger (or more aptly, spy) reporting back to the deity about his erstwhile lover; moreover, Grimm suggested that in the Old Norse case, the ravens' names set the more active intellectual processes, *animus, cogitatio,* represented by *hugr,* against the power of reason and the intellect as a whole, *mens,* represented by *munr,* thus directing our thinking about Óðinn's helpers toward a consideration of humanity's capacity for cogitation and sapience, broadly speaking, the requisite constituent functions of "the mind."[18]

Writing some decades later, E. H. Meyer took the argument in a slightly different direction and proposed, following a line of reasoning dating back to St. Augustine's attempt to analogize the concept of God to the human mind in *De Trinitate* ("On the Trinity"). In that context, Meyer wrote, the ravens would be understood as *Memoria* "memory" and *Intelligentia* "intelligence," "understanding," which, together with *Voluntas* "will," "purpose," are used by St. Augustine to explain the Holy Trinity.[19] Contemporary understandings of the raven's names have often, consciously or not, followed in the vein Meyer suggested, having been further influenced by those who, like Finnur Jónsson, would continue to relate Huginn to "thought" but now apparently derive Muninn from *muna* "to call to mind, remember" and thus gloss the name as "the remembering one" (*den erindrende*), "Remembrance," and so on.[20] In fact, the ravens are today—albeit not without controversy—commonly referred to in Anglophone contexts as "Thought" and "Memory."[21]

It is worth noting that this "thought" and "memory" perspective probably reflects many medieval Icelanders' understanding of the name-associations as well. In other words, the popular, generally held medieval view need not necessarily have been, and often was not, the same thing as the modern scientific conclusions about word histories (witness, e.g., Snorri's implied Æsir < Ásía). Thus, Sturtevant's view that the real etymologies of Huginn and Muninn are "thought" and "discernment" could well prove to be the correct understanding of the words' origins and their historical developments,[22] but that is a very different thing from what later native speakers might have believed and how they may have used the terms.[23]

The bifurcation of the mind into two partially overlapping categories by these understandings of the terms captures something essential about the way the mind was, and is, conceived. Indeed, viewing the mind in this way, as consisting of an active thinking component together with the power of recollection, has historical roots reaching back to Augustine (and even further back in time), as well as contemporary value. In modern usage, the mind is still sometimes understood to be principally composed of these same two complementary notions. The long entry for *mind* in *The Oxford English Dictionary,* for example, begins and is generally dominated by dividing the various elements into two categories, namely, those connotations touching on "senses relating to memory" and those concerned with "senses relating to thought."[24] Twinning, on the one hand, cerebration, actual mental activity, "thinking," with, on the other hand, the capacity to recall past events, "memory," is thus one means of "thinking about thinking," a problem with manifestly deep roots in Indo-European linguistic and cognitive configurations.[25] Seen in this broader historical perspective, Huginn and Muninn may then "simply" be Nordic visualizations of a much more general and much more archaic pattern for conceptualizing the human mind as necessarily twinned, or, as one scholar recently summarizes the issue, "Óðinn is anxious that Muninn will not come back, which hints at the relative superiority of

Figure 16.2 Óðinn with Huginn and Muninn, eighteenth-century Icelandic manuscript SÁM (*Stofnun Árna Magnússonar á Íslandi*) 66 (detail). By permission of the Árni Magnússon Institute for Icelandic Studies.

memory over thought. Asked rhetorically: what is thought without memory, which brings the past into the present?"[26]

Huginn and Muninn at Work

This pair of ravens serves Óðinn in similar ways in the Old Norse texts, but Huginn and Muninn are not understood to be identical or synonymous. They are, as is often the case with twin-like pairs, "the same but different." Just after his description of Óðinn's ravens (above), Snorri cites this verse, also known from the eddaic poem, *Grímnismál*:

> Huginn and Muninn
> fly each day
> over the earth;
> I fear for Huginn
> lest he not return,
> yet I fear more for Muninn.[27]

It does not, I think, strain credulity to imagine that the poet here associates Huginn and Muninn with their etymons, at least as he understands them, and actually means something by this comparative comment. But what?

Beyond the most basic and literal sense of the text, one reading would be that the poet's is an anxiety which is at once both personal and universal, namely, that he fears the loss of reasoning, of mental ability, of cogitation, of thinking—but even more so the loss of memory, the onset of dementia and the erosion of mental faculties that comes with age. This concern is natural and one which, as we know from other tales in *Snorra edda*, was current in thirteenth-century Iceland: in reflecting on Þórr's struggle with the old nurse, "Age" (Elli), during his visit with Útgarða-Loki, the text explicitly comments on age-related decline, noting that no one reaches old age who is not ruined by it.[28]

On a less personal level, the poem's lines also suggest an elegiac mode, a lamentation of sorts, an expression of concern and sorrow about pending cultural amnesia.[29] And here it is worth recalling the specific textual context for much of our knowledge of these mythological materials. The loss of memory, writ large, specifically, that is, of cultural memory—and, importantly, combating this development—is, in fact, the very purpose for the mythological handbook that is the *Prose edda*. After all, the ultimate goal of Snorri's *ars poetica* is the preservation of the tradition of skaldic poetry, a dying native art form intimately tied to metaphors drawn from the pagan past; it is a manual very explicitly addressed to "*young* poets" (<u>*ungum*</u> *skáldum*, emphasis added) for their edification and entertainment.[30] Read in this way, in a thirteenth-century Icelandic context, a stanza expressing fear for the loss of Huginn but even greater fear for the failure of Muninn to return is not just a whimsical rumination on relatively ephemeral mythological figures, but rather a poignant commentary that goes very much to the heart of the medieval Icelandic literary enterprise as a whole.[31]

A stanza preserved in another thirteenth-century Icelandic text, *The Third Grammatical Treatise*, also mentions these same twinned birds, and it too hints at their functions:

Two ravens flew
from Hnikar's [Óðinn's] shoulders;
Huginn to the hanged
and Muninn to the corpse.[32]

How, if at all, does this verse inform us about Óðinn's ravens and their wider meanings? Yet another thirteenth-century Icelandic text helps explain this anonymous stanza in *The Third Grammatical Treatise*: in *The Saga of the Ynglings*, the euhemerized opening of the massive history of the Norwegian kings, *Heimskringla*, Snorri Sturluson writes,

Óthin had with him Mímir's head, which told him tidings from other worlds; and at times he would call to life dead men out of the ground, or he would sit down under men that were hanged. On this account he was called Lord of Ghouls or of the Hanged. He had two ravens on whom he bestowed the gift of speech. They flew far and wide over the lands and told him many tidings. By these means he became very wise in his lore. And all these skills he taught with those runes and songs which are called magic songs [charms]. For this reason the Æsir are called Workers of Magic.[33]

Clearly, Óðinn has many means of acquiring knowledge; it is unlikely to be mere coincidence that Óðinn's sobriquet as "Lord of Ghouls or of the Hanged" comes just before the statement that the flesh-eating ravens are those who keep the god abreast of the news that matters. Óðinn's role as the god (or lord) of the hanged (*hangatýr, hangaguð, hangadróttin*) is generally understood in thanatological terms, according to which he seeks information from the dead and from sacrificial victims (and other hanged men) as they hover between life and death—between two worlds— much in the same way as he seems to gain runic knowledge through his own self-sacrifice, hanging on the World Tree.[34] That Huginn flies to the hanged, according to the stanza in *The Third Grammatical Treatise*, where he too will, one assumes, gather information, is very much in keeping with the projection of the more active intellectual processes associated with his etymon.[35] Muninn, on the other hand, flies to the *hræ*, which I have glossed above as "corpses," but which might equally well be translated as "carrion" or "dead bodies," and significantly, a word that can also imply the "wreck" or "fragment" of something, all senses that imply a feel for the elegiac or memorial function appropriate to a mythological bird connected to the idea of memory.[36] Far from being ambiguous or obscure in its intentions, the stanza from *The Third Grammatical Treatise* speaks directly, if with typically veiled and cryptic Norse phraseology and images, to the nature, meaning and function of the twinned Huginn and Muninn—Óðinn's "eyes in the sky."

Conclusion

Implicitly at least, I began this rumination on twins in Scandinavian mythology by suggesting that we could learn something about twinning and dyads, and their use, in the Norse world, if we began our journey with a consideration of the recently discovered, diminutive silver amulet from Lejre, as well as those from Hedeby and Nybølle, and their prominent pairs of perched birds. Whatever scholarship's ultimate disposition on the Lejre artifact, for example, its apparent concrete representation, as many believe, of Óðinn's ravens, Huginn and Muninn, provides a useful visualization for the concept of twins and twinning in the medieval Norse world. Through the Lejre figure, or more precisely, through Óðinn's ravens, we not only see the evidence for such dyads as *thought : memory* and *thinking : mind* at work in Old Icelandic literature, but are also able to come closer to understanding how "the mind" itself was represented in the Viking world and among its descendants.

Notes

I take this opportunity to thank a number of colleagues, including Tom Christensen, Pernille Hermann, Matt Kaplan, John Lindow, and Peter Pentz, for their comments, objections, and helpfulness in the preparation of this chapter, as well as to Kimberley Patton both for these reasons and for inviting me to contribute to this volume in the first instance. I note too that since this essay was originally drafted, I have had the opportunity to make related observations on memory studies and "Óðinn´s Ravens" in *Handbook of Pre-Modern Nordic Memory Studies: Interdisciplinary Approaches*, ed. Jürg Glauser, Pernille Hermann and Stephen A. Mitchell (Berlin: de Gruyter, 2018), I: 454–62.

1 "De tre amuletter har det til fælles, at de har to ravne siddende på stoleryggen, og det leder straks tankerne hen på Odin og hans to ravne" (Camilla Laursen, "Sjælden stol-amulet fundet på Lolland." Posted at *TV Øst (Seneste nyt)* on August 4, 2016; available at [last accessed March 16, 2017]; my translation). The announcement is still the most complete description of the find to date, so far as I know. For the Hedeby amulet, from no later than AD 899–911, see Hans Drescher and Karl Hauk, "Götterthrone des heidnische Nordens," *Frühmittelalterliche Studien* 16 (1982): 239, as well as the discussion in Neil S. Price, *The Viking Way: Religion and War in Late Iron Age Scandinavia* (Uppsala: Institutionen för arkeologi och antik historia, Uppsala universitet, 2002), 165–6. The Old Norse name of the god, Óðinn, is employed throughout, except where citing authors who use the Anglicized forms, Odin and Óthin.

2 The discovery of the figurine was well covered by the local press (Louise Lauritsen, "Et unikt fund af Odin fra Lejre," *Roskilde Avis*, November 13, 2009), and officially announced and interpreted in Tom Christensen, "Odin fra Lejre," *ROMU: Årsskrift fra Roskilde Museum* (2009): 7–25, and again in his "'Gud, konge eller. . .'," *Arkæologisk forum* 22 (2010): 21–5 (the latter item is an abbreviated version of the earlier article but with superior illustrations, both of the figurine itself and of the *comparanda*). See also his "A silver figurine from Lejre." *Danish Journal of Archaeology* 2, no. 1 (2013): 65–78.

3 On Lejre in medieval literature in particular, see John D. Niles, Tom Christensen, and Marijane Osborn, eds., *Beowulf and Lejre*, Medieval and Renaissance Texts and Studies 323 (Tempe, Ariz: Arizona Center for Medieval and Renaissance Studies, 2007). A comprehensive presentation of the archaeological materials is provided in Tom Christensen, ed., *Lejre bag myten. De arkæologiske udgravninger*. Jysk Arkæologisk Selskabs Skrifter 87 (Aarhus: Aarhus Universitetsforlag, 2016).

4 Debate about whether the seated figure wears characteristically male or female dress has been especially keen, although I do not see this point as being dispositive in the way many critics have. The possibility of individuals cross-dressing and in other ways "gender bending" in this otherwise profoundly homophobic warrior culture is only one of the cultural paradoxes that has fascinated modern scholarship. On this debate, especially in the light of archaeology, see Price, *The Viking Way* and Brit Solli, *Seid. Myter, sjamanisme og kjønn i vikingenes tid* (Oslo: Pax Forlag A/S, 2002). On the question of gender-identifiable dress and the Lejre figurine, see also Ulla Mannering, "Man or Woman?—Perception of Gender Through Costume," *Danish Journal of Archaeology* 2, no. 1 (2013): 79–86.

5 On the association of these two clairvoyant venues, see Vilhelm Kiil, "*Hliðskjálf og seiðhjallr*," *Arkiv för nordisk filologi* 75 (1960): 84–112.

6 E.g., Lasse Christian Arboe Sonne, "Den lille Sølvfigur fra Lejre. Bemærkninger til Tolkningen af en mulig Odin-Figur," *1066. Tidsskrift for Historie* 40, no. 3 (2010): 32–9. An early critic of the Odinic identification, Martin Rundkvist, "Odin from Lejre? No, it's Freya!" *Aardvarchaeology,* http://scienceblogs.com/ aardvarchaeology/2009/11/13/odin-from-lejre-no-its-freya/ (posted November 13,

2009; accessed most recently, March 15, 2022), objected on narrower grounds. I note that Rundkvist and Sonne enjoy excellent company in their skepticism about the Odinic identification: shortly after the find, Denmark's preeminent archaeologist, Else Roesdahl, expressed the view that although the individual on the object is most likely a deity, it is probably meant to be Freyja. She does so, however, with palpable and important reservations, going out of her way to note that female attire, if that is what we see, does not mean that it is not Óðinn ("Det er ikke umuligt, at det er Odin, selv om figuren har klare elementer af kvindedragt"). See Óluva Ellingsgaard, "Var Odin en kvinde?" *Videnskab dk,* http://videnskab.dk/kultur-samfund/var-odin -en-kvinde (posted January 27, 2010; accessed most recently, March 2, 2022). The possibility that female, rather than male, attire may be what we see on the figure tends in my view to enhance, rather than detract from, the likelihood that this object is intended to show Óðinn: textual sources ranging from Saxo's *Gesta Danorum* to the Icelandic mythological materials (as well, perhaps, as some material evidence) strongly suggest that cross-dressing was part of the magical "kit" in the Viking Age. One cannot help but be suspicious that the arguments in Price, *The Viking Way,* and Solli, *Seid. Myter, sjamanisme og kjønn* are curiously absent from most discussions among the "Odin dissenters," who tend to raise gender only in a biological sense. The first scholar to challenge some of these assumptions would appear to be Elisabeth Arwill-Nordbladh, who in several articles—for example, "Ability and Disability. On Bodily Variations and Bodily Possibilities in Viking Age Myth and Image," in *To Tender Gender: The Pasts and Futures of Gender Research in Archaeology,* ed. Ing-Marie Back Danielsson and Susanne Thedéen. Stockholm Studies in Archaeology, 58 (Stockholm: Dept of Archaeology and Classical Studies, 2012), 33–60, and "Negotiating Normativities – 'Odin from Lejre' as Challenger of Hegemonic Orders," *Danish Journal of Archaeology* 2, no. 1 (2013): 87–93—suggests a vastly more post-modern perspective, concluding, as she writes about "negotiating normativities," that "the high-ranked setting of Lejre included performative practices that were negotiating both hetero-normative and body-normative hegemonic orders." A recent important contribution to the interpretation of this figure, one that takes full account of the many possible analyses and arguments, has been the view that it represents a *völva* or seeress; see Bettina Sommer and Morten Warmind, "Óðinn from Lejre—or?", *Numen* 62 (2015): 627–38.

7   That the birds represent ravens is especially notable in their distinctive wedge-shaped tails and transversed remiges (pennaceous flight feathers); cf. Christensen, "Odin fra Lejre," 11, "På ryggen markerer nielloindlægninger de krydsende vinger lagt hen over halen på de to ens fugle. Også de kraftige næb er med til at give fuglene karakter, nok til at fastslå, at det er to ravne. . ." Whether the other conspicuous zoomorphic elements at the back of the figurine show the wolves, Geri and Freki (both names mean "the ravenous one"), or are simply decorative elements of the throne seems impossible to conclude, but the association of ravens and wolves, not only in Norse mythology, but also in nature, tends to push the interpretation in that direction. I take this opportunity to thank Matt Kaplan, science journalist at *The Economist* and 2014–15 Knight Fellow at MIT, for his stimulating discussions with me of this point in connection with his own research on wolves and ravens. A thorough examination of the figurine and its background, especially with regard to so-called farm ravens, is found in Marijane Osborn, "The Ravens on the Lejre Throne: Avian Identifiers, Odin at Home, Farm Ravens," in *Representing Beasts in Early Medieval England and Scandinavia,* ed. Michael D. J. Bintley and Thomas J.

T. Williams. Anglo-Saxon Studies, 29 (Woodbridge: Boydell Press, 2015), 94–112. Also relevant to discussion of the man-beast aspects of Óðinn's ravens are the comments in Lena Rohrbach, *Der tierische Blick: Mensch-Tier-Relationen in der Sagaliteratur*, Beiträge zur nordischen Philologie, 43 (Tübingen & Basel: A. Francke Verlag, 2009), 79, 127, 130, 232–3 *et passim.*

8 Sonne, "Den lille Sølvfigur fra Lejre," 35, for example, notes that Huginn and Muninn are known from Viking Age skaldic poetry and thus, give better reason for believing the figure is Óðinn ("her er vi derfor mere berettigede til at se en sammenhæng med Odin"), although he concludes otherwise.

9 "Hrafnar tveir sitja á öxlum honum ok segja í eyru honum öll tíðendi, þau er þeir sjá eða heyra. Þeir heita svá, Huginn ok Muninn. Þá sendir hann í dagan at fljúga um heim allan, ok koma þeir aftr at dögurðarmáli. Þar af verðr hann margra tíðenda víss. Því kalla menn hann Hrafnaguð. . ." Guðni Jónsson, ed. *Edda Snorra Sturlusonar* (Akureyri: Íslendingasagnaútgáfan, 1954), 57. The birds are widely attested in Norse literary monuments (e.g., *Heimskringla*, eddic poetry, *The Third Grammatical Treatise*). Possible iconographic treatments of the ravens have been argued for a variety of art objects, including bracteates, stone carvings, brooches and helmet plates, often from much earlier periods than the literary evidence. See Rudolf Simek, *Dictionary of Northern Mythology* (Cambridge: D. S. Brewer, 1993), 164.

10 See Peter Vang Pedersen, "Odins ravne/Odin's ravens," in *Oldtidens ansigt (Faces of the Past)*, ed. Poul Kjærum and Rikke Agnete Olsen (Copenhagen: Kongelige Nordiske Oldskriftselskab & Jysk arkæologisk selskab, 1990), 160–1, on the pair of such bird-shaped brooches from Bejsebakken near Ålborg, Denmark. I warmly thank Peter Pentz for pointing out this possibility to me.

11 See Simek, *Dictionary of Northern Mythology,* and John Lindow, *Norse Mythology: A Guide to the Gods, Heroes, Rituals, and Beliefs* (New York: Oxford University Press, 2002), 186–8. For a detailed review of the critical literature, see Gottfried Lorenz, ed., *Snorri Sturluson. Gylfaginning. Texte, Übersetzung, Kommentar*, vol. 48, Texte zur Forschung (Darmstadt: Wissenschaftliche Buchgesellschaft, 1984), 468–9, as well as the older but still relevant review of materials in Alexander H. Krappe, *Études de mythologie et de folklore germaniques* (Paris: E. Leroux, 1928), 29–44.

12 Richard Cleasby and Gudbrand Vigfusson, eds., *An Icelandic-English Dictionary*, 2nd ed., William Craigie (Oxford: The Clarendon Press, 1982) identify *hugr* primarily as "*mind,* with the notion of *thought,* answering to Germ. *Gedanke*" and as secondarily denoting "*mood, heart, temper, feeling, affection.*" *munr* too they define as "*the mind,*" and secondarily, "*a mind, longing, delight.*" Some (e.g., Finnur Jónsson) derive Muninn from the verb *muna* "to remember."

13 Cf. *Tuisto,* the proto-being of the Germanic peoples according to Tacitus in his *Germania*, whose name derives from the same root as that for *tvíburar,* "two," "twain," "twin," and so on.

14 "Geirmundr heljarskinn var sonr Hjörs konungs Hálfssonar, er Hálfsrekkar eru við kenndir, Hjörleifs sonar konungs. Annarr sonr Hjörs konungs var Hámundr, er enn var kallaðr heljarskinn. Þeir váru *tvíburar,*" [emphasis added] Guðni Jónsson, ed., *Sturlunga saga,* 2nd ed. (Reykjavík: Íslendingasagnaútgáfan, 1954), I:1. On this motif (K1921.3 *Queen exchanges own twins for slave's son*), see my "The Sagaman and Oral Literature: The Icelandic Traditions of Hjörleifr inn kvensami and Geirmundr heljarskinn," in *Comparative Research on Oral Traditions: A Memorial for Milman Parry*, ed. John Miles Foley (Columbus, OH: Slavica Publishers, 1987), 395–423. A recent evaluation of this tale and its political

(and settlement) implications for later Icelanders is given in Gísli Sigurðsson, "To Construct a Past that Suits the Present. How Sturla Þórðarson Wrote about Conflicts and Alliances of his Countrymen with King Haraldr *hárfagri* in the 9th Century," in *Minni and Muninn: Memory in Medieval Nordic Culture*, ed. Pernille Hermann, Stephen A. Mitchell and Agnes S. Arnórsdóttir (Turnhout: Brepols, 2014), 189–211.

15 Although these two deities are often represented in modern treatments as twins, there is no compelling evidence to support this view in the Old Norse materials themselves.

16 In general, the name glosses here follow Lindow, *Norse Mythology*, but in the case of Víðarr, I adopt the argument made in Albert Morey Sturtevant, "Etymological Comments Upon Certain Old Norse Proper Names in the Eddas," *Publications of the Modern Language Association* 67 (1952): 1145–62.

17 In writing "seemingly transparent," I do not mean to ignore or gloss over the very real debates about the etymologies of the names, only to note that a medieval Icelander would surely have made certain kinds of associations with them. I note too that the raven identification is clearest in the case of the Lejre amulet.

18 Jacob Grimm, *Teutonic Mythology*, trans. James Steven Stallybrass (New York: Dover Publications, Inc., 1966), 147.

19 Elard Hugo Meyer, *Germanische Mythologie* (Berlin: Mayer & Müller, 1891), 232: "Ihre abstracten Namen *Muninn* und *Huginnn* [. . .] scheinen der *Memoria* and *Intelligentia* entlehnt, die mit der Voluntas die h. Dreifaltigkeit bilden." Cf. Augustine, *De Trinitate* XIV.8, who reasons that a trinity of the mind is indicated by these three terms, "memory, intelligence, will" (*Ideoque etiam illis tribus nominibus insinuandam mentis putauimus trinitatem, memoria, intellegentia, uoluntate*).

20 Finnur Jónsson and Sveinbjörn Egilsson, eds. *Lexicon Poeticum Antiquae Linguae Septentrionalis: Ordbog over Det norsk-islandske Skjaldesprog*, 2nd rev. ed. (Copenhagen: S. L. Møller, 1931), 292, 415. "Remembrance," e.g., is used in Lee M. Hollander, trans., *The Poetic Edda* (Austin: University of Texas Press, 1928).

21 Cf. Albert Morey Sturtevant, "Comments on Mythological Name-Giving in Old Norse," *Germanic Review* 29 (1954): 68–9, who argues that this interpretation of Muninn is "undoubtedly incorrect," preferring "intelligence" or, following Gering, "discernment" (*Unterscheidungsvermögen*). If one accepts Sturtevant's view that the correct glosses are "thought" and "discernment," it is striking how by pure coincidence (and, historically, due to poetic jealousy) this paired ideology is also reflected in the late eighteenth-century motto of the Swedish Academy: *Snille och Smack* (lit., "Genius and Taste"), where one easily recognizes the same dyad, "thought" and "discernment."

22 Sturtevant, "Comments on Mythological Name-Giving in Old Norse."

23 For a recent discussion of the etymological questions surrounding the names, see John Lindow, "Memory and Old Norse Mythology," in *Minni and Muninn: Memory in Medieval Nordic Culture*, ed. Pernille Hermann, Stephen A. Mitchell and Agnes S. Arnórsdóttir (Turnhout: Brepols, 2014), 92–111, who concludes, "it seems to me on balance likely that pre-Christian poets and medieval men of letters alike could hardly have overlooked the parallel between *hugr*/Huginn and *muna*/Muninn even if one departs from a noun and the other a verb."

24 John A. Simpson and Edmund S. C. Weiner, eds., *Oxford English Dictionary*, 2nd ed. (Oxford: Clarendon Press & Oxford University Press, 1993).

25 Cf. Carl Darling Buck, *A Dictionary of Selected Synonyms in the Principal Indo-European Languages: A Contribution to the History of Ideas* (Chicago: University of Chicago Press, 1949), 1198–9, 1202–3, 1228–9.

26 Pernille Hermann, "Key Aspects of Memory and Remembering in Old Norse-Icelandic Literature," in *Minni and Muninn: Memory in Medieval Nordic Culture,* ed. Pernille Hermann, Stephen A. Mitchell and Agnes S. Arnórsdóttir, Acta Scandinavica 4 (Turnhout: Brepols, 2014), 17.

27 "Huginn ok Muninn / fljúga hverjan dag / jörmungrund yfir; / óumk ek Hugin, / at hann aftr né komi, / þó sjámk ek meir of Munin," Guðni Jónsson, ed. *Edda Snorra Sturlusonar,* 57.

28 "engi hefir sá orðit ok engi mun verða, ef svá gamall verðr, at elli bíðr, at eigi komi ellin öllum til falls." See Guðni Jónsson, ed., *Edda Snorra Sturlusonar,* 73–4, 76. Cf. Ármann Jakobsson, "The Specter of Old Age: Nasty Old Men in the Sagas of Icelanders," *The Journal of English and Germanic Philology* 104, no. 3 (2005): 297–325, especially 301–8 and the literature cited there.

29 In using the phrase "cultural amnesia," I mean it here only in the most literal sense as a sort of aggressive cultural assimilation and intend no association with the theories of the so-called catastrophist Immanuel Velikovsky.

30 Cf. "En þetta er nú at segja ungum skáldum, þeim er girnast at nema mál skáldskapar ok heyja sér orðfjölða með fornum heitum eða girnast þeir at kunna skilja þat, er hulit er kveðit, þá skili hann þessa bók til fróðleiks ok skemmtunar. En ekki er at gleyma eða ósanna svá þessar frásagnir at taka ór skáldskapinum fornar kenningar, þær er höfuðskáld hafa sér líka látit." Guðni Jónsson, ed., *Edda Snorra Sturlusonar,* 106.

31 I do not at all discount that the ancient and original sense of this verse may have been tied to a practice involving transvecting spirits; on the other hand, by the 13th century, the context—*Snorra edda*—for interpreting the phrase would have changed substantially.

32 "Flugu hrafnar tveir / af Hnikars öxlum; / Huginn til hanga, / en á hræ Muninn," Finnur Jónsson, ed. *Málhljóða- og málskrúðsrit: grammatisk-retorisk afhandling af Óláfr Þórðarson,* Historisk-filologiske meddelelser 13:2 (Copenhagen: Kgl. Danske Videnskabernes Selsk., 1927), 66. On this verse, see Tarrin Wills, ed., "Óláfr Hvítaskáld Þórðarson. Fragments," in *Poetry from the Treatises on Poetics,* ed. Kari Ellen Gade and Edith Marold. Skaldic Poetry of the Scandinavian Middle Ages, 3 (Turnhout: Brepols, 2017), 304–5.

33 "Óðinn hafði með ser höfuð Mímis, ok sagði þat honum mörg tíðendi ór öðrum heimum, en stundum vakði hann upp dauða menn ór jörðu eða settisk undir hanga. Fyrir því var hann kallaðr draugadróttinn eða hangadróttinn. Hann átti hrafna tvá, er hann hafði tamit við mál. Flugu þeir víða um lönd ok sögðu honum mörg tíðendi. Af þessum hlutum varð hann stórliga fróðr. Allar þessar íþróttir kendi hann með rúnum ok ljóðum þeim, er galdrar heita. Fyrir því eru Æsir kallaðir galdrasmiðir," Bjarni Aðalbjarnarson, ed. *Snorri Sturluson. Heimskringla I.* Íslenzk fornrit 26 (Reykjavík: Hið íslenzka fornritafélag, 1941), 18–19. The translation is from Lee M. Hollander, transl., *Heimskringla. History of the Kings of Norway by Snorri Sturluson* (1964; Austin: University of Texas Press for the American-Scandinavian Foundation, 1991), 11. Significantly, the passage immediately following these lines refers to Óðinn's knowledge of *seiðr.* On the use of ghouls and the dead in Nordic magical praxis, see my "The n-Rune and Nordic Charms," in *"Vi ska alla vara välkomna!" Nordiska studier tillägnade Kristinn Jóhannesson,* ed. Auður G. Magnúsdóttir et al., 219–29.

Meijbergs Arkiv för svensk ordforskning, 35 (Göteborg: Meijbergs Arkiv för svensk ordforskning, 2008).

34 Cf. Kimberley C. Patton, *Religion of the Gods: Ritual, Paradox, and Reflexivity* (Oxford and New York: Oxford University Press, 2009), 213–38, and Jens Peter Schjødt, *Initiation between Two Worlds: Structure and Symbolism in Pre-Christian Scandinavian Religion*, The Viking Collection, 17 (Odense: University Press of Southern Denmark, 2008), 173–206.

35 This point, and the discussion about Óðinn's ravens more generally, are also meant to push back against those looking to adduce evidence disconnecting the Lejre figurine from Óðinn (e.g., Sonne, "Den lille Sølvfigur fra Lejre," 35, when he argues that "så er ravnene imidlertid *altid* [my emphasis] knytet til kamp og krig." Clearly, that is not the case.) Suggestions of bird augury are well documented for Scandinavia; see, e.g., my *Witchcraft and Magic in the Nordic Middle Ages* (Philadelphia: University of Pennsylvania Press, 2010), 33, 218 *et passim*.

36 So Cleasby and Gudbrand Vigfusson, *An Icelandic-English Dictionary*. Cf. Johan Fritzner, ed., *Ordbok over Det gamle norske Sprog,* 4th rev. ed. (1886; Oslo, etc.: Universitetsforlaget, 1973), "1) dødt Legeme [. . .] 2) Vrag, Levningeraf noget som har taget saadan Skade, at det derved er blevet ubrugbart."

Bibliography

Ármann Jakobsson, "The Specter of Old Age: Nasty Old Men in the Sagas of Icelanders." *The Journal of English and Germanic Philology* 104, no. 3 (2005): 297–325.

Arwill-Nordbladh, Elisabeth. "Ability and Disability. On Bodily Variations and Bodily Possibilities in Viking Age Myth and Image." In *To Tender Gender: The Pasts and Futures of Gender Research in Archaeology*, edited by Ing-Marie Back Danielsson and Susanne Thedéen, 33–60. Stockholm Studies in Archaeology 58. Stockholm: Dept of Archaeology and Classical Studies, 2012.

Arwill-Nordbladh, Elisabeth. "Negotiating Normativities—'Odin from Lejre' as Challenger of Hegemonic Orders." *Danish Journal of Archaeology* 2, no. 1 (2012): 87–93.

Bjarni Aðalbjarnarson, ed. *Snorri Sturluson. Heimskringla I.* Íslenzk fornrit 26. Reykjavík: Hið íslenzka fornritafélag, 1941.

Buck, Carl Darling. *A Dictionary of Selected Synonyms in the Principal Indo-European Languages: A Contribution to the History of Ideas*. Chicago: University of Chicago Press, 1949.

Christensen, Tom. "Odin fra Lejre." *ROMU: Årsskrift fra Roskilde Museum* (2009): 7–25.

Christensen, Tom. "'Gud, konge eller . . . ,". *Arkæologisk Forum* 22 (2010): 21–5.

Christensen, Tom. "A silver figurine from Lejre." *Danish Journal of Archaeology* 2, no. 1 (2012): 65–78.

Christensen, Tom, ed. *Lejre bag myten. De arkæologiske udgravninger*. Jysk Arkæologisk Selskabs Skrifter 87. Aarhus: Aarhus Universitetsforlag, 2016.

Cleasby, Richard, and Gudbrand Vigfusson, eds. *An Icelandic-English Dictionary*, 2nd ed. Edited by William Craigie. Oxford: The Clarendon Press, 1982.

Drescher, Hans and Karl Hauk. "Götterthrone des heidnische Nordens." *Frühmittealterliche Studien* 16 (1982): 237–301.

Ellingsgaard, Óluva. "Var Odin en kvinde?" *Videnskab.dk*, January 27, 2010, http:// videnskab.dk/kultur-samfund/var-odin-en-kvinde.

Finnur Jónsson, ed. *Málhljóða- og málskrúðsrit: Grammatisk-retorisk afhandling af Óláfr Þórðarson.* Historisk-filologiske meddelelser 13:2. Copenhagen: Kgl. Danske Videnskabernes Selsk., 1927.

Finnur Jónsson, and Sveinbjörn Egilsson, eds. *Lexicon Poeticum Antiquae Linguae Septentrionalis: Ordbog over Det norsk-islandske Skjaldesprog,* 2nd rev. ed. Copenhagen: S. L. Møller, 1931.

Fritzner, Johan, ed. *Ordbok over Det gamle norske Sprog,* 4th rev. ed., 1886. Oslo, etc.: Universitetsforlaget, 1973.

Gísli Sigurðsson. "To Construct a Past That Suits the Present. How Sturla Þórðarson Wrote about Conflicts and Alliances of his Countrymen with King Haraldr *hárfagri* in the 9th Century." In *Minni and Muninn: Memory in Medieval Nordic Culture,* edited by Pernille Hermann, Stephen A. Mitchell, and Agnes S. Arnórsdóttir, 189–211. Turnhout: Brepols, 2014.

Grimm, Jacob. *Teutonic Mythology.* Translated by James Steven Stallybrass. New York: Dover Publications, Inc., 1966.

Guðni Jónsson, ed. *Edda Snorra Sturlusonar.* Akureyri: Íslendingasagnaútgáfan, 1954.

Guðni Jónsson. *Sturlunga Saga.* 2nd ed. Reykjavík: Íslendingasagnaútgáfan, 1954.

Hermann, Pernille. "Key Aspects of Memory and Remembering in Old Norse-Icelandic Literature." In *Minni and Muninn: Memory in Medieval Nordic Culture,* edited by Pernille Hermann, Stephen A. Mitchell, and Agnes S. Arnórsdóttir, 112–40. Acta Scandinavica 4. Turnhout: Brepols, 2014.

Hollander, Lee M., trans. *The Poetic Edda.* Austin: University of Texas Press, 1928.

Hollander, Lee M., trans. *Heimskringla. History of the Kings of Norway by Snorri Sturluson.* 1964. Austin: University of Texas Press for the American-Scandinavian Foundation, 1991.

Kiil, Vilhelm. "Hliðskjálf og seiðhjallr." *Arkiv för nordisk filologi* 75 (1960): 84–112.

Krappe, Alexander H. *Études de mythologie et de folklore germaniques.* Paris: E. Leroux, 1928.

Lauritsen, Louise. "Et unikt fund af Odin fra Lejre." *Roskilde Avis,* November 13, 2009; archived as https://web.archive.org/web/20091117053506/http:/roskilde.lokalavisen .dk/et-unikt-fund-af-odin-fra-lejre/20091113/artikler/711139709. Accessed March 15, 2022.

Laursen, Camilla. "Sjælden stol-amulet fundet på Lolland." Posted at *TV Øst (Seneste nyt),* on August 4, 2016, http://www.tveast.dk/artikel/sjaelden-stol-amulet-fundet-paa -lolland. Accessed March 16, 2017.

Lindow, John. *Norse Mythology: A Guide to the Gods, Heroes, Rituals, and Beliefs.* New York: Oxford University Press, 2002.

Lindow, John. "Memory and Old Norse Mythology." In *Minni and Muninn: Memory in Medieval Nordic Culture,* edited by Pernille Hermann, Stephen A. Mitchell, and Agnes S. Arnórsdóttir, 92–111. Acta Scandinavica 4. Turnhout: Brepols, 2014.

Lorenz, Gottfried, ed. *Snorri Sturluson. Gylfaginning. Texte, Übersetzung, Kommentar,* vol. 48. Texte zur Forschung. Darmstadt: Wissenschaftliche Buchgesellschaft, 1984.

Mannering, Ulla. 2013. "Man or Woman?—Perception of Gender Through Costume." *Danish Journal of Archaeology* 2, no. 1 (2012): 79–86.

Meyer, Elard Hugo. *Germanische Mythologie.* Berlin: Mayer & Müller, 1891.

Mitchell, Stephen A. "The Sagaman and Oral Literature: The Icelandic Traditions of Hjörleifr inn kvensami and Geirmundr heljarskinn." In *Comparative Research on*

Oral Traditions: A Memorial for Milman Parry, edited by John Miles Foley, 395–423.
      Columbus, Ohio: Slavica Publishers, 1987.
Mitchell, Stephen A. "The n-Rune and Nordic Charms." In *"Vi ska alla vara välkomna!"*
      Nordiska studier tillägnade Kristinn Jóhannesson, edited by Auður G. Magnúsdóttir et
      al., 219–29. Meijbergs Arkiv för svensk ordforskning, 35. Göteborg: Meijbergs Arkiv
      för svensk ordforskning, 2008.
Mitchell, Stephen A. *Witchcraft and Magic in the Nordic Middle Ages*. Philadelphia:
      University of Pennsylvania Press, 2010.
Mitchell, Stephen A. "Óðinn's Ravens." In *Handbook of Pre-Modern Nordic Memory*
      Studies: Interdisciplinary Approaches, edited by Jürg Glauser, Pernille Hermann and
      Stephen A. Mitchell I, 454–62. Berlin: de Gruyter, 2018.
Niles, John D., Tom Christensen, and Marijane Osborn, eds. *Beowulf and Lejre*, vol.
      323. Medieval and Renaissance Texts and Studies. Tempe, Ariz: Arizona Center for
      Medieval and Renaissance Studies, 2007.
Osborn, Marijane. "The Ravens on the Lejre Throne: Avian Identifiers, Odin at Home,
      Farm Ravens." In *Representing Beasts in Early Medieval England and Scandinavia*,
      edited by Michael D. J. Bintley and Thomas J. T. Williams, 94–112. Anglo-Saxon
      Studies 29. Woodbridge: Boydell Press, 2015.
Patton, Kimberley C. *Religion of the Gods: Ritual, Paradox, and Reflexivity*. Oxford and
      New York: Oxford University Press, 2009.
Pedersen, Peter Vang. "Odins ravne/Odin's ravens." In *Oldtidens ansigt (Faces of*
      the Past), edited by Poul Kjærum and Rikke Agnete Olsen, 160–1. Copenhagen:
      Kongelige Nordiske Oldskriftselskab & Jysk arkæologisk selskab, 1990.
Price, Neil S. *The Viking Way: Religion and War in Late Iron Age Scandinavia*. Uppsala:
      Institutionen för arkeologi och antik historia, Uppsala universitet, 2002.
Rohrbach, Lena. *Der tierische Blick: Mensch-Tier-Relationen in der Sagaliteratur*.
      Beiträge zur nordischen Philologie, 43. Tübingen & Basel: A. Francke Verlag, 2009.
Rundkvist, Martin. "Odin from Lejre? No, it's Freya!." *Aardvarchaeology*, http://
      scienceblogs.com/aardvarchaeology/2009/11/13/odin-from-lejre-no-its-freya/ (last
      accessed March 15, 2022).
Schjødt, Jens Peter. *Initiation between Two Worlds: Structure and Symbolism in Pre-*
      Christian Scandinavian Religion. The Viking Collection, 17. Odense: University Press
      of Southern Denmark, 2008.
Simek, Rudolf. *Dictionary of Northern Mythology*. Cambridge: D. S. Brewer, 1993.
Simpson, John A., and Edmund S. C. Weiner, eds. *Oxford English Dictionary*, 2nd ed.
      Oxford: Clarendon Press & Oxford University Press, 1993.
Solli, Brit. *Seid. Myter, sjamanisme og kjønn i vikingenes tid*. Oslo: Pax Forlag A/S, 2002.
Sommer, Bettina, and Morten Warmind. "Óðinn from Lejre—or?" *Numen* 62 (2015):
      627–38.
Sonne, Lasse Christian Arboe. "Den lille Sølvfigur fra Lejre. Bemærkninger til Tolkningen
      af en mulig Odin-Figur." *1066. Tidsskrift for Historie* 40, no. 3 (2010): 32–9.
Sturtevant, Albert Morey. "Etymological Comments Upon Certain Old Norse Proper
      Names in the Eddas." *Publications of the Modern Language Association* 67 (1952):
      1145–62.
Sturtevant, Albert Morey. "Comments on Mythological Name-Giving in Old Norse."
      Germanic Review 29 (1954): 68–9.
Wills, Tarrin, ed. "Óláfr Hvítaskáld Þórðarson. Fragments." In *Poetry from the Treatises*
      on Poetics, edited by Kari Ellen Gade and Edith Marold, 302–10. Skaldic Poetry of
      the Scandinavian Middle Ages, 3. Turnhout: Brepols, 2017.

17

Twinning and Pairing

Rethinking Number in the Roman Provincial Religious Imagery of Gallia and Britannia

♊

Miranda Aldhouse-Green

Introduction: The Good and Evil Twin

Twins and twinning are complex concepts that extend far beyond the biological actuality of birth-twins, that is, of the simple reduplication of a singleton. "Twins" involve pairs, couples, or doubles that may copy each other, but may equally present complementary or oppositional relationships. "Twinning" presents a compromise and contradiction in identities: the persona is reinforced yet divided and, potentially, each one's personality is amplified yet in some ways also diluted by the existence of the other.[1] This is especially true for identical twins, an issue addressed in Vijaya Nagarajan's chapter in this volume.

The arena for my study is a period of time on the cusp between prehistory and history, where both literature and the archaeological record can make a contribution. Medieval mythic texts from Wales and Ireland present a particular perspective on twins; more subtle and arguably more challenging, however, is evidence from the material culture of Gaul and Britain just before *romanitas* took hold and during the ensuing period when Roman and indigenous western European cultures rubbed shoulders, underwent syncretism, or appropriated and manipulated each other's traditions.

In *The Second Branch of the Mabinogi* one hears,

> Bendigeidfran son of Llŷr was crowned king over this island and
> invested with the crown of London. One afternoon he was in
> Harlech in Ardudwy, at one of his courts; he was sitting on the
> rock of Harlech, above the sea, with his brother Manawydan
> son of Llŷr, and his two brothers on his mother's side,
> Nysien and Efnysien . . . One of these was a good lad—he
> could make peace between two armies when they were

most enraged; that was Nysien. The other could cause
two of the most loving brothers to fight.[2]

This may represent one of the very few references to twins in medieval Welsh prose tales, and even here it is by no means certain that the brothers Nysien and Efnysien were actually twins. They are generally assumed to be such, partly on account of their oppositional characters. But the most positive clue to the geminal status of the Welsh mythic brothers is in their names, for "Ef" is from the Welsh word for twin (*gefell*).[3] The text quoted is the opening passage from the second of the *Four Branches*, a story that deals with violence, abuse (of both women and animals), and warfare between Wales and Ireland. The eponymous heroine of the tale is Branwen, but the story centers upon her brother Bendigeidfran (Brân the Blessed), a giant and the king of all Britain. While Branwen is the catalyst for the events that unfold, she is essentially passive; it is her brother who plays a pivotally active role in the narrative.

But there are issues concerning Nysien and Efnysien that may have relevance to the understanding of twinship in Gallo-British iconography, whilst always bearing in mind that the latter dates more than a thousand years before the *Four Branches* were compiled in written form. First, their names appear to contain an antiphonal element, as though they are two halves of a whole. Likewise, their contrapuntal natures—one a good peace-maker, the other a trouble-making war-monger—suggest two sides of the same coin, or the good and bad in all of us. Thus, in a sense, we can perceive in these two brothers a kind of Janus symbolism; it is as though the one cannot exist without the other, just as good always has to be viewed in the oppositional context of evil. The situation of these brothers resonates with the complex symbolic relationship surrounding sets of twins in Yorùbá mythical tradition, as presented by Jacob Olúpǫnà in this volume in which he discusses perceived dualities in personality in twins and their membership in both the material and spirit worlds. It is telling that, as the Welsh story progresses, it is the malevolent Efnysien whom the storyteller develops, while the righteous Nysien fades into the background. I am reminded of Shakespeare's comment in *Julius Caesar*,[4] "the evil that men do lives after them; the good is oft interred with their bones." Nysien's good conduct is rewarded by obscurity, whereas his erring brother's disruptive character earns him a stage spotlight and an enduring memory: Efnysien is the essence of disruption, trouble and nihilism.

An important point about the *Four Branches* and, indeed, about all eleven prose tales that form the *Mabinogion*, is that much of the text betrays its origin in oral tradition. Sioned Davies draws attention to the spoken performance element in the tales, as well as the role of the medieval storyteller in both handing down and shaping the stories that were transcribed probably centuries after their oral compilation.[5] In this context, the names Nysien and Efnysien take on particular resonance. Not only are they memorably similar names—in an essentially auditory world where memorability was key—but their names also convey notions of both similarity and opposition. Rather like Punch and Judy, the "goody" and the "baddy," two opposites immediately confront the listening audience, who anticipate trouble as the story progresses to its bloody and destructive climax.

In brief, the story of *Branwen*[6] unfolds thus. Matholwch, king of Ireland, requests the hand in marriage of Branwen, sister of Bendigeidfran. Bendigeidfran agrees and entertains the Irish king and his retinue to a celebratory feast. But Efnysien is angry that his half-sister has been betrothed without his permission and, as a mortal insult to her suitor, he mutilates Matholwch's horses so that they are shamed and worthless. Since, in many traditions, horses are closely linked with royal identity, it is likely that Efnysien was, in fact, attacking by proxy the Irish king himself.[7] Matholwch is justly furious at what has happened and threatens to walk away from his engagement, but Bendigeidfran manages to placate him by presenting him with a magnificent gift; a magical cauldron of regeneration that can bring dead warriors to life. The gift is significant, since cauldrons represent noble symbols of hospitality and largesse: it is fit recompense for the lost royal horses. Matholwch is apparently mollified, and the happy couple set sail for Ireland. But the insult is not forgotten, and the king's courtiers urge him to be avenged. They cause Branwen to be banished from the court and from her position as queen, forcing her to become a servant, constantly ill-treated and physically abused on a daily basis. Despite her confinement, the demoted royal consort manages to rear a starling and teach it to speak and to understand human speech. She sends it to Bendigeidfran with a letter tied to its wing, informing him of her plight, and he responds by mobilizing an army to march on Matholwch's court to avenge the insult to the royal house of Harlech.

There is apparent reconciliation between the two sides, but the Irish are treacherous. It is Efnysien who uncovers their betrayal of the peace and saves Bendigeidfran from falling into a fatal trap. But after a second truce, his tempestuous nature reasserts itself. When Gwern, the young son of Matholwch and Branwen, is introduced to the assembled company of Welsh and Irish noblemen, Nysien calls his nephew over to him and Gwern goes willingly to his uncle. Then Efnysien also calls over to Gwern, but when the boy draws near, seizes him and casts him into the feast-fire. Battle commences once again. To cut a long story short, the Welsh warriors come up against a huge obstacle, for Matholwch turns Bendigeidfran's gift of the magical cauldron against them. While his slain soldiers stay dead, the Irish ones are popped into the cauldron overnight and restored to life, to fight better than before, although they are "zombies" and cannot speak. Efnysien finally sees the error of his ways; he pretends to be a dead Irish warrior and is thrown into the cauldron. He stretches himself within the vessel so that it bursts asunder. But with the shattered cauldron, Efnysien's heart also breaks, and he dies.[8]

Nysien and Efnysien may be understood as a storyteller's construct in order to present and explore opposition, to enhance the performance-quality of the narrative, and to introduce elements of tension and risk so key to successful story-telling. The two brothers share almost the same name; in a sense, they are two halves of a single whole, reflecting the positive and negative traits that are hard-wired as part of the human condition. Their close relationship is reflected in that they are often mentioned together, as at the beginning of the tale and during the episode leading up to Gwern's destruction in the fire. Each has a necessary part to play in the tale. Once Efnysien destroys himself in the cauldron, Nysien fades out of the narrative. It is as though the one is wholly dependent upon the other as players on the stage—and, interestingly, it is the negative Efnysien who has the bigger role. By sacrificing himself in remorse, he is, in a way, merging and morphing into his brother.

These brothers need to be understood within a persistent concept in ancient European (and Indo-European) cosmologies, that of the "hostile twins."[9] In her discussion of this subject, Emily Lyle cites Donald Ward's seminal 1968 study in pointing to many parallels, including the Roman twins Romulus and Remus and, of course, the old Testament pair Esau and Jacob (Genesis 25:22). Indeed, Nysien and Efnysien would appear, on the face of it, to present just such an example of oppositional twins as those explored by Wendy Doniger in this volume in her exploration of the theme of in utero conflicts between twin fetuses in Vedic and Hindu mythologies. Contrast between twin brothers is a persistent theme; binaries and dualities are explored in relation to two beings that are the same yet are also totally different. At its most fundamental level, the *topos* of the hostile twins forces us to confront good and evil, light and darkness, in equal and tensive balance. I suspect that such confrontation was the original intention of the storyteller and perhaps still more, of the Christian cleric who may have manipulated the tales as he committed them to written texts.

What about the cognate early medieval Irish texts? To what extent do we find the theme of twinship here? As far as I can tell, references to twins in this literature are more dispersed and less substantial, meaning that they are more difficult to interpret than the oppositional Welsh brothers. But two allusions come to mind, both— interestingly—associated with a close human-horse relationship. The first concerns the queen-goddess Macha, forced to race against the fastest chariot of the king of Ulster, in order for her mortal husband, Crunniuc, to win his bet that she could outrun any horse at the annual fair. She is heavily pregnant, and, as she gives birth just after winning the race, she curses the Ulstermen, promising that whoever heard her groans in childbirth would himself suffer the pains and weakness of parturition, even when going into battle. Macha gave birth to twins, a girl and a boy, and the name Emain Macha ("the twins of Macha") was given to the place of assembly where their mother raced and produced the children.[10] The combined horse/twin-symbolism is followed through in the tales of the Ulster hero Cú Chulainn, for he alone is exempt from Macha's curse, and he, too, is bound up with horse-imagery. For at the time of his own birth, a mare stabled nearby also gives birth to twin colts, and they are given to the young boy as a present.[11] This gift may resonate with the use of these beasts as chariot-ponies: training a pair of horses to work together as a chariot-team is not easy and, for it to be successful, the pair ideally needs to be socialized together from a very early age. This in itself provides a compelling "take" on possible symbolic aspects of pairing and two-ness.[12] In the Irish material, although there is no mention of hostility or opposition between Macha's twins, there is, nonetheless, an inimical element in their birth, both in the torment visited upon the pregnant woman and in her vengeful curse on the Ulstermen.

The forgoing brief analysis provides a platform for the examination of relevant archaeological evidence. I have argued that close attention to the *Mabinogion's* two Welsh brothers surfaces concepts and principles of twins/twinning, doubles and pairs, oppositional identities, halves and wholes, partibility and completeness. (Again, note the resonance between the themes I identify in the ancient British tradition, and those foregrounded by Neolithic archaeologist Lauren Talalay in her analysis of ancient Mediterranean doubled figures.) Application of these principles to material culture in late Iron Age and the western Roman provinces, particularly iconography, forms the remainder of this chapter.

Cauldrons, Spoons, and Bodies: Paired Watery Deposition in Iron Age Europe

Llyn Fawr ("Large Lake"), near Hirwaun in the Glamorgan Uplands, remains, even today, a numinous place. In about 750 BCE, people traveled to this remote spot, on the edge of the world, from long distances to perform an act of worship and sacrifice.[13] The finds were made in 1911 and 1912 during clearance of the boggy lake for the construction of a reservoir. The archaeological significance of the site partly lies in the fact that it straddles the Bronze Age/Iron Age transition, and reveals evidence of experiments by bronzesmiths with the new metal, iron. But just as crucial is the presence of ritual deposits, offerings thrown into the water to propitiate or give thanks to the local water-spirits. These included vessels, war-gear, horse-trappings, smithing, woodcraft and farming equipment, and personal objects such as razors.[14] Some of the material from the lake was local but certain items, like the razor and some of the horse-gear, were exotic, evocative of long-distance travel and far-reaching European connections.

For present purposes, Llyn Fawr's importance is due to the inclusion in the ritual deposits of two large sheet-bronze cauldrons that were probably already over a hundred years old when they were placed in the water. In itself, the ritual interment of such heirlooms raises significant questions concerning the presentation of deliberate, perhaps ancestral, archaism. At least one of them is thought to have originally contained some of the metalwork, reflecting one major depositional event. These cauldrons were made with consummate skill by local bronzesmiths in about 900 BCE, who beat ingots of bronze into paper-thin sheets riveted together. The deposition of a pair of these rare and valuable vessels indicates the reverence in which Llyn Fawr was held but what is interesting, too, is that double cauldron water-offerings are repeated elsewhere in Britain during the Iron Age. Thus, two cauldrons formed part of the late Iron Age ritual deposit of high-status metalwork at Llyn Cerrig Bach on the island of Anglesey,[15] which dates between the second century BCE and the late first century CE. Another pair comes from the Scottish boggy site of Blackburn Mill and, as at Llyn Fawr, metalwork was contained within them. The Blackburn Mill cauldrons were found placed deliberately together, with one inverted over the other. Unlike the Llyn Fawr pair, which are very similar to each other, the two Scottish vessels were not only of different sizes but produced using different techniques, suggesting that they were made by different craftspeople and at different times: the later one was made by the Roman-period method of spinning, while the earlier one was made from a single sheet of beaten metal.[16]

Why deposit cauldrons in pairs? Could it have been that one was for the underworld gods residing beneath the surface of the water and one for the spirits of the upper air, in oppositional perspectives of dry and wet cosmologies? Could the cauldrons be considered gendered, male and female? Were they originally used for containing different substances? Were they deemed to be "twins"?

What of other paired deposits in Iron Age British and European material culture? The most prominent artifacts are the curious pairs of bronze spoons that turn up for the most part in graves (like the pair from Castell Nadolig in Pembrokeshire, West Wales[17]) but sometimes in marshy contexts. Clearly made to fit together, the two spoons in each pair are of identical size, but exhibit differences insofar as one spoon has a perforation, while the inner concave surface of the other is marked out with vertical and horizontal intersecting incised lines to form four quadrants. Individually, the spoons are "inert" or "inactive" but their pairing produced efficacy and, together, they produce a dynamic object that may have been used in divinatory practice, perhaps even by Druids. Recent experiments[18] suggest that, if the two spoons were placed with their inner surfaces together, substances could be dripped or blown through the perforation in the upper spoon onto the quadranted surface of the lower one and the patterns formed "read" or interpreted. In attempting to reconstruct how this might have worked, we used a range of modified natural "blowing/dripping tools" such as hollow bird-bones and the quills of seabirds. For the deposited substances we experimented with powders (red ochre and bone-dust) and liquids (blood and water). The details of the experiment and the function of the spoons are outside the ambit of our concern here; what *is* important is that the artifacts were made to be used as a twinned pair—deemed sufficiently valuable to receive special "burial rites" in bogs or the tombs of ritualists part of whose toolkit they might have been.[19] At least one pair of these divination spoons was discovered deliberately deposited in a marshy context at Crosby Ravensworth in Cumbria,[20] recalling the watery finds of paired cauldrons to which reference was made earlier.

Of course, the most noteworthy depositions in northern European bog-contexts are human bodies, whose startling preservation has earned them a huge amount of archaeological fame and widespread publicity. The vast majority of these are single finds, although there is evidence that those depositing bog-bodies sometimes returned to the same spot to inter the chosen dead. But occasional finds appear to represent a true pair. These include the two young men found in a marsh at Weerdinge near Bourtangermoor in the Netherlands;[21] they were discovered close together and placed as though in an embrace, one resting on the arm of the other, leading to speculation as to whether they might have been brothers, comrades-in-arms, master and servant, or even lovers. Sadly, DNA does not survive well in marshes and so it is impossible to tell if these two were related, let alone whether they might have been twins. That they met violent deaths, almost certainly simultaneously, is scarcely in doubt: a savage abdominal wound indicated that one of the pair had been stabbed in the stomach and probably disemboweled.[22] Were they killed in a sacrificial rite or as a punishment for dire misdeeds? Or were they killed together in battle and given a special, honorable burial in a sacred place? What was the relationship between them that made it obligatory for them to be interred as a couple? Unfortunately, these are questions that can never be answered with certainty. Another "twin" find may be similarly interrogated. What was the reason behind the burial of two young men close together, identically wrapped in identical woolen coats, in the Great Bog near Hunteburg in the third or fourth century AD?.[23] These two, however, were of quite different ages: one was a youth and the other a man in his thirties.[24] Despite this disparity in age, the "kinship logic" proposed for the Weerdinge deposit might still hold for the Hunteburg couple, for they may have been brothers or cousins. However, we should not rule out different interpretations for their near-identical paired burial.

The apparent connection between paired deposition and water leads to speculation concerning the nature of water as a threshold space, separating worlds but perhaps also acting as a conduit between them. It is easy to see how both the reflective surface of still water and its translucency/transparency lend themselves to inferences about double worlds or two-spirit places. Many Gallo-British Roman-period sacred sites were chosen because of the genuine or perceived healing properties of certain springs or pools, and healing is itself a transformative act that takes an individual from one state of being to another. Early medieval Irish prose mythic literature makes persistent reference to water, particularly the sea, as an entrance to the Otherworld.[25] Similar beliefs existed within Classical tradition: Virgil's graphic description of the miasmic and poisonous lake Avernus (*Aeneid* 6, 242[26]) is a case in point. The bog-bodies provide an especial refraction of "twoness": they present to us ambiguous messages about life and death,[27] and that ambiguity may well have been an intentional element in the choice of their original deposition, particularly if they were the bodies of special or "other" people, condemned, sacred, or both, whose remains had to be accorded abnormal treatment. Often perfectly preserved in the anaerobic and acidic conditions, they present dichotomous, contradictory statements about the transference from living body to corpse. Indeed, those who interred them might have been compelled to treat them in a manner that denied their full transference to ancestral status and required them to remain in stasis, neither alive nor fully dead.

Pairing in Iron Age Art

Sometime in the very late Iron Age or early post-Roman conquest period, an individual or group of people deliberately interred a large and valuable wrought-iron object in a remote boggy pool at Capel Garmon in Denbighshire, North Wales, reverently placing a large white stone at each end. It was a piece of ornate hearth-furniture, a "fire-dog" each of whose vertical shafts terminates in a highly ornate animal's head.[28] Each beast has horns but also a decorative mane, as if the blacksmith intended to construct a hybrid creature that was both ox and horse [Figure 17.1].

The stand would originally have been one of a pair flanking the hearth. It is estimated that one of them may have taken as much as three years for a single smith to make,[29] yet it was taken out of circulation and deposited in the water, presumably as an offering (what happened to the second one, I wonder?). These fire-dogs were part of a whole panoply of feasting-equipment associated with high status social relationships and engagement between communities[30] by means of commensality and exchange (of goods, stories, and information). The object had been laid on its side, as if to signify its death, and a large stone was placed at each end. At first glance, the opposing animal-

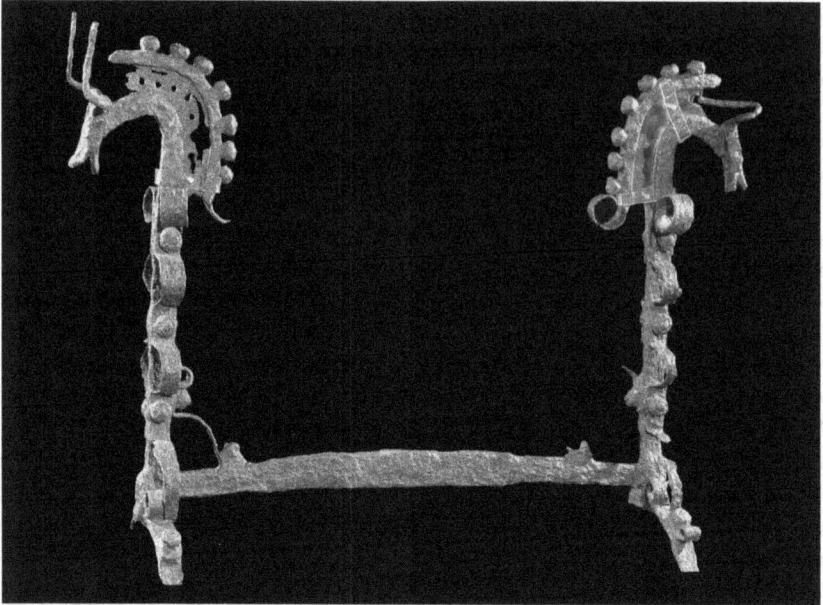

Figure 17.1 Late Iron Age wrought-iron "fire-dog" from Capel Garmon, North Wales, UK. L. 1m 7cm (3'6"). By permission of the National Museum Wales.

heads appear to be a truly twinned pair but close scrutiny reveals subtle differences between them, as if the craftsperson were intent on producing effigies of two creatures each with an individual and unique *persona*.[31] Two paired elements are present here: the doubled heads and the iconographic mixing of two animals each of whose attributes are presented in balanced reciprocity. We might add a third pairing, in so far as the fire-dog was constructed as one of a pair.

The more they are studied, the more persistent pairing or twinning appears present in Iron Age ornamented "La Tène" metalwork. Certain Iron Age swords are decorated with a pair of curious fantasy beasts, sea-monsters that look most like Moray eels, commonly referred to as "dragon-pairs."[32] Unlike the Capel Garmon creatures, which face outward, away from each other, these scabbard-beasts face each other in aggressive opposition, mouths wide-open, as if in combat. A particularly telling element in these images is their longevity and widespread distribution in Iron Age art, arguing for persistence in relevance and meaning for both artists and their high-ranking consumers. The two "dragons" are presented as equal opponents, in a perpetual, never-to-be-resolved conflict, and so may have symbolized the craft of war and the unceasing strife for supremacy against an enemy. But, as "twins" they may also, like Castor and Pollux of classical myth, have represented life and death, light and dark, the material and spirit worlds, all interdependent yet in opposition, as positive and negative dimensions of one state of being.

A metal detectorist find made in 2010 from South Cerney in Gloucestershire displays a wonderful example of oppositional twinning: it is a copper-alloy harness-mount, heavily inlaid with red and blue enameling. The central decorative feature of this piece is a pair of mirror-imaged owl-faces, one the right way up, the other one upside-down.[33] If there is a spiritual value to this imagery, it is tempting to read it as reflective of different worlds: the human, earthly realm and the divine. In early Welsh mythology, the owl is symbolic not only of night but of the nefarious twilight wherein this bird is shunned by all others as a nocturnal hunter. In the *Fourth Branch of the Mabinogi* it is into the form of an owl that the faithless conjured woman Blodeuwedd is transformed by the magician Gwydion after her betrayal of her husband Lleu.[34] (In "Barn Owl," the great twentieth-century Welsh priest-poet R. S. Thomas suggested that the cry of the barn-owl was the "voice of God in the darkness cursing himself fiercely for his lack of love."[35]) In some ways, these opposed owl-images resonate with much earlier Iron Age twinned ornament, an example of which comes from a female grave dated to the late fifth or early fourth century BCE, from Bad Dürkheim in Germany. One item of tomb-furniture consisted of a tiny sheet-gold plaque in the form of a human face: turned one way up, the visage is that of an elderly male, with a beard, baggy eyes and furrowed brow; inverted it becomes the face of a smiling young girl, with her hair piled up on her head.[36]

Contained within the numismatic collections of the National Museum Wales, Cardiff is a late Iron Age silver coin found at Maidstone (Kent) in south-east England (NMW no. C553).[37] Both the obverse and reverse of the coin bear zoomorphic motifs: the reverse die depicts a stag with exaggerated antlers apparently ridden by a small boar with similarly overlarge dorsal bristles; on the obverse, though, is twinned imagery in the form of a pair of long-necked water-birds who face each other, their necks stretched upward and their vertical beaks almost touching. The boar-imagery is carried over from the reverse: a small, uncrested but tusked boar stands beneath the birds, in between their opposed pairs of legs. Ryan Sullivan's study throws new light on this coin-die: he points out that the twinning or doubled theme is repeated in the "solar" rayed circles and concentric circles behind each crane's head. Moreover, in between the two birds is a curious segmented or beaded motif that has been identified by Sullivan as a noose. It consists of a long single vertical strip that divides in front of the birds' bodies to form two joining semi-circles, forming the "noose" itself.

Taken as a whole, the assemblage of images on this coin-face plays with singles and pairs, and this oscillation wraps around to embrace the iconography on the reverse, where there is symbolic repetition in the identical treatment of the antlers on the stag and the dorsal ridge of the boar. Thus, in the mutual acknowledgment of connections between the obverse and reverse dies (the boar and the celestial symbolism present on each), the coin itself would present the ideas of doubling and twinning.

A coda to this section refers to Iron Age sites, specifically hillforts. In a recent percipient study,[38] Mansel Spratling draws attention to the aesthetics of Iron Age Britons in a discussion of art that embraced not only metalwork and all the other usual candidates for an "art" label but also sites, like Maiden Castle. Two papers in conference proceedings[39] refer to the phenomenon of paired sites in first millennium BCE Britain: one on the pairing of hillforts in the Dorset region,[40] the other on coeval paired Wessex enclosures.[41] Both deal with the recognition that people were deliberately building monumental enclosures (defined by substantive earthworks, designed to define and enclose controlled land, and, perhaps to defend it) that related to each other, and that such signature of territory may have been associated with complex relationships between people (involving identity, belonging, exclusion, and demarcation of ritual spaces), their present kin and their ancestral past. This last point may well be reflected in the paired hillforts in Dorset since these appear to have been referencing earlier, Neolithic, monuments, reinforcing the possibility that past and present communities, respectively, were represented by the dual monuments. The other Wessex double enclosures may have been driven by different agencies, associated with separate activity-areas and/or their occupation by kin-related but discrete communities with distinct identities. These examples of monumental twinning serve to provide hints that pairing and "twinning" in later prehistoric Britain were not necessarily confined to objects but may have been "written into" both portable artifacts and monuments within the landscape.

"Twins" and Gender in Gallo-British Roman-Period Imagery

If a man and a woman stand or sit together side-by-side, the chances are that the man will be taller, having a longer torso and longer legs. Of course there are exceptions but gender dimorphism in life is usually biased, in terms of size, toward the male (the ratio being 1.22:1).[42] But this life rule is persistently flouted in the religious iconography of Roman Britain and Roman Gaul (it is particularly striking in the Gallic provinces because there is so much more surviving stone sculpture than in Britannia). Time and again couples are depicted of equal size, as though they are presented in conscious equivalence. Let us take just three examples to illustrate the point. The first is a relief of a male and female found at Dijon (Côte d'Or: Aldhouse-Green 2003, 109, fig. 18; Espérandieu 1911, no. 3441; Deyts 1976, no. 118); they sit side by side upon a high-backed bench, each turning slightly toward the other, as if in mutual acknowledgment of the relationship between them. They are of equal height, both wearing small peaked diadems on their heads, and their arms are identically positioned, with each bent at the elbow. She holds a *cornucopia* (horn of plenty) in the crook of her left arm, its wide mouth reaching to the level of her face; he carries an emblem in his left arm, in precisely the same position and of equivalent dimensions, this time a long-shafted hammer. In her right hand she holds a small dish or *patera*; his right hand is missing but (on analogy with cognate images) it may once have held a small cup. The legs and feet are also identically treated, the ankles close together, and the toes turned outward. It is as though the sculptor fully intended to depict direct equivalence between the two, almost as if the thought uppermost in his or her mind was to present a true pair, two halves of a dual-gendered partnership. This pair is probably to be identified with the Gallic-named divinities Sucellus ("he who strikes well": de Bernardo Stempel 2008, 76) and Nantosuelta (whose name might identify her as a water-deity).

The two other sculptures each depict a well-represented Gallo-British divine couple known (from a few inscriptions) as Mercury and Rosmerta. Unlike the couple from

Dijon and their fellows, this pair is distinctive in apparently representing a "marriage" between *romanitas* and *gallitas*, for the male deity's origins lie in the Roman State pantheon whilst Rosmerta's name is variously translated as associated with prosperity or queenship (De Bernardo Stempel 2008, 75). The two images are similar to one another but have widely separated provenances: one comes from Glanum in Provence [Figure 17.2], the other from Bath. Each depicts a standing female and male figure of whom the male is identified with Mercury because of the presence of this god's regular emblems of purse, winged *petasos* and caduceus (a serpent-entwined herald's staff). On both stones, the female (perhaps Rosmerta) carries a *cornucopia* in the crook of her left arm while her partner's caduceus is of similar size and is borne in precisely the same sloping angle (Aldhouse-Green 2004, 62, fig. 3.4 and 65, fig. 3.5). The sculpture from Bath is the more complex of the two and—perhaps—the more interesting, insofar as beneath the male deity's feet scurries a tiny triad of hooded beings. This serves to create dissonance in the imagery, with tension and conflict that arises from the presence of double and triple entities on the same "page." This issue is explored more fully in the next section.

Before leaving paired stone iconography, it is pertinent to consider further the relationship between them and the nature of equivalence. Given the equal size of these couples one to the other, their somatic position, and the care taken to present different emblems (such as cornucopiae and caduceus or hammer) in a precisely similar manner, how do these and other issues concerning paired Gallo-Roman images

Figure 17.2 Limestone relief of "Mercury" and "Rosmerta" from Glanum, southern France. W. 53.5cm (1'9"). Credit: G. Dagli Orti /De Agostini Pictures

inform our thinking about the meaning of partnership? Two related factors are, for me, paramount: gender and identity. The intensity of the connection between male and female images can be demonstrated by the transference or sharing of emblems between the two partners that sometimes occurs. For example, while it is to Mercury that the emblem of the purse habitually belongs, several stone sculptures from German and Alsatian sites[43] depict Mercury and Rosmerta each with a purse or, indeed, sharing a single money-bag. A significant carving from Wiesbaden[44] displays the intensity of pooled symbolism: Mercury is depicted, like a suppliant, standing in front of his female partner, who sits before him receiving the contents of the purse he offers her. But on another carving, from Mannheim[45] the transference of emblem from male to female is carried one stage further because Rosmerta alone is in possession of the purse. Exactly the same pattern can be observed with the second ubiquitous Mercury-symbol, the caduceus: one some iconography (again from the Rhineland) either both god and goddess carry the herald's staff or Rosmerta alone has it.[46]

If emblems are anything to go by, provincial sculptors in Britain, Gaul, and the Rhineland seem sometimes to have used them to challenge, manipulate or edit "traditional' gender roles. But something else may also have been going on and issues of identity may also have been played out in the iconographic arena. It is, indeed, possible that gender was employed to explore non-gender issues such as identity and belonging. In the case of Mercury and Rosmerta, we are dealing with a male deity of Roman origin and a female arguably derived from an indigenous (perhaps artificially constructed)[47] context. The sharing, swapping, or hijacking of emblems, together with deliberate isomorphism (lack of size-discrepancy between male and female bodies), seem to indicate and emphasize equivalence not simply between genders but between *romanitas* and *gallitas*. The composition of these carvings depicting gendered couples appears to represent a striving for harmony, balance, and symmetry. It is tempting to read such imagery as reflective of relationships between Rome and local people, a marriage of equals. But the dual-gendered nature of these Gallo-British "couples" should not blind us to the possibility that it is not marriage but twinship that is represented, even though same-gendered pairs do not appear in the iconographic record, as they do—for instance—in the Neolithic and Early Bronze Age iconography of the Mediterranean world (see Talalay's study in this volume). If this were to be a correct reading of the images, this kind of pairing would perhaps make the idea of equivalence between cultures even more persuasive.

However, we have an interpretative problem in so far as so many sculptures, particularly those from Roman Gaul, cannot be precisely dated, because of the lack of a secure archaeological context and because so many stones were re-used in later buildings. But some Continental scholars have attributed many Gallo-Roman sculptures—by means of style and especially by female hairstyles and clothing—to the first and second centuries CE. Even so, caution needs to be exercised, because of the time-lags involved in the adoption of fashion within the Roman Empire (particularly where trends were set by the imperial household). At least some sculptures, including those depicting paired images, may have belonged to early post-conquest horizons, at a time when new identities were still in process of negotiation and relationships between different cultural groups were being forged and developed. These twinned

Figure 17.3 Two *Dea Nutrix* white clay figurines from Roman London, depicting a mother nursing a single infant and twins respectively. First or second century CE. Height approximately 8 cm. Museum of London A 243, A 244. By permission of Museum of London.

images might well have played a role in expressing, reinforcing, and influencing such connections.

But there is another group of Roman-period Gallo-British artifacts that is highly relevant to our study of twinning. It comprises the small, mass-produced white clay figurines made principally in the Allier district of central France during the first and second centuries CE and exported to other western Roman provinces, including Britain, known as *Deae Nutrices*.[48] These were privately owned images, kept in the home, placed as votive offerings in shrines and sometimes buried with the dead. As their sobriquet suggests, the figurines represent nursing mothers; seated in high-backed wicker chairs, they suckle one or, more rarely, twin babies [Figure 17.3].

At the most obvious level, these little images represent a goddess of fertility and domestic prosperity, but their sometime sepulchral context perhaps allows us to think of them as having an extra dimension as psychopomps, guarding dead souls. The twin babies nursed by some *Deae Nutrices* may simply reflect either the actuality of twin births or, more likely, the desire to increase their power as agents for human (or animal) fecundity. But there is a further alternative insofar as the doubled symbolism could refer to the goddess's dual role in the material and spirit worlds.

Twos and Threes: Playing with Numbers

It is characteristically human to think in terms of dyadic relationships: we habitually break up a triadic relationship into a pair of dyads.[49]

We need now to consider the "numbers game" in Romano-British and Gallo-Roman figural imagery; there frequently appears to be a contrapuntal thread running through multiple-figure iconography, with the oscillation between twos and threes already noted in the Bath relief. As a case study, we might consider the collection of limestone images from Cirencester and its environs, for it includes several instances of ambiguous counting. There is a persistent theme of three plus one on four Cotswolds reliefs: Lower Slaughter,[50] Daglingworth near Cirencester[51] and two from Cirencester (Corinium) itself.[52] On each of these stones, the groups of three figures display near-identical appearance with one "odd-one-out." The three are hooded and standing, the fourth is usually seated but, on the Lower Slaughter carving, the difference between the three and the one is that the figure on the far right (to the gazer) is turned away from the others and appears to be walking away from them, while the three face to the front. In the more homogeneous group from in or around Corinium, the three hooded persons are accompanied by a definitely seated image, often interpreted as a female, although there is little detail to enable gendering of any of the figures on this group of stones. What we might be seeing, then, is not so much three plus one but one plus one, the antiphonalities between threeness and singleness being compensated for by the identicality of the triple figure. There seems almost certainly to have been attempts by the sculptor to manipulate the viewer into regarding the three as replication rather than as three distinct entities. Triplism therefore may be fulfilling particular schemata of meaning that acted alongside and as cross currents to equally important *topoi* of pairedness and doubling.

It is possible to identify further oscillation between twos and threes (or dyadism and triadism) in Gallo-Roman iconography. A prime example is that of the triple-horned bull,[53] the product of a fertile artistic or mythic imagination that was played out in small bronze figurines and the occasional stone statuette. What seems to have occurred in this iconography is the superimposition of triadism on a dyadic structure; in other words a "normal" two-horned animal is transformed into a magical creature by the addition of an imaginary extra horn. That addition further carries with it an extra dimension, that of instability or restless oscillation and irresolution between the "norm" of two and the "otherness" of three. In this way, a measure of anarchy and chaos is presented in the uneasy asymmetry that the substitution of three for two serves to create. So, a natural phenomenon (a pair of horns on an appropriate animal) becomes suddenly unnatural or weird, demanding interrogation rather than acceptance.

On a comparative note: In his renowned study of Ndembu communities in Angola,[54] Victor Turner explored both symbolic number, particularly with respect to the mystification of twinship, and color. The "default dyad" phenomenon has traditionally been reinforced in other African societies, including those of Benin and Togo, where the birth of triplets could result in the killing of one (usually the weakest or smallest), leaving the pair of dyads as survivors.[55] Turner revealed and amplified analogous Ndembu tensions associated with dyadism and triadism with respect to color-symbolism. For these communities, the three colors most saturated with spiritual meaning and power are black, red, and white, but the perceived need to impose "two-ness" on this tripartitite color system is satisfied partly by grouping red plus white— as life colors (blood, including birth-blood, milk, and semen) in opposition to black (resonant of death, decay, sterility, and maleficent spirits). The imposition of a binary system upon a triadic color-structure is also achieved by the Ndembu by the treatment of red as an ambivalent color, containing elements of both positive (white) and negative (black). Whilst the details of Ndembu cosmology need not concern us here, it is salutary to reflect on its demonstration of negotiation and engagement with tensive and contrapuntal forms of number symbolism, and on the deep relationships between two and three. Polarity (life/death, female/male, light/dark) is key to Angolan spiritual scaffolding, hence the clash, as well as the dance, of binary and trinary symbolism.

Conclusion

This chapter began with Nysien and Efnysien, the "good and evil" twins presented in medieval Welsh prose tales; the story served as a platform from which to launch discussions of twinning and pairing within later prehistoric Britain, focusing on paired watery deposition, on the one hand, and doubling in Iron Age art, on the other. The second main theme concerns the depiction of paired individuals in Roman-period Gallo-British imagery. No attempt, of course, has been made to forge direct connections between the two themes. But it is possible that generic ideas of pairing and counterpoint in cosmological thinking and presentation crossed over from pre- to post-Roman conquest religious ideologies and developed within the framework of the new "iconographic habit" stimulated in the western Roman provinces by Mediterranean traditions of human representation.

Pairing and twinning can engage with a multifaceted raft of symbolic motifs. Perhaps the most compelling of these are associated with number—and with opposition or contradiction. Intrinsic, therefore, is the capacity for contrapuntal tensions between number as reinforcement or addition, and dualism as inversion or balanced contradiction. Mirroring two-ness creates symmetry, and as humans, we are hard-wired toward this kind of order, our very bodies serving to reinforce the "rightness" of correspondent left and right halves.[56] Ideas of balance and pairing, whether exhibited in the deposition of two identical or similar objects, like a pair of cauldrons, in a lake, the doubling of motifs on art or landscapes or the twinning of images may therefore represent a subconscious default framework—whatever additional, context-dependent symbolism may have accrued. One element contained within two-ness is the notion of upside-down-ness and mutual reversal. It is tempting to relate this to ideas of double worlds: the material world and the realm of the spirits. To offer only one comparandum,[57] Richard Bradley refers to the Saami vision of the underworld as a mirror-image of earthly existence, where the dead must walk upside-down in the footsteps of the living. We find essentially similar imagery in John Milton's vision of Hell as a dark, inverted (and perverted) Paradise.[58]

Where an additional unit is put into the mix, for instance, in the triple motifs identified in Gallo-Roman and Romano-British imagery, one effect of that is to destabilize and question symmetry. A backward glance at Iron Age art reveals a persistent tradition of triplism, a theme particularly striking in Welsh decorated metalwork where the triskele is a dominant design.[59] The whole issue of triadism in art and imagery is beyond the scope of this essay. It is at least as likely that significant cosmological meaning, such as the acknowledgment of a triple-tiered cosmos,[60] was behind threeness as much as any intention to introduce instability. But when two-ness and threeness come together in apparent contradiction, as may be the case in the imagery cited earlier, it may be admissible to think of the introduction of an extra number as the result of a desire to open up and interrogate motifs and certainties.

Twinning and pairing appear to be a persistent method of referencing the supernatural world both in later western European prehistory and the Roman provincial period. There may be no connection whatever between paired deposition and double motifs in Iron Age art, and any genuine link between Iron Age practice and Roman-period iconography is certainly far from definitively established. This chapter has simply noted a recurrent phenomenon, that of doubling or twinning, and has suggested some heuristic ways of engaging with this phenomenon. The conceptual contexts that obtained at a remote lake at the beginning of the Iron Age in South Wales, where two cauldrons were placed as votive offerings and at a Gallo-Roman shrine peopled with twinned images of the divine, may, of course, be totally different. But it is at least possible that the very specific pairing present in Romano-British and Gallo-Roman imagery may incorporate some dimly acknowledged ancestral cosmology. It may even be possible that droplets of ancient folk-memory percolated down to contribute a legacy to the fateful twins of medieval Welsh myth with which this chapter began. The validity of acknowledging this kind of connectivity over time is strongly implied by the persistent iconic "Celtic" symbol of the cauldron: as we saw earlier in this paper, Iron Age cauldrons in Britain were frequently singled out for special deposition in watery contexts, sometimes in pairs. Cauldrons appear to reflect high status and communal feasting, since they were expensive and difficult to make, their size suggests they were for holding large amounts of food or drink, and they were chosen as valuable votive offerings. In both early Irish and Welsh medieval prose tales, cauldrons are persistent themes associated with plenty and with rebirth (Brân's cauldron in which Efnysien immolated himself is a case in point). While the archaeological evidence for cauldrons as special things and their treatment in texts that date over a thousand years later might be purely coincidental, it is surely more likely that cauldrons retained something of their original package of meanings over time. It may even be that the compilers of the early medieval stories, or their informants, had actually seen ancient cauldrons in shallow lakes and that, though there could be no appreciation of their true antiquity, their archaic, significant presence caused them to be woven into later myths.

The same kind of retro-referencing might make sense of the cultural prominence of the twins and pairs who march as protagonists throughout this study. Like rituals, numerical arrangements as catalysts of symbolic thought tend to persist—multiplicity of birth being one of the oldest human numerical challenges.

Notes

1 *The Times* (UK) for Monday March 7, 2011, contains a discussion concerning the development of the individual personality that might be of relevance to twinship. "The psychiatrist and psychoanalyst Carl Jung described this process as one of

'individuation' whereby the 'true self' emerges as psychological development completes itself and an individual reaches 'self actualisation'" (Tanya Byron, "I Gave Up a Man Because My Mum Didn't Like Him," *The Times T2*, March 7, 2011, 11). It may be that such a process of growing individuality could be "interrupted" or disturbed by the presence of a twin, particularly an identical twin.

2 Sioned Davies, trans., *The Mabinogion* (Oxford: Oxford University Press, 2007), 22.

3 Katie Gramich, personal communication.

4 Act 3, Scene 2.

5 Davies, *The Mabinogion*, 13–17.

6 *Branwen* is the eponymous title sometimes given to the Second of the Four Branches of the *Mabinogi*. *The Mabinogion* is the collective name given to eleven medieval Welsh prose tales, of which four (the Four Branches) have been identified as a related group (Davies, *The Mabinogion*, ix–x).

7 I am grateful to the editor of this volume, Kimberley Patton, for this observation. For a discussion of this complex identification (mare/queen and stallion/king, and cases of their recombination) in Indo-European traditions, see Wendy Doniger O'Flaherty's *Women, Androgynes, and Other Mythical Beasts* (Chicago: University of Chicago Press, 1982), especially Section IV.

8 Davies, *The Mabinogion*, 22–34.

9 Emily Lyle, *Archaic Cosmos. Polarity, Space and Time* (Edinburgh: Polygon, 1990), 105–18.

10 Jeffrey Gantz, *Early Irish Myths and Sagas* (London: Penguin, 1981), 128–9.

11 Gantz, *Early Irish Myths and Sagas*, 132; Thomas Kinsella, *The Táin* (Oxford: Oxford University Press, 1969), 22; O'Flaherty, *Women, Androgynes, and Other Mythical Beasts*, 167. It may be significant that horse/boy-child symbolism is found, too, in the First Branch of the *Mabinogi*. When the baby son born to Rhiannon and Pwyll disappears when he is three days old, he appears in the stable of one Teyrnon at exactly the same moment that Teyrnon's mare produces a foal and, like the Ulster hero and his colt, the Welsh child and the foal grow up together, almost like twins: Davies, *The Mabinogion*, 18; O'Flaherty, *Women, Androgynes, and Other Mythical Beasts*, 185.

12 I am grateful to Elizabeth Meyer, MA, Cardiff University, for this observation, drawn from her experience with horse-training in Michigan, and to Adam Gwilt, National Museum Wales, for his comments on experiments with reconstructed Iron Age chariots in Yorkshire, UK.

13 Robert Eric Mortimer (R. E. M.) Wheeler, "The Llyn Fawr Hoard," *Archaeologia* 71 (1920–21): 132–40; C. Fox, "A Second Cauldron and an Iron Sword from the Llyn Fawr Hoard, Rhigos, Glamorgan," *Antiquaries Journal* 19 (1939): 368–404; A. C. Reynolds, *The Llyn Fawr Hoard and its Legacy*. Unpublished M.A. dissertation (Newport: University of Wales, 2000); Jeffrey L. Davies and Frances Lynch, "The Late Bronze Age and Iron Age," in *Prehistoric Wales*, ed. Frances Lynch, Stephen Aldhouse-Green, and Jeffrey L. Davies (Stroud: Sutton, 2000), 183–7.

14 Davies and Lynch, "The Late Bronze Age and Iron Age," 185, fig. 4.16.

15 C. Fox, *A Find of the Early Iron Age from Llyn Cerrig Bach, Anglesey* (Cardiff: National Museum of Wales, 1946); P. Macdonald, *Llyn Cerrig Bach* (Cardiff: University of Wales Press, 2007).

16 W. H. Manning, "Ironwork hoards in Iron Age and Roman Britain," *Britannia* 3 (1972): 224–50.

17 E. L. Barnwell, "Articles Supposed to be Spoons," *Archaeologia Cambrensis* 36 (1882): 214–15; Davies and Lynch, "The Late Bronze Age and Iron Age," 213.

430 *Gemini and the Sacred*

18 Conducted by me in August 2010 in association with a film crew from BBC 2, in connection with the production of an episode of the television series *A History of Celtic Britain*. (Programme 6, screened on April 14, 2011, is where the spoon-experiments are shown).

19 Double spoons (sometimes physically joined together) are known from New Kingdom Egyptian contexts. My attention has been drawn to a particular carved wooden example, dating to 1350 BCE, from Memphis, in which the bowls are cartouches, the inner carved with lotus blossoms and birds and the handles depict near-identical facing images of the god Bes. The symbolism on these Egyptian spoons is associated with the afterlife (British Museum Acc. No. 5953: Earnest Alfred Wallis (E. A. W.) Budge, *A Guide to the Third and Fourth Egyptian Rooms* (London: Trustees of the British Museum, 1904), 178, no. 66; Madeleine Frédéricq, "The Ointment Spoons in the Egyptian Section of the British Museum," *Journal of Egyptian Archaeology* 13 (1927): 12, pl. 8. Information kindly supplied by Gill Woods).

20 Andrew P. Fitzpatrick, "Les Druides en Grande-Bretagne," in *Les Druides,* ed. Vincent Guichard et F. Perrin, L'Archéologue Hors Série 2 (2000), 49.

21 Wijnand van der Sanden, *Through Nature to Eternity: The Bog Bodies of Northwest Europe* (Amsterdam: Batavian Lion International, 1996), 101–2, 179, figs. 134, 245.

22 Ibid., 219.

23 S. Veil, "Two Bodies in Woolen Coats," in *The Mysterious Bog People*, ed. C. Bergen, Marcel J. L. Th. Niekus and Vincent T. van Vilsteren (Zwolle: Waanders, 2002), 104–6.

24 Van der Sanden, *Through Nature to Eternity*, 102.

25 Proinsias MacCana, *Celtic Mythology* (London: Newnes, 1983), 69.

26 Kitty Chisholm and John Ferguson, eds. *Rome: The Augustan Age: A Sourcebook* (Oxford: Oxford University Press/Open University Press, 1981), 231.

27 Karin Sanders, *Bodies in the Bog and the Archaeological Imagination* (Chicago: University of Chicago Press, 2009), 50.

28 Hubert Newman Savory, *Guide Catalogue of the Early Iron Age Collections* (*in the National Museum of Wales*) (Cardiff: National Museum of Wales, 1976), 62, no. 31, pl. Via.

29 According to the South Welsh blacksmith David Peterson, who made a replica fire-dog, using ancient techniques and tools, for an exhibition entitled *The Celts in Wales* at the National Museum of Wales in 1990.

30 Niall Sharples, *Social Relations in Later Prehistory* (Oxford: Oxford University Press, 2010), 112–16.

31 Miranda J. Aldhouse-Green, *An Archaeology of Images: Iconology and Cosmology in Iron Age and Roman Europe* (London: Routledge, 2004), 108–9, fig. 4.11.

32 Andrew P. Fitzpatrick, "Dancing with Dragons: Fantastic Animals in the Earlier Celtic Art of Iron Age Britain," in *The Later Iron Age in Britain and Beyond*, ed. Colin Haselgrove and Colin Haselgrove (Oxford: Oxbow, 2007), 348–52, fig. 12.

33 Davies, *The Mabinogion*, 63. Alison Brookes, personal communication. The object is part of the Iron Age collections at Corinium Museum, Cirencester, Glos.

34 "Then Gwydion caught up with her and said to her, 'I will not kill you. I will do worse. Namely, I will release you in the form of a bird,' he said. 'And because of the shame you have brought upon Lleu Llaw Gyffes, you will never dare show your face in daylight for fear of all the birds. And all the birds will be hostile to you'" (Davies, *The Mabinogion*, 63).

35 Ronald Stuart (R. S.) Thomas, *Collected Poems 1945–1990* (London: Phoenix, 2000), 319.

36 Megaw, John Vincent Stanley (J. V. S.), and Megaw, Ruth, *Celtic Art. From its Beginnings to the Book of Kells Celtic Art. From its Beginnings to the Book of Kells* (London: Thames and Hudson, 1989), 70, fig. 76; Aldhouse-Green, *An Archaeology of Images*, 196–7, fig. 7.10.

37 Miranda J. Green, "The Iconography of Iron Age Coins," in *Celtic Coinage: Britain and Beyond. The Eleventh Oxford Symposium on Coinage and Monetary History*, ed. Melinda Mays (Oxford: British Archaeological Reports British Series No. 222, 1992), 159 pl. 11:11a; R. Sullivan, *Striking the Sacred: Religious Imagery on British Iron Age Coins*. Unpublished MA dissertation (Cardiff: Cardiff University, 2010), 39, fig. 15.

38 Mansel Spratling, "On the Aesthetics of the Ancient Britons," in *Rethinking Celtic Art*, ed. Duncan Garrow, Chris Gosden, and Jeremy D. Hill (Oxford: Oxbow, 2008), 194.

39 Oliver Davis, "Twin Freaks? Paired Enclosures in the Early Iron Age of Wessex," in *Changing Perspectives on the First Millennium BC*, ed. Oliver Davis, Niall Sharples and Kate Waddington (Oxford: Oxbow, 2008), 31–42.

40 Steven Toase, "The Pairing of Hillforts: Conflict, Complementary, Coincidence Or Complex?" in *Changing Perspectives on the First Millennium BC*, ed. Oliver Davis, Niall Sharples and Kate Waddington (Oxford: Oxbow, 2008), 21–30.

41 Davis, "Twin Freaks?"

42 31 Donald Johansen and Blake Edgar, *From Lucy to Language* (London: Weidenfeld and Nicolson, 1996), 73.

43 For example from Baden (J. Alfs, "A Gallo-Roman Temple Near Bretten (Baden)," *Germania* 24 (1940): 28–40, Eisenberg (Émile Espérandieu, *Recueil Général des bas-reliefs de la Gaule romaine et pré-romaine*, vol. 8. [Paris: Ernest Leroux, 1922], nos. 6039, 6054), Nöttingen (Espérandieu *Germ.* no. 350) and Metz, Alsace (Miranda J. Green, *Symbol and Image in Celtic Religious Art* [London: Routledge, 1989], 56).

44 Émile Espérandieu, *Recueil Général des bas-reliefs de la Gaule romaine et pré-romaine*. German volume (Paris: Ernest Leroux, 1931), no. 18.

45 Ibid., no. 428.

46 Miranda J. Aldhouse-Green, "Poles Apart? Perceptions of Gender in Gallo-British Cult-Iconography," in *Roman Imperialism and Provincial Art*, ed. S. Scott and J. Webster (Cambridge: Cambridge University Press, 2003), 107.

47 By this I mean that the *persona* of Rosmerta might have been constructed as a deliberate Gallic counterpart to a deity of Roman origin.

48 Frank Jenkins, "The Cult of the Dea Nutrix in Kent," *Archaeologia Cantiana* 71 (1957): 38–46; Miranda J. Green, *Celtic Goddesses. Warriors, Virgins and Mothers* (London: British Museum Press, 1995), 112–14.

49 Victor Turner, "Colour Classification in Ndembu Ritual," in *Anthropological Approaches to the Study of Religion*, ed. Michael Banton (London: Tavistock Publications, 1996), 71.

50 Martin Henig, Graham Webster, and T. F. C. Blagg, *Roman Sculpture from the Cotswald Region,* Corpus signorum imperii Romani I, 7. Oxford: Oxford University Press, 1993, no. 98.

51 Ibid., no. 102.

52 Ibid., nos. 101 and 103.

53 Miranda J. Aldhouse-Green, "Crossing the Boundaries: Triple Horns and Emblematic Transference," *European Journal of Archaeology* 1, no. 2 (1998): 219–40.

54 Turner, "Colour Classification in Ndembu Ritual," 47–84.
55 I am grateful to Kimberley Patton for remarking on this traditional birth-custom in some West African traditions. See also the chapters by Olúpònà and Obeng in this volume for divergent attitudes to twins and triplets respectively. There is a severely practical angle on the issue of triplets: the *Times* (UK) for Tuesday March 29, 2011, ran a feature entitled: Barbara Lantin, "Trouble Trebled: How Do You Breastfeed Triplets?" *The Times T2*, March 29, 2011, 7–8.
56 In the BBC television documentary *First Life*, Sir David Attenborough refers to the paired identicality or mirror-imagery of animal (and human) bodies (BBC Two, broadcast November 5, 2010).
57 Richard Bradley, *An Archaeology of Natural Places* (London: Routledge, 2000), 12.
58 *Paradise Lost* 1 (1667): I refer to the edition by Henry C. Beeching, ed. *The Poetical Works of John Milton* (London, New York, Toronto and Melbourne: Humphrey Milford/Oxford University Press, 1914), 181–448.
59 Miranda J. Green, *Celtic Art. Reading the Messages* (London: Weidenfeld and Nicholson, 1996), 123–4.
60 Miranda J. Aldhouse-Green, and Stephen Aldhouse-Green, *The Quest for the Shaman:Shape-Shifters, Sorcerers and Spirit-Healers of Ancient Europe* (London: Thames and Hudson, 2005), 175–8.

Bibliography

Aldhouse-Green, Miranda J. "Crossing the Boundaries: Triple Horns and Emblematic Transference." *European Journal of Archaeology* 1, no. 2 (1998): 219–40.
Aldhouse-Green, Miranda J. "Poles Apart? Perceptions of Gender in Gallo-British Cult-Iconography." In *Roman Imperialism and Provincial Art*, edited by S. Scott and J. Webster, 95–118. Cambridge: Cambridge University Press, 2003.
Aldhouse-Green, Miranda J. *An Archaeology of Images: Iconology and Cosmology in Iron Age and Roman Europe*. London: Routledge, 2004.
Aldhouse-Green, Miranda J. and Stephen Aldhouse-Green. *The Quest for the Shaman:Shape-Shifters, Sorcerers and Spirit-Healers of Ancient Europe*. London: Thames and Hudson, 2005.
Alfs, Joseph. "A Gallo-Roman Temple Near Bretten (Baden)." *Germania* 24 (1940): 128–40.
Barnwell, E.L. "Bronze Articles Supposed to Be Spoons." *Archaeologia Cambrensis* 36 (1882): 208–19.
Beeching, Henry C., ed. *The Poetical Works of John Milton*. London, New York, Toronto and Melbourne: Humphrey Milford/Oxford University Press, 1914.
Bradley, Richard. *An Archaeology of Natural Places*. London: Routledge, 2000.
Budge, Earnest Alfred Wallis (E.A.W.). *A Guide to the Third and Fourth Egyptian Rooms*. London: Trustees of the British Museum, 1904.
Byron, Tanya. "I Gave Up a Man Because My Mum Didn't Like Him." *The Times T2*, March 7, 2011, 11.
Chisholm, Kitty, and Ferguson, John, eds. Rome: The Augustan Age: A Sourcebook. Oxford: Oxford University Press/Open University Press, 1981.
Davies, Jeffrey L. and Frances Lynch. "The Late Bronze Age and Iron Age." In *Prehistoric Wales*, edited by Frances Lynch, Stephen Aldhouse-Green, and Jeffrey L. Davies, 139–219. Stroud: Sutton, 2000.

Davies, Sioned, trans. *The Mabinogion.* Oxford: Oxford University Press, 2007.

Davis, Oliver. "Twin Freaks? Paired Enclosures in the Early Iron Age of Wessex." In *Changing Perspectives on the First Millennium BC,* edited by Oliver Davis, Niall Sharples and Kate Waddington, 31–42. Oxford: Oxbow, 2008.

De Bernardo Stempel, Patrizia. "Continuity, *Translatio* and *Identificatio* in Romano-Celtic Religion: The Case of Britain." In *Continuity and Innovation in Religion in the Roman West,* edited by Ralph Haeussler and Anthony C. King. Journal of Roman Studies Supplementary Series no. 67, 2 (2008): 67–82.

Deyts, Simone. *Sculptures Gallo-Romaines Mythologiques et Religieuses (Dijon Musée Archéologique).* Paris: Éditions des Musées Nationaux, Palais du Louvre, 1976.

Espérandieu, Émile. *Recueil Général des bas-reliefs de la Gaule romaine et pré-romaine,* vol. 4. Paris: Ernest Leroux, 1911.

Espérandieu, Émile. *Recueil Général des bas-reliefs de la Gaule romaine et pré-romaine* vol. 8. Paris: Ernest Leroux, 1922.

Espérandieu, Émile. *Recueil Général des bas-reliefs de la Gaule romaine et pré-romaine.* German volume. Paris: Ernest Leroux, 1931.

Fitzpatrick, Andrew P. "Les Druides en Grande-Bretagne." In *Les Druides,* edited by Vincent Guichard et Franck Perrin, 47–9. *L'Archéologue Hors Série* 2 (2000).

Fitzpatrick, Andrew P. "Dancing with Dragons: Fantastic Animals in the Earlier Celtic Art of Iron Age Britain." In *The Later Iron Age in Britain and Beyond,* edited by Colin Haselgrove and Tom Moore, 339–57. Oxford: Oxbow, 2007.

Fox, C. "A Second Cauldron and an Iron Sword from the Llyn Fawr Hoard, Rhigos, Glamorgan." *Antiquaries Journal* 19 (1939): 368–404.

Fox, C. *A Find of the Early Iron Age from Llyn Cerrig Bach, Anglesey.* Cardiff: National Museum of Wales, 1946.

Frédéricq, Madeleine. "The Ointment Spoons in the Egyptian Section of the British Museum."*Journal of Egyptian Archaeology* 13 (1927): 12.

Gantz, Jeffrey. *Early Irish Myths and Sagas.* London: Penguin, 1981.

Green, Miranda J. *Symbol and Image in Celtic Religious Art.* London: Routledge, 1989.

Green, Miranda J. "The Iconography of Iron Age Coins." In *Celtic Coinage: Britain and Beyond. The Eleventh Oxford Symposium on Coinage and Monetary History,* edited by Melinda Mays. Oxford: British Archaeological Reports British Series No. 222 (1992): 151–63.

Green, Miranda J. *Celtic Goddesses. Warriors, Virgins and Mothers.* London: British Museum Press, 1995.

Green, Miranda J. Celtic Art. Reading the Messages. London: Weidenfeld and Nicholson, 1996.

Henig, Martin, Webster Graham, and T.F.C. Blagg, *Roman Sculpture from the Cotswald Region,* Corpus signorum imperii Romani I, 7. Oxford: Oxford University Press, 1993

Jenkins, Frank. "The Cult of the Dea Nutrix in Kent." *Archaeologia Cantiana* 71 (1957): 38–46.

Johansen, Donald, and Blake Edgar. *From Lucy to Language.* London: Weidenfeld and Nicolson, 1996.

Kinsella, Thomas. *The Táin.* Oxford: Oxford University Press, 1969.

Lantin, Barbara. "Trouble Trebled: How Do You Breastfeed Triplets?" *The Times T2,* March 29, 2011: 7–8.

Lyle, Emily. *Archaic Cosmos. Polarity, Space and Time.* Edinburgh: Polygon, 1990.

MacCana, Proinsias. *Celtic Mythology.* London: Newnes, 1983.

Macdonald, Philip. *Llyn Cerrig Bach*. Cardiff: University of Wales Press, 2007.

Manning, W.H. "Ironwork Hoards in Iron Age and Roman Britain." *Britannia* 3 (1972): 224–50.

Megaw, John Vincent Stanley (J.V.S.), and Megaw, Ruth. *Celtic Art. From its Beginnings to the Book of Kells*. London: Thames and Hudson, 1989.

O'Flaherty, Wendy Doniger. *Women, Androgynes, and Other Mythical Beasts*. Chicago: University of Chicago Press, 1982.

Reynolds, A.C. *The Llyn Fawr Hoard and its Legacy*. Unpublished M.A. dissertation. Newport: University of Wales, 2000.

Sanders, Karin. *Bodies in the Bog and the Archaeological Imagination*. Chicago: University of Chicago Press, 2009.

Savory, Hubert Newman. *Guide Catalogue of the Early Iron Age Collections (in the National Museum of Wales)*. Cardiff: National Museum of Wales, 1976.

Sharples, Niall. *Social Relations in Later Prehistory*. Oxford: Oxford University Press, 2010.

Spratling, Mansel. "On the Aesthetics of the Ancient Britons." In *Rethinking Celtic Art*, edited by Duncan Garrow, Chris Gosden, and Jeremy D. Hill, 185–202. Oxford: Oxbow, 2008.

Sullivan, R. *Striking the Sacred: Religious Imagery on British Iron Age Coins*. Unpublished MA dissertation. Cardiff: Cardiff University, 2010.

Thomas, Ronald Stuart (R.S.) *Collected Poems 1945–1990*. London: Phoenix, 2000.

Toase, Steven. "The Pairing of Hillforts: Conflict, Complementary, Coincidence or Complex?" In *Changing Perspectives on the First Millennium BC*, edited by Oliver Davis, Niall Sharples and Kate Waddington, 21–30. Oxford: Oxbow, 2008.

Turner, Victor. "Colour Classification in Ndembu Ritual." In *Anthropological Approaches to the Study of Religion*, edited by M. Banton, 47–84. London: Tavistock Publications, 1996.

Van der Sanden, Wijnand. *Through Nature to Eternity: The Bog Bodies of Northwest Europe*. Amsterdam: Batavian Lion International, 1996.

Van der Sanden, Wijnand. "Wetland Archaeology in the Province of Drenthe, the Netherlands." In *Bog Bodies, Sacred Sites and Wetland Archaeology*, edited by Bryony Coles, John Coles, and Morgens Schou Jørgensen. Exeter: Wetland Archaeology Research Project (WARP) Occasional Paper 12 (1999): 217–25.

Veil, S. "Two bodies in woolen coats." In *The Mysterious Bog People*, edited by C. Bergen, Marcel J.L. Th. Niekus, and Vincent T. van Vilsteren, 104–6. Zwolle: Waanders, 2002.

Ward, Donald. *The Divine Twins: An Indo-European Myth in Germanic Tradition*. Berkeley and Los Angeles: University of California Press, 1968.

Wheeler, Robert E.M. "The Llyn Fawr Hoard." *Archaeologia* 71 (1920–21): 132–40.

Yoking the Winds

The Tears of Xanthos and Balios

♊

Kimberley C. Patton

For Gregory Nagy[1]

Introduction

A vast canvas dominates the Beal Gallery of nineteenth-century European art at the Museum of Fine Art in Boston: "Automedon with the Horses of Achilles," painted in 1868 in Rome by the twenty-five-year-old French artist Henri Regnault [Pl. 14; Figure 18.1]. Groin draped in a blood-red cloak, one leg braced on the packed earth of a riverbank, a naked charioteer springs up to restrain two massive horses. They fight him in terror, springing apart, eyes wide, veins bulging, manes flying, foam spattering their own bodies, bronze gold and chestnut.[2] The darkening sky curves to meet an ominous horizon. Regnault wrote of this work, "The horses, aware that their master [Achilles] is taking them into combat, and that this combat . . . will cost him his life, struggle and wrest with the groom [Automedon] . . . I wanted to give the picture a foretaste of disaster."[3] The painting "Automedon" depicts a scene that never takes place in the *Iliad*. Regnault's torqued vision nevertheless honors the Iliadic character of Achilles's team, inspired by their existential situation as *divine animals*.

Who are Xanthos and Balios, and does it matter that they are twins?

These immortal horses are born of the screaming winds and impossibly fast: Homer more often describes them as flying than running. Sons of Zephyros, the West Wind, and the harpy Podarge, a storm-blast,[4] they were trained by Poseidon (or perhaps, as Sarah Iles Johnston has suggested, fathered by him in a masked tradition).[5] In *Iliad* 16.144–54, we "see" them yoked and readied for battle for the first time in their main story-line as it arcs to the funeral of Patroklos in Book 23. The same two verses that describe their yoking (16.148–9) also tell us that they can fly:

Figure 18.1 "Automedon with the Horses of Achilles," 1868. MFA 90.152. Henri Regnault, French, 1843–71. Oil on Canvas. 315 X 329 cm (124 X 129 ½ in). Automedon, chariot driver for Achilles, restrains the hero's immortal twin horses Xanthos and Balios. By permission of the Museum of Fine Arts, Boston.

> . . . Patroklos
> ordered Automedon rapidly to harness the horses,
> A man he honored most, after Achilleus breaker of battles,
> Who stood most staunchly by him against the fury of the fighting.
>
> For him Automedon led **the fast-running horses under
> the yoke**, Xanthos and Balios, **who tore with the winds' speed**, (RL)
>
> [τῶι δὲ καὶ Αὐτομέδων **ὕπαγε ζυγὸν ὠκέας ἵππους**,
> Ξάνθον καὶ Βαλίον, **τὼ ἅμα πνοιῇσι πετέσθην**
> **"who 'the two of them' flew together with, at the same time as, the winds'
> blasts,"** (KP)],
>
> horses stormy Podarge once conceived of the west wind
> and bore, as she grazed in the meadow beside the swirl of the Ocean.

In the traces beside these he put unfaulted Pedasos
whom Akhilleus brought back once he stormed Eetion's city.
He, mortal as he was, ran beside the immortal horses.

—*Iliad* 16.144–54[6]

Translated as "tore," πετέσθην in 16.149 is the imperfect middle *dual* form of the verb πέτεσθαι, "to spread wings in flight, to fly"—since there are two horses. Although Homer occasionally uses the third-person plural for them, verbs describing their actions most commonly appear in the dual number. That this is not simply grammatical exigency is shown by how often the poet surrounds such verbs with other terms of doubling. The horses fly *as twins*; this sense of onrush is intensified by their synchronous flying *with the winds* ("together with, at the same time as, the winds' blasts"). The dual number, a proto-Indo-European form that has atrophied in English, and has been lost in most modern languages save a very few such as Irish, Scottish Gaelic, Lithuanian, Saami, and Slovene, once flourished as a grammatical number peculiar to duality—two-ness, in nouns, adjectives, and verbs in ancient Greek, Sanskrit, and Old English. The root *dw-* yields the Greek *dis* ("twice"), in Latin, *bis*; the Germanic *twai* and its form in Old English *twā*, "two," generating in modern English "twins." But the root metaphor of twinship, a binary state of interplay, of mutual reflection and antagonism, of wanting both to "sever and tether at the same time,"[7] leads to strange linguistic places: the Germanic *twis*, which becomes Old English *twist*; the Greek *deimos,* or fear, whose root *dwei* originally meant "to be in doubt, to be of two minds"; the Latin *dubius* ("hesitating between two alternatives"). The dual number, and duality itself, can intensify through reflexive mirroring: the twisted rope is infinitely stronger than the single strand. It can also weaken through strength-splitting and oscillation—the mighty horses are upended, their momentum destroyed when their mortal companion Pedasos is killed mid-charge, and they fall entangled in their own harness and yoke. Translators of Homer into English such as Richmond Lattimore often suppress the oddly vintage dual number, rendering, as above, Ξάνθον καὶ Βαλίον, τὼ ἅμα πνοιῇσι πετέσθην in *Iliad* 16.149 as "Xanthos and Balios, who tore with the winds' speed." But the Homeric Greek says "who 'τὼ: the two of them' 'πετέσθην: flew,' 'ἅμα: together with, *at the same time as*, less literally 'as fast as' 'πνοιῇσι: the winds' blasts'": "Xanthos and Balios, who—**the two of them**—flew **together with** the winds' blasts." By virtue of their speed, the twin horses, who are born of the winds, are also twinned with them.

That these immortals "belong" to mortals is emphasized in the poem at fraught moments, as in 16.864–6, when Hector wrenches out his bronze spear from Patroklos's wound and casts it at the retreating Automedon "as he was carried away by those swift and immortal horses the gods had given as shining gifts to Peleus." Even when the pair stands mourning at the burning pyre of Patroklos, their manes dragging in the dust just as they did at the moment of his death, Achilles recites their provenance from the gods. For him they are a supercharged inheritance, weaving a divine into a human lineage, like the scepter of Zeus that becomes Agamemnon's: "For they are immortal horses, and Poseidon gave them to Peleus my father, who in turn gave them into my hands" (*Iliad* 23. 277–8). According to second century CE writers like Pseudo-Apollodorus and Ptolemy Hephaestion, the pair were given by Poseidon as a wedding present to Achilles's father, Peleus king of Phthia, when he married the sea-nymph Thetis.[8] Claiming an older tradition, Diodorus Siculus wrote,

> according to sacred (mythical) history—κατὰ μυθικὴν ἱστορίαν—they were not horses at all, but were once Titans who betrayed their generation and fought for the Olympians, Xanthos as a companion of Poseidon and Balios of Zeus; and in the battle they asked that their shape might be changed, since they were ashamed to be seen by their brethren the Titanes, and their request was granted; and it was these horses which were given to Peleus.[9]

All traditions point to their alien nature; though sky-born, they are tethered to the earth and its mortal misery. Deeply attached to their warrior owners in every way, that misery becomes theirs in the course of the poem. They are the opposite of immune to war's agony. But death can bring them no relief.

In the *Iliad*, the twin horses' attachment to their heroes as they fall is reduplicated and performed in the symbol of the yoke (*zugón* [ζυγόν]; *hippeíon zugón* [ἱππεῖον ζυγόν], *Iliad* 5.799 in the genitive). Also yoked to one another and to a war-chariot (*hármata*; *ókhos* in the plural, or, as Gregory Nagy observes, at times simply called "the horses"), these sons of the winds must be driven, over and over, across battle-fields covered with corpses. In the epic tradition, this lets the heroes who drive them make more enemy corpses—eventually becoming corpses themselves. This in turn creates more undying memory (*kléos áphthiton*), which is the goal of the struggle, the carnage, the war, and all of it: τὸν δὲ θεοὶ μὲν τεῦξαν, ἐπεκλώσαντο δ' ὄλεθρον ἀνθρώποισ', ἵνα ᾖσι καὶ ἐσσομένοισιν ἀοιδή. "This the gods made happen, and spun ruin upon human beings, so that there would be singing for those yet to be" (*Odyssey* 8: 579–80).

The final portion of this chapter reflects on three iconic paintings spanning nearly 2600 years, inspired by, yet oddly unfaithful to, the epic tradition of the immortal twin horses of Achilles. These are: (1) Regnault's monumental work, now in Boston; (2) the Acropolis fragment of a dedicatory black-figure kantharos depicting Achilles adjusting the cheekpiece of his horses, who are called by other names, signed by Nearchos as potter and painter and dated to 560–550 BCE, still in Athens; and (3) "The divine horses of Achilles, Xanthos and Balios," by Giorgio di Chirico, perhaps the best known of his fifteen years' worth of horse-paintings, finished on Christmas Day in 1963 and now in New South Wales, Australia. All three portraits refract ways in which the *Iliad* yokes and therefore binds Achilles's two horses. All three also "scramble," and hence intensify, these horsey bonds, by portraying extra-Iliadic scenes unimagined by any later literary work in antiquity. Each of the artists visually comments on—in two cases, as I will show, in order to subvert—the horses' role as trophies. In these works of art, Xanthos and Balios are indeed magnificent war-engines. Since they are gifts from the gods, they amplify and even weaponize the charismatic power of "god-like" (θεῖος) Achilles whom they serve; their charioteer Patroklos, beloved of Achilles, whom they mourn; and Achilles's son, Neoptolemus, whose body they will ultimately carry to the Elysian Fields.[10] Yet all three artists also present the horses as autonomous *subjects*, twin brothers with their own distinct emotional worlds separate from the human theater of action. Sharing one heart, in each painting they stand in complex, dual relationship to one another and to their fate.

Híppoi Athánatoi

Xanthos and Balios are the only horses called *híppoi athánatoi* (ἵπποι ἀθάνατοι), although others, such as the horses of Hector, have divine connections.[11,12] In the wider mythological field, they are members of a tribe of such special horses, most of whom pull the chariots of gods who fly across the sky or else across the waves. Achilles's horses belong to the family of Pegasus and the horses of Helios not only by virtue of their speed, but also because they have their genesis and proper home in the sky. Of necessity, many are dual-appearing, due to the practical necessity of balancing a chariot: the two horses of Eos, goddess of the dawn; the four horses of Helios and of Ares; the eight horses of Poseidon. The eight-legged horse of the shamanic Old Norse high god Óðinn, Sleipnir, can carry the god to the gates of Hel and across the sea. It has even been suggested that Sleipnir has eight legs because at one time he was two horses. Together god and horse are a twain-kenning.[13] Occasionally, however, such special horse-pairs or dual multiples are "grounded" and belong to special humans—royal, heroic, or both—like Achilles's father King Peleus (two), King Erechtheus (two), or the Trojan kings Erichthonius and Laomedon (twelve), the latter sired by the North Wind, Boreas, Zephyros's twin.[14] They are Herakles's reward for saving Hesione from the sea-monster (*kētos*) sent by Poseidon to punish the faithless king.

In other traditions, shamanic figures often ride sky-horses. Immortal horses expand the already miraculous-seeming powers of ordinary horses. The magical horse who can fly through the heavens appears in the Islamic *Mi'rāj Namēh* tradition of Al-Burāq, who with her horse's body, eagle's wings, and woman's face, bears the Prophet from Mecca to Jerusalem then up through the seven levels of Heaven in one "night of power." As late as 1880 we know of Siberian Altai sacrifices that "launch" horses skyward,[15] just as millennia before, the *Ṛg Veda* called the bright sky the proper home of the transfigured horse-sacrifice (*Aśvamedha*): "You gods fashioned the horse out of the sun . . . From afar, in my heart I recognized your soul, the bird flying below the sky. I saw your winged head snorting on the dustless paths easy to travel."[16] The spirit-horse appears in the circling animals of the Lakota elder Black Elk's vision and Stan Jones's Apache-inspired 1948 Western ballad, "Ghost Riders in the Sky."

Like special horses, mythological twins also frequently belong to the sky. In fact, in many traditions, the sky may be the home of all twins. As Jacob Olúpọnà writes to contextualize Yorùbá views, in many African traditions one or both of any pair of mundane twins have celestial origin. If the sky-twin dies prematurely, they can seek to return and dangerously to reclaim their earthly *ibejì*, pulling their missing half back up for company. The Nuer non-metaphorically classify *all* human twins as "birds" because of their paranormal status as "children of Kuoth" (i.e., of God, whose realm is the sky).[17] Unsurprisingly, divine twin horsemen, marrying two numinous categories—twins and horses—usually operate in the sky.[18] The Vedic healer-twin Aśvins (Ashwins) are the children of Sūrya, the Sun, moving between sky and earth to heal humans and even the decapitated sacrifice, restoring its head with a pot. As mentioned in Chapter 1, their ancient Greek counterparts, the savior-twins the Dioskouroi, "suddenly appear" as fire around the masts of ships in storms,

rushing through the air with dark wings,
and at once they stop the blasts of the dreadful storm-winds,
and calm the waves on the surface of the frightened sea,
beautiful signs to sailors from their trouble.
—*Homeric Hymn* 33 (to the Dioskouroi), 12–16[19]

In sacred histories, divine beings are taller, stronger, more fertile, more compassionate and more lethal than mortal ones; they are more illustrious weavers, drinkers, archers, magicians, lovers, child-bearers, or builders of castle walls. They have odd, but still oddly recognizable powers, amplifying what is already recognized as powerful in the ordinary world. Immortal animals expand the already numinous powers of ordinary animals. "Divine twins" only intensify the numinous, uncanny features that belong to all twins, whether mortal or immortal. The theme's energy draws from the archetype of twinship—which always involves both mirroring and difference, leading either to antagonism or complementarity—and which matters a great deal in interpreting other Homeric twin-pairs. These include Castor and Pollux, already dead and buried in Sparta when their sister Helen at the Skaian gates scans the ranks of the Achaeans to identify them for her "beloved father" King Priam: "yet nowhere can I see those two, the marshals of the people, Kastor, breaker of horses, and the strong boxer, Polydeukes, my own brothers, born with me of a single mother," not knowing that "the teeming earth lay already upon them away in Lakedaimon, the beloved land of their fathers" (*Iliad* 3.343–4). Whereas any distinction between the two Aśvins has dropped away by the time we encounter them in Vedic literature, the Iliadic Dioskouroi (Gemini in Latin) share a heroic death and cultic honors (*Odyssey* 11.298–304). As discussed in the Introduction, they are given two different fathers (Zeus for Pollux and Tyndareus for Castor) in Pindar Nemean 10 and alternating afterlives in the lost *Cypria*. While preserving both paternal traditions ("sons of great Zeus"; "Tyndaridai, riders of swift horses!"), their *Homeric Hymn* collapses their unique identities as the "saviors of men on this earth and swift-sailing ships."[20] The two sons of Asklepios, Machaon and Podaleirios (*Iliad* 2.729–33), are warrior-physicians, albeit with different medical skill-sets, graves in different places, and, in later tradition, becoming different butterflies.[21] Though they are not twins, Greek tradition similarly tends to "twin" them. For example, at their birthplace in ancient Trikka (modern Trikkala) in Thessaly, where the oldest known Asklepieion was built and has possibly been found, their healing powers almost certainly persist in the nearby church of the Anargyroi ("the Unmercenaries"), Saints Cosmas and Damian, with its adjacent incubation chamber for miraculous cures.[22] Hypnos ("Sleep") and Thanatos "gentle Death" are explicitly called "twin brothers" (ὕπνῳ καὶ θανάτῳ διδυμάοσιν, *Iliad* 16.682), the winged children of primordial Nyx ("Night"), but with different gifts for human beings. Zeus sends them to carry home to Lykia the corpse of his son Sarpedon, washed and anointed by his son Apollo.

Despite their unearthly powers, Homer's Xanthos and Balios are the opposite of divinely detached from what befalls them on the plains of Troy. Since the twin horses need no *kléos áphthiton* to attain immortality, they are only briefly backlit by battle glory—and not at all by the unperishing glory of posthumous fame. While Xanthos's speech to Achilles in 19.404–17 shows that the horses share a Bronze Age code of honor, affirming the value of victory and the disgrace of defeat, in lived experience their losses only shatter them. Homer does not gloss over the cruelty of this code. Even Zeus sees their anguish, bitterly pitying them, a high god shocked into awareness of the consequences of having gifted them to a mortal king. Seth Schein poignantly writes, "Although as immortals the horses should be immune to death and the ravages of time, their tears and the language in which they are described make them seem virtually human in their suffering."[23]

And suffer they do, unforgettably, in tandem. The duality of their suffering creates resonance between them, while also providing each with much-needed companionship. Their tears bind and sustain them. For millennia, lamentation traditions have shown how the awful weight of mourning should not be born alone.[24]

Dualism and the Meaningful Yoke

The paradox of the twin horses' vulnerability is expressed throughout their story-arc in the richly generative, recurrent symbol of the ζυγόν (*zugón*, from *zeúgnūmi*), "yoke." This element attaches draft animals to whatever was to be drawn—chariot, wagon, caisson—and of necessity, coupling them to one another and making them into a single, symmetrically balanced force. In Homeric Greek, the noun can also refer to the cross-bar of a lyre, or the thwarts of a ship. The yoke joins two sides together, bridging them; but it does more. In the process, it makes them into a dual unity that is stronger than either alone, a hybrid being that resonates, sails, or runs as one. The wooden ζυγόν of Xanthos and Balios joins two creatures, then called sometimes by the singular noun ζεῦγος (*zeûgos*), "a pair" (of draft animals) (*Iliad* 18.543). This term is much more prevalent in later Greek literature than in Homeric usage, when its meaning expands to include a carriage drawn by a yoke of beasts; a chariot; the beasts themselves, especially two horses; or a pair of anything.

The yoke of the Bronze Age war-chariot, however, does not constrain Xanthos and Balios in the same way as it would two unrelated horses. Rather, it rhetorically frames their plight. This is because they are already defined by their twinship, their syzygy (συζυγία), their condition of being "yoked together." The *zugón* does not *make* them dual in their traces so much as it signals their preexisting, heartbroken duality.

The verb ζεύγνῡμι (*zeúgnūmi*), used in Homer of the readying of horses, goes on to a rich afterlife in archaic and classical Greek, recombining notions of yoking, fastening, binding, and pair-creation along a spectrum: "join together"; "join in wedlock; marry"; "set a fractured jaw" in Hippocratic writings; "bridge" (two banks of a river); even "match against one another" (two gladiators) or "make a double-reed." Exactly like twins, the two beings who are paired—or two elements that are brought into relationship in order to enable action, usually by a third party or cultural convention—tend to have some inherent resonance or complementarity between them. Also exactly like twinship, however, the verb *zeúgnūmi* and its derivative nouns like *zugón* and *zeûgos* imply a sense of compulsion, shading to violent constraint. Two beings are not only *joined* but *bound* by a third element. The yoke concretizes a preexisting affinity, but it also makes the bond inescapable. The multivalency of the word-family is clear in the *Odes* of Pindar, where forms of ze*ú*gn*u*mi can refer to readying a chariot (*Pythian* 10.65) or harnessing Pegasus (*Olympian* 13.64). But in *Nemean* 7 for Sogenes of Aigina, which begins by invoking the goddess of childbirth Eileithyia, the listener is reminded that destinies are not equally distributed, and "each is yoked to his own fate, / each constrained in his own way": εἴργει δὲ πότμῳ ζυγένθ' ἕτερον ἕτερα (*Nemean* 7.6). In Plato's renowned *Phaedrus*, the idea is built into an allegory for the moral struggle of the soul itself, which is compared συμφύτῳ δυνάμει **ὑποπτέρου ζεύγους** τε καὶ ἡνιόχου, "to the composite ("grown-together") power of a **winged pair of horses** (ones who are "**yoked together**") and a charioteer."[25] These are a tumultuous pair, one noble and one ignoble horse, which, unlike Xanthos and Balios, is mismatched. Neither horse can escape the yoke. With each pulling in a different direction, the soul-charioteer's effort to control them is made "of necessity (ἐξ ἀνάγκης) difficult and troublesome."[26] The inclusion of the ancient term ἀνάγκη, with its penumbra of force, torture, and anguish, drives home the compulsion that attends the yoke.

Together with the also-dual *h*ē*niokhos (charioteer)* and *apobat*ē*s* (the warrior who jumps off and on the chariot-board to fight)—even the name of the board (*díphros*) implies that it is a platform is designed for two—the supernatural twin animals are the power that drives a mobile, but never individual war machine.[27] As mentioned, pairs of horses (*híppoi*) are so identified with the war-chariot (*hármata*) as to be at times interchangeable with it.[28] In Book 5, as Nagy notes, Pandaros regrets that he did not heed the advice of his father Lykaon to bring horses and a war-chariot to Troy: "Somewhere in the great house of Lykaon are eleven chariots . . . and beside each chariot, [a pair of] **double-yoked** horses stand[s], champing white barley and oats (παρὰ δέ σφιν ἑκάστῳ **δίζυγες** ἵπποι ἑστᾶσι κρῖ λευκὸν ἐρεπτόμενοι καὶ ὀλύρας)." The adjective δίζυξ (*dízux*) intensifies the force of the yoking, emphasizing that the δίζυγες ἵπποι are yoked two abreast; we are given a sense of the depth of care that royal Bronze Age horses received, as well as how battle-ready they were kept, fed beside their chariots, each a unit of thought and functionality.[29,30] Later, as Achilles and his horses together mourn Patroklos, already burned on the pyre, he speaks of the elaborate care his lost beloved always took:

> But I stay here at the side, and my single-foot [hooved] horses stay with me;
> such is the high glory of the charioteer they have lost,
> the gentle one, who so many times anointed their manes with
> soft olive oil, after he had washed them in shining water.
> Therefore these two horses stand here and grieve, and their manes
> are swept along the ground as they stand with hearts full of sorrow.
>
> —*Iliad* 23.279–84

We will return to this evocative passage later.

The twin horses of Achilles are yoked in at least four interdependent ways. Their trajectory is always determined by the doubling effected by the *zugón*. First, they are physically joined in harness to the light spoked-wheel war chariots they pull, whose oldest extant forms have been found buried together with warriors and their retinues in grassy Sintashta-Petrovka kurgans east of the Ural Mountains (2100–1800

BCE).[31] Second, the brother-horses are pathetically bound to the heroes they carry into battle: beloved masters whose doom they anticipate with dread and then must grieve, struck still as a tombstone. Third and urgently, they are, like all twins, yoked to one another. Relationally expanded, the yoke of the war-chariot does not impair Xanthos and Balios as it might two other unrelated horses: they are already yoked by their twinship, both constrained and empowered by the primordial bond that joins all twins *and already renders them divine.* Fourth and finally, because of all of these associations, Xanthos and Balios, attached to mortality, are permanently caught in what Cavafy calls the "unending disaster" of death itself.[32] This is concretized even before the death of Patroklos by the accidental killing of their companion in the traces, the mortal horse Pedasos, who entangles all three of them as they fall full-tilt. The twin horses of Achilles are yoked—physically and existentially bound—in at least four interdependent ways, the last being by far the worst, overshadowing all the others.

In the *Iliad*, their main story-line, extending from Book 16 to Book 23, is defined by five moments where the *zugón*—"a symbol giving rise to thought," as Ricœur might have called it—defines both their situation and their response.

The Death of Pedasos

Once they are attached to their chariot by Automedon in Book 16—their first yoking—Xanthos and Balios are then also harnessed with the mortal trace horse, "unfaulted Pedasos" (*Iliad* 16.152–4). Captured by Achilles when the city of Eetion was taken, their "third" was so fast that he could keep up with the two divine horses as they charged. Like a spare tire, the trace horse was quickly available "on the fly" to replace a stricken horse, should one of the primary pair in the *zeûgos* fall. We find this harnessing schema depicted on vases such as the dramatic Corinthian hydria in Baltimore whose subject is the battle of Achilles and Memnon in the presence of their mothers Thetis and Eos: Xanthos and Balios are joined by Pedasos in the traces; as well as in the Nearchos fragment.[33] The story of Pedasos is so devastating that we forget his superfluity. The twin horses of Achilles cannot be killed. Why is he there?

Accidentally struck by Sarpedon's spear meant for Patroklos, poor Pedasos is wounded and dragged down, screaming "as he blew his life away" (ἔβραχε θυμὸν ἀΐσθων) (16.468) and entangling his companions in their own tack and in the gear of the chariot. The thunderous shock of the dying horse's fall is so great that even the integrity of the yoke between the immortal horses is threatened (16.470–1):

τὼ δὲ διαστήτην, κρίκε δὲ ζυγόν, ἡνία δέ σφι
σύγχυτ᾽, ἐπεὶ δὴ κεῖτο παρήορος ἐν κονίῃσι.

Here Lattimore has:

"The other horses shied apart (**διαστήτην**), the yoke creaked
(**κρίκε δὲ ζυγόν**), the guide reins (ἡνία)[34]

Were fouled together (σύγχυτ')
    as the trace horse lay in the dust beside them . . ."

Xanthos and Balios are not just "the other horses." The twin horses' τώ ("the two of them") is followed by an epic verb (διαστήτην), an aorist dual that itself emphasizes the breaking apart of two-ness, desperately "rearing in opposite directions"—just as Regnault imagined them later in Book 19—and their reins are not just "fouled" as strands but "poured out together; confounded" in a composite of the ancient Indo-European verb of libation χέω (σύγχυτ'< συγχέω). The "contrast between the horses' immortality and their forced connection with mortality" explodes.[35] All of this mingled confusion of what should be a sleek synchrony of horses, speed, direction, and reins goes on until they are desperately cut free by Automedon (16.472–6). His untethering of the corpse of Pedasos from the un-killable but frantic Xanthos and Balios restores their twinned balance:

but at this spear-famed Automedon saw what he must do
and wrenching out the long-edged sword from beside his big thigh
in a flashing stroke and without faltering cut loose the trace horse

and **the other horses were straightened out**, and pulled in the guide reins,
and **the two heroes came together** in the heart-perishing battle. (RL)

[τώ δ' ἰθυνθήτην, ἐν δὲ ῥυτῆρσι τάνυσθεν·
τώ δ' αὖτις συνίτην ἔριδος πέρι θυμοβόροιο.
and **the other [two] horses were straightened out**, and pulled in the guide
    reins,
and **the two [horses/heroes] came together** in the heart-perishing battle.]
                                                                —*Iliad* 16.472–6

Writing on the motif of the death of Pedasos in two vases by Exekias as well as a Tyrrhenian amphora in Florence and a black-figure hydria in Naples, Mary Moore tellingly misquotes (or corrects without fanfare) Lattimore's "two heroes" as "two horses."[36] Or is Lattimore's the misreading of τώ? It is not clear which "two" Homer means in 476 τώ δ' αὖτις συνίτην; it is interesting that Schein reads the phrase in the same way as Moore, as referring to the horses. In light of the iteration of τώ ("the pair, the two of them") followed by a dual verb, it is likely that Moore's version of Lattimore's translation does indeed represent the better interpretation: Xanthos and Balios are re-yoked, their sadly lost companion no longer encumbering their flight over the ground, *then* paving the way for the two heroes, Sarpedon and Patroklos, to re-engage.

The strangeness of this story is worth contemplating. Although Xanthos and Balios are tethered to a trace horse, Pedasos, who can run as fast as they do, flying "at the same time as the winds' blasts," their friend cannot replace either horse of the *zeûgos* when he is cut down. The story of Pedasos and his ghastly death therefore, seems to serve a deeper semiotic purpose. The second yoking of the *híppoi athánatoi* reveals how paradoxically un-free of death they are—how easily snarled in their traces, how bound to what can be stopped cold: halting their synchronous flight and hurling them to the unfamiliar earth.

The Death of Patroklos

In perhaps the most iconic moment of their story, the horses see the plumed helmet of Achilles worn by Patroklos roll under their feet (*Iliad* 16.795). Standing apart from the battle, they learn that their charioteer, who had that same day emerged from his tent to take the place of Achilles, *daimoni isos*, "equal to a god," is cut down like a sacrificed animal, first by the stunning blow of Apollo, the javelin of Euphorbos, and then by the bronze sword of Hector.[37] That Xanthos and Balios are sentient battle-spoils, valuable weapons of war to be stolen, emerges in the fragmentary play *Rhesus*, attributed to Euripides but still contested. Dolon agrees to spy on the Greek camp but demands of Hector the prize of Achilles's horses when the war is won.[38] The two horses are immediately paralyzed by the news of the death of Patroklos "like a grave-monument" stuck in the earth over a noble-born person's tomb.[39]

> But the horses of Aiakides standing apart from the battle
> wept, as they had done **since they heard how** their charioteer
> had fallen in the dust at the hands of murderous Hektor. (RL)

> [ἵπποι δ' Αἰακίδαο μάχης ἀπάνευθεν ἐόντες
> κλαῖον, ἐπεὶ δὴ **πρῶτα πυθέσθην** ἡνιόχοιο
> **"since the two of them had learned for the first time"**
> ἐν κονίῃσι πεσόντος ὑφ' Ἕκτορος ἀνδροφόνοιο.]

> In truth Automedon, the powerful son of Diores,
> hit them over and over again with the stroke of the flying
> lash, or talked to them, sometimes entreating them, sometimes threatening.
> They were unwilling to go back to the wide passage of Helle
> and the ships, or back into the fighting after the Achaians,
> but **still as stands a grave monument** which is set over
> the mounded tomb of a dead man or lady, . . . (RL)

> [(ἀλλ' ὥς τε στήλη μένει ἔμπεδον ἥ τ' ἐπὶ τύμβῳ
> ἀνέρος ἑστήκῃ τεθνηότος ἠὲ γυναικός
> **"just as a stele remains (in one place) fixed in the ground"**]

> they stood there holding motionless in its place the fair-wrought **chariot** (RL)

> [ὣς μένον ἀσφαλέως περικαλλέα **δίφρον** ἔχοντες
> "so they remained (there) keeping immovable the beautifully-made **chariot-on-
>   which-two-could-stand"**]

. . . leaning their heads along the ground, and warm tears were running earthward from underneath the lids of the mourning horses who longed for their charioteer, . . . (RL)

[οὔδει **ἐνισκίμψαντε** καρήατα· δάκρυα δέ **σφι**
θερμὰ **κατὰ βλεφάρων χαμάδις ῥέε μυρομένοισιν**
ἡνιόχοιο πόθῳ·
"both of them leaning their heads along the ground, and warm tears were running **from (their) eyelids down to the ground for them who were flowing with tears** because of (their) longing for (their) charioteer"]

. . . while their **bright manes were made dirty** as they streamed down **either side** of the **yoke** from under the **yoke pad**. (RL)

[. . . **θαλερὴ δ' ἐμιαίνετο χαίτη**
ζεύγλης ἐξεριποῦσα **παρὰ ζυγὸν ἀμφοτέρωθεν.**
"as their **luxuriant, loose and flowing mane was stained** (as the tears were) streaming down from the **yoke-pad** from the side of the **yoke from both sides.**"]

—*Iliad* 17. 426–40

"On account of" *póthos* for their charioteer, the twin horses are overwhelmed by the age-old feelings and traditional actions of lamentation. Mourning disfigures them, dissolving their majestic beauty and their affiliation to the sky. Everything that can flows downward from their wind-born bodies to the dark earth, the home of the dead: their tears, their mane dragging in the dirt (interestingly, given in the singular, as though speaking of it as a shared generic feature), their agency. Their twinship is emphasized in the dual form of ἐνισκίμπτω as they don't simply touch the ground, but lay or lean their mighty heads along it. As they stand apart from the battle that rages over the stolen armor of Achilles, their sorrow is catalyzed merely by the news, not even the sight of Patroklos's stripped body.

In this passage and elsewhere when the horses become the focus, Homer intensifies their duality and the use of the dual number through the use of adjectives and adverbs emphasizing doubling and two-ness. It is not enough to say that the horses' mane(s) flows down from the yoke, which would have been sufficient to paint the picture, but that it (they) do so "from both sides": two horses, two sides, one mane, one yoke-pad, one yoke: one unifying, acute grief. Hanging their heads and weeping "warm tears," soiling their bright manes, they knew that this catastrophe would trigger the death of Achilles.

When the horses stain their manes and have "longing" (πόθωι, 439) for their charioteer, these too are human actions, like Achilles' pouring dust over his head in lamentation for Patroklos at 18.23–4 and "longing" for him at 19.321 and 24.6. Generally speaking, horses in the *Iliad* are like human companions: they share the toil and danger of the heroes, who in turn care for them, address them by name, and urge them on in battle (8.185–97, 19.399–403, 23.402–17). Apart from human beings, they are the only animals said to "feel longing" (ποθέειν: 5.234, 11.161; πόθος: 17.439; cf. 23.283–4), and the only ones compared with other animals in similes (2.764, 20.495–502; cf. 10.437), a kind of comparison that normally serves to clarify some aspect of *human* existence.[40]

Schein's reflections on this episode highlight the marked power of all Iliadic horses—who feel in "human" ways, share in the trials of heroes, and are known to them by name—as well as the unique torment of Xanthos and Balios: their categorical otherness and existential bondage. As divine beings, part of the spectrum of godhood, they radiate power whenever they appear in the narrative. But as animals, battle-gear, and potential spoils of war, they are victims who are powerless to prevent what threatens them the most. Horses are by nature broken and bound, and it is perhaps not coincidental that the passage immediately preceding mentions the Trojans encircling the corpse of Patroklos by their frequent formula, "Trojans, breakers of horses." When bound horses are in the family of divinity, however, theirs is a unique anguish. Meditating on Ares in the hands of Otos and Ephialtes (χαλεπὸς δέ ἑ δεσμὸς ἐδάμνα, *Iliad* 5.391), Michiel van Veldhuizen writes, "For immortal gods that cannot be killed, being bound is the worst fate."[41]

Because they were bound to one another at birth by twinship, to the house of Peleus by the gods, and to the war-chariot by the yoke, Xanthos and Balios are also bound by loyal love to what is all too mortal. When Patroklos falls, Xanthos and Balios are as implicated as when Pedasos fell "shrieking (μακών)" but more endangered—not by death, but by despair. It is as though the clash of opposites they represent—immortal and mortal—breaks them out of the ideologies of epic heroism and sets them in a place beyond even what Homer can imagine for them.

> Thus, when the horses weep 'hot tears' for Patroklos in 17.437–8, they express the effect of his death on themselves, but at the same time the displaced θαλερή, describing their 'rich, full' manes, invokes the vitality associated with their own unaging immortality. These manes, however, are 'stained' (ἐμιαίνετο, 17.439), which powerfully expresses the contradiction between this immortality and their participation in the sorrows of human existence—the contradiction for which Zeus pities them (441–7).[42]

The ζυγόν (*zugón*) and its accessory ζεύγλη (*zeúglē*) in 17.439–40 become objective correlatives for the paradoxical tethering of Achilles's horses, not only to their external circumstances but also to their internal emotions and deepest attachments. They are yoked a third time: to Patroklos standing in for Achilles, to Patroklos slain by Hector, and the leaden grief his death visits upon them. Xanthos and Balios cannot be constrained without the express permission of the gods—but then, their constraint is absolute. Neither can they be released from bondage without divine intervention. Just as they were broken by a god, Poseidon, and given to the father of Achilles, so it is the supreme god Zeus who must rouse them from the stupor of their grief in *Iliad* 17.426–40 and get them moving back to safety. But he cannot look away from their suffering, nor fail to interrogate the gods' role in causing it.

As he watched the mourning horses the son of Kronos pitied them,
and stirred his head and spoke to his own spirit: 'Poor wretches,
why then did we ever give you to the lord Peleus,
a mortal man, and you yourselves are immortal and ageless?
Only so that among unhappy men you also might be grieved?
Since among all creatures that breathe on earth and crawl on it
there is not anywhere a thing more dismal than man is.
At least the son of Priam, Hektor, shall not mount behind you
in the carefully wrought chariot. I will not let him. Is it not
enough for him that he has the armour and glories in wearing it?
But now I will put vigour into your knees and your spirits
so that you bring back Automedon out of the fighting
safe to the hollow ships . . .'
    So spoke Zeus, and breathed great vigour into the horses,
and they shaking the dust from their manes to the ground lightly
carried the running chariot among Akhaians and Trojans.

                                                —*Iliad* 17.441–53; 456–8

In this shocking speech, it is hard not to hear echoes of Ishtar's regret for "speaking evil in the gods' assembly" and bringing on the flood in the *Gilgamesh* as she surveys the bodies who "fill the sea like fish spawn,"[43] or God's promise in Genesis 8:21 as he surveys the world He drowned. Divine remorse is rare, but like its more common human counterpart, often irremediable.

Three Paintings of the Twin Horses of Achilles

I. "Automedon with the Horses of Achilles"

With his forceful painting of a helmet-bearing Thetis in the moment she startles her son, mad with grief, passionately bending over the outstretched corpse of Patroklos,[44] the young artist Henri Regnault won the French Academy's Rome Prize in 1866. The terms called for him to send one painting each year from Rome back to Paris for three years. The first was to be a nude "displaying the student's mastery of anatomy." The Boston Museum of Fine Arts observes of "Automedon" (Fig. 18.1), "Regnault instead sent home this mammoth, operatic canvas."[45,46] Rebelling against Roman classicism and drawn to the vitalism of the Hispano-Italian school, he traveled to Spain and North Africa where he painted *Judith et Holopherne* in 1869, and then the notorious *Salomé* in 1870; painted in Tangier, his huge *Execution without Hearing under the Moorish Kings of Grenada* glows with ruby gore on marble steps. Only recently has European art history begun to recognize the affective brilliance of Regnault, one of the great Romantic painters of the nineteenth century. He was a passionate disciple of non-European faces and environments—even as he distorted and exotified their cultures—and a catalyst of what came to be known as the "Orientalist" school.

    In 1871 he volunteered for one of the last battles of the Franco-Prussian War, the doomed Battle of Buzenval. He died in the retreat from Paris on January 19. The painter Georges Clairin found him among many hundreds of the dead, shot in the head at age twenty-seven. His friend Camille Saint-Saëns dedicated his *Marche Héroïque* (1871) to Regnault's memory; his death was memorialized by the painter Carolus-Duran and the sculptor Chapu.[47] Deeply drawn to Homeric themes, Regnault sought and wove himself into an Achillean destiny—dying young, violently, and voluntarily for a glorious cause. He also earned a comparable national cultic afterlife.

Homer makes explicit that Automedon must yoke the horses together in Book 19, as he did in Book 16: ἵππους δ' Αὐτομέδων τε καὶ Ἄλκιμος ἀμφιέποντες ζεύγνυον· (*Iliad* 19.392–3). In the scene Regnault *imagines* for this scene in Book 19, the magnificent horses of Achilles see what lies ahead and resist being yoked to one another, to their chariot, and to their master. For Regnault, their foreknowledge of his death controls their action, and the entire painting. Their mood as wind-creatures is mirrored by the threatening sky, whence will come roaring their father Zephyros and his own twin brother Boreas in Book 23 to ignite the pyre of Patroklos.

Regnault's aim seems to have been to compress the complex story of the twin horses into one image, like an icon. Their trajectory is linked to Achilles's—as Nagy and Frame have each shown is true of heroes and horses—but at the same time, tragically independent of it. Never will Xanthos and Balios lie in tandem with him in the earth, accompanying their owner in death like the rare but significant heraldic skeletons in the well-known fourteenth-century BCE shaft grave at Marathon. The horses are usually two; they are always arranged in relationship to one another. Other known Mycenaean human/horse burials hauntingly pose pairs of chariot horses in explicitly twinned forms in graves found in the Argolid, and elsewhere: one above the other; facing one another as in Tumulus C at Dendra just prior to the Middle Helladic;[48] or facing in the same direction (NE), as in Tumulus B (MH-LH 1).[49] In much later geometric chamber-tombs from necropoleis at Salamis from the eighth century, horses are frequently found attached not only to one another in one or multiple pairs but also to the remains of elaborate war-chariots and funeral caissons.[50] In such burials we do not find human bones deliberately joined to horse or other animal bones, as we do in the Neolithic Mediterranean at sites like Eynan or Hatoula,[51] but the separation between the bones of the hero and his pair of war-horses, the two who pull the *biga* or dual chariot, is only slightly more attenuated. The team constituted their warrior-master's world in life: socially catalogued somewhere between companions and possessions, cherished friends but also things—like weapons—owned to achieve *kléos*, to fight over, to steal from other heroes. The funerary equine pair are part of "the hero and everything that belongs to the hero," as Nagy has expressed it, amplifying the dead warrior's identity in the regard of the living. Nine hundred years later, heraldic horseheads decorate a black-figure Athenian amphora in a grave from the early sixth century BCE; Emily Vermeule suggests continuity with noble Bronze Age burials, just as one sees in Geometric and archaic horse sacrifices in the tombs of the wealthy. If one could not have horses to accompany one in death, and perhaps, as she suggests, to mourn within the grave-house, this was a budget version.[52]

The horses of Mycenaean graves were interchangeable players in a funeral matrix that constituted a ritualized coda to the life of their warrior owner, silently linked to their chariot and to his body, armor, and weapons, to which they lie contiguous: as well as, more importantly, the social memory that his body will generate from its new home and stronghold (*oikos*, literally, "house" in ancient Greek culture, long before Herodotus used this word to describe the tomb of the hero, up through the present; the word is still engraved on modern Greek tombstones). But above all else and more than these, Bronze Age horses are linked in pairs *to themselves*—to one another—forever.

When Achilles is buried, whether in the Bronze Age shaft-grave or tholos he would have merited in history, or the golden Geometric cremation urn Stesichorus gives him because of the heroic pyres pictured by Homer in epic, this retinue of cultural value and force cannot be buried with him. These steeds, grafted into his lineage before he was born, cannot mourn for him in his tomb: they must outlive his death.

II. "Achilles Harnesses His Horses"

The charred fragments of a large black-figure kantharos from the mid-sixth century BCE were found in the debris of the Persian Sack of the Athenian Acropolis. One of them is signed by Nearchos as potter and painter (Νεαρχος με|γραφσεν κα[ι εποιεσεν). It depicts Achilles himself (Αχιλ[λ]ε[υς]) with one hand checking the cheekpiece and bit of one of his team, and with his other, grasping the horse's crest to steady him, long fingers curved into his mane [Pl. 13b; Figure 18.2]. A third horse is being led into the traces by a *hēníokhos*. In addition to the elegant precision of the design, down to the incised decorations on the horse's chest strap, the scene seems suffused with intimacy, a calm moment before the lethal churn of the battle to come. The vase cannot show the words of the conversation between hero and horses, but there can be no question of longstanding, even tender relationality. It is as though one can hear the horses breathing. What Iliadic scene is this? Is Nearchos depicting the bitter conversation between Xanthos and Achilles?

Like the Regnault painting, the Nearchos fragment depicts a scene that never takes place in the *Iliad*, but could be extrapolated from the story it tells of wonder-horses. Its most likely context is the scene in Book 19 where the solar Achilles, wearing the armor made by Hephaistos, at last prepares for a return to the fighting to avenge the death of Patroklos—whose death he has brought about, in thrall to his *mēnis*—"and the armor became as wings and upheld the shepherd of the people" (19.386). In the *Iliad*, it is not Achilles himself but again Automedon who, this time together with Alkimos, yokes and harnesses the horses.

Automedon and Alkimos, in charge of the horses,
yoked them

[ἵππους δ' Αὐτομέδων τε καὶ Ἄλκιμος ἀμφιέποντες
ζεύγνυον]

                and put the fair breast straps about them, and forced the bits home
between their jaws, and pulled the reins against the compacted

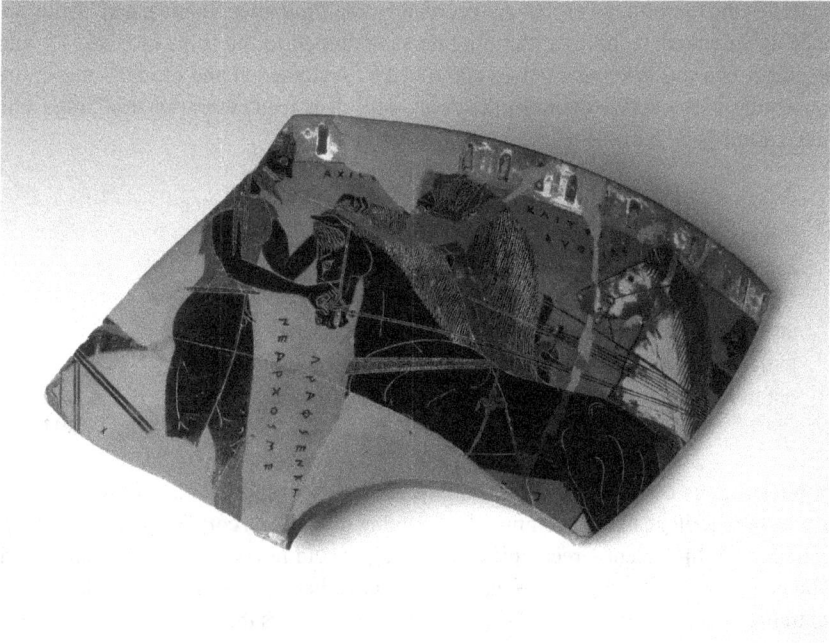

Figure 18.2 Achilles harnesses his horses. Fragment of a dedicatory black-figure kantharos signed by Nearchos as potter and painter, 560–550 BCE. National Archaeological Museum, Athens, Akropolis Collection 1.611 [NAM Akr. 1.611]; *ABV* 82.1; LIMC 1 69, s.v. Achilleus, no. 186. NEARCHOSMEGRAPHSEN KA[I EPOIESEN] Νεαρχος με|γραφσεν κα[ι εποιεσεν]. Found on the Athenian Acropolis. CAVI Collection: Athens, N.M. Acr. i, 611. CAVI Lemma: Fragmentary BF kantharos. From Athens. Nearchos. Nearchos, potter. Second quarter sixth. 560–50. CAVI Subject: A: harnessing of Achilles' chariot; woman holding his armor. B: divinities. CAVI Inscriptions: A: Χο[-. Αχιλ.[λ]ε[υς]. Νεαρχος με|γραφσεν κα[ι εποιεσεν]. Χαιτος. Ευθριας. Π[-. .Ι[-. -]ς. B: ηεφα[ι]στος, but the preliminary sketch shows ΑΙΣΤΟΣ. Χα[-. CAVI Number: 0976. "The rights on the depicted monument belong to the Hellenic Ministry of Culture and Sports (Law 3028/2002). The fragmentary Attic black-figure kantharos NAM Akr 1.611 are the responsibility of the National Archaeological Museum. Hellenic Ministry of Culture and Sports/ Archaeological Resources Fund."

chariot seat, and one, Automedon, took up the shining
whip caught close in his hand and vaulted up to the chariot. . . (RL)

—Iliad 19.392–6

The passage makes a point of the placement of the bits in the horses' mouths, which would have been followed then as now by a quick check of their position, a skilled task the archaic vase-painter Nearchos reassigns from Automedon to Achilles. *The scene restores Achilles to the role of groom and charioteer, and to the careful, tender maintenance of his own chariot team.* Deep relationship underlies this imagined moment. It could be argued that this depth of feeling between hero and horses also underlies the tumultuous exchange recorded by the *Iliad* after Xanthos and Balios are once again yoked. Achilles's immortal horses returned to the ships in Book 17 with an empty chariot. When the horses are yoked by Automedon and brought once more to the king in Book 19—their fourth yoking—his displaced bitterness, grief, rage, and dread erupt as he accuses them, screaming their names.

> . . . while behind him Achilleus helmed for battle took his stance
> shining in all his armour like the sun when he crosses above us,
> and cried in a terrible voice on the horses of his father:
> 'Xanthos, Balios, Bay and Dapple, famed sons of Podarge,
> take care to bring in another way your charioteer back
> to the company of the Danaans, when we give over fighting,
> not to leave him to lie fallen there, as you did to Patroklos.' (RL)
>
> —*Iliad* 19.397–403

Implicating his own horses in his tragedy, Achilles has fallen to a new low—not as low as the sacrilege he will commit, the dragging of Hector's corpse—but an absurdity nonetheless. In ancient Greek epic such outrage could never have gone unanswered. The charge he levies against them, that they have betrayed him and Patroklos both, so transgresses the bounds of fairness that Hera empowers the "gleam-footed" (*pódas aiólos*) Xanthos to answer with human speech.

> Then from **beneath the yoke** [ὑπὸ ζυγόφι] the gleam-footed horse answered
>   him,
> Xanthos, and as he spoke he bowed his head, so that all the mane
> fell away from the pad [ζεύγλης, **"yoke-cushion"**] and swept the ground
>   by the cross-yoke [παρὰ ζυγὸν];
> the goddess of the white arms, Hera, had put a voice in him:
> 'We shall still keep you safe for this time, o hard Achilleus.
> And yet the day of your death is near, but it is not we
> who are to blame, but a great god and powerful Destiny.
> For it was not because we were slow, because we were careless,
> that the Trojans have taken the armour from the shoulders of Patroklos,
> but it was that high god, the child of lovely-haired Leto,
> who killed him among the champions and gave the glory to Hektor.
> But for us, we two could run with the blast of the west wind
>   [Ζεφύροιο, **"of Zephyros"**]
> who they say is the lightest of all things; yet still for you
> there is destiny to be killed in force by a god and a mortal.'
> When he had spoken so the Furies [Ἐρινύες, **"the Erinyes"**]
>   stopped the voice in him . . .(RL)
>
> —*Iliad* 19.404–18

From "beneath the yoke" Xanthos answers, he whose feet are called "changeable, quick, glittering" (*aíolos*), resonant with the *Odyssey*'s lord of the winds Αἴολος. He defends himself and his brother who are speed incarnate: "we two could run with the blast of the west wind"—their own father—echoing what the poet sang of them in 16.149–50. No one could have prevailed against the raging god Apollo to save Patroklos. Xanthos then matches his master's cruelty, prophesying Achilles's doom, so close at hand. But as he does, like a lamenting widow already bereaved, he rakes the dust with his mane, just as he had done for Patroklos.

> but deeply disturbed, Achilleus of the swift feet answered him:
> "Xanthos, why do you prophesy my death? This is not for you.
> I myself well know it is destined for me to die here
> far from my beloved father and mother. But for all that
> I will not stop till the Trojans have had enough of my fighting."
> He spoke, and shouting held on in the foremost his single-footed horses. (RL)
> —*Iliad* 19.419–24

What disturbs Achilles? It is not, apparently, that his horse is suddenly talking to him, by intervention of Hera; the white-armed goddess made Xanthos "a speaking creature": αὐδήεντα δ' ἔθηκε θεὰ λευκώλενος Ἥρη· (19.407). In myth and epic, hagiography and wonder-tale, from Japan to Madagascar, human beings who are confronted with talking animals, even their own beasts who have never before uttered a word, rarely if ever puzzle over the odd fact that the animal is talking. It is *what* Xanthos is saying, and his presumption in saying it, that enrages Achilles.

Like the horses of Cú Chullain, only one of Achilles's horses can have a meaningful exchange with his mortal master; like most twins, they are distinguished from one another through different abilities. Xanthos is extraordinary for an ancient Greek horse, even one in myth. As Shapiro notes, "Growing wings is fairly mundane, for example (for a horse), compared with having the capacity for human speech, like Achilles' horses."[53] But of the twins, only one horse ever speaks in the *Iliad*: Xanthos, and only once. Balios remains, like his Irish counterpart Dub Saingland, mute, and in many ways, occulted. Sarah Iles Johnston eloquently argues that only Xanthos ever had the power of speech, since, in her view, Homer drew on an older tradition of "1) Hera's reputation as an owner of divine horses, and as one who bestowed those horses on favored warriors; and 2) an episode in which Areion, the son of Erinys, was inspired by Erinys or the Erinyes to prophesy to his master."[54] The former argument rests on a tradition possibly "lurking whereby Poseidon, not Zephyrus, was the father of Xanthus and Balius"; he bestows his horse-son Areion on Copreus in the scholiast; in fragments of Alcman and Stesichorus,[55] in which Poseidon, "having sired a horse named Xanthus and his brother Cyllarus (the mother is not named), gave them as a gift to Hera. She in turn gave Xanthus and Cyllarus to the Dioscuri, who, like Achilles, used their remarkable horses in battle. This Xanthus spoke to Castor, as Achilles' Xanthus did to him."[56] The latter argument posits that because the prophesying horse Areion, linked to Adrastus as early as the *Iliad* 23.346–7, according to the *Thebais* was sired on Erinys or Demeter Erinys by Poseidon, and because Areion carried his master after he had escaped the battle to Colonus, Argos, or Sicyon, "all of which were sites of important cults to the Erinyes . . . it is as if the horse returned to his home. Although chthonic entities could work to inspire anyone, we might imagine that those who had a special connection to them would be especially open to their manipulation. Areion—son of Erinys—would be a perfect candidate for inspiration by one or more Erinyes":[57] Ὣς ἄρα φωνήσαντος Ἐρινύες ἔσχεθον αὐδήν (19.418). Johnston even points to the earlier scene in 17.426–40, where the horses mourn in "unmistakably human ways," including the way that they "cry out" (κλαῖον), "which regularly is associated with spoken laments or cries for help (e.g., *Il.* 8.364 and 19.300, *Od.* 20.92)" rather than forms of κλάζω or μηκάομαι (e.g. *Il.* 10.276, *Od.* 14.30), which, as she points out, belong to animals like goats, oxen, and ordinary horses.[58] In other words, Homer signifies the elevated nature even of their cries, their weeping, by using verbs reserved for human beings.

> ἵπποι δ' Αἰακίδαο μάχης ἀπάνευθεν ἐόντες
> **κλαῖον** . . .

> But the horses of Aiakides standing apart from the battle
> **wept** . . .

> —*Iliad* 17.426–7

Nearchos's scene has another anomaly. Strangely, the two lead horses are not given their Homeric names, but are instead named Chaitos (Χαίτος) and Euthoias (Εὐθοίας). The presence of a third horse makes it more than likely that this is indeed the Iliadic scene but transposed into sixth-century Athens. Alan Shapiro comments, "The Painter Nearchos, however, when he depicted Achilles harnessing his horses on a kantharos about 560, knew other names for the horses . . . He does nevertheless show familiarity with the Homeric version, for he depicts the hero with three horses, the two immortal and one mortal, Pedasos."[59] Gregory Nagy suggests that Nearchos was drawing from a performative Iliadic tradition outside what we have inherited in the text.[60] Alternatively, others, such as Erika Simon, suggest that the horses' names, Chaitos and Euthoias, are borrowed by the painter from names of famous racehorses of his day. "It was in these years the chariot race probably became a major event at the Panathenaia."[61] Since the kantharos was a votive dedication on the Acropolis, this would imply that the dedicator chose either to commemorate a victory or to ask Athena for one by yoking his own pair of horses into Achilles's chariot—depicting them in the line of their owner's intense gaze, heads bent beneath his elegant, patrician grasp.[62] In doing so, like Regnault, he stepped through the image into the force field of Achilles.

The horses of the ancient Greek heroes have their old Irish counterparts in the Celtic hero Cú Chulainn's magical team Liath Macha ("Macha's Grey") and Dub Sainglend ("Black of Saingliu"), "two horses, swift, high-springing, big-eared, beautiful, bounding, with flaring nostrils, with broad chests, with lively heart, high-groined, wide-hoofed, slender-legged, mighty and violent."[63] In the Ulster Cycle they appear to him from the otherworld beneath the pool of Linn Liaith at Sliab Fúait, a gift from either Macha, a horse goddess, or her sister the Morrígan. Yet as with Xanthos and Balios, despite their intrinsic bond, the twin horses are not interchangeable: they are different colors, they are differently endowed with speech. The Celtic horses even have different responses to his violent last *agōn*, called *ríastrad* ("contortion"; "warp-spasm"), with the Gray of Macha fighting more extremely even than Xanthos does under the reins of Achilles's terrible *kholos*, when at the hero's death, the Gray's twin, the Black of Saingliu, flees to the pool whence he arose.

On the day of Cú Chulainn's death, "when Cú Chulainn's foes came for the last time against him," the hero tells his charioteer Láeg to harness the Gray of Macha to the chariot. On the night before, the Morrigu had broken the chariot, for she liked not Cú Chulainn's going to the battle, for she knew that he would not come again to Emain Macha.[64] The horse refuses. Says Láeg, struggling like Regnault's Automedon with a clairvoyant horse, "I swear by my people's god, even if Conchobor's province surrounded Liath Macha, they could not drag him to the chariot. He has not opposed you until today. The spirit that always delighted me has not appeared today. If you wish, go call the gray yourself. . . . Cú Chulainn went to him, and three times the horse turned his left side toward Cú Chulainn."

Then Cú Chulainn reproaches his horse for his inconstancy:

"'Never, Liath,
        You beauty
have you
        turned to me
your left side
        in savage anger
so I will not
        act against you
I will forgive
        death's due
my intent did not falter
        on a great plain
when I drove you about
        though reins were red
horses and hosts
        were kept off.
Smashing chariot-frames
        and yokes and pads
where we sat
        a pleasant seat
Badb struck us
        in Emain Macha
never.'"

"At that Liath Macha came to CuChulainn and let great round tears of blood fall on his feet.

CuChulainn leapt into the chariot and made a dash to the south along the Midluachair road."[65] Liath Macha relents only for Cú Chulainn himself, but like Xanthos, weeps tears of blood for his short life.

After the killing of Láeg ("the king of charioteers"), Liath Macha is pierced by Lugaid mac Con Roí's spear, intended for Cú Chullain: "CuChullain snatched the spear away, and each said farewell to the other. Liath Macha left with half the yoke about his neck." He is met by Conall Cernach, "all bloodied going to Linn Leith. Conall Cernach spoke:

> No yoke guides him
>   to Linn Leith
> he goes off
>   with wounds
> wrecked chariot
>   under left jaw
> with bloodstains
>   of man and horse.'"

Although the *Táin* gives the Gray of Macha a mortal, heroic death, the tradition could not leave him slain, but had to reassert his immortality through an act of ritual renewal in its source. "He went to Linn Leith, the Gray's Pool, in Sliab Fuait. Out of it he had come to CuChullain, and to it he went after he was wounded. At that CuChullain spoke [echoing a prophecy], 'Your horse will pull a single yoke here today.'"[66,67] With Dub Sainglend still yoked and harnessed, Cú Chulainn is finally pierced by the third magical king-killing spear of Lugaid. "[H]is bowels came out on the cushions of the chariot . . . his only [remaining] horse went away from him, the Black Sainglain, with half the harness hanging from his neck, and left his master, the king of the heroes of Ireland, to die upon the plain of Muirthemne."

But a dominant tradition has the Grey of Macha arising a second time from the magical pool in order to return to the stone Clochafarmore where Cú Chulainn had tied himself. The horse himself becomes a berserk, assuming the dreadful power of his master's *ríastrad*:

> Then Liath Macha returned to CuChulainn to guard him while his soul was in him and his warrior's light remained shining from his brow. Liath Macha made three bloody charges around him so that fifty fell by his teeth and thirty by each of his hoofs. That is the number of the host he killed. From that slaughter there is [the saying], no more fierce were Liath Macha's victorious onslaughts [than] when CuChullain was slain.

> Then a raven flew onto CuChullain's shoulder. "That pillar did not usually hold birds," said Erc mac Coirpri.

> Then Conall Cernach and Liath Macha went off and circled through the carnage. They saw CuChulainn by the pillar. Liath Macha went and put his head on CuChullain's breast. "Liath Macha cares about that corpse," Conall said.[68]

It is no accident that Liath Macha is Cú Chulainn's first mourner. The Gray's relationship to the hero as his spirit-animal and vehicle of war is even more significant than his tender, fraught relationship with his wife. Between the martial and the domestic spheres, as with Achilles, there can be no doubt which is the theater of greater existential import in the arc of Cú Chulainn. It is Liath Macha who is first widowed by his death.

Macha makes his way back to Eamhain Mhacha, where Cú Chulainn's widow Emer greets him in deep sorrow. The yoke that bound the slain hero's otherworldly chariot horse to him and to his twin the Black of Saingliu, who arose from the same pool, is literally shattered in battle, as are the bonds it represents. The destruction of the bond between husband and wife resonates with the destruction of the yoke joining the immortal horses of Cú Chulainn. The organizing image of the *caoineadh* (traditional Irish lament) of the widowed Emer is the dissolution of the chariot-team— the wreckage of the quaternity of warrior, charioteer, and dual horses. Bereaved, unhusbanded, Emer addresses her lament to her direct counterpart: the unmastered, untwinned Liath Macha.

> *Misery!*
> Liath Macha[,]
> he has not come
> with two matched horses
> before his chariot
> *great grief!*[69]

Socially dual figures in the epic, their power and stature defined by their binding allegiances, the solitary Emer and Liath Macha now stand in truncated parallel. There could be no greater emblem of grief, no greater sympathetic audience for her lament than Liath Macha. Ritual substitute and chief mourner for Cú Chulainn, mirror to his lost horse-brother, he ends his role in the Ulster Cycle as a lone immortal creature now stranded in human tragedy. Severed by the glory of heroic ordeal into unnatural solitude—half of a pair of twins, as much the hero's widow as his human widow— Liath Macha pays a terrible price for loving Cú Chulainn and fighting his battles, as does his twin Dub Sainglend, in his way, for his flight. So too Xanthos and Balios. In the end, heroes destroy all who love them. Their cults alone remain.

Central themes resonate between these two ancient cycles: the twin horses of origin, who are defined by their role as a chariot-team talismanic to the hero, with whom they have an uncanny bond; their interchangeability with the hero, his chariot, and one another; their counterpoint differentiation by color and degree of speech or relationality to the hero; their intimate knowledge of the fate of the hero; the stubborn reluctance of the more powerful and prominent horse of each pair, the one who stands up to the hero and refuses to carry him to his death (Xanthos and Liath Macha, respectively); their ruthless participation in the hero's episode of murderous battle mania; the traditions of heartbreaking equine grief when the hero falls. Finally, there is the divine twin animals' inclination to flee in response to the hero's death from the hyper-masculine, murderous realm of war to the womb-like sacred lake or the far-off fields of the maternal wind "in the meadow beside the swirl of the Ocean," the place of their origin. This longing resolves the oscillation between immortal and mortal realms for the twins Liath Macha and Dub Sainglend by delivering one from the strife forever while resurrecting the other to fight on, ultimately stranding him in the human world of grief and loneliness. For Xanthos and Balios, this shared longing, expressed in Quintus Smyrnaeus, appears as the only antidote to the hell of war that entangles them.

The Threshing-floor of Corpses

Fresh-fed by a broken heart, his *mēnis* unsaid but possessed by *kholos*, Achilles drives his team into battle despite Xanthos's warning.[70] His avenging onslaught depends on, but also fuses with, the might of his horses; he sweeps like θεσπιδαὲς πῦρ (*thespidaés pûr*, "god-kindled fire"), once again δαίμονι ἶσος (*daímoni ísos*, "equal to a daimon") so that "the black earth flows with blood." But there is a more chilling metaphor to follow:

as when a man **yokes together** male oxen with broad foreheads
(ὡς δ' ὅτε τις ζεύξῃ βόας ἄρσενας εὐρυμετώπους)
to crush white barley on a well-founded threshing floor,
and quickly the barley is stripped under the feet of the loud-bellowing oxen,
so under great-hearted Achilles the single-footed horses
were trampling corpses and shields alike, **and the axle beneath
was all splattered with blood,**
                    [αἵματι δ' ἄξων
νέρθεν ἅπας πεπάλακτο καὶ ἄντυγες αἵ περὶ δίφρον][71]

and the rims which went around the chariot,
were being struck with drops from the horses' hooves
and from the chariot wheels.

—*Iliad* 20.495–502[72]

Schein's insight into the tragedy of Xanthos and Balios is piercing: "In one other significant passage, at the end of Book 20, the horses of Achilles are associated with a kind of defilement and with the contradictions inherent in the human condition and especially in Achilles himself."[73]

The immortal horses, which should be living easily a life of unaging immortality, are instead imaged as labouring oxen. They also resemble Hektor's mortal horses at 11.531–7 bloodily carrying his chariot through the Greeks and Trojans, trampling corpses and shields (11.534–7 ~ 20.499–502), rather than the immortal horses of Poseidon, who skim his chariot lightly over the waves, and the bronze axle beneath the chariot is not even wet (13.29–30). Like the oxen to which they are compared, the horses of Achilles are associated with a particular kind of human toil. In a sense, at the end of Book 20 they become as savage as their master as he presses on 'to win the boast of triumph / . . . and his unconquerable hands were splattered with gore' (20.502–3).

"The immortal horses, which should be living easily a life of unaging immortality, are instead imaged as labouring oxen." It is the yoke that is, to invoke Ricœur's words, "the symbol that produces thought." It is the yoke of the war-chariot becomes the yoke of field oxen, trampling human barley on the threshing floor, pounding the blood from once-living, newly destroyed enemy bodies.

The Funeral Games of Patroklos: Twin Horses in Stasis

Book 23, which opens with the mourning of Troy for Hector, finds the horses of Achilles and all the horses of his men still in thrall to him and his raging grief. He "will not allow the Myrmidons to be scattered" (Μυρμιδόνας δ' οὐκ εἴα ἀποσκίδνασθαι Ἀχιλλεύς, *Iliad* 23.4) among the ships, but reminds them that they must remain active warriors, discharging death's duty:

> "Myrmidons, you of the fast horses (Μυρμιδόνες ταχύπωλοι), my steadfast companions,
> **We must not yet slip free of the chariots our single-footed horses,**
> **but with these very horses and chariots we must drive up close up**
> **to Patroklos** and mourn him, since such is the privilege (of the perished).
>
> Then, when we **have taken full satisfaction from the sorrowful**
> **dirge we shall set our horses free**, and all of us eat here." (RL)
>
> [αὐτὰρ ἐπεί κ' **ὀλοοῖο τεταρπώμεσθα γόοιο**
> "when we have taken our fill of the deadly lament"
> **ἵππους λυσάμενοι** δορπήσομεν ἐνθάδε πάντες.]
>
> —*Iliad* 23.6–11

All of the horses must be bound not only to one another and to their chariots in harness, but also to ceremonial grief itself: tethered to the mourning for Patroklos by their owners, his companions. Only after the need for sorrowing has been met "to full satisfaction," a common term for describing the course of ritual mourning in ancient Greek thought, can the horses be unyoked and unharnessed.

A jarring ritual crisis attends the monumental funeral sacrifice Achilles carefully curates for Patroklos.[74] After placing the corpse at the peak, piling the hundred-square-foot pyre with the bodies of skinned sheep and "shambling horn-curved cattle," placing "two-handled jars of oil and honey (23.170), driving "four horses with strong necks," and cutting the throats of two of the "nine dogs of the table that had belonged to the lord Patroklos" (173–4) and finally, horribly, killing the final victims to join Patroklos in death, "twelve noble sons of the great-hearted Trojans" (175), he finds that "the pyre of dead Patroklos would not light": Οὐδὲ πυρὴ Πατρόκλου ἐκαίετο τεθνηῶτος·(192).

There are catalytic powers missing and sore-needed, supernatural forces that must be summoned: the great winds Boreas and Zephyros, the North Wind and West Wind. According to Hesiod, along with Notos, the South Wind, they are the children of Eos (Dawn) and Astraios (Starry).[75] Although they are two brothers of triplets in *Odyssey* 5.295, in the *Iliad* they are only mentioned together as a pair, who "rise to shake the sea where the fish swarm," who "blow from Thraceward, suddenly descending, and the darkened water is gathered to crests, and far across the salt water scatters the seaweed; so the heart in the breast of each Achaian was troubled" (*Iliad* 9.4–8). In other words, in the *Iliad*, the named, deified winds are twins. They are also the father and uncle of Xanthos and Balios, the source and prototype of the horses' ability to run "like the winds." With theurgic focus, Achilles summons the father and uncle, twin ancestors of his immortal twin horses:

> He stood apart from the pyre and **made his prayer to the two winds**
> **Boreas and Zephyros,** north wind and west, and promised them splendid
> offerings [στὰς ἀπάνευθε πυρῆς **δοιοῖς ἦρᾶτ' ἀνέμοισι**
> **Βορέη καὶ Ζεφύρῳ,** καὶ ὑπίσχετο ἱερὰ καλά·] and much outpouring from a
>   golden goblet entreated them
> to come, so that the bodies might with best speed burn into the fire
> and the timber burst into flame.
>
> —*Iliad* 23.194–8

Having up until this moment hoarded the corpse of his beloved friend and *therápōn*, refusing his release by fire—the subject of Regnault's "Thetis Brings the Arms Forged by Vulcan to Achilles"—Achilles can only fulfill his vow to the desperate *psūkhē* of Patroklos with unearthly help. His plea must be conveyed to the feasting wind-gods by Iris, who is on her way to a sacrificial feast with the Aithiopians. Hearing this, the wind-ancestors of the horses "with immortal clamour rose up, and swept the clouds in confusion before them" (23.212–13).

> They came with a sudden blast upon the sea, and the waves rose
> under the whistling wind. **They came** to the generous Troad
> and **hit** the pyre, **and a huge inhuman blaze rose, roaring**. (RL)
>
> αἶψα δὲ πόντον ἵκανον ἀήμεναι, ὦρτο δὲ κῦμα
> πνοιῇ ὕπο λιγυρῇ· Τροίην δ' ἐρίβωλον **ἱκέσθην.**
> ἐν δὲ πυρῇ **πεσέτην,** μέγα δ' ἴαχε θεσπιδαὲς πῦρ.
>
> —*Iliad* 23.214–16

But if we attend to the twinship of the Zephyros and Boreas, whereas Homer uses the third-person plural form of ἱκάνω ("to come"), as the brother winds approach the Troad, the dual number emerges in 23.214–15:

> "They [both] reached [**ἱκέσθην,** aor. ind. mid. 3rd dual of **ἱκνέομαι**]
>   the fertile Troad.

[Together] they cast themselves down [πεσέτην, aor. ind. act. 3ʳᵈ dual of πίπτω] into the pyre, and **a great god-kindled fire roared**."

Were Xanthos and Balios among these still-harnessed horses of the Myrmidons, driven to the bier of Patroklos? The poem does not tell us, although we later learn that the pair is entirely set apart from the mortal horses in their mourning for Achilles's beloved. As on the battlefield of Troy where he fell and they saw him die, they stand once more frozen, weeping, self-defiling in their grief like human mourners, only this time near the roaring pyre fueled by their divine father and his brother. Achilles mentions their special relationship to their fallen charioteer, announcing that neither he nor his horses will participate in the funeral games—chariot-races—that he institutes for Patroklos. Strangely, it is the first time, so close to the end of the poem, that he himself speaks of their origin in his father's house, and how he came to own them:

> Now if we Achaians were contending for the sake of some other
> hero, I myself should take the first prize away to my shelter.
> You know how much my horses surpass in their **speed**
>   [ἀρετῇ = aretē: "virtue, excellence"]) all others:
> yes, for they **are immortal [horses]** [ἀθάνατοί τε γάρ εἰσι],
>   and Poseidon gave them
> to Peleus my father, who in turn gave them into my hands.
> But I stay here at the side, and my single-footed horses stay with me;
> such is the high glory of the charioteer they have lost,
> the gentle one, who so many times anointed their manes with
> soft olive oil, after he had washed them in shining water.
> **Therefore these two [horses] stand here and grieve**
> [τὼ δ' ἕστατον ἀχνυμένω κῆρ], and their manes
> are swept along the ground as they stand with hearts full of sorrow.
> But take, the rest of you, places in field, whichever Achaian
> has confidence in his horses and his compacted chariot.
>
> —*Iliad* 23. 274–86 (RL)

In a typically Achillean address, at the same time magnanimous and aggrieved, superior and wounded, victorious and victimized, the owner of Xanthos and Balios makes it known to the Achaeans that any victory in the games he has established is already illegitimate, won by default and are due to the tragedy of the circumstance. He reminds them that his horses are immortal, a talisman of Poseidon's favor to his family and an extension of his own superiority. But he is also compelled to acknowledge their complicated grief, and publicly to lament it himself. Their beautiful manes, for which Patroklos cared so lovingly, washing and oiling them (23.280–2), again sweep the dirt of the ground. Xanthos and Balios have relapsed in their grief; this resurrects their stance as funeral monument in Book 17. They are paralyzed at the funeral bier of Patroklos, perhaps also remembering Achilles's stinging blame at 19.403 for abandoning their gentle *hēniokhos* to his doom.

Lattimore has once again tried to soften the insistent poetic repetition of *two*-ness in 23.283–4, Achilles's description of the grieving Xanthos and Balios. A translation that allows the dual number its full poetic force would read:

τὸν **τώ** γ᾽ἑσταότες **πενθείετον**, οὖδεῖ δέ σφι
χαῖται ἐρηρέδαται, **τὼ δ᾽ ἔστατον ἀχνυμένω κῆρ**.

"The two (**τώ**), standing here, both mourn him (**πενθείετον**, dual form of
    πενθέω), their manes dragged through the earth;
the two of them stand (**ἔστατον**, dual of **ἵστημι**), their [**one, shared**] heart
    (nom. singular of **κῆρ**) grieving in both of them (**ἀχνυμένω**, dual present
    participle of **ἄχνυμαι**)."

Though there is no plural for the epic Greek κῆρ (heart), the juxtaposition of the singular term with the plural horses makes it clear that they share one bitter affect.

Even the chariot race in honor of Patroklos will be a controlled *agốn*, replicating in many ways the dynamics of the battlefield. The heroes' horses are featured actors, named and elevated, their histories alluded to, and their yoking figuring prominently: "After him [Eumolpos] rose the son of Atreus, fair-haired Menelaos, the sky-descended, and led beneath the yoke the swift horses (ὑπὸ δὲ ζυγὸν ἤγαγεν ὠκέας ἵππους), Aithe, Agamemnon's mare, and his own Podargos" (23.293–5). As on the battlefield, the gods interfere with this contest, but particularly with horsemanship. When Apollo, angry with Diomedes, strikes "the shining whip from his hands" as his stallion, "the Trojan horses" close in on Eumelos, and "seemed forever on the point of climbing his chariot, and the wind (πνοιή: here, the horses' 'breath, panting') of them was hot on the back and on the broad shoulders of Eumelos," Athena sweeps down to restore Diomedes's whip and "inspired strength [battle-rage] into his horses (μένος δ᾽ ἵπποισιν ἐνῆκεν)" (23.390). Then she delivers the most powerful coup de grâce one can deliver to a chariot-team, short of outright killing them:

and she, a goddess, **smashed ("broke, shivered") his chariot yoke**
    [ἵππειον δέ οἱ ἦξε θεὰ ζυγόν], and his horses
ran on either side of the way, the pole dragged, and Eumelos
himself was sent spinning out beside the wheel of the chariot.

—*Iliad* 23.392–4

By smashing the *zugón*, Athena sunders the link between the chariot's two running horses, thus destabilizing the assemblage of horses-chariot-charioteer. Its rocketing momentum forward is ruined.

To an almost unbearable degree, *Iliad* 24.265–81 repeats and amplifies the theme of the yoke, of the activity of yoking and unyoking of draft animals to one another—and to the appropriate wheeled vehicle for their task. Destroyed by the loss of Hector, Priam prepares to go in person to ransom the body of his son. Cursing his other sons as "wicked children, my disgraces . . . the liars and the dancers, champions of the chorus, the plunderers of their own people" (24.253), his instructions to his terrified sons to "get my wagon ready and be quick about it" are followed by a passage dominated by the yoke:

> They took away from its peg the mule **yoke** made of boxwood
> with its massive knob, well fitted with guiding rings, and brought forth the
> the **yoke** lashing (together with the **yoke** itself) of nine cubits.
>
> —*Iliad* 24.268–70
>
> Then they carried out and piled into the smooth-polished mule wagon
> all the unnumbered spoils to be given for the head of Hektor,
> then **yoked** the powerful-footed mules who pulled in the harness
> and whom the Mysians have once as glorious presents for Priam;
> but for Priam they led under the **yoke** those horses the old man
> himself had kept, and cared for them at his polished manger.
> Now in the high house the **yoking** (ζευγνύσθην) was done for the herald
> and Priam, men both with close counsels in their minds. And now came
> Hekabe with sorrowful heart and stood close beside them.
>
> —*Iliad* 24.281–3

The ζῦγός emerges as an embodiment of the constraint of grief upon autonomy, freedom, power, and pleasure: it signifies the heavy cost of being king, father, statesman, warrior, horseman, and, most of all, of losing one's favorite child, one's best beloved.

The Afterlife of Xanthos and Balios:
Quintus Smyrnaeus, *Posthomerica*

Just as Diodorus, "following the account preserved in the myths," gives Xanthos and Balios a prequel as Titans, so Quintus Smyrnaeus in his third-century CE *Posthomerica* gives them an afterlife. Zephyros and Boreas will again be dispatched, this time by the wind-god Aeolus to hasten the burning of the body of the dead Achilles, just as Achilles summoned them to burn the body of Patroklos.

> Aeolus obediently lost no time in summoning bitter Boreas and the gusting blast of Zephyrus and sending them off to Troy in the form of a swift whirlwind. They swiftly took storm-force flight over the sea; land and sea together roared as they hurtled onward, and all the clouds rushing through the air's vast expanse massed beneath them. In accordance with the will of Zeus, they soon **swooped together** on the pyre of the dead warrior Achilles.
>
> [δαϊκταμένου Ἀχιλῆος αἶψα πυρῇ ἐνόρουσαν ἀολλέες **"together, in warlike throngs"**]
>
> —*Posthomerica* 3.699–710

Once again, Xanthos and Balios will be catatonic in their grief. But now their grief causes them to yearn to flee the work of war altogether—to return home—to their mother's world, to the place of their birth, "in the meadow beside the swirl of the Ocean."

> The **immortal horses** of fearless Aeacides were by the ships.
> They were not **unaffected** by his death:
> they too wept for their king's death in battle.

> [Οὐδὲ μὲν **ἄμβροτοι ἵπποι** ἀταρβέος Αἰακίδαο
> μίμνον **ἀδάκρυτοι**, "lacking tears" παρὰ νήεσιν, ἀλλὰ καὶ αὐτοὶ
> μύροντο σφετέροιο δαϊκταμένου βασιλῆος·]

> In the extremity of their grief they wished not to mix any longer with wretched men or with the horses of the Argives, but to remove far away from miserable mankind beyond the streams of Ocean and the caves of Tethys to the place where divine Podarge once gave them birth, storm-footed steeds, after mating with sounding Zephyrus. And they would have carried out their intention if the will of the gods had not restrained them so that when Achilles' spirited son came from Scyros to the army they could be there for him, in accordance with the threads of fate spun for them at their birth by the Moirae, daughters of Chaos: immortal though they were, since their birth they had been destined to be broken in by Poseidon, then to have as their masters bold Peleus and unwearied Achilles, and then fourthly greathearted Neoptolemus, whom they would bear at Zeus' command to the Elysian plain in the Land of the Blessed. And so even though they were afflicted with hateful sorrow they remained by the ships, their hearts **grieving for one master and longing to see another [τὸν μὲν ἀκηχέμενοι, τὸν δ' αὖ ποθέοντες ἰδέσθαι]**.
>
> —*Posthomerica* 3.743–65

Neoptolemos's relationship with Xanthos and Balios is one of solar restoration and recovery of their purpose: "mounted behind his father's immortal horses" (ἵπποισιν ἑοῦ πατρὸς ἀθανάτοισιν), he advances on the Trojan army like Sirius, and they "bore him along, eager to drive the enemy away from the ships; they had been brought to him by Automedon, who was their driver. The horses in turn were glad to be carrying a master so like Aeacides: they felt in their immortal hearts that he was no less a man than Achilles" (8.33–8). Like his father, he is given the opportunity to recite their genealogy, this time to Eurypylus before they fight to the death: "The horses that carry me are my godlike father's (ἵπποι δ' οἳ φορέουσιν ἐμοῦ πατρὸς ἀντιθέοιο), offspring of Harpyia and sired by Zephyrus: they can gallop over the barren sea barely touching it with their hooves, borne along quick as the wind" (8.154–7). And as they bore the murderous Achilles like threshing oxen, so, flying again (ἐπέτοντο) through bodies, they expedite the rampage of Neoptolemos (9.215–24):

> With instant obedience he used his whip to direct the power of those immortal horses toward the fray, and they flew swiftly through the carnage bearing their

mighty master [οἳ δ' ἐπέτοντο ῥίμφα διὰ κταμένων κρατερὸν φορέοντες ἄνακτα]. Just as Ares enters murderous battle mounted on his chariot, the earth trembling as he passes, the divine armor ringing out on the god's breast: just so the mighty son of Achilles advanced against noble Deïphobus, and clouds of dust rose from his horses' feet.

Xanthos and Balios can never die. Yet their destinies, spun for them at birth by the Fates, who Quintus reminds us are the "daughters of Chaos," they are indentured by the will of Zeus to the male members of the Phthian royal lineage who can and do die in the epic tradition:

> since their birth they had been destined to be broken in by Poseidon, then to have as their masters bold Peleus and unwearied Achilles, and then fourthly greathearted Neoptolemus, whom they would bear at Zeus' command to the Elysian plain in the Land of the Blessed.

> τέτρατον αὖτ' ἐπὶ τοῖσι Νεοπτολέμῳ μεγαθύμῳ,
> τὸν καὶ ἐς Ἠλύσιον πεδίον μετόπισθεν ἔμελλον
> Ζηνὸς ὑπ' ἐννεσίῃσι φέρειν μακάρων ἐπὶ γαῖαν.

> —*Posthomerica* 3.757–62

In Quintus's vision, perhaps based on older traditions, the twin horses' final interaction with mortals will be eschatological: Zeus will command them to carry the son of Achilles, Neoptolemos, to the Elysian Fields. Xanthos and Balios will assume their ultimate and perhaps inevitable role as shamanic spirit-animals, crossing the boundaries between the realms of the living and the dead to safely deliver the last Myrmidon—and perhaps the most volatile—to his final, appropriately heroic home, one of a number of possible Homeric afterlives.

The Divine Horses of Achilles: Yoked in Sorrow

A third portrait of the immortal twin horses of Achilles depicts another moment that appears nowhere in the *Iliad* nor anywhere in the Epic Cycle, but seems instantly credible: Giorgio di Chirico's portrait of them as they walk alone on the beach at Troy [Pl. 15; Figure 18.3]. One of the original artists of *pittura metafisica*, di Chirico (1888–1978), of Greek heritage but culturally Italian, influenced surrealism with his enigmatic, visionary work. Trained in the impressionist style, he was transformed by his encounter with Nietzsche and Schopenhauer during his studies at the Academy of Fine Arts in Munich. By 1919 he was openly criticizing modern art, advocating a return to classicism. A neo-Baroque style came to dominate his work, and many of his portraits, while referencing sculpture, have at the same time an eerily animate quality. For close to two decades later in his life, he painted a series of horses, sometimes solitary, sometimes in pairs, and very often by the sea. A few pairs he called "The Divine Horses of Apollo," but these, while spirited, do not begin to approach the dreamlike, searing portrait he finished on Christmas Day in 1963—"The divine horses of Achilles, Xanthos and Balios."

In richly saturated shades, the sea heaves in the restless, polychromatic blues of the Mediterranean. There are the ἵπποι ἀθάνατοί, walking by the same shores of the Hellespont where Regnault imagined them. But DeChirico renders our twins elegiacally. There is no Automedon, no Patroklos or Achilles, no Neoptolemos. There are no humans to feed or harness them, no one to oil their manes. There are no gods to pity them. There are no Achaean ships. There is no Trojan War. There is no Troy: the artist shows it in ruins, with a column drum projecting, almost floating, in the surf offshore. One, on the beach, lies directly in the horses' path. Most of all, there is no yoke; there is no chariot. They were once yoked to one another by the kinetic structure of the war-chariot. They are finally free forever from mortal ownership; at the same time, they are invisibly yoked in their grief, yearning. Lost in their memories, the heroes they loved long since perished, they nuzzle one another, as two bonded horses do, in reassurance and greeting. Dominant as always is Xanthos, whose entire luminous body DeChirico shows in motion, one leg raised mid-step, eyes half-lidded in sorrow. Eclipsed, at his side as always, is Balios, pausing to brace his brother, eyes wide. Their necks and heads arch symmetrically. They are heraldic in their two-in-oneness.

Figure 18.3 Giorgio di Chirico, "The divine horses of Achilles, Xanthos and Balios," 1963. Oil on canvas, 96.5 x 87 cm. Art Gallery of New South Wales 178.2006. Photo: AGNSW. © Giorgio de Chirico/SIAE. Licensed by Copyright Agency.

The artist has painted two cloaks by their hooves as they walk sadly in the sand—Achilles, Patroklos. Red and blue, distinguished from one another, as are the horses themselves, golden and bay. Di Chirico wants to show a time beyond the *Iliad* or even the *Iliupersis* when the wooden yoke has long fallen from their necks. Sorrowing still, Xanthos and Balios stay bound to one another, walking the shore where they lost their mortals, able to comfort only one another. Their yoke is invisible but no less powerful than one made of wood. It is made of their shared trauma when all that can perish around them has done so, leaving them in the vast loneliness of immortality. As twin brothers, their only lasting yoke remains to one another. Each serves as a repository of the other's memory.

On Sunday, July 26, 2020, the body of civil rights giant Congressman John Lewis crossed the Edmund Pettus Bridge in Selma, Alabama, one final time. The route was strewn with red rose petals to signify the blood shed during his first peaceful march there on behalf of voting rights on March 7, 1965, when he was nearly beaten to death by state troopers. A caisson driven by a driver dressed in morning-coat and top hat bore the casket, pulled by two dark chestnut horses joined by a wooden yoke. The historian and journalist Crystal deGregory wrote, "With a top hat held high to his breast, the tradition connected him—and through him, all of us—to free and enslaved black hack drivers of yesteryears long ago."[76] In silence, the driver stopped his horses in the middle of the bridge, and again at a place where Lewis family members waited to accompany the caisson on foot for the last part of the journey. "'Stand there. Stand there, boy,' directed the driver to his laboring horses once on the foot of the bridge on the other side."[77] Stopped and standing in the rising heat of summer morning, the two horses turned and nuzzled one other.

Conclusion

Automedon's yoking of the divine horses of Achilles, twin sons of the West Wind, at Patroklos's own order (ἵππους δ' Αὐτομέδοντα θοῶς ζευγνῦμεν ἄνωγε) in Book 16 ignites the long Iliadic arc of the *agṓn*, death, and funeral of his beloved "other," twin, and ritual substitute (*therápōn*). As dual, yet differentiated, actors in the story, Xanthos and Balios both accelerate and interpret the events that span Books 16–23 of the *Iliad*. They are emotionally complex, with a profound attachment to particular heroes, and a supernatural relationship to Zeus, the future, and to Fate. Yet they also remain glorious slaves, their living bodies fiercely contested as spoils by fighting heroes, as though their loyalties could easily be transferred to an enemy owner. Sons of the West Wind and a Harpy, of the lineage of the sky, especially its savage gusts, they fly like birds; they are battle-taxis, murderous oxen, mourners, and prophets. But when entangled in the death of a beloved, they freeze like a grave monument, bound to the earth and unable to move at all. And when accused, they passionately and memorably defend themselves. Although other heroic horses figure in the epic, only Xanthos and Balios are full characters in the Iliadic theater, with an active, shared role as significant as that of gods on both sides of the war, demigods, and heroes. But they also play a passive, inert role as contested as the armor of Achilles, or, arguably, as that of stolen enemy consorts, widows, and corpses. That is their paradox, and why they are so much more than possessions.

The twin horses of Achilles are physically joined to one another before each battle by the ζυγόν (*zugón*), creating a chariot pair—a cultural image so iconic as to be re-created in the symmetrical arrangement of beloved, sacrificed horses in Bronze Age tholos tombs and the shaft graves of warriors. In 16.152–4 they are tethered to the mortal trace horse Pedasos, their "third." He is killed by Sarpedon and dragged down, entangling his immortal companions in the gear of the chariot as he dies in agony. The twins are separated and their yoke is threatened, creaking (κρίκε δὲ ζυγόν). The guide reins tethering perishable to imperishable creatures must be swiftly and brutally severed by their charioteer.

Xanthos and Balios are just as powerfully bound to Patroklos, *therápōn* of their moody master, who excelled at "the management and the strength of immortal horses" (*Iliad* 16.476) when Automedon compares Alkimedon to Patroklos and asks him to take over "the whip and the glittering guide reins" (16.479) while he descends from the chariot to do battle. They are all the more entangled in his death when, struck by Apollo in the back and Hector in the front, he falls in the dust; and at that spot, the fighting raging around them, they stand immobile, paralyzed in grief until Zeus, deeply sympathizing with their plight, re-animates them and sends them back to the ships. The immortal horses are Achilles's possessions; they are horse-twin slaves whose omnipotence is culturally constrained when they are gifted by gods to heroes, or inherited by their explosive sons and grandsons; yet they can run like birds, as fast as the wind itself, and are not in thrall to death itself. They are divine animals, with consciousness and agency, yet are compelled to serve warriors whose purpose is to die a glorious death and win *áphthiton kléos*. They have a ghastly knowledge of the future reserved for oracles and prophets, while remaining powerless to change it. They are yoked to the humans they love, to whom they have socially defined affinities, and whose violent, sudden deaths consume them in grief. In Cavafy's version of *Iliad* 17.442–7, Zeus, full of regret for the gods' role, sees their pain. But Xanthos and Balios, τὰ δυὸ τὰ ζῶα τὰ εὐγενῆ —"the two, the animals ("living ones"), the nobly-born"—can only "pour out" (ἐχύνανε) their tears: a modern Greek form of a verb of great antiquity, meaning "to offer liquid sacrifice", "to offer liquid sacrifice."

" . . . Σεῖς ποὺ οὐδὲ ὁ θάνατος φυλάγει, οὐδὲ τὸ γῆρας
πρόσκαιρες συμφορὲς σᾶς τυραννοῦν. Στὰ βάσανά των
σᾶς ἔμπλεξαν οἱ ἄνθρωποι." – Ὅμως τὰ δάκρυά των
γιὰ τοῦ θανάτου τὴν παντοτεινὴ
τὴν συμφορὰν ἐχύνανε τὰ δυὸ τὰ ζῶα τὰ εὐγενῆ.

—from *Τα άλογα του Αχιλλέως*, "The Horses of Achilles,"
Constantine P. Cavafy

" '. . . You—whom neither death nor old age constrain—
Fleeting calamities torture you.
Men entangle you in their trials.'
Nevertheless, because of the unending disaster of death,

the two animals, nobly-born,
poured out their tears."[78]

None of the imagined experiences in these three images of the immortal horses of Achilles, nor in any of the ancient sources where they appear, can be interpreted apart from the affective category of twinship. The twin horses are a chariot-team, inexorably defined by their yoke. In later tradition, when one king is gone and his son not yet arrived, they yearn only to escape their situation in Troy and return to the meadow of their motherland.

De Chirico's painting implies that they never could. Trapped in the theater of a war that is over yet never ends, only their mirrored sorrow and single broken heart remain.

Notes

1 With deep respect and affection, this chapter is dedicated to Gregory Nagy, Francis Jones Professor of Classical Greek Literature and Professor of Comparative Literature at Harvard University, a brilliant scholar and teacher. Throughout his lifetime, he has joyfully opened the way to so many who imagined that the world of classical antiquity was closed to them. My debt to him is endless. The errors are all mine.

2 Xanthos (ξανθός) is the color gold or yellow, of various shades, often with a tinge of red or brown; it is also the epithet of Achilles himself in *Iliad* 1.197 and 23.141. "Xanthos" is also the gods' special name for the River Scamander (20.74). Balios (Βαλίος) seems to mean "piebald"; "spotted, dappled: two-colors, typically black and white." In the view of Karin Hornig, the horses' contrasting colors (light, luminous; and dark, occulted) express a solar/lunar binary chromotype in animal pairs, particularly horses and camels, of cultural importance in both Western and Eastern antiquity: "Die Farben der Pferde: Ein Beitrag zur Dualitätssymbolik in Ost und West," in *Der Weise geht leise: im Gedenken an den Begründer der Freiburger Sinologie Professor Dr. Peter Greiner,* ed. Harro von Senger and Haiyan Hu-von Hinüber, Freiburger fernöstliche Forschungen, Bd. 10 (Wiesbaden: Harrassowitz Verlag, 2016), 229–74.

3 Sourced in Henri Cazalès, *Henri Regnault: sa vie et son oeuvre* (Paris, 1872), cited in the Boston MFA catalogue description. The title of his rough study for the painting, now in the Musée d'Orsay, "Automédon ramenant les coursiers d'Achille des bords du Scamandre," makes clear that the body of water is the river rather than the Hellespont.

4 Podarge is given sisters by Hesiod: Aëllo and Ocypetes, who with their swift wings (ὠκείης πτερύγεσσι) follow, keep pace with (ἅμ' ἕπονται) both the wind-blasts of the winds (ἀνέμων πνοιῇσι) and the birds, specifically the vultures whose relatives they are (καὶ οἰωνοῖς). Hesiod, *Theogony*, 266–9.

5 Sarah Iles Johnston, "Xanthus, Hera and the Erinyes (Iliad 19.400–18)," *Transactions of the American Philological Association* 122 (1992): 86–7.

6 Homer, *The Iliad of Homer*, trans. Richmond Lattimore (Chicago: The University of Chicago Press, 1951, 2011). Alternate translation for 16.149 and emphasis of particular terms in Greek and English in bold font by the author. Throughout, "RL" refers to Lattimore's text, which for some verses is followed by the Greek, followed by author's suggested translation, indicated by (KP) in the first instance, emphasizing the original themes of duality, yoking, etc. that Lattimore at times downplays through more generic word choice.

7   Tegan Quin, interviewed by Jenn Pelly and Liz Pelly, "Nine Albums Later, Tegan and Sara Are Finally Ready to Discuss High School," *New York Times*, September 24, 2019, https://www.nytimes.com/2019/09/24/arts/music/tegan-and-sara-high-school.html, accessed December 7, 2020.

8   Pseudo-Apollodorus, *Bibliotheca* 3. 170; Ptolemy Hephaestion, *New History* Book 6 (in Photius, *Myriobiblon* 190).

9   Diodorus Siculus, 6.3.1 [Eustathius Il. 19.400].

10 Quintus Smyrnaeus, *Posthomerica* 3.760–1, ed. and trans. Neil Hopkinson, Loeb Classical Library 19 (Cambridge, Mass and London: Harvard University Press, 2018).

11 The two horses of the Dioskouroi, named Kyllaros and Xanthos in Alcman (Frag. 25), share the same windy parents as Xanthos and Balios; by the time of Stesichorus (Frag. 178), they are joined by Phlogeus and Harpagos in a quadriga.

12 "The horses of Achilles, offspring of the Harpy Podarge and the West Wind, Zephyros (16.150), are described as 'immortal' at 16.154, 17.444, and 23.277 (cf. 10.402–4). Their immortality distinguishes them from other horses in the poem with divine connections: those of Eumelos, 'swift-footed like birds, /. . ./ which Apollo of the silver bow bred and reared . . ." (2.764–6), and those given by Zeus to Tros in recompense for his son Ganymede, 'the best / horses there are, East or West' (5.266–7). There is no indication in the text that the remarkable horses of Rhesos, 'whiter than snow and running like the winds' (10.437), have anything to do with the gods." Seth Schein, "The Horses of Achilles in Book 17 of the Iliad," in *Homeric Epic and its Reception* (New York: Oxford University Press, 2015), 16, n. 12. Although other divine horses exist in Greek myth, only Xanthos and Balios are such in the *Iliad* and the Epic Cycle. A thousand years later in Quintus Smyrnaeus they are called ἄμβροτοι ἵπποι.

13 In the Old Norse *Heithreksgátur* (*Heithrek's Riddles*), no. 36, trans. Lee Hollander, Óðinn disguised as the thane Gestumblindi taunts King Heithrek.

> Gestumblindi said:
> "Who are the twain
> that on ten feet run?
> three eyes they have,
> but only one tail.
> Alright guess now
> this riddle, Heithrek!"
> Heithrek said:
> "Good is thy riddle, Gestumblindi,
> and guessed it is:
> that is Odin riding on Sleipnir."

14 In *The Best of the Achaeans*, Gregory Nagy comments, "The verb *théō* 'run, speed', as we see it applied to the speeding *Íphiklos* (θέεν: Hesiod fr. 62.1 MW), also applies to speeding ships (*Iliad* I 483, *Odyssey* ii 429, etc.) and to speeding horses (*Iliad* X 437, XIX 415, XX 227, 229) . . . In the case of horses, we may be more specific: their speed is by convention compared directly to the speed of wind, by way of the verb *théō*. At X 437, the horses of Rhesos are 'like the winds in speed [θείειν].' At XIX 415, Xanthos, the wondrous horse of Achilles, says that they, the hero's horse team, could run [θέοιμεν] as fast as the gust of Zephyros the West Wind, described as the fastest of all. *Despite their speed, however,* Achilles is fated to die 'by *ís* [ἶφι], at the hands of a god and a man" (*Iliad* XIX 417). Finally, at

XX 227, the wondrous horses fathered by Boreas the North Wind are described as so swift that their feet barely touch the tips of the grain stalks as they race [θέον] across fields of grain. Also, at XX 229, their feet barely touch the tips of the waves as they race [θέεσκον] across the surface of the sea." Gregory Nagy, *The Best of the Achaeans*, 2nd ed. (The Johns Hopkins University Press, 1999): 50.

15 Wilhelm Radloff, *Aus Siberien. Lose Blätter aus einem Tagebuche eines reisenden Linguisten* (Leipzig: T. O. Weigel, 1884), vol. 2, 18, and description on 20 ff.; reproduced and discussed in Marianne Görman, "Influences from the Huns," in *The Problem of Ritual: Based on Papers Read at the Symposium on Religious Rites Held at Åbo, Finland, on the 13ᵗʰ–16ᵗʰ of August 1991*, ed. Tore Ahlbäck. Scripta Instituti Donneriani Aboensis XV(Åbo, Finland: The Donner Institute for Research in Religious and Cultural History, 1993), 292–3.

16 "Hymn to the Horse," *Rig Veda* 1:162, in *Rig Veda*, trans. and ed. Wendy Doniger O'Flaherty (New York: Penguin Classics, 2005).

17 In 1970, the anthropologist James Littlejohn cogently rejected the metaphorical explanation by Evans-Pritchard and elaborated by Lévi-Strauss of the Nuer identification of twins with birds: "The Nuer state that twins and birds and birds twins, *not that one is like the other if they wanted to create that meaning*" (91). James Littlejohn, "Twins, Birds, Etc", in *Bijdragen tot de Taal-, Land- en Volkenkunde* Deel 126, 1ste Afl., ANTHROPOLOGICA XII (1970): 91–114. Remarking that the Nuer classify individuals in two major ways, by unilineal descent groups and communities, "The same two principles confer identity on twins, and by the first they are descended from Spirit or a spirit . . . This is no more a figure of speech than any other Nuer statement classifying creatures, *for twins have a component in their identity which they do not owe to their mother's husband.*" (93) [emphasis mine].

18 In his revelatory study *Hippota Nestor*, Douglas Frame has shown the centrality of horses and horsemanship to twinship in the solar mythology of the twin-brothers the Aśvins, horse children of the sun, and the linked Greek Dioskouroi, hidden but recoverable in the figure of Nestor. He writes in his Introduction, "The name Nestor contains the verbal root of *nóstos*, namely **nes-* . . . Vedic has a cognate of the Greek name *Néstōr* which goes to the heart of the Indo-European twin myth, and this cognate is relevant to Nestor as an epic figure. The cognate is the name *Nā́satyā*, which belongs to the twin gods of the Vedic pantheon.. . . . .Nestor's epithet *hippóta*, 'the horseman,' is part of the comparison . . . The Vedic twins are also called 'horsemen'; this is the meaning of their second and more common name, *Aśvínā*. There is thus a double comparison between the *Aśvínā Nā́satyā* in Vedic and *hippóta Néstōr* in Greek. To interpret this double comparison, and to reconstruct Nestor's myth, the Greek Dioskouroi are also taken into account. The basic myth of this paradigmatic pair of Indo-European twins completes the picture for both Vedic and Greek." Douglas Frame, *Hippota Nestor*. Hellenic Studies 37 (Washington, DC: Center for Hellenic Studies, Trustees of Harvard University; Cambridge, MA: Distributed by Harvard University Press, 2009). http://nrs.harvard.edu/urn-3:hul.ebook:CHS_Frame.Hippota_Nestor.2009 *Hippota Nestor*.

19 Translated here by Apostolos Athanassakis, *The Homeric Hymns*, 3rd ed. (Baltimore: Johns Hopkins, 2020).

20 "She mingled in love with Kronion, loud of dark clouds,
Under the peak of Taygetos, that lofty mountain,
and bore these children as saviors of men on this earth

and of swift-sailing ships, whenever wintry storms
sweep along the pitiless sea. Then men go
to the edge of the stern and with offers of white lambs
they pray and call upon the sons of great Zeus.
When great winds and the waves of the sea
bring the ship under water, they suddenly appear,
having sped through the air with rushing wings,
and forthwith they calm the cruel windy storms
and level the waves of the foaming high seas.
For the sailors' labor these are fair signs, and when they see them
they rejoice and quit their toilsome struggle.
Hail, Tyndaridai, riders of swift horses!"

Hesiod, *Homeric Hymn* 33: "To the Dioskouroi," in *The Homeric Hymns*, 3rd ed., trans. Athanassakis.

21 Commenting on the differentiation between medical pairs of brothers, such as Saints Cosmas's and Damian's differing advice on performing surgery (see James Skedros's chapter in this volume), Douglas Frame comments, "In Greek Machaon is a surgeon, Podalirius an internist and psychiatrist (he diagnosed Ajax's madness from the crazed look in his eyes)" (Correspondence, 2017). Machaon is slain by Eurypylus in Quintus Smyrnaeus 6.408, and buried in Gerenia in Messenia, where he received cultic honors; a marble torso from the 2ⁿᵈ c. BCE is identified as belonging to both of them. Of Podaleirios, Strabo (6.3.9) writes, "In Daunia, on a hill by the name of Drium, are to be seen two hero-temples: one, to Calchas, on the very summit, where those who consult the oracle sacrifice to his shade a black ram and sleep in the hide, and the other, to Podaleirios, down near the base of the hill, this temple being about one hundred stadia distant from the sea; and from it flows a stream which is a cure-all for diseases of animals." Both brothers share in Asklepios's cult as their father evolves from "blameless physician" to compassionate god. Podaleirios's name is attested on a votive potsherd from the Asklepieion at Corinth. Machaon becomes the Old World Swallowtail (*Papilio machaon*) and Podaleirios, the Scarce Swallowtail Butterfly (*Iphiclides podalirius*).

22 Strabo (8.360 and 9.437) says that the Asklepieion at the city of Trikka, known to Homer (*Iliad* 2.729) as the home of the hero Asklepios and one of the cities held by Machaon and Podalirius, was reputed to be the oldest in Greece; in 1903 Kastriotis excavated a building in the city center that he took to be the Asklepieion, but which turned out to be from the Roman Imperial period. See P. Kastriotis, τὸ ἐν Τρίκκῃ Ἀσκληπιεῖον (1903). There is, however, reason to speculate that a later Hellenistic building found in the same area may have incorporated the older sanctuary, as Theocharis observed in 1958, because decrees were found there, which were usually kept in the main sanctuary of the city. The church of the Anargyroi is close by, set on the city's small acropolis (D. Theocharis, *Praktika* [1958]: 64–80).

23 Schein, "The Horses of Achilles," 197.

24 Margaret Alexiou, *The Ritual Lament in Greek Tradition* (Cambridge: Cambridge University Press, 1979).

25 Plato *Phaedrus* 246a.

26 Plato *Phaedrus* 246c.

27 As Nagy elucidates, the constant, kaleidoscopic substitution of a charioteer for a warrior in this arc from *Iliad* 16–23 begins with the fatal, ritually significant

self-substitution of Patroklos for Achilles as apobatic warrior and Automedon for Patroklos as charioteer; after Alkimedon in turn becomes the charioteer for the now-fighting Automedon. Gregory Nagy, "The Failed Apobatic Adventure of Pandaros the Archer: A Bifocal Commentary on *Iliad* 5.166–469," *Classical Inquiries: Studies on the Ancient World from the Center for Hellenic Studies*, May 20, 2015, https://classical-inquiries.chs.harvard.edu/the-failed-apobatic-adventure-of-pandaros-the -archer-a-bifocal-commentary-on-iliad-5-166-469/.

28 Ibid. In referring to *Iliad* 5.192, Nagy observes, "Occasionally, as here, Homeric diction refers to a chariot by way of combining the nouns *hippoi* 'horses' and *harmata* 'chariot.' More often, however, *hippoi* 'horses' can refer not only to the horses but also to the chariot pulled by the horses. Examples in the passage we are reading can be seen at verses 227, 249, 255.. . . [So at 5: 227] "ἐγὼ δ᾽ ἵππων ἀποβήσομαι ὄφρα μάχωμαι 'I [= Aeneas] will leap off from the chariot [literally, the horses] in order to fight [on foot]'."

29 This phrase appears later once in the gruesome episode at *Iliad* 10.465–514 in which Odysseus and Diomedes slaughter the sleeping Thracians and their king, Rhesos, in order to steal his magnificent horses. Odysseus takes care to drag each corpse out of the stolen horses' path as he was killed, "that the bright-maned horses might pass easily through and not be shaken within them at stepping on dead men" (*Iliad* 10.488–92). Understatedly, the poet tells the listener, "These horses were not yet used to them."

30 Nagy cites G. S. Kirk, ed., *The Iliad: A Commentary. Vol. 2, Books 5–8* (Cambridge: Cambridge University Press, 1990). "About the responsiveness of horses to a chariot driver who knows them well, I refer to Kirk 1990:84, commenting on *Iliad* 17.475–6, who notes what Automedon says about Patroklos: that the horses of Achilles especially heeded Patroklos as their chariot driver."

31 See the summary of excavations near Kazakhstan in David S. Anthony, *The Horse, The Wheel and Language: How Bronze Age Riders from the Eurasian Steppes Shaped the Modern World* (Princeton, N.J.: Princeton University Press, 2007), 397–405; the very recent identification of these grave vehicles as carts by Aleksandr Semenenko (2020) has failed to convince most. Three similar Bronze Age graves with chariots were discovered in 2018 in Sinauli, Uttar Pradesh. See the report of T. S. Subramanian in "Royal burial in Sanauli," *Frontline*, September 28, 2018.

32 Constantine P. Cavafy, Τα άλογα του Αχιλλέως, "The Horses of Achilles." Translation from modern Greek by the author, with inspiration in the work of Peter J. King and Andrea Christofidou, *Cavafy Bilingual Anthology, from Poems 1896–1904*, https://www.ellopos.net/elpenor/greek-texts/modern/cavafy_achilles.asp.

33 "Hydria with the Fight of Achilles and Memnon," Walters Art Gallery 48.2230, Baltimore, *c*. 575–550 BCE (Archaic Late Corinthian). Inscriptions in the Corinthian alphabet identify the figures.

34 In post-Homeric Greek, ἡνία can mean bridle or reins; but it clearly means reins in Plato's *Phaedrus* εἰς τοὐπίσω ἑλκύσαι τὰς ἡνίας (254). The struggle of Xanthos and Balios against what joins them anticipates the famous black and white horses in Plato's *Phaedrus* whose charioteer cannot control them as they fight one another for control of the soul ascending to heaven.

35 "Earlier, the contrast between the horses' immortality and their forced connection with mortality had been expressed in their being yoked together with the trace horse Pedasos, 'who although he was mortal kept up with the immortal horses' (ὃς καὶ θνητὸς ἐὼν ἔπεθ᾽ ἵπποις ἀθανάτοισι, 16.154). When Sarpedon accidentally kills

Pedasos with an errant spear-cast intended for Patroklos, and the horse 'fell in the dust, bellowing' and 'lay dead in the dust', the reins of the two immortal horses become entangled as they rear in opposite directions (16.467–71). Their helpless confusion in the face of Pedasos' tangible mortality is relieved only by Automedon's quick action in cutting away the dead trace horse, so that they can again move coordinatedly (τὼ δ' αὖτις συνίτην, 16.476). This incident is especially striking because normally 'in duels in the *Iliad* it is . . . the eventual victor who misses with his first spear-cast', but here Patroklos, not Sarpedon, will conquer." Schein, "The Horses of Achilles," 194.

36 Mary Moore, "The Death of Pedasos," *American Journal of Archaeology* 86, no. 4 (1982): 580.

37 On the sacrificial death of Patroklos, see Steven Lowenstam, *The Death of Patroklos: A Study in Typology*, Beiträge zur klassischen Philologie, Heft 133 (Königstein/Ts.: Hain, 1981).

38 "(Hector): 'Then what greater prize than these will you ask me for?' Dolon: 'Akhilleus' horses. The prize must be worth the toil when one stakes one's life on Fortune's dice.' Hector: 'Ah! but your desires clash with mine about those horses; for they are immortal and born from immortals, who bear the son of Peleus on his headlong course. Poseidon, lord of the ocean [salt sea], broke them and gave them to Peleus, so runs the legend.'" Attributed to Euripides, *Rhesus*, 181–8, trans. Phillip Vellacott (London and New York: Penguin Classics, rev. ed. [1954; 1973]).

39 See the memorable discussion of this paralysis and its relationship to the stele and the tomb, meaningful markers of death, in Michiel C. van Veldhuizen, "Divining Disaster. Signs of Catastrophe in Ancient Greek Culture," PhD Dissertation (Providence: Brown University, 2018), 299–300: "One parallel passage later in the *Iliad* sheds further light on the connection between immobilizing and death. At the death of Patroclus, the immortal horses he had borrowed from Achilles are so distraught that they are completely motionless. The opening formula is nearly identical to Poseidon's stunning of Alcathoos: 'But just as a *stele* remains steadfast (ἀλλ' ὥς τε στήλη μένει ἔμπεδον), one that is placed over a tomb mound (τύμβῳ) of a dead man or woman, so they remained motionless (ὣς μένον ἀσφαλέως) holding the well-built chariot' (*Il.* 17.434–6). While the point of the comparison is the fact that both *stele* and horses stay in place (μένει, μένον), the funerary connotation (the *stele* as grave marker and the context of Patroclus' death) is equally significant. As the horses stand motionless, they neither want to retreat 'to the wide Hellespont' (ἐπὶ πλατὺν Ἑλλήσποντον) nor go back into battle. This effect is similar to the stunned Alcathoos, who is said to be unable to retreat or evade. The inclusion of the formulaic line ending ἐπὶ πλατὺν Ἑλλήσποντον (ἐπὶ πλατεῖ Ἑλλησπόντῳ) is significant: the formula occurs twice more in Homer to refer to the tomb that will contain the bones of Achilles, which will in fact be mixed with those of Patroclus (*Il.* 7.86, *Od.* 24.82; cf. *Il.* 23.125–6). The immobilization of the horses and their unwillingness to return to the Hellespont, then, foreshadows the death of their master, Achilles."

40 Schein, "The Horses of Achilles," 17–18.

41 "There is indeed a close semantic connection between binding and taming, since bonds are an important means of taming or subduing (δαμνάω, δαμάζω, δάμνημι), including of wild animals such as the horse, an animal that has a special connection to Poseidon. In his treatise on horsemanship, Xenophon describes a method of breaking in horses through a figure-of-eight maneuver known as πέδη, 'fetter' or, in equestrian terms, 'ring' (X. Eq. 3.5, 7.13). Poseidon is typically said to 'tame'

ships through storms and gales, as the formulaic line ending Ποσειδάων ἐδάμασσεν testifies (e.g. Od. 11.399, 24.109). In a passage from the Iliad, Poseidon tames not a ship but a warrior, and he does so by magically rooting him to the spot, or binding him. The Greek hero Idomeneus battles with Alcathoos when Poseidon comes to Idomeneus' aid (Il. 13.434–8):

> But now, at the hands of Idomeneus, Poseidon subdued him (ἐδάμασσε),
> and, having bewitched (θέλξας) his flashing eyes, he bound (πέδησε) his shining limbs
> so that he could neither retreat nor evade,
> but like a stele (ἀλλ᾽ ὥς τε στήλην) or a tree with towering leaves
> he stood there, motionless (ἀτρέμας ἑσταότα)."

Van Veldhuizen, *Divining Disaster*, 299.

42 Schein, "The Horses of Achilles," 17–18. Prior to this, Schein writes, "It is no accident that in 17.437–8, δάκρυα is modified by θερμά ('hot'), which is a frequent epithet of tears when, for metrical reasons, a plural form of δάκρυα is desirable rather than a singular (7.426, 16.3, 18.17, 235). At the same time, the phrase 'hot tears' intensifies the pathos of a death (18.17, 235) or a funeral (7.426) for the one who is weeping, or, in the case of Patroklos in 16.3, the pathos of the defeat of the Greek army considered as a kind of collective death." (17).

43 Gilgamesh XI. iii, trans. Stephanie Dalley, *Myths from Mesopotamia: Creation, The Flood, Gilgamesh, and Others* (Oxford: Oxford University Press, 1991), 113.

44 "Thetis apporte à *Achille* les armes forgées par Vulcain" ("Thetis Brings the Arms Forged by Vulcan to Achilles"), École nationale supérieure des beaux-arts, Paris.

45 https://collections.mfa.org/objects/31014, accessed September 29, 2020.

46 This tone was anticipated by the *Encyclopedia Britannica* in 1911, which called it "a lively recollection of a carnival horse-race." *Encyclopedia Brittanica* (1911) s.v. "Regnault, Henri," vol. 23, 46.

47 See Marc Gotlieb's *The Deaths of Henri Regnault* (Chicago: University of Chicago Press, 2016), and the review by Margaret MacNamidhe review by Margaret MacNamidhe in *Nineteenth-Century Art Worldwide* 16, no. 2 (2017). https://doi.org/10.29411/ncaw.2017.16.2.7.

48 "Catalogue of Horse Sacrifices" no. 1, in Elizabeth Kosmetatou, "Horse Sacrifices in Greece and Cyprus," *Journal of Prehistoric Religion* 7: 31–41 (Jonsered: Paul Åstroms Förlag, 1993); Evangelia Protonotariou-Deilaki, "The Tumuli of Mycenae and Dendra," in *Celebrations of Divinity and Death in the Bronze Age Argolid*, ed. Robin Hägg and Gullög C. Nordquist, Proceedings of the Sixth International Symposium at The Swedish Institute at Athens, Series 1, 40 (Stockholm: Svenska institutet i Athen; Göteborg, Sweden: Paul Åströms Förlag, 1990), 85–102, Figs. 11–12; S. Payne in idem., "Appendix: Field Report on the Dendra Horses," 103–6.

49 Kosmetatou, "Catalogue of Horse Sacrifices," no. 2; Protonotariou-Deilaki, "The Tumuli of Mycenae and Dendra," Figs. 13–15.

50 Ibid., Catalogue of Horses Sacrifices nos. 13–23. In the case of no.14, two asses lie apart from one another in a secondary burial in a chamber tomb in Salamis; "it seems that the second animal tried to free itself at the sight of the first animal being put to death."

51 Hatoula (PPNA): Old woman and bos bucranium burial, as discussed by Anna Belfer-Cohen and Nigel Goring-Morris. See Monique Lechevallier, Avraham Ronen, and Patricia C. Anderson, *Le Gisement de Hatoula en Judée Occidentale, Israel* (Paris: Association Paléorient, 1994).

52 Boston Museum of Fine Arts 63.1611. This horse-vase would be for "the simpler archaic Athenians who wished to be buried with a horsehead amphora." Emily Vermeule, *Aspects of Death in Early Greek Art and 10 Poetry* (Berkeley: University of California Press, 1979), 60, fig. 15. In this touching vase, the horses are shown facing one another, their eyes wide and foreheads touching, a sight taken from real life. Vermeule argues that the idea seems to be about the horse mourning the owner: "the focus seems to remain on the burial, and not on providing transportation to the hereafter. If epic tradition intended that human captives, dogs, and horses should accompany the dead man on his road, it does not care to exhibit this funeral throng; the sacrificed alien and the soul-less animal have slipped away" (61).

53 Harvey Alan Shapiro, *Art and Cult Under the Tyrants in Athens* (Mainz am Rhein: Phillip von Zabern, 1989), 110.

54 Sarah Iles Johnston, "Xanthus, Hera and the Erinyes (Iliad 19.400–18)," 98. Drawing from Statius's *Thebaid*, in which Areion prophesied in order to warn Adrastus as he drove away from Eteocles and Polyneices's fateful duel (*Thebaid* 11.442–23), Johnston argues *pace* Dodds, Nilsson and others who maintain that the Erinyes are needed to "disrupt the natural order" whereby horses do not speak. She notes that "they [the Erinyes] did not stop Xanthus' voice until he had finished his statement to Achilles. The fact that Xanthus' statement was complete and uninterrupted is confirmed by the phrase Ὡς ἄρα φωνήσαντος, which always follows a finished statement in Homer, never an interrupted one" (91). She continues with a key comparative argument: "speaking warriors' horses are not actually contrary to the 'natural' order of the mythic or epic world . . . We know that horses spoke not only to Achilles but to Castor and Adrastus as well, and also that Jason was spoken to by a wooden figurehead—the closest thing to a warrior's steed that this hero had" (ibid.). Hence "the Erinyes did not intervene to stop Xanthus from warning Achilles, but rather inspired the horse's prophecy, stopping it only when it was completed . . . the Erinyes, like many chthonic deities, had general prophetic functions" (97).

55 Stesichorus fr. 178 Campbell; Alcman fr. 25 Campbell; Alcman fr. 76 Campbell = Aelian, HA 12.3. "Aelian presumed that Alcman was copying Homer in making a horse talk to its master." Johnston, "Xanthus, Hera and the Erinyes," 86, n. 3. Nikolas Yalouris posits that because "Hera was sometimes Poseidon's partner in cults associated with horses . . . Hera was the mother of such wonder horses in earlier, lost traditions" (Nikolas Yalouris, "Athena als Herrin der Pferde," *Museum Helveticum* 7 [1950], 79–88). Cited and discussed in Johnston, "Xanthus, Hera and the Erinyes," 86, n. 4.

56 Johnston, "Xanthus, Hera and the Erinyes," 86.

57 Ibid., 97.

58 Ibid., 88.

59 Shapiro, *Art and Cult under the Tyrants in Athens*, 110.

60 Gregory Nagy argues that "the Iliadic tradition as performed at the Panathenaia in preclassical times was in many ways different from what we have in 'our' version." *The Ancient Greek Hero in 24 Hours* (Cambridge, MA: Harvard University Press, 2013).

61 See Erika Simon, photographs by Max and Albert Hirmer, *Die griechischen Vasen* 2 (Hirmer Verlag: Munich, 1981), cat. nos. 64, 80. "Nearchos hat wohl Namen berühmter Rennpferde seiner Zeit auf die mythischen Rosse übertragen." More

in Shapiro, *Art and Cult under the Tyrants in Athens*, 110, n. 89; for Simon on the Panathenaic chariot-race in the sixth century, see her chapter 2, esp. 40.

62 The round, widened eyes of the horses and Achilles are a convention of black-figure vase painting, yet lend to this particular scene a kind of tension and urgency for what is to come, not unlike the Regnault painting.

63 Description of Liath Macha and Dub Sainglend in the *Táin Bó Cúailnge* ("The Cattle-Raid of Cooley"), an epic cycle of Irish stories recorded in the eighth century. CE. Cecile O'Rahilly, ed. and trans., *Táin Bó Cúalnge from the Book of Leinster* (Dublin, 1967; repr. 1970, 1984: Dublin Institute for Advanced Studies), 218. "In one shaft of the chariot was a grey horse, broad-thighed, small stepping, long-maned. In the other shaft a black horse, flowing maned, swift-coursing, broad-backed. Like a hawk to its prey (?) on a day of harsh wind, or like a gust of the stormy spring wind on a March day across a plain, or like a furious stag newly roused by hounds in the first chase—so were the two horses of Cú Chulainn in the chariot, as if they were on a bright, fiery flagstone, so that they shook the earth and made it tremble with the speed of their course." My gratitude to William Bradford Guild for his assistance with the horses of Cú Chulainn.

64 The fort Eamhain Mhacha in Northern Ireland, whose name may mean "Macha's twins" or "Macha's pair."

65 *Táin Bó Cúailnge*, "The Death of CuChulainn," in *Two Death Tales from the Ulster Cycle*, trans. Maria Tymoczko (Dublin: Dolmen Press; Atlantic Highlands, NJ: Humanities Press, 1981), 42–3.

66 Ibid., 58.

67 Anon, *Chulain, The Hound of Ulster: The Chronicle of the Life of Chulain* (Abela Publishing, 2018). "This witnessing, the Black Steed [Dub Sainglend] neighed in mournful wise, and went back to the glen in Donegal, and no man dared to seek or follow him, nor ever found they trace of him again."

68 *Táin Bó Cúailnge*, "The Death of CuChulainn," 61. The raven is likely the Morrígan herself.

69 *Táin Bó Cúailnge*, "The Death of CuChulainn," 77.

70 On the three kinds of heroic anger and their significance in the *Iliad*, see Gregory Nagy, "A Sampling of Comments on the *Iliad* and *Odyssey*," https://chs.harvard.edu/curated-article/gregory-nagy-a-sampling-of-comments-on-the-iliad-and-odyssey/. These are established as early as the speech of Kalkhas the seer (1.74–83); whereas *mēnis* (citing the work of Muellner) is "a kind of divine sanction," *kholos* "is a kind of explosive anger that is generally instantaneous," and *kotos* is "an anger that is timed to go off only in the fullness of time."

71 Παλάσσω is an epic verb meaning "besprinkle, defile," as in Athena's dire prediction to Odysseus that the suitors who eat up his substance will "besplatter the earth with blood and brains" αἵματί τ' ἐγκεφάλῳ τε παλαξέμεν . . οὖδας in *Odyssey* 13.395; in the middle voice, it can mean "shake, i.e., draw lots from an urn," so κλήρῳ νῦν πεπάλαχθε διαμπερές "determine fate by lot," *Iliad* 7.171.

72 Here I use Seth Schein's translation.

73 Schein, "The Divine Horses of Achilles," 25.

74 A ritual crisis might belong to the same spectrum as a ritual failure; the former is less serious, but nevertheless requires a kind of hyper-focus to set the right processes in motion, or to jump-start them if they have stalled. See the thought-provoking essays in *Ritual Failure: Archeological Perspectives*, ed. Vasiliki G. Koutrafouri and Jeff

Sanders (Leiden: Sidestone Press, 2013). *The advent of divine twins to the scene would represent the reduplication of supernatural power necessary for such an intervention*: the summoning of the brother-winds to light a pyre. In a resonant case, in the *Aitareya Brāhmaṇa, Kaushitaki Brāhmaṇa*, and *Pravargya Brāhmaṇa*, the Aśvins are summoned by the gods to heal a sacrifice that has been mutilated when the ants behead the vainglorious Makha. Without a head, the sacrifice of Makha, even with three pressings, brings no blessings to the gods. The gods summon the Aśvins, who replace the head of the sacrifice with the *Pravargya* pot, compensating from that point on for the decapitation. See my discussion in Chapter 1 of this volume, 5–6.

> (The gods) said to the Aśvins:
> 'You are doctors; put back the head of the sacrifice.'
> —*Taittirīya Āraṇyaka* 5:1

75 Hesiod, *Theogony*, 378–9.
76 Crystal A. deGregory, "Congressman John Lewis Remembered in Selma, Alabama with Carriage Ride Across Edmund Pettus Bridge," *The Atlanta Voice*, July 26, 2020. https://www.theatlantavoice.com/articles/congressman-john-lewis-remembered-in-selma-alabama-with-carriage-ride-across-edmund-pettus-bridge/, accessed August 9, 2020.
77 Ibid.
78 Constantine P. Cavafy, *Τα άλογα του Αχιλλέως*, "The Horses of Achilles." Translation from modern Greek by the author, with inspiration from the work of King and Christofidou, *Cavafy Bilingual Anthology, from Poems 1896–1904*.

Bibliography

Alexiou, Margaret. *The Ritual Lament in Greek Tradition*. Cambridge: Cambridge University Press, 1979.
Anthony, David S. *The Horse, The Wheel and Language: How Bronze Age Riders from the Eurasian Steppes Shaped the Modern World*. Princeton, N.J.: Princeton University Press, 2007.
Athanassakis, Apostolos N., trans. *The Homeric Hymns*, 3rd ed. Baltimore: Johns Hopkins, 2020.
Dalley, Stephanie, trans. *Myths from Mesopotamia: Creation, The Flood, Gilgamesh, and Others. The World's Classics*. Oxford and New York: Oxford University Press, 1991.
deGregory, Crystal A. "Congressman John Lewis Remembered in Selma, Alabama with Carriage Ride Across Edmund Pettus Bridge." *The Atlanta Voice*, July 26, 2020. https://www.theatlantavoice.com/articles/congressman-john-lewis-remembered-in-selma-alabama-with-carriage-ride-across-edmund-pettus-bridge/. Accessed August 9, 2020.
Fontenrose, Joseph. "Daulis at Delphi." *California Studies in Classical Antiquity* 2 (1969): 107–44. Accessed August 8, 2020. doi:10.2307/25010584.
Frame, Douglas. *Hippota Nestor*. Hellenic Studies 37. Washington, DC: Center for Hellenic Studies, Trustees of Harvard University; Cambridge, Mass.: Distributed by Harvard University Press, 2009. http://nrs.harvard.edu/urn-3:hul.ebook:CHS_Frame.Hippota_Nestor.2009.
Gotlieb, Marc. *The Deaths of Henri Regnault*. Chicago: University of Chicago Press, 2016.
Görman, Marianne. "Influences from the Huns." In *The Problem of Ritual: Based on Papers Read at the Symposium on Religious Rites Held at Åbo, Finland, on the*

13th–16th of August 1991, Scripta Instituti Donneriani Aboensis XV, edited by Tore Ahlbäck, 292–3. Åbo, Finland: The Donner Institute for Research in Religious and Cultural History, 1993.

Hankoff, Leon D. "Why the Healing Gods are Twins." In *The Yale Journal of Biology and Medicine* 50 (1977): 307–19.

Hesiod. *Theogony*. Translated and edited by Glenn W. Most. The Loeb Classical Library, no. 57. Cambridge, Mass.: Harvard University Press, 2019.

Homer. *The Iliad of Homer*. Translated by Richmond Lattimore. Chicago: The University of Chicago Press, 1951, 2011.

Homer. *The Odyssey of Homer*. Translated by Richmond Lattimore. New York: Harper & Row, 1967, 2007.

Hornig, Karin. "Die Farben der Pferde: Ein Beitrag zur Dualitätsymbolik in Ost und West." In *Der Weise geht leise: im Gedenken an den Begründer der Freiburger Sinologie Professor Dr. Peter Greiner*, edited by Harro von Senger and Haiyan Hu-von Hinüber, 229–74. Freiburger fernöstliche Forschungen, Bd. 10. Wiesbaden: Harrassowitz Verlag, 2016.

Iles Johnston, Sarah. "Xanthus, Hera and the Erinyes (Iliad 19.400–18)." *Transactions of the American Philological Association* 122 (1992): 85–98.

King, Peter J., and Andrea Christofidou. *Cavafy Bilingual Anthology, from Poems 1896–1904*. https://www.ellopos.net/elpenor/greek-texts/modern/cavafy_achilles.asp.

Kosmetatou, Elizabeth. "Horse Sacrifices in Greece and Cyprus." *Journal of Prehistoric Religion* 7 (1993): 31–41. Jonsered: Paul Åstroms Förlag.

Koutrafouri, Vasiliki G., and Jeff Sanders. *Ritual Failure: Archeological Perspectives*. Leiden: Sidestone Press, 2013.

Lechevallier, Monique, Avraham Ronen, and Patricia C. Anderson. *Le Gisement de Hatoula en Judée Occidentale, Israel*. Paris: Association Paléorient,1994.

Lévi-Strauss, Claude. "The Structural Study of Myth." In *Myth: A Symposium*, edited by Thomas A. Sebeok, 81–106. Bloomington: Indiana University Press,1972.

Littlejohn, James, "Twins, Birds, Etc." *Bijdragen tot de Taal-, Land- en Volkenkunde Deel 126*, 1ste Afl., ANTHROPOLOGICA XII (1970): 91–114.

Lowenstam, Steven. *The Death of Patroklos: A Study in Typology*. Beiträge zur klassischen Philologie, Heft 133. Königstein/Ts: Hain, 1981.

MacNamidhe, Margaret. "Review of *The Deaths of Henri Regnault* by Marc Gotlieb." *Nineteenth-Century Art Worldwide* 16, no. 2 (2017). https://doi.org/10.29411/ncaw .2017.16.2.7.

Moore, Mary B. "The Death of Pedasos." *American Journal of Archaeology* 86, no. 4 (1982): 578–81, Figs. 1–4.

Nagy, Gregory. *The Best of the Achaeans; Concepts of the Hero in Ancient Greek Tradition*, 2nd ed. Baltimore: The Johns Hopkins University Press, 1999.

Nagy, Gregory. *The Epic Hero*, 2nd ed. Washington, DC: Center for Hellenic Studies, 2006 http://nrs.harvard.edu/urn-3:hlnc.essay. The 1st ed. (printed version) of "The Epic Hero" appeared in 2005, in *A Companion to Ancient Epic*, edited by J. M. Foley (Oxford), 71–89.

Nagy, Gregory. *The Ancient Greek Hero in 24 Hours*. Cambridge, Mass.: Harvard University Press, 2013.

Nagy, Gregory. "The Failed Apobatic Adventure of Pandaros the Archer: A Bifocal Commentary on *Iliad* 5.166–469." *Classical Inquiries: Studies on the Ancient World from the Center for Hellenic Studies*, May 20, 2015. https://classical-inquiries .chs.harvard.edu/the-failed-apobatic-adventure-of-pandaros-the-archer-a-bifocal -commentary-on-iliad-5-166-469/.

Nagy, Gregory. *A Sampling of Comments on the Iliad and Odyssey*. Washington, DC: Center for Hellenic Studies, 2017. https://chs.harvard.edu/curated-article/gregory-nagy-a-sampling-of-comments-on-the-iliad-and-odyssey/.

Payne, S. "Appendix: Field Report on the Dendra Horses." In *Celebrations of Divinity and Death in the Bronze Age Argolid*, edited by Robin Hägg and Gullög C. Nordquist, 103–6. Proceedings of the Sixth International Symposium at The Swedish Institute at Athens. Series 1, v. 40, 85–102. Stockholm: Svenska institutet i Athen. Göteborg, Sweden: Paul Åströms Förlag, 1990.

Platte, Ryan. *Equine Poetics*. Hellenic Studies, 74. Washington, DC: Center for Hellenic Studies, 2017.

Protonotariou-Deilaki, Evangelia. "The Tumuli of Mycenae and Dendra." In *Celebrations of Divinity and Death in the Bronze Age Argolid*, edited by Robin Hägg and Gullög C. Nordquist. Proceedings of the Sixth International Symposium at The Swedish Institute at Athens. Series 1, v. 40, 85–102. Stockholm: Svenska institutet i Athen. Göteborg, Sweden: Paul Åströms Förlag, 1990.

Quintus Smyrnaeus. *Posthomerica*. Edited and translated by Neil Hopkinson. Loeb Classical Library, no. 19. Cambridge, Mass. and London: Harvard University Press, 2018.

Rig Veda. Translated and edited by Wendy Doniger O'Flaherty. New York: Penguin Classics, 2005.

Schein, Seth. "The Horses of Achilles in Book 17 of the Iliad." In *Homeric Epic and its Reception*. New York: Oxford University Press, 2015; Oxford Scholarship Online, 2016, DOI:10.1093/acprof:oso/9780199589418.003.0003.

Shapiro, Harvey Alan. *Art and Cult under the Tyrants in Athens*. Mainz am Rhein: Phillip von Zabern, 1989.

Simon, Erika. *Ausnahmen von Max und Albert Hirmer*. Die griechischen Vasen 2. München: Hirmer Verlag, 1981.

Van Veldhuizen, Michiel C. "Divining Disaster. Signs of Catastrophe in Ancient Greek Culture." PhD Dissertation. Providence: Brown University, 2018.

Vermeule, Emily. *Aspects of Death in Early Greek Art and Poetry*. Berkeley: University of California Press, 1979.

Walker, Henry John. *The Twin Horse Gods: The Dioskouroi in Mythologies of the Ancient World*. London: I.B. Tauris, Ltd, 2015.

Part Seven

Epilogue

19

Epilogue

Dialogue

Ⅱ

Joseph O. Garrity and Philip S. Garrity

Figure 19.1 Joseph and Philip Garrity, 1989. By permission of the Garrity Family.

JG: Four faces gaze at me, side by side across two photographs, Polaroids snapped in a heat wave the year after we were born [Figure 19.1]. We are crouched in the backyard lawn at dusk, wearing only our diapers, hair slicked from the sprinkler spitting at the end of a hose. From our eyes, our four fiery blue eyes, beams the steady bewilderment of wild animals being observed, interrupted by onlookers. We appear remarkably similar, remarkably at ease, remarkably natural with one another. Studying the photos, I move between the faces, resting in each gaze, waiting for a spark of recognition to arise, for the veil of anonymity to lift. I experience the same phenomenon I always have in these early photos: I sense your quizzical expression, some essence beyond appearance call up to me. Then I move to the face beside yours, the one that by default is mine, realizing, in this case, that I can only find myself by process of elimination. Then I realize that in every case, in every sense, I am because you are. There was no me before you, no you before me. There was only our one at the same time, who was *YaYa.*

Until we were five, we didn't use our given names. I called you "YaYa," and you called me the same. We were YaYa. "YaYa" meant "you and me and we, all at once."

No one else referred to us this way, nor would we have responded—the name was ours alone, emerging from a proto-language that preceded, and almost certainly blocked, our uptake of English. Linguists call it "cryptophasia." It was like the Yorùbá *Àṣẹ*, the "sacred unconscious energy with which spoken words arise . . . [and which] twins themselves embody."[1]

Mom wrote her observations in our baby album, its puffy yellow cover emblazoned with *HERE I AM*:

> When they were babies and Philip would cry for a toy Joseph had, Joseph would give the toy to Philip while making a squeaking sound (somewhere between a cat's meow and a mouse noise). Eventually the sound became soothing for Philip to hear. Later when Philip would cry for Joseph's toy, Joseph only needed to make "the sound" to stop Philip's crying. Joseph would not need to give up the toy. I saw this strategy in action today when Philip wanted to keep the fishing rope to himself. Joseph made his squeaking sound and Philip said "OK" and they shared the rope.

The sound, loosely translated, meant: *Remember, I give for you.*

Even as we assimilated English into our lexicon, YaYa remained. At four years old, helping Mom prepare breakfast, you asked me, "YaYa, why aren't there any birds in these eggs?" I explained: "That's another country that has birds in their eggs. Our country doesn't have any." Before our parents, before our older siblings, we were each other's poor teachers. Our definitions, limits, boundaries were all determined by our committee of two, and were therefore porous, malleable, and subject to change.

Because of our congruence, we tended to repeat, rather than learn from, our mistakes. At three years old we escaped onto the first-story roof from the window of our bedroom. Despite Mom's repeated attempts to prevent us, we later summited the second story. Multiple times we had to be given ipecac to purge the medicine we binged in the hall closet. The hardwood floors of the kitchen had to be resurfaced not once, but twice—first, when we trampled the drying resin and received a hellacious warning from Mom, and later, when we trespassed again in order to report back to her that the floors really weren't dangerous, "only sticky." You were my terrible influence, and I was yours, but this grew into our greatest strength: boundless, leapfrogging curiosity. Taking one step further than the other, inventing and mutually defying boundaries, we mapped a vast territory. We asked foolish questions of our world and together, foolishly answered them. No single child could have deviated so far from common sense. We created and amplified our own rules, those foundational myths that were more convincing than anything that came afterward in our lives.

Entering kindergarten, our classmates quickly noticed our moniker, YaYa. They didn't understand that it was ours alone, but that simultaneously we had our other names, too, for them to identify us, if they could. I remember it was you who yielded to their teasing, telling me on the walk home from school one day that we had to stop saying "YaYa," and make a hard switch to only our given names. We were five years old and I had never heard you say my name. You spoke it aloud then for the first time—"Jo-seph"—and the sound of it in my ear was cold, alien. For months, forming yours in my mouth took conscious effort—"Phil-ip"—like using my opposite hand to write. The feeling was something new, a distant sensation I would later name "grief."

§§§§§§§§§§§§§§§§§§§§§

PG and JG: We are 25 years old and find ourselves again in an Ohio town originally called Millsville, purchased and renamed as Twinsburg in the early nineteenth century by renowned brothers. Moses and Aaron Wilcox were identical twins who married sisters, had nine children each, lived and worked together, held all property in common, fell ill of the same disease, and died within hours of each other on September 24, 1827. They were even buried together in the same grave. The interconnectedness of the Wilcoxes lives on in Twinsburg as a pilgrimage site for thousands of twins and other multiples from around the world who convene at the annual Twins Days Festival.[2] Like the ancient Yorùbá cities of Ilobu, Igbo Ora, and Ile-Ife, Twinsburg repeated their paradigmatic celebrations: "Cities that were traditionally founded or inhabited by twins not only collectively honor twins . . . but recount their founding myths and festivals and rituals associated with the town."[3]

We are embedded in the mile-long twin parade wearing matching vintage powder blue suits trimmed in blood red. A film crew follows us in the August swelter amid

Figure 19.2 Philip and Joseph Garrity, appearing in *Twinsburg*, a short film by Joseph (Joe) Garrity, 2016. Photo by Teresa Castro. Jog Films.

the thousands of other twin pairs, aiming cameras and microphones, lugging makeup kits and fresh costumes. The spectators lining the street notice this smaller spectacle within the larger one. They murmur: *Are they famous? Will we be on TV? Or in a movie?* They project a false reality onto the powder-blue twins, but the deception is mutual; shrouded in artifice, we play roles that are realer than either of us can fathom [Figure 19.2].

JG: We are shooting a short film that I am writing and directing. I play "Jerry" and you play "Paul," brothers who have attended the Twinsburg festival for as long as they can remember, first brought there in diapers by their parents. As young adults now living on opposite coasts, Jerry still clings to their childhood tradition, while Paul's enthusiasm has waned. The film's premise: this is the year they will confront the fact that the feeling is no longer mutual.

PG: On the set, a meta-plot unfolds, blurring art and reality. I begin to take on features of my character, resisting the demands of your production the same way Paul resists Jerry's festival. Toward the end of one long day of filming, I refuse to do any more takes, leaving the set and disappearing for several hours. I am pressure-testing the production and the disruptions exacerbate an already fragile set. The script is in flux as you rewrite dialogue—at night in the hotel, during the car ride to set, even between setups while the lights are being moved. Your distress mirrors Jerry's, afraid that your show of unity may be falling apart.

We are filming the climactic fight scene. Paul has just sabotaged the final event of the festival, and Jerry erupts in the midday heat.

Jerry: "Why did you come?!"

Paul: "Because you're still terrified of being alone!"

Jerry: "And you can't be with people—what happened?"

Between tense takes, you pace with your arms folded, eyes fixed on the ground, diving deeper into Jerry.

We reenter the frame to repeat the scene again and again. The crew looks on in strained silence as the emotions build with each successive take. I am agitated and concerned as I struggle to separate Jerry from Joe. My polyester suit is stifling in the humidity and I desperately want to step out of the scene, to say something to you, to ask if you are OK. But instead I remain silent as my character Paul continues to shout his lines.

JG: This is where the filming ends, with the script unfinished, the story unresolved. Jerry and Paul shed their matching blood-red trimmed, powder blue suits, becoming Joe and Phil once more. In bitter silence, we leave Twinsburg and return to opposite coasts.

§§§§§§§§§§§§§§§§§§§§§

PG: A few years after we finished filming *Twinsburg*, when I was a graduate student in Boston and you were back in California continuing with filmmaking, I stumbled on a course in the catalogue with the subtitle of this volume: "Twins and Twinship in Mythology and Religion." It was the last thing I expected to find at divinity school. Somehow, though, it seemed fitting that the topic of twinship might have a place among Christian mysticism, Buddhist philosophy, and Sufi poetry, the things that had drawn me to study theology and philosophy in the first place. To me our twinship had always seemed mysterious, defying easy analysis.

Despite being intrigued, I was reluctant to enroll. The complexities of filming *Twinsburg* and the turmoil that followed made me wary of retreading that terrain. Plus "twin studies" seemed more your thing than mine; you had immersed yourself in research for years leading up to the production. You would send me arcane books and articles on archetypal twin personalities and twin psychology: I browsed them with lukewarm interest. But here was a whole course that the universe had sent me like another book, giving me another chance to read it. With ambivalence, I agreed. Some part of me felt that I was doing it for you.

I knew you'd be thrilled to hear how, when I told Professor Patton about *Twinsburg*, she had the class watch it—and how surreal it was for me to witness a classroom full of students critically discussing its motifs and character arcs, drawing parallels between the film and the twin legends and sacred histories we were reading. How had our misadventures in filmmaking made their way into a Harvard classroom? It was the beginning of a clash of realms—of modern art and millennia-old traditions, of self-created fiction and eternal truth, colliding. Mythology, as I was learning, is the quintessential arena for this kind of collision. This resonated with another convergence I encountered at divinity school, between the transcendent realm of ideals and the immanent realm of my own experience. Esoteric mysteries and universal truths, enshrined in the spiritual traditions I venerated yet held at a safe distance from life's entangled messiness, would gradually be subsumed into partial, finite realities. In search of wisdom figures like Christ and Buddha who could offer clear and absolute principles by which I could meaningfully live, I would instead find flawed, complicated characters in my daily path, hidden teachers who offered murky, harder lessons about love and life that more often challenged than consoled me. More than anyone, you were one of these hidden teachers.

In her introduction to *Gemini and the Sacred,* Patton asks this: "How are 'real' twins related to those of sacred history, if they are in fact at all?" We set out to address this question, drawing on our own experience as identical twins. As we read the myths chronicled here, separated at times by thousands of miles, I came to see how the light of religion and mythology could illumine the subtleties and particularities of our dynamic— the interchange of consonance and dissonance, intimacy and alienation, recognition and non-recognition—which often felt capricious and beyond our control or understanding. But writing this *Epilogue* was not a simple matter of listing what about being "real" twins was illuminated by the mythology of twinship. Like *Twinsburg*, even this project was far more fraught than we anticipated. I now recognize a certain seasonality in those movements of resonance and dissonance, a natural ebb and flow that situates us in a broader pattern of human experience spanning places, cultures, and histories. I see clearly that at the root of our lived experience as twins—the narratives about twins that we've encountered outside ourselves, as well as those we've created from within—is something eerie and recurrent. "That there is an invisible plane supporting the visible one" is what Joseph Campbell called "the basic theme of all mythology."[4]

JG: We tried for a long time to "co-write" this piece in a ghostly shared voice, congealing our perspectives into an omniscient narrator that sounded exactly like neither of us. Perhaps it sounded like whoever our "singleton" might have been, had our zygote not divided to form us as distinct people, what they call "identical" twins. In this voice we attempted to relate each of our experiences and the personal myth enacted in our short film *Twinsburg*, as well as the broader legacy of twin myth this anthology divulges, echoing up from antiquity so many of the dynamics we instinctually recognize but have struggled in the past to articulate. The result was an amalgamation I eventually couldn't stomach, as I tried in successive attempts to make clear to you, eventually by yelling through the phone from a street corner in Mexico City. It's funny and sad how a project revisiting this complicated past could transport us right back to that time—but this is the story of our condition, funny and sad, tragic and absurd, what many wish in ignorance that they had, too. You are my living biography, and I am yours, for better or worse.

PG: During the year after college I lived in Cusco, Peru, the oldest city in the Americas and the seat of the Incan empire a thousand years earlier. I would walk the narrow, cobbled streets, passing the great Spanish cathedrals on my way to work. As elaborate as the churches were with their towering spires, the foundations upon which they stood were even more impressive. The massive stones had been carved and fitted so precisely that mortar was unnecessary. They were the remnants of Incan temples upon which the Spanish had built their churches—one god supplanted by another in a brutally literal display of cultural and religious dominance. I would see a Quechuan woman standing by the church, dressed in traditional garb with a llama in tow, offering to take photos with tourists for a fee. When dusk would fall she would walk into the foothills, headed to some outlying village, to the descendants of those who had built the foundations of this place.

Sometime during that year I learned that the term "Yaya" in Quechua translates as "wise one," "elder," or "shaman." The translation seemed to be more than coincidental. I imagined us as five-year-old boys discreetly invoking our sacred title, guarding the mystery from the uninitiated, from the "civilizing" forces that pressed in from all sides. Olúpònà explains how cultural factors gradually eclipsed the Ibeji's traditional kingly names of *Táyéwò* and *Kẹ́hìndé* to fall out of use in Yorùbá society, citing a campaign against these names "in an effort to normalize and desacralize twins."[5] Ultimately, we ourselves succumbed to a similar pressure—whether real or perceived—to assimilate to a culture of individual people with individual names, to supplant the shamanic *YaYa* with our Christian names.

Nearly three decades later, I wonder how my five-year-old self came to that decision, what sort of logic framed the dilemma in such starkly binary terms: either remain in our private world and be ostracized from the outside world, or sacrifice the intimacy of YaYa in return for integration with wider society. Like the Yorùbá Ibeji and the Vodou Marasa who act as liminal figures mediating between the realm of social life and the realm of wilderness, or the human and the spirit realm, as YaYa we seemed to be standing on our own threshold between two worlds.[6] YaYa was wild and undomesticated, primordial, while "Philip and Joseph" were tame and orderly, domesticated and above all, distinguishable.

Could I have made another calculus, one in which the value of our twinned intimacy outweighed any loss of connection with the wider group? Might I have then been strong enough to ignore their mocking, to resist the colonizing power of individualism? Even so, how long would that have lasted? When would have been an "appropriate" time to start using our given names with each other? This speaks to a fundamental dilemma: Was the "natural" course to maintain a fused identity and the "unnatural" one to individuate—or vice versa? Did I give into fear when we were five, and tarnish some sacred bond? Did I break our unity for the sake of acceptance by the wider world? Or did we simply outgrow a juvenile phase as we rightly should— indeed, *must* have?

Someone told me recently that motivations are never pure; they are alloys of different emotions. Perhaps the two countervailing forces—one toward convergence and the other toward divergence—were both natural. Just as there was a desire to merge with the wider group, evidenced by the retiring of YaYa, there was another desire to affirm the anomaly of our twinship. But perhaps both were sourced in a deeper need to feel accepted, to feel connected to something larger. While that need was at first met within our dyad, increasingly we looked beyond it to the attention and special treatment we received from others. After all, we wielded a unique power, even if in our earliest years we weren't aware of it.

I have hazy memories of us as three-year-olds venturing down the street to our neighbors' house, standing on their front porch and alternately parroting "cookie, cookie" until they opened the door with those cookies. Yorùbá Ibeji traveled "from house to house and place to place, dancing the twin dance and collecting gifts."[7] Our "dance" was not rehearsed or premeditated; it was driven by a simple desire shared by all children: to reach out to the world and taste it. Had we been not two children but one, we would likely have had neither the courage to venture away from home nor the charm to endear our neighbors. It was they, not we, who saw it as a dance.

Mom's friend saw it that way, too. She worked for a talent agency and encouraged Mom, against her reservations, to audition us for commercials around age four. Identical twins were highly sought after in film and television, as labor laws limited child actors to work no more than four hours per day; with twins playing the same role, production could go for twice as long. We were unaware of this economy, the commodification of twins to achieve greater productivity. To us, the auditions were just adventures in San Francisco where we would go into brightly lit rooms and strangers would tell us to play with a toy or put on socks or eat some pork product and parrot back phrases in tandem. *It's delicious!* Mom got us out of the business before we were old enough to understand that what had been for sale was us.

The line between unsolicited and solicited attention is a subtle one. A kind of Pavlovian response can develop to others' attention; the feeding produces a hunger for more of the attention even if unsought in the first place. Moving into elementary school, we came to learn twin tropes and stereotypes, playing into other people's intrigues and indulging their perennial questions about telepathic powers, shared pain, and synchronous dreams. We developed gimmicks like the "word game," reciting in unison a seemingly random list of words to the amazement of our peers; the sleight was that we had memorized them beforehand. Obeng writes of orphaned twins in Ghana who "develop their mystique to fend for themselves."[8] While never in dire straits, we, too, developed our mystique half-consciously, blending the authentic and the artificial to put on a show in exchange for social sustenance.

JG: Strangely, we grew up next door to a family with identical twin boys our same age. We weren't the best of friends with them—our four parents didn't get along well—what was odd was that I didn't sense that we were all, collectively, twins. The neighboring boys were fiercely competitive with one another, their arguments often erupting into violent assaults. You and I were mostly averse to confrontation, inclined to make truces and return swiftly to cooperation. Perhaps the difference was related to the deliberate ambiguity of the neighbor twins' seniority. They defended their mother's outlandish claim that neither one was older, that they had been born at the exact same time.[9] Though it couldn't be disproven, I remember struggling to imagine the anatomical scenario.

The fact was that both pairs of look-alike brothers were told many things about who we were as twins. Just like our given names, the explanations and lore of our twinship were just that—*given*, prescribed by outsiders. Yes, I understood that we were seen differently than other children, but only by being largely unseen as individuals. The casual observer couldn't or wouldn't see past our veil of sameness, and even some relatives were prone to mistaking us for one another. To allay their embarrassment, we offered up to them our spiel of the usual cues, somehow always stemming from you: your ears stuck out more, you had a brown birthmark in your right eye, and beneath that, a scar from a leap onto a coffee table when we were two. By default, I was the other one, the blank slate. From within our twinship, the partial anonymity became routine. I could blend into our two-ness, fade to the background when it suited me, and when it didn't, I could try—often in vain—to speak out.

I have to trust all those who have told us we are alike, because I am largely blind to it. Even in the doubled confusion of our earliest photos, it isn't that I see my likeness in you; it's that before a certain age, I simply disappear among the two faces. I study the expressions, read the gestures, and always discover—without fail—your face first. Out from that fog of uncertainty, the ambiguous face that remains, I adopt as myself.

Likewise, I have to trust the doctor who declared me three minutes older than you (unless of course a fateful "twinversion" had occurred, a permanent swap). Growing up I never intuitively sensed my 180-second seniority over you, regardless of that trivial fact being ingrained in me through sheer repetition of the most inane of all questions asked of twins: "Who's older?" To be honest, I often felt you were the older one, more capable and pragmatic, more ruthless. At times I was quietly thankful that by mere minutes, in this one department, I had bested you. I sometimes imagined what it would have been like had you held the title of first-born. You might have lorded it over me, not heeded my cat-mouse sound of compassion. I was oddly comforted to hold the title, to show to you that a slightly older brother could defer to his younger, could demonstrate forgiveness. The universal names applied to first-born and second-born twins of the Yorùbá, Táyéwò and Kẹhìndé, simplify the dilemma, and the arrangement resonates with me: as Olúpònà writes, the first-born serves the second-born, is sent out by her or him into the world "on an errand," to report on it. That I arrived first, ounces lighter than you and banged-up in the journey—my nose cartilage bent, my ankles turned inward—seems to prove that you sent me on ahead as scout, taking one for the team. From a young age we seemed to fit this model: while I would venture out to test the waters among others, I often allowed you to navigate the waters among us.

On rare occasions I can see what they see, catching a glimpse of me in your image: at an odd angle, in a far mirror, when you wear my clothing, in low lighting, when you are dancing. In these passing moments, I suddenly get it, and just as suddenly, I don't again. Our vacillation between recognition and non-recognition is found among the *Lwa*: "As a divided unity, the Marasa are their own mirror image; thus, they stand on both sides of the cosmic mirror, making them uniquely capable of *sonde miwa* (fathoming the mirror) simultaneously from both sides."[10] All our lives we have been fathoming the mirror, its reflections and distortions.

PG: There is an image seared in my memory: I see you on your knees, your face contorted and howling at the ground as you clutch the carpet with your fists. I am startled by the intensity of the white-hot rage and sorrow that has engulfed you. Mom has just told us that she put the house on the market again, despite promising us a few months earlier that we would stay in our hometown. Someone has bought it and we will be moving within a few weeks. It is the climactic end to several years of dislocation that had begun as small tremors with our parents arguing, with Dad moving out and in and back out again. Nearly all of my memory of that time—the separation, the divorce, the move—is fused with that one visual: a ten-year-old boy on the floor, shaking from the pain of being uprooted and, even worse, betrayed. I'm sure I was crying, too, but I can't remember. As I search for my own feeling, all I find is a reflection of yours.

The move was more than a loss of place; it was a loss of the land from which YaYa had emerged. Grim writes of "ecological imaginaries" of Native American cultures, which he describes as "the deep, attractor relationships between place and people that activate the affective, cognitive, and creative forces at the heart of cultural life."[11] An integral part of myth-making is land-claiming by which "an indifferent landscape is transubstantiated, turned into an icon, and the elementary idea is established in a local habitation."[12] The fluidity and intimacy of our connection as twins seemed fused—appropriately, entangled—with our relationship to the natural environment of 1870 Tanglewood Way. There was the bed of deep green ivy in the side yard that ran up the walls of the house, the trees on the other side that we scaled like the twin *ẹdun* (colobus monkeys) of the Yorùbá, the forts we would build out back from logs and branches and planks from an old fence, the two great walnut trees towering over the front yard, standing like sentinels keeping guard. Every autumn they would blanket the lawn with a mosaic of brown, red, and yellow—a sea of color in which we buried ourselves. We didn't need toys. We had our hands, our imagination, the trees, and each other. In the weeks before we moved, the realtors had one of the walnut trees cut down, claiming it was diseased. The yard looked bare, unbalanced. "When the homelands of indigenous peoples are literally cut down or mined away . . . the whole possibility of imaging oneself and one's community in place and in words is fragmented and subverted."[13] The spirit of YaYa stayed buried in the land we would soon leave.

I helped Mom look for houses near Sacramento where she had found a new job, while you opted out in protest. You always seemed more embittered by the experience, more hung up about letting go and moving on. Our three older siblings would go in separate directions: one to college, another to live with a family friend, and the third to live with Dad. You and I would go with Mom to a one-story, cookie-cutter house with a barren backyard of dirt. A year earlier we had been a family of seven; now we were scattered across hundreds of miles of dusty California farmland.

JG: From our earliest experiments with the family camcorder, stopping and rewinding the tape to get the moment right, we were natural stand-ins for one another. The boundaries between actor, writer, and director were porous, and ultimately the subject was always the same: exploring our strangely conjoined humor, our congenital curiosity that propelled ideas into action. When Mom gave us a rudimentary digital camera with its own editing software in junior high school, our cinematic universe exploded. Our freewheeling creations proliferated with sound effects and stock music, ricocheting across genres from action to horror, commercial parody to stop-motion fantasy, many with cameos by Peter, our runty, surly dachshund.

In the classroom we discovered another creative pursuit, developing a mutual interest in biology, specifically the unit on genetics. We learned about the genetic code that united all living organisms, distinguishing one from another through tiny mutations carried over generations. Every once in a while, that code would be repeated in a rare, but persistent, phenomenon: identical twinning, the unexplained splitting of a days-old zygote. Rarer still, we learned, we were mirror image twins— opposite-handed, our hair whorling in reverse directions. We were electrified by these insights into our strange origins. For the first time we were learning about ourselves in absolute terms, an empiricism that was as alluring as it was misleading. There was knowledge there, secrets we believed could tell us who we were, and we were hungry for them.

PG: Of Achilles and Patroklos, the warrior and his sacrificial substitute whose name means "healer" (*therapōn*), Gregory Nagy highlights "an uncanny mix of intimacy and alienation that only twins will ever truly understand."[14] As children, everything in our lives had been public domain to one another. Only with adolescence did our social landscape begin to fragment as increasingly large tracts of our world became sequestered into private realms, hidden from each other's sight. Our social circles began to diverge ever so slightly and romantic interests were kept hidden from the other. Perhaps, as might have been true for our older siblings, Catholic shame muted us, but I suspect that the silence between us was deeper than theirs. The price of the new intimacy we found in relationships seemed to be the intimacy we had once shared.

As twins, I suspect, we may have felt the burden of being "models of enhanced human interaction and communication."[15] There was a painful mismatch between our reality and the expectations the world had about us being symbiotic best friends. Vijaya Nagarajan wonders about the dissonance felt by devout Hindu Indian-American parents between the harmonious portrayal of Lava and Kusa and the more fraught dynamics of their own twin children.[16] It may be that this very ideal of a sublime connection inevitably brings with it the double of disillusionment, and the risk of an even steeper fall into disconnection and discord. Occasionally I would confide in Mom about my darker feelings, my melancholy, and my romantic woes. She would gently encourage me to talk to you about it, hinting that you, too, had revealed to her much the same sentiments. It would be years later when we would finally would tread into those sequestered realms. Until then, we would keep our silence.

Later in high school I would scold you for making mistakes during lacrosse practice. Under helmets and pads, the coaches couldn't tell us apart. I remember shouting at you after practice—"You're making me look bad!"—and demanding that you work harder and get better. Of course, I made mistakes too, and yet you didn't seem to complain. I was channeling a sense of indignation at the fact that my identity was tied so inextricably with yours—that your weaknesses could be my own.

And then there were times we got into real fights. We would punch each other in alternating succession with increasing force. It was as if we were fencing—you would attack as I retreated, I would attack as you retreated. But then there would be a moment, perhaps when the blows got too hard, when one of us would say the other's name in some sort of tone or frequency—maybe like that toddler squeak. It was like a whistle that indicated we had crossed a line and needed to stop. The other, who would have won, had to concede, because the plea was earnest, irrefutable. In an instant, we would lower our fists and walk away.

Nearing graduation, we found ourselves retreading these territorial disputes more frequently. In the heat of it all, I insisted that we attend separate colleges. I knew you were hurt, but too proud to say it. I felt I needed to live on my own, to be my own person for the first time in my life.

JG: Once we separated for college, I staved off loneliness by writing loose scripts for us to shoot on holiday breaks, enlisting our high school friends to act in the supporting roles. I could direct you like myself, because in our lifetime together I had memorized your every sound and gesture. You were capable of everything I was, and more.

Late in college, I used the media lab to digitize our family's earliest home videos, from a time before we moved behind the camera, when we were still peering into the lens from walkers and playpens. Watching us on the monitor, I could see our resemblance the way others did, how strikingly similar the infant faces were, often uncertain which belonged to me. I remembered Mom describing a recurring nightmare she had in the months after we were born: entering the nursery, she would discover two truly identical babies, no longer able to distinguish them. As I watched the tapes copy over, her nightmare didn't seem so surreal. Could we have been mistaken in infancy, one for another—permanently? I scoffed at the idea. After a lifetime of minor identity swaps, many of which we either instigated or exploited, what would a major one even mean? Probably nothing. But the question nagged, the laugh caught in my throat, and I entertained conspiracy theory.

In our last year of college, I cast you in a short film, "Twinversion," in which future versions of ourselves discover that they had been switched at birth. By bizarre legal mandate, our hapless characters are forced to trade identities as adults—Joe becomes Phil, Phil becomes Joe. Throughout the deadpan mockumentary I scattered the home video footage, those two ambiguous faces searching in the lens as our future selves searched back, looking in vain for the fateful moment where it all went wrong. It was moronic. It was oddly prescient.

With the short film completed, the "twinversion" premise lingered in my mind, a satirical, but sobering, question of our identities. I wanted to take the idea further, bring it to a bigger stage. Where could we raise the alarm on this hidden (fictious) epidemic? I searched online for twin conventions and discovered one almost immediately: Twinsburg, Ohio, a city founded by twins who lived and died together, and home to the annual Twins Days Festival, the world's largest gathering of multiples. *Twinsburg* would be our most ambitious project yet. I bought plane tickets from our opposite coasts to reunite us in Cleveland. Tepidly, you obliged. Approaching each other in the airport, as was the custom, we exchanged bashful smiles and a stiff hug. Introductions were always unnatural to us—we'd never had one to begin with.

In the city of Ondo, Jacob Olúpọ̀nà—his middle name forever Kẹhìndé even though Isaac Táyéwò was long dead—reports, "Everywhere I turned during the three-day celebrations I saw twins—twins of various ages, identical twins, fraternal twins both of the same and opposite genders—twins, twins, twins!"[17] There is a word we first heard in Twinsburg, Ohio: *singleton*. You laughed at how coarse the term sounded, like a slur—and in a way, it was. A pejorative for those born with individuality, for whom the experience of being twinned could never be truly fathomed. We heard it often in the banter of the festivalgoers, dressed in matching outfits: "Singletons would never understand." The truth was, I didn't understand either, and at this stage, I felt closer to a singleton than a twin. Among the spectacle of the Twins Days Festival, I didn't sense I had found my people; instead I felt the alienation of someone who wasn't twin enough, not card-carrying or flag-waving, the kind who never knew how to answer the benign question, "Are you close?" In reply, my mind always ricocheted in defense: did they mean, could we be closer? Or, should we be? I had internalized the belief projected onto us since we were infants, that we were automatically and forever united, and that anything less would be an aberration.

PG: After college, I didn't come home. There was some guilt around that, as if I was meant to rectify my hasty and rash decision to part ways with you after high school. I had assumed I would move closer to home, perhaps to the Bay Area where you had been all that time. Instead, I went even further away, to volunteer doing humanitarian relief work in Peru for a year before moving to Boston to work for a global health nonprofit. My immersion in efforts to alleviate poverty and disease led me into deeply existential and spiritual questions about suffering, hope, and God. The vulnerability I saw around me was reflected back at me, showing me that I, too, was implicated in the forces of disease and chaos that I confidently thought I controlled. As Nietszche warned, I had been gazing into the abyss, and now the abyss was gazing into me.

It was an intensely solitary journey living on my own the following year in Boston, deluged in spiritual and philosophical reading, struggling to find answers to help assuage the anxiety that would well up and overtake me. I would sporadically reach out to our family in fits of existential angst, the depths of which I couldn't seem to communicate. I remember I called you once, desperately trying to articulate the questions that amazed and tormented me. In response, I heard mostly stunned silence.

A deeper problem would reveal itself: a rare and aggressive bone cancer had been developing in my right leg. In the wake of the diagnosis—and the news that I would need to immediately start an intensive, year-long regimen of chemotherapy and surgery—I might have expected the mental and spiritual anguish that had plagued me for the past year to ratchet up; strangely, the cancer had the opposite effect. Instead of terror, I felt a profound kind of assurance, an unshakeable trust that things would be alright regardless of how the illness unfolded. As difficult as it had been to articulate the mysterious existential crisis of the past year, harder still to communicate was the sense of awe and peace following the diagnosis.

JG: Lying in the radiology room across the country from you, I secretly hoped for the technicians to call up in my bones whatever had been found in yours, to make us identical again. You had called me on my lunch break earlier that week. The knee pain you noticed after a run was something more. In a routine X-ray at a sports clinic, the technician had discovered a lemon-sized mass at the end of your right femur. A biopsy confirmed its malignancy: stage II osteosarcoma, six months old, no signs of metastasis. On the call I remained calm, calculated, listening to you describe the uncertainties, asking you pointed questions, hanging up and returning to work. I made an appointment for my own scans. I was tranquil as the technician left the room, the machine imaging my body in successive bursts. If I were sick and doomed, I thought, then we would do as we always had done: endure whatever came together. The alternative was unthinkable, standing by as you endured a gauntlet alone, with the potential of total loss. The radiologist returned with my results—clear—and that's when it hit me, the deferred disbelief, panic, despair.

We were on opposite sides of it now.

My well-being was always ritually linked with yours, conditioned upon it. As a child I vaguely understood that as long as you were OK, I would be, too. In the top bunk at night, alongside the other bedtime prayers, I would add something like, "and keep Philip safe." Watching you suffer was in some ways more visceral to me than my own discomfort, more unbearable. Perhaps it was the anxiety of being helpless to alleviate your distress. The cat-sound Mom had observed had its limits. Homer's tale of Patroklos sacrificing himself in battle as the *therapōn* of Achilles rings true. I was more comfortable with the idea of this substitution into your role than playing my own as helpless spectator. Leaving the radiology room that day, a disk of grainy images in hand, my lifetime of braiding our fates together began to unravel.

PG: That year of chemotherapy is mostly a blur to me now. I remember you coming to visit me in Boston a few times, slouching into a chair across from my hospital bed. You were mostly silent. We would exchange some sarcastic banter or stumble into petty arguments. I knew that you were having a hard time, but I didn't have the energy or patience to be the spillway for your bottled feelings. I felt mostly aggravated by your persistent melancholy and passive aggression, the negative energy you seemed to bring into the hospital room. It was hard for me to sympathize with your struggle since it seemed to be smothering my own.

The chasm that had separated us during my year of spiritual angst divided us again; only now, I was on the side of some incommunicable hope while you were stranded in a private despair. And yet that hope was fragile, threatened by that despair. There was something about your grimace that reflected back to me a hollowness to my supposed contentment. Here was the ten-year-old boy howling on the carpet, mirroring back pain I had buried deep, that I couldn't—or refused—to feel.

Nearly a year later, when I finished treatment and had returned to good health, I went to Ireland to spend a summer on my own before the start of divinity school, taking time to reflect on the previous years of upheaval and healing. It was deliberately solitary—a chance to get off the grid, to slow down, and to sift through my experiences in the hopes of writing a spiritual memoir. After a year of being so utterly dependent on others—to eat, to bathe, to walk—venturing into a new country with only a hiking backpack was a radical assertion of self-sufficiency, of my hard-won independence.

I remember when your calls came, like the tug of a leash. You were pressing me to wrap up my travels by early August. You had been getting things in place for us to return to Twinsburg and film once more, this time with a crew and a script and budget. This was the year to do it, you said. But I demurred, saying I couldn't promise I'd be able to make it this year. To me, *Twinsburg* was just another video project, an inconsequential lark—like the homespun videos we had made as teenagers with the family camcorder. Beneath my apathy was annoyance. Your continued fixation on our twinship seemed worn-out and pathetic, like our gimmicks to impress our classmates. But I also sensed, to you, my time away in Ireland was just another vacation, not a vital pilgrimage of sorts. You didn't seem to care that I was working on my own project, one whose creation didn't depend on you. I wished that yours didn't depend on me, but I knew it did—your insistence told me as much—so I gave in.

A few days before I would fly from Ireland to Ohio to begin filming, I had a dream:

> You and I are driving to meet friends for lunch. I'm sitting in the passenger seat as you drive, your face rigid and expressionless. As we approach the restaurant, you keep passing open parking spaces, as if ignoring them on purpose. I point out several spaces but you don't respond. Exasperated, I say, "Pull over the car. Clearly you're not capable of doing this." You stop the car in the middle of the road and I walk around to the driver's side door. You just sit there, staring out the windshield. I try pulling you out of the car, but you won't budge. I then reach into the backseat and retrieve a green, cloth-bound book. It is an anthology of Shakespeare's plays we had at home as children. It doesn't belong to you, but

you have claimed it like one of the many family albums or keepsakes that you have rummaged through over the years. I am holding the book hostage, trying to lure you out of the car when you suddenly pull out a brown book with gold-lined pages which I recognize as my Bible. I freeze, speaking slowly. "Don't . . ." You suddenly hurl it out the window and down into a deep gulch beside the road. After a moment of shock, I scream at you to get it. The decline is too steep for me to retrieve it myself, as my leg is post-surgery. You seem to understand my outrage and my physical limitations and you begrudgingly get out of the car and climb down into the gulch to retrieve the Bible. There is a man on the far side who is approaching through the trees, so I tell you to hurry up. Then the dream ends.

JG: The farcical comedy that had been gestating since our first trip to Ohio was steadily transforming itself during your cancer. The mockumentary about Phil and Joe championing a meaningless cause became the dramatic comedy of Jerry and Paul learning to articulate a long-buried grief. While Jerry contended with shedding his idealized twin identity, Paul accepted his desire for individuality. Each of these characters, I told you, was a part of me. But I needed your help to enact the myth.

The *Gospel of Thomas* was named for the Christian apostle who was given another epithet, *Didymos*, meaning simply "twin": Jesus says to his twin brother Thomas that to enter the kingdom we must become a "single or solitary one." To do this, one must make the one two, and the two one again—make peace with his otherness, with the strange truth that he is not simply *one* self. Yet one must also remain whole, encompassing his duality. This was the other secret aim of *Twinsburg*: to reconcile the one and the two, the half and the whole—the division within each of us, twin or singleton. We had to root out our assumptions about who we were as two in order to redefine what being someone, anyone, meant.

PG: I arrived in Ohio, barreling onto the set with reckless abandon. Like Junajpu, the fiery "overzealous trickster" of the *Popol Wuj*, both my character Paul and I interchanged continually, upending the scripted order both on and off the set. "It's a *game*," Paul says derisively of Jerry's ritual in Twinsburg. During a scene in which Paul is meant to be tipsy, you caught me sneaking drinks between takes with another actor. I knew it was a cardinal rule not to drink on set, lest it slow production, and I argued that it was to get into character. Really it was to break free of the tedium of the shooting schedule. You scolded me and I laughed, goading you to go ahead and fire me. I was chafing at the constraints of a production in which I was an integral but unwilling participant.

You continued tuning the dialogue to our dynamic darkening in real time—a mirror of life in art, the unresolved tensions between us coloring the longing and anguish you wrote into Jerry, and the apathy and hostility emerging in Paul. As the shoot went on, I began weighing in on the script, deciding what was authentic or inauthentic to Paul's character, and let you know with increasing fervor: Paul's love interest Nancy was too thinly developed; his character arc was stunted; the dramatic lows and comedic highs of the story were out of proportion. For years you had encouraged my input into your projects, but I had demurred; now you were suddenly overwhelmed by my aggressive attempts to reshape the script and set.

JG: We each had our stories to tell. On the car ride to the Cleveland airport after we had wrapped filming, we argued loudly, hurling grievances at one another. I said you had deliberately hindered an already stressful production. You said I had handcuffed you, manipulated you, inviting everyone involved to act in my public therapy. You reminded me that I had mentioned your cancer as part of a fundraising appeal in pre-production. You said it wasn't my story to tell. "Well, this is *my* cancer story," I said.

In the weeks following the film shooting, we hardly spoke. Our attempts at conversation devolved quickly into impasse and more silence. One night, as the argument strayed far beyond *Twinsburg*, you told me you wished I had better controlled my emotions during your cancer treatment. You said my grief wasn't helpful, and that you would have been better off without me there.

Something shifted then, a final piece clicked into place, because as I left the call, I felt ready to let you go. To let everything go. I looked up late night bus routes to the Golden Gate Bridge.

I stayed awake, made deals with myself, waiting for it to pass. It broke like a fever in the morning, thinking of Dad.

PG: "I don't know how you spent so many nights in a place like this," you said. You spoke from the darkness, an eye mask covering your face. The hospital room was dim, with only the fluorescent hallway light breaking in at the edges of the drawn curtain. I sat at the side of your bed in a plastic chair.

"I would have just been a hollow shell," you said.

I could hear the depression in your voice. You pulled the eye mask up to your forehead and some of the light caught your face. I had never seen you look so old. Your eyes were empty, deadened. You didn't look like my twin. It struck me then, the weight of all the years that we had lived apart, the time and circumstance that had carved us, imperceptibly, glacially, into different people.

It had been six months since our argument on the phone that had pushed you nearly over the edge. You told me about it a week later, in the middle of another knock-down, drag-out fight over the phone. I was laying into you about something when you interjected with some kind of whimper, maybe something like that old sound. Or maybe your voice cracked. It forced a pause, and in the silence you told me. I thought we were in a wrestling match. I didn't realize how close we were to the edge of the abyss—of absolute alienation and mortal disconnection.

I had moved back to the Bay Area for the summer for a hospital chaplaincy internship, in large part to be closer to you. Earlier that night I had been at a bar in San Francisco when I got a call from Mom telling me to get to Kaiser Oakland. You were having a suicidal episode, believing that nearly everything around you was a weapon. When I arrived you were in a bed in the ER, trying to self-calm in the dark. Sitting beside you, I felt helpless knowing that you might succumb to something far beyond my control. It struck me that you had sat in this same kind of chair, looking across another hospital bed at a brother you hardly recognized, one who might slip away. Even now, the mirroring is hard to fathom. But this is where mythology becomes useful, when the invisible world can break into the visible one.

Of the Marasa, McGee says, "Should one die before the other, it imperils the life of the still-living twin, who may be pulled to the other side to restore the balance of the pair."[18] I see us now tethered to one another, oscillating in alternating motion, following the same trajectory, just out of sync. I venture into the underworld of chaos in the shantytowns of Peru, spiraling into my own existential crisis that manifests in my body as cancer. As I mirror your mortality back to you, you descend into the underworld of chaos, which manifests in your mind as suicidal depression. Maybe it was your desire to unite with me that, like a self-fulfilling prophecy, pulled you down into the lethal realm from which you had initially been denied when the radiologist failed to make us identical again. Or maybe it was the universe's intolerance of imbalance, of the dangerous instability that ensues when life circumstances treat twins differently. In Vodou, "ritual propitiation" is needed to restore the balance of the pair. Was this ours?

Perhaps your creation of *Twinsburg*, all of your archaeology into old family videos and memorabilia, was your preemptive creation of an Èrè Ìbejì or a *plat Marasa*, in case you lost me. Perhaps you believed that this transformation of pain into art would conjure healing, like the Diné Stricken Twins, whose weeping turned into a song affirming their restoration to health. Maybe that's what provoked the resistance in me and the turmoil between us, particularly in the wake of cancer: you seemed to be eulogizing me before I was gone. And perhaps it stoked a death anxiety that was smoldering even before cancer. I wonder if I unconsciously equated "unity" with "death," with the annihilation of the self as it merges with another. Maybe "I" didn't want to disappear inside "us."

Between two who are entangled, as twins must always be, what looks like conflict can actually be love. There is a courtship ritual among eagles called a "talon lock" or "death spiral" in which they interlace their talons mid-air and spiral chaotically to the ground, letting go at the last moment. An act of seeming struggle and mutual destruction is rather a stunning display of intimacy. With us, it's often hard to sense the love that abides beneath the strife and silence that have often littered the surface of our relationship. But others see it, even when we don't. I think of Mom's deep intuition as a young mother that each of us would have had a harder time losing our twin brother than losing her.

There's something terrible about that kind of love. Like a magnet, it's both attractive and repulsive. It explains your pull toward unity and my push toward independence. I resisted the entanglement and the vulnerability that comes with having an aspect of my identity outside of my control, like having my heart go walking around outside my body. It is why I insisted we retire YaYa, why I scolded you on the lacrosse field, why I demanded we go to different colleges. The vulnerability persisted through the cancer experience, and beyond it. While holed up in my hermitage in Ireland, I asked *Why do you need me for* Twinsburg? But there was a deeper question beneath that: *Why do you need me in order to tell your story?* And beneath that, one that touched bedrock: *Why do you need me?*

It is a question meant not really for you, but for the universe or God or whomever wove us together as two-in-one, whomever stitched us into the fabric of everything and everyone else. I pull at the threads to free myself, insistent on finding security in selfhood, safety in self-sufficiency, but find it only unravels us both. Your downfall could be mine, and mine yours.

JG: Editing the film each night after work, eventually I reached the part I had been long avoiding: the fight scene. Months had passed since the filming in Ohio ended, yet it still made me queasy to watch the footage from that scene, to relive how raw and explosive we were. Filming the moment had been hard enough, but to have to sift through take after take in order to assemble the scene overwhelmed me. It was too much to enter that moment again on loop, watching myself explode in tears that I knew were all too real—real anger, real grief at having you almost disappear from me. If I was going to complete the film, I needed some separation. As a sort of optical sleight of hand, I tried applying a flop effect across the footage, flipping left and right. For most images without clear giveaways (like an "F" facing the wrong way), a flop effect can be difficult to discern. The slight asymmetries in the face, however, give the subject a subtle alteration, recognizable as themselves but somehow distorted. With us, the result was transfixing—we appeared less like ourselves and more like each other. For the first time, I could see myself in you, and you in me. The mirroring solved my hang-up, and now I could cut the scene with a degree of objectivity, tune it to make the conflict of Jerry and Paul impactful. In the finished film, I decided to leave the fight scene flopped, feeling the slightly disorienting effect was merited. No one ever seemed to notice the change. Did you?

PG: There is something extraordinary about identical twins, what Nagarajan describes as "a sense of supernatural 'abundance.'"[19] We had lived this. But reading the chapters of *Gemini and the Sacred* has caused me to ask whether the myth of our twinship had become too grandiose. We had created—or bought into—the idea of ourselves as members of a priestly or royal class set apart from and above singletons, like Yorùbá *ibeji*, "surrounded by an aura of sacredness."[20] We had built a religion around that primal, mystical unity, believing more in the structure than the substance: a vast cathedral around an oasis, a wellspring that had once surged but had since dried up. The plaques on the wall told its story. We greeted the guests who strolled by, curious, peering in. "This must be a holy place," they would say. "Yes, quite holy," we would say. But they would leave feeling as parched as we were.

We are left now to face the potential hollowness of our special bond, calling everything into question. We are drawn back to our origin, to the spark of creation. What if the dawning event of identical twins—of one zygote becoming two—is as ordinary as any other cellular division? What if we are as alone and random as everyone else? What if, in the final analysis, all are singletons?

Perhaps these doubts don't erase the mystery, but release it beyond the confines of a self-satisfied identity, destabilizing the way we view all other cellular events as merely ordinary. The spark of mystery is there within each: the fusion of two gametes to become one zygote, the differentiation of one pluripotent stem cell into any number of cell types, the division of one skin cell into two. The mystery expands, permeating all facets of reality, "transubstantiating an indifferent landscape"[21] into something supernatural. Martin Luther wrote, "If you could truly understand a grain of wheat, you would die of wonder." In the *Popol Wuj*, as Vincent Stanzione notes, a single maize kernel symbolizing the skull of the First Fathers germinates into all of creation, into the maizeland. The apparent simplicity of a seed reveals an elegant complexity that would enrapture or even rupture the mind if only we could "truly understand."

The boundaries between the miraculous and mundane, extraordinary and ordinary, twin and singleton become porous. The *Gospel of Thomas* moves beyond binaries to a place of non-duality where movement and repose paradoxically coexist. This is what is so scandalous about the secret gnosis that Jesus imparts to the disciple Thomas when he says, "I am you." But it is not a simplistic equation of the two; with the *unus-ambo*, duality is not subsumed by the unity.[22] Otherness and non-recognition are still honored. When Jesus asks his disciples to tell him who he is like, Thomas says he is "wholly incapable of saying whom you are like" (§13) and Jesus commends this response. Admitting the other's ineffability shows the depth of one's intimate knowledge of him.

JG: We stumbled our way into this world foraging for words and their meanings, scouting the territory beyond our nation of two for larger and more exotic words, flocks of phrases, whole species of thought. These names entered our nation like specimens to inspect as we pleased, to test and mutate, to bat back and forth, to interbreed and concoct novel varieties. What grew was a brother-tongue that short-circuited itself, rife with misuse, malapropism, and private vernacular so malleable as to be meaningless. Remnants of our jabbering persist to this day in the voices we use to speak to animals, as we spoke to Peter the dog, whose own name metastasized into more derivations than we could catalogue. Until middle school, I managed to retain our personal definition of "approximately" to mean "exactly," failing numerous math tests and forever stunting my mastery of fractions. But did you know we are a fraction? To this day I haven't mastered this concept, how one human being can be divided into two halves and become two whole human beings. How can these once-halves who were so admired for their halfness, fawned over and ogled so persistently, magically assume their separate wholeness? I am still doing the math. What I know is that this no-man's land between your personhood and mine is wired and treacherous.

So we've cleaved the text and chosen this chosen this epistolary format, something like open letters to one another. Looking back over this all today, June 26, 2020, in the very town where a central part of our story is set, Twinsburg, I admit your letters don't always feel very lettery. Perhaps mine don't either. But I forget, once again, that we aren't in our private, assumed language anymore. There are others looking in at us. I will greet them, that great singleton world, and the sprinkling of twins, too—on behalf of both of us.

Do you remember the tattered *Oxford American Dictionary* that floated around the Tanglewood house, with its red paperback cover cover? I have it. It has two contradictory definitions of the word "identity." The first, more common, reads: "the condition of being a specified person or thing." The second, more specific, peculiar to us, is: "the state of being identical, absolute sameness." Side by side, those two vastly different definitions. Like you and I—and YaYa too—our absurd paradox.

PG: You and I had largely denied our differences, seeing them as shameful signs of a fall from grace, from the "sacred intimacy" and unity we once had. We romanticized the idyllic time during the reign of YaYa when we lived in the trees of Tanglewood Way, before the fall when we were banished from the garden. We've tried to return to that place through art and spirituality, to find a common voice, only to be frustrated when we've found ourselves out of sync, stepping on the other's story. It's why we resorted to writing separate sections for this epilogue, as we were unable to speak in a unified voice, despite our best efforts.

   Yet the tales told in *Gemini and the Sacred* show how differences between twins, even divine ones, are not only inevitable but in fact necessary. Having vanquished the death-lords of Xibalba, Junajpu and XB'alamkiej, are reborn to become opposites of each other, the sun and the moon. The Navajo-Diné Stricken Twins compensate for each other's deficits, the blind one carrying his crippled brother on his shoulders. Olúpònà, Doniger, and nearly every author in this book describes how, despite their entanglement and the impossibility of perfect spiritual freedom from one another, each twin of a pair has his own *orí-destiny* and karma; each has her own role to play and their own path to follow.

   Perhaps the "sacred intimacy" of twinship is as fragile and at times as volatile as all human relationships. Perhaps there is a relief in this. It means that you and I are invited to descend our pedestal—built as much by us as by the cultural forces from which we emerged—to rejoin the wider human family. In releasing our sacrosanct relationship as twins, perhaps we are welcomed into another kind of kinship altogether, that of mere brothers—to accept the work of negotiating differences and flaws, of learning to love the other as neither mirrored nor contested self, but instead as truly "other" [Figure 19.3].

Figure 19.3 Philip and Joseph Garrity as Paul and Jerry in the final scene of *Twinsburg*. Photo by Teresa Castro. Jog Films.

This work will not be effortless, as it seemed to be in the Tanglewood garden, when that mysterious unity poured forth from the wellspring into which we were born. It will take patience and humility, a trust that the water will flow again, even in these dry and dusty lowlands.

§§§§§§§§§§§§§§§§§§§§§

JG and PG: YaYa has made 5.1 revolutions around the sun. It is early autumn and they are in a kindergarten classroom full of singleton children, individually named. The singletons have taken notice of their mutual utterances of "YaYa" and begin to tease them. *YaYa?* they laugh. *You are Philip! And you are Joseph!* YaYa feels a sense of shame and separation from the singletons. YaYa are walking the three short blocks home. As they turn down their street, YaYa stops YaYa.

"We can't use "YaYa" anymore," YaYa says.

YaYa, confused, picks delicately through the words that are like shards of glass. He doesn't reply, so YaYa continues.

"They notice us. We have to use our real names," YaYa says. "You have to call me Phil."

YaYa has never heard YaYa utter this name before.

"Promise," Phil insists.

The other is silent and motionless, trying to understand.

"Joe, OK?"

YaYa has never heard YaYa say this name before either. He has never felt this kind of distance. A gap opens up between them. He hesitates, then speaks.

"OK," says Joe, who once was *YaYa.*

§§§§§§§§§§§§§§§§§§§§§

Notes

1   Jacob Olúpọ̀nà, "The Code of Twins: Ìbejì in Yorùbá Cosmology, Ritual, and Iconography," in *Gemini and the Sacred: Twins and Twinship in Religion and Mythology*, ed. Kimberley C. Patton (London: Bloomsbury Academic, 2022), 84.

2   Estimated between 20,000 and 30,000 in 2019. Katherine Dill, "Annual Twinsburg Twins Days Festival Injects Millions into Local Economy," June 25, 2019. https://twinsdays.org/economic-impact/. Accessed June 17, 2020.

3   Olúpọ̀nà, "The Code of Twins," 87.

4   https://billmoyers.com/content/ep-3-joseph-campbell-and-the-power-of-myth-the-first-storytellers-audio/. Last accessed 5.25.22.

5   Olúpọ̀nà, "The Code of Twins," 73.

6   Olúpọ̀nà, "The Code of Twins"; Adam Michael McGee, "Marasa Elou: Twins and Uncanny Children in Haitian Vodou," in *Gemini and the Sacred: Twins and Twinship in Religion and Mythology*, ed. Kimberley C. Patton (London: Bloomsbury Academic, 2022), 127–53.

7　Olúpọ̀nà, "The Code of Twins," 86.

8　Pashington Obeng, "Twins: Welcome and Unwelcome Danglers in African Religions," in *Gemini and the Sacred: Twins and Twinship in Religion and Mythology*, ed. Kimberley C. Patton (London: Bloomsbury Academic, 2022), 114.

9　This could well be read as this family's attempt to triage what Olúpọ̀nà calls a crisis of "two individuals occupying the same niche in the lineage webs . . ." by lionizing that crisis, rather than attenuating it through remembering which twin was born first. Adam McGee writes of how "the Marasa's mystical power" disrupt social norms of birth order by opening up "a dangerous mystical and epistemological space where chaotic social forces are unleashed. By restoring age-normal social order, the parents are believed to be protecting their children and their family by returning them to the good graces of society" (McGee, "Marasa Elou," 140).

10　McGee, "Marasa Elou," 132.

11　John Grim, "Twins in Native American Mythologies: Relational Transformation," in *Gemini and the Sacred: Twins and Twinship in Religion and Mythology*, ed. Kimberley C. Patton (London: Bloomsbury Academic, 2022), 168.

12　Joseph Campbell, *The Way of the Animal Powers*, Historical Atlas of World Mythology, vol. 1 (San Francisco: Harper & Row, 1983), 248, quoted in Grim, "Twins in Native American Mythologies," 169, and n. 25.

13　Grim, "Twins in Native American Mythologies," 168.

14　Gregory Nagy, "Achilles and Patroklos as Models for the Twinning of Identity," in *Gemini and the Sacred: Twins and Twinship in Religion and Mythology*, ed. Kimberley C. Patton (London: Bloomsbury Academic, 2022), 283.

15　Philip M. Peek, Introduction, in Philip M. Peek, ed., *Twins in African and Diaspora Cultures* (Bloomington, IN: Indiana University Press, 2011), 27, quoted in Obeng, "Twins," 122, and n. 47.

16　Vijaya Nagarajan, "Twins in Hindu Mythology and Everyday Life in the California Diaspora," in *Gemini and the Sacred: Twins and Twinship in Religion and Mythology*, ed. Kimberley C. Patton (London: Bloomsbury Academic, 2022), 235.

17　Olúpọ̀nà, "The Code of Twins," 71.

18　McGee, "Marasa Elou," 133.

19　Nagarajan, "Twins in Hindu Mythology and Everyday Life in the California Diaspora," 232.

20　Olúpọ̀nà, "The Code of Twins," 93.

21　Campbell, *The Way of the Animal Powers*, 248, quoted in Grim, "Twins in Native American Mythologies," 169, and n. 25.

22　Charles Stang, "The Divine Double in Late Antiquity," in *Gemini and the Sacred: Twins and Twinship in Religion and Mythology*, ed. Kimberley C. Patton (London: Bloomsbury Academic, 2022), 387.

Ọ̀rọ̀ tó rin méjì o ò   Spirit Children who walk in pairs!

—Yorùbá *Orin Ìbejì* (twin songs)

Contributors

♊

Miranda Aldhouse-Green is Emeritus Professor of Archaeology at Cardiff University. Her research interests lie in the fields of ancient religion and ritual in Iron Age and Roman Europe; her particular specializations include cult-iconography, sacrifice, priesthood, mythology, and religious art, especially as revealed in material culture, although she draws heavily upon Classical literary sources, where relevant. She has published a number of books and research monographs, among them *Symbol and Image in Celtic Religious Art* (1989), *Celtic Goddesses* (1995), *Dying for the Gods* (2001), *Caesar's Druids* (2010) and, most recently, *Sacred Britannia* (2018). Her book *Bog Bodies Uncovered* (2015) won two major US awards: the Society for American Archaeology Book of the Year Award (Popular Category) 2016 and the Archaeological Institute of America Felicia A. Holton Book of the Year Award 2017.

Wendy Doniger is the Mircea Eliade Distinguished Professor of the History of Religions, Emerita, at the Divinity School at the University of Chicago. She is a scholar of Sanskrit and Indian textual religions, and, more broadly, of comparative religion, mythology, and philosophy. She is the author of over fifty books, several of which deal with twins and doubling, including *Dreams, Illusion and Other Realities* (1984), *Splitting the Difference: Gender and Myth in Ancient Greece and India* (1999), *The Bedtrick: Tales of Sex and Masquerade* (2000), *The Woman Who Pretended to Be Who She Was* (2005), and *The Ring of Truth: Tales of Sex and Jewelry* (2017).

Douglas Frame is Senior Fellow of the Center for Hellenic Studies in Washington, DC. He served as Associate Director of the CHS from 2000 to 2012. His publications include *The Myth of Return in Early Greek Epic* (1978) and *Hippota Nestor* (2009); the latter work, which locates the Homeric figure of Nestor "the horseman" in the Indo-European twin myth that includes the Vedic Aśvins and the Greek Dioskouroi, inspired his chapter in this volume.

Joseph O. Garrity is a writer and filmmaker of narrative, nonfiction, and audiovisual projects. His short film *Twinsburg,* a personal comedy-drama set at the annual Ohio twin convention in a town by the same name, was selected by fifty film festivals and has won nine awards. He was lead editor and assistant director of *Watergate*, a six-part documentary series by Charles Ferguson that screened at Telluride, New York Film Festival, and Berlinale. During four years at Pixar Animation Studios, he was an assistant editor on *The Good Dinosaur, Inside Out*, and *Finding Dory*. While earning a BA in Molecular Biology from UC Berkeley, his short film *Lettering* was awarded the Eisner Prize in Film. Currently he is pursuing an MFA in Creative Writing from UC Riverside's program at Palm Desert.

Philip S. Garrity is Program Director for Global Oncology, a nonprofit organization that works to expand access to cancer and palliative care services in Latin America and Africa. He previously worked for Partners in Health, another global health organization that strengthens health systems in low- and middle-income countries. He has lectured on the intersection of global health, spirituality, and illness at numerous universities and conferences and his writing has appeared in, among others, *The New York Times, The Lancet, The Huffington Post,* and two anthologies on writing by Oxford University Press. He holds a Master of Divinity degree from Harvard Divinity School and a Bachelor of Arts degree in International Development Studies and Spanish from UCLA.

John Grim is Senior Lecturer and Research Scholar at Yale School of Forestry and Environmental Studies and Yale Divinity School. He is an Environmental Ethicist-in-Residence at Yale Interdisciplinary Center for Bioethics. He teaches courses on religion and ecology, Native American and indigenous lifeways, and the thought of Thomas Berry. He is the author of *The Shaman: Patterns of Religious Healing Among the Ojibway Indians* (1983), and with Mary Evelyn Tucker, *Ecology and Religion* (2014), the Emmy Award–winning film *Journey of the Universe* (2011), and *Thomas Berry and the Arc of History* (2019). John is a past President of the American Teilhard Association.

Adam Michael McGee is the Arts Editor and Managing Editor of *Boston Review*. He holds a PhD in African and African American Studies from Harvard University and a Master of Theological Studies from Harvard Divinity School. His scholarly work has been published in *Studies in Religion/Sciences Religieuses, Dreaming: Journal of the Association for the Study of Dreams*, and the *Journal of Haitian Studies*. Learning to serve the Marasa, the twin *lwa* (spirits) of Vodou, was among McGee's earliest encounters with the religion. Later he would be initiated into a priesthood lineage with a strong connection to the Marasa, and move into an apartment in Boston that turned out to be on the route of an annual Roman Catholic devotional parade for Ss. Cosmas and Damian. These strong connections to spiritual twins exist in spite of his having almost no biological twin relations.

Stephen A. Mitchell is the Robert S. and Ilse Friend Professor of Scandinavian and Folklore at Harvard University. He has been a fellow of The Radcliffe Institute for Advanced Study and The Swedish Collegium for Advanced Study and is the author of *Heroic Sagas and Ballads* (1991) and *Witchcraft and Magic in the Nordic Middle Ages* (2011); in 2000, he co-edited with Gregory Nagy the second edition of Albert B. Lord's *The Singer of Tales*. His recent projects include the co-edited volumes *Minni and Muninn: Memory in Medieval Nordic Culture* (2014), *Old Norse*

Mythology—Comparative Perspectives (2017) and *Handbook of Pre-Modern Nordic Memory Studies: Interdisciplinary Approaches* (2018). Not without relevance to the present volume, his oldest children, Erik (1985–2021) and Katrina, are fraternal twins.

Vijaya Nagarajan is Associate Professor in the Department of Theology/Religious Studies (Dept. Chair 2018–20) and in the Program of Environmental Studies at the University of San Francisco. Her fields of research, teaching, and writing/activism focus on Hinduism, gender, ritual, ecology, commons, climate, energy, and ethics. She is active in the American Academy of Religion and in environmental movements in the United States and in India. Her book *Feeding a Thousand Souls: Women, Ritual and Ecology in India—An Exploration of the Kolam* (2019) is an extensive exploration of a popular women's ritual art, the kolam, and the multiple ways in which beauty embodies ethics (feedingathousandsouls.com). Becoming a mother of twins in 2000, she wondered how twins are imagined in Hinduism and the ethnographic realities of how Hindu mythology impinges on parenting.

Gregory Nagy is Francis Jones Professor of Classical Greek Literature and Professor of Comparative Literature at Harvard University, where he continues to teach. From 2000 to 2021 he served as Director of the Harvard Center for Hellenic Studies in Washington DC. He is the author of *The Best of the Achaeans: Concepts of the Hero in Archaic Greek Poetry* (1979; 2nd ed., with new Introduction, 1999). Other publications include *Homer the Preclassic* (2010; paperback ed. 2017) and *The Ancient Greek Hero in 24 Hours* (2013). With Stephen A. Mitchell, also a contributor to this volume, he co-edited the second edition (2000) of Albert Lord's *The Singer of Tales* (1960), co-authoring a new Introduction.

Pashington Obeng is Professor of African Studies, Dean of Arts and Sciences and the Head of Department of Humanities and Social Sciences at Ashesi University in Accra, Ghana. He specializes in the anthropology of religion on continental Africa and New World Afro-Atlantic areas, Indian Ocean and Transatlantic African Diaspora studies, and cultural communication with a focus on Black filmic representations. He is the author of *Asante Catholicism: Religions and Cultural Reproduction among the Akan of Ghana* (1996); *Shaping Membership, Defining Nation: The Cultural Politics of African Indians in South Asia* (2008); and *Rural Women's Power in South Asia: Understanding Shakti* (2014). He has also published numerous articles on anthropology of religion, culture, and African Diaspora studies. His present work researches the cosmologies and lifeways of West African Hindus and Jews. Obeng was raised in a nation with a long history of religious and political response to twins; he is also the son of a twin. His father was Jacob Atta Adu Kumi, whose twin brother, Obeng's uncle, was called Essau Atta Adu Kumi.

Jacob Ḳẹ́hìndé Olúpọ̀nà is Professor of African Religious Traditions at Harvard Divinity School and Professor of African and African American Studies in the Faculty of Arts and Sciences at Harvard University. He specializes in the comparative study of Islam, Christianity, and traditional religions in Africa, with a special focus on the

Yorùbá people of southwestern Nigeria. He is currently working on a study of the explosive growth of evangelicalism across all branches of Christianity (including but also beyond Pentecostalism) in the larger context of Nigerian Christianity and society. Among his numerous books are *Kingship, Religion and Rituals in a Nigerian Community: A Phenomenological Study of Ondo Yoruba Festivals* (1991) and *The City of 201 Gods: Ile-Ife in Time Space and the Imagination* (2011). Born a twin, Jacob Kẹ̀hìndé sadly lost his brother Isaac Taiwo in childhood, and grew up immersed in Yorùbá *ìbejì* (twinship) traditions. Drawing on both his academic expertise and his life experience, his chapter in *Gemini and the Sacred* is his first full-length study of this rich subject.

Kimberley C. Patton is Professor of the Comparative and Historical Study of Religion at Harvard Divinity School. Her fields of research include ancient Greek religion and archaeology, particularly ritual studies, sanctuaries, and iconography. She also works in the history of world religions and in cross-cultural religious phenomenology. She is the author of *Religion of the Gods: Ritual, Paradox, and Reflexivity* (2009), which won the American Academy of Religion Book of the Year Award in 2010 (Analytical-Descriptive Category). Her research on hybrid identity in the context of maternal mortality at the Neolithic site of Çatalhöyük, co-authored with forensic archaeologist Lori Hager, appears in *Religion in the Organization and Transformation of a Neolithic Society: Vital Matters*, ed. Ian Hodder (2014). *Gemini and the Sacred* is inspired by her interest in cultural responses to twins, long-standing since the birth in 1992 of her brother Geoffrey's and sister-in-law Karen's identical twin children, Alycia (now Lee) and Caitlyn.

Gregory J. Riley is John Wesley Professor of New Testament and Christian Origins at the Claremont School of Theology. Until recently he was also Professor of Religion at the Claremont Graduate University and Professor of New Testament at Bloy House, the Episcopal Theological School at Claremont. His areas of interest include the history of ideas that contributed to the rise of Christianity, Greco-Roman religion and philosophy, Gnosticism, and their influence on the rise and development of the early Church. He also works in many areas of New Testament studies, especially the Pauline and Johannine literature. His book *One Jesus Many Christs* was the first choice in religion of the Book of the Month Club and the British Book of the Month Club, and his book *The River of God* was a History Book Club selection. The chapter in this volume arises from his many years of work on the *Gospel of Thomas.*

James C. Skedros is the Michael G. and Anastasia Cantonis Professor of Byzantine Studies at Hellenic College and Holy Cross Greek Orthodox School of Theology in Brookline, Massachusetts. His teaching and research areas include popular religious practices in Late Antiquity, Byzantine Christianity, early Christian and Byzantine hagiography, pilgrimage, and Christian-Muslim relations. He was awarded two Fulbright Fellowships, both for the study of Byzantine saints in Thessaloniki, Greece. In addition to his book on the historical development of the veneration of the early Christian martyr Demetrios, *St. Demetrios of Thessaloniki: Civic Patron and Divine*

Protector, 4ᵗʰ–7ᵗʰ c. CE (1999), he has published several articles as well as entries in reference works on early Christianity.

Prods Oktor Skjærvø is Aga Khan Professor of Iranian Emeritus, formerly at Harvard's Department of Near Eastern Languages and Civilizations. His fields of research include the pre-Islamic languages and Zoroastrian literatures of Iran with special focus on epigraphy and philology, as well as the Zoroastrian and Manichean religions, on all of which he has published extensively. A separate field of research of his is the Iranian language spoken in Khotan in southwestern Xinjiang, where he authored the catalog of the Khotanese manuscripts in the British Library (2002) and edited the Khotanese translation of the Buddhist *Sutra of Golden Light* (2004). Intended for a more general public were his *The Songs of Zarathustra* in Norwegian (2004) and *The Spirit of Zoroastrianism* (2011) with translations of Old Iranian texts. He is currently working on numerous projects from a range of Old Iranian studies. His article on twins in ancient Zoroastrian cosmology is based on a chapter in a book on an old Iranian weaving myth.

Charles M. Stang is Professor of Early Christian Thought and Director of the Center for the Study of World Religions at Harvard Divinity School. His research and teaching focus on the history and theology of Christianity in Late Antiquity, especially Eastern varieties of Christianity. More specifically, he is interested in the development of asceticism, monasticism, and mysticism. His first book, *Apophasis and Pseudonymity in Dionysius the Areopagite: "No Longer I"* (2012), won the Manfred Lautenschläger Award for Theological Promise in 2013. His most recent book, *Our Divine Double* (2016), examines the idea in early Christianity, Manichaeism, and Neoplatonism that each person has a divine counterpart, twin, or alterego, and that to encounter one's divine double is to embark on a path of deification that closes the gap between image and archetype, human and divine.

Vincent James Stanzione is a historian of religion, ethnographer, and master storyteller who has lived in the Guatemalan Highlands since 1990 and worked with the Tz'utujil Maya in Santiago Atitlán for over twenty years. An expert on Mayan sacred histories—especially the *Popol Wuj*, to whose preservation he is devoted—he speaks frequently in colleges and universities throughout North America, and in many cultural settings in Guatemala. His areas of research include ancient and contemporary Mayan cosmology and theology; rituals of divination, initiation, and pilgrimage; syncretism; forms of resistance; and the impact of transculturation. He is the author of a number of books, including *Rituals of Sacrifice: Walking the Face of the Earth on the Sacred Path of the Sun: A Journey through the Tz'utujil Maya world of Santiago Atitlán* (2003) and *Los Nawales: The Ancient Ones (Merchants, Wives, and Lovers: The Creation Story of MaXimón)* (2016). His long life with Junajpu and XB'alamkiej, the Hero Twins of the *Popol Wuj*, has, like them, taken many forms; he is grateful to be part of the re-memberment of the Maya Day-keeping ritual with Maya K'iche' Day-Keepers, with whose contemporary lives and trials the sacred tale is tightly bound.

Most recently, he has completed an original translation of the *Popol Wuj*, a ten-year project inspired by indwelling his contribution to *Gemini and the Sacred.*

Lauren Talalay is Curator Emerita and Research Associate at the Kelsey Museum of Archaeology, University of Michigan. Her research focuses on the Neolithic period of the Mediterranean, primarily Greece, with an emphasis on figurines, gender, and the human body as a symbol. She also publishes on contemporary issues, particularly the use of archaeological images in modern advertising and political cartoons. She has written or collaborated on numerous articles and seven books, including *Deities, Dolls, and Devices: Neolithic Figurines from Franchthi Cave, Greece* (1993); *Prehistorians Round the Pond: Reflections on Prehistory as a Discipline* (2005); *The Prehistory of the Paximadi Peninsula, Euboea* (2013), and ". . . *What These Ithakas Mean*": *Readings in Cavafy* (2002), which was voted one of the best books of 2002 by the *Times Literary Supplement.* An identical twin, she and her "better" half have occasionally switched identities, secretly standing in for each other when necessity (or mischief) called.

Figure Con.1. "Gemini," the Hunterian Psalter, folio 3r (detail). Glasgow University Library, MS Hunter 229 (U.3.2), *c.* 1170 CE. Scotland/Bridgeman Images.

Index

NOTE: Page references in *italics* refer to figures. Page references followed by n. refer to notes.

Names of twins are presented together, e.g. Achilles and Patroklos/Patroclus (Greek mythology); Nakula and Sahadeva (Hindu mythology)

www.ingramcontent.com/pod-product-compliance
Lightning Source LLC
Chambersburg PA
CBHW071351290326
932CB00045B/1424